THE FORMATION
OF THE CHRISTIAN BIBLE

THE FORMATION
OF THE CHRISTIAN BIBLE

BY

HANS von CAMPENHAUSEN

TRANSLATED BY

J. A. BAKER

PHILADELPHIA
FORTRESS PRESS

Library of Congress Catalog Card Number 73-171495

ISBN 0-8006-1263-9

First Paperback Edition 1977

6579E77   Printed in U.S.A.   1-1263

VENERANDO ORDINI THEOLOGORUM UNIVERSITATIS

SANCTI ANDREAE APUD SCOTOS

NEC NON

VENERANDO ORDINI THEOLOGORUM UNIVERSITATIS UPSALENSIS

AB UTROQUE SUMMO THEOLOGIAE DOCTORIS HONORE ORNATUS

HUNC LIBELLUM

PERGRATI ANIMI SIGNUM DONAT

MEMOR VETUSTAE NECESSITUDINIS

QUA ET CUM SCOTIS MATERNAE GENTIS ORIGINE

ET CUM SUECIS PATERNI DOMICILII CAUSA CONIUNCTUS EST

AUCTOR

CONTENTS

FOREWORD

THIS BOOK is not meant as yet another treatment of the favourite topics covered in textbooks on the history of the Canon. My purpose is not to trace when and where the various books of the Bible first emerged, were quoted, grouped together, and disseminated, and finally found their place in the Canon. These are questions which, taken by themselves, belong rather to the science of biblical Introduction than to Church history; and it is hardly likely that any further substantial discoveries will be made in this area. My own interest lies in the great historical process of the formation of the Canon as such, the problem of the Christian canon, the pressures which motivated and the resistances which obstructed its emergence, the outcome of the controversies and the theological significance of that outcome. In previous presentations of the history of the Canon this aspect of the subject has at best been merely touched upon or treated in outline; it has never been made the central theme.

It may perhaps seem presumptuous to attempt anything of the kind. It was the view of Theodor Zahn, whose immense *Geschichte des neutestamentlichen Kanons* remained a fragment, that a history of the 'dogmatic ideas', a history, so to speak, of the dogma of the Canon, would be virtually impossible to write; and that in any case such an enterprise would be unrewarding (I, p. 84). He justified his position on the grounds of the nature and incompleteness of the extant early Christian literature, and concluded that in the early Church the Canon never at any time became the 'object of serious dogmatic thinking or of real doctrinal formation'.

The first difficulty lies in the facts of the situation. Everyone knows how scanty are our extant sources for the first, crucial centuries in particular, and how easily they tempt one to fill the gaps with more or less fantastic hypotheses, or to overstrain the little evidence we have by violent interpretation. In my view, however, it is possible nevertheless, given the requisite caution, to reconstruct the main lines of the formation of the Canon. The man who wants to know too much loses the thread, and in the end learns nothing; the man who turns his attention to what is actually there perceives to his astonishment that the links are by no means so obscure as had at first appeared. The right course is not to concentrate simply on isolated individual texts but—more in the manner of the historian than of the literary critic—to observe those lines which link up and finally form a discernible pattern.

In the same way it has to be admitted that the direct statements
about the Canon, taken by themselves, offer for the most part little
illumination. But here again the important thing is to see them not as
isolated statements but in the context of the problems and difficulties
of their time, and accordingly to assess them in their relevance to other
issues. Of course, the theological conflicts of the early Church were not
fought out over the Canon as such; but from the start they relate to
the already existing Old Testament and to the testimony concerning
Christ and his words and works; and they thus both demand and stimulate the 'canonical' consolidation and defence of the new tradition
and of the ancient scripture, until we finally arrive at the incorporation
of these elements in the bipartite Bible. In this process even casual
remarks may be extremely instructive and of fundamental importance.
In fact, however, it is not even true to say, as Zahn believed, that we
are never dealing with any but incidental and 'fairly indefinite ideas and
terms'. Paul's statements about the old Scriptures, and the use which he
makes of them, are of great importance on matters of principle; and
what Justin and Irenaeus, Tertullian and Origen also have to say from
time to time about their canon is definitely based on 'serious dogmatic
thinking'. The concept of what constitutes dogmatic thought should
not be restricted by formalistic criteria; it needs to be understood in
terms of essential character and content.

In the present work I have deliberately concentrated on the history
of the concept of Scripture and of the Canon. From this the questions
of the significance and effect of the contents of Scripture, of the history
of exegesis and of hermeneutics cannot indeed be rigorously separated,
and in certain passages it will be necessary to discuss them or at least to
touch upon them; but they do not constitute the objective or the real
subject-matter of my presentation. On the other hand, I have not
taken the concept of the canonical in too narrow a sense. It has to
correspond to the actual history of the Canon. It is purely arbitrary to
make liturgical use, or formal definition, or the concept of inspiration,
or, worse still, official ecclesiastical confirmation the only criterion,
according to one's taste, of what is canonical. The fundamental idea—in
keeping with the meaning of the word—is the status of a standard or
norm which some writing or collection of writings has acquired for
faith and life. Its binding character must be universally and definitively
recognised. As a result of this the demarcation of the canonical from
non-canonical material in the course of time follows to some extent
automatically; and because the Canon testifies to the divine revelation,
and because its authority is of divine, not human origin, further reflection attributes it almost at once to a special, direct intervention or
inspiration of God. The final regulations concerning the contents and
arrangement of the Canon have to be enacted by ecclesiastical authority.

But this, the last stage in the formation of the Canon, lies outside the period with which I shall be concerned.

The book is arranged as follows: the first three chapters describe the relation of the Church to the traditional Old Testament, and the struggles for its recognition; the next three deal with the emergence of the New Testament; and the last chapter is devoted to the earliest theological interpretations of the new bipartite Bible, which was established by the beginning of the third century. I have endeavoured to cite the relevant historical literature pretty completely. On the other hand I have declined to enter into debate with the more recent work in systematic theology on the subject of the Canon, though not quite without misgivings. This would have quite intolerably enlarged the scope of the book. Nevertheless, I have summed up the essential conclusions in a Postscript in such a way that the significance of the historical study for matters of principle will be made clear to the reader who is interested in this latter aspect, though he will not be saved the trouble of reading the whole work. Possibly the results of my investigation may in this way command assent even among those who would prefer to evade their theological implications. It was not my ambition to write a sensational work; but neither did I write it from the *inane studium supervacua discendi*.

The relevant material has occupied me for many years. It is impossible for me to thank all those who have helped the work forward with their advice and co-operation—beginning with those colleagues in my Faculty who did me the kindness to listen to this or that chapter, when it was far enough advanced, and to give me the benefit of their queries and suggestions. The patience of my secretary, Frau Anna Maria Traumann, has been inexhaustible; and in the final stages the heaviest burden fell on my generous Assistant Professor, Dr Gerhard May, who checked the innumerable references with a critical eye, prepared the Indexes, and also on many occasions shared with me the strain of proofreading, for which my eyesight is no longer adequate. During my work on the history of the Canon I have often, to my great advantage, taken advice of that sage of the Apocrypha, Ben Sira: 'If thou seest a man of understanding, get thee betimes unto him' (Ecclus 6,36). I am now ready to learn the further truth of the canonical saying, that it is better to hear the rebuke of the wise than the praise of fools (Eccles. 7,5).

Heidelberg,   H. VON CAMPENHAUSEN
31 October 1967.

ABBREVIATIONS

ACW	Ancient Christian Writers
AnalBoll	Analecta Bollandiana
BJRL	Bulletin of the John Rylands Library
BZ	Byzantinische Zeitschrift
CQR	Church Quarterly Review
CSCO	Corpus Scriptorum Christianorum Orientalium
DACL	Dictionnaire d'Archéologie chrétienne et de Liturgie
DTC	Dictionnaire de Théologie Catholique
EvTh	Evangelische Theologie
GCS	Die griechischen christlichen Schriftsteller
HNT	Handbuch zum Neuen Testament
HTR	Harvard Theological Review
HZ	Historische Zeitschrift
JBL	Journal of Biblical Literature
JEH	Journal of Ecclesiastical History
JRel	Journal of Religion
JTS	Journal of Theological Studies
LCC	Library of Christian Classics
MelScRel	Mélanges de Science religieuse
N.F.	Neue Folge
NovTest	Novum Testamentum
N.S.	New Series
N.T.	New Testament
N.T. Apocrypha	New Testament Apocrypha, (ed.) E. Hennecke and W. Schneemelcher: E.T., R. McL. Wilson *et al.*, 2 vols, 1963–
NTS	*New Testament Studies*
O.T.	Old Testament
RAC	Reallexikon für Antike und Christentum
RB	Revue biblique
RevBen	Revue Bénédictine
RevSR	Revue des Sciences religieuses
RGG	Religion in Geschichte und Gegenwart
RHPR	Revue d'Histoire et de Philosophie religieuses
RHR	Revue de l'Histoire des Religions
RivAC	Rivista di Archeologia Cristiana
RivBibl	Rivista biblica
RSR	Recherches de Science religieuse
RTAM	Recherches de Théologie ancienne et médiévale
SJT	Scottish Journal of Theology
StudEvang	Studia Evangelica
StudPatr	Studia Patristica

StudTheol	Studia Theologica
ThBl	Theologische Blätter
TheolStud	Theologische Studien
ThStKr	Theologische Studien und Kritiken
TLZ	Theologische Literaturzeitung
TR	Theologische Rundschau
TU	Texte und Untersuchungen
TWNT	Theologisches Wörterbuch zum Neuen Testament
TZ	Theologische Zeitschrift
VC	Vigiliae Christianae
ZAW	Zeitschrift für die alttestamentliche Wissenschaft
ZKG	Zeitschrift für Kirchengeschichte
ZNW	Zeitschrift für die neutestamentliche Wissenschaft
ZTK	Zeitschrift für Theologie und Kirche

CHAPTER ONE

Jesus and the Law in the Gospel Tradition

THE CHRISTIAN Bible is not a completely new formation. Through its 'Old Testament' it is linked with Judaism, whose 'Scriptures' Christianity took over at the very moment of its emergence, and has retained ever since. This was something which happened long before it was possible to speak of a 'New Testament'. Consequently the first chapters of the present work will have to deal with the question of the adoption and status of the Old Testament Canon within the Church.

For Christianity the Old Testament is no longer a canonical book in the same sense as it once was for the Jews. In the synagogue the Torah and the 'Scriptures' had been the absolute authority, the exhaustive revelation, which God had given to his people. In the Church Christ himself accompanies and takes precedence over the ancient book. Christianity is no longer a 'religion of a book', in the strict sense of that phrase, since Christians believe in the lordship of the living Christ and in the present reality of the Spirit. Hence even the authority of the Old Testament has to be experienced and understood in a new and different way. This new perspective was given simultaneously with the birth of the Church—in the experience of the Resurrection and in the affirmation of the death of Jesus as a saving event 'in accordance with the Scriptures'. From now on the ancient Scriptures are related to Christ, and it is on the basis of Scripture that Jesus Christ is understood as Lord.

What does this imply for the understanding of the Old Testament Canon and for its authority? This is an enormous question. It was only gradually that its full import became apparent to the Church. The answers propounded were many and various, nor was any definitive solution ever reached, though in the process of seeking one the whole of theological thought was drawn into the debate. The present work will be limited to tracing developments only so far as they impinge upon the concept of the Canon itself, define that concept theologically, and lead to directly identifiable results. Nevertheless, the fact is that the problem with which we are concerned did not arise for the first time with faith in Christ. It began with the historical activity of Jesus himself, if indeed he was more than just another scribe or prophet. The authority mani-

fested in his words and actions is a new kind of authority, which made
it inevitable that the whole problem of the Canon should be taken up
and seen in a fresh light. It is with Jesus, therefore, that we shall begin
—with him and with the earliest portrayals of him and ongoing thoughts
about him in which the image of his person was preserved for posterity
and through which it continues to influence the life of Man.

Jesus must be seen against the background of the *Judaism* of his time.
It is, however, virtually impossible to define with precision the concept
of Scripture held in his environment. The reasons for the difficulty are
threefold: the relevant sources are extremely sparse; the views on the
subject held by the various parties within Judaism at the time were still
widely divergent; and the Old Testament Canon itself had not yet been
closed, but was, in part at any rate, still fluid. Nevertheless, what was
settled was the idea of a normative collection of sacred writings, the
concept of a 'canon' as such. It had already been in existence for a long
time, and nowhere met with resistance.[1] It is already clearly attested in
the second century B.C. Thus, the Greek Prologue to Ecclesiasticus
(c. 130 B.C.) speaks of the noble inheritance which Israel has been given
in 'the Law and the Prophets and the other writings'.[2] Similarly, Philo
of Alexandria (ob. A.D. 49–50) mentions 'the Laws, and the words
foretold by the prophets, and hymns and the other writings, by which
knowledge and piety are multiplied and perfected'.[3] It was still some
time before the limits of the last group, the 'writings', was finally
determined; but there is no doubt about the principal section of this
canon—the *Tora* or 'Law', as the Pentateuch was now regularly termed.
It was on this foundation that the total structure of the Canon was
built. The canon of the Samaritans, who separated from the Jews c.
300 B.C., consisted solely of the five books of Moses; and the Sadducees
(in opposition to the Pharisees) were right to the last prepared to allow
unqualified validity to this portion of Scripture alone. It is probable
that by about 200 B.C. the collection of the Major and Minor Prophets
had already been added to the Law. It appears that the prophets were
primarily understood as tradents and interpreters of the Tora, and that
canonical respect was accorded to their writings on this basis.[4] According to the well-known saying of one of the later Rabbis, if Israel had

[1] On what follows cf. O. Eissfeldt, *Introduction to the O.T.*, 1967, pp. 562ff.;
R. Meyer, 'Kanonisch und apokryph im Judentum', *TWNT* III, 1938, pp.
979ff.; A. Jepsen, 'Sammlung und Kanonisierung des Alten Testaments',
*RGG*³ I, 1957, pp. 1123ff.; 'Zur Kanongeschichte des Alten Testaments',
ZAW 71, 1959, pp. 114–136; A. C. Sundberg, *The Old Testament of the Early
Church*, 1964; R. Mayer, *Einleitung in das Alte Testament* I, 1965, pp. 15–25.
[2] BS prol. 1; cf. in the text of the book itself, which is, of course, earlier, chh.
44ff.
[3] *De vita contempl.* 25,
[4] Cf. O. Plöger, *Theocracy and Eschatology*, 1968, p. 45.

not sinned, she would have been given no Scripture save the Tora and the Book of Joshua (the latter on account of the directions for the allocation of the Promised Land).[5] In the messianic age, when sin has been done away, the Prophets and the Writings will consequently lose their validity, and only the Tora 'will not cease'.[6]

These data and statements already indicate where we are to look for the principal concern behind the question of the Canon: it is a concern with the 'Law' and with the exposition of the legal prescriptions regulating Jewish life. Hence the term Tora is not always strictly confined to the Pentateuch, but frequently denotes the whole of Scripture (including, indeed, even the rabbinic tradition). When set against the original content of the texts, such a designation undoubtedly betokens a degree of narrowness and distortion. The material of the five books of Moses is by no means restricted to legal regulations. One of its main constituents is history—the story of the election of Israel, the covenant making, the promises and mighty acts of God in the conquest of the land. This salvation-history was continued in the various instances of God's governance and judgment which his people experienced; and the prophets were the messengers of the divine will in the contemporary situation. At one time Israel lived by virtue of her historical vocation, and understood and maintained her own identity by means of this historical credo.[7] Now, however, the raging torrent of the past is seen as dried up and 'brought to a standstill'.[8] The history of Israel becomes a 'collection of historical examples for human behaviour in the face of the Law and its implications'.[9] There is no vital inner renewal, the community produces no more prophets;[10] and though the sacred book which tells her story does, it is true, foretell an eschatological messianic age still to come one day, yet its hold on the life of the devout here and now is exercised almost entirely through the demands of the definitive Law.

This idea of the 'Law and the Prophets' is confirmed by the New Testament polemic against the 'Pharisees and scribes',[11] and became

---

[5] Rabbi Ad(d)a bar Chanina (4th cent. A.D.), Ned. 22b: cf. [Strack]-Billerbeck, IV, 1, 1956[2], p. 435.

[6] Rabbi Johanan (3rd cent. A.D.), Meg. 1, 70d, 51: cf. [Strack]-Billerbeck IV, 1, p. 435.

[7] Cf. G. von Rad, Old Testament Theology I, 1962, pp. 121ff.

[8] R. Bultmann, Primitive Christianity, 1956, p. 70.

[9] M. Noth, 'Die Gesetze im Pentateuch', Gesammelte Studien zum Alten Testament[3], 1966, p. 115.

[10] The characteristic assertion of the Syriac Apocalypse of Baruch 85.3, that 'the prophets have been laid to rest', is, however, to be understood as a dogmatic proposition, and does not do justice to the whole truth of the contemporary situation: cf. Sundberg, op. cit., pp. 114ff.

[11] And also by corresponding positive references: Matt. 5:17; 7:12; 11:13; 22:40; cf. Lk. 16:29, 31. The 'normative aspect' in the concept of revelation is

B

decisive for the concept of the Jewish canon as ultimately determined.[12] But it by no means exhausts the possibilities for understanding and expounding Scripture which were live options in the time of Jesus. The picture was much more complex and more fluid, and we can still discern some theological groups at least which had their own distinctive approach.

The canon of Alexandrian–Hellenistic Judaism probably differed in no essential point from that of the Jews of Palestine.[13] Here too the Torah formed the centrepiece of Scripture;[14] but under the influence of the environment the attempt was made with the help of allegorical interpretations to construct a speculative exegesis and to extract from it every brand of philosophic wisdom of a moral and dogmatic kind.[15] A universal interpretation of the Law, comprising all 'truth', is also found among the Qumran sect,[16] though here there is not the slightest trace of Greek philosophy. The main object, however, for which they searched the Scriptures—displaying a devotion not merely to the Law

thus constantly 'in the foreground', and must not be underplayed, as W. Trilling, *op. cit.* (n. 49 below), tends to do.

[12] G. Östborn, *Cult and Canon. A Study in the Canonisation of the Old Testament*, Uppsala-Leipzig, 1950, prefers to think in terms of cultic motives: the actualisation of 'Jahwe's activity' in worship exercised decisive influence on the development of the canon. I cannot discover, however, that such an interpretation, which springs from the presuppositions of the Uppsala school, and which quite unjustifiably claims the support of G. von Rad, has any basis in the sources relevant to our period.

[13] The opposite, traditional assumption that Alexandria did have a so-called 'canon' of its own has been strongly controverted by A. Sundberg, 'The Old Testament of the Early Church—A Study in Canon', *HTR* 51, 1955, pp. 205–226, and in the work mentioned in n. 1 above.

[14] This is true even of Philo, in whose writings 'passages from the non-Pentateuchal books are never given an exegesis of their own in the true sense of the word, but are simply adduced in the course of expounding sections of the Torah' (N. Walter, *Der Thoraausleger Aristobulos*, 1964, p. 31 n. 1.

[15] Cf. Walter, *op. cit.*, pp. 129ff. It is possible to enlarge the rather limited relevant source material to a certain extent, if we are allowed to draw conclusions from Christian literature—though these are not always very compelling ones. In particular we can examine both Paul and his Jewish opponents for indications of earlier presuppositions behind their concept of Scripture: cf., e.g., D. Georgi, *Die Gegner des Paulus im 2. Korintherbrief*, 1964, pp. 265ff.: 'Das Alte Testament als Archiv des Geistes', and the essay by the same author in Eckert-Levinson-Stöhr, *Antijudaismus im N.T.?* 1967, pp. 82–94; also K. Baltzer, *Das Bundesformular*, 1964², pp. 128ff.

[16] This statement is based on O. Betz, *Offenbarung und Schriftforschung in der Qumransekte*, 1960; J. A. Fitzmyer, 'The Use of explicit Old Testament quotations in Qumran literature and in the N.T.', *NTS* 7, 1960/1, pp. 297–333; W. Foerster, 'Der Heilige Geist im Spätjudentum', *NTS* 8, 1961/2, pp. 117–134; H. Braun, *Qumran und das Neue Testament* II, 1966, pp. 301–325.

but also to the Prophets—apart from their peculiar regulations concerning conduct and purity, was eschatological predictions; and they interpreted the ancient texts as referring directly to the fortunes and experiences of their own community. Scripture afforded references to the 'Teacher of Righteousness', to the events of the most recent past, and to the messianic future. What enabled the theologians of Qumran thus to unravel the Scripture was the 'Spirit of God'. All this is reminiscent of the typological-prophetic use of the Old Testament in the Christian Church. The difference, however, is that in Qumran revelation derives exclusively from the exposition of the ancient Scriptures as such, and knows no living source of the knowledge of God to place alongside them. Even the Teacher of Righteousness becomes Master and Prophet only in virtue of his scriptural learning. A third, widespread element in the religious background of the time of Jesus is that of apocalyptic.[17] Its writings and ideas influenced Christianity from the very moment of its birth. Here, however, in contrast to Qumran and even more to the later institution of the Christian Church, there was a complete lack of a definite historical starting-point which could provide the basis for a new, concrete authority. The trend to apocalyptic did nothing to further the development of the canon. The apocalyptists normally hide behind age-old biblical names, and by using this means to secure greater respect for their numerous productions rather diminish than increase the importance of the earlier, canonical writings. The formation of a clearly defined canon was thus held back, or at most stimulated in a negative way as a result of hostility to these 'apocrypha'. For it is well known that the Rabbinic councils of Jerusalem (c. A.D. 65) and Jabne (i.e., Jamnia, c. A.D. 90) which finally closed the Jewish canon were wholly dominated by the spirit of strict Pharisaic–Rabbinic orthodoxy. The Jewish canon was limited to the ancient writings of the distant classical period, and thus the Old Testament as we know it today came into being, in opposition to every kind of sectarianism, to hellenism, to apocalypticism, and last but not least to the newest and most dangerous heresy, the church which proclaimed Christ as Lord.

The activity of Jesus antedated this period by two generations. The tradition of his teachings does not enable us to define his attitude to the ancient Scriptures in detail. But three points of some importance can, it seems to me, be established. It must suffice here to list them briefly as a starting-point for our investigations without entering into a discussion of the question of the historical 'genuineness' of individual sayings, a problem which is not of decisive importance in the present

[17] The origins and setting of apocalyptic still present many problems. For a general survey cf. P. Vielhauer in *N.T. Apocrypha* II, pp. 582ff.; G. von Rad, *O.T. Theology* II, 1965, pp. 301ff.; D. S. Russell, *The Method and Message of Jewish Apocalyptic*, 1964.

context.[18] First of all, *Jesus* acknowledged, as any pious Jew of his time
inevitably did, 'the Law and the Prophets' as a witness to the will of
God. Hence there were times when he will have appealed to 'Scripture',
though not in the one-sided way and with the anxiety-ridden concern
over particular texts which was characteristic of legalistic Judaism.
'Jesus is familiar with the will of God in a way that has not been
mediated through the Torah',[19] and for that reason he does not speak
like a Pharisaic rabbi or a Qumran scribe but simply as an expositor of
Scripture, and that in an independent, direct, and non-derivative
manner.[20] This is the second decisive trait which puts him in a class
apart; and it is wholly consonant with the distinctive character of his
preaching. It is true that Jesus never weakened the seriousness of God's
demand, but rather intensified it; but his call to men to be converted
in view of the coming kingdom of God and his judgment was primarily
concerned with the liberating possibility of a new beginning, and
brought with it the divine 'forgiveness'. The 'Gospel' takes precedence
over the Law, and establishes a saving immediacy of access to God
which the Law and its interpreters could never bring about. Hence
at the same time the message is inseparable from the mystery of
the 'authority' and the person of Jesus. This is the third fundamental
datum. At first this mystery remains unresolved. Jesus justifies himself neither by a direct statement about himself nor by appealing to an
official status or to a particular role which he has to play in the eschatological event. Only after the resurrection does faith in Christ decisively
break through this barrier. Consequently, it is only then that the question of Jesus' relation to the predictions of the prophets and to the
authority of the old Law is posed inescapably, and demands an answer.
But in a very short time both these things—the question and the
answer—are retrojected into the earthly life of Jesus, and then, in
conjunction with the primitive corpus of sayings and traditions, are
expanded, extended, and transformed until the whole forms a complex
but indissoluble unity.

The earliest source of which we can ask our questions is the *Logia-
source* common to Matthew and Luke, and known as 'Q'.[21] Its contents

[18] What follows is based on the presentation adopted in the first chapter
of my book, *Ecclesiastical Authority and Spiritual Power*, 1968, entitled 'The
Authority of Jesus'.
[19] E. Käsemann, 'Zum Thema der urchristlichen Apokalyptik', *Exegetische
Versuche und Besinnungen* II, 1964, pp. 105–131.
[20] It was a feeling for this fact about Jesus which 'restrained even the later
period, which was so fertile in creating legends, from anywhere attributing to
Jesus a command to his disciples to compose a Gospel or any other kind of
written teaching' (A. Jülicher and E. Fascher, *Einleitung in das Neue Testament*[7],
1931, p. 453).
[21] The material is conveniently collated in A. Harnack, *The Sayings of Jesus*,
1907; cf. also T. W. Manson, *The Sayings of Jesus*, 1919.

stem in the main from the sphere of the primitive Palestinian community. Here the problem of Jesus' authority *vis-à-vis* the ancient
Scriptures and the Law seems as such to be as yet almost unnoticed.
But from the very first there is no doubt of the unqualified lordship of
Jesus and of the binding force of his words. It is utterly clear that with
his advent a new and final epoch has begun. Profession of belief in him
and in his words is decisive for salvation;[22] for Jesus, the Son of Man, is
something greater than Jonah and Solomon.[23] Yet no scriptural proof,
properly so called, is provided for this statement; demonstration of this
kind is adduced only for John, who prepares the way for Jesus,[24] and
whom 'the Law and the Prophets' had prophesied as the last of the line.[25]
This is remarkable, since there can be no doubt that the assertion that
the crucifixion and resurrection of Jesus were in accordance with the
Scriptures is extremely old;[26] but these events have not yet been treated
in the Logia source. This source is essentially concerned with conveying
sayings material, which has little need of justification of this kind.
Nevertheless, the opposition of Jesus to the legalistic piety of the
Scribes is clear throughout. Their attitude is seen as the extreme
perversion of that true obedience which God requires.[27] This condemnation, however, is nowhere directed against the Law itself, not even,
indeed, against the pettifogging 'traditions' of the Scribes as such.[28] In
the Temptation narrative Jesus three times appeals emphatically to the
sacred Scripture.[29] Its validity is taken for granted; manifestly there is
as yet no critical consideration of its authority.

When we pass from Q to Mark, the picture changes completely. Not
only is Mark writing his Gospel at a later date, he is writing in a Gentile
Christian spirit for Gentile Christians, to whom the presuppositions of
Judaism are no longer automatically comprehensible. At the heart of
all stands a hellenistic christology: Jesus, Son of David and Son of
Man, is the Son of God who gives his life as a sacrifice for the redemption of mankind;[30] he is the Lord who coerces the demons, and who
proclaims a 'new teaching with authority'.[31] But this Jesus Christ is
also the one unambiguously prophesied by Scripture, as is proved by

[22] Matt. 7:13f., 21, 24–27 and parr.; 10:32f. and parr., 37, 39 and parr.
[23] Matt. 12:41 = Lk. 11:31f.   [24] Matt. 3:3 = Lk. 3:4–6.
[25] Matt. 11:12f. = Lk. 16:16. It is, however, as is well known, extremely
difficult to arrive at an assured exegesis of this saying.
[26] I Cor. 15:3f.; cf. pp. 106f. below. There is no need to discuss here how far
this is a matter of a *fully worked out* proof from Scripture on the prediction and
fulfilment model or how far it merely 'postulates' an O.T. connection. Cf. the
mutually conflicting treatments by J. Jeremias, *TWNT* V, 1954, pp. 703ff.,
and A. Suhl, *Die Funktion der alttestamentlichen Zitate und Anspielungen im
Markusevangelium*, 1965, pp. 37ff., 123ff.
[27] Lk. 11:39–52 and parr.   [28] Matt. 23:23 = Lk. 11:42.
[29] Matt. 4:4, 7, 10 = Lk. 4:4, 8, 12.   [30] Mk 10:45.
[31] Mk 1:27.

repeated, programmatic quotations and references.[32] The conflict with the religious leaders of contemporary Judaism has now intensified, and appears in a new group of sayings, the conflict dialogues between Jesus and the Scribes. Here the mischievous nonsense of their ceremonial laws, their sabbath practice, and their purity, regulations is sharply condemned.[33] There is no longer any question of tolerating these ancient ordinances and 'traditions'. It must be asked whether this polemic does not inevitably touch the Law itself, to which the Scribes so often appeal, and thus in turn the Scriptures in which this Law is transmitted. Nevertheless, it is clear that Mark is not prepared to go that far. Certainly it is no accident that he avoids using the actual term, 'Law', to refer to this ancient material which for his churches is now obsolete. On the other hand, however, he represents Jesus as going back in his disputes with his opponents, who 'do not know the scriptures',[34] to these very texts—and not merely to the 'Prophets', but directly to 'Moses', who rightly taught the commandment of God. But the scribal exegetes have perverted the true sense of the Scripture with their additions.[35]

On one occasion only does Jesus appear to dissociate himself directly from a regulation of the Mosaic Law: he rejects, explicitly and categorically, the right of a man to divorce his wife. This ordinance, it would seem, does not correspond to the primal will of God, who created man and woman for permanent, absolutely indissoluble partnership;[36] but Moses, in view of the people's 'hardness of heart', required the attestation of the divorce by a writ, confirmed by witnesses. The passage, however, ought probably not to be taken to mean that in making this regulation Moses was allowing divorce against the express command of God. The writ of divorce is here thought of simply as a punitive compromise to deal with a culpable action by 'bringing it out of secrecy and anonymity, and establishing it before God and the world'.[37] Most exegetes, of course, take these words in the sense of a

---

[32] Mk 1:2f.; 7:6f.; 12:10f., 36f.; 14:27 (15:24, 34, 36). Mark is already making use of the 'prediction and fulfilment pattern', but he has not yet, generally speaking, organised it into a formal proof: cf. Suhl. op. cit., pp. 43f.

[33] Mk 2:1ff., 23ff.; 3:1ff.; 7:1ff.; 10:1ff.; cf. 11:17.

[34] Mk 12:24.   [35] Mk 7:5–13; cf. 11:17.   [36] Mk 10:2–12.

[37] So, in agreement with K. H. Rengstorf, and in my view convincingly, H. Greeven, 'Zu den Aussagen des Neuen Testaments über die Ehe' (ZEE I, 1957, pp. 109–125) pp. 114f. On this view, the phrase πρὸς τὴν σκληροκαρδίαν ὑμῶν (Mk 10:5) is equivalent to εἰς μαρτύριον ὑμῖν τῆς σκληροκαρδίας (cf. Mk 1:44; 6:11). Unfortunately Matthew took Moses' injunction as a concession, because of his own more legalistic and casuistic understanding of the prohibition of divorce, and consequently referred to the command to draw up a writ of divorce in terms of 'permission' (ἐπέτρεψεν), whereas Mark puts the matter the other way round. (The points to note in the text are these: in Mark Jesus refers to Moses' regulation in terms of 'command' (10:3, 5), while the

'concession', which for Jesus' disciples is no longer to apply in practice; 'but even then they can hardly be understood as a reproach against Moses. In fact the early tradition, found also in Q, of Jesus' prohibition of divorce, and the fact that the practice of the early Church was in conformity with this, meant that this passage had to contain a rejection of the hitherto obtaining rule; and Matthew, despite his even more decisive affirmation of the Law, drew this consequence equally, indeed more emphatically.[38] The saying should not, however, be understood for this reason as a deliberate critique of the Law, nor used as a hermeneutical starting-point for assessing Mark's attitude to Law and Scripture in general.[39] Later, to be sure, the passage was to play a large part in gnostic criticism of the Old Testament;[40] but Mark, while certainly an anti-Judaist, was equally certainly no Gnostic.[41]

If we are looking for a ruling in principle on the question of the Law, then we will do better to consider a different text from the Gospel: Jesus' dispute over the rubbing of the ears of corn on the Sabbath.[42] Here, indeed, we are not offered a more, or less radical answer to the problem, but rather a succession of different arguments, competing with and yet complementing one another.[43] Jesus first counters the charge against his disciples by appealing to David's similar behaviour, when he consumed the priestly shewbread. Scripture itself, therefore—in this case a text from the 'former Prophets'—does not back up the legalistic formalism of the Pharisees. To this is linked a second pro-

---

Jews use the language of 'permission' (10:4); in Matthew Jesus speaks of Moses' ruling as 'permission' (19:8), while the Jews see it as a command (19:7)—Tr.).

[38] Matt. 5:31f.

[39] Mark is not, as many expositors think, here deliberately setting one passage of Scripture against another: cf. Suhl, *op. cit.*, p. 74.

[40] Cf. p. 83 below.‎"

[41] On this point I find myself in emphatic disagreement with the views of S. Schulz, 'Markus und das Alte Testament', *ZTK* 58, 1961, pp. 184–197. It is true that Schulz, no more than myself, wishes to stigmatise Mark as a Gnostic; but he does think that Mark, as Jewish and Christian 'Gnostics' were later to do, adopted a 'critical selection, a residuum of particular divine commands and sayings within the Old Testament, a canon within the Jewish O.T. canon of Scripture' (p. 193), and regarded 'the commandments and prohibitions of the Law' as 'human enactments, or Mosaic concessions', 'theologically indifferent' for Christians, or even, on occasion, to be actively rejected (p. 195). The words of Mark himself afford no grounds for thinking that he was here enunciating a principle of such a universal and radical sort.

[42] Mk 2:23–28.

[43] In Mk 2:25ff. we have a consciously arranged presentation of arguments which are put forward in a different but comparable way in Matt. 12:5–7: cf. R. Bultmann, *History of the Synoptic Tradition*, 1967, pp. 16*ff.; and F. W. Beare, 'The Sabbath was made for Man,' *JBL* 79, 1960, pp. 130–136; also Suhl, *op. cit.*, pp. 82–87.

nouncement, carrying conviction simply by virtue of what it says, and again referring to the primal will of God: the Sabbath was made for Man, not Man for the Sabbath. Elsewhere Jesus repeatedly makes similar direct appeal to men's capacity to judge for themselves, and to arrive at the right answer: 'Is it lawful on the sabbath to do good or to do harm, to save life or to kill?'[44] Here it is men's ordinary, straight-forward moral sense which is competent to judge the issue, and which gives its verdict for helpful action. But even now there is more to be said. The passage closes with an appeal to the authority of the 'Son of Man', that is, of Jesus himself. He is the final, supreme authority, and 'Lord even of the sabbath'. The disciples who follow Jesus know what they have to do to obey the will of God;[45] they do not sew new-woven material on to old garments,[46] that is to say, they refuse to be forced back into obsolete Jewish legalism. The sequence of these steps in the argument could indeed be reversed. We could say, that under the guidance of Jesus his Church had rejected all Pharisaic scrupulosity and all holy-seeming but purely external behaviour, and had found the way to true freedom. She was now in a position to grasp directly the primal will of God for Man, and to fulfil it without restriction. And she knows that the meaning and real intention of the ancient biblical revelation, so far from being overthrown by this, in fact corresponds to it.

Nevertheless, in defining the interrelation of the individual sayings in this way we have already gone beyond what Mark directly states, and may have overestimated the degree of conscious reflection in the arrangement of his ideas. Hellenistic Christians were in general quite unworried in dealing with the problem of the Law;[47] for them it was no longer a living issue. Only where Judaistic Christianity clashed with the Gentile church was the problem still real. It is in some such environ-ment, for example, the borderland between Palestine and Syria, that we are to look for the provenance of the Gospel of *Matthew*. Here the question, what significance the old Law, valid for the Fathers, was to have alongside the authority of the Lord, is once more given an answer, and this time a final and profound one, fully conscious of the importance

---

[44] Mk 3:4, in the story of the man with a withered hand, which follows imme-diately on the passage under discussion. Matthew, in his corresponding account (Matt. 12:11f.), refers to the everyday experience of pulling a sheep out of a pit into which it has fallen, even when this occurs on the Sabbath, and al-though a sheep is far inferior to a human being: cf. Lk. 13:15; 14:5.

[45] I see no reason to regard the christological argument as 'a manifest narrow-ing and weakening of the previous one', since the Christian community 'might well allow their Lord, but not anyone, the liberty which he took' (E. Käsemann, 'Das Problem des historischen Jesus', *Exegetische Versuche und Besinnungen* I, 1964³, p. 207).

[46] Mk 2:21.   [47] Cf. p. 23 below.

of the decision involved, within the framework of a 'Gospel', and making use of Jesus' words as preserved in the tradition. Matthew refuses to be subservient to any ecclesiastical school of thought, and champions neither Jewish nor Gentile Christian interests simply as such. His purpose is, in opposition to false guides, known to him personally, who seek to relax the stringency of the commandment,[48] to hold fast to that which Jesus in fact taught, and by conscientious reflection to work out the true spiritual relationship which even now still obtains between the freedom of discipleship and the old order of the biblical Law.[49]

Matthew emphasises more strongly than anyone before him the inner coherence which links Jesus to the ancient salvation-history. All the prophets, indeed the whole of sacred Scripture, point to him. The proofs from prophecy which he adduces presuppose fairly long and methodical study on these lines. The whole life of Jesus, from the proclamation of his birth to his death on the cross, proves to be a fulfilment of ancient prophecy. In the counsel of God everything comes to pass as it does, point by point, 'in order that' the old oracles may be fulfilled. The whole Gospel is studded with these quotations, with their characteristic introductory formulas, which bear witness to Jesus.[50] Jesus himself, as the Lord who demands and promises, stands

---

[48] Matt. 5:17ff.; 7:15ff.; 24:11ff. The question of the validity of the Law arises spontaneously as a result of the confrontation with Judaism and of scholastic discussion within Christianity itself. It is, in my view, hardly possible to define the 'heretics' against whom Matthew is fighting any more precisely, and, for example, following Bultmann, *Theology of the New Testament* I, 1952, p. 54, to connect Matt. 5:19 with Paul, or, as Schoeps, *Theologie und Geschichte des Judenchristentums*, 1949, p. 120 n. 1, 127 n. 1 *et al.*, does, to see Matt. 13:25 as referring to the same apostle. In a discussion angled directly at Gentile Christians who were free of the Law, such passages would be virtually meaningless: J. Munck, *Paulus and die Heilsgeschichte*, Aarhus, 1954, p. 249. Be that as it may, the 'antinomians' or 'libertines' whom Matthew must have had in mind are not yet characterised as gnostics: cf. G. Barth, *op. cit.* n. 49 below, p. 149; R. Hummel, *op. cit.* n. 49 below, pp. 64ff.

[49] Of recent years the Gospel of Matthew has repeatedly been studied from precisely this point of view: cf. esp. G. Bornkamm, G. Barth, H. J. Held, *Tradition and Interpretation in Matthew*, 1968; R. Hummel, *Die Auseinandersetzung zwischen Kirche und Judentum im Matthäusevangelium*, 1963; W. Trilling, *Das wahre Israel—Studien zur Theologie des Matthäus*³, 1964, and *TLZ* 90, 1965, pp. 433–437 (discussing the views of Hummel). Also P. Nepper-Christensen, *Das Matthäusevangelium ein judenchristliches Evangelium?* Aarhus, 1958; and G. Strecker, *Der Weg der Gerechtigkeit*², 1962, neither of whom, however, can I follow when they dub Matthew a true hellenist.

[50] On this subject cf. R. V. G. Tasker, *The Old Testament in the New Testament*², London, 1954, pp. 41–48; K. Stendahl, *The School of St Matthew*, Uppsala, 1954, pp. 20ff.; *id.,Quis et unde?* An analysis of Mt. 1–2', *Judentum, Urchristentum, Kirche* (Festschrift für Joachim Jeremias), 1960, pp. 94–105; Strecker, *op. cit.,* pp. 49ff.; B. Lindars, *New Testament Apologetic. The Doctrinal Signi-*

before his own who believe on him,[51] learn from him,[52] and are guided
and directed by his command and example.[53] In this way the external,
limited righteousness, which the Pharisees both lived out themselves
and required of others, is radically overthrown and surpassed.[54] What
now becomes of the old Law? The answer to this question is complicated by the fact that on this very point Matthew has carefully collated
and combined various divergent traditions, and that therefore the
material which he provides is far from unitary. But Matthew has not
merely collected material; he has also arranged it in a significant way;
and he not infrequently adds new, programmatic statements which
illuminate and interpret the whole context. By starting from these
passages we can, in my view, establish his own position beyond reasonable doubt.[55]

All this applies pre-eminently to that great Matthaean composition,
the 'Sermon on the Mount'. The Sermon is the solemn proclamation of
God's ultimate command by Jesus himself. It offers the new law of life
to the poor, persecuted community of disciples to whom their master
shows the way which alone leads to blessedness, the way of following
him. To this extent the Sermon is the new Christian Torah, and it is no
accident that it is promulgated from a mountain, as the old Torah once
was from Sinai.[56] By the commands which Jesus proclaims the ancient
Torah is not merely surpassed, but superseded. That is why, in the
first part of the Sermon, we have the great series of antitheses which
sets the demands of the new and better 'righteousness'[57] in thoroughgoing and emphatic opposition[58] to what was 'said to the men of old.'[59]

---

ficance of the Old Testament Quotations, London, 1961, pp. 259–265; R. H. Gun-
dry, The Use of the Old Testament in St Matthew's Gospel, Leiden, 1967.

[51] Matt. 18:6; cf. 27:42; also G. Bornkamm, 'Enderwartung und Kirche im
Matthäus-Evangelium,' op. cit. n. 49 above, p. 25.

[52] Matt. 11:29.   [53] Matt. 23:8, 10.

[54] Matt. 5:20; cf. Strecker, op. cit., pp. 137ff.; 151f.

[55] In their new, more carefully thought out context even sayings derived
from Mark or Q acquire a greater and more radical significance.

[56] So B. W. Bacon, Studies in Matthew, New York, 1930; J. Jeremias, art.
Μωυσῆς, TWNT IV, 1942, p. 875; G. D. Kilpatrick, The Origins of the Gospel
according to St Matthew, Oxford, 1946, p. 118. To this extent the disputed
Moses–Christ typology (Schoeps, Theologie, pp. 87ff.) is undoubtedly correct.
On the other hand, Bacon's theory that the Gospel of Matthew, with its five-
part structure was as a whole intended as a counterpart to the Torah, seems to
me, as to Bornkamm 'Enderwartung', p. 32 n. 2, unconvincing.

[57] Matt. 5:20; 6:33: cf. Trilling, op. cit., pp. 183f.

[58] Matt. 5:21–48: cf. V. Hasler, 'Das Herzstück der Bergpredigt. Zum Verständnis der Antithesen in Mt. 5, 21–48', TZ 15, 1959, pp. 90–106. The anti-
thetic pattern may already have been traditional in some of the material, but has
manifestly been imposed for the first time by the Evangelist himself on the
antitheses which derive from Q (5:31ff., 38ff., 43ff.): E. Klostermann, Mat-

As Lord of his people Jesus thrusts aside the limited commands of the existing law with his mighty, 'But I say to you', in order to replace them root and branch with a new and extreme demand. Obedience, purity, and love, as he teaches them, tolerate neither dilution nor qualification. They must be practised completely or not at all; and by them alone will men be saved in the day of judgment.[60] There can be no doubt about it: in face of Jesus' superior authority the Law can no longer be invoked as a court of appeal.[61] At the same time it becomes clear that this new norm set up by Jesus is of its very nature something that can no longer be fully covered by rules and regulations, since it consists in the absolute surrender of the egoistic will. What Matthew has in view in the Sermon on the Mount is not a new nomism, but a new life in a new bond of fellowship which brings suffering and blessedness in one. For Matthew, 'perfection and fulfilling the commandments are aims that can be realised only in following Jesus'.[62]

Surprisingly, however, the fact that the Law is thus outstripped means not that it is abolished but precisely that it is reaffirmed.[63] Matthew has not made the slightest attempt to delete the conservative sayings, which assert the continued validity of the Law; on the contrary, he has retained them and given them solemn emphasis. Without the Torah there can be, in his view, 'no righteousness at all, and

---

*thäusevangelium*³, 1938, p. 42. This fact, together with the salient position which he gives to the whole series, shows what importance he attached to it.

[59] The concept of the 'men of old', taken in isolation, might have more than one meaning. In the context there can be no doubt that Jesus intends to direct his criticism not only against Later Judaism, but 'even against the Old Testament itself': J. Schniewind, *Das Evangelium nach Matthäus,*¹¹ 1964, p. 57.

[60] Matt. 7:24–27.

[61] This is the real claim implicit in the words, ἐγὼ δὲ λέγω ὑμῖν: W. G. Kümmel, 'Jesus und der jüdische Traditionsgedanke,' *Heilsgeschehen und Geschichte. Gesammelte Aufsätze 1933–1964,* 1965, pp. 31ff. Cf. E. Fuchs, 'Jesu Selbstzeugnis nach Matthäus 5', *Zur Frage nach dem historischen Jesus*², 1965, p. 114: 'That this [sc. the O.T. reference of the Gospel] is not a matter of stupidly exalting the Old Testament to dogmatic status may be seen clearly enough from the antitheses in particular'; also Trilling, *op. cit.,* pp. 207ff. I cannot concur with the statement of Bornkamm, 'Enderwartung', p. 32, that in Matthew the Law 'legitimates' Jesus' teaching and messianic ἐξουσία, and find no trace of such an idea in the text (on the exegesis of Matt. 12:8 cf. below). Even in Matthew Jesus is more than a mere 'exegete' of the Law. That Matthew, as Bornkamm stresses in opposition to Bacon and Kilpatrick, does not yet make use of the concept of the *nova lex* may have less to do with the continued existence of the old Law than with the point, brought out by Bornkamm himself (*op. cit.,* pp. 35ff.), that Jesus' lordship is personal and in no way 'legalistic' in character.

[62] Bornkamm, *op. cit.,* p. 26.

[63] So H. Braun, *Spätjüdisch-häretischer und frühchristlicher Radikalismus* II, 1957, p. 13 n. 4; p. 97 n. 2; cf. *TR* 28, 1962, pp. 110f., in opposition to the view of E. Percy, *Die Botschaft Jesu,* Lund, 1953, pp. 163–165.

certainly not one better than that of the Scribes and Pharisees'.[64] The
Law, down to the last flourish on the last letter, will remain in force
'so long as the earth endures';[65] and only the man who takes it seriously,
'teaches' it and 'does' it, in even its smallest details, shall 'be called
great' in the kingdom of heaven.[66] Indeed, even the rabbinic exegeses,
which Mark had already rejected,[67] come, on this way of looking at the
matter, closer to the Law, and thus catch something of its value. The
scribes and Pharisees sit 'on Moses' seat', and what they teach is good
in itself, and must be acted upon.[68] All that is wrong is their own
conduct, their 'hypocrisy', and their conceited urge to impress others
with their own importance, a trait which must never find its way into
the Christian community.[69] But concern for the Law as such is still
important,[70] and the man who intends to enter into life 'keeps the
commandments'.[71]

Nevertheless, Matthew passes on all Mark's narratives in which
Jesus breaks the prevailing sabbath and purity regulations, and he
explicitly defends this behaviour. It is clear, certainly, that in comparison
with his source he rather weakens the seriousness of the formal breach

[64] Hummel, *op. cit.*, p. 69.
[65] A. M. Honeyman, 'Matthew V, 18 and the Validity of the Law', *NTS* I,
1954, pp. 141f. E. Schweizer, 'Matth. 5, 17–20. Anmerkungen zum Gesetzesverständnis des Matthäus,' *Neotestamentica. Deutsche und englische Aufsätze
1951–1963,* 1963, pp. 399–406, takes 5:18 to mean rather that this goal has
already been reached since Jesus has brought both Law and Prophets to their
fulfilment by laying down the new commandment of love of neighbour. A similar view is taken by H. J. Schoeps, 'Jésus et la loi juive', *RHPR* 33, 1953, pp.
1–20.
[66] Matt. 5:18f. There is general agreement that these astonishingly reactionary
formulations cannot be the work of the Evangelist, but must derive from an
older tradition which wished to retain the Law in a strictly literalist sense. It
was only with difficulty that such statements could be made to accord with his
own view. The redactional 'caption' (Bultmann, *Synoptic Tradition*, p. 150)
in 5:20 is a move in the desired direction. For a detailed discussion cf. Trilling,
op. cit., pp. 167–186.
[67] Cf. p. 8 above.
[68] Matt. 23:2f. This passage is placed as a preamble to the succeeding denunciation of the Pharisees, as being the point of primary importance, By contrast,
however, Matt. 15:2–6 follows Mk 7:9–13 in retaining the appeal to the 'word
of God' against the 'tradition of the fathers'.
[69] Matt. 23:2–12; cf. 6:1.
[70] Matt. 13:52; 23:3. Trilling, *op. cit.*, p. 209, pertinently remarks concerning
the antitheses of the Sermon on the Mount: 'The heart of the matter is not the
proclamation of a new law in place of the old, but the indication to Jesus'
disciples of a goal of superabundant righteousness, a realisation of the Decalogue and of the great commandment which is new in the sense that is radical
and, by the same token, perfect.' In Matt. 13:52; 23:34, Christ, who is 'wisdom',
'sends' not only prophets and wise men but also scribes to Israel: cf. E. Haenchen, 'Matthäus 23', *Gott und Mensch. Gesammelte Aufsätze,* 1965, pp. 44f.
[71] Matt. 19:17.

of the law, and would like to exclude altogether any idea that the law might be abolished on principle;[72] but equally there is no suggestion in what he writes of a mechanical adherence to the letter of the law.[73] How are we to understand this apparent contradiction? Jesus himself, at various points in the Gospel, supplies the answer to this question. That good on which life depends must at all times be done without reserve or qualification.[74] On this point there can be absolutely no conflict as a result of the requirements of the Law. The man who lovelessly and arrogantly seeks to hide from the manifest will of God behind formal detailed regulations such as the sabbath commandment is acting directly contrary to the true meaning of the Law. This thought, which already appears in Mark's tradition,[75] Matthew has taken up and exalted into a principle. The ultimate meaning of the Law is not 'legalism'. It is true that in the particular formulation which is given to this idea in connection with the Q material even the least commandments are not overlooked; but the vital, 'weightier' matters, on the fulfilment of which everything depends, are the fundamental demands of justice, mercy, and faithfulness.[76] That one should do to one's fellow-man the good which one expects from him constitutes an absolutely precise description of what 'the Law and the Prophets' taught;[77] they 'hang' on the double commandment to love God and one's neighbour.[78] It is thus this commandment which controls the exegesis and application of the individual regulations, and not the other way round. Exegesis on this principle does not destroy the Law. On the contrary, if the Law is understood in accordance with its deepest meaning and with the mind of God and his Messiah, it genuinely affirms it and puts it into practice for the first time. This definitive,

[72] Cf. Bornkamm, *Enderwartung*, pp. 23f.

[73] Especially significant in both these respects is, once again, the story of the rubbing of the ears of corn, which Matthew has taken over (12:1ff.) from Mark with characteristic variations: cf. V. Hasler, *Gesetz und Evangelium in der alten Kirche bis Origenes*, Zurich, 1953, pp. 18f. First, in Matthew's version the situation in which the disciples rub the ears is, so to speak, a special emergency, because they are 'hungry' (12:1); and secondly, in Jesus' answer the fact that their behaviour is consonant with the O.T. is even more strongly emphasised by introducing a reference to sabbath-breaking by the very priests in the Temple (12:5). Furthermore, the idea that God himself intends a limitation to the sabbath commandment (Mk 2:27) is now presented as a quotation from Scripture (Matt. 12:7). On the other hand, the greatness of Jesus' authority is also underlined even more strongly: he is, as Messiah, greater even than the Temple (12:6). It is, of course, true that this makes Jesus superior only to the cultic order and not to the Law as such; but Matthew also maintains his sovereign Lordship over the sabbath (n.b. the γάρ in 12:8).

[74] Matt. 12:12.   [75] Mk 3:4f.   [76] Matt. 23:23 = Lk. 11:42.

[77] Matt. 7:12. Cf. also the double citation of Hos. 6:2 ('mercy and not sacrifice'): Matt. 9:13; 12:7.

[78] Matt. 22:40.

perfect understanding of the Law was taught by Jesus and adopted by Christians; and it was to make this point that Matthew coined the exaggerated formula, that Jesus had not come to destroy the Law but to fulfil it.[79]

This is a spiritual attitude, particularly suited to Matthew, which finds externalism or 'hypocrisy' in the acceptance of Jesus' message profoundly hateful. But it is an attitude which comes fully to life only when we see it against the background of the situation which we must assume to have obtained at the time and in the milieu from which his Gospel came. The congregations in which Matthew taught, and in which the traditions which he handed on were formed, were conditioned by Judaism, and had not as yet finally abandoned the connection with Judaism and its traditional religious associations.[80] These Christians were still struggling under attacks and calumnies against their sect and its law, and so they too set their 'understanding of the Torah consciously within the Jewish scribal tradition'. No one must be able to charge them with levity. They remain faithful to the Law, though in fact they understand the ancient requirement of 'righteousness' better than do the Pharisees and Scribes;[81] and, having been won for the kingdom of heaven by the Messiah, Jesus, they bring out of the treasures of the Scripture 'things new and old'.[82] In order to give offence to no man they are prepared to forgo privileges to which, as the liberated children of God, they are strictly entitled,[83] just as their Master too was humbly prepared to fulfil all the demands of righteousness.[84] His claim to supreme authority, however, they will never forgo. They know whose disciples they are, and they are determined to confess him in all circumstances.[85] No one shall dare to misinterpret the peace and the 'easy yoke',[86] the forgiveness of sins[87] and the new blessedness which he

---

[79] Matt. 5:17. The sentence opens the discussion in the Sermon on the Mount of the problem of the Law, and appears to be a Matthaean formation. There is no need to relate it one-sidedly to Jesus' conduct *or* to his teaching, for it is men's relationship to the Law as a whole and *as such* that is in mind. Thus far one can agree with the remarks of H. L. Ljungmanns, *Das Gesetz erfüllen*, Lund, 1954, and G. Delling, art. *TWNT* VI, 1959, pp. 292f. By contrast, the extended christological exegesis of the saying by the yardstick of the Messiah's own fulfilment of the Law is constructive over-interpretation. The comment of Trilling, *op. cit.*, p. 210, though somewhat too schematised, is to the point: 'The three essential aspects, under which the Matthaean view of "fulfilment" is to be understood, are the interpretation of the Torah by reference to the will of God, its concentration, and its perfecting.'

[80] On this point cf. esp. Hummel, *op. cit.*, pp. 28ff., 159–161.

[81] Matt. 5:20.   [82] Matt. 13:52.

[83] Matt. 17:26f.; cf. Hummel, *op. cit.*, pp. 103–106. The saying about fasting (Matt. 9:15 = Mk 2:20) ought, at least in Matthew, to be taken in the sense of an *ex post facto* justification for Christians of the Jewish custom of fasting. Matthew also assumes this custom in 6:16–18.

[84] Matt. 3:15.   [85] Matt. 10:17–39.   [86] Matt. 11:28–30.   [87] Matt. 26:28.

brings,[88] to mean a comfortable discharge from moral obligations or a revolutionary abrogation of hitherto valid norms. On the contrary, to follow Jesus is to take up the cross,[89] and the rejection of any sort of antinomianism is a constantly repeated burden of the Gospel. The gate is still strait and the way still narrow; but this is still the only way that leads to life, however few they be that walk in it.[90]

Matthew has thus given a grand unitary presentation, consciously aimed at a thorough clarification of the relationship between obedience to the Law and being a disciple of Christ. One cannot, however, help asking how long this readiness for suffering, this stringent humility, could be maintained and affirmed in the midst of Jewish persecution and, most of all, in the altered conditions of the hellenistic world. The situation is reminiscent of the problems faced by conservative Lutheran theology, standing between the Catholic and the Reformed positions in the sixteenth century. The old laws are to remain in force, even though a new faith is now confessed, even though on the one hand the old guardians of the law do not recognise the new exposition of it, and on the other events are already pushing forward and expanding into realms where reference to the old system has lost any kind of practical significance. Matthew stands on the borderline between two eras. He is the last witness to a Christian faith which sought truly to follow Jesus and to live by his promises, and yet at the same time to be sincerely loyal to the old law. But this was an untenable position. One day Christians were going to have to take a decision and choose: either the old commandments of the biblical Law, or the new fellowship of a church which held it sufficient to confess the one Lord who calls and redeems his faithful out of all nations.

The groups which were not prepared to make this choice later became encapsulated in what is known as Ebionism. 'Those Jews who believe in Jesus', wrote Origen, 'have never abandoned their ancestral law'.[91] For the sake of this Law Ebionite *Judaeo-Christianity* cut itself off from Paul and from the whole Gentile Christian universal Church. Unfortunately the state of our sources on this subject is so complicated that it is not possible to write the history of Ebionism with any confidence.[92] We shall therefore confine ourselves to the final stage of its development, that which is represented pre-eminently in the Judaeo-

---

[88] Matt. 5:3–12.   [89] Matt. 10:37–39.
[90] Matt. 7:13f.   [91] Contra Celsum II, 1.
[92] On the whole problem of Judaeo-Christianity in its relation to orthodoxy cf. the study by G. Strecker in the supplementary chapter to the new edition of W. Bauer, *Orthodoxy and Heresy in Earliest Christianity*, 1972, pp. 241ff., esp. pp. 270ff. The most comprehensive presentation of the Theology and History of Judaeo-Christianity is to be found in the work of that title by H. J. Schoeps, 1949; its conclusions, with critical revisions, are summarised in the same author's *Urgemeinde, Judenchristentum, Gnosis*, 1956.

Christian sources of the Pseudo-Clementines. These sources are to be dated in the first half of the third century, but certainly comprise in part older material.[93] Here we can discern at least the outlines of a theological system which attempts to correlate the authority of Jesus and the authority of the old Law, and to enable them to co-exist on an equality. Judaeo-Christian Gospels have come down to us only in modest fragments.[94] But even the 'basic stratum' of the Pseudo-clementines frequently operates by appealing to dominical sayings; and these sayings have to be accepted in all circumstances.[95] In this respect they retain the earliest form of the controversy, that in which it is still linked to the tradition about Jesus; and as such they may fittingly conclude this chapter.

For the Ebionites Christ is above all a 'prophet',[96] the last true prophet in the long series of prophets before him.[97] He is the one before all others to whom men must hearken. 'The true prophet must be sought above all things; for without him it is not possible for men to enjoy secure possession of anything at all.'[98] There can be no question of Moses or any other teacher or revealer taking precedence or control over Jesus in his perfection;[99] but, like Moses, he is a teacher of the

---

[93] Since the basic study by O. Cullmann, *Le problème littéraire et historique du roman pseudo-Clémentin*, Paris, 1930, this much has been almost universally acknowledged. Beyond this point critical opinion differs: cf. B. Rehm, 'Clemens Romanus II', *RAC* 3, 1957, pp. 197ff.; G. Strecker, 'The Preaching of Peter' in *N.T. Apocrypha* II, pp. 102ff.; and J. Irmscher, 'The Pseudo-Clementines', *ibid.*, pp. 532ff.

[94] Cf. the survey by P. Vielhauer, *ibid.*, vol. I, pp. 117ff.

[95] They are used especially to establish the Ebionite thesis of the permanence of the Law: cf. Hom. 51, 55–57. Peter drives Simon into a corner with his ταῖς γραφαῖς χρῆσθαι, ὡς Ἰησοῦς ἐδίδαξεν (*ibid.*, 58, 1); cf. Schoeps, *Theologie*, pp. 172f.

[96] In the Pseudo-clementines Jesus' 'constant title, formulated on the basis of Deut. 18:15 is ... ὁ ἀληθὴς προφήτης, or, ὁ τῆς ἀληθείας προφήτης; μόνος ἀληθὴς προφήτης also occurs (Hom. III, 21)' (Schoeps, *Theologie*, p. 100).

[97] From this starting-point we eventually arrive at the gnosticising conception of the prophet who was seen by the patriarchs and thereafter constantly manifested afresh under an altered appearance: Hom. V, 13, 5f; cf. E. Molland, 'La thèse, "La prophétie n'est jamais venue de la volonté de l'homme" (2 Pierre I, 21) et les Pseudo-Clémentines', *Stud Theol* 9, 1955, pp. 78ff.; G. Strecker in *N.T. Apocrypha* II, pp. 107f.

[98] Hom. I, 19, 8.

[99] It is true that Jesus is frequently coupled—and far more emphatically than in Matthew (cf. n. 56 above)—with Moses, but he is never described directly as a 'new Moses'. He simply testifies to the eternal validity of the Mosaic Law: *Ep. Petri ad Jac.* 2, 5. The two are set on a par only in the unique passage, Hom. 5, 6f. Because in each case it is only a question of *doing* the good which both of them taught, Moses fulfils the same role for the Jews as Jesus for the Gentiles. On the other hand, an explicit assertion of Jesus' superiority to Moses is found only in Rec. I, 59: he was not merely, like Moses, a prophet, but also the Christ.

Law, and the purpose for which his words were uttered, and the reason why they are indispensable, is that they disclose the divine will in the Scriptures.[100] All those elements which in hellenistic theology emphasise Jesus' significance as Saviour and Redeemer are now played down or treated as peripheral: his miraculous birth, the atoning effect of his death, the new power which springs from his resurrection, and the guidance of the Church by his Spirit play no important part.[101] The dominating concepts are those of the Law as the revelation of God's requirements and of the divine truth which controls the world.

This last is reminiscent of the speculations of hellenistic Judaism, and is moving toward gnostic conceptions.[102] Small wonder, then, that Ebionitism at once encounters the same difficulties as arise in these other systems. If what is wanted is an ideal revelation of perfect truth, then the Torah in its concrete actuality can no longer suffice, and the offensive elements in the ancient writings are, if not allegorised, impossible to stomach. The result is that even in Ebionite Judaeo-Christianity a certain critique of the Law is inescapable; and this has of necessity to go further than Matthew's attaching relatively greater or less importance to individual regulations, an expedient which is the result of thinking not in legalist but in evangelical terms. In connection, therefore, with the sayings of Jesus which are critical of the Law[103] the Ebionites develop a fantastic theory concerning the more or less sound or false elements within the sacred Scripture. It is now observed, or asserted, that this Scripture was not written down until after the time of Moses, and in the process was manifestly falsified.[104] In this way the believer can disembarrass himself in particular of the whole sacrificial cultus, now indefensible; and in the historical parts of the Torah anything morally offensive is deleted[105]—indeed, the process ends up with the wholesale rejection of every prophet between Moses and Jesus

---

The statement is made in quite general terms: non ideo credendum esse Jesu, quia de eo prophetae praedixerint, sed ideo magis credendum esse prophetis, quod vere prophetae sint, quia eis testimonium Christus reddat (I, 59, 4). Jesus is identified only with the sinless primal Man, Adam: Hom. XIII, 21; V, 10; cf. Molland, *op. cit.*, p. 78.

[100] The same applies to the words in which the Apostles interpret the Scriptures: *Ep. Petri ad Jac.* 2f.

[101] Cf. Schoeps, *Theologie*, pp. 71ff.

[102] Schoeps' almost completely non-gnostic interpretation of Ebionitism has rightly been rejected; cf. esp. the reviews by G. Bornkamm, *ZKG* 64, 1952–3, pp. 196–204; R. Bultmann, *Gnomon* 26, 1954, pp. 177–189; W. Kümmel, *ThR* 22, 1954, pp. 147–151.

[103] Matt. 13:17 and parr.; 15:2ff. and parr.; 19:4ff. and parr.; 22:29 and parr.; Hom. III, 50f., 53.

[104] Cf. Hom. II, 15f., 50–52; III, 22f., 47, 51; cf. Molland, *op. cit.*, pp. 80ff.

[105] Hom. II, 52. On the hostility to the cult cf. Schoeps, *Theologie*, pp. 219ff.

C

himself, not excepting John the Baptist. Ebionite Christianity restores the genuine Law as given by Moses, and is the re-establishment of the primal religion of Adam. Because the Christian 'reformed' Judaism, which is the result of this process, seeks to express Jesus Christ and the ancient Law in terms of a common religio-philosophical denominator, in the end it is satisfied with neither one nor the other, and is compelled to correct them both. Even the old canon of Scripture is not preserved, but destroyed.[106]

The fact is that if the canon was to be preserved within the Church, then this would have to be accomplished on quite a different basis. The way ahead had already been indicated long before, and it is prima facie paradoxical that it should be the Gentile church which had taken it. It was because this church had freed itself from the Law that it was able to keep the Scripture. The decision to do so was taken in a completely altered situation. Men were no longer much disposed to clutch at individual sayings of Jesus, which knew nothing of the fresh problems that were arising, and therefore could not directly supply the answers; but despite this there was no sense of disloyalty to or alienation from either the Lord or the ancient Scriptures. It was recognised that the Law was obsolete in a new situation where the Church had her own understanding of the new age of salvation and her own duty to hearken to the new 'Spirit'. But it is not enough to refer to this development in such general terms. We must try to trace in detail how it came about that the validity of the Jewish Law was set aside in practice and over-ruled in principle, and yet the ancient Scriptures were retained in the new community.

[106] Cf. Braun, *Qumran* II, pp. 226f. Yet the relevant passages hardly point to a critically emended version of the O.T., but to a special (? secret) teaching and knowledge of what is true and what is false. This interpretation is supported by the fact that even Symmachus, who was an Ebionite, translated the O.T. in full.

CHAPTER TWO

Law and Scripture in the Gentile Church of the First Century

THAT THE first Christian congregations should have retained 'the Law and the Prophets' as sacred Scripture and divine revelation is natural enough, and calls for no elaborate explanation.[1] They consisted of Jews, who remained Jews, and whose desire it was to constitute the true Israel of the final age of salvation. It was to this that they knew themselves called in the name of Jesus, and for this reason that they appealed to the Scriptures. It is true that faith in Christ did not derive from the ancient writings; it was rooted in direct encounter with Jesus, and arose from the experience of his resurrection. But an understanding of what it meant that Jesus was Messiah or Son of Man or the present and future Lord, a theological interpretation of his nature, could be arrived at only in the context of earlier prophetic and apocalyptic hopes, through the ever valid testimony of 'the scripture'. In the Christian faith from the very first both elements, Jesus and the Scripture, were mutually and inseparably related.[2]

[1] It is important to realise that there was at first no attempt to provide any justification for taking over the old Jewish Bible and allowing it authority There was not the slightest occasion to give the matter thought: cf. F. Mildenberger, *Gottes Tat im Wort. Erwägungen zur alttestamentlichen Hermeneutik*, 1964, p. 94 n.6. When W. G. Kümmel (in: Feine-Behm, *Einleitung in das Neue Testament*[14], 1965, pp. 350f.) remarks: 'Both in the case of Jesus himself and of the primitive church this "sacred scripture" was, as regards its validity and meaning, subject to the *critical* authority either of Jesus or of the Spirit of God, bestowed upon the church by the Risen Lord', this is a perfectly correct statement of the case. But to say this is to describe only the facts of the situation; it does not catch the underlying principle or the theological sense of the primitive community. On this subject cf. further H. von Campenhausen, 'Das Alte Testament als Bibel der Kirche', *Aus der Frühzeit des Christentums*, 1963, pp. 159f.

[2] For the same reason there was no immediate need to provide an extended 'proof from Scripture'; this was required at an early stage only in connection with the surprising fact of Jesus' 'Passion'. The conviction that the old hopes and predictions had been fulfilled was a 'postulate', implicit in belief in the crucified and risen Lord from the start. To this extent I am in agreement with A. Suhl, *Die Funktion der alttestamentlichen Zitate und Anspielungen im Markusevangelium*, 1965.

Seen in this light, the 'prophetic', christological exegesis of the Old Testament is as old as the Church itself. But the Scripture did not consist solely of prophets and texts susceptible of interpretation as prophecy. It also contained—in Jewish eyes, as its prime feature—the 'Law', the sacred and binding code for human life, which God had once laid upon his people, and which every Jew had a duty to follow. At first it was taken for granted that this part of the ancient Scripture also remained in force for Christians who were Jews. It is true that Jesus had adopted an attitude of great freedom with regard to the Law, and that this was not the least of the reasons for the hostility which he had drawn upon himself from his opponents; moreover, his largely Galilean following certainly did not belong to the strict observance. Nevertheless, there was not the least occasion to think in terms of a radical abolition of the Law. Why should not the first Christians continue to live in accordance with the rules and institutions hitherto in force? Consequently the Law was not the subject of the first Christian theological reflections, nor of the earliest controversy with Judaism.[3] This assessment would seem to be confirmed by the wholly unpolemical tradition of the words of Jesus in the Logia-source.[4]

But the situation quickly changed. Indeed, it was bound to change in the very moment when Christianity outgrew the milieu of Judaism, and expanded into new, heathen areas. Here the assumptions which hitherto had been taken for granted were lacking. On the one hand, Christians in the mission field had no desire to renounce the Old Testament, nor, indeed, was it practicable to do so; its religious and ethical content had already proved successful in Jewish propaganda, and in addition there could be little hope of 'teaching' the new salvation in Christ, and making it comprehensible to the heathen without making use of the 'Scripture'. On the other hand, however, it at once became clear that to take over the 'Law', lock, stock, and barrel, as a practical norm simply was not feasible. The Torah was not just a historical work, and a book of theological instruction and edification, but also an actual code of law currently in force. There could be no objection to taking over certain ethically illuminating passages; but to retain the plethora of detailed regulations, frequently obsolete, in the cultic and ceremonial field, the rules relating to purity, clean and unclean foods, sabbath observance, and the like, was out of the question, if Christian preaching was not to be saddled from the start with an intolerable burden. Jewish missionary propaganda had already run into difficulties

---

[3] E. Käsemann, 'Zum Thema der urchristlichen Apokalyptik,' *Exegetische Versuche und Besinnungen* II, 1964, pp. 113f., rightly makes this point in opposition to E. Fuchs, 'Über die Aufgabe einer christlichen Theologie', *ZTK* 58, 1961, p. 256.

[4] Cf. p. 7 above.

in this very area, and had resorted to all kinds of relaxations and re-interpretations. Only from the strictest of all requirements, the command of circumcision, was dispensation never given; without that a proselyte could never achieve membership of the people of God, and a share in the blessings of salvation. By contrast, the Christian mission exhibited from the start a new broad-mindedness and freedom; the starting-point and decisive content of its preaching was not the Law, nor any sacral system, but Jesus Christ. Circumcision and many other regulations could thus be left aside, and Christ given full play as the only bringer of salvation. In practice, therefore, Christ and the Law at once parted company.

What was the significance of this change for the status of the holy Scriptures? On the prevailing Jewish understanding of them it was in the Law that their centre of gravity and their authority were to be found. How could they now be taught and commended as God's inviolable word, when their concrete commands were ignored, and men were content with baptism and confession of Jesus as Lord and, as regards other matters, with what he himself had taught his disciples? At this point a problem arose from which the Church could not in the long run escape, even if at first she hardly appreciated its full significance. On finding a solution to this problem depended whether and in what sense the Old Testament could really become a Christian bible. Theory and practice were at odds. On the one hand, the Scripture ought to retain the sacred status it had always enjoyed. On the other, the suspension of the Law in the life of the Gentile churches was by now an irreversible fact. The resistance which conservative Judaeo-Christian circles had put up to any form of Gentile mission could not be maintained.[5] Even in Jerusalem men did not shut their eyes to the necessity of admitting the heathen to the newly given salvation. Circumcision, therefore, at least was waived, and other problems, which were bound to arise, were left more or less in the air.[6] But events soon left this solution far behind. Before long, sabbath and food regulations were playing no part in the life of the Gentile Christian church. This development can be traced in the way in which Mark emphasises the liberty of Jesus and his disciples, and noticeably plays down the question of principle with regard to the Law. By contrast, the profound,

---

[5] Matt. 10:5, 23 seem to be a last echo of this resistance. This resistance, by the way, was not connected in the first instance with the dangers that threatened the Law, but with the old promise of the prophets that the conversion of the nations attendant upon the restoration of the Davidic kingdom was to be the work of God alone. Human efforts should not seek to anticipate this eschatological miracle: cf. F. Hahn, *Das Verständnis der Mission im Neuen Testament*, 1963, pp. 43ff.

[6] It is in this context that Peter's vacillating conduct in Antioch (Gal. 2:11ff.) is to be understood.

but nevertheless somewhat artificial, solution which Matthew put forward was able to achieve a degree of success principally in Judaeo-Christian or Judaeo-Christian dominated churches.[7]

That in this situation the church did not content itself with purely pragmatic decisions, but sought and found a basis in principle for the new freedom, stands essentially to the credit of one man: Paul. Moreover, his solution of the problem of the Law also proved determinative for the future history of the canon. It is true that his approach did not survive entire or unchanged; but in certain fundamental features it was in the end universally accepted. Of any pre-Pauline essays hardly a trace is to be found. All that we can discern at all clearly are the efforts at resistance on the part of the 'Judaisers', who clung to circumcision, and tried to prevent a radical abandonment of the system of the Law. These attempts, however, if we discount certain Judaeo-Christian groups, quickly came to grief, and had hardly any effect on the Gentile church. There will be no need here to undertake the difficult task of reconstructing the teachings (in any case, far from unified) of the 'Judaisers'; and we shall content ourselves with following the main lines of the development which comes to light in the extant documents, above all in Paul and his disciples. For it was not the defence and preservation of the Law, but its nullification which in the end made it possible for the Church to regard the whole Old Testament, including the Torah, as God's word, to understand it in a Christian sense, and to keep it as part of her own Canon.

I

In the life-work and lifelong struggles of Paul are mirrored the fortunes of the primitive Christian mission to the Gentiles during the first generation of the Church. Here the problem of the validity of the old Law was an urgent issue of daily life which demanded a decision. Paul was a missionary through and through, and although other missionary work among the Gentiles had preceded his and continued alongside it, as he himself acknowledges, he felt himself to be the Apostle of the Gentiles *par excellence*. From this standpoint the problem of the Law was above all a practical problem. There can be no doubt that whenever Paul turns to discuss the question of the Law he is thinking of the requirements of the Gentile mission, that is, of the necessity for the preaching of the Gospel to be free from the trammels of the Law. But the problem of the Law was also the decisive issue of his personal life; at this point his own faith and the success and significance of his apostolic ministry coincide. By his own admission Paul had been 'zealous for the Law', and on this very account a persecutor of the

[7] Cf. pp. 16f. above.

Christians, until Christ by compelling him of all people to become a preacher of the Gospel among the Gentiles had as it were taken the place of the Law in his life. The calling of Paul was at the same time a conversion. The total fulfilment of his commission is both the ultimate probation and the redemption of his own person in its new fellowship with Christ the Lord. In rejecting the Law which had hitherto determined his life, therefore, two things were at stake: the success of his mission, embracing all nations, and the truth of faith in Christ as he had understood and preached it, 'his' Gospel.[8]

This central importance of the problem of the Law does not imply, however, that Paul's preaching must all the time have been encumbered with discussing it. His faith in Christ was strong and direct enough to be expressed freely, and to be effective, without any reference to its Jewish presuppositions. The earliest extant Pauline epistle says nothing either about the Law or about the whole justification doctrine which is its counterpart. It seems possible, therefore, that Paul was compelled to turn to these questions in detail, and to make them known to the Gentile Christians, only at a later stage as a result of hostile judaising propaganda.[9] This does not mean, however, that there is anything secondary or trivial about the content of his 'polemical teaching'; it is precisely this which in giving a logical interpretation of his missionary procedures and attitudes reveals the fundamental presuppositions of Pauline faith. The same applies to his attitude toward the ancient sacred Scriptures. There are Epistles, deriving either from him or from his school, which omit all mention not only of the Law but of the whole of sacred Scripture in general.[10] Yet it would certainly not be correct to conclude from this that Paul regarded Scripture as dispensable in a Gentile church, or that he had of set purpose been 'extremely guarded' on the subject.[11] The merest glance at his major Epistles is enough to convince one of the contrary. The picture which these texts present of Paul's relationship to Scripture in general is neither vacillating nor self-contradictory nor obscure, but unequivocal, unified, and impressive in its systematic coherence.

[8] Cf. on this point pp. 105ff. below.
[9] Cf. W. G. Kümmel, 'Das literarische und geschichtliche Problem des Ersten Thessalonicherbriefes,' *Heilsgeschehen und Geschichte, Gesammelte Aufsätze 1933–1964*, 1965, pp. 406–416.
[10] The Epistles in question are those to the Philippians and Colossians, the two to the Thessalonians, and the letter to Philemon.
[11] So A. von Harnack, *Das Alte Testament in den paulinischen Briefen und in den paulinischen Gemeinden*, 1928, p. 128. According to E. Lohmeyer, *Grundlagen paulinischer Theologie*, 1929, p. 104, Paul deliberately developed two different presentations of his Gospel—one with and one without appeal to Scripture. Both positions are rightly refuted by O. Michel, *Paulus und seine Bibel*, 1929, pp. 116ff.

Whatever assessment we may make of the religio-historical back-ground to the Pauline epistles or of the theological formation which Paul underwent, this much is clear: for him 'Scripture' was the infallibly revealed 'Word of God', and could not err. As a Christian he still remained faithful without qualification to this conviction. Renounce the use of Scripture he could not if he would. Recollections of and allusions to the biblical texts permeate the great Epistles, appearing in sentence after sentence; and in addition there are dozens of explicit quotations.[12] Every section of the old canon is represented, and even works which we regard as 'apocryphal'.[13] Generally speaking, the manner in which the quotations are introduced agrees with the technical forms employed in the Mishnah;[14] and the methods of exegesis, which to our way of thinking are highly arbitrary, are also to a great extent scholastic and traditional.[15] For Paul, Scripture does not merely pro-claim God's will and commandments; everything which it says is absolutely true, and this makes it an inexhaustible source of every kind of knowledge. Paul does not use its words only to underline the points he wishes to make to his congregations when declaring to them God's salvation and the divine praises, or when giving them spiritual exhorta-

[12] The reader will find a full compilation of the evidence in J. Bonsirven, *Exégèse rabbinique et exégèse paulinienne,* Paris, 1939, pp. 276ff.

[13] In addition to I Cor. 2:9 cf. the table of 'apocrypha' in the narrower sense in A. C. Sundberg, *The Old Testament of the Early Church,* 1964, pp. 54f.

[14] Cf. B. M. Metzger, 'The Formulas introducing Quotations of Scripture in the NT and the Mishnah', *JBL* 70, 1951, pp. 297–307; J. A. Fitzmyer, 'The use of explicit Old Testament quotations in Qumran literature and in the New Testament', *NTS* 7, 1960–1, pp. 297–333.

[15] In addition to the work of Bonsirven already quoted (n. 12 above) cf. L. Goppelt, *Typos. Die typologische Deutung des Alten Testaments im Neuen,* 1939; 'Apokalyptik und Typologie bei Paulus', *TLZ* 89, 1964, pp. 321–344; H. J. Schoeps, 'Paulus als rabbinischer Exeget', *Aus frühchristlicher Zeit* (Gesammelte Aufsätze), 1950, pp. 221–238; J. W. Doeve, *Jewish Hermeneutics in the Synoptic Gospels and Acts,* Assen, 1954; *Christian Origins and Judaism,* London, 1962; W. D. Davies, *Paul and Rabbinic Judaism²,* London, 1955; D. Daube, *The New Testament and Rabbinic Judaism,* London, 1956; E. E. Ellis, *Paul's Use of the Old Testament,* Edinburgh, 1957; B. Lindars, *The New Testament Apologetic. The Doctrinal Significance of the Old Testament Quota-tions,* London, 1961, pp. 222ff.; J. Coppens, 'Les arguments scripturaires et leur portée dans les lettres pauliniennes', in: *Stud. Paulin. congressus internat. cathol. 1961* II (= *Anal. Biblica* 17/18, 1963), pp. 243–253. According to J. Pépin, *Mythe et allégorie. Les origines grecques et les contestations judéo-chrétiennes,* Paris, 1958, p. 252, the use of allegory in Paul ought also to be attributed to a palestinian rather than a hellenistic milieu (?). On the issues of theological principle involved cf. J. Schmid, 'Die alttestamentlichen Zitate bei Paulus und die Theorie vom sensus plenior,' *BZ* NF 3, 1959, pp. 161–173; H. Müller, *Die Auslegung des alttestamentlichen Geschichtsstoffs bei Paulus* (Diss. Halle 1960); L. Buisson, 'Die Entstehung des Kirchenrechts,' *Zeitschrift der Savigny-Stiftung für Rechtsgeschichte* 83 (Kanonist. Abt.) 1966, pp. 63ff.

tion. When he is offering them revelations of a wide-ranging theosophical and speculative kind—concerning, for instance, the special
character of the resurrection body[16] or the destiny of the Jews[17]—
he supports his case either explicitly or implicitly with Old Testament
texts. In evaluating these he pays no heed to the possible influence of
human mediators, he does not rate one scriptural source as higher or
more valid than another, there are no qualifications from the standpoint
of 'naturalistic' or 'rationalistic' philosophy. Scripture, both in its
totality and in each individual word, is as such sacred, divine, miraculous. Small wonder then that Paul, who grew up with this book and
who lives in its world of thought, continues even after his conversion
to follow the Jewish-rabbinic methods of understanding and expounding
Scripture. It would be quite impossible for anyone to be a greater
believer in Scripture than he.[18]

For all that, in his relationship to Scripture as a Christian Paul does
undergo a profound change, and radically parts company with every
variety of belief in Scripture to be found within Judaism. For Paul
reads the Scripture from the standpoint of Christ, and therefore in a
new spirit. This is not simply to say that the biblical statements are now
interpreted, with appropriate pains and skill, as referring to Christ
and to Paul's own community; Qumran had already done as much.[19]
Rather does it mean that now the historical experience of Christians
and the new life which flows from this are consciously understood and
affirmed as a new and unique starting-point, an independent way-in to
the ancient Scriptures. The Spirit which searches all things, even the
depths of the godhead,[20] did not derive from the Scriptures, but was
given for the first time as something quite new, with belief in Christ.
Paul turns to the one who 'raised from the dead Jesus our Lord', and
finds—as the Jew had found in the Torah—that now in Christ 'are hid
all the treasures of wisdom and knowledge'.[21] To this extent the
Christian has become spiritually independent, and in his relationship
with God is, so to speak, a law to himself.

Precisely for this reason it is now also possible for Paul, through faith
in Christ, really to read the Scripture aright, and to understand its
profoundest purposes. All the promises which God has made find their
fulfilment and their goal only in Christ.[22] Hence the Scripture, and
everything which it relates or teaches, refers properly to 'us, upon

---

[16] I Cor. 15:44f.   [17] Rom. 9–11.

[18] H. Ulonska, *Die Funktion der alttestamentlichen Zitate und Anspielungen in
den paulinischen Briefen* (Diss. Münster, 1963) seeks to controvert this perfectly
plain state of affairs by modernising interpretations, but succeeds only in artificially creating difficulties which in fact do not exist.

[19] Cf. p. 5 above.   [20] I Cor. 2:10.

[21] Rom. 4:24; Col. 2:3.   [22] II Cor. 1:20.

whom the end of the ages has come'.[23] The Scripture itself 'foresaw'[24] the present moment, was, so to say, waiting for it, and was written less for the sake of earlier generations than for that of the Christians now alive.[25] Hitherto its profoundest mysteries have remained hidden, as indeed for the Jews they still do whenever the Scripture is read. But for Christians, who 'with unveiled face' behold the glory of Christ, that which was hidden has been revealed, revealed indeed in a surpassing splendour which abolishes the old Mosaic dispensation of the 'letter' of the Law in favour of a new, spiritual freedom.[26] The attitude which, from this standpoint, Paul adopts toward the beginnings of the christological 'proof from Scripture' is highly significant. He knows of it, and acknowledges its validity; but for himself makes little use of it, and certainly does nothing to develop it.[27] Certainly, Paul too maintains that the sending of Christ is in accordance with the divine plan of salvation, and thus with the 'Scriptures'; and he can cite to this effect the earlier Christian formulas which stress this idea.[28] But the later, typical form of the proof from Scripture, which confirms the claims of Christ by demonstrating the oracular agreement of particular details from the life of Jesus with the corresponding prophecies of the Old Testament, does not occur in Paul. Paul, moreover, does not envisage that the old prophets or Abraham would have 'seen' or known the person of Jesus in advance. Such prescience is the property only of 'Scripture' itself, and even here what is foreseen is not the details of the story of Jesus but the fact of the coming salvation, namely that God

[23] I Cor. 10:11; II Cor. 6:2. On this point cf. K. H. Schelkle, 'Hermeneutische Regeln im Neuen Testament', *Wort und Schrift* (Gesammelte Aufsätze) 1966, pp. 31–44, esp. pp. 34f.

[24] Gal. 3:8.

[25] Rom. 4:23f.; 15:4; I Cor. 10:6; cf. 5:6ff.

[26] II Cor. 3:6–18. These few remarks are not, of course, intended as a complete exegesis of a passage as pregnant as it is problematic, and one moreover which in its pointed polemic is concerned not strictly with the Scripture but with the Law and the nature of the apostolic ministry and vocation: cf. W. C. Van Unnik, ' "With unveiled face——" ' an Exegesis of II. Corinthians III 12–15', *NovTest* 6, 1953, pp. 153–169; S. Schulz, 'Die Decke des Moses,' *ZNW* 49, 1958, pp. 1–30; J. Jervell, *Imago Dei—Gen. 1, 26f. im Spätjudentum, in der Gnosis und in den paulinischen Briefen*, 1960, pp. 173ff.; D. Georgi, *Die Gegner des Paulus im 2. Korintherbrief*, 1964, pp. 246ff.; and finally, J. Roloff, *Apostolat—Verkündigung—Kirche*, 1965, pp. 100–103; and H. Ulonska, *op. cit.*, pp. 132–140. Cf. also H. Conzelmann, 'Paulus und die Weisheit', *NTS* 12, 1965–6, pp. 233f.

[27] In this respect there is a greater difference between the real-life Paul and the Paul described in Acts than C. H. Dodd, *According to the Scriptures*, 1952, pp. 16ff., allows.

[28] Nevertheless, he does so only twice in all: Rom. 1:3, and I Cor. 15:3f. In each case he is seeking to back up and commend something to his readers by appealing to older tradition: in the former instance his own person, with which they are as yet unacquainted, in the latter, his views.

would justify the Gentiles by faith.[29] It is therefore hardly possible that Paul himself could have written, as the spurious ending of Romans has it, that the mystery of Christ 'through the prophetic writings is made known to all nations'.[30] The only route he knows runs from Christ to knowledge of the Scriptures, and its direction cannot be reversed.

All this forms the background to the great controversy over the validity of the Law, a controversy with which the texts cited are already in part concerned. An inexorable belief in the validity of Scripture makes any compromise solutions impossible, and exerts strong pressure toward a radical solution based on fundamental principles. There is no need here to go into every aspect of the significance of this controversy; it will be sufficient to consider those few positions which are normative for our present subject.

In every instance when Paul speaks of the 'Law', he is thinking of the particular, divinely revealed Law of the old covenant, and of its concrete demand of 'righteousness'.[31] It is true that the sense of what Paul has to say can to some extent be transferred to Christian 'legalism' or to any other kind; but it is important not to confuse this conceptual extrapolation with what Paul actually says, and with the only things which, in that particular situation, he had in mind. Paul regarded the Pentateuchal Law as a strictly indissoluble unity. Admittedly, when he is speaking of the holiness of the Law, it is the moral commands which involuntarily obtrude themselves,[32] and when he wants to emphasise that the Law is obsolete, he conversely seems to be thinking primarily of the ritual and ceremonial prescriptions.[33] Nevertheless, this distinction is nowhere

[29] Gal. 3:8.

[30] Rom. 16:26. Inasmuch as it is now the Scripture which is to make Christ known, this verse goes even further than the formula adopted by Paul in Rom. 1:2f. In this respect it is akin to the later apologetic or possibly Lukan theology: cf. pp. 47ff. and 88ff. below. It is significant that apart from Acts these two texts are the only ones which St. Porúbčan can adduce in support of his thesis: 'The Pauline Message and the Prophets', *Stud. Paulin. congressus intern, cathol. 1961* I (= *Analect. Biblica* 17–18, 1963) pp. 253–258.

[31] So far from being controverted by that much-debated passage, Rom. 2:14f., this statement is in fact confirmed by it. On the other hand, the νόμος χριστοῦ (Gal. 6:2) and the νόμος τῆς πίστεως (Rom. 3:27), of which Paul speaks, are not relevant in this connection. These expressions make use of a common idiom to describe the power of the new life as that which takes the place of the old Law, and thus makes it possible to be in essence equal or comparable in righteousness without the Law.

[32] Rom. 13:8–10; Gal. 5:19ff.

[33] It was rules of this kind which underlay that problem of table-fellowship which led to the clash between Paul and Peter in Antioch (Gal. 2:11ff.); but in the life of the Pauline churches they appear to have played very little part. Belief in astral spirits, and the observance of particular days and seasons in Galatia, will have been connected with judaising propaganda, but are stigmatised by Paul as a relapse into heathenism: Gal. 4:8–11. By contrast, Col. 2:16, 21 must refer to O.T. and Judaistic regulations.

explicit nor consciously worked out as such.[34] To differentiate in this way between individual prescriptions, and to assign a higher value to some than to others, is, however, pre-eminently the mark of those who, like Matthew, wish to rescue the Law in principle;[35] and in a different way it is also characteristic of the later dogmatic standpoint which interpreted the Law as in essence the religious and moral commands and nothing more.[36] In the same way, it would seem, the judaisers in Galatia demanded first and foremost only the circumcision of Gentile Christians.[37] It is not they but Paul who adds the assertion—a necessary corollary by rabbinic standards—that anyone who allows himself to be circumcised is then under an obligation to keep the whole Law without exception.[38] But his reason for pressing the matter to this extreme alternative is that he is determined to controvert absolutely the validity of the Law for Gentiles, and to refuse to allow it to be brought into consideration in any way.

If anyone still wants to keep the Law in any sense whatever, then for him Christ died in vain; and any Gentile turned Christian who accepts that ancient token of salvation, circumcision, has denied Christ. The harshness of this thesis, which Paul develops especially in the Epistles to the Galatians and to the Romans, can no longer be explained simply in terms of contemporary conflicts and the practical necessities of the Gentile mission. It has deeper roots. It is, moreover, no merely theoretical matter, but radically determines the whole life of the churches founded and trained by Paul. Paul orders their affairs without taking the 'Law of Moses' as his guide, even on occasions when unequivocally binding regulations of a 'canon law' type are involved.[39] At most, the

[34] Despite this fact C. Haufe, 'Die Stellung des Paulus zum Gesetz,' *TLZ* 91, 1966, cols. 171–178, tries to establish that in Paul's writings there is a radically different evaluation of 'the Jewish cult and ceremonial law' on the one hand, and of 'those commandments which group themselves around the command to love God and one's neighbour' (col. 172)—believing that otherwise the 'inherent contradictions' (col. 171) in Paul's doctrine of the Law cannot be removed. This alleged self-contradictory character, however, is the product—not to mention numerous inaccuracies in the interpretation of particular texts—of nothing more than the author's failure to understand the inner coherence of the movement of Paul's thought.

[35] Cf. pp. 10ff. above.

[36] This process begins, though not without problems, in the writings of Ptolemaeus and Justin: cf. pp. 82ff., 92ff. below.

[37] Gal. 6:12; cf. 2:14, and n. 33 above.

[38] Gal. 5:3.

[39] In this connection the reader may be referred to my own earlier treatment of this question: H. von Campenhausen, *Die Begründung kirchlicher Entscheidungen beim Apostel Paulus*[2], 1965. Even in Paul's general moral exhortations recourse to the Old Testament is strikingly rare: cf. L. Nieder, *Die Motive der religiös-sittlichen Paränese in den paulinischen Gemeindebriefen*, 1956, p. 106; W. Schrage, *Die konkreten Einzelgebote in der paulinischen Paränese*, 1961,

analogous regulations of the Mosaic Law may provide additional confirmation of decisions already arrived at;[40] but when compared with the rest of the material on which a Christian's spirit-given capacity for judgment had to work—the apostolic teaching, the word of the Lord, the example of his predecessors in the Church—the Law itself no longer had any independent importance. It was no longer in force; it had been abrogated. On the other hand, it never occurs to Paul to forbid the Jewish-Christian congregations to observe the ancient legal prescriptions. Any attempt to do so would in the nature of the case have been, of course, completely hopeless. Paul rightly reckons it a great enough success that the apostles in Jerusalem have tolerated the absolute freedom of the Gentile church from the Law, and have not broken with them over the matter. But equally clearly he has no desire to apply the requirements of his missionary situation to Jewish Christians.[41] The practical implications of his position are as clear as its basis in theological theory.[42] So far as the crucial problem is concerned, minor inconsistencies of this sort are of no significance.

---

p. 233. A different view is put forward by Buisson, *op. cit.*, pp. 74ff., who understands the legal decisions in Paul's writings as largely 'O.T. exegesis of Jesus' words' (p. 75 n. 228). He therefore considers that we can detect in Paul 'fragmentarily and from time to time' an analogy between the old Law and the organisation of the Church; the only difference between Paul and 'later thinkers' is that Paul has not as yet broken through to a 'systematic synthesis'. Personally I cannot possibly accept so incoherent a picture of Paul's doctrine of the Law.

[40] I Cor. 9:8; 14:34. Other examples, which I myself do not find convincing, are suggested in Schrage, *op. cit.*, pp. 234, 238. The problematic passage I Cor. 4:6 is best left out of account, since it is questionable, first of all, whether it refers to the O.T. at all, and secondly because it is quite impossible to arrive at an assured exegesis: for a recent view cf. M. D. Hooker, ' "Beyond the things which are written": An Examination of I Cor. IV, 6', *NTS* 10, 1963–4, pp. 127–132. Those who regard Ephesians as Pauline may also cite Eph. 6:1–3, where the command to love one's parents is based on Ex. 20:12. Even in this instance, however, as P. Bläser, *Das Gesetz bei Paulus*, 1941, p. 230, rightly emphasises, the command is so wholly incorporated into the demand of Christ that it is from this very much more than from the Decalogue that it derives its authority.

[41] In Judaism and its religious traditions, including even circumcision, Paul still sees a great privilege, which he has given up only for the sake of Christ: Rom. 3:1f.; 9:4f.; II Cor. 11:22; Gal. 2:15f.; Phil. 3:4ff.

[42] Hence even the Jewish Christian may no longer boast of his advantages, since he too is redeemed only by faith in Christ (Gal. 2:16). Circumcision 'is of value' to him only so long as he actually fulfils the will of God; and conversely, the Gentile who does God's will also finds complete acceptance with God even without circumcision (Rom. 2:25ff.). In fact, the relative standing of the two can positively be inverted: those who want to impose circumcision on the Gentile Christians have thereby become 'mutilators of the flesh', while by contrast the uncircumcised become the true circumcision (Phil. 3:2f.), the seed of Abraham (Gal. 3:7), and the spiritual 'Israel' (Gal. 4:26, 28; 6:16). The ancient sacral requirement has here become a mere image, and the Jewish Christian's

The question naturally arose, how freedom from the Law, even if restricted to Gentile Christians, was to be justified in view of the plain demands of the Bible itself. Unless it proved possible to find a clear answer to this question, the Pauline 'Gospel' could properly be stigmatised as a lie and a distortion. If, on the other hand, an attempt to judaise the Gentile church misfired, then the more or less wholesale abandonment of the Jewish Bible would inevitably seem the only solution open.[43] In either case Paul's life work would be destroyed.

The seemingly obvious way out, namely that of watering down, or reinterpreting the Law, or giving it only a relative importance, Paul never even contemplated. Not only did he believe in Scripture in general; in the Law in particular, as he had learned and practised it, he saw still the unalterable standard of the righteousness which God demands, a standard never to be surpassed. In this he remained—as surely as ever Matthew did—a faithful Jew.[44] Moreover, Paul never complains about the burden of the many external, legalistic requirements—either on his own behalf or on that of his congregations. He never says that the Law is too oppressive or too complicated a load to be laid on the Gentile Christians, nor does he normally argue from some alleged impossibility of fulfilling the Law's demands.[45] The critique which he puts forward is far more radical and central: at no time or place was the Law itself, however good or complete it might be, capable of truly bringing men to God, or of enabling them to enjoy

---

regulation of his life by the Law a convention of no significance for salvation. Paul still accepts a church made up of Jews and Gentiles as an established fact which is to continue; but it is already clear in his writings that any distinction between these two branches can in fact be no more than an interim arrangement which one day is bound to disappear in a 'catholic' community which will unite both groups.

[43] The conclusion which Marcion did in fact later draw.

[44] Even the way in which Paul concentrates attention on the moral command (Rom. 13:8; Gal. 5:14) recalls the carefully worked out solution of the problem in *Matthew*: cf. pp. 15ff. above.

[45] Such an idea is completely lacking in Galatians, and clearly played no part whatever in Paul's personal life: I Cor. 4:4; Phil. 3:6. It appears only in Romans, and this is linked with the fact that here the Jew in his relationship to the Law is included with the Gentile in a systematic examination. The reason why Paul seeks to present the contradiction between pretensions and performance in the harshest possible light is that his remarks are aimed not at the Gentile, but at the Jews' conceited conviction of their own perfection by the standard of the Law: Rom. 2:17ff.; 7:15ff. But even in Romans it is expressly stated that Abraham, even if he did attain perfect righteousness in his works, nevertheless thereby acquired something to boast about only before men, not before God: Rom. 4:2. To take the path of fulfilling the Law by works done in one's own power as opposed to the path of faith is perverse from the very start and accompanied by no divine promises, and therefore comes to grief not simply because it is impossible of achievement.

God's good pleasure—nay more, instead of helping men in the effort to achieve this goal, it simply made their position all the more wretched and hopeless. This, as Paul expressly emphasises, is the fault not of the Law but of Man, who in his 'fleshly' sinful nature is in no position effectually to meet the requirements of God.[46] The Law as such is completely 'holy, and just, and good';[47] but this makes no difference to the fact that it was precisely by means of the Law that Man was driven into the delusion of a self-made righteousness, and thus to impenitence and that death which is the wages of sin. Christ alone rescues men from this predicament. Faith in him and in his Gospel brings the gift of the Spirit, which actively creates love, and thus genuinely and abundantly fulfils the demands of the Law and of the Good in freedom. This apologetic and paraenetic concept is manifestly essential for Paul, since he propounds it twice in virtually the same words.[48] In his efforts to rebut any suspicion of hostility to the Law he is even capable of the audacity of claiming that he—with his Gospel of freedom from the Law—is in fact upholding the Law.[49] What he means is that it is precisely the Gospel which succeeds in realising the true purpose of the Law. But it is not some power inherent in the legal demand itself which brings this about, but the grace of the one Man, Jesus Christ. Christ has satisfied the demands of the Law by his death, and the new freedom in his Spirit belongs only to those who have died to the world and all its lusts. It is this which for the first time reveals the whole seriousness of the Law: Christ did not simply override it, but by the agency of the Law was made a curse in our stead for our sins, and by his dying he has ransomed and redeemed us. This means, however, that any route by which men might return to the Law has been cut off: 'Christ is the end of the Law', and the righteousness which he effects is the possession only of the one who 'believes'.[50]

Paul is therefore distinguishing between the abiding truth and holiness of the content of the Law, and the Law as a means of attaining salvation. At this latter point the Law breaks down, while its requirements, for what they are in themselves, remain true and justified. That is why Paul can, on the one hand, present the Law as divine, and, on the other, simultaneously reject its pretensions and any acknowledgment of them. The train of thought as such is entirely clear; but in this form it is by no means adequate to cover Paul against the attacks of his opponents. Does not such a conception of the Law contradict everything that the Old Testament itself teaches about it? Anyone who wants to exclude

---

[46] Rom. 7:13f.   [47] Rom. 7:12.
[48] Rom. 13:8–10; Gal. 5:13f.; cf. 6:23.   [49] Rom. 3:31.
[50] Rom. 10:4. I shall spare the reader a debate about the interpretation and significance of these well-known texts in detail. The best available survey is that of R. Bultmann, *Theology of the N.T.*, I, pp. 259ff., 288ff.

the Law completely, manifestly has 'the Scriptures' against him, and is demonstrably an innovating apostate and traitor. If Paul is to hold his own, therefore, he must also bring positive proof that his gospel is in fact taught in the Old Testament, and that even there the sacred, God-given Law[51] is already presented in a negative light, abandoned, or relegated to an inferior and subordinate position.

This is the significance of the strange typological exegeses in which Paul contrasts Mount Sinai with Jerusalem, Sarah with Hagar, Isaac with Ishmael, and attempts to interpret these pairs in terms of the old divine covenant of the Law and the new one of the Spirit.[52] The splendour of the death-dealing Mosaic Law, which was written on tablets of stone and passes away, is nothing compared with the new, abiding splendour of the Gospel and of the living Spirit of Christ, which endows the heart with liberty.[53] The Scripture itself teaches that 'by works of the Law no flesh is justified'. These artificial exegeses are, however, far less important than the positive testimony which Scripture affords in support of an 'evangelical' interpretation of the venerable figure of Abraham. To this Paul appeals with unshakeable resolution. Of the patriarch Abraham, who knew nothing of the Law, it is stated that he believed the promises of God, and that on account of this faith alone God attributed 'righteousness' to him.[54] Here, therefore, Scripture itself demonstrates that in fact it is not the Law but faith which wins God's approval, and thus points ahead to the coming Gospel, and to the Christians, who are Abraham's true, spiritual children. Paul goes into great detail in order to confirm and justify this exegesis of his, concentrated as it is on one single text.[55] In Abraham, the prototype, the righteousness that is by faith was proclaimed long—four hundred and thirty years—before the Law and even before the command to circumcise were promulgated. Already, therefore, Paul asserts, these

[51] The divine origin of the Law is not disputed even in Gal. 3:20, however 'gnostic' the depreciatory feature of mediation by angels may seem in view of the way in which the problem of the Law developed in the second century: cf., e.g., Chr. Maurer, *Die Gesetzeslehre des Paulus, nach ihrem Ursprung und in ihrer Entfaltung dargelegt* (Diss. Zürich, 1941), p. 27; also, less dogmatically, H. Schlier, *Der Brief an die Galater*[13], 1965, pp. 157f. R. Bring, 'Der Mittler und das Gesetz—eine Studie zu Gal, 3,20', *Kerygma und Dogma* 12, 1966, pp. 292–309, goes too far in a positive direction.

[52] Gal. 4:21ff.; the same applies to the arbitrarily selected quotations in Rom. 10:5ff.

[53] II Cor. 3:7ff.; cf. n. 26 above.   [54] Gen. 15:6; Rom. 4; Gal. 3:6ff.

[55] Particularly striking is the fact that he makes no reference to Gen. 22, a passage which for Jews had always been, and for Christians was later to be, basic for the understanding of the figure of Abraham. On this point cf. R. Le Déaut, 'La présentation targumique du sacrifice d'Isaac et la sotériologie paulinienne,' *Stud. Paulin, congressus internat. cathol. 1961* II (= *Analecta Biblica* 17–18, 1963) pp. 563–574.

later regulations are of far less importance, and cannot cancel the prior dispensation. Moreover, from the very first they were never thought of as a permanent institution. The period during which the Law applied was meant to be a temporary time of slavery, which was to last only until the appearing of Christ and the age of final liberty. His explanation of why this sombre interlude was necessary at all, however, is not very successful.[56] Paul seems to think that God wished to make sin all the more powerful by means of the Law, in order that he might then destroy it all the more completely.[57]

For our present purpose, however, there is no point in discussing in further detail where Paul's argumentation is obscure or strained. What is important is that the 'Law' and the 'Scripture', which rabbinism had virtually equated, are now separated once more, and that even in the Old Testament the Gospel takes the dominant place. This is an objective advance in the understanding of the subject with which we are concerned in the present work. The way forward to a realistic Christian understanding of the Scriptures is now open. The individual commands of the Mosaic Law need no longer be a cause of disquiet, for they belong to a past which since the appearing of Christ has lost its authority. Recognition of the difference in historical significance between the past and the present has become of crucial importance; for only where this is recognised, is it possible to maintain without qualification the unity of

[56] This is significant. In later sketches of the salvation-history the emphasis is above all on the meaning and purpose of the divine plan of salvation; and, given such an approach, the need for the era of the Law has to be explained in terms of education. Paul, by contrast, starts from his experience of the opposition between the Law and the Gospel, and all his enthusiasm is concentrated on showing that the Law has now been superseded and no longer applies. His own picture of the salvation-history develops from this. In history as such, and in 'understanding' its inner rationale, he has absolutely no interest; and of a theodicy he has no need. For these reasons it seems to me that recent discussion about Paul's concept of history and his thinking on salvation-history is highly problematic. The statements which Paul does make are inevitably pressed too far, when they are divorced from their starting-point and interpreted as general answers to systematic questions of 'meaning'. They may properly be considered only as the starting-point of a development in thought which is certainly necessary, but which inevitably leads far beyond Paul, considered in his historical actuality.

[57] Rom. 5:20; Gal. 3:19. That the παιδαγωγός of Gal. 3:24 was no kindly and beneficent 'tutor', must by now be universally agreed; cf. Schlier, *Galaterbrief*, pp. 168ff. 'There are no parallel Jewish conceptions to such an evaluation of the Law', observes with justice H. J. Schoeps, *Paulus*, 1959, p. 181. The same applies, however—though Schoeps denies this—to Paul's assumption that the validity of the Law was purely transitory, and was to come to an end with the old aeon: cf. U. Wilckens, 'Die Bekehrung des Paulus als religionsgeschichtliche Problem', *ZTK* 56, 1959, p. 291; Goppelt, *Apokalyptik und Typologie*, pp. 325f.; E. Bammel, Νόμος Χριστοῦ, in: *Studia Evangelica* III, 1964, pp. 120–128.

D

God's saving purpose and of the Scripture that bears witness to it, without having to dispute the independent and supreme importance of Christ and the Church. A 'christological' exegesis, in the narrower sense, of the Old Testament, or the formal synthesis of scriptural proof in every detail, is not fundamentally necessary to justify recognition of this double truth. Paul does not rest his case exclusively on typological exegeses—indeed, in his basic definition of the faith of Abraham they play almost no part. What is decisive is the discovery that the ancient Scripture as a whole, even though in a hidden and prefatory manner, yet speaks of the same faith and the same salvation which Christ in the end brought to men and realised among them. Only when this point has been reached, can the Old Testament be truly understood, from within, as a Christian Bible.

This was not the goal which Paul had directly in mind, when he was developing the relevant part of his thought. The intention behind these ideas of his is patently polemical and apologetic. Paul makes less use of them to defend the Christian sense of Scripture than he does of the Scriptures, which both he and his opponents equally acknowledge to be authoritative, to fight for his Gospel, that is, for the freedom of Gentile Christians from the Law. By the next generation interest in this struggle against the demands of Judaism had already largely died, since freedom from the Law for Gentile Christians had in essentials been achieved. Paul's arguments thus lost their immediate relevance, and their deeper significance was no longer understood. Already by the time of Ephesians, which goes under Paul's name and which was unquestionably written under the controlling influence of Pauline thought, the abolition of the Law is no longer seen as victory over an almost demonic power which had directly strengthened the arm of sin, but supremely as an act of spiritual peacemaking, enabling the unification of Jew and Gentile to take place within the Church.[58] Hebrews tackles the problem from a quite different angle, and other writers lose sight of it altogether.[59] But the consciousness that the Law was fundamentally obsolete, and that there was a difference as well as a coherence between the Old and New 'Testaments' was never lost. In essence, of course, a salvation-history pattern of thought was bound up with belief in Christ from the very first; for one of the presuppositions of such belief is that, under the dominion and guidance of the ancient God, a new and final salvation has been inaugurated, at once the end and the predicted consummation of the ages. But Paul was the only one to propose on this basis a definite, concrete distinction between the epochs, because it was the central problem of the Law which drove him to do so, and compelled him to certain 'historical' reflections. In doing so he was following no earlier conception, nor indeed was he setting out to develop a general

[58] Eph. 2:14ff. [59] Cf. pp. 67ff. below.

theory of 'salvation-history'; but the result of his reflections on the significance of Abraham and of Jesus, and of the Law which in point of time came between them, was in fact to establish and initiate such a theory. Paul created the presuppositions which made it possible to take over the ancient Scriptures, and to set a 'New' Testament alongside the 'Old' but clearly distinct from it. In this respect the full significance of his thought became apparent only a century later, in the critical period between Marcion and Irenaeus, the period in which the 'New Testament' as such emerged. It is true that this development did not take place solely under Pauline influence; and the principal theologians who support the new bipartite canon are often enough in disagreement with Paul at the very points on which they explicitly appeal to him. But it is a sheer historical fact that the permanent basic assumption of the Christian Bible is a Pauline conception, or at least one inaugurated by Paul, and to that extent the Christian Bible is inconceivable without him. Thus far, therefore, the ideas and intentions of Paul did effectually prevail within the Church despite all the dislocation, dilution and distortion to which they were subjected. For this, however, we are indebted not only to the influence of his Epistles but perhaps even more to that of the work of his greatest disciple in mediating his thought, namely to the Gospel and above all to the Acts of Luke.

II

That the author of the twin works handed down to us under the name of Luke was in fact none other than the companion and colleague of the apostle, mentioned several times by Paul himself and in the deutero-Pauline writings, is for me personally beyond question. There is, however, no need in our present context to defend Luke's personal contact with Paul, since it is not of decisive importance for an understanding of the Lukan writings and thought. Their general background is clear without coming to a conclusion on this point. Luke is a Gentile Christian of the second generation.[60] He sees in Paul the greatest of all missionaries, and knows that he himself is committed to Paul's cause as his life's work. The burning ecclesiastical questions with which Paul had struggled have by now passed away, and are in general no longer debated. The Gentile Christian church, freed from the Law, has expanded mightily; its congregations are now spread throughout the

---

[60] Recently the attempt has been revived to give a late date, in the middle of the second century, to the Lukan writings. This seems to me completely impossible. On the problem of dating cf. most recently: H. Conzelmann, 'Luke's place in the development of Early Christianity', in: (ed.) E. Keck and J. L. Martyn, *Studies in Luke–Acts* (Festschrift Paul Schubert), New York, 1967, pp. 298–316, which suggests a date c. A.D. 100.

Roman Empire. In Christian eyes Judaism, now that its Temple and nationhood have both been destroyed, has been the object of divine judgment, and, what is more, no longer possesses the capacity to persecute the Church directly. Furthermore, Jewish Christianity, which had only reluctantly tolerated the liberty of the Gentile church, has lost its controlling influence. In retrospect the troubles and anguished decisions which had once beset the Church now appear in a brighter light. It was in this frame of mind that Luke created his great diptych. The apologetic and edifying tendencies to which he gave rein in doing so were further reinforced by what was in any case a harmonising view of his subject.

Nevertheless, Luke has not forgotten the past. He seeks to hold fast to the memory of crises and 'battles long ago', and to make them fruitful for the present. And so he takes the bold decision to supplement and continue the Gospel compiled by him[61] with a second volume, this time on the history of the Church. Such an attempt was unique. It gave Luke the chance to pose once more the question of the validity and supersession of the Law within the Church, and in portraying former events to discuss and answer it in his own way. Luke writes as an 'historian';[62] and this gives his treatment of the problem of the Law, as compared with Paul's, from the start a distinctive importance of its own. But we must be on our guard against over-hastily making a difference in intention and situation into an opposition on matters of substance.

The Gospel begins with the story of the birth of Christ[63]—in traditionalist Jewish circles, holding to an intensely Old Testament piety, a world of simple, 'righteous' people[64] who, 'in accordance with the Law of Moses,'[65] 'walk in all the commandments and ordinances of the Lord blameless'.[66] The purity and poetry of this vanished world are sketched with patent sympathy. Luke takes a lively interest in the old

[61] On this point cf. pp. 123ff. below.

[62] 'The first Christian historian' (Dibelius) was as such naturally also a 'theologian'. 'He did not state these principles' (sc. in the Prologue) 'as an historian or as a theologian, for he knew nothing of such a distinction', writes P. Schubert, 'The structure and significance of Luke 24', in: *Neutestamentliche Studien* (Bultmann-Festschrift)[2], 1957, p. 171.

[63] The essential coherence of these chapters with the overall plan of the two-part Lukan work is rightly emphasised by H. H. Oliver, 'The Lucan Birth Stories and the Purpose of Luke-Acts', *NTS* 10, 1963–4, pp. 203–205, and W. B. Tatum, 'The Epoch of Israel: Luke I–II and the theological plan of Luke–Acts,' *NTS* 13, 1966–7, pp. 184–195. Cf. also P. S. Minear, 'Luke's use of the Birth Stories,' in: (ed.) Keck and Martyn, *Studies in Luke-Acts* (Festschrift Paul Schubert), 1967, pp. 111–130. Recognition of this fact does not depend on any particular solution of the problem of sources.

[64] Lk. 1:6; 2:25.   [65] Lk. 2:22f.

[66] Lk. 1:6.

historic customs and ordinances,[67] the picture of which he derives from earlier sources.[68] There is absolutely no suggestion that the regulation of life by the Law is felt as religiously oppressive or painful. The conflict stories which Luke takes over from Mark are not here directed against the Law,[69] the free exposition of which by Jesus is resisted only by the 'hypocrisy' of the Pharisees.[70] As yet, however, all this ancient world of Judaism has not reached its goal; it is a waiting world, looking with a yearning but patient hope for the day when God will fulfil his promises[71] and redeem his people, so that 'delivered from the hand of their enemies, they may serve him without fear in holiness and righteousness all the days of their life'[72]—a day which still tarries. And although this hope at first is still clothed entirely in the old forms of Israel's national expectations,[73] yet there is already an intimation that the paradoxical course[74] of its fulfilment will in the end give 'all peoples' a share in the salvation.[75]

With the coming of Jesus the time of fulfilment has begun. He is the light, whose rising[76] opens a new age of salvation. Nevertheless, Jesus' first sermon, which proclaims the joyful message with explicit reference to olden prophecy,[77] discloses a sombre reaction: the ancient, elect people of God refuses to be converted, and in the person of its leaders sets itself in avowed and mortal opposition to Jesus.[78] Here is the first statement of a theme which recurs constantly throughout the Gospel, and which supplies the background to the coming catastrophe of Judaism and to the Gentile mission. Jews have the first claim on the new salvation. To them, therefore, it is first offered—even Paul, in Luke's presentation, regularly begins by preaching in the Jewish synagogues.[79] But the people of God proves itself unworthy of its privilege;[80] it rejects eternal life. Hence salvation finally passes it by, and turns instead to the Gentiles.[81] In the last chapter of Acts Paul, in

---

[67] Lk. 2:27, 42.

[68] In view of Lk. 23:56, Acts 1:12, etc., the intense pleasure in such details portraying the Jewish milieu and its laws cannot be ascribed entirely to the sources; it is characteristic of Luke himself.

[69] On the contrary, the Law points the way to life: Lk. 10:25-28; 16:29.

[70] Lk. 12:1. The long dispute over questions of purity (Mk 7:1ff.) is almost entirely omitted.

[71] Lk. 1:55, 70, 72f.   [72] Lk. 1:74f.

[73] Lk. 1:32f., 51ff., 71, 74; cf. 24:21; Acts 1:6.   [74] Lk. 2:34f.

[75] Lk. 2:30ff.   [76] Lk. 2:32.

[77] Isa. 61:1f. In the quotation the phrase about the 'day of vengeance' on the heathen has been tacitly omitted: cf. M. Rese, *Alttestamentliche Motive in der Christologie des Lukas* (Diss. Bonn), 1965, pp. 213ff.

[78] Lk. 4:16–30.   [79] Acts 17:2.

[80] For a more detailed study of this point cf. H. Conzelmann, *Theology of Luke*, 1960, pp. 145ff.; H. Flender, *St Luke: Theologian of Redemptive History* 1967, pp. 107ff.   [81] Acts 13:45-49; 26:19f.

his speech to the Roman Jews, draws the line across the page to close the account. The heart of the people, he declares, is hardened, and its destruction can no longer be averted, as Isaiah rightly foresaw long ago: 'Let it be known to you then that this salvation of God has been sent to the Gentiles; they will listen'.[82]

In all this the problem of the Law seems to play no part. Luke presents the matter as though at bottom it was only the stiff-necked jealousy of the Jews which begrudged the Gentiles salvation, and therefore sought to obstruct missionary work among them[83]—an idea which is already to be found in Paul.[84] In Acts Paul himself before his conversion appears not really as one zealous for the Law of his fathers but simply as a blind tyrant who persecutes Christians for no discernible reason.[85] In reality, however, Luke knows very well that from the start the Jews charged the Christians with breaches of the sacral ordinances: both Stephen and Paul are accused of apostasy from the Mosaic Law, with blasphemy, and with desecrating the Temple.[86] Luke, however, wishes to make these accusations out to be mere calumny. In his version Paul, even as a Christian, is a loyal and punctilious Jew who, whenever he is in a Jewish community, conducts himself in accordance with its rules.[87] Likewise, the accusers of Stephen are 'false witnesses', giving evidence from malice and at the instigation of the Jews.[88] But

---

[82] Acts 28:25–28.

[83] Acts 13:45; 17:5; 22:21f. I cannot agree with E. Haenchen (*Die Apostelgeschichte*[5]/[14], 1965, p. 102), who instead sees the preaching of the Resurrection 'from beginning to end' as the principal cause of offence which led to the breach. It is certainly true that for Luke the Resurrection stands at the heart of the Christian preaching, but he sees it as a perfectly rational occurrence and one, moreover, which corresponds exactly to an ancient Jewish hope: Acts 23:6; 24:21; 26:8. Hence to a certain extent it proves positively helpful, in that it can serve to attract and not only to offend both Gentiles (Acts 17:32) and Jews. Paul deliberately exploits the conflict which on this point existed between the Pharisees and the Sadducees: Acts 23:6; 24:21; 26:8; cf. 4:2.

[84] I Thess. 2:16; cf. O. Michel, 'Fragen zu I Thessalonicher 2, 14–16: Antijüdische Polemik bei Paulus', in: W. Eckert *et al.*, *Antijudaismus im N.T.?* 1967, pp. 50–59; cf. also Rom. 11:31.

[85] Acts 8:3; 9:1f., 13f. In any case, at this point Luke could hardly do otherwise, since he places the beginning of the offensive Gentile mission only very much later. But even when addressing the Apostolic Council Paul makes no mention of the problem of the Law, but testifies only to the success of the Gentile mission: Acts 15:4, 12, 25f.; cf. 21:19. A hint of the true situation occurs in Acts 22:3f.; cf. 21:28.

[86] Acts 6:11, 13f.; 18:13; 21:27–30; 24:6. Since these questions might prove to be of no interest to the Roman authorities (Acts 18:14f.; 25:18f.), Paul was also falsely accused of political crimes: Acts 17:7; 25:8. All three accusations occur together Acts 25:7f.

[87] Acts 16:3; 18:18; 21:23ff.; 23:3–5; 24:10, 20; 26:3ff. Cf. P. Vielhauer, 'Zum "Paulinismus" der Apostelgeschichte,' *EvTh* 10, 1950–1, pp. 2ff.

[88] Acts 6:11, 13.

this makes no difference to the fact that the whole ancient legal system is now ripe for destruction, and will collapse—not from any fault of the Christians but because of the Jews themselves, who again and again have despised and abused it. This is the truth which Stephen brings out with terrifying trenchancy in his last speech. Moses passed on to the Jews the words of life;[89] but they rejected and denied him, and never themselves kept their holy law.[90] 'Uncircumcised in heart and ears',[91] they offered their sacrifices not to God but to idols and to the stars;[92] and when, in place of the old tabernacle, a Temple was built, once again they failed to grasp that the Most High, as his own prophets had testified, does not dwell in a house constructed by human hands.[93] Every prophet sent to them they murdered,[94] and from time immemorial resisted the Holy Spirit. Finally, they betrayed and slew even the 'Righteous One' predicted from of old.[95]

The readers of these words well know what they imply: the measure of sin has been filled up, and judgment has not tarried.[96] Henceforward there is for the Jews no longer either Temple or sacrifice or even a commonwealth of their own within which the laws of Moses are observed. A new religious order is beginning, which has no need of such aids, and the heathen are to possess the salvation which Israel has

---

[89] Acts 7:35ff.; cf. Deut. 32:47.   [90] Acts 7:35, 53; cf. 23:3.

[91] Acts 7:51.   [92] Acts 7:41ff.

[93] Acts 7:48f.; cf. 17:24. I cannot associate myself with the view, which since Wellhausen has dominated critical study, that this text is intended to justify a total rejection of a temple of any sort. Personally I regard the opinion of Wendt, Bauernfeind et al. (rejected by Haenchen, op. cit., p. 237) as correct, namely that the purpose is to stress in opposition to the Jews that God is exalted far above the sacral τέμενος, and that the Temple possesses only 'relative value'. J. Bihler, Die Stephanusgeschichte, 1963, pp. 71–77, 161–178, and T. Holtz, 'Beobachtungen zur Stephanusrede Acta 7', in: Kirche—Theologie—Frömmigkeit (Festschrift Gottfried Holtz), 1865, pp. 102–114, have done nothing to shake me in this conclusion. (Holtz considers that behind the speech lies a Jewish original friendly to the Temple, which Luke has worked over in a contrary sense. But the reading τῷ θεῷ, which he adopts in v. 46, in my view makes such a reconstruction impossible). Despite the abrupt attack of v. 51, which comes as a surprise, the text does not call for so 'radical' an exegesis, and Luke could not possibly have stigmatised the accusation of hostility to the Temple (Acts 6:13) as a slander, and then confirmed its truth by the mouth of Stephen himself Furthermore, a hostile attitude to the Temple cannot be reconciled with Luke's other statements, either in the Gospel or in Acts (Bihler, op. cit., pp. 161ff.). Nevertheless, it must be admitted that by its violence Stephen's speech bring to light a hidden tendency and a suppressed problem with which Luke was in fact involved. At bottom he has outgrown the ancient sacral order, and certainly does not want it renewed; but on the other hand, he has no doubt of its divine origin and authority, and is therefore obliged to affirm it for the Jewish past, even though it no longer applies to the Gentiles (luckily for them) and has by now become absolutely impracticable.

[94] Acts 7:52f.; cf. Lk. 13:33.   [95] Acts 7:52.   [96] Cf. Lk. 21:20–24.

disdained. We cannot but be aware that Luke himself belongs spiritually to this new, universal human order of God, and welcomes it; but
his immediate concern is to attack not the Law but the Jews. The
Temple and sacrificial worship are not regarded as corrupt in themselves. If the time for them is now past never to return, yet the immediate occasion of their downfall is to be sought less in the inadequacy or
obsolescence of the Law than in the misuse which the Jews have made
of it, and in the crimes which they have committed against Christ
and the Christians, and which have called down judgment upon them.
As a result the Law has for ever lost its old significance, limited as this
was in time and to one particular people. But this is only one aspect of
the way in which salvation-history has developed. Already before the
end of the Jewish nation and quite independently of that, developments
within the Church have led to a limitation of the Law and the victory
of a new freedom which has given the Gentiles access to the Gospel. It
is this spiritual process, corresponding to the historical events, with
which Luke is chiefly concerned. In the chapters that follow its course
is described in detail and with superlative artistry. In all this the leaders
of the Church do not act arbitrarily or at their own discretion, nor is
it any sort of immanentist process which creates this new situation. It
is God himself who by his marvellous Providence guides his own eternal
counsel of salvation to a successful conclusion without the people most
involved being able at first to realise at all what is happening.[97]

The first dispersion and expansion of the Church is the direct
consequence of the Jews' crime against Stephen.[98] At first, however, it
reaches no further than the heterodox Judaism of Samaria,[99] and the
Ethiopian eunuch who, as a 'God-fearer' acquainted with the Scriptures,
is likewise not to be reckoned as properly a Gentile.[100] The Christian
mission does not stop at those boundaries which had always for Jews
been impossible to cross; but it remains still within the Jewish ambit,[101]
and its attachment to the Jerusalem community therefore raises no
serious difficulties.[102] The decisive transition into the world of heathenism is signalised by the Cornelius story.[103] Here the dramatis personae are

[97] On what follows cf. esp. M. Dibelius, 'Das Apostelkonzil', and 'Die Bekehrung des Cornelius', *Aufsätze zur Apostelgeschichte*[4], 1961, pp. 84ff. and 96ff.;
also the relevant sections of Haenchen's great commentary.
[98] Acts 8:2ff.; cf. 11:19.   [99] Acts 8:5ff.
[100] Acts 8:26ff. Even this encounter is brought about by direct instructions
from God.
[101] Cf. Acts 9:31.   [102] Acts 8:14ff.; 9:32; but cf. 11:1ff.
[103] It is true that Cornelius too is portrayed as a pious 'God-fearer', but at the
same time he is explicitly numbered among the 'Gentiles': Acts 10:28, 45.
There is here a tension with the contrasting evaluation of the eunuch which
Luke could not remove, because both stories were part of the tradition, and he
had to work with the material at his disposal. Moreover, in Luke's eyes the way

miraculously brought together by means of an angel, visions, and inspirations.[104] Peter cannot avoid—even though a violation of the Jewish Law is supposedly involved[105]—entering the Gentile's house, and even before he has finished preaching Christ, the spirit of God, to the astonishment of the Jewish Christians present, falls on all his Gentile hearers.[106] There is, as it were, nothing left for him to do but to draw the unavoidable conclusion, and to administer baptism to them.[107] He now perceives 'that God shows no partiality, but in every nation any one who fears him and does what is right is acceptable to him.'[108] Within the Church the distinction between 'clean' and 'unclean' human beings has no validity whatever;[109] everyone who believes in Jesus Christ receives the forgiveness of his sins.[110] This is also the answer which Peter gives when the Jerusalem Christians remonstrate with him for having disregarded the food laws;[111] the Spirit has fallen on the Gentiles 'just as on us at the beginning . . . Who was I that I could withstand God?' When those 'of the circumcision' heard this, 'they were silenced. And they glorified God, saying, "Then to the Gentiles also God has granted repentance unto life".'[112] God is the one who is really active here, bringing about the new situation. Where he has gone ahead, men are bound to follow.

With this the rightness of the mission to the Gentiles has been in principle decided. But the question how the Gentile Christians can be incorporated into the Church is left open. As Luke represents it, this matter came up for discussion only years later,[113] and in the meantime the Pauline mission had achieved its first great successes, thus justifying the earlier decision.[114] Only a particular group of Jewish Christians, and especially those who had once been Pharisees, refuse to acquiesce in the situation. They demand that all new converts should be circumcised and made to obey the Mosaic Law.[115] This is the occasion of the 'Apostolic Council', at which Peter once more brings in the Cornelius episode: God, 'who knows the heart', bestowed on the Gentiles the gift of the Holy Spirit, and by so doing 'bore witness to them'. There can be no going back on God's decision. Moreover, against the alleged necessity for salvation of keeping the Law a further argument is now

---

to this miraculous conversion was better prepared if the subject were a devout man (Acts 10:22) and not a completely godless heathen.

[104] Acts 10:3ff., 10ff., 19ff.   [105] Acts 10:28.   [106] Acts 10:44f.

[107] Acts 10:47.   [108] Acts 10:35.

[109] Acts 10:28; cf. 10:15; 15:9.   [110] Acts 10:43; cf. 11:17.

[111] Acts 11:3. In my opinion, and despite the objections of Haenchen, *op. cit.*, pp. 306f., Peter's vision in 10:9ff., the account of which is now repeated (11:4ff.) in this new context, relates to the same offence (cf. 10:10a).

[112] Acts 11:15–18.   [113] Acts 15:7.   [114] Cf. Acts 15:4, 12.

[115] Acts 15:1, 5. It is noticeable that Luke, in contrast to Paul, is at pains to clear the first apostles of any suspicion of judaising.

advanced: it has in any case never been possible truly to keep it. It would therefore be tempting God, should they seek to burden the newly converted heathen with a yoke 'which neither our fathers nor we have been able to bear.[116] But we believe that we shall be saved through the grace of the Lord Jesus, just as they will.'[117] James supplements these remarks with a proof from Scripture, based not only on the prophets but also on Moses, who not for nothing 'from early generations . . . has had in every city those who preach him'.[118] So, in the end, the decision is arrived at to annul the illegitimate demands of the judaisers, and not to lay any further burdens on the souls of the heathen who turn to God,[119] that is to say, formally to grant them freedom from the Mosaic Law. The modest conditions attached to this decision, enumerating certain requirements still regarded as 'necessary', are not seen by Luke as a limitation of this freedom; for by his time they had long been a universally recognised moral code for Christians, the validity of which was therefore in his eyes something taken for granted which no one could find oppressive.[120] Thus the new freedom of the Gentile church is

[116] Cf. Acts 13:38f.
[117] Acts 15:10f.; cf. 10:43; 13:38; 20:24. In this smooth and simple form the Pauline faith lives on, not just in Luke but as a standard Christian profession.
[118] Acts 15:21. This is, however, a sentence 'which, though linguistically and textually free from any sort of problem, yet as regards context and meaning is one of the most difficult in the whole New Testament' (Dibelius, op. cit., p. 87.)
[119] Acts 15:19, 24.
[120] This is the crucial discovery of Haenchen, op. cit., pp. 412ff., who rightly regards the 'Apostolic Decree' as Luke's own composition. The prohibitions themselves 'will have come to be accepted as binding in a mixed Dispersion community, where Jewish demands were more moderate, and the Jewish members of the congregation contented themselves with requiring the observance of these four rules, laid down by Moses himself for the heathen' (p. 413). Reference should also be made here to the early study of K. Böckenhoff, Das apostolische Speisegesetz in den ersten fünf Jahrhunderten, 1903. To 'the admittedly scanty material', which Haenchen adduces to illustrate the later dissemination of the decree in the Church may be added Pliny, Ep. X, 96, 10: cf. A. Ehrhardt, Social Problems in the Early Church. The Framework of the New Testament Stories, 1964, pp. 276–290, esp. 281ff. Cf. also E. Molland, 'La circoncision, le baptême et l'autorité du décret apostolique (Actes XV, 28sq.) dans les milieux judéo-chrétiens des Pseudo-Clémentines', StTh 9, 1955, pp. 1–39, on the dissemination of these or similar regulations in the light of the Jewish Christian sources of the Pseudo-Clementines; also: R. Arbesmann, art. 'Fasten', RAC VII, pp. 484f. In fact these prohibitions correspond to the rules which 'in the Old Testament itself are imposed even on the heathen, should they be living in a Jewish community': Haenchen, op. cit., p. 392 n. (cf. Lev. 17f). It would seem that Luke himself was still aware of this fact, in view of his reference (Acts 15:21) in this context to Moses, who is preached in every town: cf. n. 118 above. But if this illuminating interpretation of the passage, given by Haenchen, op. cit., p. 391, is correct, then we must add that Luke by no means made the point clear, but rather left it intentionally obscure. In the crucial passage (Acts 15:28) he speaks only in quite general terms of the 'necessity' of observing these points,

realised in practice, the apostles confirming what the Holy Spirit has indicated. Joy is universal. From henceforward there is, in Luke's version, no further conflict with the Judaisers;[121] it is only the Jews who fight against the freedom of the Gentile Christians, and in particular persecute Paul with the help of Gentile mobs whom they have incited.[122] The life of the Gentile Christian church, as Luke knows it, has finally been put in order. Within it the Mosaic Law has no further standing.

Thus Luke, taking a historian's route, arrives at the same destination that Paul, in the light of his own call-experience, had desiderated on, so to say, dogmatic grounds. His claim to be the sole apostle of all the Gentiles Luke suppresses. The most important decisions in the debate about the Law are arrived at without any intimation being given of his significant role in the matter. Luke is concerned to portray the overall development, and to reserve the dominant position for the first apostles in Jerusalem. Nevertheless, in his evaluation of the Law in principle he largely agrees with Paul; and in the practical consequences for the life of the Church he is absolutely at one with him.[123] For both, the factor that sets the whole discussion in motion, is the same. 'For both Paul and "Luke" the crucial problem is the freedom of the Gentile mission from the Law';[124] and it was this which called in question the universal recognition of the Jewish Law. Both are convinced that the Law was given 'spiritually' and by God himself to the nation; but both also affirm that it has had its day, and that the grace which has been manifested in Christ has now put an end to its dominion. Furthermore,

---

and in 21:25 refers merely to the 'judgment' of the Apostles. The word 'Law', is the very one which he does not use. Conzelmann, op. cit., p. 198 n. 2, is therefore not expressing Luke's view of the matter when he writes: 'The apostolic decree is indicative of continuity, in that the Law, even though reduced to an absolute minimum, is applied to the Gentiles.'

[121] But cf. 21:20ff.

[122] Acts 17:5ff.; 18:12ff.; 21:27; 22:22; 24:5ff.; 25:3.

[123] W. Mundle, 'Das Apostelbild der Apostelgeschichte', ZNW 27, 1928, p. 50, writes: 'Because for Luke there are no longer any struggles or rivalries between the apostles, he is deprived of any opportunity to emphasise Paul's independence in the way that Paul himself does. The historical picture which we are offered in Acts is one of a Paulinism that has been victorious all along the line.'

[124] Haenchen, op. cit., p. 99. Haenchen continues, however: 'But "Luke" is unaware of the Pauline solution.' By 'the' Pauline solution of the problem Haenchen, like so many, understands simply the narrow polemical thesis that the Law leads 'not to God but to sin'. I am very far from wishing to weaken in any way the theological importance of this distinctively Pauline idea; but if we are concerned with actual historical connections, then such an assessment is extremely one-sided. Not one single primitive Christian writer in fact adopted this particular Pauline thesis. If, therefore, we wish to make this the yardstick for our evaluation, then Paulinism played absolutely no part whatever in the problem of the Law.

in the firm opinion of both, this dominion could never have been the basis for an effective order of salvation; and for that reason also it ought not to be forced upon the heathen. Finally, both appeal in support of the new freedom and of the historical fact that the Law is obsolete to the explicit testimony of sacred Scripture.

Nevertheless, as retailed by Luke Paul's ideas lack bite. They have lost their abstruseness, but at the same time also their original profundity, and have been flattened out into colourless generalities, easy to grasp but lacking definition. The disciple has never had personally to battle through either the outward or the inward conflicts in which Paul was engaged. He has never experienced the demonic power of the Law, which separates men from God precisely in virtue of the truth of its demands; and he is quite satisfied that it can be dismissed simply on the grounds of its misuse by the Jews and of the impossibility of fulfilling it.[125] Subsidiary ideas, of which Paul does indeed make use, have here been given fundamental importance. On the other hand, whereas Paul regarded any acceptance of the Law by Gentiles as a denial of Christ, for Luke it would simply have meant subjecting them to an unreasonable burden.[126] Similarly, the concealed problems in the concept of salvation history are also identified differently in each writer. For Paul, it remains hard to conceive why the fatal Law was ever permitted at all, if it could do no more than multiply sin; for Luke, who judges it less harshly, and indeed regards it with some sympathy, it seems more reasonable to ask whether in it there were not in fact certain limitations and defects which have been done away by the new, better order. The ideas that the Temple and the sacrificial cultus are dispensable, and that cultic purity regulations are a matter of indifference to God, who is near to every human being,[127] point in this direction. Lukan Christianity has clear traces of 'humanistic' spiritualisation and universal morality. Nevertheless, he has not drawn the logical conclusions which inevitably follow from such a position. For him it is enough that in the contemporary Gentile Church the Law has lost its power; his assessment of it in itself is as little critical as that of Paul.

Luke, too, still understands the Law as a unity and does not divide it into essential, permanent truths and transitory, ceremonial pre-

[125] These two reasons are in fact not wholly compatible, and either one or the other tends to be given prominence according to the context.

[126] It may well be that when he refers to the impossibility of fulfilling the Law Luke is thinking of the 'vast quantity of commands and prohibitions, which no man could hope to cope with', which is 'the way in which the matter would have struck a Gentile Christian'; but he never explicitly advances this banal justification for regarding the Law as intolerable. In my view, we have no right to attribute this to him, as Haenchen, *op. cit.*, p. 100, wants to do, simply on the grounds that it must obviously have been one of his leading ideas.

[127] Acts 17:27f.

scriptions.[128] Moreover, he has no hesitation whatever about allowing Jewish Christians their observance of the Law as an obvious right. This attitude, which by the standards of later solutions of the problem is very nearly self-contradictory, is the very thing which shows how close he is to Paul. Equally, Luke absolutely rejects the idea of a 'new, Christian Law'.[129] He abstains as firmly as Paul from adopting any Old Testament regulations as such for the Church; and at the very point where such a transfer in fact takes place, that is, in the conditions attached to the Apostolic Decree, so far from emphasising the point, he takes pains to camouflage it.[130] This agreement with Paul is all the more noteworthy in that Luke, in contrast to Paul, takes a definite historical and theological interest in particular ordinances, offices, and regulations within the community.[131] Yet he never derives such regulations from the old laws but always and only from Jesus, the apostles, or the Spirit at work in the Church.[132]

In his conception of the Law, therefore, Luke, taking him all in all, stands to Paul in a relationship much more of either kinship or dependence than of difference or variation. The same applies to his attitude to Scripture,[133] though here he shows more theological independence, and faces new questions. For Luke, as well as for Paul, the Old Testament as a whole is God-given, and consists exclusively of divine revelation. But the Law has become for him, far more than for Paul, a matter of 'historical' interest only, and has receded very much into the background within Scripture as a whole. The Prophets, however, have acquired correspondingly greater significance; and this element in the Scriptures has become virtually the determinative factor in their Christian use.[134] In contrast to Paul, Luke has adopted the traditional

---

[128] Goppelt, *Christentum und Judentum im ersten und zweiten Jahrhundert,* 1954, p. 232, remarks that Luke 'is the only N.T. writer to single out the ceremonial ordinances from the νόμος by giving them the special designation of the " ἔθη of Moses".' This distinction is certainly significant. But it does not justify us in saying that a lower value is placed on these elements; cf. Lk. 16:17. The conjecture that by using this phrase Luke may have intended to help the congregation to understand 'what in the O.T. Law was of permanent directive value for them', goes far too far.

[129] Conzelmann, *op. cit.,* p. 147, sees a clear contrast here between Luke and the developments of Early Catholicism.

[130] Cf. n. 120 above. Even the presbyteral constitution of the congregation is presented as an innovation and not as an O.T. Jewish tradition: Acts 14:23.

[131] He is in no sense, however, searching for rigid norms but simply for historical prototypes and examples.

[132] The one exception (Acts 23:5) proves the rule: here Paul is speaking as a Jew in the presence of the Jewish authorities.

[133] On this subject cf. the careful survey in Conzelmann, *op. cit.,* pp. 146ff., where, however, the emphasis is placed very differently.

[134] Nevertheless, the wealth of scriptural citation in Luke is not yet—as it is in Justin—fully covered by the pattern of prediction and fulfilment: Rese,

christological proof from Scripture, and developed it.[135] In the Gospel, citations from the Prophets accompany the whole life of Jesus from its beginnings to the Passion and Resurrection, and even find their way into the first basic data of the history of the Church.[136] Every part of the Bible—Moses, the Prophets, the Psalms and the other 'Writings'— is pressed into service.[137] The men of the old covenant not only agree in faith with Christ, apparently they had already 'foreseen' the details of his destiny—in fact it is this prevision which is the essence of their prophetic role.[138] In Paul it was only Scripture as such which possessed this mysterious power of prophetic vision. It is true that in Luke the formal oracular method is not carried to such lengths of precision as in Matthew. We are no longer 'in the realm of the clear and naïve' but in that of solemn mysteries, 'beyond the understanding of the profane';[139] but on the other hand, so far as the meaning is concerned, Luke offers simple correspondences, illuminating to the reason. The Greek-educated Gentile Christian no longer has a mind to the dark, typologising and hair-splitting exegesis of Paul. But Luke knows as well as Paul that the meaning of the prophets really becomes clear only in the light of the present, that is, of Christ.[140] It is Christ himself who has to open the eyes of those who believe in him, if they are to perceive the meaning of the ancient prophecies. This applies particularly to that hardest of all the riddles of history, the Passion and death of the Son of God, the necessity of which can be understood only on the basis of Scripture. This process of comprehension through hindsight is unforgettably described in the Emmaus story. His identity hidden from them, the Risen Lord takes his disciples through all the relevant passages, awakening their sluggish minds to faith by expounding to them what the

op. cit., p. 204. T. Holtz, Untersuchungen über die alttestamentlichen Zitate bei Lukas (Habilitationsschrift, Halle, 1964, TS only) appears to be concerned essentially with questions of provenance and textual variants only; cf., his own comments, TLZ 90, 1965, cols. 863f.

[135] Acts 1:16, 20; 2:16ff. This however, represents all that O.T. prophecy could predict, in Luke's view. The preaching of the coming Kingdom and judgment is still something deriving from Christ alone: cf. Conzelmann, op. cit., pp. 16ff., 150ff.

[136] Cf. Lk. 24:25, 44. Special emphasis had already been given to the Psalms in Philo. To these predictions should now be added those made by the Lord himself: Lk. 21; 24:6, 44; Acts 1:4; 11:16; 20:35.

[137] Cf. Acts 2:30f.

[138] This means that for Luke the words of Scripture are themselves 'drawn into the concept of divine predestination' (Acts 1:16; 2:31; 3:18; 7:52; 13:24): Flender, op. cit., p. 129.

[139] A. von Ungern-Sternberg, Der traditionelle alttestamentliche Schriftbeweis 'de Christo' und 'de evangelio' in der alten Kirche bis zur Zeit Eusebs von Caesarea, 1913, pp. 286ff.

[140] Cf. Acts 8:30f.

prophets had said beforehand concerning his Passion, until joy at this new understanding begins to burn in their hearts.[141] In the farewell scene at the conclusion of the Gospel the importance of such an understanding of Scripture is affirmed once again. The Lord reminds them of his own words that 'everything written about me in the Law of Moses and the prophets and the psalms must be fulfilled. Then he opened their minds to understand the scriptures.' Only when this has been done have these future world-missionaries become 'witnesses' in the fullest sense.[142] This retrospective reference to words spoken on an earlier occasion by Jesus himself is all the more striking in that the Gospel has said nothing about any such previous instruction.[143] The fact is, of course, that dogmatic requirements are at work here. Faith in Christ rests on the proof from prophecy, which reveals the inner, salvation-history meaning of the story of Christ. Hence Jesus must have taught his disciples this proof from the start. The truth of the message about Christ can be checked only by reference to Scripture.[144] The Jews, who reject this message, thus prove themselves to be obdurate also as regards the Scripture;[145] Christians, however, understand what is involved, and believe the Scripture.[146]

Alongside the Scripture, however, there now emerges a second and powerful factor. This is the Holy Spirit, and the new authority of the disciples, which is responsible for the fact that the testimony and the message are indeed believed. The Spirit, as 'power from on high',[147] gives the ability to proclaim the Gospel of Christ openly and effectively. Moreover, in the power of Jesus' name the disciples themselves work 'miracles of healing, signs and wonders',[148] which vouch for them in the same way that Jesus himself was 'attested' and legitimated in his authority by 'mighty works'.[149] Luke emphasises this element far more strongly than Paul, who also knows and acknowledges this type of argument.[150] But there is no reason to condemn Luke's sometimes rather naïve pleasure in obvious miracle-stories as a regrettable lapse into half-heathen habits of thought—in his presentation there is always a theological meaning.[151] For Luke, there is no Christian preaching

---

[141] Lk. 24:25–27, 32.   [142] Lk. 24:44–48.

[143] This is still true even if Jesus' words are to be understood strictly 'as indicating the content of the final teaching of the Risen Lord': H. von Baer, *Der heilige Geist in den Lukasschriften,* 1926, p. 77.

[144] Acts 17:11, 18:28.   [145] Acts 13:27.

[146] Acts 24:14; 26:22f.   [147] Lk. 24:49.

[148] Acts 2:43; 4:7, 10, 30; 5:12; 6:8; 14:3; 15:12; 19:11.

[149] Acts 2:22; Lk. 24:19.

[150] Rom. 15:18f.; I Cor. 2:4; II Cor. 12:12; Gal. 3:5; on the subject of this palpably traditional conception cf. E. Käsemann, 'Die Legitimität des Apostels', *ZNW* 41, 1942, pp. 61ff.

[151] Baer, *op. cit.,* p. 203: 'Just as there was no clash between the moral seriousness of the Person of Jesus and his miraculous power, so also there could be no

which, on the one hand, is not spiritually attested by the living, miraculous power of its effects, and on the other, cannot be checked and confirmed as to its rightness by the agreement of its testimony with ancient prophecy.[152] Herein lie the truth and power which create belief. Only in this way are the proof from Scripture, and the ancient Scriptures themselves, whose importance Luke stresses more strongly than does any other New Testament writer, brought into a proper theological equilibrium with faith in Christ and the spirit of Christ. Testimony to Christ stands on its own feet, and is alive with directly overwhelming power; but at the same time it looks back to Scripture, the ultimate meaning of which it uncovers, and with the testimony of which it can never dispense.

This immense stress laid on the testimony of Scripture as an indispensable confirmation of faith and of the preaching is something consciously thought out, and in this respect goes beyond Paul, and moves some way toward those later apologetic theories which occasionally make Scripture the exclusive basis for conversion to Christianity.[153] But Luke is far removed from the unguarded rationalism of this false biblicism. Luke not only frees the Jewish Bible from the Law; at the same time he achieves the positive task of defining theologically the place which it is to occupy within the Christian Church. In his own way he brings the understanding which Paul created to its proper conclusion.

III

One step further and we find ourselves in 'John'. Here the question of the contemporary standing of the Law has been almost forgotten. Only weak and obscure reminders of former controversies still echo through the text, attracting little or no attention. We are at the end of the period when men's attitude to the old Bible was motivated and determined by the conflict over the Law and its validity in practice. Instead, new questions are looming up, concerned no longer with this

---

feeling that the mighty outward operations of the Spirit of the Lord were incompatible with the spirit of moral renewal.' It should be pointed out, however, that the 'mighty operations' are never, in Luke, ascribed directly to the Holy Spirit.

[152] This does not mean, however, that Luke would have regarded it as necessary to refer back constantly to the Old Testament. Those mission sermons which he presents as addressed not to Jews but to Gentiles make virtually no use of the Old Testament: cf. U. Wilckens, *Die Missionsreden der Apostelgeschichte*, 1961, pp. 96ff. In this again Luke is in agreement with Paul: cf. pp. 24f. above.

[153] Cf. pp. 87f. below.

single point but with the authority of the traditional 'scriptures' as a whole.

Our remarks will be based on the Gospel of John in the final form in which it has come down to us.[154] This Gospel quite certainly cannot be regarded as expressing a standard Christian piety of an ecclesiastical type, even though it is not in the strict sense 'heretical'. It probably reflects the spirit and the theology of particular, spiritually highly developed circles and conventicles, based in Asia Minor or Syria. We shall refrain in this context from discussing the obscure problems of the Gospel's origin.

It is obvious that the Gospel represents a working over of earlier texts and traditions, which it has taken as the basis for its own very different thought and idiom. Among these earlier elements there was certainly a Gospel which was to some extent akin to the Synoptists. It is from this traditional material that the few traces derive of those discussions about the Law which were once so typical. They are now seen through the haze, as it were, of a completely different mode of thought, and are not introduced for their own sake. They are now no more than an illustration of the fundamental opposition between Jesus and the Jews. Moreover, in the presence of Jesus, the Son of God, 'the Jews' are representatives of the godless world; and the Law of Moses to which they appeal, 'their' Law, as it is termed over and over again, thus becomes virtually a symbol of a world of faith which Jesus has rendered obsolete.[155]

In two healing stories we are told that Jesus has broken the commandment concerning the Sabbath, and thus aroused the opposition of the Pharisees and the 'Jews': first, in the healing of the lame man at the Pool of Bethesda,[156] and secondly, in that of the man born blind.[157] On each occasion this detail is not related immediately but only brought in later, and not very skilfully at that.[158] It serves simply as a starting-point for the discourse, which forthwith turns to the Person of Jesus, and concentrates on him and on his superhuman claims. What matters is to acknowledge the Son of God; and because 'Moses' disciples' fail to do this, Moses himself becomes a judgment upon them.[159] In the traditional manner they seek to turn the old Law against Jesus;[160] but the Evangelist no longer bothers to discuss in detail how far the Law,

[154] The Epistles, in my view, are the work of the 'Redactor', or at least of someone in his immediate circle. On the Apocalypse, with its very different character, cf. pp. 215ff. below.
[155] The relevant material on this point has been collected by, e.g., W. Bauer, *Das Johannesevangelium*³, 1933, p. 31. That occasionally the concept still occurs in John with a different, somewhat more concrete significance, has been rightly stressed by W. Gutbrod, art. Ἰσραήλ κτλ., *TWNT* III, 1938, pp. 378–381.
[156] Joh. 5:1–9.   [157] Joh. 9:1–7.   [158] Joh. 5:9; 9:14.
[159] Joh. 9:28f.; cf. 5:45.   [160] Joh. 9:39; cf. 5:27.
E

despite the external breach of its commandments, is nevertheless fulfilled or surpassed or superseded by the Redeemer. Only once does Jesus attempt himself to appeal to the Law in his own defence, and to justify his actions by reference to it as in the Synoptic Gospels. When occasion arises, he says, the rite of circumcision, which Moses commanded, is carried out on the Sabbath; how much more permissible, therefore, must it be to make a man's whole body healthy on the sabbath![161] As a means of establishing the primacy of the command of love this example is not, it must be admitted, particularly well chosen. The Jews, it has been alleged earlier, themselves did not observe the Law: 'none of you keeps the Law'[162]— but again, the argument is not pressed. Traditional ideas stand side by side, and there is no attempt to reconcile them;[163] they are no more than touched upon, because the real interest is not at all in the 'Law of Moses' but in Jesus. The central concern is to affirm him and his divine origin.

Christ is the Light of the World, the Way, the Truth, and the Life; no one experiences the truth and comes to the Father except through him.[164] John's real opinion of the Law becomes apparent only when it is no longer a question of individual regulations but of the crucial claim of the Law to mediate salvation to men, and when this claim is confronted with Jesus. Here the judgment is unequivocal: the Law, that is, the essence of the Jewish revelation and religion, does not lead to God: 'the Law was given through Moses; grace and truth came through Jesus Christ'[165]—meaning, only through Christ, for the first time through Christ, who truly knew the Father,[166] and absolutely never at any time through Moses and the Law. In thus setting the two side by side the author certainly does not imply a 'synthetic parallelism' with the old revelation;[167] this is a clear antithesis, with the emphasis appropriate to a programmatic declaration.[168] The Jews do indeed

---

[161] Joh. 7:22–24.   [162] Joh. 7:19; cf. 5:47.
[163] R. Bultmann, *Gospel of John*, 1971, p. 277, notes the same phenomenon, though interpreting it somewhat differently, in accordance with his own presuppositions: the 'clear line of argument has been confused by the Evangelist's treatment'.
[164] Joh. 8:12; 9:5; 10:9; 12:35; 14:6, etc.   [165] Joh. 1:17.   [166] Joh. 1:18.
[167] As suggested by J. Jeremias, art. Μωυσῆς, *TWNT* IV, 1942, p. 877; similarly W. Eltester, 'Der Logos und sein Prophet', in: *Apophoreta* (Haenchen-Festschrift), 1964, p. 133, and many others. N. A. Dahl, 'The Johannine Church and History', in: *Current Issues in N.T. Interpretation* (Festschrift O. Piper), 1962, p. 133, writes: 'The Johannine contrast is that between the law, given through Moses, which is a testimony, and the reality to which Moses bore witness, the true grace and gracious truth, which came through Jesus Christ.'
[168] So too, though with some reservations, W. Gutbrod, art. νόμος, *TWNT* IV, 1942, pp. 1075f., and most of all, Bultmann, *Gospel of John*, p. 00: 'The question whether there exists any sort of positive relationship between the Old Testament and the revelation in Jesus is not even considered here . . . all that the writer has in mind is their opposition. . . .'

imagine that Moses supplied a sign to guarantee his authority when he gave them 'bread from heaven' to eat; but the true 'bread of life' is given not by Moses but by the Father, and this bread is Jesus himself.[169] He is no accuser, like Moses, but a redeemer of those who believe in him; whoever sets his hope on Moses instead of Jesus is lost.[170]

These are ideas which in their contrast between law and grace, Moses and Christ, are reminiscent of Paul. In John, however, the same thesis is essentially harsher in its effects, because all the considerations which in Paul still strive to justify the Law as such and to safeguard its intrinsic value have disappeared. John does not emphasise the divine origin of the Law, which is seen as the law of Moses and the Jews only. He says nothing about the permanent validity of its demands, nor does he distinguish within the Old Testament between an era of the Law and a previous period during which faith was already dominant. All relative values, all qualifications and distinctions have vanished in the transcendent clarity of the light which radiates from Jesus, who from of old has enlightened the world, and who now bestows only grace upon grace.[171]

In such circumstances, however, there is also no explicit rejection or condemnation of the Law. It has become a thing indifferent. The question may be asked, whether the 'Jews', when they turn the Law against Jesus, are not in fact simply abusing it and acting contrary to its real meaning—even to the point of that terrible cry with which they cut themselves off from their 'king': 'We have a Law, and by that Law he ought to die'.[172] And indeed there is one passage in the Gospel where the Law comes directly to the help of Jesus against 'the High Priest and the scribes'. Some time before the final disaster the pious Nicodemus objects to the precipitate and legally improper attempts to secure Jesus' destruction, with the words: 'Does our law judge a man without first giving him a hearing, and learning what he does?'[173] It may be doubted, however, whether this reference should be taken to signify anything more than an appeal to universal standards of justice and righteousness. The appeal to the Mosaic Law in force at the time serves, therefore, only to express the traditional idea that the condemnation of Jesus was 'unjust' in every sense, and his execution a judicial murder.[174] That the Torah has special significance as a document of divine revelation is hardly in mind here; the Law figures only as an

---

[169] Joh. 6:31–35.   [170] Joh. 5:45; cf. 7:19.   [171] Joh. 1:9, 16.
[172] Joh. 19:7.
[173] Joh. 7:51 Cf. Bultmann, Gospel of John, p. 311: 'Nicodemus' cool objectivity allows us to see' that revelation does not simply contradict the Law, but that it is the misuse of the Law which makes the world deaf to the Revealer.'
[174] Cf. Joh. 18:23; 19:6.

'example', not in its 'unexampled' importance.[175] John is not interested in the question, what the theological significance of the Law may have been before Jesus was manifested. All that matters is this: to know that he has 'come', that through him as a result his disciples 'have life, and have it abundantly',[176] and 'abide' in him and in his teaching alone.[177] John anyway never even considers any adoption of the old norms by the Church;[178] the 'new commandment' of love, which controls the Church, makes external regulations, it would seem, absolutely superfluous. Even in paraenetic contexts, therefore, there is hardly an mention of the Old Testament.[179] Jesus, his word and his teaching only are decisive.

In the circumstances it would not really be surprising if together with the 'Law', which in John is treated as one entity with the 'Scripture', the old Jewish Bible as a whole had become an object of indifference, a mere relic from the past. This is not, however, what happened. There was one thread linking the Old Testament positively with Jesus which even John was not prepared to sacrifice, namely the 'proof from scripture', which was possible only by using the Old Testament. The Old Testament quotations in the Fourth Gospel—and· there are not many—are almost all to be accounted for on this basis;[180] this is the relationship on which all the stress is laid. That this should be so is, of course, in line with early Christian tradition; but the picture presented

[175] The use of this play on words (in German, 'beispielhaft' . . . 'beispiellos': Tr.) to point up the situation in this passage was made by E. Käsemann during the discussion on a lecture given in 1955 by N. A. Dahl on 'John and the Old Testament', the ideas in which have since appeared in print in the article listed in n. 167 above.

[176] Joh. 10:10.   [177] Joh. 8:31; 15.   [178] Joh. 13:34.

[179] Explicit citations from the O.T. are never used for this purpose. The reference to Cain in I Joh. 3:12 does no more than evoke a memory, and it is in any case the only such instance. The idea of νόμος never occurs; and the Jewish concept of τηρεῖν τὰς ἐντολάς is paradoxically given a new twist by making it refer (in Joh. 14:21) to the new command of love, and in I John to the commands of Jesus: I Joh. 2:3f.; 3:22, 24; 5:3; cf. 2:5; on this point cf. H. Riesenfeld, art. τηρέω, TWNT VIII, 1965-, pp. 144f. That the formula, ἀπ' ἀρχῆς, and the appeal to the 'old teaching' refer in this Epistle not to the O.T. but to the beginnings of the Church has been demonstrated by H. Conzelmann, ' "Was von Anfang war" ', in: Neutestamentliche Studien für R. Bultmann², 1957, pp. 194–201.

[180] On this subject as a whole cf., e.g., C. K. Barrett, 'The Old Testament in the Fourth Gospel', JTS 48, 1947, pp. 155–169; B. Noack, Zur johanneischen Tradition, Copenhagen, 1954, pp. 71–89. According to Dahl (op. cit., n. 167 above) the quotations occur in all strata of the Gospel except in what Bultmann calls the 'revelationary discourses'. Bultmann himself thinks that in this connection we have to reckon with secondary glosses and additions. E. Hirsch, Das vierte Evangelium in seiner ursprünglichen Gestalt verdeutscht und erklärt, 1936, for obvious reasons regarded almost all O.T. quotations as additions by the redactor.

by the proof from Scripture within the Fourth Gospel is not homogeneous. Even at the level of purely formal classification very varied types of proof are found side by side: the appeals to Scripture may be made explicitly within the framework of a controversy between Jesus and the Jews, they may occur as terse or extended allusions, as editorial reflection, or in the form of typology. The Fourth Gospel is here manifestly the inheritor of a richly developed tradition with many branches.[181] In addition—and with even more emphasis than in Luke—predictions of Jesus' own occur alongside the old Scriptures.[182] The quotations themselves, moreover, are not on a par with one another as regards their relevance or importance. It will be necessary to examine these differences a little further, since they are extremely significant for the Johannine attitude to the Old Testament. In this context the problem of sources is not of decisive importance; but the general differentiae between the traditional and the specifically Johannine material are in any case impossible to overlook.

A first stratum of simple, direct scriptural proofs, which in essence are undoubtedly traditional material, occurs within the Passion narrative. It was from this setting that scriptural proof originally sprang, and here pre-eminently that it remained a potent factor. The entry into Jerusalem,[183] the casting of lots for the clothes at the foot of the Cross,[184] the drink of vinegar,[185] and the omission of the crurifragium[186] are supported by accompanying quotations from the Old Testament. Again, the testimony of the Baptist, now put into his own mouth, is traditional in character.[187] This naturally does not imply that such argumentation was taken less seriously by the Evangelist, only that for him it is by now a conventional theological exercise which is taken for granted. In the very first chapter he has Jesus being proclaimed as the one 'of whom Moses in the Law, and also the prophets wrote'.[188] The biased Jewish conviction that in the Scriptures they have eternal life is perfectly correct to the extent—and only to the extent—that these actually refer to Jesus, and are to be read from that standpoint.[189] If the Jews had really believed Moses, they would also believe Jesus; for it was of Jesus that Moses wrote.[190] 'Had they been open to the words of Moses they would also have been open to the words of Jesus.'[191] Furthermore, for John the unveiling of the old prophecies is possible only *post eventum*, starting from encounter with Christ and

[181] Cf. von Ungern-Sternberg, *op. cit.*, pp. 268.; B. Lindars, *New Testament Apologetic*, 1961, pp. 265–272.
[182] Joh. 2:19–22; 18:9–32; cf. 12:33f.; 13:19. That in 17:12 a saying of Jesus is adduced as 'scripture' is the very odd assumption of E. Freed, *Old Testament Quotations in the Gospel of John*, Leiden, 1965, pp. 51ff., 119f., 129.
[183] Joh. 12:13–15.   [184] Joh. 19:24.   [185] Joh. 19:28f.
[186] Joh. 19:36f.   [187] Joh. 1:23.   [188] Joh. 1:45.
[189] Joh. 5:39.   [190] Joh. 5:46f.   [191] Bultmann, *Gospel of John*, p. 272.

experience of him. 'What stands written' is disclosed to the disciples of Jesus only in retrospect, after the glorification of the Lord;[192] and, as in Luke, they cannot believe the Resurrection until they have grasped and understood afresh the relevant words of Scripture.[193] The process of prediction itself is now—in a manner made easier by the concept of Jesus' pre-existence—understood in a most exaggerated sense: Abraham himself was already exulting that he was to see the coming of Jesus, and he did see it, with joy;[194] and 'Isaiah saw his glory, and spoke of him'.[195]

Nevertheless, the links for which the Evangelist is really looking are not to be found in the traditional, miraculous coincidences discernible here or there. His most important proofs from Scripture are concerned rather with the deeper, religious significance of the Redeemer himself, his destiny and his person. The saving meaning of these things is not so much substantiated by the old quotations, as hinted at and given mysterious emphasis. Christ, it is asserted in dependence on Isaiah, is the Lamb of God,[196] who takes away the sin of the world; hence—like Moses' bronze serpent[197]—he must be 'lifted up', both on the cross and from the earth altogether, 'that whoever believes in him may have eternal life'.[198] The divinity of the Son cannot be contested, if the Scripture, which 'cannot be broken', has already described as 'gods' mere men who have heard God's word.[199] It is to Jesus that the words of the Psalmist apply: 'Zeal for thine house will consume me',[200] that is, bring him to his death;[201] and it is in his followers that the old

---

[192] Joh. 2:22; 12:16; cf. 14:26.

[193] Joh. 20:9. The exposition of this verse in the context of the grave-narrative is, however, difficult. Perhaps we are here dealing, as Bultmann, *John*, p. 685, thinks, with a gloss due to church redaction. What the words have in mind would then be the situation of the disciples up to the moment when they enter the empty tomb, after which they are 'convinced by the evidence of their own eyes'. Since, however, the phrase applies only to the mysterious 'other disciple' and not to Peter, it must certainly be intended to pay honour to his livelier faith.

[194] Joh. 8:56.

[195] Joh. 12:41; cf. Dahl, *op. cit.*, pp. 131f. According to Bultmann, *John*, p. 452 n. 4, this is only a 'footnote' by the Evangelist. A similar conception to that in these passages, though expressed somewhat more guardedly, is to be found in I Pet. 1:10–12; cf. K. H. Schelkle, 'Hermeneutische Regeln im Neuen Testament,' in: *Wort und Schrift* (Gesammelte Aufsätze), 1966, p. 40.

[196] Joh. 1:29, 36; cf. Isa. 53:7. On this topic cf. most recently F. Gryglewicz, 'Das Lamm Gottes,' *NTS* 13, 1966–7, pp. 133–146; B. Murmelstein, 'Das Lamm in Test. Jos. 19, 8', *ZNW* 58, 1967, pp. 273–279.

[197] Num. 21:8f.   [198] Joh. 3:14f.

[199] Joh. 10:34f.; cf. Ps. 82:6. Bultmann, *John*, p. 389f. prefers to regard Joh. 10:34–36 as an interpolation, or to understand the text, with its argument *a minore ad maius*, as a parody of Jewish biblical theology. This hardly seems to me a possible interpretation.

[200] Joh. 2:17; cf. Ps. 69:10.   [201] Bultmann, *John*, p. 124.

prophetic word is fulfilled, 'They shall all be taught by God',[202] for the man who has learned from the Father now comes to Jesus.[203] What is more, even the unbelief which Jesus comes up against has been foretold in the Scripture.[204] It is clear that in these 'scriptural proofs' we are dealing more with fairly loose connections of ideas than with proofs in the strict sense. These are not verifiable oracles, but solemn indications of the greatness of Jesus and of his sacrificial death. The words of the ancient Scripture set the new salvation in a deepened perspective, as it were, and enable men to understand it as the eternal counsel of God. In this mode 'scriptural proof' avoids one danger which very easily attaches to it in its traditional form. It is true that John did not reject the traditional testimonies associated with the Baptist and with the Passion narrative. Nevertheless, it is no accident that he did not accumulate further 'proofs' of this sort, but for his own part adopted a different style in his appeal to the Old Testament.

Scripture is therefore capable of throwing the miraculous light of divine promise upon Jesus, but that is not sufficient to bring men to faith. For this to happen Jesus must himself enlighten them, and this enlightenment occurs only when at the same time the offence which the humility of Jesus' earthly manifestation inevitably gives to the unenlightened vision is overcome. To wish to rely completely on a method by which the mystery of the hidden revelation was converted point by point into a recognisable divine plan would be to miss the meaning of faith in Christ, because such a desire for proof and certainty would simultaneously be a rejection of decision and of genuine encounter with the Word made flesh. This would no longer be the way of faith but of the world, which instead of believing prefers to demand unambiguous 'signs' in the illusion that thus it can be in control of the criteria by which we can be certain of recognising revelation correctly.[205] To bring this out is the purpose of a third group of 'scriptural proofs' which are intentionally put into the mouths of Jesus' opponents, and adduced not in support of him but against him. The 'Jews' and the 'Pharisees' also appeal to Scripture, but not in order to believe. On the contrary they do so precisely in order to justify their obdurate rejection of the Saviour present in their midst, and to explain it as 'in accordance with the scriptures'.

To start with, it is a cause of offence that Jesus comes from Galilee, from the despised town of Nazareth. This is Nathanael's immediate reaction, when Philip invites him to come to Jesus as the predicted

---

[202] Isa. 54:13. [203] Joh. 6:45. [204] Joh. 12:37-40.
[205] Bultmann, *John*, p. 228. The whole commentary again and again elaborates this insight, thus bringing out a vital element in the Johannine conception of faith. The reader is referred to the work in question for a full treatment of what follows here.

Saviour. But, being 'the true Israelite, in whom is nothing false', he bows before the presence of the Lord and, inwardly overcome, recognises him spontaneously as Son of God and King of Israel.[206] For others, however, these unseemly origins of Jesus become an insuperable obstacle: 'Has not the scriptures said that the Christ is descended from David, and comes from Bethlehem, the village where David was?'[207] The Pharisees, being learned in the Scriptures, know at once 'that no prophet is to rise from Galilee'.[208] Another thing that in their eyes tells clearly against Jesus is that it is known who his father and mother are;[209] for, as is well known, in John's Gospel Jesus is 'the son of Joseph'.[210] But 'when the Christ appears', they allege in opposition, 'no one will know where he comes from'.[211] To them it seems downright insanity that Jesus should assert notwithstanding that he has been sent by his divine 'Father', and has come down from heaven.[212] And when Jesus speaks of his being 'lifted up', that is, of his crucifixion, departure from the world, and glorification, the common people react violently against him because they 'have heard from the Law that the Christ remains for ever'.[213]

The paradoxical and ironic significance of such scriptural proofs is obvious. The scribes, who think that, unlike Jesus[214] and the accursed uneducated common people,[215] they know their Bible, in very truth pass sentence on themselves. Of course, in a superficial, external sense their arguments are 'correct'; but precisely for that reason they fail to see what is really important, and block the path by which they might arrive at a faith based on a true understanding. Jesus does come from Nazareth and not from David's town of Bethlehem—but for all that he is still the Messiah. He was indeed conceived in the ordinary natural manner—and yet he comes not of flesh and blood,[216] but from heaven and from God. He is truly to be crucified and to die—but it is precisely his death which is the entrance to a new and greater life. Everything is turned upside down, just as it is in the case

---

[206] Joh. 1:45–51. The miracle of Jesus' telepathy and clairvoyance, which is the decisive external factor in the story, is dismissed by Jesus himself as nothing more than a preliminary: Nathanael is to see heaven open above the person of Jesus, and to experience his union with the Father—'the angels of God ascending and descending on the Son of Man.' On the origins of this image cf. G. Quispel, 'Nathanael und der Menschensohn (Joh. 1, 51),' *ZNW* 47, 1956, pp. 281–283; also W. Michaelis, 'Joh. 1, 51, Gen. 28, 12 und das Menschensohn-Problem', *TLZ* 85, 1960, cols. 561–578.

[207] Joh. 7:42.   [208] Joh. 7:52.   [209] Joh. 6:42.

[210] Joh. 1:45; cf. H. von Campenhausen, *Die Jungfrauengeburt in der Theologie der Alten Kirche,* 1962, pp. 10ff.

[211] Joh. 7:27.   [212] Joh. 6:38f.   [213] Joh. 12:34.

[214] Joh. 7:15.   [215] Joh. 7:49.

[216] The same is true of all who believe in him: Joh. 1:13; cf. von Campenhausen, *Jungfrauengeburt*, pp. 11f.

of that descent from Abraham which the Jews bring up in support of their own position. Looking at the matter purely externally, of course they are descended from Abraham; only this natural descent is quite irrelevant to the question of their true nature—on the contrary, as enemies of Jesus it is no longer Abraham but the Devil who is their Father.[217] In every instance we are concerned with the same typical misunderstanding which crops up at every step, so to speak, in the Fourth Gospel. The Jews, indeed all men, even the disciples, are constantly inclined to take literally and in a material sense what is spiritually meant, and to demand palpable confirmation and proof where instead what matters is to take Jesus himself seriously in the humility and ordinariness that conceals him, and by listening to what he has to say to become truly certain of his divine glory.[218] One can only be completely dumbfounded at the naïveté of those exegetes who fail to detect the significance of John's irony, and proceed to take seriously the scriptural proofs directed against Jesus, seeking to draw the sting of these supposedly dangerous arguments by introducing from other Gospels facts which are omitted here, as that Jesus did indeed come from Bethlehem, was of Davidic descent, and was born of a virgin. In this way the unbelieving opponents of Jesus are involuntarily transformed into doughty biblical scholars who simply had the bad luck not to be in possession of adequate information about the life of Jesus—a situation for which they cannot really be blamed.

The only question which matters (and it is one which modern misunderstandings have only made more urgent) is this: against whom is John really directing his mockery of these learned methods of scriptural proof? Can it still be the Jews? To me this seems out of the question. By the time the Fourth Gospel was written, the Jews must have known for almost as long as the Evangelist himself of the Christian assertion of Jesus' Davidic descent, origin from Bethlehem, and birth of a virgin. But if so, then their objections will inevitably have been both couched and answered in forms different from those used here. Furthermore, the requirement that the Messiah should not be of known or natural origin is virtually impossible to explain on the assumptions of contemporary Judaism.[219] We are forced, therefore, to assume that John's target is not the Jews but his own Christian contemporaries, who had altered the earlier data in order to be able to

---

[217] Joh. 8:39–44.

[218] A similar dialectic is involved here to that which characterises the question of signs and wonders. In themselves the latter are no more rejected by the Evangelist than are proofs from Scripture; but they must lead to faith, and are not to be taken as neutral demonstrations, gratifying even the unbelieving and 'blind'.

[219] I take it for granted that we are not here dealing with actual speeches made during Jesus' lifetime on earth.

mount a supposedly compelling proof from Scripture.[220] The relevant legends, as is well known, have come down to us in the Gospels of Matthew and Luke. John is directing his attack not against these stories as such but against the spirit which he believes he can discern behind such biblicistic argumentation.[221] Nor, when the purport of his theology is understood, can it be said that this is a superfluous or peripheral exercise. John is here consciously fighting for a vital feature of his faith in Christ, which does indeed know and accept the 'signs' but refuses none the less to put its trust in mere 'signs', for assurance of salvation is to be found only in hearkening to the spirit-filled word of Jesus.

In our present context the point of chief importance is that this polemic is nevertheless patently not yet directed against the Scripture as such but only against a narrow and unspiritual understanding of its true meaning. John allows even scriptural 'proof' to remain for what it is; he is opposed only to according it too high a value, or, more correctly, to the attitude which attaches a false value to details that, whether right or wrong, are in any case disputable, and are not the stuff by which true faith lives. In his view the Old Testament does not exist in order that men may rummage through it looking for arguments which are then alleged to decide the truth or otherwise of Christ. Faith in Christ is established by Christ; he lives through his Spirit and his Word. The ancient Bible does indeed bear witness concerning him, and can lead men to him. But the decisive factor is only and always Christ himself. Beside him all else is stripped of its glory, and even the Scripture possesses continuing value only on his account.

Consequently, for all his distinctive characteristics, John is an Evangelist who still shares the orientation of primitive Christianity. What he has to say about the Old Testament still belongs wholly within

---

[220] That the text of Joh. 7:42 fits neither the O.T. nor rabbinic expectations, and, generally speaking, can be understood only with reference to Christian traditions, has been impressively demonstrated by Freed, *op. cit.*, pp. 39ff. Although his own concerns, and his attempt at a solution of the problem tend in a direction different from that of the present work, he does on one occasion come near to the view put forward here, when he writes (p. 48): 'John's conception of Jesus as "the Christ, the Son of God" (11:27) surpassed the common Jewish-Christian concept of his Davidic descent and the Christian tradition of his birth at Bethlehem. The Messiah of John is a more sublime figure. The physical descent of Jesus and the place of his birth are at most secondary compared to Jesus' real origin as the λόγος that was ἐν ἀρχῇ and σάρξ ἐγένετο, and even now is ἐκ τῶν ἄνω and not ἐκ τοῦ κόσμου τούτου. The presentation of two conflicting views may be only a device on John's part to portray the ignorance of Jesus' Jewish critics and even that of those Christians who fail to perceive the real meaning of Jesus. For this reason both views are left unanswered.'

[221] The same attitude underlies his refusal to identify John the Baptist with Elijah in accordance with Mal. 3:23 (cf. Justin, Dial. 8, 4; 49, 3): Joh. 1:21 as opposed to Matt. 11:14; 17:12 parr.

the sphere of primitive Christian thought, and is quite distinct from the very different approaches to the problem developed in the second century. Despite its diminished importance the Scripture remains a unique document, and one at unity in itself. Only out of the Old Testament can Christians speak seriously about Christ. John shows no inclination whatever to set additional testimony from other religions, from the poets, or from philosophy alongside the Old Testament, and so to put all these sources on the same religio-historical level. Despite his criticism of particular proofs from Scripture he nowhere attempts to subject the Scripture to 'critical' analysis by disintegrating it into strata of differing importance.[222]

The general validity of the ancient Bible is thus presupposed, not contested. But the inward, spiritual affinity with Scripture is wearing thin.[223] Now it is only the one thread, none too strong at that, of prophetic prediction which links the Old Testament with faith in Christ. In contrast to Paul, and even to Luke, this Gospel, despite a not inconsiderable series of Old Testament quotations, no longer displays anywhere a living appreciation of the spirit and content of the ancient Scriptures. The quotations cannot be combined to form even rudimentarily a recognisable picture of salvation-history.[224] The Scripture as a document of the past has for John become almost completely devoid of significance; nor does he really take it any more into consideration as a work of moral edification and instruction. Yet this has nothing in common with gnostic criticism of the Scriptures or with Marcionite hostility toward them. It is simply the radical nature of faith in Christ which has put so great a gulf between John and the Old Testament.

In conclusion, however, we must remind ourselves once more that the Gospel of John, as we stressed at the outset, undoubtedly does not represent the average piety of the wider Christian community. The general line of development ran in a different, almost indeed in the opposite direction. After the Law had been dealt with, and the immediate threat from Judaism was past, the Old Testament was read, taught, and used with all the greater interest and delight; and at the close of the period we have been considering it was virtually taken for granted as the Bible of Christians.

[222] The isolated comment of Joh. 7:22 is not intended 'critically' in this sense of the word. As Bultmann, *John*, p. 278 n. 3, says, it is 'clearly of only academic interest', and does not serve to diminish the importance of circumcision: cf. Gutbrod, *TWNT* IV, p. 1076 b. 280.

[223] This opinion is not necessarily affected by one's judgment on the particular question of the relation of its contents to Judaism or Jewish Christianity, which we can afford to leave open.

[224] Cf. the remarks to similar effect of E. Käsemann, *The Testament of Jesus*, 1970.

CHAPTER THREE

The Crisis of the Old Testament Canon
in the Second Century

THE PREVIOUS chapter has shown how the principle that the Old Testament Law did not apply to Christians, though implemented only as the result of fierce conflicts, was soon universally felt to be self-evident. In the Gospel of John the Scripture is regarded almost exclusively as a prophetic document for those who believe in Christ, and its importance as a normative guide for living has virtually been forgotten. There are some writings indeed which—as some Pauline Epistles had already done at an earlier date[1]—pay the Old Testament absolutely or as good as no attention at all.[2] But silence in these instances should not be taken as deliberate rejection. In principle 'the Books'[3] are everywhere known and recognised; it is simply that it was not felt necessary to make them the exclusive nourishment of one's religious life. Early Christianity is positively not to be regarded as a 'religion of the Book';[4]

---

[1] Cf. pp. 24f. above.

[2] Despite numerous biblical echoes Revelation and Hermas contain no quotation, in the proper sense of the word. This is in line with the distinctive claim of apocalyptic to prophetic status in its own right. But neither are there any direct quotations in I–III John (the only O.T. reference is to Cain in I Joh. 3:12). The Didache provides two O.T. quotations (14, 3; 16, 7) and a general reference to the 'prophets of old' (11, 11), Ignatius in his Epistles at most three (cf. p. 72 n. 63 below), while the Pastorals, though they solemnly stress the utility of knowledge of the Scriptures (II Tim. 3:14ff.), are content with a single O.T. quotation, I Tim. 5:18 (on II Tim. 2:19 cf. M. Dibelius and H. Conzelmann, *Die Pastoralbriefe*[3], 1955, p. 84); and even in Polycarp, who delights to quote, the O.T. allusions and explicit quotations (indisputable only in 12, 1) are lost in the abundance of N.T. material.

[3] A. von Harnack, 'Über das Alter der Bezeichnung "Die Bücher" ("Die Bibel") für die Heiligen Schriften in der Kirche,' *Zentralbl. für Bibliothekswesen* 45, 1928, pp. 337ff., rightly concludes from II Clem. 14; II Tim. 4:13 that this designation is as old as the Church itself. H. Köster, *Synoptische Überlieferung bei den Apostolischen Vätern*, 1957, pp. 67ff., though with some reservations, agrees. As regards the Testimony of the Scillitan Martyrs, which was Harnack's starting-point, the question can, if necessary, be left undecided whether in fact by *libri* here the O.T. is still meant and not, as in later recensions of the text, *libri evangeliorum*: so G. Bonner, 'The Scillitan Saints and the Pauline Epistles', *JEH* 7, 1956, pp. 141–146, esp. 144f.; cf. further Optatus, V, 6.

it is the religion of the Spirit and of the living Christ. 'He himself prophesies that "He himself dwells in your midst" ', declares the Epistle of Barnabas.[5] This new spiritual self-awareness has therefore profoundly altered the function which the Old Testament had in Judaism, because the centre of gravity of faith itself has been shifted. Nevertheless, the ancient Bible is still held in honour, and now as in earlier days is regarded as the book of divine revelation. Hence the at first sight paradoxical fact that for more than a hundred years the Church possessed the same 'canon' as the synagogue. The situation is perfectly clear, and should not be disguised: there is still absolutely no 'New Testament' which might be placed alongside the 'Old Testament' as a collection of documents of similarly binding force. The ancient Jewish Bible is and at first remains the single scriptural norm of the Church, and—even if with varying emphasis—is everywhere recognised as such.[6]

Special, theologically oriented explanations of this state of affairs are quite unnecessary; they merely confuse the simple facts. It is quite wrong to say that the Old Testament had no authority in its own right for the first Christians, and that it was taken over purely because people saw that it 'treated of Christ' or pointed toward him.[7] The critical problem, to which Luther's well-known but much misused formula supplies an answer,[8] had not yet been posed.[9] The situation was in

[4] It still did not seem to be so to Celsus in the second half of the second century: cf. W. Völker, *Das Bild vom nichtgnostischen Christentum bei Celsus*, 1928, pp. 79f. [5] Barn. 16, 9.
[6] On what follows the reader is referred to my own essay, 'Das Alte Testament als Bibel der Kirche vom Ausgang des Urchristentums bis zur Entstehung des Neuen Testaments', in: *Aus der Frühzeit des Christentums. Studien zur Kirchengeschichte des ersten und zweiten Jahrhunderts*, 1963, pp. 152–196, the conclusions of which are here summarised. Of works dealing with the subject more broadly may be mentioned the study by L. Diestel, *Geschichte des Alten Testaments in der christlichen Kirche*, 1869, which though obsolete has never been replaced, and the popular survey by H. Karpp, *Das Alte Testament in der Geschichte der Kirche. Seine Geltung und seine Wirkung*, 1939. (A great deal of relevant material on this general field will now be found in the *Cambridge History of the Bible* (3 vols), 1965–70: Tr.)
[7] Cf. A. Jepsen, 'Kanon und Text des Alten Testaments', *TLZ* 74, 1949, col. 73; similarly, though intended more cautiously as a general principle, K. H. Rengstorf, *The Resurrection of Jesus*, 1972. Even W. G. Kümmel gives the following as his opinion in the new edition of Feine-Behm, *Einleitung in das Neue Testament*[14], 1965, pp. 350f.: 'This [sc. O.T.] "sacred scripture" was, as regards its validity and interpretation, already subjected to the *critical* authority of Jesus during his lifetime, and in the primitive Church to that of the Spirit as given by the Risen Lord (cf. Matt. 5:21ff.; II Cor. 3:12ff.; Joh. 5:39ff.; 10:35f.; II Tim. 3:15; Heb. 8:13), and therefore had no intrinsic authority of its own.'
[8] *Deutsche Bibel* VII, 385; cf. H. Bornkamm, *Luther und das Alte Testament*, 1948, pp. 128f.
[9] In substance it appears for the first time in Valentinian theology (cf. pp.

fact quite the reverse. Christ is certainly vindicated to unbelievers out of the Scripture; but the converse necessity, to justify the Scriptures on the authority of Christ, is as yet nowhere even envisaged. The exegesis of the Old Testament in terms of Christ is carried out with naïve simplicity. But the liberty taken in so expounding it is never claimed as some special new privilege; there is just the simple conviction that in so doing Christians have really understood the true ultimate meaning of the testimonies. In fact, of course, such free or arbitrary exegesis was nothing unheard-of, given the exegetical assumptions of the age. Similar methods had long been employed in ancient Homeric studies, and had become even more frequent in hellenistic Judaism in the exposition of the Torah. As early as the second century B.C. Aristobulus, the exegete of the Torah, and after him pre-eminently Philo, had developed on the grand scale the method of eliminating offensive material and mere 'externals' from the text by substituting a new, more profound meaning, arrived at by allegorical interpretation.[10] Christians needed to adapt these methods only to the extent that their interpretation was tuned no longer to philosophical or theological insights but to Christ who was predicted in the Old Testament. And even this practice of actualising the text in terms of one's own community was not completely new in Judaism, since it had already been used copiously by the Qumran sect.[11] The interpretations of the first Christians may seem to us so uninhibited as to verge on the fantastic, but to them their

---

84f. below), then in Clement of Alexandria (cf. pp. 297f. below) and in the Muratorian Fragment (cf. p. 250 below). The comment of W. Wrede, *Untersuchungen zum Ersten Klemensbriefe*, 1891, p. 75 is pertinent: 'Historically it would be a wholly unsatisfactory description of the case to say that the O.T. was *still* valid—either in whole or in part—for Christians, as though recognition of its validity had been a matter calling for some thought instead of what was the truth of the situation, namely that the possession of this miraculous and infallible book was in Christian eyes an advantage of the new religion which proved one of its greatest sources of enlightenment and strongest recommendations.' Cf. further A. von Harnack, *Lehrbuch der Dogmengeschichte* I⁴, 1909, pp. 194ff.

[10] Cf., e.g., R. M. Grant, *The Letter and the Spirit*, 1957, pp. 31ff.; J. Pépin, *Mythe et allégorie*, 1958, pp. 221ff.; N. Walter, *Der Thoraausleger Aristobulos*, 1964, pp. 124ff.

[11] Cf. pp. 4f. above. Nevertheless, the distinctions to which attention is drawn by J. A. Fitzmyer, 'The use of explicit Old Testament quotations in Qumran literature and in the New Testament', *NTS* 7, 1960–1, p. 331, should not be overlooked: 'At Qumran many of the Old Testament texts were applied to events in the recent history of the sect; in this respect there is some similarity to the backward glance of the New Testament writers. But the messianic hope at Qumran shifted the emphasis much more to a *coming fulfilment* of the Old Testament scriptures. Again, common to both was the implicit desire to enhance some recent event in their histories or some idea or person with an Old Testament association, as a result of a certain analogy which they saw between the event and some event in Israel's history.'

understanding of the ancient writings seemed for that very reason to be quite simply enlightening and virtually compelling. The Jews, who refused to accept this understanding, prove themselves by that very fact to be obdurate.[12]

That the precise scope of the Christian as of the Jewish canon is not yet fully decided in no way detracts from its authority.[13] Attempts at exact enumeration of the normative Scriptures do not begin until later.[14] Quotations in primitive Christian literature show that the borderline between canonical and what on later classification were to be extra-canonical books has not yet been clearly drawn;[15] but the concept of holy Scripture as a totality invested with authority is nevertheless already established. This is another point on which there is no distinction between Jews and Christians. The insignificant discrepancies in the composition of the canon which exist right up to the last[16] are never taken very seriously.[17]

The Church's use of the Old Testament is dominated above all by a concern with scriptural proof relating to both Christ and the Church. The Old Testament is the book that prophesies Christ, indeed, it is in the strict sense the 'Book of Christ', and in everything that it teaches and reveals, as Paul had already stated,[18] it has Christians in mind. An extremely simple and exaggerated notion of the way in which prophecy

---

[12] Cf., e.g., Acts 7:52.; Joh. 5:46f.; 9:28ff.

[13] Cf. p. 2 above.

[14] The question of the τῶν παλαιῶν βιβλίων ἀκρίβεια, namely, πόσα τὸν ἀριθμὸν καὶ ὁποῖα τὴν τάξιν εἶεν, is, so far as I am aware, taken up and answered for the first time by Melito of Sardis: Eusebius, HE IV, 26, 13f.; cf. A. C. Sundberg, The Old Testament of the Early Church, 1964, pp. 133ff.

[15] Cf., e.g., the extremely careful collation by A. Oepke, 'Βίβλοι ἀπόκρυφοι im Christentum,' TWNT III, pp. 987ff., and the table in Sundberg, op. cit., pp. 54f. The latter disputes that any demarcation of the 'Writings' (as distinct from the Law and the Prophets) had been generally made before the end of the first century A.D.

[16] 'There is in fact no early Christian list of canonical books which exactly corresponds to the Jewish canon. . . . Later, only Lutheran orthodoxy and even more explicitly the Reformed Churches after the Synod of Dordrecht hold to the Masoretic canon as the inspired word of God' (Jepsen, art. cit., col. 70). A detailed treatment of this development in the early Church will be found in Sundberg, op. cit., pp. 129ff. Reference to the Jewish canon constantly plays a part in these developments even at this early stage.

[17] By contrast the charge of 'falsifying the text' plays a very prominent part from the time of Justin (Dial. 71: 72; 73; 84) onwards, just as it does in the polemic against false teachers. Cf. H. Köster, Septuaginta und synoptischer Erzählungsstoff im Schriftbeweis Justins, 1963; on the heretics, A. Bludau, Die Schriftfälschungen der Häretiker, 1925. On the problem of the LXX cf. J. Leipoldt and S. Morenz, Heilige Schriften, 1953, pp. 71ff., and on 'the standing of the LXX in the early Church' cf. esp. H. Karpp, ' "Prophet" oder "Dolmetscher"? ' Festschrift für Günther Dehn, 1957, pp. 103–117.

[18] Cf. pp. 27f. above.

worked was universal at this period. No one had any doubt that Moses, David, and the prophets had all of them been confidently assured of the coming of Christ, and had clearly foreseen both his person and many of the details of his life.[19] Indeed, Christ himself, either as 'Logos' or through his Spirit, already speaks to men in the Old Testament.[20] This conception opened up a whole new approach to the ancient Scripture, and the proof-texts in which such connections and coincidences were seen constantly increased in number. The significance of Scripture was therefore no longer limited to providing in opposition to Jewish doubts miraculous confirmation of belief in Christ and of the mystery of God's plan of salvation. By means of this book Christ himself enlightens, instructs, and guides his Christian people. And so the Old Testament comes to be acknowledged as an inexhaustible source of practical exhortation and instruction, as well as of theological reflection and speculation on deeper questions, 'profitable for teaching, for reproof, for correction, and for training in righteousness'.[21]

I Clement affords an excellent sample of this accepted method of using the Bible. In its eagerness to dispense edification this document cites the Old Testament some hundred times,[22] and also praises the enthusiasm which its readers evince for the book:[23] 'Strive and contend, brethren, over everything which pertains to salvation! You have looked into the scriptures, which are true, which were given by the Holy Spirit; and you know that nothing unrighteous or perverse is written in them.'[24] God or Christ or the Spirit—in this context no value is attached to distinctions between them—speak out of its pages to the elect,[25] and the latter are in humility to practice whatever is written therein.[26] The concerns of practical morality predominate. It is impossible to identify any definite opponents against whom edifying

[19] Cf., e.g., I Pet. 1:10f.; Barn. 5, 6; 9, 7; Ignatius, *Magn.* 9, 2; Melito, Frag. 11; and, from a somewhat later period, the particularly detailed list of prophetic documents in Asc. Isa. 4, 20–22.

[20] In addition to Luke (cf. pp. 47f. above) and John (cf. p. 56 above) cf., e.g., Did. 14, 3; Heb. 2:11ff.; 10:5; Barn. 5, 6; I Clem. 16, 3ff.; 22, 1; II Clem. 3, 5; Justin, *Apol.* 36; *Dial.* 7; 56, 11, etc.; and, earlier than any of these, I Cor. 10:4.

[21] II Tim. 3:16.

[22] Wrede, *Untersuchungen*, p. 60, reckons 'more than 70 genuine quotations' and in addition more than 20 allusions to O.T. stories or adaptations from such stories; A. von Harnack, *Einführung in die alte Kirchengeschichte. Das Schreiben der römischen Kirche an die korinthische . . .* , 1929, p. 66 n. 2, speaks of 'about 120 O.T. quotations and allusions'.

[23] Similarly *II Tim.* 3:15; *Ep. Polyc.* 12, 1.

[24] I Clem. 45, 1–3; cf. 53, 1; 62, 3.

[25] I Clem. 50, 7. On the close but colourless link between the Spirit and Scripture cf. H. Opitz, *Ursprünge frühkatholischer Pneumatologie*, 1960, pp. 38ff.

[26] I Clem. 13, 1.

THE CRISIS OF THE OLD TESTAMENT CANON

observations of this sort might be directed. Jews or Jewish Christians no longer come into the picture; and for this very reason there is complete freedom to use the ancient words and prescriptions as models or examples in any way the reader wishes. Clement, in accordance with the particular concern of his letter, also refers, as is well known, to the excellent way in which the ancient priestly worship was ordered, and argues that the Church with her system of bishops and deacons ought not to fall short of this model.[27] The latter were appointed by the apostles just as the priests were appointed by Moses[28]—and this did not happen by chance, for the Scripture had already spoken prophetically long ago of the appointment of bishops (overseers) and servants in righteousness.[29] The quotation which is thus put to use against the contemporary troublemakers in Corinth has been not inconsiderably altered to make it fit; but this does not imply malicious 'falsification'. All it shows is that at this period such 'scriptural proofs' were handled with freedom because they were thought of more as edificatory than as legalistic or dogmatic. The Old Testament is not thereby converted into a source of 'canon law'; it simply supports and confirms from its own side what is already seen as a religious duty on independent grounds.[30] Very popular too, in accordance with Jewish precedent, is the listing, either as awful warnings or to give comfort, of Old Testament instances of God's control of events.[31] And, of course, as soon as we include typological and allegorical exegesis, which had already been a favourite with Paul, the possibilities become endless. The writer of I Clement is still fairly restrained in this respect;[32] but in other material from this period such exegesis occurs virtually everywhere that the Old Testament is used. The earliest extant Church sermon,[33] the so-called II Clement, already makes somewhat extravagant use of this current method.[34] Yet even this is done less on the basis of a worked-out conception of the meaning of the Old Testament than as the result of the naïve, more or less arbitrary and *ad hoc* employment of a recognised procedure which can be applied, extended and varied at will.

It is still necessary as in earlier days to defend the Christian under-

[27] I Clem. 43f.   [28] I Clem. 43f.   [29] I Clem. 42, 5.

[30] For a more detailed discussion of this point cf. H. von Campenhausen, *Ecclesiastical Authority and Spiritual Power*, 1969, pp. 87ff.

[31] In addition to the innumerable examples in I Clement these occur in a variety of forms esp. in Hebrews (ch. 11), and Acts (7; 13:17ff.), and in isolated instances in James (5:10f.), Jude (5ff.; cf. II Pet. 2:15f.), and I John (3:12). Cf. K. Beyschlag, *Clemens Romanus und der Frühkatholizismus*, 1966, pp. 48ff.

[32] The sole instance is his interpretation of Rahab's scarlet thread in terms of the blood of the Lord (12, 7f.).

[33] Possibly based on an O.T. lesson which will have preceded it (Isaiah); cf. the literature cited in H. Köster, *Synoptische Überlieferung*, p. 62 n. 2.

[34] Cf. II Clem. 2, 1–3; 14. On the exegesis of the latter passage cf. G. Krüger, 'Zu II. Clem. 14, 2,' *ZNW* 31, 1932, pp. 204f.

F

standing of the Bible against the claims of Judaism. But this defence has
lost much of the urgent topicality which it once possessed. Hence in I
Clement Judaism is in fact completely ignored; here it is Christianity
which is regarded without question as the revealed religion of the Old
Testament.[35] The Christian community is the true people of God, and
the Bible is exclusively their book. But even where Judaism is directly
in mind, as in Hebrews or Barnabas, the result of the confrontation is
not so much a piece of straight polemic as of Christian introspection on
the bases of their own belief, an exercise in intellectual reflection—one
might almost say, of 'theology'.[36] Of the various parts of the Old
Testament it is prophecy and the 'Law' which in the course of this
exercise of themselves come once more to the forefront. Faith in
Christ and freedom from the Law, the two fundamental innovations
by which the Church had been distinguished from Judaism, had both
to be shown to be 'scriptural', if the new biblical people of God was to
be 'scriptural', if the new biblical people of God was to be vindicated
against the synagogue. These two concerns, however, gradually converge and interfuse. On the one hand, the old Law and its ceremonial
regulations are interpreted typologically, that is, as christologically
prophetic; and on the other, Christ comes to be regarded as the new
Teacher of the Law, the one who does not so much abrogate the old
Mosaic law as purify it and reveal its ultimate meaning in terms of
moral freedom.

In this connection Hebrews shows itself to be still strongly conditioned by Pauline concepts. The Law had been valid only for a limited
period, and was destined from the outset to be abolished and superseded by Christ. Hence the strongest possible emphasis is laid on its
provisional character and on its weakness and inadequacy.[37] But the
'Law' here no longer denotes the whole corpus of God's commands
and requirements. First and foremost, it is the priestly cultus and the
Temple services which are in mind; the 'Law' is understood as the
ceremonial law, and this in turn is seen in terms of the expiation and
sanctification which it strove but failed to achieve. This ultimate goal
is attained only through the perfect sacrifice of Christ, and to this
extent the old Law contains no more than merely 'a shadow of the good
things to come instead of the true form of these realities'.[38] The assessment is, however, not purely negative. Precisely by virtue of their
imperfection the old, obsolete arrangements were a constant pointer to
the future true atonement in Christ, which has now been effected. In
this prophetic function of witnessing beforehand to the Christian

[35] Cf. Harnack, Einführung, p. 70.
[36] On what follows cf. R. Bultmann, Theology of the New Testament, I, pp.
108ff.
[37] Cf. esp. Heb. 7.   [38] Heb. 10:1.

salvation lies their only real meaning; the Law is, as it were, a prototype version of that which faith proclaims: 'Just why all this prefiguration of Christ's deed of salvation, which no one in the time before Christ could understand, should have been instituted at all, it would probably be fruitless to ask the author in his satisfaction over his interpretation'.[39] At the very point where Paul had seen a fundamental opposition, Hebrews discerns a genuine if imperfect analogy. In this way the Old Testament as a whole takes on for the writer an 'evangelical' meaning of promise.[40] The examples, consolations, and exhortations to be found in it still have something to say, and now more especially are they worthy of the attention of Christians; for as the latter go forward on their pilgrimage of faith the Old Testament surrounds them with a 'cloud of witnesses',[41] it addresses them with words of comfort, 'as sons',[42] and it holds over them a threat which is all the more severe, inasmuch as through Christ they have received higher gifts and promises.[43]

The Epistle of Barnabas goes one step further in the acceptance of the old Law. For this writer too the whole Old Testament is full of types pointing forward to Christ; and Christians, whose ears have been 'circumcised',[44] consequently perceive on every page the glory of Jesus, in whom and as referring to whom all things are to be understood.[45] 'For the Master made known to us by the prophets things past and things present, and gave us a foretaste of things to come'.[46] In contrast to Hebrews, however, Barnabas abandons a literal interpretation of the Law even for the past; in addition to the prophetic-christological he recognises only a general moralising allegorical interpretation of its prescriptions. The wisdom and knowledge which God has given to Christians understands the meaning of the ancient text,[47] and keeps them, in simple faith, from following after Jewish error.[48] Circumcision, sacrifice, the sabbath, the fasts, the dietary laws—the true meaning of

---

[39] Bultmann, *Theology* I, p. 111. The whole Epistle is concerned not at all with the salvation-history problem as such but simply with the biblical backing for contemporary faith. What matters to him is 'to justify the new revelation . . . out of the existing scriptures, and thus to present its inner truth as something already rooted in the salvation-history which has gone before': O. Kuss, 'Der Verfasser des Hebräerbriefes als Seelsorger,' in: *Auslegung und Verkündigung* I (*Aufsätze zur Exegese des Neuen Testaments*), 1963, p. 355.
[40] Heb. 4:2.   [41] Heb. 12:1.   [42] Heb. 12:5.
[43] Cf. Heb. 2:2f.; 3:7ff.; 10:28ff.; 12:18ff. The same typical argument *a minore ad maius* occurs in I Clem. 41, 4 (cf. J. Klevinghaus, *Die theologische Stellung der Apostolischen Väter zur alttestamentlichen Offenbarung*, 1948, p. 61) and II Clem. 6, 9.
[44] Barn. 9, 3.   [45] Barn. 12, 7.   [46] Barn. 1, 7.
[47] Barn. 6, 10. On 'gnosis' in Barnabas cf. H. Windisch, *Der Barnabasbrief* (*HNT* suppl. vol. III, 1920), pp. 307ff.; P. Meinhold, 'Geschichte und Exegese, im Barnabasbrief', *ZKG* 59, 1940, pp. 255ff., esp. 258f.
[48] Barn. 3, 6.

all these is nothing to do with any 'carnal' actions, but signifies rather those interior attitudes and that moral conduct which God wished to lay as an obligation on mankind.[49] Moses, David, and the prophets naturally were aware of this truth and expressed it.[50] But the Jews from the very beginning failed and to this day still fail to understand it, 'because they did not hearken to the voice of the Lord'.[51] Their literal interpretation of the Law was therefore one enormous misconception. Christians are the only people who rightly read, understand, and act upon the ancient Bible 'as the Lord willed',[52] that is, in the true and original meaning which God intended.[53]

Barnabas represents, if we may put it this way, the most thorough-going attempt to wrest the Bible absolutely from the Jews, and to stamp it from the very first word as exclusively a Christian book.[54] But a weapon honed that sharp soon acquires a jagged edge.[55] It is not surprising that his attitude toward the Old Testament was nowhere adopted without qualification.[56] It not only makes any reasonable exposition of the older revelation in its own context impossible, but completely destroys any notion of continuity in salvation-history or of divine governance;[57] and this was the very last thing which the Church in its current missionary situation was prepared to sacrifice. Thus in its turn the Epistle of Barnabas confirms the impression that the Church of the early second century had without misgivings taken possession of the Bible and was making full use of it, but had not as yet

[49] Even in Barn. 7 and 8 it is not assumed, as Windisch, *op. cit.*, p. 343 thinks that 'the procedures of the Temple, the sacrificial ritual, and the custom of fasting are all based on positive divine commands'; the question of their legiti-macy is not even considered.
[50] On the problem of the *testimonia* and *florilegia* of which Barnabas apparently made use cf. P. Prigent, *L'Épître de Barnabé I-XVI et ses sources*, Paris, 1961, pp. 29ff.
[51] Barn. 8, 7.   [52] Barn. 10, 12.
[53] Only one passage, Barn. 5, 2, seems to envisage a straightforward meaning of christological prophecy, valid for the Jews alone. But this passage, being both obscure and an isolated instance, must not be allowed to blur the clear picture given by the Epistle as a whole.
[54] For a different view cf. L. Goppelt, *Christentum und Judentum im ersten und zweiten Jahrhundert*, 1954, pp. 218f.
[55] The writer of Barnabas himself is not always able to carry his exegetical principle through quite consistently: cf. Windisch, *op. cit.*, pp. 357, 393ff.; Klevinghaus, *op. cit.*, pp. 41ff.; A. Oepke, *Das neue Gottesvolk in Schrifttum, Schauspiel, bildender Kunst und Weltgestaltung*, 1950, pp. 52f.
[56] Least of all, of course, by the gnostics, who take the diametrically opposite view, and make the gap and the disparity between the O.T. Law and Chris-tianity the starting-point of their thinking.
[57] W. Maurer, *Kirche und Synagoge*, 1953, p. 20, writes: 'This radical chris-tianisation of the Old Testament means, however, at bottom the total destruc-tion of its historical character.'

been able to develop a theory of scripture sufficiently worked out to match this use.

Nevertheless, as a permanent arrangement this unreflecting adoption and recognition of Scripture by Christians simply would not do. Jewish opposition, however, was very little of a disturbing factor here. It is true that throughout the second century and even later Judaism was an adversary to be taken seriously, and that again and again it proved necessary to counter Jewish arguments drawn from the Bible. But the secure self-confidence which Christians themselves had acquired in relation to the Scriptures could no longer be challenged effectively from that quarter. It was too clear that they were sensible of their spiritual superiority, of the new treasures and the living truth of their faith in Christ, which was proof against the Old Testament and which could no longer be shaken by criticisms of a legal or formalist kind. It was rather the controversies within the Church which inevitably forced development along. It was precisely in a situation where the divine authority of the Scripture was taken absolutely seriously, and where any opinion or arrangement might be justified, as occasion required, out of the sacred text, that the difficulties inherent in having so wide and ambiguous a norm became apparent as soon as problems were raised, the answers to which had not been agreed in advance, but were called in question and made matters of controversy by some party or group. In these circumstances it is at first a matter of complete indifference which particular contentious issue is the subject of debate.

An interesting picture of such situations has come down to us from as early as the beginning of the second century in the Epistles of Ignatius of Antioch. The bishop tells us how he fared in a disputation in the church of Philadelphia with opponents who challenged his views with false, apparently docetic propositions about Christ.[58] Both sides appealed directly to the Old Testament. The false teachers went so far as to assert that they were able to accept only what was specifically stated in the Old Testament 'documents'—the Gospel message by itself was not yet sufficient proof.[59] Ignatius is disgusted by such

---

[58] They were not in fact 'judaisers', but were stigmatised as such by Ignatius purely for polemical purposes on account of their stubborn biblicism. This is the view put forward, in my opinion convincingly, by E. Molland, 'The heretics combatted by Ignatius of Antioch', *JEH* 5, 1954, pp. 1–6.

[59] *Philad.* 8, 2: ἐπεὶ ἤκουσά τινων λεγόντων, ὅτι ἐὰν μὴ ἐν τοῖς ἀρχείοις εὕρω, ἐν τῷ εὐαγγελίῳ οὐ πιστεύω· καὶ λέγοντός μου αὐτοῖς, ὅτι γέγραπται, ἀπεκρίθησάν μοι, ὅτι πρόκειται· ἐμοὶ δὲ ἀρχεῖά ἐστιν Ἰησοῦς Χριστός, καὶ ἄθικτα ἀρχεῖα ὁ σταυρὸς αὐτοῦ καὶ ὁ θάνατος καὶ ἡ ἀνάστασις αὐτοῦ καὶ ἡ πίστις ἡ δι᾽ αὐτοῦ, ἐν οἷς θέλω ἐν τῇ προσευχῇ ὑμῶν σωθῆναι. For the translation cf. C. C. Richardson, *Early Christian Literature* (LCC), *ad loc.*, and W. Bauer, *Lexicon of N.T. Greek*, p. 111a.—The term, τὰ ἀρχεῖα, is striking, and seems to have been adopted simply for this specific occasion

excessive 'Judaism',[60] notwithstanding the fact that he too attempts at
first to defend his own position on the points in question by asserting
that they are 'written', that is, that they have in very truth already been
proclaimed and taught by the biblical prophets.[61] But this gets him
nowhere, for it is precisely this which seems to his opponents to be the
'question' in dispute. So, instead of attempting a direct proof from
Scripture, he finally falls back on the oral Gospel of his church,[62] and
rejects any further investigation of the Old Testament: 'For me Jesus
Christ is the "primary source"; the inviolable documents are his Cross,
his death, his resurrection, and the faith which he creates.'

It would be perverse to read into such a profession a deliberate
depreciation of the ancient Scriptures. It is true that the tendency to
quote and to advance scriptural proof is not very pronounced in
Ignatius;[63] but he is in no doubt, nevertheless, that the witness of the
Old Testament is on his side,[64] and in another passage he recommends its
study specifically as a defence against heresy. Not only the Church's
Gospel and the witness of her martyrs but even Moses and the Prophets
by themselves ought to have been enough to recover the false teachers

---

in order to emphasise the 'documentary' character. That the ordinary designation for the O.T., γραφή, does not occur in Ignatius must be accidental,
since he uses the corresponding verb, γέγραπται, both here and in Eph. 5, 3;
Magn. 12. It is not possible, however, to make ἀρχεῖα refer to written Gospels,
Apocalypses, or other 'archival' documents instead of to the O.T. There is no
longer any need today to controvert such interpretations, of which some have
been wilder than others: cf. Campenhausen, 'Altes Testament', p. 163 n. 51.
Why the contrasting of the O.T. and the εὐαγγέλιον in this passage should
'suggest that a written Gospel is meant', I am unable to understand; for a different
view, however, cf. O. Michel, art. 'Evangelium', *RAC* VI, col. 1125, cf. 1122.

[60] Philad. 6, 1; cf. Magn. 8, 1, etc.; for the interpretation of these passages
cf. Molland, 'Heretics', *ad loc*. There is absolutely no question of a contrast between literal and allegorical exegesis, for which C. Schmidt, *Gespräche Jesu
mit seinen Jüngern nach der Auferstehung*, 1919, p. 393 n. 3, wished to find evidence in Philad. 8, 2.

[61] These are the 'prophets' referred to in Philad. 9, 2.

[62] It makes no difference for our present purposes whether the following words
represent a later summary or still belong to the report of the debate itself, as
E. Flesseman-van Leer, *Tradition and Scripture in the Early Church*, Assen,
1954, p. 35, with less probability, conjectures.

[63] Ignatius' sole concern is constantly to exalt the decisive, overwhelming
significance of the oral Gospel in face of a one-sided over-valuation of the O.T.
on the part of the heretics: Magn. 9; 13, 1; Philad. 5; 9; Smyrn. 5, 1; 7, 2, etc.
The importance of the O.T. for Ignatius is perhaps somewhat underestimated
by H. Rathke, *Ignatius von Antiochien und die Paulusbriefe*, 1967, pp. 23–26.

[64] Explicit citations from the O.T. occur on only three occasions, but two of
these are introduced with the solemn formula, γέγραπται: Eph. 5, 3; Magn.
12; Trall. 8, 2; cf. Köster, *Synoptische Überlieferung*, p. 25. Furthermore, it
should be noted that neither does Ignatius ever appeal directly to the authority
of the 'Lord': cf., *ibid.*, p. 60.

from their disgraceful defection.[65] For the Prophets were 'disciples of Christ', filled with his grace,[66] who believed in the Gospel,[67] and who like the Apostles and the whole Church have together with Abraham, Isaac and Jacob entered through Christ into salvation.[68] Perhaps the reason for such an emphatic statement is that Ignatius, more than his opponents, was a man who habitually preached under the direct inspiration of the Spirit, but who nevertheless had no wish to be thought of as one who despised the 'Scripture'. The picture which emerges from his Letters is in any case perfectly clear: despite the strenuous theological controversy both parties agree in affirming the fundamental character of the biblical 'documents', and neither knows of any canon other than these holy 'archives' of the past to put alongside the oral preaching.[69] But it is also becoming clear that the Old Testament cannot possibly suffice permanently as the one norm for the teaching of the Church.

Such difficulties within Christianity increase in importance in the succeeding period in proportion as the Church becomes more firmly settled in its new environment, and a process of inner hellenisation follows on the earlier, more external one. For the first generation of the Church the Old Testament was what it had been for the synagogue, a sacred datum whose divine authority needed no proof. At first the Christian missionaries, like those of Judaism, had encountered virtually no problems in the hellenistic world. The incomparable majesty of the ancient and mysterious divine book exercised a compelling effect, and with its monotheism, its moral commands, and its supposedly 'spiritual' character it seemed to measure up completely to the expectations which were brought to it. But as soon as men were no longer content to consider only a limited selection of impressive passages and sayings,[70] but determined henceforward to become properly acquainted with the whole

[65] Smyrn. 5, 1; 7, 2. On the interpretation of these passages cf. N. Brox, *Zeuge und Märtyrer*, 1961, pp. 211ff.
[66] Magn. 9, 2.
[67] Magn. 8, 2; Philad. 5, 2.
[68] Philad. 5, 2; 9, 1.
[69] The argument that gnostic Docetists could never have supported the O.T. so emphatically (T. Zahn, *Ignatius von Antiochien*, 1873, p. 380, followed by Klevinghaus, *op. cit.*, pp. 99f.) is circular, since it rests on a general presupposition that the gnostics were hostile to Scripture. Nor does it at all follow that the requirement that the Gospel should be proved by the testimony of the O.T., and that without this support it should not be believed, is 'impossible' in the mouth of Christians (Klevinghaus, *op. cit.*, p. 99). On the contrary, this is the assumption on which is based the whole christological proof mounted from Scripture against the Jews. In the circumstances there is no reason why the epigrammatic formulation in the text should not also be attributed to Ignatius.
[70] It is obvious that this was very largely what happened at the beginning: cf. C. H. Dodd, *According to the Scriptures*, 1952, pp. 61ff., 126f.

enormous mass of the Scripture, and to expound it in accordance with the Christian teaching and message, inevitably problems and stumbling-blocks arose which had to be dealt with. Not every alien concept, cruel demand, and peculiar practice could be accepted without question; and even the allegorical interpretation proved unable to convince and satisfy in every case. Above all, the whole complex of cultic and ceremonial commandments—sacrificial worship, circumcision, fasting, the sabbath, and so on—presented special difficulties. For all this afforded the most striking contradiction to the very quality in Christian propaganda which exerted the greatest appeal—the vision of an enlightened, 'philosophical' religion of spiritual freedom and inward-ness in contrast to the 'superstition' and immorality of the heathen cult of idols and temples. Thus the old problem of the 'Law', seemingly dealt with long since, became once more the centre of attention and a matter of painful and topical urgency. The issue was no longer whether the old regulations were still binding on Christians themselves—this was no longer contemplated by anyone—but the supreme claim of the Law to be God's perfect revelation, and with this the authority of sacred Scripture as such. Were these commands not unworthy of a Christian God? How could it be said of them that they had ever been in keeping with his perfect will, holy, righteous, and good?[71] As compared with Paul's day the battle was now facing, so to speak, in the opposite direction. Now it was no longer a matter of vindicating faith in Christ in face of the ancient Scriptures, and of confirming it with proof-texts understood in a prophetic sense. Now the problem posed was the reverse one: how, starting from the newly established Christian stand-point, could the old Law ever have been a true revelation of God, and on what assumptions could its problematic regulations ever have had a tolerable meaning? What was at stake was the righteousness of the Law, and with it of holy Scripture itself,[72] in other words, its traditional claim to be divine and perfect. How could this be vindicated? The question, once put, could not be ignored. An answer had to be found.

In all this there was a general acceptance of the supposedly self-evident assumption that the Old Testament must be something like an ideal manual of virtue, of religious duties, and of correct ideas about God. It was this presupposition, dictated by the thinking of the con-temporary world, which called in question the perfection of Scripture and of the Law; and it was from this angle that they had to be defended.

---

[71] This is the same problem with which 'Barnabas' had been faced—though he had not suspected its scope—but which had been unknown to earlier Chris-tianity. The exaggerated position adopted by the Pastoral Epistles (I Tim. 1:8f.) belongs to an even later period: cf. pp. 181f. below.

[72] The Law is always to the forefront not only in the relatively harmless discussions in Hebrews and Barnabas but also in Ptolemaeus, Justin, etc.

In this situation the simplest available solution might seem to be to qualify and to limit to some extent the hitherto extremely rigid assertion of Scripture's authority in view of the new knowledge vouchsafed to Christians. The Old Testament might be regarded as a kind of preliminary revelation, and as such both contrasted with the final revelation of Christ, and also justified and even retained, though only when it had been reinterpreted and purified by means of a more or less strictly anthologised version. The preparatory stage represented by the Old Testament could then be associated in a positive way with the witness of the rest of Man's religious and intellectual history. It must not be forgotten that at this period such relativising attempts were an innovattion; but at the same time they were to a certain extent in keeping with related 'philosophical' efforts in Christian propaganda, and they went half way to meet the syncretistic tendencies discernible in every quarter, tendencies which certainly did not stop at the threshold of the Christian churches. And herein from the start lay a danger. It is no accident that the critical approach to the canon began in circles and groups which were the most open to alien influences, and which had from the outset been furthest removed from the ideas of primitive Christianity, that is to say, in the camp of those who were rightly characterised by later orthodoxy as heretical, and whom we today know as 'gnostic' theologians. The crude syncretism and the arbitrary and undisciplined character which their semi-mythological criticism displayed, especially in the early days, makes the severity of the reaction from within the Great Church easily understandable. But it would be fallacious to conclude that the gnostics had invented the problem. It was simply that with their presuppositions they were bound to be the first to notice it; and they then proceeded to deal with it in accordance with their own ideas. Sooner or later, however, the catholic theologicans had to address themselves to the same problem; and they did so by rejecting the draft solutions of the gnostics and substituting their own.

It would be a false understanding of the relativising 'exegeses' which the Old Testament underwent in gnostic circles to suppose that fantastic religious visionaries had set out deliberately from the start to discredit the Old Testament. Before Marcion there were hardly any 'anti-biblical gnostics'[73] in the strict sense. The view which dominated earlier scholarship, that 'the gnosis' had more or less rejected the Old Testament from the start,[74] is today no longer tenable—indeed, it has

[73] E. de Faye, *Gnostiques et gnosticisme²*, Paris, 1925, pp. 353, 355ff.

[74] Cf., e.g., Harnack, *Dogmengeschichte* I, p. 373; Leipoldt, *op. cit.*, I, p. 14. Even Bultmann, in the relevant section of his *Theology of the N.T.* (pp. 109f.) cannot adduce a single example in support of this view. W. Bauer, *Orthodoxy and Heresy in Earliest Christianity*, pp. 195ff., confessedly argues from later evidence; but even this does not prove as much as he believes and would like it to do.

very nearly been reversed. Certainly in the earliest sources such an intention is nowhere expressed.

Even the ecclesiastical polemists assert nothing of this kind, and their silence on this point cannot be merely accidental. In general what they condemn in the gnostics is not the rejection but the arbitrary exegesis of holy Scripture, by which its true witness is twisted and falsified,[75] the adulteration of its message with the language of heathen philosophy and poetry, and the preference given to the gnostics' own revelational writings, out of which their own fantastic assertions are exclusively proved.[76] It is also alleged that they bring shocking and blasphemous charges against the Creator God, the 'Elohim' of the Old Testament; but at first all that is meant by this is that they do not regard him as the supreme God, and consider his revelation, judged by the standard of Christ, to be prefatory and limited. The full, pneumatic knowledge of the gnostics goes far beyond not merely the Old Testament but also the ordinary Christian preaching. This can lead to a corresponding emphasis on, indeed, to an exaltation of their own superiority which has nothing but contempt for others; and this tendency to despise the God of the Creation and of the Law is undoubtedly illuminating for the peculiar, specifically 'gnostic' element in their spirituality.[77] To the gnostic it seems simply 'laughable', therefore, that the Old Testament 'Lawgiver' and Demiurge should have been able so to deceive himself as to his own limitations and those of his commandments.[78] But quite apart from the fact that naturally a very great deal is made of such

---

[75] Cf. Bludau, *op. cit.*, pp. 22ff.

[76] Cf., e.g., Hippolytus, Elench. V, 1ff., and esp. 7 and 8.

[77] H. Jonas, *Gnosis und spätantiker Geist* I[3], 1964, pp. 227ff., has clearly demonstrated this in principle.

[78] So, e.g., according to Clem. Alex., Strom. III, 9, 2f., in the Carpocratian book, 'On righteousness', which was read in a syncretistic sect and erroneously attributed to the gnostic 'Epiphanes': H. Kraft, 'Gab es einen Gnostiker Karpokrates?' *TZ* 8, 1952, pp. 434–443. In this context too belongs the 'Apocryphon of John', used by Irenaeus, *Adv. haer.* I: cf. C. Schmidt, 'Irenäus und seine Quelle in adv. haer. I, 29', in: *Philothesia* (Kleinert-Festschrift), 1907, pp. 315ff. The fantastic creation story which the Apocryphon puts into the mouth of Christ repeatedly corrects Moses' statements ('not, as Moses said, . . .': 45, 8ff.; 58, 15ff.; 59, 17ff.; 73, 4ff.), but at the same time constantly borrows from him (cf. esp. 48, 8ff.), and uses the words of Scripture in its argumentation (59, 1ff., cf. Isa. 6:10). Especially characteristic is 44, 13ff.: 'And he said to them, "I am a jealous God; beside me there is none" (Ex. 20:5)—by saying which he already indicated to the angels who were under him that there is another God. For if there were not another God, of whom would he have to be jealous?' (this quotation follows the edition of the Berlin MS. by W. C. Till; the three further versions published by M. Krause and P. Labib in 1962 exhibit no variations of substance in this passage). Similarly, but more with the idea of a self-deception of which he himself subsequently becomes aware, the Archigenetor in the 'Unnamed Coptic Gnostic Text', published by A. Böhlig and P. Labib in 1962, appeals to Isa. 46 in the LXX version (151, 12f.; 155, 30f.; 160, 28f.).

expressions by the polemical writers, and that the number of radical, antinomian sects was not great, and that their doctrine even at this stage may already have been dependent on Marcion,[79] it would be a mistake to think that such polemic rendered any positive evaluation of the Old Testament impossible from the start. It is precisely the gnostics who have a special interest in all ancient writings and thus in the Jewish traditions as well. Indeed, they have a partiality for appealing to the Old Testament in order to justify their special doctrines; whole gnostic works 'are by and large nothing more than gnostic exegesis of Old Testament texts'.[80] The fact that at the same time they assess the Scripture 'critically' by the standard of the Gospel, and regard its God, on an evaluation which combines the mythological with the religio-historical approach, as less than perfect, does not as yet entirely destroy the credibility of the sacred book. This is still true to a certain extent even in the case of Marcion, who made the decisive break with all 'preparatory stages' leading to the Christian revelation. Only his disciple, Apelles, so far as we know, dared to dismiss the Old Testament as nothing more than an untrustworthy collection of lies and fables.[81]

Although, therefore, the relationship of pre-Marcionite gnosis to the Old Testament is admittedly paradoxical, yet it is not incomprehensible, and may, *mutatis mutandis*, be seen as parallel in some respects to the use of the Canon by liberal theologians in modern times. The heretics, like the rest of the early Church, had at first simply taken over the Jewish bible, and therefore strove—by misunderstanding, allegorisation and correction—to find their own insights within it. But even they recognise a certain authority in this old revelatory document as basically self-evident; and this authority can still assert itself even where men subject the content of the biblical statements to derisive criticism, and dissociate themselves from it.

Some examples from the early period of the gnostic movement may illustrate what has just been said. The Simonians, who are indeed thoroughly Jewish in origin, appeal in support of their speculations explicitly to the words of Scripture, which, for those souls who have

[79] Cf. de Faye, *op. cit.*, p. 371; R. M. Grant, *Gnosticism and Early Christianity*, New York, 1959, p. 149; a different view is put forward by H. C. Puech in *N.T. Apocrypha* I, pp. 231f. (on the Cainites). Later works—the *Pistis Sophia*, the *Books of Jeu*, and the 'Unknown Gnostic Work'—are no different, in their 'solemn formulas' of citation, from the catholic Church of the third century: C. Schmidt, *Gnostische Schriften in koptischer Sprache aus dem Codex Brucianus*, 1892, pp. 539ff.

[80] K. Rudolph, *TLZ* 91, 1966, col. 101, in reply to J. Maier, *Vom Kultus zur Gnosis*, 1964, p. 24.

[81] Cf. A. von Harnack, *Marcion. Das Evangelium vom fremden Gott*[2], 1924, pp. 178f.; *id.*, 'Sieben neue Bruchstücke der Syllogismen des Apelles', *TU* VI, 3, 1890, pp. 111ff.

been trained for higher things, are fully sufficient to instruct them.[82] Their fantastic exegesis of the creation story does, it is true, call on heathen texts as well—syncretism is a constant tendency of all the gnostic schools—and their opponents complain that in this way Moses has been abominably distorted;[83] but they themselves are convinced that he already meant his words in their sense, and simply expressed himself allegorically.[84] Similarly, just like the catholics, they hear the 'Logos' speaking in the Prophets, although they have a very different conception of this Logos from the catholic one.[85] The Naassenians appeal in support of their principal figure, the 'Man' Adamas, the heavenly prototype of Adam, to Isa. 53:8,[86] and back this up with numerous other passages from Scripture.[87] The Book of Baruch, by the gnostic Justin, allegorises the creation story, and cites both Moses[88] and various prophets.[89] The creation story also enjoys especial popularity in later gnostic writers.[90] Thus, the work, 'On the Nature of the Archons', for all its derogatory polemic against the Archons who made the world and their 'Captains', nevertheless provides a paraphrase—in places word for word—of the creation story and primal history, which, though critically assessed, yet retains intrinsic validity.[91]

[82] Hippolytus, Elench. VI, 10, 2.   [83] Hippolytus, Elench. VI, 9, 3.
[84] Hipplytus, Elench. VI, 14, 7.   [85] Hippolytus, Elench. VI, 13.
[86] Hippolytus, Elench. V, 7, 2; for a further catena of O.T. quotations combined with an allegorical interpretation of words from Homer cf. ibid., 7, 34f.
[87] Hippolytus, Elench. V, 7, 32; 7, 39; 8, 19; 9, 6. Here the N.T. already plays a part alongside the Old.
[88] Hippolytus, Elench. V, 26, 11.
[89] Hippolytus, Elench. V, 26, 36; 27, 4; cf. E. Haenchen, 'Das Buch Baruch', in: Gott und Mensch (Gesammelte Aufsätze), 1965, pp. 265–298.
[90] Cf. Irenaeus, Adv. haer. I, 18, and esp. Tertullian, Adversus Hermogenem. Clement Alex., Eclog. proph. 56, 2, clashes with Hermogenes over the correct exegesis of Ps. 18:6. On Heracleon and Theodotus cf. nn. 104, 107 below. The Psalter was a favourite source for establishing the doctrine of aeons; Ps. 84 is quoted for this purpose in the Pistis Sophia (Schmidt-Till, pp. 76ff.), and a whole series of Psalms in the 'Unknown gnostic work' (ibid., p. 342). The 'Apocryphon of John' too is particularly interested in the opening chapters of Genesis: cf. W. C. van Unnik, 'Die jüdische Komponente in der Entstehung der Gnosis', VC 15, 1961, p. 78. Further texts may be found in A. Böhlig. 'Der jüdische und judenchristliche Hintergrund in gnostischen Texten von Nag Hammadi', Studies in the History of Religion (suppl. to Numen) 12, 1967, pp. 119ff. The preference for using Genesis was not confined to the gnosis in these early centuries, but was quite general: cf. G. Kretschmar, Studien zur frühchristlichen Trinitätstheologie, 1956, p. 31; G. T. Armstrong, Genesis in the Early Church, 1960, The 'Unnamed Coptic-Gnostic Work' appeals (58, 30) to a further ἱερὰ βίβλος, which elaborates on the Tree of Knowledge in Paradise.
[91] Cf. secs. 134–136, 143, in the translation by H. M. Schenke, TLZ 83, 1958, cols. 661–670. Similar efforts to give a detailed interpretation of this material from Genesis occur in the 'Fragment of a Conversation between John

Where contradictions occur, the multiplicity of aeons and angelic beings means that there is no difficulty in allowing for higher or lower degrees of inspiration,[92] and consequently in distinguishing within the Old Testament different parts or stages of revelation. In all probability Judaism had already anticipated the Christian gnostics on this point, when it occasionally allowed within its bible for 'repetitions' of inferior value[93] and for the intrusion of secondary elements into the sacred text.[94] Theories about the 'false pericopes' were developed especially in gnosticising Jewish Christian circles. Here Moses is retained, but the witness of the prophets is rejected and qualified either in whole or in part.[95] But even here there is not a complete breakaway from the Bible; indeed, to the best of our knowledge, no sect ever went so far as to construct a new text, purged of 'false pericopes'.[96] Such a group simply had its own ἐπίλυσις, differentiating between various elements

---

and Jesus', published by W. E. Crum, which, according to Puech, op. cit., p. 244, is very closely related to the 'Apocryphon of John'.

[92] The Ophites, for example, reckon that there are seven spirits who between them inspire the sacred text (Irenaeus, Adv. haer. I, 30, 11); the Simonians, who boast that they are able to bring back the souls of the prophets (Tertullian, De anima 57), according to another source hold that these souls are inspired a mundi fabricatoribus angelis: Irenaeus, Adv. haer. I, 23, 3; Hippolytus, Elench. VI, 19, 7. According to Saturninus the Jewish God is one of the angels who made the world, among whom Satan opposed him as an enemy (Irenaeus, Adv. haer. I, 24; Hippolytus, Elench. VII, 28). The gnostic Justin allows for a conversion of the Demiurge (Hippolytus, Elench. V, 26, 18), while Heracleon holds that he was already inspired by the Logos in the creation (Origen, Comm. Joh. II, 14, 102), and on the other hand takes ἐκ προσώπου in Ps. 69:10 to refer to the conquest of the δυνάμεις by the Saviour (ibid., X, 34, 223).

[93] On the concept of δευτέρωσις cf. H. Bietenhard, art. 'Deuterosis,' RAC III, 1957, pp. 842–849.

[94] Cf. G. Hölscher, Kanonisch und Apokryph, 1905, pp. 60f. On the attempts to 'conceal' (גנז), i.e., to exclude, certain passages recognised to be post-canonical, cf. G. Quispel, VC 2, 1948, p. 39; R. Meyer, TWNT III, p. 980.

[95] This may be seen from the statements of the Pseudo-Clementines, though in detail the meaning of these is fiercely debated: cf. esp. E. Molland, 'La thèse "La prophétie n'est jamais venue de la volonté de l'homme" (2 Pierre I, 21) et les Pseudo-Clémentines,' Stud. Theol 9, 1955, pp. 67–85; for a different view, H. J. Schoeps, Theologie und Geschichte des Judenchristentums, 1949, pp. 148ff. It may be that the heretics of the Pseudo-Epistle of the Corinthians to Paul may belong to the same grouping with their assertion, οὐ δεῖν προφήταις χρῆσθαι (10). It is very striking that even where the prophets are rejected the authority of Moses remains unimpaired. Is the critique of the prophets, which by now, indeed, is carried on more with an eye to the uniqueness of the true Prophet, Christ himself, connected with the fact that the prophets appear to reject the 'Law'? If so, then they would have been rejected in these circles on the same grounds as those on which Justin exalts them above Moses: cf. p. 97 below.

[96] On the way in which this criticism worked in detail, and particular texts were rejected as false, cf. Hom. Clem. II, 52; III, 17.

in the Scripture, whereas the catholics derived it all uniformly from
the one Holy Spirit.[97] In other circles the solution was to stress that the
true meaning of Scripture was actually discernible only to gnostic
pneumatics.[98]

In the case of the great gnostics—Basilides, Valentinus, and the
Valentinians—the Old Testament is, however, perceptibly inferior in
status to the New Testament texts.[99] But this does not yet mean that
men were prepared to renounce its testimony altogether. It is true
that, according to the extant fragments, Basilides hardly quoted the
Old Testament at all;[100] but in Isidore, who as an ex-Christian takes
over the theory that the Greeks had plagiarised the Old Testament,[101]
the picture is already changing, and in a Basilidean treatise described
by Hippolytus numerous, more or less critical quotations from the Old
Testament occur once more alongside sayings from the New Testament
'scriptures'.[102] Valentinus, the pneumatic, speaks in his own name, and
for his explicit quotations seems to have drawn almost exclusively on
New Testament texts.[103] But, as the attitude of his disciples shows,

[97] II Pet. 1:19–21; cf. Molland, 'La thèse', pp. 69f., and Bauer, *Orthodoxy*,
p. 199. On the ἐπιλύσεις of the *Pistis Sophia* cf. C. Colpe, 'Die Thomas-
psalmen und die Gnosis', *JAC* 7, 1964, p. 88. In the Epistle of Jude I myself—
unlike Bauer, *op. cit.*, p. 201, who concurs with the view expressed in Jülicher-
Fascher, *Einleitung in das Neue Testament*[7], 1931, p. 214—can detect no clear
instance of polemic against a rejection of the O.T. revelation.

[98] Irenaeus, Adv. haer. I, 3, 5; 8, 1; Hippolytus, Elench. V, 26, 6.

[99] In the succeeding period this naturally does not apply only to the 'great'
exponents of the gnosis; one may compare, for example, the Naassenian work
described in Hippolytus, Elench. V, 6–8, which positively luxuriates in both
Old and 'New' Testament quotations alongside others from its own secret
writings. By contrast it is asserted, of the Ququeians, who may have been a
splinter group of the Valentinians: novum testamentum auferentes aliud sibi
commenti sunt. duodecim apostolis barbara imposuerunt nomina, vetere tamen
testamento integro retento—though this statement does, it is true, come from a
late oriental source (Abraham Ecchellensis): cf. A. von Harnack, 'Der Ketzer-
katalog des Bischofs Maruta von Maipherkat', *TU* XIX, 1, 1899, p. 16; Puech,
op. cit., pp. 187f.

[100] Apart from certain allusions there is only one quotation (from Job) and
that is neutralised by a veneer of literary elegance: Clem. Alex., Strom. IV,
83, 1.

[101] Cf. n. 163 below.

[102] Cf. Hippolytus, Elench. VII, 22, 3f.; 15; 23, 1; 23, 6; 25, 3f.; 26, 2.

[103] On this point cf. pp. 140f. below. The so-called *Gospel of Truth* from the
Codex Jung (ed. Malinine–Puech–Quispel, Zurich, 1956) may be not by Valentinus himself, but nevertheless of Valentinian provenance. This again contains
many New Testament echoes, especially of John and Paul, but no explicit
quotation, and in particular there is nothing which demands unambiguously
to be referred to the Old Testament. The points of contact rightly noted by the
editors at 19, 35f. with Ps. 69:29, and at 32, 29 with Isa. 60:19f.; III Esdras 2:35,
are quite general; for a different view cf. K. H. Schelkle, 'Das Evangelium veritatis als kanonsgeschichtliche Quelle,' *BZ* N.F. 5, 1961, p. 90. The *Gospel of*

despite an unequivocal preference for the words of Jesus and the material of the New Testament, it is impossible to speak of a radical rejection of the Old Testament Bible in the Valentinian tradition.[104] 'He approves one part of the Law and the Prophets, and rejects another,' as Pseudo-Tertullian puts it.[105] Heracleon too, for all his criticisms, quotes Moses and the Scriptures,[106] and appeals to the creation story, allegorically understood.[107] According to Theodotus the 'psychic Christ' at least had been announced by the Prophets and the Law;[108] and he must therefore be acquainted with a christological proof from Scripture. In short, the old procedure of criticising the Old Testament and yet calling upon its witness is still in force.[109] Jesus alone is the true Word. As such he is something greater than the 'Voice' that was

---

Philip, which likewise is closely related, at least in part, to the Valentinians, also exhibits only general conceptual links with the Old Testament (Adam, Paradise, the Ark, etc.). The *Gospel of Thomas* is even further removed from the O.T.: Van Unnik, 'Die jüdische Komponente,' pp. 75f.; J. Munck, 'Bemerkungen zum koptischen Thomasevangelium', *StudTheol* 14, 1960, pp. 138f. The writer draws upon a great many N.T. texts, but 'the O.T. he simply ignores' (E. Haenchen, *ThR* 27, 1961, p. 326). A different view is taken by G. Quispel, 'Das Thomasevangelium und das Alte Testament', in: *Neotestamentica et Patristica* (Cullmann–Festschrift), 1962, pp. 243–248, and *Makarius, das Thomasevangelium und das Lied von der Perle*, Leiden, 1967, pp. 77f. He regards the Gospel as Encratite, and thinks that it made use of the LXX, and, through the Jewish-Christian source, of the Hebrew Bible. Yet here again it is entirely a matter of problematic 'allusions' and echoes.

[104] A point rightly taken by G. Heinrici, *Die valentinianische Gnosis und die heilige Schrift*, 1871, pp. 182f.; Zahn, *op. cit.*, vol. I, pp. 730–732; also Bludau, *op. cit.*, pp. 24f., who adduces Tertullian, *Praescr.* 28; Irenaeus, Adv. haer. I, 3, 6; III, 12, 12. W. Foerster, *Von Valentin zu Herakleon*, 1928, p. 66. ascribes a total rejection of the O.T. only to the 'Valentinians of Hippolytus', among whom he assumes there to have been a 'reworking' of the original Valentinian deposit (p. 100). But he fails to distinguish between an emphatic depreciation of the earlier revelation and an assumed 'rejection' of the O.T. Bauer's thesis (*Orthodoxy*, p. 197) that 'Ptolemaeus was the only one to find his way out of the purely negative attitude' to the O.T. (which he assumes for Valentinus and Heracleon) seems to me to throw light on the matter. Moreover, Bauer himself demonstrates elsewhere (p. 48) that according to Tertullian, Adv. Valent. 4 the Valentinian Theotimus undoubtedly must have adopted a more positive attitude. Theodotus, too, quotes the O.T., and includes Genesis among the προφητικαί γραφαί (Clem. Alex., Excerpt. ex Theodoto 50, 3; cf. 47, 3).
[105] Ps.–Tertullian, Adv. omnes haer. 4, 6.
[106] Hippolytus, Elench. VI, 32, 7f.; 36, 2; Origen, Comm. Joh. II, 14; XIII, 60.
[107] Hippolytus, Elench. VI, 30, 9.
[108] Clem. Alex., Exc. ex Theod. 59, 2f.
[109] Cf. Basilides in Hippolytus, Elench. VII, 25, 4 (here with a version of his own of Ex. 6:2f.; likewise Heracleon, *ibid.* VI, 36, 2); 22, 3; 22, 15; 26, 2; Clem. Alex., Strom. IV, 83, 1.

John the Baptist, and *a fortiori* he is something greater still than the 'echo' of the old prophets.[110]

Such analytical formulations indicate that the hermeneutical free-for-all is coming to an end, and that conscious theological reflection on the problem has begun. The great gnostics made a start by basing their theological argumentation on the words of Jesus, and by seeing in them directive authority. The murky efforts of syncretistic Bible criticism are now examined, and brought out into the clear light of scholarly awareness. A lucky chance has preserved for us at least one text which gives a coherent treatment of this theme. The famous *Letter to Flora* of the Valentinian Ptolemaeus[111] is a small, self-contained treatise on the question, how is a Christian to assess the 'Law', if he wishes to read and understand the Old Testament aright? This short work is written on an unusually high intellectual and literary level, and shows the advanced state of theological education which Valentinianism had attained by the middle of the second century. The solution which it offers is still a gnostic one; but the crude and unconsidered ideas of earlier gnosis are now clarified and systematised and given a lively presentation within the framework of a 'popularising' but well thought out and elegant discussion.

The immediate subject under consideration is not the ancient Scriptures in general but the Law promulgated by Moses.[112] Once again, therefore, the Law emerges as the central problem, decisive for a right understanding of the Old Testament. The Law—and this is the essential thesis—is not homogeneous, but comprises diverse elements of varying value: 'First of all, it must be realised that that law contained in the Pentateuch of Moses does not all derive from one lawgiver, by which I mean not from God alone'.[113] The perfect God cannot have directly promulgated the Law, because the Law 'is imperfect and needs to be fulfilled by someone else—indeed, it contains prescriptions which are not conformable to the nature and will of such a God'.[114] Behind the Law, therefore, stand different 'authors', and according to which is responsible at any given point so the Law will have a quite different significance and authority. The question of the binding force of the

---

[110] Origen, Comm. Joh. VI, 20, 108 and 117.

[111] Epihanius, *Panar.* 33, 3–7. Cf. the edition, with detailed commentary, by G. Quispel, *Sources chrétiennes* 24², 1966; and *id.*, 'La lettre de Ptolémée à Flora', *VC* 2, 1948, pp. 17–56.

[112] 3, 1.

[113] 4.1: πρῶτον οὖν μαθητέον, ὅτι σύμπας ἐκεῖνος νόμος ὁ ἐμπεριεχόμενος τῇ Μωσέως πεντατεύχῳ οὐ πρός ἑνός τινος νενομοθέτηται, λέγω δὴ οὐχ ὑπὸ μόνου θεοῦ, ἀλλ' εἰσί τινες αὐτοῦ προστάξεις καὶ ὑπ' ἀνθρώπων τεθεῖσαι.

[114] 3.4: οὔτε γὰρ ὑπὸ τοῦ τελείου θεοῦ καὶ πατρὸς φαίνεται τοῦτον τεθεῖσθαι (ἑπόμενος γάρ ἐστιν), ἀτελῆ τε ὄντα καὶ τοῦ ὑφ' ἑτέρου πληρωθῆναι ἐνδεῆ, ἔχοντά τε προστάξεις ἀνοικείας τῇ τοῦ τοιούτου θεοῦ φύσει τε καὶ γνώμῃ.

Law coincides for the gnostic with the question of its origin and of the provenance of its respective stipulations. As a rule men will advocate either of two mutually opposed opinions, which—says Ptolemaeus—are both equally false: one party wish to attribute the whole Law directly to God the Father, and to acknowledge it *en bloc* as right; the others—he has the Marcionites in mind—ascribe it conversely to the devil, whom they also make responsible for the creation of the world, and reject it *in toto*.[115] In fact what matters is to follow a middle course, and such a course can be found with certainty, if only men will 'hold fast the words of our Redeemer', which 'alone are capable of guiding us unerringly to an understanding of what is right'.[116]

Having reached this point the letter plunges at once *in medias res*. The words of the Saviour, to which Ptolemaeus repeatedly appeals,[117] not only supply the general standard of objective guidance, they also specifically authorise the methodological principle which he follows, namely that of distinguishing critically between the ingredients of the one Scripture. When Jesus rejects divorce, he explicitly states that Moses instituted it only with an eye to the 'hardness of heart' of those who received the command; in view of their 'weakness' he could not do otherwise. But, strictly speaking, the command was absolutely 'contrary' not only to God but even to Moses' own wishes.[118] Jesus' words about the contributions of the 'Elders' go even farther. The perverse traditions of these men, their Mishna, so to speak, found their way into the text at a later stage, and are equated by Jesus with unrighteousness. Jesus, like Isaiah before him, rejected this interpolation with the utmost rigour.[119]

So far Ptolemaeus has betrayed nothing of his gnostic starting-point, but in the spirit of a sober and objective criticism has in fact restricted himself to the traditional words of Jesus. But his examination now goes a stage further. Even the revealed Law, that namely which has been purged until it is free of all human concessions and interpolations, is not all of a piece; as regards its content it has to be analysed yet again, this time into three parts. First, there are those elements which Jesus himself accepted and 'fulfilled' by his exposition of them in the Sermon on the Mount. Secondly, there are those, like the laws relating to revenge and murder, which are not actually 'unrighteous'; but they contradict the essential goodness of the true God, and instead make allowances for the weakness of men. While it is true, therefore, that

---

[115] 3, 2f.

[116] 3, 8: . . . (τῶν) ῥηθησομένων ἡμῖν τὰς ἀποδείξεις ἐκ τῶν τοῦ σωτῆρος ἡμῶν λόγων παριστῶντες, δι' ὧν μόνον ἔστιν ἀπταίστως ἐπὶ τὴν κατάληψιν τῶν ὄντων ὁδηγεῖσθαι. Cf. 7, 9.

[117] On this point cf. pp. 85, 141 below.   [118] 4, 2–10.

[119] 4, 11–14. The exegesis is incorrect, but consistently follows a 'literal' sense.

G

Jesus the Son of God affirmed such laws in the abstract, in effect he nullified them.[120] Finally, there is a third group, the 'typical' laws, consisting of images and symbols, that is, the ceremonial regulations concerning sacrifices, circumcision, the sabbath, fasting, and the Passover, which were once meaningful as pointers to spiritual truths, but which are now obsolete. The materials of true sacrifice are not brute beasts nor externals such as incense, but the giving of praise and glory and thanks to God, fellowship, and doing good to one's neighbour. The true circumcision is the circumcision of the heart, the true fasting is the turning of the soul from evil, and so forth.[121] Here Ptolemaeus swings into line with the traditional Jewish allegorising of the Law, which presents no difficulties. It should be noted, however, that his critical analysis does not always stop at these ceremonial 'externals', but includes the moral commands. Even the Decalogue, which he is the first in the history of the Church to elevate to a special position as God's 'pure law, free from inferior additions', is in fact imperfect, and still requires a final fulfilment by the Saviour.[122] In this way, moreover, are resolved all those difficulties which the statements about the Law in Paul's writings seem to raise, statements to which Ptolemaeus appeals in this context; for if the Apostle at one time rejects the Law, and at another approves and accepts it, then the explanation must be simply that he has different parts of this complex entity in mind at different times.[123]

If we now review Ptolemaeus' comments so far, the really important new idea, and the one to which he himself gives especial prominence, at once becomes apparent: the Law is to be assessed by the words of Jesus. It is binding for Christians only in so far as it is acknowledged by Jesus and confirmed by his perfect teaching. Nevertheless, in Ptolemaeus —in contrast to Paul or Luke—the relationship between Jesus and the old Law is no longer understood in terms of salvation-history. There is absolutely no mention in his treatise of the Israelites or Jews as the ancient people of God;[124] and in his typological exegesis of the Law it is not christological prophecy but general religious and moral truths which

---

[120] 5, 1–7; 6, 1–3.   [121] 5, 8–15; 6, 4f.

[122] 5, 3: καὶ ἔστι μὲν ὁ τοῦ θεοῦ νόμος, ὁ καθαρὸς καὶ ἀσύμπλοκος τῷ χείρονι, αὐτὴ ἡ δεκάλογος, οἱ δέκα λόγοι ἐκεῖνοι οἱ ἐν ταῖς δυσὶ πλαξὶ δεδιχασμένοι, εἴς τε ἀπαγόρευσιν τῶν ἀφεκτέων καὶ εἰς πρόσταξιν τῶν ποιητέων, οἳ καίπερ καθαρὰν ἔχοντες τὴν νομοθεσίαν, μὴ ἔχοντες δὲ τὸ τέλειον, ἐδέοντο τῆς παρὰ τοῦ σωτῆρος πληρώσεως. Cf. against this view Irenaeus, Adv. haer. IV. 16, 3.

[123] 6, 6: ταῦτα δὲ καὶ οἱ μαθηταὶ αὐτοῦ καὶ ὁ ἀπόστολος Παῦλος ἔδειξε, τὸ μὲν τῶν εἰκόνων, ὡς ἤδη εἴπομεν, διὰ τοῦ πάσχα δι' ἡμᾶς καὶ τῶν ἀζύμων δείξας, τὸ δὲ τοῦ συμπεπληγμένου νόμου τῇ ἀδικίᾳ, εἰπών "τὸν νόμον τῶν ἐντολῶν ἐν δόγμασιν κατηργῆσθαι", τὸ δὲ τοῦ ἀσυμπλόκου τῷ χείρονι "ὁ μὲν νόμος" εἰπών "ἅγιος καὶ ἡ ἐντολὴ ἁγία καὶ δικαία καὶ ἀγαθή".

[124] Even in his paraphrase of Jesus' saying in Matt. 19:8 any mention of the Jews is rigorously avoided: 4, 5–10.

he has principally in mind,[125] as in Philo. The Law, therefore, does not lead men nor 'drive' them toward Christ. But his timelessly valid words provide the standard by which it is to be judged; they are the key which opens the Old Testament, the only guidelines by which Christians can learn how to read it, and know what to affirm and what to reject. The same kind of approach is found in Heracleon,[126] Theodotus,[127] and even in Valentinus himself,[128] so that we are certainly dealing here with a settled basic principle of the Valentinian school.[129] This principle is manifestly superior not only to the unbridled caprice of other gnostic schools but also the naïve and total lack of method of popular Christian use of the Scriptures. The hitherto undifferentiated unity of the Scripture is shattered; but the assessment of its component parts is not to be left simply to human preference. It is to be subject to Christ and his word alone.

The importance of this proposition and of the hermeneutical advance which it effects is obvious. We have no right to doubt the seriousness and subjective integrity with which Ptolemaeus lays such stress upon it. But it must be asked how far his critical conclusions really follow, as he believes, from the exegesis of the words of Jesus. At the close of his argument he exhorts the lady to whom his Letter is addressed (who appears to be a catholic) not at first to trouble herself any more about the further problems of unity and multiplicity in the Godhead.[130] Let it suffice her that she can be sure that the instruction which she has

[125] The one—ambiguous—exception (5, 15; also 6, 6) depends on the reference to Paul (I Cor. 5:7).

[126] Cf. n. 106 above; also Origen, Comm. Joh. XIII, 27, 164: προσεδέχετο ἡ ἐκκλησία τὸν χριστὸν καὶ ἐπέπειστο περὶ αὐτοῦ, ὅτι τὰ πάντα μόνος ἐκεῖνος ἐπίσταται and ibid. XIII, 53, 363 (on Joh. 4:42): οἱ γὰρ ἄνθρωποι τὸ μὲν πρῶτον ὑπὸ ἀνθρώπων ὁδηγούμενοι πιστεύουσιν τῷ σωτῆρι, ἐπὰν δὲ ἐντύχωσιν τοῖς λόγοις αὐτοῦ, οὗτοι οὐκέτι διὰ μόνην ἀνθρωπίνην μαρτυρίαν, ἀλλὰ δὶ αὐτὴν τὴν ἀλήθειαν πιστεύουσιν.

[127] Clem. Alex., Exc. ex Theod. 3, 1: ἐλθὼν οὖν ὁ σωτὴρ τὴν ψυχὴν ἐξύπνισεν, ἐξῆψεν δὲ τὸν σπινθῆρα. δύναμις γὰρ οἱ λόγοι τοῦ κυρίου. Cf. 74, 2.

[128] Cf. esp. in the Epistle to Rheginos, which may be by Valentinus, the introductory remarks at XXII[K], 25ff., about the 'rest', which we, in contrast to the problem-ridden sophists, 'received from our Redeemer, our Lord Christ, which we received when we learned the truth and calmed our minds on the subject'; and the similar thought at the close of XXV[K], 37ff.: 'These things I have received from the ungrudging generosity of my Lord, Jesus Christ' (translation by R. McL. Wilson, Epistle to Rheginos, London, 1970). As yet, however, there is no mention of the words of Jesus.

[129] Quispel, Sources, p. 78, refers to a similar expression in Apelles (Epiphanius, Panar. 44, 2): ὑποδείξας ἡμῖν (sc. ὁ χριστός ἐν ποίᾳ γραφῇ ποῖά ἐστιν τὰ φύσει ἐξ αὐτοῦ εἰρημένα καὶ ποῖά ἐστι τὰ ἀπὸ τοῦ δημιουργοῦ and to Hom. Clem. III, 49, 2: . . . οὗ τῇ διδασκαλίᾳ πειθόμενος γνώσεται τίνα ἐστὶν τῶν γραφῶν τὰ ἀληθῆ, τίνα δὲ τὰ ψευδῆ. Reminiscent of the Pseudo-Clementine δευτέρωσις is Ptolemaeus' concept of the δεύτερος νόμος (5, 6); cf. p. 19 above.

[130] 7, 8–10.

received flows from the apostolic tradition and has been tested by the words and teaching of the Saviour.[131] Unlike the anti-gnostic polemists Ptolemaeus prefers not to parade the speculative elements of his system, but rather seeks to camouflage them in accordance with the purpose of his work, which is to woo converts.[132] Nevertheless, in the end he formulates the real result of his enquiry: the Old Testament Law, even as regards its divine elements, can be derived neither from the devil nor from the perfect God, but must have been promulgated by an intermediate being, the creator of the world.[133] Yet even this is perhaps a simplification; in fact, according to Valentinian teaching, the three different elements of the divine Law derive instead from three different divine powers: the pneumatic seeds, the Sophia, and the powers of the Demiurge.[134] Ptolemaeus, therefore, rates the value of the Old Testament in part higher, in part even lower than his summary suggests. Furthermore, his view of the Son of God is hardly as simple as it appears: in the context of Jesus' recognition of the divine Law it is in fact the 'pneumatic Christ' whom he has in mind, and who is decidedly not to be identified with the real Redeemer.[135] None of this any longer has anything to do with the tradition of Jesus' words which Ptolemaeus quotes. Either it derives from secret special traditions, or it may be the result of an uncontrollable allegorical exegesis of the parables and of the

[131] 7, 9: . . . ἀξιουμένη τῆς ἀποστολικῆς παραδόσεως, ἣν ἐκ διαδοχῆς καὶ ἡμεῖς παρειλήφαμεν μετὰ καὶ τοῦ κανονίσαι πάντας τοὺς λόγους τῇ τοῦ σωτῆρος ἡμῶν διδασκαλίᾳ . . . The word κανονίσαι here has, of course, nothing to do with a 'canonical' collection, as I myself unfortunately mistranslated it in an earlier work (Ecclesiastical Authority, p. 158). The correct rendering is that of Quispel, Sources, p. 69: 'nous confirmerons nos conceptions par les paroles du Sauveur.' On the Valentinian concept of tradition cf. pp. 140f., 167 below.

[132] This tactical angle should not be over-emphasised; cf. K. Müller, Nachr. Gött. Ges. d. Wissensch., 1920, p. 205: 'There can no longer be any doubt that the special character of the gnosis does not reside in the so-called systems, to which the anti-heretical writers give such prominence.' H. Langerbeck, Aufsätze zur Gnosis (ed. H. Dörries), 1967, would like to regard these speculations as very largely secondary, though he concedes (p. 65) that it would be wrong to conclude from the fact that 'in Ptolemy's Letter to Flora the cosmogonic myths are wholly omitted' that therefore 'they played no part in the thinking of Ptolemy himself'. W. Foerster, 'Die Grundzüge der ptolemäischen Gnosis', NTS 6, 1959–60, pp. 16–31, takes rather the opposite line, bringing out the importance of the speculative element, but (p. 29) he sees the meaning of the 'allegorical exegesis of scripture' in Ptolemy, nevertheless, as an attempt 'to demonstrate from the words of scripture, and especially of Jesus, the gnosis which he has to offer'.

[133] Mention of attributing the Law to the devil must be a reference to Marcion: cf. Quispel, Sources, p. 72; also M. Hornschuh, ZKG 78, 1967, pp. 356f. Significantly, the assertion that the φθοροποιὸς διάβολος himself is regarded as the author of the Law and of the world (3, 2) caricatures Marcion's teaching in exactly the same way as the Church polemists do.

[134] Quispel, VC, pp. 40ff.; Sources, pp. 84ff.; cf. Irenaeus, Adv. haer. I, 7, 3.
[135] Quispel, Sources, pp. 89f., commenting on 5, 7.

Fourth Gospel, of a kind known to be particularly characteristic of Valentinian theology.[136]

In the case of these speculations we are not dealing with peripheral matters which an objective assessment of the Valentinian position could, if necessary, ignore. Instead, with their hierarchical sequences and distinctions they reflect an absolutely fundamental feature of Valentinianism (and, to a greater or lesser degree, of all gnostic systems) which likewise makes its appearance in the similarly structured cosmology and anthropology, christology and ecclesiology. This pattern of thought is at the opposite pole to the harsh concrete alternatives which dominate primitive Christianity and the Old Testament. Nevertheless, by means of these distinctions and reinterpretations it succeeds in building theoretical bridges even between itself and the Old Testament. The newness of the central truth of Christianity was one of the things about it which the Valentinians most highly prized,[137] but that did not mean that they wanted simply to abandon the Old Testament. In defending it against Marcion's radical criticism, indeed, Ptolemaeus evaluated it more kindly than was customary in the earlier gnosis.[138] Yet it is precisely at this point that it becomes clear that on gnostic assumptions any genuine recognition of the Canon is impossible. Even in Ptolemeaeus, who wants to safeguard it, the Canon as a normative entity in the strict sense is already disintegrating.

It is impossible to remain in doubt for very long that the gnostic understanding of holy Scripture cannot be reconciled with the use which the Church had hitherto made of it. The dismembering of the sacred text among a number of different beings who were held to have inspired it or acted as mediators of revelation was from the start completely unacceptable to her on account of the polytheistic character of this method of interpretation. Moreover, any concession was bound to have the effect of compromising with the even more dangerous assault of Marcion, who had totally rejected the Scripture of the Demiurge and banned it from his church.[139] On the other hand, however, it was also impossible to persist in the belief and practice which had obtained hitherto, and to assert the uniform perfection of the whole Scripture. The differences between the Old Testament on the one side and the 'doctrine' of Christ and the moral views which Christians

[136] Cf. pp. 168, 193, 196 below.

[137] Evidence for this will be found in the so-called 'Gospel of Truth' (on which cf. n. 103 above and p. 140 below).

[138] The alleged diabolic origin of the O.T. is more harshly rejected by Ptolemaeus than the opposite catholic position: Quispel, VC, pp. 29ff. This is not just another aspect of his desire to win converts. It is clear that in the Valentinian camp Marcion's total rejection of the O.T. was regarded as more dangerous than its uncritical acceptance in the Great Church.

[139] On Marcion cf. pp. 149ff. below.

upheld on the other could no longer be ignored. What was needed, therefore was a completely new initiative, if the Scripture was to be rescued, and the Old Testament was to retain its traditional 'canonical' status.

Neither tradition nor practice suggested any way in which this might be done. Indeed, it seems that until the outbreak of the gnostic crisis no one had really even tried to look for one. Ptolemaeus may not in substance have been exaggerating when he rejected the unqualified catholic acceptance of the Law as a somewhat primitive notion which had never been properly thought through. In the struggle with the Jews over scriptural proof no one had felt the need for a critical examination of the Scripture; indeed, unqualified acceptance of it formed the only basis on which dialogue was possible.[140] Even when dealing with the heathen, who knew nothing about it, the custom was to appeal without a qualm to the immemorial and infallible sacred Scriptures. It is precisely in the apologetic literature that we find the most exaggerated reliance on its miraculous inerrancy.[141] Christians, it is claimed, make no arbitrary assertions, for their beliefs can be discovered and checked in their Scriptures.[142] 'We opened'—so runs the apocryphal mission sermon of Peter—'the books which we have of the prophets, we found their predictions correct, and we understood that they were ordained by God. We say nothing without the scripture.'[143]

It was, so far as one can tell, the unaided achievement of Justin finally to take the thinking on this subject beyond this traditional standpoint, and to try to establish the old confidence in the Scriptures with new arguments, dealing squarely with the objections that had been raised for so long. Justin was the first orthodox theologian to possess what may be called a 'doctrine of holy scripture'. In evolving such a doctrine he was not thinking only of the Jews. Although his anti-gnostic and anti-Marcionite writings have been lost, the extant *Dialogue with the Jew Trypho* clearly indicates how strongly he was influenced by opponents within Christianity,[144] when he takes his stand

[140] This is axiomatic even for the author of Barnabas, however much he contests the Jewish exegesis as misinterpretation. Aristides in his brief remarks about the Jews (Apol. 14) does not discuss the scripture or the Law. It seems, however, that he regards circumcision, the sabbath, and the rest of the ceremonial law as a mixture of misunderstanding and apostasy, and connects them, in a way not unlike that of Colossians, with the Jewish worship of angels.

[141] Among the early Apologists only the *Epistle of Diognetus* and Minucius Felix do not make confirmatory use of the formal authority of Scripture. Jewish apologetic, as the *Letter of Aristeas* in particular demonstrates, had already shown Christian apologists the way in this.

[142] Aristides, Apol. 16, 3.

[143] Clem. Alex., Strom. VI, 128; cf. Acts 26:22f.

[144] Cf. esp. Dial. 30, 1; 80. On the problem of sources cf. P. Prigent, *Justin et l'Ancien Testament*, Paris, 1964, esp. pp. 74ff

decisively on the side of a *tota scriptura* biblicist orthodoxy against scepticism and criticism.

Justin certainly did not take this decision purely for tactical reasons. The defence of the ancient Scriptures was more to him than an urgent apologetic necessity which he could not evade. It was a central concern of his own personal faith. His Christian belief is built on the Old Testament. If we may take him at his word, then he was converted simply by reading the prophetic writings, and only then joined the living community of the 'friends of Christ'.[145] Be that as it may, the Scripture alone gives him the certainty that his understanding is based not on opinion but on God's truth. 'I cannot make up my mind to follow men and human dogmas; I prefer to follow God and what he has taught'.[146] After his conversion, therefore, Justin puts his powers as a philosopher and teacher exclusively at the service of the holy Scripture. The ability to understand Scripture is, according to himself, the only gift of grace which he has received from God.[147] The real misfortune of the philosophers, with whom he had so long been associated, was that they engaged in discourse about God, although they had no information from God himself.[148] Consequently, philosophy was bound to split up into a mêlée of conflicting schools of thought.[149] The same slavery to doctrines delivered by men made it impossible for the Jews to follow Christ.[150] And finally it is belief in individual teachers which has been the principal source of all divisions within the Church of Christ.[151] In the holy Scripture, on the other hand, God himself speaks to us, that is to say, his Logos or his Spirit which of old filled the prophets.[152] Justin is not concerned to distinguish more precisely which powers inspired men at different times; for in contrast to the gnosis, inspiration for him means precisely the assurance that in every word of holy Scripture we really are in touch with God himself.[153] It is this

---

[145] Dial. 8, 1. Similar statements are made by Tatian, Theophilus and even Hilary.

[146] Dial. 80, 3; cf. I Apol. 10, 6 on the impotence of ἀνθρώπειοι νόμοι.

[147] Dial. 58, 1.   [148] Dial. 3, 7.

[149] Dial. 2, 2; cf. 6, 1; 35, 6; I Apol. 26, 6.

[150] Dial. 48, 2; 140, 2. Justin uses the word παράδοσις only once (Dial. 38, 2) for these Jewish traditions. His sparing use of the verb παραδιδόναι is also to be explained by his strict scriptural principle; cf. the examples collated in Flesseman–van Leer, *op. cit.*, pp. 83ff.

[151] I Apol. 26, 6; Dial. 35, 6.

[152] Cf. I Apol. 33, 6; 59, 1; also C. Andresen, 'Justin und der mittlere Platonismus,' ZNW 44, 1953–3, p. 182 n. 96.

[153] The detailed evidence for this statement will be found in W. A. van Es, 'De Grond van het Schriftgeloof bij de "Apologeten" van de tweede Eeuw', *Gereformeerd Theol. Tijdschrift* 34, 1933, pp. 194ff., esp. 287ff. Justin did not, however, develop any very exact psychological theory of the process of inspiration; such a theory occurs first in Athenagoras, Suppl. 9, 1, and then notably in

which gives the words of the Bible their incomparable power to threaten and restore.[154] Strictly speaking, the holy scriptures need no exegesis. All that is necessary is to listen—and then one cannot but assent.[155]

Nevertheless, Justin does not omit to supply one proof of the truth of that word of God on which all his work is based—a proof which, he is convinced, is absolutely compelling, and one such as no heathen philosopher ever adduced for the truth of his own teaching.[156] This proof consists in the consonance of the christological texts in Scripture with the facts, a consonance which in Justin's eyes is as miraculous as it is patent and incontrovertible. In his view it is quite obvious that all the predictions relating to the first coming, that is, the earthly life of Christ, have been fulfilled point by point. One can only conclude, therefore, that as regards the remainder of the prophecies still outstanding and, indeed, everything that it states or teaches Scripture can rationally claim one's belief.[157] This, for Justin, is a genuine, absolutely conclusive proof which cannot be evaded: 'We have shown that everything which happened had already been proclaimed beforehand by the prophets. Consequently one must feel the same confidence with regard to that which has likewise been prophesied, but has not yet come to pass, as to that which has already occurred.'[158] Thus the holy Scripture is confirmed as an infallible source of divine truth, and a firm foundation is laid on which one can proceed to build with confidence.[159]

Theophilus (e.g., Ad Autol. II, 9f.) and in Montanism (cf. Campenhausen, *Ecclesiastical Authority*, pp. 187ff.).

[154] Dial. 8, 2; cf. 121, 2. The context makes it clear that this characteristic of the τοῦ σωτῆρος λόγοι can once again refer directly only to the O.T.

[155] Dial. 55, 3. According to 7, 2 they can dispense with even a competent ἀπόδειξις.

[156] I Apol. 20, 3 (μόνοι).

[157] Justin thus discovers within history the actual fulfilment which the Jewish apocalypses had attempted to create by literary artifice with their antedated *vaticinia ex eventu*, in order to inspire confidence in their own predictions; cf. P. Vielhauer in: *N.T. Apocrypha* II, p. 586.

[158] I Apol. 52, 1; cf. 12, 9f.; 30, 1; 31, 7; 33, 2; 44, 11; 53, 12; similarly, e.g., Dial. 110, 117, etc. Cf. Mart. Just. 2, 6. Theophilus, Ad Autol. I, 14; II, 9, repeats the method of proof developed by Justin, as later do Irenaeus, Dem. 42; 86; Tertullian, Apol. 20, 2f. In the *Preaching of Peter* (cf. n. 143 above) it is already an established principle. By contrast, the similar argument in Barn. 1, 7 is as yet aimed at a different conclusion: Barnabas sees 'the correctness of the predictions guaranteed not by the fact that prophecies relating to the past and present have been fulfilled . . . but by the fact that even the μέλλοντα (the eschatological events . . .) have begun to be realised' (Windisch, op. cit., p. 307). In Dial. 7 Justin uses the personal conduct and miraculous powers of the prophets as additional support for their credibility.

[159] The rationalism of this argument has often been censured. Nevertheless, the importance of the concept within the totality of Justin's theology should not be over-estimated. Justin is well aware that for a genuine, spiritual understanding of Scripture spiritual illumination is necessary: cf., e.g., Dial. 7, 3; 44, 2;

With this historical scheme of prophecy and fulfilment Justin gives a place of central importance to a concept which in Ptolemaeus had receded completely into the background. This concept derives from earlier Christian tradition;[160] but now characteristically its purpose has been altered. Now the aim is not so much to demonstrate the validity of faith in Christ from the Scripture as conversely to re-establish the threatened authority of Scripture in the light of Christ.[161] With the christological proof from Scripture Justin links the proof of the antiquity of Scripture, which derives from Jewish missionary propaganda, and according to which the standard philosophers of ancient times acquired their wisdom from the Bible.[162] Hence Scripture is superior to all heathen philosophy—a conclusion in striking contrast to that of the gnostic Isidore, who used the same idea for a different purpose, namely to put the heathen on an equality with Scripture as witnesses to truth.[163] This form of scriptural proof, which Justin simultaneously uses in the traditional manner against the Jews, was to remain a well-nigh invariable and certainly, with the abundance of examples which it later accumulated, the supreme ingredient of the apologetic and didactic literature.[164]

78, 11; 92, 1; similarly Barn. 6, 10. This is a point which was bound to make itself felt in relation to Judaism. The Jews do not possess this illumination (cf., e.g., I Apol. 31, 5; 36, 3; Dial 9, 1; 14, 2; 29, 2; 34, 1; 55, 3), and have therefore forfeited their claim to their, or now no longer their 'but rather our scriptures' (Dial. 29, 2). It should also not be overlooked that the fulfilment of the prophecies does not, in Justin's view, absolutely establish the faith and Christian truth. To achieve this the proof is constructed in broader terms: cf., e.g., Dial. 11; 35, 7; van Es, op. cit., vol. 35, 1934, pp. 300ff. The same point is rightly emphasised by Oepke, Das neue Gottesvolk, p. 253, though with a somewhat arbitrary bias toward his own theme of the 'popular concept of God'. In this way the consonance of scriptural testimony and reality, of the γραφαί and the πράγματα, acquires, as it does in Luke, fundamental and living significance.

[160] On the difference between Justin's thought on this point and that of the N.T., which is aimed primarily at the Jews, cf. S. Amsler, L'Ancien Testament dans l'Église, Neuchâtel, 1960, pp. 95f.

[161] This does not mean, of course, that the O.T. ceases to give its witness to Christ as it has always done; both the Apology and the Dialogue equally make this clear.

[162] I Apol. 44; 46, 3; 59f.; Dial. 7, 1. It is clear that the traditional, somewhat external concept of a 'theft' on the part of the Greeks—an idea which does not occur in Justin himself—is at once restricted and deepened by his own conception of the activity of the λόγος σπερματικός: I Apol. 5; 8; 46; II Apol. 10, 2; 13; cf. M. Pellegrino, Gli Apologeti Greci del II. Secolo. Saggio sui rapporti fra il Cristianesimo primitivo e la cultura classica, Rome, 1947, pp. 82ff. For a fair assessment of this apparently rather wild notion cf. H. Chadwick, Early Christian Thought and the Classical Tradition, 1966, p. 141 n. 52.

[163] Clem. Alex., Strom. VI, 53, 3f. (cf. pp. 139f. below). Valentinus takes a radically different view: ibid., VI, 52, 3f. (cf. p. 140 n. 167 below).

But however impressively this procedure developed, it was still not adequate to solve the problem with which we are concerned. The proof from Scripture makes it clear that the Old Testament must be a miraculous and superhuman divine book, and to that extent worthy of men's belief. But it suggests no way of justifying or interpreting in a tolerable manner its strange and alien elements, and the less than 'Christian' character of its legal provisions.

Justin feels this difficulty more keenly than anyone else, for he is a 'philosopher'. In the writings of Plato he has come to know the reality of the one, unchangeable True and Good so decisively that even as a Christian he cannot accept any revelation as perfect which belies this knowledge.[165] God is One, and what was once good and true in his sight remains, to all ages and in all lands,[166] for ever unchangeable and the only valid goodness and truth.[167] The teaching of Jesus is the perfect manifestation of this truth, and Justin finds witness to it even in the prophets of the Old Testament. But the 'Law' appears patently to contradict this ideal truth. Justin is thus confronted with the same question which Ptolemaeus posed, and answered in his own way. For Justin, however, the answer is not open to discussion. He is familiar with the gnostic criticisms of the scripture;[168] but he is determined not to yield them one inch of ground. With extreme, polemical harshness he formulates his counter-principle, one which in this respect allies

---

[164] Cf. A. von Ungern-Sternberg, *Der traditionelle alttestamentliche Schriftbeweis "de Christo" und "de evangelio" in der alten Kirche bis zur Zeit Eusebs von Caesarea*, 1913, p. 233. In my own opinion, in the light of the material presented by this author, Justin's importance in opening up this method ought to be assessed even more highly than he is prepared to do.

[165] I have no doubt that Justin's rightly celebrated Introduction to the Dialogue does not contain the materials for an exact biography but is in a very high degree 'stylised'; cf. N. Hyldahl, *Philosophie und Christentum. Eine Interpretation der Einleitung zum Dialog Justins*, Copenhagen, 1966, esp. pp. 140ff. But what this section has to tell us about his 'philosophical beliefs' and his relationship to Plato can and must, in my view, be taken more seriously as positive evidence than Hyldahl is prepared to allow. Justin may indeed have been more of an eclectic than a Middle Platonist in the strict sense, but the strong link between his presuppositions and Platonist theory has been demonstrated, despite Hyldahl's objections, convincingly by Andresen, *op. cit.*, pp. 157ff.; R. M. Grant, 'Aristotle and the Conversion of Justin', *JTS* N.S. 7, 1956, pp. 246ff.; H. Chadwick, 'Justin Martyr's Defence of Christianity,' *BJRL* 47, 1965, pp. 293f., and *Early Christian Thought*, pp. 20ff., cf. p. 16. There is no need to deny him an independent reading of Plato. On Justin's 'level of education' cf. W. Schmid, 'Die Textüberlieferung der Apologie des Justin,' *ZNW* 40, 1941, pp. 128ff., and 'Frühe Apologetik und Platonismus. Ein Beitrag zur Interpretation des Prooms von Justins Dialogus,' in: *Hermeneia* (Festschrift O. Regenbogen), 1952, pp. 163–182.

[166] I Apol. 39, 2ff.; II Apol. 9, 3f.; Dial. 23; 28, 4.

[167] Dial. 11, 1; 23, 1; cf. 30, 1.

[168] Cf. esp. Dial. 80, 4.

him once more with his Jewish opponents:[169] 'I am absolutely convinced that no passage of scripture can contradict any other, and will
rather concede that I do not understand what is said' than admit the
possibility of the least contradiction; 'and I will go to any trouble to
bring the man who considers that there are in scripture mutually
contradictory passages to accept this conviction of mine.'[170] But how
is this to be done in face of that contradiction which is theologically the
most significant because it touches the very substance of the Scriptures,
namely that between the ancient ceremonial law and Christian philosophical perfection? Can Justin make common cause with Judaism even
on this question?

What Justin actually does is to make abundant use of that method of
expounding the Law, approved in Judaism, which had originally been
allegorical but by now had in Christian hands been largely converted
into the typological method;[171] and he uses it more especially in defending the faith against the Jewish exegesis. The hidden prophetic meaning
which, in his view, attaches to many of the regulations of the Law then
proves that with the coming of Christ these have lost their significance,
and, contrary to Jewish practice, are no longer to be observed.[172] Justin
feels, however, that this explanation is not adequate to deal satisfactorily
with the awkward fact of the old Law in its entirety. In this he is more
penetrating than the writer of Hebrews, and parts company with
Barnabas, which he knows and uses.[173] Against the gnostic criticism of

[169] In this context differences arise only over the validity of the LXX translation, which for Justin is normative, and over alleged falsifications of the text
by the Jews: Dial. 71, 2; 72, 3; 73, 1; 73, 5f.; 84, 3f.; 120, 5. This may be linked
with the fact that the limits of the Jewish canon were more narrowly drawn:
cf. Sundberg, op. cit., pp. 159, 171f. These controversies continued down into
the Middle Ages: cf. B. Blumenkranz, Juifs et chrétiens dans le monde occidental
430–1096, Paris, 1960, pp. 225f., 237f. But the question of the Canon played
as such hardly any part in the debate.

[170] Dial. 65, 2. Cf. Josephus, Contra Apionem I, 38, on βιβλία ἀσύμφωνα and
μαχόμενα. This idea naturally also takes a leading part in Justin's fight against
gnostic theories.

[171] Allegorical exegesis appears significantly in those very parts which bring
out the original, concrete sense of the ritual commands and then contrast this
with the new, Christian morality: Christians no longer know a circumcision of
the flesh, but only that of the heart (Dial. 19, 2; 28, 4), no longer mere external
washings but that inner purification which is the effect of baptism (Dial. 14;
29), etc. But even here it is impossible to draw a clear boundary-line between
this and typological exegesis.

[172] Justin, however, is extremely brief in his application of this proof, particularly with regard to the Law, and contents himself with only one or two examples: Dial. 42, 4. The main source for his typological analogies is not the
legal but the narrative parts of the Torah, and indeed of the whole O.T. For
his hermeneutical concepts cf. Dial. 114, 1.

[173] Even Dial. 29, 2—ἡμεῖς γὰρ αὐτοῖς (sc. ὑμετέροις γράμμασι) πειθόμεθα,
ὑμεῖς δὲ ἀναγινώσκοντες οὐ νοεῖτε τὸν ἐν αὐτοῖς νοῦν—does not mean that Justin

the Law such a way out would have been too easy. It would have meant that in the interpretation of the ceremonial law—though only of the ceremonial law—Justin would very possibly have compromised with Ptolemaeus while at the same time completely failing to make his case via-à-vis Marcion, who rejected any sort of allegorical interpretation. Therefore, precisely in those contexts where he has the false teachers in mind, Justin determines upon an exegesis of these texts which is exclusively 'historical', and takes their original, literal meaning entirely seriously, that is to say, it affirms their validity as divine ordinances.[174] Nevertheless, the ceremonial law constitutes no contradiction of the eternal and essential will of God, for it is an *ad hoc* law, framed solely for the Jews. The wicked stubbornness, the spiritual crudity, and the constant disobedience of the Jewish people compelled God to take appropriate counter-measures.[175] Thus, 'circumcision, which derives from Abraham', was ordained simply in order that, even in dispersion, the Jews might remain identifiable, and not escape their merited punishments.[176] Sacrifices and the Temple were established to exclude the persistent worship of idols,[177] and the sanctification of the sabbath became necessary in order that, despite their sins, the nation might at least be reminded again and again of their God.[178] Similar reasons are given for the dietary laws,[179] ritual washings,[180] and so on.

---

ever adopted the radically spiritualising reinterpretation of the Law, as Flesseman-van Leer, *op. cit.*, p. 79, suppose. Hyldahl, *op. cit.*, p. 260, wishes to deny any influence on Justin by Barnabas.

[174] The relevant section of the Dialogue is a self-contained treatise (Dial. 10–29) which must originally have been aimed at gnostics and Marcionites: cf. Dial. 23, 1f.; 30, 1; and Prigent, *Justin*, pp. 74f. These ideas are not forgotten, however, in the succeeding sections, where Justin's polemic is turned against the Jews (Dial. 92), and are able to be combined with the typological interpretation and with the demonstration that the Law contains eternal norms: Dial. 44, 2: . . . λέγω δέ, ὅτι τὶς μὲν ἐντολὴ εἰς θεοσέβειαν καὶ δικαιοπραξίαν διετέτακτο, τὶς δὲ ἐντολὴ καὶ πρᾶξις ὁμοίως εἴρητο ἢ εἰς μυστήριον τοῦ χριστοῦ ἢ διὰ τὸ σκληροκάρδιον τοῦ λαοῦ ὑμῶν These divisions correspond to the very similar tripartite arrangement of Ptolemaeus (cf. pp. 83f. above). In Justin, however, all parts of the Law, despite their differing meanings, are attributed equally to the one God. In my earlier essay (cf. n. 6 above), p. 189, I had as yet not clearly grasped the connection between the 'historical' interpretation of the Law and the anti-gnostic polemic, and wrongfully reproached Justin with lack of logic—something which can happen all too easily under the influence of his highly diffuse style.

[175] Dial. 27, 2–4; 46, 5. Frag. 20 (Otto, vol. II, p. 264) also emphasises the rebelliousness of the Jews in contrast to all other nations. According to G. Mercati, 'Un frammento nuovo del Dialogo di S. Giustino', *Biblica* 22, 1941, pp. 354–362, who provides a more complete version, this fragment may well be genuine.

[176] Dial. 16, 2f.; 19, 2; 19, 5; 23, 5; 92, 3.

[177] Dial. 19, 6; 22, 1; 22, 11.

[178] Dial. 19, 6; 21, 1.   [179] Dial. 19, 2; 20, 1.4.

Naturally Justin constantly appeals in support of his interpretation to the criticism of the cult in the early prophets; he mentions even 'the statutes that were not good and ordinances' which, according to Ezekiel, God imposed on his people as a punishment.[181] The strongly hostile feelings which the Church of that period without exception entertained toward the Jews who were fighting and denouncing her, forms the background to his astonishing exegesis and makes it possible. But its real point is aimed less at the Jews than at the gnostics. Despite all the limitations made necessary by the behaviour of the Jews the Law had always been intended as a way of salvation for them, and was there to lead them to repentance.[182] For Moses too taught 'what Nature itself shows to be pious and righteous',[183] and made it possible even then for the devout to attain to blessedness, if only they understood him aright. The abandonment of the ceremonial law was for the purpose of rescuing the real, moral law from the attacks of the gnostics; otherwise, says Justin quite explicitly, their critique of the Law would in fact succeed.[184] The Jews may justly be reproached that by their external interpretation of the ordinances they encouraged the drawing of false conclusions, which turn 'those who have no understanding', that is, the heretics, against the law God has given.[185] Furthermore, even the pettiest regulations of the ceremonial law are 'harmless' in themselves,[186] and it would therefore certainly be no sin to keep them. 'We ourselves', Justin explains, 'would observe bodily circumcision, sabbaths, and feast days without question, were it not that we know the reason why they were imposed on you in olden times, namely for your wickedness and obduracy'.[187] The real, spiritual order, appropriate to God, is something quite different. It is not dependent on externals such as

---

[180] Dial. 43, 1.

[181] Dial. 21, 4. The reference is to Ezek. 20:25. 'This utterance, which is quite unique in the O.T.' does not, of course, refer to the whole ritual and ceremonial law, but probably has in mind the sacrifice of human firstborn: W. Zimmerli, *Ezechiel*, 1960–, p. 449. The quotation, however, is introduced only to expound one particular point in connection with a longer quotation on the question of the sabbath. Justin gives this remarkable passage no special significance.

[182] Dial. 27, 2; 30, 1.   [183] Dial. 45, 3.   [184] Dial. 23, 1.

[185] Dial. 30, 1.   [186] Dial. 18, 3.

[187] Dial. 18, 2; cf. 27 2; similarly Irenaeus, Adv. haer. IV, 15; 16, 3.5; 2, 1; 28; Dem. 8. In a weakened, less vindictive and more pedagogic presentation a similar idea occurs in Tertullian, Adv. Marc. II, 18f., 22. In the O.T. only Ezekiel contains a first tentative move in this direction: cf. n. 180 above. In the Rabbis the view is occasionally found that the five books of the Torah (or, alternatively, the Torah and Joshua) would have sufficed, if Israel had not sinned: cf. F. Michaeli, 'Tradition et canon des Écritures.' À propos du canon de l'Ancien Testament,' *Études théol. et relig.* 36, 1961, p. 80. The naive reference to Gal. 3:19 and Heb. 10:3 in W. A. Shotwell, *The Biblical Exegesis of Justin Martyr*, London, 1965, pp. 10f., simply obscures what Justin says and means.

these; its aim is the circumcision of the heart, purity of mind, true, inner obedience. 'The prophecy which arose after Moses' death is valid for ever; and the Psalms say the same.'[188] God's true will is spiritual, moral, human, and universal. Thus, he was already well known to Abel, Enoch, Noah, Abraham and the rest of the patriarchs, 'who had received no fleshly circumcision, who kept no sabbaths, nor any of the other commandments' which were promulgated for the first time by Moses.[189] But this does not justify the 'nonsensical and laughable assumption' that in the Law one is not dealing with one and the same God throughout, or that this one God did not will that one unchanging righteousness should be practised in all ages and by all peoples.[190] These considerations are then combined with the old concept of the fulfilment of salvation-history. The particular 'law given on on Horeb' has finally become obsolete, ever since Christ 'came as an eternal law and as a new covenant for the whole world'.[191] 'For I have . . . read, that at the end there will be a law and a covenant, which will surpass all other laws. This all men must now keep, if they wish to have a share in God's election.'[192]

Justin's doctrine of Scripture is manifestly complex, and contains inner tensions. This arises from the necessity to uphold the traditions of earlier teachers, and at the same time to meet the problems posed in a new and changing era with these traditional ideas. For him, as for his predecessors, the point at which all the difficulties converge is the Law. Justin is here fighting on three fronts. The same arguments which were once developed against the Jews, and then also proved serviceable for the Gentile mission, now have to be turned against the gnostic and Marcionite critics; and for this they simply are not adequate. They have to be reshaped and supplemented; but they cannot be jettisoned, because they are still needed for the fight on the first two fronts. The result is that they appear in quite a different light and with different functions according to the point of view from which they are regarded and the opponents whom they are supposed to counter. And finally, they now also have to justify themselves before the judgment-

---

[188] Dial. 30, 1f.
[189] Dial. 23, 1; similarly 11, 5; 10, 4; 20, 1; 23, 4; 27, 5; 43, 2; 44, 2; 45, 4; 92, 2. Justin seems to regard the setting up of the Golden Calf as the event which brought about the giving of the Mosaic law: Dial. 19, 5f.; 20, 4. This idea occurs also in Irenaeus, Adv. haer. IV, 15, 1, and was to have a long history: cf. P. G. Verweijs, *Evangelium und neues Gesetz in der ältesten Christenheit bis auf Marcion* (Diss. Utrecht 1960), p. 225 n. 11 (with an incorrect reference to Adv. haer. IV, 14, 2), who refers to W. C. van Unnik, *De beteeknis van de Mozaïsche Wet voor de Kerk van Christus volgens de Syrische Didaskalie*, Amsterdam, 1952.
[190] Dial. 23, 1; 30, 1.   [191] Dial. 11, 2; 43, 1.
[192] Dial. 11, 2; 67, 10; 122, 5.

seat of Platonism, which Justin cannot give up. The Scripture, and within the Scripture the Law, reveal God's truth. Against the Jews, they are to be the prophetic allies of the faith of Christ, but to Christians themselves the Law is no longer to apply; nevertheless, it must have been promulgated by God, and was meant to be taken seriously, not just in a typological and prophetic sense but also literally. This then is the key to the violent solution on which Justin is set. He holds fast to the divine origin of the whole Law; but he puts the ceremonial sections in a special category, in that he does not interpret them purely prophetically, as has been done hitherto, but as a particular pattern of life applying to the Jews alone. One is reminded of Luther comparing Moses to the lawgiver of mediaeval Saxony, and commenting that at times we must 'know and take heed to whom God's word is addressed'.[193] But Justin does not start from the conviction that there is a variable factor in law which makes different demands on those of different periods, nations, or circumstances; on the contrary, he just as much as Ptolemaeus measures the Jewish Law by an ideal norm, which in his view can and must be valid everywhere. Hence the special feature of the Law is merely that it deviates from a truth which is eternal and otherwise universally valid. But this deviation in its turn calls for a special explanation which, being, as it is, harshly anti-judaistic, can hardly be regarded as satisfactory.

This, however, is not the essential heart of Justin's scheme, nor the element of significance for the future. What is really important is that Justin—like Paul and Luke before him—has once more found the answer to the problem of the Law, and with it of the whole Old Testament Canon, by means of a 'historical' approach, that is, by organising the Old Testament material specifically in accordance with the great epochs of salvation-history. A pre-legal epoch, down to the time of Moses, an epoch of the Law, conditioned by the obstinacy of the Jews, and then an epoch once more free of the Law but now universal to the whole human race, form a sequence which, despite the diversity of its component elements, stands wholly under the dominion of the one God, who is the God of Jesus Christ. Within this scheme the emergence of the prophetic theology, which Justin especially values as already revealing the 'eternal', purified law of God, free of all limitations and going beyond Moses, forms an additional caesura in the line of salvation-history.[194] Moreover, this picture of salvation-history is not sketched out for its own sake, but is wholly polemical and dictated by Justin's particular purposes.[195] The only difference is that now it is

[193] Sermon of 27 August 1525 (*Coll. Works* XVI, p. 384); 'Wider die himmlischen Propheten,' *ibid.* XVIII, p. 81; cf. Bornkamm, *op. cit.*, pp. 104ff.
[194] Dial. 30, 1; cf. 7, 1.
[195] It is from this point of view that I myself would prefer to interpret—and so

supremely Marcion and the gnostics who have joined the Jews as his opponents, and that vis-à-vis these new adversaries the real question is no longer the defence of the claims of Christ in accordance with the Scripture, but the rescue of the Old Testament.

It may be asked how far this picture of salvation-history, despite the change of front, is determined by earlier models. Hitherto it is precisely in their conceptions of salvation-history that both Paul and Luke seem to have exerted the least influence. The task to which they devoted themselves had apparently come to nothing. The popular use of the Old Testament in the Church very definitely did not have a 'salvation-history' orientation in any strict sense of that term. It was only the critique of the gnostics, who themselves did not think in 'historical' terms either, which reopened the question of the validity of the Law in the past. In dealing with them Paul would have been an extremely dangerous ally, since his peculiar doctrine of the multiplication of sin by the Law was as little suited as anything well could be to ward off the gnostic attacks. It is therefore understandable that Justin logically ignores Paul altogether. Nevertheless, Justin's concept of salvation-history does exhibit certain points of contact with Paul which can hardly be accidental. Paul too had allowed for a pre-Mosaic order of salvation which had no need of the Law; and both Paul and Justin vindicate Christian freedom from the Law on this basis against the Jews. Vis-à-vis Judaism Christianity is valid as a renewal of the original condition of man, which had already once been the object of God's approval, and was better than the Law which was promulgated later. Paul's argumentation on this point was entirely concentrated on the one patriarch Abraham,[196] whereas Justin emphatically includes the whole pre-Mosaic period with its various holy men.[197] But Justin too can on occasion confine himself to Abraham, and when he does, it is striking that, like Paul, he appeals precisely to the saying about faith, without mentioning Abraham's other merits.[198] It seems likely, therefore, that

---

limit the importance of—the 'salvation-history' element in Justin's thought, which B. Seeberg, 'Die Geschichtstheologie Justins der Märtyrers', ZKG 58, 1939, pp. 1ff., and C. Andresen, op. cit. (n. 152 above), so strongly emphasise: it is simply the inevitable result of his standing by the O.T. Chadwick, 'Justin Martyr's Defence', p. 297, approaching the matter more from the angle of the presuppositions of the Logos-concept, evaluates 'Justin's theology of history as a distinctive and personal achievement'. Hyldahl, op. cit., pp. 52ff., 62ff., disputes the allegedly unphilosophical and purely Christian derivation of Justin's 'historico-theological' approach in Seeberg and Andersen.

[196] C. Dietzfelbinger, Heilsgeschichte bei Paulus? 1965, pp. 41ff., has rightly emphasised this feature in Paul.

[197] As Luke had already done: cf. N. A. Dahl, 'The story of Abraham in Luke-Acts' in: Studies in Luke-Acts (Festschrift Paul Schubert), Nashville-New York, 1967, pp. 139–158.

[198] Dial. 11, 5; 23, 4; 92, 3 (44, 2).

at this point we should assume some Pauline influence, since Justin must in any case have been acquainted with the Epistles. The point of contact remains, however, completely superficial, and has nothing to do with the deeper motivation of Paul's critique of the Law.[199] For Justin, opposition to the old Law is dictated not by the Gospel nor by faith but by that ideal law which was known to the patriarchs, which the prophets had proclaimed, and which was finally embodied perfectly and with redeeming power in Jesus the new lawgiver.[200] Whereas Paul made the Law into a curse both for the Jews and, in a transferred sense, for the Gentiles as well, Justin restricts its negative significance to the ceremonial law, and sees even this as a comprehensible measure of penal education. So far as the Jews are concerned, he allows, if we may put it this way, a *usus politicus legis*. His interpretation is thus quite differently oriented and, seen as a whole, has absolutely nothing in common with Paul.

Luke is undoubtedly closer to Justin in character.[201] Like Justin, he exhibits a clear tendency to see Christianity as the world religion of the consummation of history, a faith of universal human values; and he too understands the sacrificial worship of the Temple, and all the ritual regulations of the old covenant, as a system specific to the Jewish nation. But Luke is unable to follow this train of thought to its logical conclusion, because he still regards the old Law as a unity, and, despite a certain anti-Jewish feeling which again is reminiscent of Justin, he is in this context more strongly controlled by the legacy of Paul and by the continuing presence of Jewish Christianity. Consequently, in his eyes it is not the institution but the abrogation of the Law which is the punishment, and the patriarchal period as a time when men were free from the Law does not come into consideration. Even less, therefore, can we speak of Justin's being influenced at all strongly by Luke.

It is clear that Justin blazed his own trail under pressure from the new questions that were being posed. The one theologian with whom he can seriously be compared is the Valentinian Ptolemaeus. And when we do compare them, we become aware not only that their starting-points are the same, and their intellectual equipment very similar, but equally that their theological intentions and their final solutions are

[199] So also Verweijs, *op. cit.*, pp. 240f.
[200] As the new Law (or new Lawgiver) Jesus is by no means understood in purely 'legalistic' or 'moralistic' terms: Dial. 11, 4; 12, 2; so also Hyldahl, *op. cit.*, p. 269 n. 26. The further question, whether or to what extent Justin's Christianity itself deserves such a reproach does not fall to be considered here. The decisive consideration is the way in which he brings the concrete demand for repentance to bear on his time and on his world. It should not be forgotten that we possess only two explicitly apologetic writings of Justin's, whereas his oral and literary activity extended far more widely.
[201] Cf. Hyldahl. *op. cit.*, pp. 260ff.

H

completely and utterly different. Neither of them any longer adopts a naïve attitude to the Law, that is to say, they no longer accept it without question as a datum of relevation, but they measure it against a moral and religious ideal which for them is the real law of God. Both of them derive this ideal norm from Jesus Christ and from his prophetic forerunners—though Justin is more decided than Ptolemaeus on this latter point. Both of them inevitably find the Mosaic Law, when measured by this standard, to be imperfect; but Justin overcomes this problem to some extent by an idealising interpretation of its content, from which only the ceremonial law is excepted, while Ptolemaeus—equally not without difficulty—lays the law summarily at the door of the Demiurge. Both of them make their task of exegesis somewhat easier by treating the cultic and ceremonial law as *sui generis*, and subjecting it to a special interpretation: for Ptolemaeus it is pure allegory (though an allegory enacted in practice), while for Justin it is more a christological prophecy (though at the same time a concrete system for the education of the Jews). Finally, both of them equally regard the Law as no longer in force since the coming of Christ.

The essential difference between the two positions is to be seen in their concepts of God. Justin holds unshakeably to the old belief in one God. This gives his anti-gnostic standpoint an inner affinity to the Old Testament, which Ptolemaeus lacks; but at the same time it compels him to lay on this one God the whole heavy burden of a historically dead revelation and an obsolete law. The gnostic, by contrast, can take the law in his stride by splitting it up and distributing the various parts among different divine and human authors. As a result Justin inevitably has a quite different view of the historical difference between the two eras, of the old and of the new covenant, from that of Ptolemaeus. It is true that Ptolemaeus also recognises that historical circumstances have to be taken into account, and that they have produced an impaired 'second law', in which revelation is obscured; but because it is not God, or at any rate not the supreme God, but only Moses or the Elders whom he makes responsible for this second law, this failure is devoid of any profounder interest. He pursues the problem no further. The historical explanation serves the purely negative purpose of removing an awkward fact, and thus obliterates the real question. Justin, on the other hand, has to face it all the more squarely. So, instead of resorting to simple excisions from the text, with which it was possible for Ptolemaeus to be satisfied, he sketches the outline of a historical development corresponding to the plan of salvation of a single God. This allows him to incorporate the Scriptures *en bloc*, and to explain the varying statements which they contain in terms of different eras without losing hold on the sovereignty of God. This is a decisive victory. While the canonical significance of the Old Testament within gnosis is becoming problematic and, indeed, vanishing altogether, the Church has affirmed the Old Testament as her own against Judaism, and has justified and preserved it in a new way against the even more dangerous attacks of the heretics.

Yet we must not overlook the deficiencies of Justin's outline. It is true that he is in fact successful to a large extent in answering the urgent questions with his division of salvation-history into epochs; but this success is dearly bought. For at the same time he puts the most stringent ban on any attempt to go further and draw critical distinctions. The hermeneutical principle which he follows is not the authority of the word or the teaching of Jesus but the *a priori* assumption that the divinely inspired holy Scripture constitutes an absolute, monolithic unity, free from any internal contradiction. A Jewish conception which till his time had been adopted without serious reflection is thus exalted into a principle of Christian theology. At first, of course, this applied only to the Old Testament. Moreover, the theology of the early Church, seen as a whole, was less harassed and hampered by it than we with our modern, rationalistic outlook would expect. In practice not only Jerome but even Julius Africanus handled the Old Testament with a fair degree of freedom, and other theologians were for the most part unaware of the problems lurking beneath the surface. This was not due merely to a lack of critical sense or of interest in critical questions. The salvation-history and christological approach did as such open up a valuable line of approach to the issues that motivated the Old Testament. Despite the fact that as a dogma it went much too far, it did make possible a genuine understanding of the content of the Old Testament, whereas the 'critical' efforts of the gnosis subordinated the ancient scriptures to a kind of speculative and mythological thought alien to their nature, and thus destroyed their meaning. To this extent Justin's instinct as a practical theologian, and his 'orthodoxy', rightfully gained a victory over an opponent who for all his training and formal acuteness never had the slightest sympathy for the actual material on which he worked.

Justin's conception of salvation-history set in motion the following train of development. The hard anti-judaistic line of his teaching about the Law was relaxed, and in its place the idea of divine education became the dominant concept. This was certainly not contrary to the sense of Justin's Christianity, and indeed found its first openings in his own writings.[202] The eternal and the transitory meanings of the Law were

---

[202] This is true even of his view of Judaism (cf. pp. 94f. above); but it is, of course, the concept of the λόγος σπερματικός which should above all be borne in mind here. It does not, however, by any means follow that the permanent truths of religion and righteousness revealed to the Jews in the Mosaic law were, according to Justin, also 'revealed to the rest of mankind in the natural laws of

more carefully and, in part, differently defined; but the fundamental
analysis into epochs was all the less likely to disappear in view of the
fact that it had also been taught by Paul. In Paul it had countered Jewish
criticism of the Gospel; in Justin, given a new significance, it opposed
the hellenistic critique of the Old Testament. (Though Paul would
have been of no direct use at all to Justin in this matter.) Justin's
scheme remained indispensable just so long as, on the one hand, in
addition to the attacks of paganism there was gnostic and Marcionite,
and later Manichaean polemic to counter, and, on the other, the
starting-point for all concerned was an ideal and unalterable concept of
truth, the creation of Greek philosophy. Even the pioneering theologian
of the next generation, Irenaeus, despite a fresh and important fertilisa-
tion by Paul, kept wholly, so far as the salvation-history interpretation
of the Law and of the Old Testament was concerned, to the lines laid
down by Justin.[203]

In another respect, however, there is already beginning to be a change
and a shift in the context of debate in Irenaeus' writings. In the battle
against the gnosis the pressure is sensibly reduced by the formation of
the New Testament; from this point on, the problems connected with
the Old Testament lose a great deal of the burning urgency they once
had. Dealing with them becomes more an internal theological exercise—
one, indeed, which continues to this day. The coming of the New Testament means that there is now a viable basis on which the debate about
the meaning and content of Christian doctrine can be conducted far
more securely than it every could when every argument had to take a
laborious and roundabout route through the Old Testament. Justin
himself had already on occasion attempted to supplement his Old
Testament demonstrations suitably with 'brief sayings of our Saviour'.[204]
But take him for all in all, he is one of the last representatives of that
era in Christian history which from the standpoint of the history of the
Canon may still be termed 'primitive', when there was no other 'scripture' to which men could appeal in their preaching of Christ except the
traditional Old Testament. The changeover had already begun in his
time. But it was to take another generation before a 'New' Testament
genuinely emerged alongside the 'Old', in status seemingly its equal, but
in fact from the very first enjoying a far superior importance which
radically transforms and deepens the whole problem of the Canon.

---

morality, religion and justice', as V. E. Hasler, *Gesetz und Evangelium in der
alten Kirche bis Origenes,* Zurich, 1953, p. 39, believes.
    [203] Cf., e.g., Adv. haer. IV, 16, 3ff. Verweijs, *op. cit.,* p. 359, who rightly cites
this passage, is wrong to see in it the effects of 'the basic concept of the post-
apostolic age'. It is the result of the influence of Justin, who for his part had, to
the best of our knowledge and belief, no predecessors in this regard. Verweijs
overlooks the anti-gnostic character of the conception.
    [204] Dial. 18, 1; cf. further pp. 166ff. below.

CHAPTER FOUR

The Pre-history of the New Testament Canon

IN THE early Church the term, the 'christian bible', signifies, as we have seen, simply the Old Testament, taken over from the synagogue and given a Christian interpretation. As yet there is no mention of a New Testament canon, for the thing itself does not exist. This is the thesis which it will be the purpose of the present retrospective chapter to establish. The thesis is not new; but it is by no means generally accepted. The dominant opinion is that the beginnings of the New Testament can be traced back into the first century or at least into the first decades of the second. It is customary to talk of a 'canon of the Four Gospels', a 'canon' of the Pauline Epistles, and an 'apocalyptic canon', even before the time of Marcion. Our sources certainly do nothing to justify such ideas. But the situation is further confused by the fact that there is no one agreed definition of the concept of the canon, and that its use is often very hazy indeed. To make my own position clear: by the beginnings of the canon I do not understand the emergence and dissemination, nor even the ecclesiastical use and influence of what were later the canonical writings.[1] One can, in my view, speak of a 'canon' only where of set purpose such a document or group of documents is given a special, normative position, by virtue of which it takes its place alongside the existing Old Testament 'scriptures'. Nothing of this kind is to be observed before the middle of the second century; and the assertion that something of the sort must, nevertheless, already have begun and existed is neither provable nor probable. The fact that a work which later became a 'New Testament' book is occasionally echoed or utilised or alluded to is not 'canonisation'; indeed, taken for what it is and no more, it is not even a move in that direction—even without taking into account the uncertain and problematic character of most of these slight references and conjectured 'quotations'.

Given this formal definition of the concept of 'canon', the present chapter is bound to be predominantly negative in its significance: it

---

[1] A. Souter, *The Text and Canon of the New Testament*[2], 1954 (revised by C. S. C. Williams), p. 140, emphasises that the attestation of a particular book has to be distinguished from its recognition as part of the Canon, and adds pertinently: 'Unfortunately it is not possible entirely to separate these two things.'

interposes an emphatic 'Not yet' to all the attempts to find early beginnings for a binding 'New Testament'. Nevertheless, the essential substance of that which was one day to form the New Testament is, of course, earlier. This is the historical testimony to Jesus Christ and to what he signifies, his salvation, his truth, and his word. This from the very first possesses especial sanctity and special authority to control men's lives. To this extent the force and authority of the tradition belong in a positive sense to the pre-history of the New Testament Canon. The tradition is taught with authority, and demands the response of faith. At first it is exclusively oral, but being of supreme spiritual importance is by no means to be presented in any way the preacher may choose; on the contrary, because it strives to attain permanent validity, it tends toward a more or less fixed and permanent form. Now, once such a tradition has acquired a fixed and definite form, and is finally standardised and made binding in that form, then it may almost be called 'canonical'; for in that case it would be the stage immediately prior to the later Gospels or New Testament in general, the text of which will have added hardly anything new of substance. The only question is whether, and if so to what extent, such a possible consolidation within the earlier history of the tradition did in fact take place, and was recognised and accepted.

In order to answer this question there is no need to raise, much less discuss, all the problems of the synoptic and other Gospel traditions as such.[2] Even the difficult question of *Sitz im Leben* can be left aside. We are hardly to think here in terms of actual mission preaching, but rather of catechetical instruction by various missionaries and teachers, possibly of the conscious cultivation of this tradition in particular circles and 'schools', and finally of recital within a more or less liturgical framework and of early preaching in the context of worship. The situation must have varied considerably in accordance with time, place, and circumstance, and the character, size and composition of the congregations. There is no need to think poorly of the faithfulness and conscientiousness of the earliest mediators of the tradition; but equally it is certain that even in the most favourable instances absolute reliability in the preservation of what was handed on was both unattainable and manifestly not attained. In particular, a consistent arrangement of the material in the course of oral transmission is, in the nature of the case, hardly possible; and this means that the most important safeguard

[2] Of the abundant literature on this subject only the following can be mentioned here: M. Dibelius, *Die Formgeschichte des Evangeliums*[6], 1966; R. Bultmann, *History of the Synoptic Tradition*, 1965; K. Stendahl, *The School of St Matthew*, Uppsala, 1954; H. Köster, *Synoptische Überlieferung bei den apostolischen Vätern*, 1957; B. Gerhardsson, *Memory and Manuscript. Oral Tradition and Written Transmission in Rabbinic Judaism and Early Christianity*, Uppsala, 1961.

against additions, abbreviations, transpositions and alterations is missing even where—it may be—there is a desire to avoid anything of that kind. It is no accident that all the efforts to establish a fixed 'apostolic' confession of faith, or a definable 'primitive christian catechism', have come to grief. All the convergences and all the formal agreements which we possess alongside the variations and deviations only attest a certain toughness and trustworthiness in the tradition, but no more than that.

The question whether and how far an intention of 'canonising' the tradition existed at all or was effective is therefore not easy to answer. Analogies, deductions, and general form-critical considerations can at the most indicate possibilities; they do not take us to our goal. Only definite statements about the mind and intentions of the collectors and tradents or their hearers might help us; and where these are lacking we must resign ourselves, and in doubtful cases allow for the possibility that a 'canonising' intention and the kind of thinking that goes with it had not yet emerged. Fortunately, however, our meagre sources do not quite fail us in this respect. What can be said, either positively or negatively, about the pre-history of the concept of canon is little enough; but that little is illuminating and, so far as it goes, clear and definite. And with that we must be content.

The only documents we possess coming directly from the first generation of the Church are the Epistles of the apostle Paul. We certainly may not generalise from their evidence without further investigation; but they do warn us against over-estimating the universal importance of the original tradition in the life of the Gentile Christian congregations. The Pauline churches plainly did not live by the mere appropriation and preservation of traditional teaching material. On the contrary, they were proud of their own 'knowledge' and 'freedom' and the abundance of miraculous 'gifts' with which they knew themselves endowed, and by which they were enlightened and guided. Paul himself defends this freedom, even when he is aware and critical of its spiritual dangers. By his passionate rejection of the 'Law' he even gives it a special significance, both as a matter of principle and for polemical purposes. Nevertheless, though this emphasis on freedom is indeed directly opposed to the Law, it is not antagonistic to an acceptance of particular traditions. Even Paul acknowledges an older tradition, deriving from Christ and relating to him. This for him is authoritative and demands recognition, even though its scope, from the point of view of subject-matter, is small enough. This is the background against which we should see the new liveliness and independence of his churches. This fact, which cannot be contested, becomes even more important when we remember that, as regards his own person, it is precisely the independence and autonomy of his commission, derived directly from Christ, which he loves to emphasise. Although he knows that he owes no allegiance to any church authority or to any of the earlier apostles, and that Christ himself appeared to him, nevertheless in bearing witness to Christ he deliberately associates himself with an existing tradition, which he passes on, and which he also desires his congregations to respect and obey. We may, if we wish, regard this as a manoeuvre in 'church politics', designed to ensure peace for his work and a continuing link with the primitive community and the Church as a whole; but this gives us no right not to take seriously what he has to say.[3]

The basic evidence for what has been said is the celebrated passage in the fifteenth chapter of I Corinthians: 'Now I would remind you, brethren, in what terms I preached to you the gospel, which you received, in which you stand, by which you are saved, if you hold it fast—unless you believed in vain. For I delivered to you as of first importance what I also received, that Christ died for our sins in accordance with the scriptures, that he was buried, that he was raised on the third day in accordance with the scriptures, and that he appeared to Cephas, then to the twelve. Then he appeared to more than five hundred brethren at one time, most of whom are still alive, though some have fallen asleep. Then he appeared to James, then to all the apostles. Last of all, as to one untimely born, he appeared also to me.'[4] It is of no concern to us at the moment, how far back the 'traditional' formula may go or what its pre-history may have been. The nucleus of it is certainly an old[5] and, for Paul, established piece of normative 'tradition'. It would be impossible to stress its importance more than is done in this passage. Paul terms this received text *tout court* as 'the Gospel'. On this, as he emphasises, the whole Christian faith rests, and without the reality here attested would be a thing of nought and 'vain'. Naturally it is not a matter of the precise words as such, but of the content of the tradition, that is, of the fact of the death and resurrection of Christ, which may not be called in question. Paul does not treat the text as a sacral formula; he does not hesitate to interrupt and expand it with his own

[3] There is no need to load this brief sketch with references to the inexhaustible Pauline literature; my own view of Paul's basic attitude to the questions here discussed will be found in: H. von Campenhausen, *Ecclesiastical Authority*, pp. 29ff., and *id., Die Begründung kirchlicher Entscheidungen beim Apostel Paulus*[2], 1965.

[4] I Cor. 15:1-8. For detailed exegesis cf. H. von Campenhausen, *Der Ablauf der Osterereignisse und das leere Grab*[3], 1966, pp. 8ff. and the literature listed there.

[5] For the 'original semitic text' cf. most recently J. Jeremias, 'Artikelloses χριστός—zur Ursprache von I. Cor. 15, 3b-5', *ZNW* 57, 1966, pp. 211-215; B. Klappert, 'Zur Frage des semitischen oder griechischen Urtextes von I. Kor. XV 3-5', *NTS* 13, 1966-7, pp. 168-173.

words (it should be remembered that it was already known to his readers). What is originally communicated and then permanently recorded by this text is the reality of the 'thing'. This was 'among the first things' which Paul taught, in Corinth as in all his churches, and he had his converts learn it by heart.[6] He takes it for granted that the same thing happens everywhere, whenever Christ is preached: 'Whether then it was I or they, so we preach and so you believed.'[7] Certainly the passion with which all this is emphasised is heightened and intensified by the actual situation, the danger of a fatal distortion of the faith in Corinth. But the idea of the fundamental and universal importance of this piece of tradition cannot be attributed to this; the practice to which Paul refers is already presupposed.

Paul, is clearly reminding his readers of the instruction which he gave, possibly before baptism, to newly converted Christians at the founding of his churches. The concepts of 'delivering' and 'receiving' which he uses are not chosen by accident. They are connected with Jewish ideas of tradition, and have a ceremonial and technical meaning which describes the special act by which fixed traditions are formally handed on. It is a matter of the reliability of what is attested in this way. Paul's emphasis on the age, the universal dissemination and the incontestable validity of the text serve the same purpose. Because the words relate to an event which is as real as it is unprecedented, a list of persons who as eye-witnesses can guarantee the truth of the content, was attached to the formula even before Paul's time. Paul includes himself in his own words as the last of the list; for he too has seen the risen Lord. It is a matter of great moment to him that he was involved at the start in the story of the Church; and for his congregations his own testimony is naturally of special significance. But the validity of what is handed down here does not depend on this additional guarantee.

Taking this text by itself, the most attractive suggestion might seem to be that it is a kind of confession of faith, a self-contained formula of teaching or tradition which contains the primitive christological creed of the Church. The unique importance of the death and resurrection of Christ for the Church's existence, and for the early Christians' understanding of their own position, might seem to justify such an interpretation. Nevertheless, it is hardly possible to isolate this passage so completely within the history of the tradition. Some chapters earlier Paul

[6] V. 3: ἐν πρώτοις. The meaning is either, 'at the start of his instruction', or, 'as the most important element in it'. (The RSV, quoted in the text above, adopts the latter: Tr.) A definite decision between the two renderings does not seem to be possible. In the end, indeed, they come to the same thing: the most important point is taught 'before' anything else, and the 'first' thing taught (which is the way III Corinthians already takes it: cf. n. 35 below) is also the most important.

[7] I Cor. 15:11.

cites another text, which is equally well known to his congregation, and of which he states in exactly the same way that he himself had 'received' it. There is no occasion to conceive or interpret the process implied here any differently from that obtaining in the first example. It is true that this second passage does not deal with 'the Gospel', pure and simple; but nevertheless it does refer once again to an event of the greatest importance, and provides information indispensable to any Christian congregation, the account of the institution of the Lord's Supper by Jesus 'on the night, when he was betrayed'.[8] In this admonitory reminder Paul again has in mind the first, fundamental instruction of the congregation, in which this binding 'delivery' of the tradition was carried out. Moreover, the liturgical text itself must already have been known to the Corinthians from their celebration of the Lord's Supper: 'For as often as you eat this bread and drink the cup, you proclaim the Lord's death until he comes.'[9]

We have, therefore, at least two passages which Paul has taken over word for word from the earlier tradition, and taught to his congregations.[10] Are we to suppose that these two major items have in fact exhausted the content of the traditions handed on to him? That is not very probable. If I Corinthians had not been preserved we would have known nothing either about these passages or about any clear citation of the words of Jesus in Paul. The echoes of the resurrection formula in his letters would have been unrecognisable to us, and a purely 'enthusiastic' interpretation of his preaching of Christ would have been virtually unavoidable. Indeed, the attempt to establish such an interpretation is occasionally still made even today, despite the evidence to the contrary. The occurrence of our texts in I Corinthians was determined by special occasions; the absence of further passages of the same kind, either here or in other Epistles, consequently proves nothing. We are therefore justified in asking whether there may not have been other pieces of tradition which Paul regarded as basic and indispensable when giving instruction. One might, for example, conceive of a text relating to baptism, which certainly was not inferior to the Lord's Supper in importance. A trustworthy statement about the return of Christ would likewise have been virtually essential.[11] Such conjectures must, of course, always be tentative; but the existence of other elements of

[8] I Cor. 11:23–25. For detailed exegesis cf. esp. G. Bornkamm, 'Herrenmahl und Kirche bei Paulus,' *Studien zu Antike und Urchristentum (Gesammelte Aufsätze* II)², 1963, pp. 146ff.

[9] I Cor. 11:26.

[10] We are dealing, in fact, as E. Käsemann, 'Konsequente Traditionsgeschichte?' *ZTK* 62, 1965, p. 141, emphasises, with 'catechetical tradition'. I Cor. 15 is concerned 'less with conveying than with establishing the faith'.

[11] I Thess. 4:15ff. cannot, of course, be such a statement, since its detailed description of the End was previously unknown to the recipients.

tradition no longer extant must be regarded as a probability. On the other hand, there can hardly be a case for greatly increasing their number. Paul would in any case not have needed further historical particulars on which to base the preaching of Christ, as he practised this and understood it, and he could well have been content with no more than those 'texts' which we have examined or conjectured. Here and there, of course, the material calls for illustration. The formula about the death and resurrection of Christ mentions neither the Jews nor the cross, and the opening of the Last Supper passage[12] requires to be supplemented, if it is to be understood, by some sort of 'Passion narrative', however short. But it does not follow from this that such a narrative had already been handed on to Paul in a fixed version; and above all it was not yet one of those established pieces of tradition which he taught and 'delivered' to his congregations.

The most striking feature of all is that the words of the Lord, which must have been collected and handed on in the primitive community and elsewhere from the earliest days, played no, or at least no vital, part in Paul's basic instruction of his churches. Paul himself is already acquainted with a series of these sayings, and he employs them in the same sort of context as primarily controlled their use elsewhere, it would seem, in the early period: in his writings too they occur exclusively in connection with hortatory or consolatory paraenesis, and as aids to deciding practical and moral questions in the life of the community. It may be that the sayings which Paul quotes came to him by way of an earlier, possibly oral collection. (The parables appear to have been missing from this collection; at any rate they are never mentioned by him.) But nothing requires us to conclude that in his turn Paul taught these words to his churches, and formally handed them on to them. On the contrary, the manner in which in I Corinthians he adduces the sayings of the Lord about divorce[13] and about the maintenance of missionaries[14] in support of his view, and in a third instance, the case of the unmarried, regrets the lack of any word of the Lord,[15] shows either that these sayings were not at that time known to the community or at least that he could not assume such knowledge. It follows that he had not 'delivered' them nor caused them to be remembered in a fixed form.

Even more straightforward is the reference to a saying of a different kind, but one equally ascribed to Jesus himself, namely a prophecy, in I Thessalonians. The Thessalonians have been disquieted by certain 'premature' deaths, and are afraid that those Christians who have

---

[12] That the words ἐν τῇ νυκτὶ ᾗ παρεδίδοτο are themselves an illustrative addition by Paul is possible but hardly probable.
[13] I Cor. 7:10.   [14] I Cor. 9:14.   [15] I Cor. 7:25.

fallen asleep, and who therefore will be unable to experience the Parousia, may have lost all hope of sharing in the future glory. Paul demonstrates to them, 'by the word of the Lord',[16] that their anxiety is unfounded, and puts them in a position to comfort one another in future 'with these words'.[17] It is clear that these Christians—admittedly not long converted—were not yet acquainted with the text mentioned in this passage. Other allusions to sayings of Jesus, which on the whole are by no means frequent (though there is a concentration of them in the paraenetic sections of Romans[18])[19] are not indicated as such. It must remain an open question to what extent, nevertheless, they were recognised by the recipients.[20] We could, of course, assume that Paul was counting on other persons competent for the purpose, for example, the 'teachers', to instruct the community in these sayings of Jesus. But bearing in mind the normative importance which he attaches to his own apostolic teaching, such an arrangement would be no less significant; it would mean that the faith of Christians plainly rested on the bare data of the story of Christ, as attested by the tradition, and delivered by the apostle to each newly founded community. By contrast, the words of the Lord would indeed be quoted, perhaps even 'taught' and committed to memory; but they would not possess the same kind of fundamental importance, or be decisive for men's salvation.

How are we to imagine this personal instruction given by Paul? Paul himself refers constantly to what he has taught and delivered to his

---

[16] The phrase τοῦτο γὰρ ὑμῖν λέγομεν (I Thess. 4:15) must be taken to mean that for the statement which follows Paul is appealing to an apocalyptic word of Jesus, even though such a word is unknown to us, and it is impossible to determine its precise form and extent with certainty from Paul's rendering of it: cf. M. Dibelius, An die Thessalonicher I. II.³, 1937, pp. 25f. P. Nepper-Christensen, 'Das verborgene Herrenwort,' StTh 19, 1965, pp. 136–154, thinks that there may have been a 'collection of words of Jesus' to which Paul is appealing in this passage.

[17] I Thess. 4:15–18.

[18] In an Epistle of ideas, addressed to an unknown congregation, this is perhaps no accident, and is in keeping with the adoption of an equally traditional formula, Rom. 1:3f.; cf. F. Hahn, Christologische Hoheitstitel, 1963, pp. 251ff. W. G. Kümmel, 'Jesus und Paulus', ThBl 19, 1940, col. 212, prefers to argue from this evidence to the use of sayings of Jesus in the mission preaching (?).

[19] Rom. 12:14, 17; 13:8ff.; 14:13, 14; 16:19; I Cor. 4:12; I Thess. 5:2. Further, somewhat problematic echoes, and the literature relating to them, are listed in W. Schrage, Die konkreten Einzelgebote in der paulinischen Paränese,1961, p. 243.

[20] H. Riesenfeld, The Gospel Tradition and its Beginnings, London, 1957, p. 15, on the contrary assumes precisely this. He states (p. 14): 'There can be only one explanation of this strange fact, namely, that the primitive Christian letter-writers, and among them Paul, took express pains to avoid citing the sayings of Jesus in the context of their original utterance.'

congregations by virtue of his apostolic authority.[21] He wishes his churches to follow the example which he has given,[22] and to remain faithful to the 'standard of teaching' which has been handed on to them by him[23]—not infrequently in conjunction with an emphatic rejection of other false doctrines and of teachers who wish to establish the Law.[24] Also part of his teaching are the simple moral ground-rules of the new life. Because of the summary nature of such reminiscences it is hardly possible to be certain about points of detail. That in instructing his 'children' Paul did not proceed without a plan of any kind, and that inevitably he must have mentioned some things regularly and in more or less unvarying order and form, is obvious. It is possible that even where he was not dealing with earlier testimony he made use of 'customary phrases' and formulas.[25] But this is by no means definitely proven; and that his instruction as a whole would simply have followed a traditional scheme seems out of the question. His consciousness of his own apostolic status and vocation, and the originality and spontaneity of his nature, were both too strong to allow of any such thing. The direct 'demonstration of the Spirit and of power', which distinguished his preaching, fired his hearers, and banished all trace of formalism or systematic organisation from his letters, will not have been absent from his missionary preaching.

If we review the whole range of Paul's utterances from the point of view of the history of the Canon, a remarkable picture emerges. All the elements which the New Testament was one day to include and to invest with its unified authority are discernible here. There is the historical testimony to the person and saving significance of the Lord; there are sayings from his mouth; and last but not least, there are the teachings and the example of the apostle himself. All these items already have sacred and binding force and significance. They are not, however, all on one level, but their relative prominence and importance change from one occasion to another. Considered as formal norms, they are not of equal scope, nor do they have, so to speak, one and the same state of aggregation.

[21] I Cor. 11:2, 23; 15:1, 3; Gal. 1:9, 12; Phil. 4:9, Col. 2:6; I Thes. 2:13; 4:1; II Thess. 2:15; 3:6.

[22] I Cor. 4:16f.; 10:33; 11:1; Phil. 3:17; I Thess. 4:1.

[23] Rom. 6:17. According to R. Bultmann, 'Glossen im Römerbrief', *Exegetica*, 1967, p. 283, this text would not be Pauline. This view is rejected by H. Greeven, 'Propheten, Lehrer, Vorsteher bei Paulus,' *ZNW* 44, 1952–3, pp. 20f.; J. Kürzinger, ΤΥΠΟΣ ΔΙΔΑΧΗΣ und der Sinn von Röm. 6, 17f.,' *Biblica* 39, 1958, pp. 156–176.

[24] Rom. 16:17f.; II Cor. 11:3f.; Gal. 1:6ff.; 6:12f.; Phil. 3:2f.

[25] L. Goppelt, 'Tradition nach Paulus', *Kerygma und Dogma* 4, 1958, pp. 213–233. Gerhardsson, *op. cit.*, pp. 288ff., goes much too far in this direction; for a different view cf. Schrage, *Einzelgebote*, pp. 187ff.

1. For Paul, the word and the person of the apostle are still a single reality; they are—even when his exhortations have to be by letter—his direct presence. The arena in which he fights to win acceptance for them is limited to the Gentile world, and within that world to those churches in particular which have been founded by him. Together with his converts Paul expects the near return of the Lord, and does not think in terms of long tracts of time. His Gospel and his teachings have a clear and definite meaning; but they have not yet been cast in permanent form. The letters are genuine letters, occasional pieces.[26] In such cirumstances it is hardly possible to speak of a universally valid apostolic norm, or of a 'canonical status of the apostle' himself[27]—quite apart from the remarkable fact that a one-sided exaltation of apostolic authority is precisely what Paul himself tries to avoid in his own churches.[28] A completely 'authoritarian' interpretation of the apostolic jurisdiction would very likely be inappropriate for the apostles in Jerusalem also: living apostles are not 'canonised'. Nevertheless, for lac!. of unequivocal evidence this question may perhaps have to be left open.

2. All the sayings of Jesus known to Paul already have a fixed form and uncontested validity. 'The Lord' is infallible, and in everything that he says or demands enjoys a status far superior to that attaching to the opinion even of an apostle.[29] For Paul, moreover, there is as yet no question of doubting the genuineness of the tradition. Nevertheless, these sayings fall outside the established canon of tradition. Even if elsewhere, for example, in the Jewish Christian churches, such a process of 'canonisation' was already under way, Paul does nothing to advance it. Only occasionally—one might almost say, when compelled to do so—he appeals to such a saying in order with its help to arrive at

---

[26] This is in no way contradicted by II Thess. 2:15. As against J. Ranft, *Der Ursprung des katholischen Traditionsprinzips*, 1931, p. 256; O. Cullmann, *Die Tradition als exegetisches, historisches und theologisches Problem*, Zurich, 1954, pp. 42f. with n. 1; and P. Lengsfeld, *Überlieferung*, 1960, p. 49, the comment of J. Beumer, 'Die mündliche Überlieferung als Glaubensquelle', *Handbuch der Dogmengeschichte* I, 4, 1962, p. 8, is correct: Paul's intention here is 'simply to emphasise the importance of instructions backed by his apostolic authority, whether given by word of mouth or in letters. He has no notion of enduing what is written with additional value, namely that which attaches to the inspired word of God recorded in holy scripture, and is in no way seeking to draw comparisons between oral and sacral-literary paradosis. . . .'

[27] As against E. Lohmeyer, *Die Briefe an die Philipper, an die Kolosser und an Philemon*[13/12], 1964, p. 176, on Phil. 4:9. In an even more general sense, A. Jülicher-E. Fascher, *Einleitung in das Neue Testament*[7], 1931, p. 456, describe the 'multitude of prophets, speakers with tongues, teachers', in primitive Christianity as an 'abundance of living, "canonical" elements'.

[28] Cf. Campenhausen, *Ecclesiastical Authority*, pp. 46ff.

[29] I Cor. 7:12.

a decision on some practical or pastoral problem. Of course, this does not mean that in the rigid acceptance of the Jesus tradition Paul saw a moral problem or a difficulty which might restrict true spiritual freedom. That would be a more than merely anachronistic misconception. Nevertheless, the fact that the sayings of Jesus recede into the background is no accident. They do not contain that which, for Paul, is the basic 'Gospel'—Christ himself as the crucified and risen Redeemer, in whose saving destiny Christians have a share, and in whom they 'believe'.

3. The genuinely 'canonical' tradition which he upholds is solely the testimony to Christ in terms of salvation-history. This is the starting-point of his preaching. Although Paul cites the only two formulas known to us in this connection without pedantry, yet he takes good care not to alter them arbitrarily or to adapt them to the immediate requirements of the context. In order to substantiate the disputed resurrection of Christians, he quotes the testimony relating to the undisputed resurrection of Christ, which of course says nothing directly to the point. He refers to the Institution narrative not to justify the long established observance of the Lord's Supper but as a basis for demanding appropriately spiritual behaviour.[30] This is very significant. We are already familiar with the characteristic relationship between a fixed, canonical 'text' and an 'exegesis' which actualises it by means of consequential additions.[31] The original form of the tradition is therefore deliberately retained. In this way it acquires an element of permanence and 'authenticity' which clearly suits Paul not simply as teacher and guardian of his churches but on principle. As we have

[30] Similarly, the 'miniature apocalypse' (P. Vielhauer in N.T. Apocrypha II, p. 611) quoted in I Thes. 4:15ff. is used to establish not the Parousia as such but confidence in the resurrection of Christians who have already died. Even more marked is the extension of Jesus' ban on divorce (I Cor. 7:10f.) to cover the wife as well. Yet this supplementation by analogy is probably quite unintentional. Moreover, it is not certain that it is not earlier than Paul: cf. Schrage, Einzelgebote, pp. 241f.

[31] This kind of thing occurs in the succeeding period only with regard to O.T. quotations; with 'Gospel' texts it is found hardly at all before the middle of the second century. They have not quite as yet become 'canonical'. This fact is correctly observed in the case of Justin by R. M. Grant, The Letter and the Spirit, London, 1957, p. 77, but is wrongly explained in terms of the historical character of the Gospels: 'Justin does not give exegesis of the gospels, probably because as historical works they need no exegesis. They speak for themselves.' On the absence of an exact exegesis cf. also E. Massaux, Influence de l'Évangile de saint Matthieu sur la littérature chrétienne avant saint Irénée, Louvain-Gembloux, 1950, p. 650, and W. A. Shotwell, The Biblical Exegesis of Justin Martyr, 1965, p. 25. Naturally, this kind of interpretation by Paul stresses the authority of the tradition, and does nothing to weaken it as K. Wegenast, Das Verständnis der Tradition bei Paulus und in den Deuteropaulinen, 1962, p. 104 and elsewhere, repeatedly alleges.

already noted, Paul's loyalty to the existing and 'traditional' form of the Christian message may be seen either as a tactical manoeuvre, or better as the expression of an 'oecumenical' attitude, which prefers to maintain the unity of the churches with one another and, above all, with the primitive community in Palestine. Christ is one, and his body is not to be torn apart by cliques and party opinions.[32] Hence there is no 'other' Gospel than as Paul proclaims and understands it, and such as the apostles before him have explicitly acknowledged and confirmed.[33] That is why the original form of the testimony to Christ, which is the medium of the Gospel and can, therefore, itself be called 'the Gospel', is preserved. By using this description for it Paul to some extent anticipates the later changeover from the one, preached Gospel to the fixed, 'canonical' Gospel texts.

What is striking is the strictly 'historical', as it were, documentatory significance which the Christ-tradition thus acquires as regards not only its content but also its form. Especially significant in this respect is the citing of the witnesses of the resurrection by name: the list has already—before Paul's time—been arranged in chronological order, and takes no notice whatever of the rank of the persons involved. Quite apart from the large number of witnesses, the age, the universal dissemination, and the fixed form of the testimony all argue for the trustworthiness of its content, and make it rationally unassailable. Paul in fact demonstrates that the whole Christian message must collapse, if the historical basis of the resurrection is not reliable, and that it is indispensable for everyone who believes in Christ to take the old resurrection testimony seriously and to affirm it;[34] but he offers no safeguards of a sacral or authoritarian kind in support of this clear and enlightening datum. Such guarantees would actually be of little use as backing for a historical fact.

Today it is often thought necessary to give this down-to-earth character, which marks the Pauline (and not only the Pauline) concept of tradition some assistance by introducing apostolic or even christological authority as a theological confirmation of the early testimony. This authority is to back up the historical text, and bestow on it a kind of higher infallibility. But this is directly contrary to what Paul in fact says. Paul does not once tell us from whom the old formulas originally derive, or from whom he himself received them.[35] This is all the more remarkable, since it goes against Jewish practice. It may

---

[32] I Cor. 1:10ff.   [33] Gal. 1f.   [34] I Cor. 15:12ff.

[35] III Corinthians, which comes from the second century, has carefully supplied this deficiency: ἐγὼ γὰρ ἐν ἀρχῇ παρέδωκα ὑμῖν, ἃ καὶ παρέλαβον ὑπο τῶν πρὸ ἐμοῦ ἀποστόλων, γενομένων τὸν πάντα χρόνον μετὰ ᾿Ιησοῦ Χριστῷ (4). Reacting in the opposite direction Marcion even deleted ὃ καὶ παρέλαβον from I Cor. 15:3, in order to leave Paul his independence in splendid isolation: cf. A. von Harnack, *Marcion. Das Evangelium vom fremden Gott*[2], 1924, p. 47.

be that here the special considerations of the objections to his position and authority play some part. It is not accidental that Paul emphasises that he received the Gospel 'neither from men nor by the agency of men', but was called directly by Christ himself. Perhaps he is afraid that doubts will be cast on his apostolic independence, if he names the personages from whom he received his tradition, and so to that extent appears to be dependent on them.[36] Perhaps the whole question of derivation seemed to him a matter of indifference; or it may even have been that the origin of the formula was no longer known. But whatever the reason, Paul could never have taken the line he did, if the truth and importance of the 'canonical' text depended, in his view, in the very least on the authority of its originator. The formulas are old and have been binding for a long time. It is enough that their content is guaranteed and worthy of belief. Taken as they stand, they require no further warrant, either from men in general or from the apostles in particular.[37]

Even more reckless is the assumption that the tradition to which Paul appeals as a natural, historical tradition, mediated by men, was in his eyes simultaneously mediated by the exalted Lord himself, and only thus guaranteed as veridical. Christ himself, it is said, is present and at work in the tradition, and in this way is its real guarantor.[38] Now, it

[36] A different view is expressed by U. Wilckens, 'Der Ursprung der Über-lieferung der Erscheinungen des Auferstandenen', in: *Dogma und Denkstruc-turen* (Festschrift E. Schlink), 1963, p. 62 n. 12: 'This biographical question will have to be disregarded in any interpretation of I Cor. 15:3a, because when Paul speaks, in the context of his own thought, about his receiving the tradition, it is entirely to prove that the Gospel in question is everywhere one and the same.'

[37] Against this view it may certainly not be objected that it was Paul himself who, as an apostle, provided the required guarantee for his own churches. For on the contrary, in both I Cor. 11 and I Cor. 15, what he is trying to do is precisely to provide more, 'historical' safeguards of the truth, by emphasising the age of the tradition, than seemed possible on his own unsupported testi-mony. G. G. Blum, *Tradition und Sukzession. Studien zum Normbegriff des Apostolischen von Paulus bis Irenäus*, 1963, pp. 31, 35, 37, is also wrong in his repeated assertion that this text is, for Paul, 'a major expression of *apostolic* tradition' (p. 31, italics mine).

[38] O. Cullmann, 'Paradosis et Kyrios. Le problème de la Tradition dans le Paulinisme', *RHPR* 30, 1950, pp. 16–30; and *Tradition*, pp. 8ff., esp. pp. 11, 20, 24; also P. Lengsfeld, 'Tradition innerhalb der konstitutiven Zeit der Of-fenbarung', in: ed. J. Feiner–M. Löhrer, *Mysterium Salutis* I, 1965, p. 277; also, in a different way, J. N. Bakhuizen van den Brink, 'Traditio im theologi-schen Sinne', *VC* 13, 1959, pp. 73f. J. R. Geiselmann, *Jesus der Christus*, 1951, pp. 83ff., and G. Bornkamm, *op. cit.*, p. 148, followed by K. Wegenast, *op. cit.*, pp. 97f. and F. Hahn, *op. cit.*, p. 93, although they dissent from Cullmann's position, all try to salvage some element of truth from this view. Any such at-tempt, however, presses the text further than it will go. Goppelt, *Tradition*, p. 223, and in a purely dogmatic sense P. Neuenzeit, *Das Herrenmahl*, 1960, pp. 81f. (assistentia spiritus sancti), express themselves more cautiously.

I

is true that Paul says that he received the Last Supper tradition 'from the Lord'; but this implies no more than that the tradition derives from Jesus, refers and testifies to him.[39] The 'enthusiastic' interpretation of this statement, namely that Paul 'received' it by inspiration, has today rightly been abandoned.[40] Even less does the text lend itself to the task of proving a continuing activity of Christ within the tradition to guarantee it. If Paul had had any such idea, he would inevitably have expressed it clearly. Above all, he could not possibly have omitted it when repeating the resurrection testimony in the same epistle, for here he amasses every argument which might in any way support and confirm the truth of the formula. It is clear that behind all such modern extrapolatory interpretations lies an awareness, sound enough in itself, that the very real effect of the Gospel and of faith is not to be comprehended purely in rationalistic terms, but involves an activity of God in which Christ, or more correctly the spirit of Christ, has its share. Christ is attested by the old-established word, and on the basis of that word is proclaimed in spiritual power and becomes the object of faith. But the question of the effectiveness and appropriation of salvation should not be confused with that of the witness to Christ and the reliability of that witness; for the two are not the same thing. Whenever Paul refers to that which was originally handed down, and which is permanently valid, his primary concern is simply with the fact that by all the external criteria of proof this tradition is assured and trustworthy. Where, therefore, he abides by the traditional formulas, passes them on, and urges that they be preserved, this makes him in essence the first theologian of a new canon based on the story of Christ.

In this concern Paul is an heir of Jewish thought and its highly-trained respect for tradition. As such he is certainly not alone in his day and generation, as he himself testifies. But the young hellenistic church, of which he more than anyone else was the founder, did not in this respect follow in his footsteps. The joyful sense that the salvation

---

[39] I Cor. 11:23: ἐγὼ γὰρ παρέλαβον ἀπὸ τοῦ κυρίου, ὃ καὶ παρέδωκα ὑμῖν κτλ. . . . There are a number of possible interpretations of the much disputed ἀπὸ, and too much should not be built on it. I do not believe that Paul meant to imply nothing less than 'that the chain of tradition goes back without a break to the words of Jesus himself', as J. Jeremias, *The Eucharistic Words of Jesus*[2], 1966, p. 101 thinks; for Paul nowhere speaks of '*chains* of tradition', and in this instance we are dealing with more than an isolated 'word of the Lord' (Dibelius, *Formgeschichte*, p. 242). Because the account really does derive from the Lord, in the sense that it accurately preserves his words and actions, it can also be said to start from him, without compelling us to regard the κύριος formally 'as the originator of the tradition', as, among others, does W. G. Kümmel in: H. Lietzmann, *An die Korinther I. II*[4], 1949, p. 185 (with reference to p. 57).

[40] Cf. the survey and detailed refutation of such views in Geiselmann, *op. cit.*, pp. 67-78.

which had been proclaimed to the churches, and whose power they daily experienced, was here and now most assuredly near at hand, overwhelmed all concern or precautions for keeping the traditional testimony unaltered. The concepts of 'receiving' and 'delivering' lose their fixed, technical meaning, and in the end almost completely disappear.[41] No one doubts that the truth of Christ as presented by his spiritual leaders and teachers contains the original truth and passes it on in the form in which the first disciples, apostles and prophets had once preached it.[42] The great salvation 'was declared at first by the Lord, and it was attested to us by those who heard him, while God also bore witness by signs and wonders and various miracles and by gifts of the Holy Spirit distributed according to his own will.'[43] 'One Lord, one faith, one baptism, one God.'[44] No need seems to be felt for a more precise definition of the Christian message by means of a binding norm which would guarantee uniformity. The crisp phrases in which Paul had testified and taught have gone altogether or dwindled into mere catchwords, used by the believer to profess his faith.[45] On the other hand, stories and legends about Jesus, his heavenly origin and redemptive work, luxuriate uncontrolled. It is precisely the resurrection, the event for which Paul attached such importance to the original testimony, that is given endless variations in new narrative versions, of which not one agrees in content with the list of names supplied by him. Legends about the earthly manifestation or the birth of the Lord proliferate even more mischievously.[46] Only the Passion narrative, despite accretions, retains a more marked uniformity both in the order of events and in the style. Nevertheless, it is clear that commitment to a fixed version of the christological data of salvation, such as Paul had accepted and required of his churches, is no longer the rule anywhere.

But the Christian Church is a unique entity; and this fact also

[41] Cf. Beumer, *op. cit.*, pp. 16f.

[42] Eph. 4:11ff.; Heb. 13:7, 17; Did. 15, 1; II Clem. 17, 3, 5; Hermas 13, 1 (Vis. III, 5, 1); 92, 4 (Sim. IX, 15, 4); 93, 5 (Sim. IX, 16, 5); 102, 2 (Sim. IX, 25, 2); II Pet. 3:2. The concept in I Clement (42) is constructed in accordance with a somewhat more definite theory, and in a different way the same is true in Ignatius (Magn. 13, 1; Philad. 9, 1).

[43] Heb. 2:3f.

[44] Eph. 4:5f. It is, in my opinion, by no means 'obvious' that this confident formula is directed against schism, as E. Käsemann, 'Das Interpretationsproblem des Epheserbriefes', *Exegetische Versuche und Besinnungen* II, 1964, p. 256, and *The Testament of Jesus*, 1969, believes.

[45] This is the case in Ignatius; cf. also the material in F. Kattenbusch, *Das Apostolische Symbol* II, 1900, pp. 312ff., and more generally in O. Cullmann, *Die ersten christlichen Glaubensbekenntnisse²*, 1949. Relevant too are the 'theological summaries of history' discussed by E. Stauffer, *New Testament Theology*, 1949, pp. 239ff.

[46] Cf. H. von Campenhausen, *Die Jungfrauengeburt in der Theologie der alten Kirche*, 1962, esp. pp. 16ff.

becomes clear in the history of her tradition. This is immediately consolidated in new forms, which are not to be explained simply in terms of pressures from the environment or of purely inherited material. While the old salvation-history formulas are falling into desuetude, a different complex of tradition is coming to the forefront, not only in Jewish Christian but also in Gentile churches.[47] This is the tradition of the sayings of Jesus, which are cherished to the extent that they can be used for exhortation, instruction, and regulation of church life.[48] Texts from the 'Sermon on the Mount' are especially popular. In suitable selections the words of Jesus now appear as a part of the

[47] It seems to me that there is in fact a kind of inverse proportion here. Where the Pauline tradition is absent or has withered away, the sayings tradition increases in importance. By contrast, the Paulinist Ignatius, who insists on the great facts of salvation, whether adorned with legend (Eph. 19; Smyrn. 3, 2) or in established formulas (cf. n. 45 above), seems to make almost no use of the tradition of the sayings of the Lord. At most one might point to Eph. 14, 2; Pol. 2, 2; but whether, even in these cases, it is really words of Jesus which are being quoted remains doubtful: cf. Köster, op. cit., pp. 42f.

[48] The tendency of the material which we are about to consider is correctly characterised by Massaux, op. cit., p. 650: 'What above all they are looking for is that part of Christ's teaching in which he founds the new religion, and defines a rule of life in conformity with it.' Quotations of Jesus' words for a different purpose are virtually non-existent. In the Apostolic Fathers a speculative use, such as we find in Barn. 6, 13, is very much the exception. On the other hand, a practical and moral application is now given even to sayings which originally can hardly have been meant in this sense, e.g., Barn. 4, 14; Ignatius, Eph. 14, 2; II Clem. 2, 4. Cf. further I Pet. 3:9; Acts 20:35; (21:14?); Did. 1, 2–2, 3; 8, 2; 9, 5; I Clem. 13, 2; 46, 8; II Clem. 4, 2.5; 5, 2–4; 6, 1f.; 8, 5; 9, 11; 12, 2; 13, 2; Ignatius, Pol. 2, 2; I Tim. 5:18; Polycarp, Phil. 2, 3; 7, 2; cf. also the summary of the baptismal vow in Pliny, Ep. X, 96, 7. (For a detailed critical discussion cf. Köster, op. cit.) The 'dogmatic' approach to the words of Jesus is not found before the controversy with the gnosis and its speculative treatment of the parables, while the historical elements relating to the 'life of Jesus' recede further and further into the background. The moral and catechetical line does not, however, break off because of the new dogmatic interest, but continues through Aristides and Justin down to Cyprian: cf. A. J. Bellinzoni, The Sayings of Jesus in the Writings of Justin Martyr, Leiden, 1967, pp. 140f. It may, therefore, be debated whether W. Schmithals, 'Paulus und der historische Jesus', ZNW 53, 1962, pp. 156f., is even partially correct, most of all as regards the 'historical material' in the narrower sense, when he asserts: 'The whole of Christian literature down to Justin . . . knows or uses hardly any traditions concerning the historical Jesus'; and E. Haenchen, 'Die frühe Christologie', ZTK 63, 1966, p. 146, is certainly wrong when, in support of Schmithals, he explicitly describes the 'Logia'–tradition as 'minimal'. Against Schmithals cf. W. G. Kümmel, 'Paulus und Jesus, Jesus und Paulus', in: Heilsgeschehen und Geschichte: Gesammelte Aufsätze 1933–1964, 1965, pp. 452f. At the most, the question may be asked, why the words of Jesus are not quoted more often and more clearly. In my own opinion this is partly connected with the character of the extant documents, but above all with the fact that 'the whole of christian literature', apart from the O.T., is non-canonical (though not, as Schmithals, p. 157, says, 'markedly apocryphal').

'glorious and venerable rule of our tradition,'[49] by which Christ has taught Christians right conduct and nobility of mind.[50] 'Forsake not the commandments of the Lord, but keep that which thou hast received, neither adding anything nor taking anything away.'[51] The instruction of converts had always emphasised the moral demands of the new teaching;[52] now, it would seem, these commandments are generally undergirded with sayings of Jesus. They are carefully impressed on the minds of the believers,[53] so that they can be appealed to, and Christians 'reminded' of them.[54] Yet the 'commandments of the Lord' by no means include only sayings of Jesus. They comprise the whole of Christian moral tradition, which does not distinguish at all sharply on the basis of provenance between its various constituent sayings and instructions.[55] The particular use determines the arrangement and the form. Thus, words of Jesus are incorporated by way of example into the ancient pattern of the 'Two Ways', and put forward together with the traditional material of this teaching as 'ordinances of the Lord'.[56] The so-called 'Teaching of the Lord through the Twelve Apostles'[57] does not make the claim either to contain only verbatim instructions of Jesus himself or to be directly written by the apostles;[58] but it conceives of the Christian way of life as a unity, and deliberately introduces it

[49] I Clem. 7, 2; cf. E. Flesseman–van Leer, *Tradition and Scripture in the Early Church*, 1954, pp. 23f.

[50] I Clem. 13, 1; cf. 7, 3. [51] Did. 4, 13; cf. Barn. 19, 11.

[52] I Thess. 2:14; 4:1–9; II Thess. 3:4ff.; Eph. 4:20ff.; Heb. 6:1f.

[53] I Clem. 2, 1.

[54] Acts 20:35; I Clem. 13, 1; 46, 7; Polycarp. Phil. 2, 3; 12, 1.

[55] Cf. I Pet. 3:9, and above all the collected sayings-material in James and the Didache. On James cf. G. Kittel, 'Der geschichtliche Ort des Jakobusbriefes', *ZNW* 41, 1942, pp. 71–105, and 'Der Jakobusbrief und die apostolischen Väter,' *ZNW* 43, 1950–1, pp. 54–112, esp. 83–109 (against Kittel's untenable early dating, however, cf. K. Aland, 'Der Herrenbruder Jakobus und der Jakobus, brief', *TLZ* 69, 1944, pp. 97–104); and E. Lohse, 'Glaube und Werke—zur Theologie des Jakobusbriefes', *ZNW* 48, 1957, pp. 1–22; on the Didache cf. esp. Köster, op. cit., pp. 239ff.

[56] Barn. 21, 1. According to G. Kretschmar, 'Ein Beitrag zur Frage nach dem Ursprung frühchristlicher Askese', *ZTK* 61, 1964, p. 47, it is possible that the basic document underlying the Teaching of the Two Ways was not Jewish but Christian, and would then have been 'the earliest rule of life written for Christians'.

[57] On the question of the original title of the 'Didache' cf. J. P. Audet, *La Didachè—instructions des apôtres*, Paris, 1958, pp. 91ff.; 247ff.; G. Klein, *Die zwölf Apostel*, 1961, pp. 80–83.

[58] Cf. A. Ehrhardt, 'Apostolische Kirchenordnungen als Beispiele früh-byzantinischer Interpolationen', *Zeitschr. der Savigny-Stiftung für Rechtsge-schichte* 67, Romanist. Abt., 1950. pp. 405f.; A. F. Walls, 'A Note on the Apos-tolic Claim in the Church Order Literature', Stud Patr II, 1957, pp. 83–92; and, more carefully, W. Speyer, 'Religiöse Pseudepigraphie und literarische Fälschung im Altertum', *JAC* 8–9, 1965–6, pp. 122f.

with a superscription which will bind the reader.[59] Frequently the commands[60] of the Lord given in the Gospel[61] occur cheek by jowl with Old Testament commandments, in so far as these were taken over.[62] This conjunction presented absolutely no problems: Jesus had already spoken in the old covenant, and on occasion, by a reverse process, his words are cited as words of Scripture.[63]

[59] This is all the more striking in view of the fact that, to all appearance, the Didache is already aware of the existence of a written book of the Gospels: cf. Köster, op. cit., p. 11; Audet, op. cit., p. 442.

[60] This concept occurs again and again in the usage of the early church: δικαιώματα: I Clem. 2, 8; 58, 2; Barn. 2, 1; 10, 11; 21, 1; Hermas 49, 4 (Mand. XII, 6, 4); δόγματα: Did. 11, 3; Ignatius, Magn. 13, 1; ἐντολαί: Barn. 4, 11; 16, 9; Did. 4, 13; Ignatius, Eph. 9, 2; II Clem. 17, 6; ἐντάλματα: II Clem. 17, 3; νόμος: Barn. 2, 6; Hermas 59, 3 (Sim. V, 6, 3); cf. James 1:25; 2:12; προστάγματα: I Clem. 2, 8; 58, 2.

[61] Did. 8, 2. The phrase does not refer to a book of the Gospels, but simply describes the teaching and message of Jesus—μνημονεύοντες ὧν εἶπεν ὁ κύριος διδάσκων—Polycarp, Phil. 2, 3; cf. the examples cited in Köster, op. cit., pp. 6ff. If in Did. 15, 3f. and II Clem. 8, 5, it is, as it would appear to be, a written Gospel which is in mind, nevertheless the reference is from a literary point of view quite indefinite. This fact hardly supports a late dating of the Didache, such as that argued for by F. E. Vokes, 'The Didache and the Canon of the New Testament', Stud Evang III, 1964, pp. 427–436. Moreover, this earlier custom of not making references specific to any one Gospel, which Marcion may have been the first to abandon (cf. p. 155 below), continued for a long time, notably in Clement of Alexandria, but also in other writers.

[62] Cf., e.g., I Clem. 13, 1f.; Did. 8, 2; Barn. 10, 12; II Clem. 13, 2ff.; and Köster, op. cit., pp. 69f. L. Buisson, 'Die Entstehung des Kirchenrechts,' Zeitschr. der Savigny-Stiftung für Rechtsgeschichte 83, Kanonist. Abt., 1966, p. 99, remarks with reference to Did. 13: 'Such an equation of priestly law from the Torah with Jesus' words to his disciples is possible only because Jesus' words were put on a level with the Torah.' The analogical utterances of the latter thus appear to be 'sanctioned by Jesus' words'.

[63] Barn. 4, 14 and II Clem. 2, 4 are, however, the only even moderately certain examples of this. Too much importance should not be attached to these much-discussed passages. In Barn. 4, 14 there is a reference to Matt. 20:16, πολλοὶ κλητοί, ὀλίγοι δὲ ἐκλεκτοί, to which the words ὡς γέγραπται are expressly appended. More recent exegetes, however, as against Zahn, op. cit., vol. I pp. 847f., reckon inter alia with the possibility of an O.T. quotation (IV Esdras 8:3; 9:15), or, more probably, of a lapse of memory; cf. Köster, op. cit., pp. 125f. II Clem. 2, 4 combines with Isa. 54:1 the text of Matt. 9:13, characterised explicitly as ἑτέρα γραφή. But it is precisely in combinations of quotations that such a description can easily occur, suggested by the O.T. passage. The explanation given by A. von Harnack, Origin of the N.T., 1925, pp. 27f., when referring to associated lections of both Old and New Testament texts, is illuminating in this context also. Massaux, op. cit., p. 74, on Barn. 4, 14 and II Clem. 2, 4, sums up the situation in even more general terms: 'A word of Jesus, once written down, is γραφή, not as coming from a Gospel which, taken as a whole, would itself be γραφή, but because it has been uttered by Jesus, the Prophet speaking in the name of God, or rather, himself the Word of God.' But here as in II Pet. 3:16 (where Paul's Epistles are lumped together with the

This, however, remains the exception, and does not imply that these words were considered valid because they appeared in sacred books. The authority behind them is still—as in Paul—the authority of the Lord himself, not the authority of a particular literary work, regarded as 'canonical', in which his words were preserved and made available.[64] Where the mediation of his teaching is in mind, the custom is to refer not to documents, which would be cited as such, but always and only to the living witnesses to his truth and person: the apostles and prophets, the teachers, the 'old' and the elders, who preached and preserved the original message and teaching. These are the real mediators of his power and of Church authority. This fact is very significant. In contrast to Judaism and its Law, the 'Gospel' by which the Church lives is an immediately present reality; and so far from the oral word's being subordinate to the written, it is by being oral that the word demonstrates its real meaning and power. It is this which simultaneously determines the character of the tradition and endangers its continuance. The words of Jesus are applied rather than quoted, in the strict sense of that word; and never are they explained and 'expounded' in their fixed form like a sacred text. Alongside the synoptic sayings words of Jesus are impartially quoted which we, from their provenance and meaning, are compelled to describe as apocryphal.[65] In the first one and a half centuries of the Church's history there is no single Gospel writing which is directly made known, named, or in any way given prominence by quotation. Written and oral traditions run side by side or cross, enrich or distort one another, without distinction or even the possibility of distinction between them.

Against this background the immense importance which attaches to the Gospel of Mark becomes clear.[66] It was certainly not the author's intention to put an end to oral instruction or to tie it exclusively to his

---

λοιπαὶ γραφαί!) the question of date also needs to be considered. That 'around the middle of the second century, words of the Lord transmitted in writing' could already count 'as γραφή' can hardly be doubted (Bultmann, *Theology*, II, p. 140). This, in my view, is also relevant to the Pastorals (cf. p. 181 below) Nevertheless, in both I Tim. 5:18 and II Tim. 3:14–17 the term γραφή in all probability refers simply to the O.T.: cf. M. Dibelius–H. Conzelmann, *Die Pastoralbriefe*[4], 1966, pp. 62, 89f.

[64] Cf. the instructive list of 'citation formulas for synoptic quotations' in Köster, *op. cit.*, pp. 64ff. There is no indication even of the kind of 'collection' of Jesus' words which one would have thought natural. E. Freed, *Old Testament Quotations in the Gospel of John*, Leiden, 1965, pp. 53ff., for all his collation of Old and 'New' Testament scriptural quotations in the Apostolic Fathers, has failed to take sufficient account of this.

[65] Barn. 6, 13; Did. 1, 6; II Clem. 12, 2.

[66] I find this adequately emphasised only by S. Schulz, 'Die Bedeutung des Markus für die Theologiegeschichte des Urchristentums', Stud Evang II, 1964, pp. 135–145.

own text. But the Gospel in book form was, when compared with the methods of the Jesus-tradition till that time, something new, and possible only in literature. The various elements and strands of tradition are here brought together within the framework of a story of Jesus, and subjected to the controlling theme of the christological preaching of salvation, in other words, of the 'Gospel'.[67] It is only the fact that on the one hand Mark makes the deeds, words, and prophecies of Jesus all point forward to the Passion, Resurrection, and Return of the Lord, but on the other projects these traditional data of salvation back on to the concrete figure, story and preaching of Jesus, which effectively safeguards the message of the exalted Saviour and Lord from changing beyond recognition or evaporating into nothingness,[68] and at the same time liberates his 'teaching' from the narrowness of mere moralism.[69]

The rapid spread of this new literary genre shows what a deep and universal need it supplied. In the course of this development earlier tendencies too revived to some extent. The Gospel of Matthew greatly expanded its Markan source with sayings (and stories), and did more to satisfy the long-standing catechetical desire for a teachable 'Gospel' in the old style.[70] By contrast, other, 'gnosticising' Gospels—among which in this respect John must be reckoned—blurred the concrete teachings and features in the picture of Jesus, recast his words in line with their current theological concerns, and strengthened the supernatural and mythological elements.

As regards the formation of the Canon, the only question of interest is whether, and if so in what way, the authors of the Gospels invested their works with a claim which did not simply assert the independent authority attaching to any genuine tradition but demanded special status precisely for this particular book. In the case of the traditional Four this never happens. The majority of them are completely silent

[67] That only a selection of the sayings-material was taken over by Mark, and that the message of salvation as such was not elaborated (Dibelius, *Formgeschichte*, pp. 259ff.) does not alter the fundamental importance of this step.

[68] Paul by himself could never have provided an effective counter to this danger. The history of gnosticism proves it.

[69] If the development of the Gospel had proceeded predominantly along the lines of catechetical collections of sayings, then from the point of view of the history of the Canon a quite different outcome would have been possible, namely that 'alongside the O.T. would have emerged merely a collection of normative sayings of Jesus, either in looser or in more organised form, and supplemented at most by eschatological visions': Harnack, *Origin*, p. 8 n. 3. In Syria it did in fact happen for a time that only 'the Gospel' was cited alongside the ancient scriptures: cf. p. 167 n. 92 below.

[70] Despite its kinship with the catechism in the Didache, Matthew as a whole can best be understood not as a catechism but rather as 'an attempt to supersede a catechism': Kretschmar, *op. cit.*, p. 57 n. 69. Cf. the cautious approach to the problem of form in Matthew in W. Trilling, *Das wahre Israel*[3], 1964, pp. 216–219.

concerning what it was made them undertake their task, or the importance and function of their work. We can only conjecture that from the
first the Gospels were intended for reading aloud in the congregation.[71]
But it is not until a hundred years after Mark that we hear of this as a
practice taken for granted.[72] Naturally any work intended for church
use would like to have as wide recognition and acceptance as possible;
but the earlier Gospels clearly did not claim exclusive validity, and
certainly did not acquire it. The widest distribution was achieved by
Matthew, which may be regarded as an 'enlarged and improved'
version of Mark. Later Gospels, such as the Gospel of Peter, which was
used even in catholic circles, drew upon and quoted even more sources,[73]
but were no more successful in ousting all rivals. It is highly questionable whether the idea is correct, that originally each individual Gospel
had its own territorial domain.[74] A classification into groups according
to purpose and tendency might also be considered, but no Gospel fits
exclusively into any one group. Thus, it may be that the Fourth Gospel
was originally intended for a particular circle of readers, being written
'that you may believe that Jesus is the Christ, the Son of God'. But in
the same breath it explains that 'Jesus did many other signs in the
presence of his disciples, which are not written in this book',[75] and so,
consciously or unconsciously, leaves the way clear for further presentations.

Only one evangelist is known to us who has given more precise
indications of the purpose and import of his record, and of the basic
principles on which he proceeds. This is Luke, in the preface to his
two-volume work, which stands at the beginning of the Gospel and is
referred to in the introduction to Acts.[76] Luke's unique position in this
respect is no accident, but is linked with the aim which he is pursuing.
Luke writes not, or at any rate not only for the Christian community

[71] Various indirect indications and traces of liturgical use are listed in O.
Michel, art. 'Evangelium', *RAC* VI, 1966, cols. 1142–1144.
[72] Justin, I Apol. 67; for apocalyptic writings there is earlier evidence: cf.
Rev. 1:3; Hermas 8 (Vis. II, 4).
[73] The only writer, however, to make an explicit reference to his predecessors
is Luke. His Gospel, like that of Matthew, may be described almost as an early
harmony of the Gospels: cf. Leipoldt, *op. cit.*, I, p. 135.
[74] Even the Gospel of the Egyptians may never have been 'the' Gospel of all
Christians in Egypt, but at most the Gospel preferred by Gentile Christians
there. The Egyptian Jewish Christians probably used the *Gospel of the Hebrews*:
W. Bauer, *Orthodoxy and Heresy in Earliest Christianity*, 1964, pp. 49–53;
cf. W. Schneemelcher in *N.T. Apocrypha* I, p. 117.
[75] Joh. 20:30f.; cf. 16:12. The phrase is, of course, stereotyped, and a popular literary tag in other writings: cf. Bultmann, John, 1971, p. 697 n. 2; also
K. Thraede, 'Untersuchungen zum Ursprung und zur Geschichte der christlichen Poesie I,' *JAC* 4, 1961, pp. 117ff. on the tag, 'pauca e multis'.
[76] Acts 1:1.

but for a wider public. His work is to appear on the open market, and therefore calls for an introduction. The dedication to the 'most excellent Theophilus' is to commend it to the heathen public, and to catch their interest. Luke presents himself as a historian. He affects the style of the prefaces customary in contemporary historical works. This, judged by the content of the Gospel, is a concession to the taste of the 'world'; but this does not, of course, imply that Luke did not intend to take seriously the principles to which he refers. His whole presentation shows that he really does want to be a historian. He believes in the divine direction of the saving history which reaches its consummation in the story of the Church, and he seeks to commend faith in Christ to his readers from this angle.[77]

'Inasmuch as many have undertaken,' runs the famous passage,[78] 'to compile a narrative of the things which have been accomplished among us, just as they were delivered to us by those who from the beginning were eyewitnesses and ministers of the word, it seemed good to me also, having followed all things closely for some time past, to write an orderly account for you, most excellent Theophilus, that you may know the truth concerning the things of which you have been informed'. Luke is thus aware that he has had predecessors in his undertaking. Even if the statement that there have been 'many' of them may be rhetorical and boastful exaggeration,[79] it cannot refer simply to Mark.[80] And though he forbears to engage in explicit polemic against earlier compilers, as heathen historians often did on such occasions, nevertheless it is clear that his predecessors have failed to satisfy him. He wants to provide something better, and so 'it seemed good' to him to make a fresh attempt. This time the work is to go right back to the beginning—Luke, as is well known, begins with the announcement of the Baptist's birth[81]—and to give a complete account, in the correct order and sequence, of all the relevant events.[82] As his

[77] That this was Luke's intention is not disproved by the fact that, as E. Haenchen, *Die Apostelgeschichte*[5], 1965, p. 105 n. 4, emphasises, it could not be immediately comprehensible to a heathen, and that the problem of safeguarding the historical tradition was very much an 'internal Christian' one: cf. G. Klein, 'Lukas 1, 1–4 als theologisches Programm', in: *Zeit und Geschichte* (Bultmann-Festschrift), 1964, pp. 211ff.

[78] Lk. 1:1–4: cf. the fundamental studies by F. J. Foakes Jackson and K. Lake in: *The Beginnings of Christianity* I, 2, London, 1922, pp. 133ff., and H. J. Cadbury, *ibid.*, pp. 489–510; E. Trocmé, *Le 'Livre des Actes' et l'Histoire*, Paris, 1957, pp. 41–50; 78–82; 125ff.; further literature in Klein, *op. cit.*

[79] Cf. J. Bauer, 'Πολλοί Luk. 1, 1', *NovTest* 4, 1960, pp. 263–266.

[80] As Cadbury, *op. cit.*, pp. 492f. rightly pointed out.

[81] Mark had already seen the 'beginning of the Gospel of Jesus Christ' in the Baptist's later emergence to undertake his public ministry (Mk 1:1): cf. E. Lohmeyer, *Das Evangelium des Markus*[16], 1963, pp. 9ff.

[82] This cannot, as E. Lohse, 'Lukas als Theologe der Heilsgeschichte',

ultimate source Luke takes into account only the traditions of the old apostles and evangelists themselves, here seen, in the best historian's manner, as 'eyewitnesses', but at the same time also as fellow-workers, actively involved in the life of the Church.[83] That as regards the events which have happened 'among us'[84] Luke partly counts himself as a witness, is not stated,[85] but implied at the appropriate moment in the text.[86]

The whole story of Jesus and the early Church is thus seen as 'contemporary history' in the wider sense. The aim of the presentation is apologetic and practical: Theophilus, who has himself already received some 'instruction',[87] and who is addressed as the representative of all well-disposed heathen, is to conclude from the book that the Christian preaching rests on sure historical premises, and may therefore demand and receive unreserved confidence. Luke therefore does not intend to repeat the Christian missionary preaching, nor to set out once again material with which the neophyte is familiar from his baptismal instruction (this, as we know, was in general *not* arranged in a historical pattern),[88] but he proposes to state the historical presuppositions of the

---

EvTh 14, 1954, pp. 260f., and U. Wilckens, *Die Missionsreden der Apostelgeschichte,* 1961, p. 69 n. 1, believe, be simply a matter of geographical arrangement, but must also at the same time involve a chronological one, as Acts 1:1 already proves. Klein, *op. cit.,* pp. 210f., would prefer to emphasise 'the linking of different phases'.

[83] Dibelius, *Formgeschichte,* p. 11: 'It is plainly not the writer's intention to refer to two completely separate groups, since he links them by using one article for both; but equally it cannot be his view that the two groups are identical. . . . But, as regards the earliest period, it seems to him quite certain that those who lived through it also proclaimed it, as "ministers of the word" '; similarly, A. M. Ramsey, 'The Gospel and the Gospels', *StudEvang* I, 1959, p. 35. Primarily, no doubt, it is the twelve apostles who are here in mind, since they supremely were 'eyewitnesses' and preachers in one.

[84] As against Klein, *op. cit.,* p. 197, I see not the slightest difficulty in taking this phrase in the wider sense, current until well on in the second century, of 'in our time', even though ἡμῖν in the next verse is used with a more specific reference.

[85] The παρηκολουθηκότι in 1:3 does not, however, justify us in concluding that Luke was personally present at the events he describes.

[86] Despite all objections this still seems to me the most straightforward interpretation of the much-discussed 'we'-passages in Acts.

[87] The term κατηχήθης (1:4) can, however, be taken of outsiders in the non-committal sense of a neutral 'having been informed': cf. Gerhardsson, *op. cit.,* p. 211, and the RSV translation, quoted p. 124 above.

[88] Cf. M. Dibelius, *Formgeschichte,* p. 14. That the material of Theophilus' instruction consists, instead, of 'the writings mentioned in 1:1', as U. Wilckens, 'Kerygma und Evangelium bei Lukas', *ZNW* 49, 1958, p. 228, believes (and likewise, apparently, Lohse, 'Lukas', p. 270; Klein, 'Lukas 1, 1-4', pp. 213f.), is impossible. If it were true, then everything which Dibelius has to say on this point would be not merely 'stated somewhat too categorically' (Wilckens, *op. cit.,* p. 229 n. 17; *Missionsreden,* p. 69 n. 2) but actually false.

Christian message and of the Church and its life. In this way its divine origin will be demonstrated, and the truth of its preaching guaranteed. By doing this, however, Luke in fact provides a new presentation of the historical content of the Christian faith and of the whole 'tradition', including the words of the Lord.

Consequently, the first part of his work corresponds completely to the now traditional form of a 'Gospel'. The relationship to the old tradition of the words and the 'Word' is no different from what it always has been. Luke does as he thinks fit with the traditional texts, regrouping, editing, and providing new settings as the plan of his work made essential. But he is in no doubt that what he creates in this way simply repeats the substance of the old message—except that now, for the first time, this expanded presentation offers the assurance of a really comprehensive and reliable version. The trustworthiness of the tradition is here assumed from the start. Jesus himself appointed the apostles (who are identical with the 'Twelve') as public witnesses to his story and teaching. Luke shows how the preaching of Christ, starting from Jerusalem, strikes out along entirely new paths and forges irresistibly ahead, but at the same time never escapes from the oversight and control of the apostles.[89] Even the Pauline mission to the Gentiles involves no breach, but is recognised and confirmed in Jerusalem. In the one, growing Church the dominant note is a continuity of preaching as well as a continuity of order and life. But this unbroken advance of teaching and learning is not to be equated with a supposed commitment to an inviolable canon of received texts and dogmas[90]—any more than the organic spread of Church offices in Luke is meant to prove a definite, sacrally unalterable form of constitution and succession.[91]

Even Luke, therefore, has not developed the 'canonical' growthpoints in Paul. His Gospel is not intended to forge and fasten on men an 'iron' version of unshakeable traditions, but, as he himself emphasises, is compiled in accordance with his own judgment from a wide range of oral and written traditions, and published under his own name of Luke.[92] In these circumstances Luke was not in a position to establish

[89] Acts 8:14ff.; 9:26ff.; 32; 1of.; 15 (21:18ff.).

[90] Here Gerhardsson, *op. cit.*, pp. 208ff., for the sake of his rabbinic parallels, has once more 'radicalised' and over-interpreted Luke's in itself constructive presentation: cf. W. D. Davies, 'Reflections on a Scandinavian Approach to "the Gospel Tradition",' in: *Neotestamentica et Patristica* (Cullmann-Festschrift), Leiden, 1962, pp. 14–34; E. Lohse, *TZ* 18, 1962, pp. 60–62; W. G. Kümmel, *TR* 31, 1965–6, pp. 25f.

[91] Cf. Campenhausen, *Ecclesiastical Authority*, pp. 153ff.

[92] That Luke was named in the title of his work dedicated to Theophilus, as M. Dibelius, 'Der erste christliche Historiker', in: *Aufsätze zur Apostelgeschichte*[4], 1961, p. 119, has rightly emphasised, 'can almost be taken for gran-

an authoritative version. The reliability and superiority which he claims for his work resides solely in the diligence with which he has collected, and perhaps in the care with which he has checked, the material which he now puts out in ordered form. At one point, however, he does go beyond Paul. Luke is concerned to stress the apostles as the original eyewitnesses and mediators of the word, whereas Paul keeps their names much more in the background in such contexts.[93] In Luke their position and authority now appear in a new, transfigured light: they are the leaders, chosen and vested with authority by Christ, of the first Christian church, and are portrayed as 'holy men', filled with the Spirit. As regards tradition, however, they are valued chiefly as 'witnesses' to the story of Jesus, and first and foremost to his resurrection,[94] not as a new source of sacred tradition. What Luke offers in his work on the basis of their testimony (and not only theirs) is guaranteed most decidedly not by sacral but by rational and 'natural' means[95]—exactly as Paul had done with his 'Gospel'.[96] In Luke's case this does not at all

---

ted'; for 'it would be strange if, when the person to whom the dedication is addressed is mentioned by name, the one making the dedication should be anonymous'. This carefully formulated hypothesis is confirmed by the literary practice of the whole ancient world. It is astonishing with what assurance E. Haenchen asserts the contrary ('Das "Wir" in der Apostelgeschichte und das Itinerar', *ZTK* 58, 1961, pp. 335f. = *Gott und Mensch* [Ges. Aufs.], 1965, pp. 233f.; also *Apostelgeschichte*, p. 105 n. 4). The points made by A. D. Nock, *Gnomon* 25, 1953, pp. 497–506 (while, moreover—something which should not be suppressed—explicitly agreeing with Dibelius on the question of authorship) and J. Dupont, *Les sources du Livre des Actes*, Bruges, 1960, pp. 132f., against Dibelius on this question are quite insufficient to shake his thesis. On the contrary, it would be an outstanding confirmation of it if in fact no more than three exceptions could be found in the whole of antiquity to the rule that a dedication by name presupposes the naming of the author. And what is more, when we come to examine these three alleged exceptions we find that they dwindle to two, if not one. The *Rhetorica ad Herennium* did indeed appear with a dedication, but without nameing Cornificius, who nevertheless was well known to be the author. On the other hand Hebrews, adduced by Nock and Dupont, is utterly irrelevant, since it contains no dedication (in my own view, it would be read, as the conclusion indicates, as a letter of Paul's); and their final example, also a Christian work, the Epistle to Diognetus (so named by the editor), ascribed to Justin Martyr, has come down to us only in a single MS, now damaged by fire, is never mentioned nor cited by any other ancient author, and is altogether so surrounded with riddles that it seems hazardous to draw any far-reaching conclusions from it. Cf. further n. 101 below.

[93] Cf. pp. 114f. above.

[94] Lk. 24:48f.; Acts 1:8, 21f.; 2:32; 3:15; 4:33; 5:30ff.; 10:39ff.; 13:31.

[95] Significantly enough, this was later felt as a defect; and various Old Latin (and Gothic) MSS, borrowing from Acts 15:28, add 'et spiritu sancto' after the 'mihi' of Lk. 1:3.

[96] For this reason it is impossible to agree with Klein, 'Lukas', pp. 206f., that it is simply Luke's personal tendency which makes him substitute 'his own discovery of the truth' for 'recourse to the apostolic tradition'.

mean that he wished to justify the faith itself purely historically and on naturalistic lines. The believer grasps the truth of Christ by on the one hand understanding Jesus, on the basis of the Scripture, as 'objectively' fulfilling the ancient salvation-history,[97] and on the other hand he is 'subjectively' convinced by the miraculous effects of the Spirit. But the content of belief, all that the story of Christ comprises and implies, cannot just be lightly asserted and affirmed as mere assertion; it has to be mediated and guaranteed by a trustworthy tradition. Faith is inevitably bound up with this historical communication and mediation, and to supply the proof necessary to confirm what is taught in this way no one, in Luke's opinion, is better fitted or in a better position than the educated Christian historian, conscientiously pursuing his calling.

In the event, however, Luke did not gain any advantage over the earlier Gospels. On the contrary, at first its standing was strikingly inferior to that of Mark and, above all, of Matthew.[98] Acts is not attested at all before Irenaeus. Justin certainly knows Luke's Gospel,[99] but uses it relatively little. Papias and Hegesippus do not mention him.[100] There may be various reasons for this. At first Luke–Acts may have attracted little notice among Christians because of the manner in which it appeared,[101] and its relatively worldly character. In many circles, too, its connection with Paul will have been no recommendation. Later, the Gospel in particular may well have seemed discredited by the use

[97] The purpose of scriptural proof in Luke is primarily to demonstrate this, and in this respect it is markedly different from the 'oracular' pattern of proof in Matthew: cf. Lohse, 'Lukas', p. 264 n. 30, and the excellent observations of P. Schubert, 'The Structure and Significance of Luke 24', *Neutest. Studien für R. Bultmann*[2], 1957, pp. 176ff.

[98] Cf. J. Knox, *Marcion and the New Testament*, Chicago, 1942, pp. 124ff., with whose further theories on the history of Luke's Gospel, however, I cannot concur; Massaux, *op. cit.*, pp. 651ff. H. Greeven, 'Erwägungen zur synoptischen Textkritik', *NTS* 6, 1959–60, p. 289, writes: 'Of the three, Matthew must have come the earliest and most completely under the influence of preservative forces. We have seen that this is most usually the case with a text which is in use in a closed community, where there is considerable interchange and internal circulation. The text-critical evidence thus points to Matthew as the synoptic gospel "with the longest service", that is to say, the one most widely preferred for church use.'

[99] Dial. 103, 8 not only uses material peculiar to Luke, but also is clearly describing Luke himself in the reference to the 'followers' of the apostles.

[100] Cf. n. 106 below.

[101] It was, as Dibelius, *Aufsätze*, pp. 118f., has shown, intended from the outset for a literary public, 'for the commercial market'. Haenchen, *op. cit.* n. 92 above, wrongly claims the support of H.-I. Marrou, 'La technique de l'édition à l'époque patristique', *VC* 3, 1949, pp. 222ff., in objecting to this conclusion, since Marrou had emphatically confined his doubts about current notions on the subject of ancient book production to a later, 'patristic' period; cf. more recently L. Koep, art. 'Buch I', *RAC* II, 1954, cols. 676f.

which Marcion and other heretics made of it.[102] But these are conjectures, which can hardly be confirmed because, as has already been said, it is not yet the general practice to cite particular Gospels by name.[103] 'The Gospel', to which appeal is normally made, remains an elastic concept, designating the preaching of Jesus as a whole in the form in which it lives on in church tradition.[104] The normative significance of the Lord's words, which is the most important point, is thus directly dependent upon the person of the Lord, and is not transferred to the documents which record them.

Yet another literary preface which provides illuminating evidence in support of this view is a fragment excerpted by Eusebius from the five books of 'Exegeses of the Words of the Lord' by Papias. Unfortunately, it is very difficult to date the composition of this work.[105] Eusebius wants to place Papias in the post-apostolic age; but every consideration of content and style suggests rather that he should be pushed further back, perhaps into the second or third decade of the second century. It is certain that he cannot be earlier than the last decade of the first

---

[102] Origen, Hom. Luc. 16 (Rauer², p. 97, 12f.): innumerabiles quippe haereses sunt, quae evangelium secundum Lucam recipiunt; cf. 20 (Rauer², p. 120, 7–10). The Gospel of Thomas also gives Luke the preference over the other synoptists: O. Cullmann, 'Das Thomasevangelium und die Frage nach dem Alter der in ihm enthaltenen Tradition', TLZ 85, 1960, col. 333; cf. the evidence in the index of W. Schrage, Das Verhältnis des Thomasevangeliums zur synoptischen Tradition usw., 1964, p. p. 210: passages dependent on Matt., 6; on Mark, 1; on Luke, 9.

[103] Except in Papias (Eusebius, HE III, 39, 15f.) there is no instance of the mention of any Gospel by name before Theophilus, who refers to the Gospel of John (Ad Aut. II, 22). When, in Justin, Dial. 106, 3, it is said of Jesus, μετωνομακέναι αὐτὸν Πέτρον ἕνα τῶν ἀποστόλων, καὶ γεγράφθαι ἐν τοῖς ἀπομνημονεύμασιν αὐτοῦ γεγενημένον καὶ τοῦτο . . ., the word αὐτοῦ does not refer to the Gospel of Peter, still less to Jesus (as suggested by Leipoldt, op. cit. I, p. 131), but in all probability should be emended to αὐτῶν, as proposed by Otto, Justini Opera³, 1877, vol. I, 2, p. 380 n. 10. That Justin should describe the Gospels as ἀπομνημονεύματα τῶν ἀποστόλων, and especially that he should stress them as 'sources' of his own presentation, is in keeping with the apologetic character of his extant writings; cf. p. 184 below.

[104] R. Heard, 'Papias Quotations from the New Testament', NTS 1, 1954–5, p. 133, pertinently comments: 'As long as the chain of oral tradition lasted, however, its authority for the teaching of Jesus seems to have remained paramount, and such Gospels as circulated to have been of only confirmatory importance.'

[105] On this question cf. most recently the very full discussion by J. Munck, 'Presbyters and Disciples of the Lord in Papias', HTR 52, 1959, pp. 223–243, which gives an account of all the modern attempts at a solution. According to R. Annand, 'Papias and the Four Gospels', SJT 9, 1956, pp. 46–62, Papias was earlier than Luke, and was included by Luke in his preface among the predecessors of his own work. Quite apart from anything else, however, this flight of fancy completely misunderstands the character of Papias' work.

century. Papias mentions Matthew,[106] and has most to say about Mark; in addition he also makes use of 1 John and 1 Peter,[107] and possibly the Apocalypse.[108] Nevertheless, he is far from regarding the Gospels as the final or canonical form of the Jesus-tradition; indeed, he declares with feeling his belief in the superiority of the oral tradition. 'That which comes from books', he writes, 'seems to me not to be of such service as that which begins as living speech and remains so'.[109]

[106] That his mention of a record of the Lord's words, alleged to be in Hebrew (III, 39, 16), may quite definitely be a reference to our Gospel of Matthew, has in my view been most illuminatingly proved by J. Munck, 'Die Tradition über das Matthäusevangelium bei Papias', in: *Neotestamentica et Patristica* (Cullmann—Festschrift), 1962, pp. 249–260, and, in a different way, by J. Kürzinger, 'Das Papiaszeugnis und die Endgestalt des Matthäusevangeliums', *BZ* N.F. 4, 1960, pp. 19–38, and 'Irenäus zur Sprache des Matthäusevangeliums', *NTS* 10, 1963–4, pp. 108–110. Eusebius has preserved no statement by Papias about the Gospels of John or Luke. As is well known, interpretations of this remarkable fact vary widely, and a definite decision seems hardly possible.

[107] Eusebius, *HE* III, 39, 17.

[108] Andreas Caes., *Praef. in Apoc.* (= Funk–Bihlmeyer, *Frag.* V); cf. F. Loofs, *Theophilus von Antiochien Adversus Marcionem und die anderen theologischen Quellen bei Irenäus*, 1930, pp. 325ff.

[109] Eusebius, *HE* III, 39, 4: οὐ γὰρ τὰ ἐκ τῶν βιβλίων τοσοῦτόν με ὠφελεῖν ὑπελάμβανον ὅσον τὰ παρὰ ζώσης φωνῆς καὶ μενούσης. The fundamental importance of this attitude is not to be disputed, as R. P. C. Hanson, *Tradition in the Early Church*, 1962, pp. 38f., would like to do, nor misunderstood as polemic against supposedly heretical literature, as in A. F. Walls, 'Papias and Oral Tradition', *VC* 21, 1967, pp. 137–140. It is specifically characteristic of early Christianity, though it is also found elsewhere in similar form. Gerhardsson, *op. cit.*, pp. 205f., refers to rabbinic parallels, and Philo emphatically exalts the importance of oral tradition as compared with the sacred scriptures: *Vita Mosis* I, 4; cf. Munck, 'Presbyters and Disciples', p. 229. As late as the 13th century the Arab historian, Abu-el-Qasim ibn 'Asakir writes: 'My friend, strive zealously and without ceasing to get hold of (traditions). Do not take them from written records, so that they may not be touched by the disease of textual corruption': K. Koch, *Was ist Formgeschichte?* 1964, p. 86, quoting H. Birkeland, *Vom hebräischen Traditionswesen*, Oslo, 1938 (but cf. also G. Widengren, *Literary and Psychological Aspects of the Hebrew Prophets*, 1946, for a different view of the Arab evidence). In the early Church the example that at once springs to mind is Clement of Alexandria, who appeals to Plato to support his argument for the indispensability of oral tradition and instruction as a matter of principle: cf. pp. 299ff. below. The text of the baptismal creed was for a whole century transmitted by word of mouth alone—a practice which is not to be explained simply by the requirements of a real or supposed 'disciplina arcani'. On the whole question cf. H. Karpp, 'Viva Vox,' in: *Mullus* (Festschrift T. Klauser, 1964), pp. 190–198. 'That by the word "books" Papias was referring directly to the writings of'—what was later—'the New Testament', or, at any rate, that they were included in the works he had in mind, seems to me, as against Beumer, *op. cit.*, pp. 18f., in view of the context indisputable, and I personally would like to emphasise this even more strongly than does Flesseman–van Leer, *op. cit.*, p. 65.

Consequently, in his own work, which illustrates the Lord's words from the 'unwritten tradition',[110] he likes to adduce everything which 'he has learned from the Elders and preserved'. With a rather affected self-complacency he himself goes bail for their trustworthiness,[111] for he has not followed any old gossips, but only good informants, who would have mentioned only such commands as 'were given for faith from the Lord, and derive from the truth itself'.[112] He has taken every opportunity to ask those men who knew the old fathers, what the latter in their time had themselves heard from 'the disciples of the Lord':[113] 'What did Andrew say, or Peter, Philip or Thomas or James or John, Matthew or any other disciple of the Lord, and what did Aristion say, or John the Elder, the disciples of the Lord?'[114]

Although Papias does not present himself as a historian, as Luke does, but seems to be interested simply in the transmission of words and teaching as such, yet for this very reason he attaches especial value, in what he has to communicate about the 'commands' of the Lord, to that which goes back to the original eye-, or rather aural, witnesses.

[110] Eusebius, *HE* III, 39, 11 (cf. n. 123 below). As the emphasis on ἐντολαί (39, 3) shows, it is really the words of the Lord with which we are concerned here. It is to these that the interest, be it ethical or 'dogmatic', attaches, even when the utterances are set in a narrative framework (cf. the quotation in Irenaeus, Adv. haer. V, 33, 3f. = Funk–Bihlmeyer, *Frag.* I). Hence the phrase κυριακὰ λόγια is primarily to be understood as a one-sided description of the content of *Mark* (*HE* III, 39, 15), and not so much as an example of a looser usage, which can indeed cover 'deeds' as well, λεχθέντα ἢ πραχθέντα: for a different view cf. G. Kittel, art. λόγιον, *TWNT* IV, 1942, pp. 144f., followed by Munck, 'Presbyters', p. 228, and Kürzinger, 'Papiaszeugnis', pp. 36–38. That Papias was at the same time himself interested in miracle stories, and constantly retailed them (cf. Eusebius, *HE* III, 39, 8f., and the account of the end of Judas, Funk–Bihlmeyer, *Frag.* III), is, of course, by no means incompatible with this.

[111] Cf. Dibelius, art. 'Papias', *RGG* IV², 1930, pp. 892f.

[112] Eusebius, *HE* III, 39, 3: οὐ γὰρ τοῖς τὰ πολλὰ λέγουσιν ἔχαιρον ὥσπερ οἱ πολλοί, ἀλλὰ τοῖς τἀληθῆ διδάσκουσιν, οὐδὲ τοῖς τὰς ἀλλοτρίας ἐντολὰς μνημονεύουσιν, ἀλλὰ τοῖς τὰς παρὰ τοῦ κυρίου τῇ πίστει δεδομένας καὶ ἀπ' αὐτῆς παραγινομένας τῆς ἀληθείας.

[113] In my view the πρεσβύτεροι are to be distinguished from the κυρίου μαθηταί, and cannot include them. In opposition to G. Strecker, *Der Weg der Gerechtigkeit²*, 1966, pp. 192f., I would wish to stress the improbability of the opposite assumption even more decisively than Munck, 'Presbyters', pp. 236ff., has already done with his detailed argument; cf. further G. Bornkamm, art. πρεσβύτερος, *TWNT* VI, 1959, p. 676 n. 165, and Blum, *op. cit.*, pp. 74f.

[114] Eusebius, *HE* III, 39, 4: εἰ δέ που παρηκολουθηκώς τις τοῖς πρεσβυτέροις ἔλθοι, τοὺς τῶν πρεσβυτέρων ἀνέκρινον λόγους· τί Ἀνδρέας ἢ τί Πέτρος εἶπεν ἢ τί Φίλιππος ἢ τί Θωμᾶς ἢ Ἰάκωβος ἢ τί Ἰωάννης ἢ Ματθαῖος ἢ τις ἕτερος τῶν τοῦ κυρίου μαθητῶν, ἅ τε Ἀριστίων καὶ ὁ πρεσβύτερος Ἰωάννης, τοῦ κυρίου μαθηταί, λέγουσιν. There is no reason to think that the text has been corrupted or cut: cf. Munck, 'Presbyters', pp. 240ff.

K

These are primarily the well-known figures of the circle of the Twelve,[115] but here they are described not as 'apostles' but as 'disciples of the Lord'.[116] To these are now added Aristion and 'the Elder' John.[117] There is no need to discuss here the historical problems raised by these names. It is clear that Papias does not consider restricting the circle of witnesses to the twelve Apostles, as Luke does.[118] To him all information about Jesus is welcome, provided that it can be traced back to some 'disciple' who genuinely knew the Lord.[119]

In view of this, even written sources are not rejected by Papias on principle. As already stated, he mentions by name both Mark and Matthew—on the authority indeed of earlier tradition which recognised

[115] Papias' selection is reminiscent of John, but this may be coincidence: cf. W. Bauer, 'Das Apostelbild in der altchristlichen Überlieferung', in: N.T. Apocrypha II, pp. 12f.

[116] This description is already found in Acts 9:1, and later is a favourite with Irenaeus and Clement of Alexandria: cf. Munck, 'Presbyters', p. 232. In other passages too Papias apparently avoids the title of 'apostle', and speaks only of 'disciples' of the Lord, presumably because he is 'as yet unfamiliar with the concept of "apostolicity"' (Blum, op. cit., p. 74). In the circumstances it is superfluous to look, as does B. H. Streeter, The Four Gospels[8], 1953, p. 21, for a special explanation of the allegedly 'extraordinary fact' that in Papias 'the earliest allusion in Christian literature to the Gospels is an endeavour to minimise their accuracy and Apostolic authority'.

[117] With no compelling reason W. Larfeld, 'Ein verhängnisvoller Schreibfehler bei Eusebios', Byzant.-Neugriech. Jahrbuch 3, 1922, pp. 282–285, with the aid of a violent emendation (τοῦ Ἰωάννου μαθηταί), wishes to make these two into disciples of the Beloved Disciple. E. Bammel, art. 'Papias', RGG V[3], 1961, p. 48, adopts the same emendation but makes it refer to the Baptist. The interval (of time?) between these two and the preceding names is marked by the alteration in the pronoun and the change to the present tense: cf. John F. Bligh, 'The Prologue of Papias', Theol. Stud. 13, 1952, pp. 234–240. A definite distinction between apostles and disciples is found in the Gospel of Philip 35 (p. 107, 27f.).

[118] Strangely enough, K. Beyschlag, 'Herkunft und Eigenart der Papiasfragmente', StudPatr IV, 1961, p. 279, asserts the opposite, despite the fact that he himself, ibid., n. 4, points out that all the authorities whom Papias names elsewhere specifically do not belong to the apostolic group.

[119] I cannot see that, as G. Bornkamm, art. 'Evangelien, synoptische', RGG II[3], 1958, col. 761, asserts, the later 'increasingly strong tendency to affirm if not direct, at any rate indirect apostolic authority for the Gospel of Mark' is 'clearly' discernible in Papias; similarly K. Niederwimmer, 'Johannes Markus und die Frage nach dem Verfasser des zweiten Evangeliums', ZNW 58, 1967, p. 177. Papias in any case does not say what is alleged in later accounts, namely that Peter for his part checked and 'sanctioned' or 'confirmed' Mark's Gospel (Eusebius, HE II, 15, 2; Jerome, Vir. Ill. 8); he merely names the reliable source on which Mark drew. Clement of Alexandria, in a passage of the Hypotyposes quoted by Eusebius (HE VI, 14, 6), repeats a similar tradition, which positively denies any direct Petrine authorisation: Peter's listeners had encouraged Mark to write the Gospel, ὅπερ ἐπιγνόντα τὸν Πέτρον προτρεπτικῶς μήτε κωλῦσαι μήτε προτρέψασθαι. On Irenaeus cf. pp. 203 below.

their work. Mark, he says, recorded the sayings and stories of th.
Lord, somewhat untidily, it is true. But then, he was not an eyewitness;
he had to derive them from Peter's sermons, in which they came up as
occasion required. He was concerned simply to reproduce with accuracy
what he heard, and so is free from blame.[120] Papias did not, it would
seem, mention any other Gospels.[121] It is clear that in explaining the
words of the Lord he does not feel himself tied to definite Gospel texts;
instead he was ready to add new material from the 'unwritten tradition',
which he regarded as equally genuine and binding. Thus, he tells a
story of Jesus and the Adulteress, which later appeared in the *Gospel
of the Hebrews*, and was probably identical with the narrative interpolated into our present Fourth Gospel.[122] In general, however, the
parables and teachings which he passed on inspired no confidence, but
struck men, in Eusebius' phrase, as alien and legendary in character.[123]

[120] Eusebius, *HE* III, 39, 15: καὶ τοῦθ' ὁ πρεσβύτερος ἔλεγεν· Μάρκος μὲν
ἑρμηνευτὴς Πέτρου γενόμενος, ὅσα ἐμνημόνευσεν, ἀκριβῶς ἔγραψεν, οὐ μέντοι
τάξει τὰ ὑπὸ τοῦ κυρίου ἢ λεχθέντα ἢ πραχθέντα· οὔτε γὰρ ἤκουσεν τοῦ κυρίου
οὔτε παρηκολούθησεν αὐτῷ, ὕστερόν δε, ὡς ἔφην, Πέτρῳ, ὃς πρὸς τὰς χρείας
ἐποιεῖτο τὰς διδασκαλίας, ἀλλ' οὐχ ὥσπερ σύνταξιν τῶν κυριακῶν ποιούμενος
λογίων, ὥστε οὐδὲν ἥμαρτεν Μάρκος, οὕτως ἔνια γράψας ὡς ἀπεμνημόνευσεν·
ἑνὸς γὰρ ἐποιήσατο πρόνοιαν, τοῦ μηδὲν ὧν ἤκουσεν παραλιπεῖν ἢ ψεύσασθαί τι
ἐν αὐτοῖς. The passage has an apologetic ring; yet, in my view, it does not suggest that the critics against whom Mark is being defended were measuring the
lack of system in his Gospel by the standard of Luke or John. It is also not impossible that behind the formal objections there were also differences on matters
of fact. On the other hand, that Mark was attacked precisely because he added
what were still oral reminiscences to the written teaching of Peter, seems to me,
as against T. Y. Mullins, 'Papias on Mark's Gospel', *VC* 14, 1960, pp. 216–224,
in no way indicated in the text. On the stereotyped character of the concluding
sentence cf. W. C. van Unnik, 'Zur Papias-Notiz über Markus', *ZNW* 54,
1963, pp. 276f.

[121] For Mark and Matthew he appeals to the testimony of an 'Elder', to whom
quite possibly Luke and John were simply unknown. It is also possible that the
two last-named seemed to him to inspire less confidence, and to be discredited
by heretical use: Bauer, *Orthodoxy*, p. 204. It seems to me, on the other hand,
less probable that Papias did in fact have something to say about Luke, but
that it was so disparaging that Eusebius hesitated to include it in his Church
History (*ibid.*, pp. 184f.).

[122] Eusebius, *HE* III, 39, 17: ἐκτέθειται δὲ καὶ ἄλλην ἱστορίαν περὶ γυναικὸς
ἐπὶ πολλαῖς ἁμαρτίαις διαβληθείσης ἐπὶ τοῦ κυρίου, ἣν τὸ καθ' Ἑβραίους
εὐαγγέλιον περιέχει. Cf. U. Becker, *Jesus und die Ehebrecherin*, 1963, pp. 92–105.
As against his view, pp. 99f., it seems to me, with Zahn, *op. cit.* I, p. 854, to
follow clearly from the words of Eusebius that the reference to the Gospel of the
Hebrews comes from him and not from Papias.

[123] Eusebius, *HE* III, 39, 11: καὶ ἄλλα δὲ ὁ αὐτὸς ὡς ἐκ παραδόσεως
ἀγράφου εἰς αὐτὸν ἥκοντα παρατέθειται, ξένας τέ τινας παραβολὰς τοῦ σωτῆρος
καὶ διδασκαλίας αὐτοῦ καὶ τινα ἄλλα μυθικώτερα. Eusebius viewed Papias with
little sympathy, because he supposed him responsible for the millenarianism of
many of the early Fathers: *HE* III, 39, 12. Nevertheless, his verdict that the
man was narrow-minded and of a low intellectual level (39, 13: σφόδρα γάρ τοι

We have, on the available evidence, no reason to mistrust this judgment.[124]

What is new is that Papias, despite all his preference for the oral, is obliged to distinguish his information expressly from 'different', falsified traditions, and will give credence only to those mediators of tradition who teach and preserve the 'truth' of the original commandments, that is to say, who have remained orthodox.[125] The tradition is no longer regarded as a univocal entity, the 'genuineness' of which can be assumed without question; and even its exegesis has become matter for dispute. Significantly, what Papias collects is not simply sayings of Jesus, but that which can be adduced from the earliest days to help toward a right understanding of them.[126] The question of what was originally right and valid reflects an advanced stage of development of the tradition and of controversy about it, such as we do not yet find, for example, in the time of Ignatius.[127] It is this change in the situation which one day is going to make it necessary formally to sift and fix the tradition in a way binding on all, that is, to establish a canon of the New Testament. But Papias himself seems to be still a hundred miles from such a regularisation, and, with his enthusiasm for the oral tradition, almost to be working in the opposite direction. Paul had still been able to appeal to fixed, recognised texts, by which the crucial data of the story of Christ were laid down in a clearly defined sense. Luke had clearly marked out the starting-point of all those traditions which were already undergoing a broader development, and had tried to set the whole within the firm framework of a historical work which was to serve as a reliable source of instruction both for the contemporary world and for posterity. In Papias everything is sinking back into the flood of chaotic tradition, whether written or oral, which despite his alleged sifting is at most only a little restricted by his own theological judgment,

---

σμικρὸς ὢν τὸν νοῦν, ὡς ἂν ἐκ τῶν αὐτοῦ λόγων τεκμηράμενον εἰπεῖν, φαίνεται) will not have been based on this alone.

[124] Because of the lack of genuine material, however, there is absolutely no justification for the conclusion of Bammel, *op. cit.*, col. 48, that Papias' claim to have pursued his own independent researches is demonstrably 'a mere literary form of words'.

[125] Eusebius, *HE* III, 39, 3 (cf. n. 112 above); also 39, 15 (μηδὲν ψεύσασθαι). These texts are not to be understood as implying no more than the usual literary convention, as Munck, 'Presbyters', p. 230, believes; and the ἀλήθεια—as against Blum, *op. cit.*, p. 78—denotes more than just historical reliability; cf. on this point, e.g., E. Schwartz, 'Über den Tod der Söhne Zebedaei' (1904) = *Gesammelte Schriften* V, 1963, pp. 48–123, esp. pp. 59ff.

[126] That Papias' aim was not 'to collect the sayings of the Lord', but primarily to expound them with the help of the paradosis, is rightly emphasised by Schwartz, *op. cit.*, p. 58; but this does not mean that his efforts were solely in connection with the Gospels we now possess.

[127] Cf. pp. 71ff. above.

and is mostly in practice uncontrollable, bursting all banks and defences and spreading far and wide. 'It is as if an attempt had been made to keep the immediacy of the original revelation as a present reality by clinging to the living word, not to the dead, transient written text.'[128]

It is certainly not to be assumed that conditions within the early gnostic groups were essentially different from and more favourable than those which obtained among the communities which were later called orthodox and catholic.[129] Our information about them derives only from the time after Marcion, whose 'canon' inevitably furthered such developments everywhere; but the very definite impression is that the earlier 'sects' in fact lagged behind the great Church in developing a 'New Testament', and certainly nowhere outstripped it. This is not really surprising, if we recall what was said in the preceding chapter. The same tendencies which inevitably loosened and undermined the authority of the Old Testament 'scriptures' within all gnostic groups were hardly likely to be foremost in encouraging the formation of a new canon. Pleasure in the proliferation of syncretistic mythology and speculation sorted ill with the old Jesus-traditions, so alien to their spirit. Jesus Christ becomes a timeless symbol or principle of redemption, and what matters is to emphasise this. The old sayings and stories are converted into mythical signs and images, which have to be expounded with the gnostic key, if their mystery is to be deciphered.[130] Jesus did not give away his highest revelations to the public at large, but entrusted them to a narrow circle of chosen disciples. Their knowledge was passed on to the gnostic conventicles.[131] Further efforts were made to relativise and discredit the texts of the Church's tradition about Jesus by treating them—like the Old Testament—no longer as a unity, but dividing them into different levels. According to the pedagogic intention and the varying degree of inspiration which produced them, they therefore contain elements of widely differing value, and can by no means be regarded as binding without further question.[132]

[128] F. C. Baur, *Lehrbuch der christlichen Dogmengeschichte*[3], 1867, p. 96.

[129] Cf. on this point Knox, *op. cit.*, p. 26 n. 11; B. F. A. Westcott, *A General Survey of the History of the Canon of the N.T.*, 1855, pp. 249ff., and esp. 281f.; N. Brox, *Offenbarung, Gnosis und gnostischer Mythos bei Irenäus von Lyon*, 1966, pp. 56ff. The view of Harnack, *Growth*, p. 22, was that a collection of N.T. scriptures grew up 'first among the Marcionites and gnostics—naturally enough; for having rejected the Old Testament they felt the urgent necessity to replace it with another "litera scripta".' But the assumption behind this conclusion, by no means applies to the gnostics (apart from Marcion), as the preceding chapter has shown; on Marcion, cf. pp. 143ff. below.

[130] Irenaeus, Adv. haer. II, 23, 2; III, 2, 2.

[131] Cf. e.g., Irenaeus, Adv. haer. I, 3, 1; 8, 1; Clem. Alex., Exc. ex Theod. 66.

[132] Irenaeus, Adv. haer. I, 7, 3; III, 2, 2; IV, 35, 1, 4; Hippolytus, Elench. X, 9, 2. Cf. Brox, *op. cit.*, p. 61; but the explicit reference to the deficient know-

In such circumstances there can hardly be any conscientious attempt
to safeguard the traditions and their literal authority. New texts are
constantly being produced with fresh variations on the gnostics'
favourite ideas, which, though they are supposed to rest on old revelations, claim no really exclusive authority. Significantly, the Church's
written Gospels—regardless whether they are used or ignored—are
hardly ever attacked or criticised.[133] This, however, is symptomatic not
only for the gnostic but also for the catholic Gospels, if one compares
this situation with the constant critique of the Old Testament. Even
within the camp of the Great Church the Gospels are still not a recognised norm, to be referred to as such. They may be accepted or ignored,
anthologised in any way that seems appropriate, expanded or
improved.[134] Only the Old Testament has truly 'canonical' status, and,
as we have seen, its validity for this very reason constitutes a problem
which is taken up and passionately debated again and again.

Some texts which have come down to us from the earlier gnosis may
be used to illustrate what has just been said. A strange Simonian book
of revelations, the 'Great Apophasis', has been excerpted in fair detail
by Hippolytus.[135] The book solemnly promises to reveal ultimate
truths, such as may be understood only by those who have been exalted
to the image of God.[136] For this purpose it appeals to the Old Testament,[137] in which the supreme, seventh Power makes itself heard
'allegorically' through Moses and the Prophets.[138] Heathen philosophers and poets are brought in to supplement the Scripture.[139] By

---

ledge and powers of comprehension of the apostles (Adv. haer. III, 1, 1; 12,
12, etc.) must derive primarily from Marcion.

[133] Outside Marcionism no example of this is known to me, even from a later
period.

[134] It is clear, however, that dogmatic corrections, except in the case of Mar-
cion, were not very frequent: cf. A. Bludau, Die Schriftfälschungen der Häre-
tiker, 1925; L. E. Wright, Alterations of the Words of Jesus as quoted in the
Literature of the Second Century, Cambridge, Mass., 1952; and in general:
M. A. Siotis, Αἱ δογματικαὶ παραλλαγαὶ τοῦ κειμένου τῆς καινῆς διαθήκης,
Athens, 1960.

[135] Elench. VI, 9–19. The particulars in these sections should not be lumped
together with the further details which Hippolytus takes over from Irenaeus,
Adv. haer. I, 23.

[136] Elench. VI, 9, 4; 10, 2; 18, 2.

[137] Elench. VI, 10, 1. 2; 14, 4. 6f.; 17, 5.

[138] Cf. esp. the striking parallel to I Pet. 1:24f. (Elench. VI, 10, 2), where,
after quoting Isa. 40:6f., the text reads: ῥῆμα δέ φησιν ἐστὶ κυρίου τὸ ἐν στόματι
γεννώμενον ῥῆμα καὶ λόγος, ἄλλη δὲ χωρίον γενέσεως οὐκ εστι. The statement in VI, 19, 7, repeated from Irenaeus, Adv. haer. I, 23, 3, that the prophets were inspired only 'a mundi fabricatoribus angelis' (cf. Tertullian, De
anima 57, 7), can therefore hardly be correct.

[139] The examples cited, however, do not completely justify Hippolytus'
indignation (Elench. VI, 9, 3; 19, 1), inasmuch as they do not really put the

contrast, references to the Gospel texts are extremely scanty and unemphasised.[140] These belong, one might say, to the wider group of sacred and edifying writings in general. Of a New Testament canon, therefore, there is not the least indication.

The *Book of Baruch* by the gnostic Justin[141] displays similar pretensions to those of the 'Great Apophasis'. The readers are bound by an oath to observe the strictest secrecy as to its teachings.[142] This voluminous work enjoyed especial prestige in the circle of its adherents; but there were several other books, professing to reveal mysteries, associated with it,[143] which therefore certainly cannot as yet have been combined into a new 'canon'. In contrast to the Simonian work, which was almost completely 'Jewish' in its appeal, there is here an extensive development of syncretistic mythology which, indeed severely shakes the authority of the Old Testament Scripture,[144] though this is still quoted.[145] Hosea, it is asserted, could not prevail with his message against the evil of the Naash (serpent),[146] and 'all the prophets' who came before Jesus failed in their mission.[147] Jesus was a son of Joseph and Mary, and kept the lambs at Nazareth, when at the age of twelve he was called by Baruch.[148] He overcame the temptations of the Naash, and underwent crucifixion as a means of separating his higher from his lower substance.[149] These phantasies are also linked with ancient myths, and incorporate Omphale, Aphrodite, Heracles, Leda, and Ganymede into their 'allegorical' interpretation of the universe. It is naturally difficult to say what Gospel 'sources' may have been used. Certain points of

---

heathen writers on the same level as the Scripture. The words of Plato, Aristotle (VI, 9, 6) and Empedocles (VI, 11) serve only as parallels, and to elucidate certain abstract ideas; and the quotation from Homer (VI, 15, 4) is meant to endorse what the Bible has to say as a universal truth κατὰ τοὺς ποιητάς.

[140] There is one quotation from the synoptic account of the Baptism of Jesus (Elench. VI, 16, 6 = Matt. 3:10/Lk. 3:9), and one further echo of the same passage (VI, 9, 10 = Matt. 3:12/Lk. 3:17). It is possible that Luke was the writer's source; but unfortunately the mention of the 'lost sheep' (VI, 19, 2 = Lk. 15:6) appears in the final, unreliable chapter of the account, and does not permit of any certain conclusions. This theme, variously presented, enjoys great popularity in other gnostic writers: Zahn, *op. cit.* I, p. 740; cf. further the so-called Gospel of Truth 31f.

[141] Hippolytus, Elench. V, 23–27; cf. E. Haenchen, 'Das Buch Baruch. Ein Beitrag zum Problem der christlichen Gnosis', *ZTK* 50, 1953, pp. 123–158 = *Gott und Mensch* (Ges. Aufs.), 1965, pp. 299–334.

[142] Elench. V, 27, 1; cf. 24, 1; 26, 6.

[143] Elench. V, 27, 5; cf. 24, 2.

[144] Cf. the reply to the speech of 'Elohim', Elench. V, 26, 15f.

[145] Once again, of course, in its allegorical significance, as Moses himself had intended for the purposes of secrecy: Elench. V, 26, 6.

[146] Elench. V, 27, 4.   [147] Elench. V, 26, 29.

[148] Elench. V, 26, 29.   [149] Elench. V, 26, 31f.

agreement with Luke and John appear to be not entirely coincidental.[150] But naturally they imply nothing as to the existence of a New Testament 'canon'.[151]

Among the Naassenians, on the other hand, the Fourth Gospel is clearly a favoured text, in addition to Matthew; and Luke and Mark are also familiar.[152] This may point to a later period, when the catholic Four Gospel canon was perhaps already in existence or in process of formation. But the sectaries are far from confining themselves to these four. Hippolytus complains that they were much more prone to base their scriptural proofs on their own, secret writings; and in this connection he names the Gospel of the Egyptians,[153] and on another occasion a Gospel according to Thomas.[154] Moreover, their enthusiasm for quotation is not limited to Christian texts.[155] Ancient philosophers and poets, heathen myths and mysteries, are continuously cited. The constant interweaving of the various pieces of evidence, among which the Old Testament is included, shows that this syncretistic, allegorising *mélange* of all mythologies and religions is a matter of deliberate theological intent. The gnostic revelation both uncovers all secret sources of truth and itself transcends them all. It draws on every religious document and every 'canon'; but precisely for this reason it is logically impossible that it should ever establish its own, ultimate canon.

The 'great' gnostics prior to and contemporary with Marcion come markedly closer to the 'catholic' tradition. Significant of this tendency are the collections of the words and parables of Jesus, such as we find in the Gospel of Thomas.[156] 'The synoptic material serves as a basis, in

---

[150] The agreement with Luke in the rough indication of time, ἐν ταῖς ἡμέραις Ἡρώδου τοῦ βασιλέως (Elench. V, 26, 29), the detail of Jesus being twelve years old, and the location in Nazareth, do not seem to me, as against Haenchen, *op. cit.*, p. 134 (= 310) n. 11, of great importance; but V, 26, 32, clearly recalls Lk. 23:46. The saying about the prophets has a 'Johannine' ring (cf. Joh. 10:8), and there is some connection between V, 26, 32 and Joh. 19:26.

[151] Haenchen, *op. cit.*, p. 139 (= 315) takes a different view: 'This use of scripture may be interpreted as evidence for a canon such as must *de facto* have been in existence in the middle of the second century. It is possible that Justin was also familiar with extra-canonical writings' (!). In my opinion these are baseless assumptions. The most that the texts prove is that Luke, John, and the Pauline Epistles may also have been read in gnostic sects 'in the middle of the second century'—which did not need to be proved.

[152] Hippolytus, Elench. V, 6–8. The texts (e.g., 7, 26) are contaminated in a way that makes exact attribution difficult. The citation of Joh. 3:6 in 7, 40 is actually introduced as a 'quotation from scripture': τοῦτ᾽ ἔστι ... τὸ γεγραμμένον.

[153] Elench. V, 7, 8f.   [154] Elench. V, 7, 20.

[155] On Paul cf. pp. 143ff. below.

[156] This on the assumption that the Gospel of Thomas is also more or less gnostic in character. According to G. Quispel, 'Das Thomasevangelium und das Alte Testament', in: *Neotestamentica et Patristica* (Cullmann-Festschrift), 1962, pp. 243–248, and, *Makarius, das Thomasevangelium und das Lied von der*

fact, so to speak, as a canonical text, of which the gnostic sayings or additions are the exegesis.'[157] Of Basilides it is alleged that he wrote a Gospel of his own, and then a commentary on it in twenty-four books.[158] Unfortunately, on the scanty evidence available we can form no definite idea of its character.[159] Possibly it borrowed from various Gospels, not only from those which were later classed as 'canonical', but also 'apocryphal' ones such as the 'Words of the Lord according to Matthias'.[160] It would appear that the Gospel of Basilides remained in use for a long time among his followers.[161] Yet this did not rule out the use of other Gospels alongside it.[162] The voluminous exegesis by the master is reminiscent of Papias. Yet it would be naïve and fallacious to argue from this to the 'canonisation' of this Gospel; for then, the 'Prophet Parchor', who was expounded by Basilides' son, Isidore,[163] perhaps

---

Perle, 1967, pp. 65–113, however, it is Jewish Christian and Encratite in character, and made use of none of the canonical Gospels; cf. p. 80 n. 103 above.

[157] A. Adam, *Gnomon* 34, 1962, p. 360, on the *Gospel of Thomas* in a review of the edition by Guillaumont, Puech, and Quispel, Leiden, 1959; similarly H. C. Kee, ' "Becoming a child" in the Gospel of Thomas', *JBL* 82, 1963, p. 314.

[158] Agrippa Castor in Eusebius, *HE* IV, 7, 7.

[159] In particular, we do not know how far it made use of the earlier Gospels. Hippolytus, Elench. VII, 27, 5 ascribes to Basilides a citation of Joh. 2:4 and Matt. 2:1f. (but cf. n. 162 below), Epiphanius, Panar. XXIV, 5, 2, one of Matt. 7:6. In any case, according to *Act. Arch.* 67, 5, it apparently contained the story of the Rich Man and Lazarus (Lk. 16:19ff.), but also made use of the Matthaean 'eunuch'-saying (Matt. 19:12) in a variant or edited version: Clem. Alex., Strom. III, 1; cf. Bludau, *op. cit.*, pp. 22ff. This information does not allow of such definite conclusions as are often drawn from it. W. Sanday, *The Gospels in the Second Century*, 1876, pp. 188–196; 298–301, envisaged considerable points of contact with all four canonical Gospels; Zahn, *op. cit.* I, pp. 763ff., in his study on 'Basilides und die kirchliche Bibel', thought in terms of a collation 'from the Gospels of Matthew and Luke, and probably also of John' (p. 773). H. Windisch, 'Das Evangelium des Basilides', *ZNW* 7, 1906, pp. 236–246, considered that Basilides' Gospel was a new edition of Luke, while F. M. Braun, *Jean le Théologien et son évangile dans l'église ancienne*, Paris, 1959, p. 106, sees it as a compilation from the four canonical Gospels and other, legendary elements—something on the lines of the 'Unknown Gospel'. Further, more or less barren hypotheses are listed by H. C. Puech, in *N.T. Apocrypha* I, pp. 257f. He himself regards the use of Matthew and Luke as probable, but at the same time emphasises the uncertainty of all these conjectures.

[160] Hippolytus, Elench. VII, 20, 1. Cf. also the fantastic details about Simon of Cyrene in Irenaeus, Adv. haer. I, 24, 4, which call to mind the biographical notices in Papias.

[161] In all probability it was at first, as Agrippa Castor says (cf. n. 158 above), referred to by them simply as 'the Gospel'. The designation κατὰ Βασιλείδην εὐαγγέλιον (Origen, Hom. Luc. 1:1: Rauer², p. 5, 3) may not originally have been attached to it.

[162] This follows from the account in Hippolytus, who explicitly refers to several Gospels (Elench. VII, 22, 4).

[163] Clem. Alex., Strom. VI, 53, 2. The reference may be to a pseudiepigraph of the deacon Prochorus, mentioned in Acts 6:5.

also the 'Prophecy of Ham', designated by him as a source of Greek philosophy,[164] or 'Barcoph and Barcabbas', must all have belonged to the Basilidean 'canon'.[165] All these 'apocryphal' texts reflect only the general gnostic delight in secret revelations and ancient traditions, which they interpret, allegorise and expound in the spirit of their own theology. Isidore again made use of heathen authors, and for the first time had recourse to the well-known Jewish theory of Greek plagiarism.[166] (This gave him a right to discover secret truths even in these writers, and was thus less polemically than apologetically intended, in order to defend the utilisation of such sources against the scruples of a stricter 'Christian' feeling.)[167]

Valentinus too is supposed to have written his own 'Gospel of Truth'.[168] But this piece of information is very doubtful. Even if the document of the same name, discovered at Nag Hammadi, is the one meant, there must certainly be a misunderstanding somewhere.[169] This is no Gospel, in the literary sense of the term, but an enthusiastic discourse or meditation on the basic ideas of the Valentinian doctrine of redemption. Its date of origin is still uncertain,[170] and for this reason it is difficult to make much use of the text for the purposes of a history of the Canon.[171] It is true, however, that at a later period the Valen-

[164] Clem. Alex., Strom. VI, 53, 5; cf. Rec. Clem. IV, 27.

[165] Barcoph and Barcabbas are, however, certainly thought of as sons of Noah, and their revelations—like those of the 'Prophecy of Ham'—would have belonged rather to the Old than in a 'New' Testament: R. Liechtenhan, *Die Offenbarung im Gnosticismus*, 1901, pp. 20ff.

[166] Clem. Alex., Strom. VI, 53, 3f.

[167] The customary exploitation of the proof from antiquity seems to be present in the Valentinian, Julius Cassianus: Clem. Alex., Strom. I, 101, 2. On the other hand, Valentinus himself plainly interpreted the supposed agreements between Christian and heathen authors in the light of Rom. 2:15 as a natural theology proceeding from the common source of the human heart: Strom. VI, 52, 4; cf. Zahn, *op. cit.* II, pp. 953ff.

[168] Irenaeus, Adv. haer. III, 11, 9.

[169] Cf. p. 197 below.

[170] In common with H. Ringgren, 'The Gospel of Truth and the Valentinian Gnosticism', *StudTheol* 18, 1964, pp. 51–65, I consider the general Valentinian character of the text indisputable; on the other hand, there is nothing to prove either the alleged authorship of Valentinus himself or a pre-Marcionite origin for the work, and in my view both these are less probable.

[171] What is more, its supposed allusions to N.T. texts are not remotely so clear as is often alleged. It is possible to be reasonably certain that the author was acquainted with Luke or Matthew, with John and the Apocalypse, and certainly with some Epistles of Paul; further points of contact are possible, but could equally well be the result of coincidence or of mediation through other works. I can accept neither the methods nor the results of those who are prepared to go further than this, sometimes with great dogmatism. This applies above all to W. C. van Unnik, 'The "Gospel of Truth" and the New Testament' in: F. L. Cross (ed.), *The Jung Codex*, London, 1955, pp. 79–129,

tinians used all the Gospels of the Great Church.[172] The Gospel of John, on which Heracleon, in fact, wrote a 'Commentary',[173] enjoyed especial popularity.[174] But their basic principle, to accord the words of Jesus alone supreme, unquestionable authority,[175] rather entailed a critical approach to the canonisation of the Gospels as such, and was more sympathetic to the earlier form of a sayings-tradition than to an

---

and K. H. Schelkle, 'Das Evangelium Veritatis als kanongeschichtliches Zeugnis', *BZ* N.F. 5, 1961, pp. 90f. (These two writers have been followed, largely without reservations, by R. M. Grant, *Gnosticism and Early Christianity*, 1959, p. 129; Hanson, *op. cit.*, pp. 189f., and L. W. Barnard, 'The Epistle ad Diognetum, two Units from one Author?' *ZNW* 56, 1965, p. 137.) Any echo, even the most modest, of a 'New Testament' work is taken as a sure sign that that work was known and used; what is still missing is then explained as the result of chance; and it is then stated categorically that the later catholic canon was 'in substance' (Schelkle, *op. cit.*, p. 91) already present in its entirety in Valentinus in the pre-Marcionite period—indeed, that his canon was 'absolutely identical' with that of Tertullian (Van Unnik, *op. cit.*, p. 123). Van Unnik is even prepared to go so far as to say (p. 122) that the N.T. writings which the text never mentions by name or cites verbatim can, nevertheless, be seen, from the way in which they are treated, to have already possessed canonical authority for Valentinus. The editors of the Evangelium Veritatis, M. Malinine, H. Ch. Puech, and G. Quispel (Zurich, 1956), also refer (p. xiv) to the importance of the text for the history of the Canon, but express themselves with more caution, and emphasise the uncertainty of the dating: 'Furthermore, if the date attributed to the redaction is exact, then the Gospel of Truth, which appeals so frequently to scripture, and refers notably to the Apocalypse of John and the Epistle to the Hebrews, constitutes a document of the first importance for the history of the N.T. Canon.'

More important, it seems to me, is what can be deduced from the Epistle to Rheginos, which in fact must have been written by Valentinus. Here (XXIV^v 6–10), in the context of an explicit emphasis on the 'Gospel' as something 'read', we find a reference to the Transfiguration story: 'For you remember from your reading in the Gospel that Elias appeared and Moses with him . . .' (cf. Pennard, *Epistle to Rheginos*, 1970, ad loc.). Unfortunately it cannot be determined which gospel is here meant. That the precise formulation is rather more akin to Mark (9:4: Ἠλίας σὺν Μωϋσεῖ) than to Matthew (17:3) and Luke (9:30: Μωϋσῆς καὶ Ἠλίας) tells us nothing. It is clear that apocryphal gospel texts are used in the Epistle, as well as the Gospel of John: cf. Quispel and Puech, in: *De resurrectione (epistula ad Rheginum)*, (ed.) Malinine, Puech, Quispel, and Till, 1963, pp. xxxff., and the notes on the passage in question, p. 38.

[172] This can be demonstrated for Matthew and John from the Letter to Flora, of Ptolemaeus, and is confirmed in general by Irenaeus, Adv. haer. III, 12, 12, and Tertullian, Praescr. 38, 8 (Valentinus integro instrumento uti videtur). On the other hand, the echoes of Matthew which Massaux, *op. cit.*, pp. 425f., thinks to find in Valentinus himself are extremely indefinite.

[173] The fragments preserved by Clement and Origen will be found in W. Völker, *Quellen zur Geschichte der christlichen Gnosis*, 1932, pp. 63ff.

[174] Cf. W. von Loewenich, *Das Johannes-Verständnis im zweiten Jahrhundert*, 1932, pp. 74ff.; M. F. Wiles, *The Spiritual Gospel: The Interpretation of the Fourth Gospel in the Early Church*, 1960, pp. 96–111.

[175] Cf. pp. 81f. above.

ascription of normative status to particular 'apostolic' accounts.[176]

The examples from gnosticism which we have quoted contain no direct statements about the importance of the old tradition or of the Gospel literature. It is clear, nevertheless, that these were handled with even greater freedom than was customary in the 'catholic' camp. But even in the latter circles men did not always shrink from simply inventing Jesus-sayings. This is proved by the orthodox work, 'Conversations of Jesus with his Disciples after the Resurrection', whether this is dated in the period before or, as is more probably correct, after Marcion.[177] The same picture is presented by the Apocalypse of Peter, which to begin with borrows well-known sayings from the Gospels, but then gives an entirely fresh version of the Transfiguration story, to suit its own taste.[178] In general, the catholic church may have been stricter in the selection of her texts than the majority of 'heretical' groups; but basically the picture is the same on either side: the sayings of Jesus and the tradition about Jesus are in themselves authoritative, and they are continuously expanded at discretion from a variety of sources, including oral ones, in accordance with tradition or current requirements. Among written sources the 'canonical' Gospels, or at any rate Matthew, have by now attained a certain ascendancy;[179] but we can hardly be more precise than that. All that can be said without fear of contradiction is that in fact not the slightest trace has survived to suggest that these four 'canonical' Gospels already possessed special status, as is often alleged, and were formally grouped together. All speculations about the emergence of a Four-Gospel canon, whether in Asia Minor or in Rome, prior to the time of Marcion, are without foundation, and rest simply on the arbitrary retrojection on to this period of an anachronistic idea. This is shown by the fact that the provenance of such 'quotations' as can be identified follows no clear pattern and is constantly changing, by the vague way in which they are introduced, and by the only direct statements on the subject which we have from the early period, namely

[176] It is well known that the 'Sayings-Gospel' form persisted chiefly within gnosticism. But this is due primarily to a lack of interest in history and to a one-sided preference for the revelation discourse not to a predilection for the archaic form as such.

[177] Cf. M. Hornschuh, *Studien zur Epistula Apostolorum*, 1965, pp. 9ff. ('Die Stellung zur evangelischen Tradition und zu den kanonischen Büchern des Neuen Testaments'), who argues against the traditional ascription of an early date, not least on grounds connected with the history of the Canon (p. 116); cf. p. 217 n. 38 below. Doubts of the 'orthodoxy' of the Epistula Apostolorum, regarding it as 'Jewish Christian', do not seem to me to have been made out by A. Ehrhardt, 'Judaeo-Christians in Egypt, the Epistula Apostolorum and the Gospel to the Hebrews', *StudEvang* III, 1964, pp. 371ff.

[178] Apoc. Pet. 15 (Eth.). By contrast, 4 (Eth.) gives a quotation from the ancient 'scriptures' (Ezek. 37:4ff.) as such and completely correctly.

[179] Cf. n. 98 above.

those of Luke and Papias. Against this we have nothing to set save a traditional prejudice, supported by great names, and, so it would seem, ineradicable by reason or evidence.[180]

Hitherto we have confined ourselves to the Jesus-tradition and the Gospel literature. This complex forms the starting-point of 'canonical' development, and will later constitute the first centre of gravity of the 'New Testament'. But from the time of Marcion—and that means, already in the oldest 'New Testament' known to us—the Gospel is linked with an 'apostolic' element, the letters of the Apostle Paul. This section too has its pre-history in the period before the Canon. To conclude the present chapter, therefore, we shall examine the position which the Pauline Epistles won for themselves in the earliest days of the Church. It is a commanding one, unique in fact, and was not simply the work of Marcion—a point which is not always sufficiently noted. Almost all the New Testament Epistles which are definitely pre-Marcionite bear the name of Paul, or are clearly dependent on his model.[181] The only exceptions are I Peter and I John,[182] but, as regards the respect in which they are held, both are far inferior to the Pauline letters, and indeed in comparison with them hardly receive any attention at all. Papias is said to have cited them;[183] but even Irenaeus, who is acquainted with both, nevertheless makes no use of them when he is concerned to give reliable examples of the teaching of the apostles.[184] Paul is 'the Apostle' *par excellence*—that is how he is referred to throughout the second century.[185] It is clear that his Letters were collected at an early stage,[186] and were soon well known everywhere. That they were

---

[180] On this point cf. further pp. 171ff. below.

[181] This is true, however the question of genuineness is answered, in the case of Ephesians, Colossians, and II Thessalonians. Hebrews, too, in my opinion is meant to be taken as a Pauline letter. The Pastorals (and, of course, 'III Corinthians' also) are, like II Peter, in my opinion post-Marcionite. James, which is dependent on Jewish models, may date from the beginning of the second century, but is not attested by Origen, and in form can hardly be considered an Epistle at all.

[182] The former, however, as is well known, stands completely within the Pauline tradition.

[183] Eusebius, *HE* III, 39, 17: κέχρηται δ' ὁ αὐτὸς μαρτυρίαις ἀπὸ τῆς 'Ιωάννου προτέρας ἐπιστολῆς καὶ ἀπὸ τῆς Πέτρου ὁμοίως. Cf. Jülicher-Fascher, *op. cit.*, p. 477: In such cases 'it need not exactly be a case of formal references, as to sacred scriptures; in his interesting statistics Eusebius does not distinguish between use and genuine citation.'

[184] Cf. p. 194 below.   [185] Cf. p. 212 below.

[186] More precise than this we cannot be. The daring hypotheses of W. Schmithals, 'Zur Abfassung und ältesten Sammlung der paulinischen Hauptbriefe', *ZNW* 51, 1960, pp. 225–245, are unfortunately completely unprovable; cf. in reply, e.g., N. A. Dahl, 'Welche Ordnung der Paulusbriefe wird vom muratorischen Kanon vorausgesetzt?' *ZNW* 52, 1961, p. 50 n., and 'The Particularity of the Pauline Epistles as a Problem in the Ancient Church' in: *Neo-*

also read liturgically is probable. 'Take up the epistle of the blessed Paul the Apostle', we read in I Clement. 'What wrote he first to you in the beginning of his Gospel?'—the reference is to I Corinthians.[187] And in the letter which Ignatius of Antioch sends to the Pauline church at Ephesus he explicitly refers to the supremely high example which Paul left behind.[188] In the letter to Rome Peter's name, it is true, is coupled with Paul's, but not as an author.[189] Paul remains the only New Testament 'author' who is mentioned and quoted as such.

Around the middle of the second century there was a falling-off in esteem for Paul in orthodox circles. This is connected with the fact that he was held in such high regard by the heretics and especially by Marcion, and was treated by them virtually as one of themselves.[190] It may be doubted whether the quotation of I Cor. 11:32 in the 'Great Apophasis' in fact derives from the Epistle direct;[191] but the Book of Baruch plainly knows and uses the great Pauline letters.[192] The Naassenians too base their secret doctrines on Pauline texts.[193] Basilides,

---

testamentica et Patristica (Cullmann-Festschrift), 1962, pp. 261–271; Bauer, *Orthodoxy*, pp. 220ff.; and the survey by C. F. D. Moule, *The Birth of the N.T.*, 1962, pp. 199–206.

[187] I Clem. 47, 1f. There is no need to discuss here the further questions raised by this strange expression. It is possible that I and II Corinthians are here treated as a unity.

[188] Eph. 12, 2: ... Παύλου συμμύσται, τοῦ ἡγιασμένου, τοῦ μεμαρτυρημένου, ἀξιομακαρίστου, οὗ γένοιτό μοι ὑπὸ τὰ ἴχνη εὑρεθῆναι, ὅταν θεοῦ ἐπιτύχω, ὃς ἐν πάσῃ ἐπιστολῇ μνημονεύει ὑμῶν. The final statement is manifestly false, and is to be regarded, with W. Bauer, *Die Briefe des Ignatius von Antiochia und der Polykarperbrief* (HNT supp. vol. II), 1920, p. 212, as 'an exaggeration which in Ignatius is at least surprising'; cf. the similarly boastful exaggeration of the anti-Montanist Apollonius in Eusebius, *HE* V, 18, 4: δοκεῖ σοι πᾶσα γραφὴ κωλύειν προφήτην λαμβάνειν δῶρα καὶ χρήματα. Ignatius' exuberant remark certainly does not justify the conclusion drawn by W. Schneemelcher, 'Paulus in der griechischen Kirche des zweiten Jahrhunderts', *ZKG* 75, 1964, pp. 5f., that ïgnatius had 'very little knowledge of the Pauline Epistles', and indeed possibly may have 'known or read none of them'. Another question is, of course, how many Epistles and which ones were in fact familiar to him; the use of I Corinthians, at any rate, appears 'quite certain' (so Bauer, *Orthodoxy*, pp. 217f.). H. Rathke, *Ignatius von Antiochien und die Paulubriefe*, 1967, pp. 21f., connects the text with the 'Pauline' Ephesians (1:15ff.), and rightly concludes that 'Ignatius knew several Pauline letters'. More problematic are the 'clear quotations' and 'briefer echoes' discussed pp. 28–39.

[189] Ignatius, Rom. 4, 3; cf. H. Lietzmann, 'Petrus, römischer Märtyrer' (1936) = *Kleine Schriften* I, 1958, p. 112; O. Cullmann, *Peter: Disciple, Apostle, Martyr*, 1962, pp. 110ff.

[190] Cf. pp. 176ff. below.

[191] Hippolytus, Elench. VI, 14, 6. The same phrase occurs in the writings of the Peratae (Elench. V, 12, 7).

[192] Hippolytus, Elench. V, 24, 1; 26, 16 (I Cor. 2:9?); 26, 23 (II Cor. 11:30; 26, 25 (Gal. 5:17; cf. 26, 27: ἀκροβυστία).

[193] Cf. esp. Hippolytus, Elench. V, 7, 19.

who likes to appeal to 'the Apostle',[194] develops his discussion about eating meat offered to idols.[195] The Epistle 'de Resurrectione' to Rheginos, of which Valentinus may be the author, is based on the chapter about the resurrection in I Corinthians.[196] It is precisely the teaching about resurrection which illustrates very clearly why Valentinian gnosis was able to claim the Apostle as an ally. In contrast to 'orthodox' theology, which still, in an almost Jewish manner, had no real function for resurrection and judgment save that of acting as an inducement and a threat, Valentinian theologians were concerned with spiritual resurrection as a present reality, with faith and freedom, in a way which, though admittedly one-sided, did nevertheless preserve Pauline ideas in a living and effective form. The Church had herself first to rediscover Paul, before she could overcome gnostic Paulinism.[197]

Nevertheless, we cannot speak of a 'canon' of Pauline Epistles even in gnosticism, before Marcion. For the concept of a canon to exist, there must first be the concept of a canonical Gospel, and this, as we have seen, was even more remote from gnosticism than from the great Church.[198] Even the apocalyptic writings nowhere form a new 'canon',

[194] Clem. Alex., Strom. III, 2, 1; Origen, Comm. Rom. V, 1 (Lommatzsch VI, 336f.); cf. H. Langerbeck, *Aufsätze zur Gnosis*, 1967, pp. 56, 64, 80.

[195] Irenaeus, Adv. haer. I, 24, 5. Despite E. C. Blackman, *Marcion and his Influence*, 1948, p. 30, it is not safe to assume on the basis of Hippolytus' account that Basilides cited Paul as γραφή in the sense of 'sacred scripture': cf. Zahn, *op. cit.*, I, p. 765 n. 4.

[196] 'As the Apostle said' (45, 24f.)—though this is followed by a heavily contaminated quotation; cf. Quispel-Puech in the Introduction to the edition cited n. 171 above, pp. xiii, xxxi. It is well known that the Valentinian tradition about Theudas was believed to derive from Paul himself: Clem. Alex., Strom. VII, 106, 4. The Valentinian Ptolemaeus used Pauline texts to support his doctrine of aeons: Irenaeus, Adv. haer. I, 3, 1.4; 8, 5; for further examples cf. Zahn, *op. cit.* I, pp. 751ff. According to Langerbeck, *op. cit.*, pp. 81, 141, 167, and passim, Valentinianism and the great gnostic schools were all in essence the product of the encounter between Paulinism and Platonism.

[197] This was first done by Irenaeus, and then, in a different way linked with gnostic traditions, by Clement.

[198] It may, of course, be argued that the unequivocally literary character of the Pauline deposit made him from the start a better candidate for 'canonicity' than the originally fluid tradition about Jesus, which basically was tied to a single document. Nevertheless, it is hardly possible to say, with Hanson, *op. cit.*, pp. 195f., simply: 'We are not therefore justified in saying that the four gospels were the earliest part of the New Testament to receive recognition as canonical. A better case could be made for assuming that a collection of St. Paul's epistles was the first part of the canon of the New Testament to circulate as a collection of documents with special authority.' The collection of the Pauline Epistles remains, as A. Vögtle, *Das Neue Testament und die neuere katholische Exegese* I, 1966, p. 16, strikingly expresses it: 'a corpus Paulinum—non canonicum.' The possibility of a Pauline canon in heretical communities is also discussed by Knox, *op. cit.*, pp. 26f.

for all that a high value is set on their special, pneumatic authority.[199] It is not by chance that the whole idea of a new canon to complement the ancient 'scripture' is missing from the sources; and we have no right to supply it. To ask whether this or that writing or group of writings enjoyed canonical status is wholly premature. The power and trustworthiness of the living tradition are still the dominant factors; and the literary documents of the early period, though certainly effective and important in their preservative and regulatory function, remain nevertheless an almost invisible and anonymous element in the spiritual life of the Church. Within the totality of a received tradition which is taken for granted, believed in, and supported, and which makes itself felt with direct authority, they still have no unique status of their own.

[199] Cf. pp. 214ff. below.

CHAPTER FIVE

The Emergence of the New Testament

THE COMMON feature characterising the whole epoch which we have just reviewed is the lack of any formal authentication of the tradition which derives from and witnesses to Christ, in short, the lack of a New Testament. To this extent the pre-Marcionite church still belongs to the era of 'primitive Christianity'. Her Bible is the Old Testament, which apparently suffices her for the demonstration and confirmation of her faith. The Christian knows, and imagines that he always will know, Christ himself exactly as he was known and attested by the first disciples. Indeed, it seems obvious that this must be so; for the word of the old apostles, prophets and fathers of the Church still lives on, mediated by the Spirit. What is taught, preached, and believed in the congregation is therefore accepted without question as authentic and original, even when, as occasion demands, it is expounded, amplified, abbreviated or supplemented.[1] There is no sense of any break between the present and the early period; and where 'alien' teachings occur, they are decisively rejected—at first only with a reference to the moral deficiencies of the false teachers,[2] but later with a demonstration of the dangerous character of their views, which do not accord with earlier exegesis of the Lord's words.[3] But there is something chancy and imprecise about such refutations; they appeal simply to what is familiar, what has always been known. Christians just 'know' the original truth; no one refers in support of it to texts and documents, regarded as an acknowledged and established norm.

It is certainly true that this state of unreflecting confidence in one's own stock of religious beliefs could not last for ever; and it may be thought strange that it persisted as long as it did. But this does not give us the right to correct and reconstruct the actual course of development

---

[1] A paradigm case is what I Clement has to say about the appointment of officials by the apostles: I Clem. 44; for this an O.T. but not an N.T. 'scriptural proof' is provided: 42, 5. Cf. pp. 66f. above.

[2] Matt. 7:15ff.; Acts 20:29–35; Did. 11, 8–10; Herm. 43 (Mand. XI); I Tim. 6:3ff.; II Tim. 3:1ff.; Tit 1:10ff.; yet even at this stage there is some indication of contrasts in the content of doctrine, e.g., I Tim. 4:1–5; Tit. 3:9.

[3] This stage is reached in I John, Ignatius, and indeed in Papias as well (cf. pp. 134f. above.).

to suit our own impatient fancy. What is decisive is the witness of the extant sources, not the conjectural extrapolations we may like to make from them. And their witness is unambiguous. But if in the two preceding chapters we have shown that the idea of a normative Christian canon, of a new collection of writings, or 'scripture', is as yet nowhere to be found, we must now explain why it was that this idea came into existence at one stroke with Marcion and only with Marcion, and, what is more, why all its logical implications were there from the start in his presentation. The way in which the Church reacted to this development by creating a New Testament makes the proof complete. From every side we converge on the same result: the idea and the reality of a Christian Bible were the work of Marcion, and the Church which rejected his work, so far from being ahead of him in this field, from a formal point of view simply followed his example.[4]

Because of the unequivocal way in which Marcion worked out his position, and the great effect he achieved, we constantly forget that we know absolutely nothing directly—that is, nothing which is drawn from any source other than the perspicuity of his teaching and work—about the personal assumptions, character, and development of the man himself. These have, it is true, not been completely obliterated, though they do come to us only through the reports of embittered opponents. But if there is one fundamental objection to be made to Harnack's classic presentation it is this, that he all too quickly changes the dogmatic phenomenon that is Marcion into the picture of a particular man, and interprets it as a psychological expression of his personality and beliefs. In this respect the very silence of the material must indicate a quite definite and deliberate self-discipline on Marcion's part. Probably, with his strongly emphasised doctrine of two gods, his dogmatism, and his harsh asceticism, he was more deeply involved in the trends and passions of his time and of his teachers than we today realise.[5] But there is no need to go into these questions. Whatever the facts, the first Christian canon remains his peculiar and unique creation, one in which neither churchman nor gnostic anticipated him. Marcion made it the foundation of his mission and of his church, and the latter followed him with unswerving loyalty in observing it. In quite a new sense Marcion's whole preaching was consciously 'New Testament' biblical theology, that is, it is based exclusively on the canon which he drew up. This was no by-product of his theological endeavours but their normative and most important result. In this section we shall follow

[4] The main features of the view of Marcion developed here have already been outlined in my essay, 'Marcion et les origines du Canon Néotestamentaire', *RHPR* 1966, pp. 213–226.

[5] Cf. U. Bianchi, 'Marcion: Théologien biblique ou docteur gnostique?' *VC* 21, 1967, pp. 141–142.

Harnack's study, though on certain points of detail, and in general with regard to Marcion's place in the history of the Canon, it will be necessary to place the emphasis differently.[6] Questions of textual reconstruction, which are always debatable ground, and the complex problems of the original versions and text-historical effects of Marcion's bible fortunately need not occupy us here.[7]

The stimulus to set up the new canon did not come to Marcion from an analysis of what the uncertain state of Church tradition in general might suggest or require, much less from any neutral, scientific examination of its elements, but was theologically conditioned. It followed from the conflict in which Marcion's fundamental conviction found itself with the whole Christian preaching to date, and from the uncompromising determination with which he took up the fight and waged it to the end. Marcion is simultaneously an antinomian and an ascetic who despises the world. His Christianity is polemical. The 'Gospel', which he passionately espouses, of the pure goodness and mercy of God stands, in his eyes, in a double, indissoluble opposition to 'this world'. There is, on the one hand, an opposition to everything which may be called 'law' or legalistic righteousness, and, on the other, the surrender of all earthly blessings and desires which can fetter Man to the world and keep him there. To the extent that Marcion experiences the Gospel once more in its true nature as the redemption of the lost, his theology is primitive Christian in the spirit of Jesus; and in his understanding of faith as freedom from the Mosaic law he is directly akin to Paul. But the tension between law and faith, which dominates Paul's theology, has in Marcion become simple contradiction; and the redemption of those lost in the world becomes hatred toward the creation, toward all the gods at work 'in Nature',[8] and toward the cruelly-just Creator of this world himself. This God of the world is the God of the old cove-

[6] A. von Harnack, *Marcion: Das Evangelium vom fremden Gott. Eine Monographie zur Geschichte der Grundlegung der katholischen Kirche*[2], 1924 (referred to in this chapter simply as Harnack). In my opinion, Harnack unnecessarily weakened his position by the unfounded assumption that there was a Four-Gospel canon before Marcion. The refutation of this theory by J. Knox, *Marcion and the New Testament*, 1942, pp. 140–157, has rightly superseded Harnack on this point (Knox's remarks on this issue are independent of his more far-reaching hypothesis concerning the original form and post-Marcionite history of the Lukan work). The majority of scholars, however, seem still to prefer to follow Harnack, in that they continue to maintain that Marcion's bible did not evoke the establishment of the catholic N.T. but merely accelerated a development in this direction which had already begun.

[7] On these subjects cf. Harnack, pp. 149*ff., 183*ff., and, in addition to Knox, *op. cit.*, also E. C. Blackman, *Marcion and his Influence*, 1948, as well as those sections of general studies on the history of the N.T. text which relate to Luke and Paul.

[8] Εἰ οὖν τοῖς ἐν τῇ φύσει οὖσι θεοῖς δουλεύετε is Marcion's reading at Gal. 4:8: Harnack, p. 75*.

nant and of the Jewish 'scripture'. With him the Father of Jesus Christ has nothing in common and nothing to do. The latter is a strange and mysterious being, a God unknown to the world, and faith in the Gospel of Jesus therefore means absolute separation from the world and its ordinances. This attitude of moral and cosmic 'desecularisation' may be interpreted as a nihilistic 'radicalising' of tendencies common to all gnostics;[9] only it should not be overlooked that in fact no gnostic before Marcion ever went so far as he does. The implacable logic with which Marcion thought through his basic ideas to their conclusion, and the practical consequences which he deduced from them, explains a great deal of the power and enthusiasm of the movement founded by him. It is only in the light of this that its consequences for the history of the Canon are to be understood.

To some extent criticism of the Old Testament Bible had, as we have seen, already begun before Marcion's time.[10] Thus, not to mention lesser groups, the Valentinians had discerned in the Old Testament the voices of a variety of persons, aeons, and gods, whose revelation was to be not so much fulfilled as corrected and superseded by the coming of Christ. But just as they interpreted their own distinctive position vis-à-vis the ordinary believers of the Church not as one of opposition but as a higher, spiritual stage, so too they were able to arrange the words of Scripture and the powers that inspired them in a scale of importance, and thus to accord them still some degree of recognition and validity. A useful tool for this purpose, whenever it was necessary to overcome difficulties in the Biblical text in a meaningful manner, was the ambiguity of allegorical exegesis, as this was universally practised. By it words were reinterpreted, acquiring in the process a greater profundity and wisdom, now appreciated for the first time. No one was in the least interested in rejecting the ancient Scripture altogether. It was only Marcion for whom such compromises had at one stroke become impossible. He rejected allegory, typology, and the exegesis of the Old Testament in terms of 'mysteries', as impermissible and misleading, a camouflage of the real meaning.[11] In his eyes the biblical prophecies proclaimed a Messiah different from Jesus Christ, and the commandments contradicted what Jesus had taught his followers and required of them. If hitherto the Old Testament had been idealised and made spiritual in order to raise its meaning to the level of the dominant contemporary views, now with Marcion it was caricatured and made carnal and no less unhistorically demoted to the very lowest level in order to present

[9] So H. Jonas, The Gnostic Religion[2], 1963, pp. 137ff.; 320ff.; and similarly H. J. Schoeps, Aus frühchristlicher Zeit, 1950, pp. 255ff.
[10] Cf. pp. 73ff. above.
[11] Marcion, himself, however, 'allegorised' the parables of Jesus: R. M. Grant, The Letter and the Spirit, 1957, p. 65.

it as in its entirety a fitting document of that petty despotism which was the cruelly punitive and crudely this-worldly system of the Creator God. Though for the world and for the Jews the Old Testament might retain some relative validity, because it was after all the gift of God the creator and not simply of the Devil,[12] and though Marcion himself was not always completely rigorous in expunging the Old Testament allusions from his own bible,[13] yet as a standard of what Christians should believe and teach it was no longer of any account.

What this inevitably meant for the second-century Church it is now hardly possible to appreciate. She had lost her 'scriptures'; at one and the same moment her proud claims to be the religion of the most ancient wisdom and the religion of historical fulfilment were both rendered invalid. The 'archives' from which for so long she had confidently drawn the highest knowledge, and had refuted and convinced both Jews and heathen, were now to be burnt. The one sacred document of the Christian revelation was apparently the work of a different God; the foundation on which Christians had believed themselves to stand had sunk into the abyss.

Yet this was but one aspect of this monstrous revolution. The Christian message and doctrine, the living preaching by which men had hitherto lived with full assurance, were also to be rejected at Marcion's behest. This was an inescapable conclusion which he was bound to draw, and did draw. Not only was there the emphatic moralism of the Church, which had supplemented the commands of Jesus from the Old Testament, and thrust them into the foreground as the main element in the new way of life, but nowhere could one find a Christian gospel which had freed itself, as Marcion wished it to do, wholly from the Old Testament, 'the Law and the Prophets'. For him this meant that the true meaning and the original message of Jesus had not been preserved in their early purity, but had everywhere been falsified, distorted, and virtually turned upside down. It is the comprehensiveness of this condemnation, tolerating no exceptions, that makes Marcion's onslaught in fact something new, something to shake the very foundations. There had for a long time been false teachers, who changed the ancient truth, and 'mixed gall with honey'.[14] They had been countered by referring—in addition to the Old Testament—to the word of the early witnesses, and to the convictions which the Church had from the very beginning, as it was thought, retained and taught unaltered. For Marcion, this primary confidence in the Church's message had been destroyed. Even the first disciples had plainly not understood the Lord's words, and had unsuspectingly adulterated them with Jewish views

[12] Harnack, pp. 67, 113f., 116f.   [13] Harnack, pp. 66, 113ff.
[14] Papias in Irenaeus, Adv. haer. III, 17, 4.

which destroyed their meaning. The tradition of the Church, and her allegedly holy faith, had simply perpetuated this. All the more, therefore, was she undeserving of further belief. With the 'scripture' the tradition too had collapsed.[15] What was left to hold on to? That was the question with which Marcion now saw himself unavoidably confronted.

Many gnostics, when they were compelled to contradict the prevailing belief, had appealed to 'secret' traditions, which the Lord was supposed to have confided to individual, selected disciples in preference to the rest.[16] In the free composition, whether oral or written, of such 'revelations' in support of one's own opinion it was not usual to be over-scrupulous.[17] If Marcion had been a humbug or an enthusiast, as he was reckoned by his enemies, he might have taken this line. But he did not. Marcion was convinced that in constructing his doctrine he was not following his own inspirations and convictions but the authentic and original teaching of Jesus, which he had rediscovered, and which it was vital to proclaim in pure and undistorted form. That is to say: Marcion regarded himself neither as the founder of a religion nor as a prophet but as a reformer. He is the first, and for a long time was the only, Christian theologian to prove, from a formal viewpoint, an absolutely pure and thoroughgoing embodiment of this particular religio-historical type. It is in the light of this fact that the establishment of the new Canon is to be understood. In Marcion's eyes the Old Testament was finished, and no longer valid in any sense whatever. Everything turned on the Gospel—and this had been betrayed, and was no longer to be found in the contemporary Church. It was therefore necessary to retrace one's steps, not in search of traditions, which even in the most favourable circumstances were still dubious and unconfirmed, but of definite written documents, which might possibly have preserved the original truth safe through all error and confusion, and which could therefore teach and safeguard it still. If the truth was again to be held in honour, and to be more permanently effective in future, then there was only one way to achieve this: the ancient documents must once more be set upon the lampstand as the genuine and trustworthy witnesses to the message of Christ, and be exalted to the status of the normative rule, the 'Canon' of the Church. That is why Marcion's bible contains no new dogmatic, catechetical, or edifying texts of any

---

[15] It is therefore incorrect to regard Marcion's N.T. as simply a substitute formation for the existing O.T. Bible, on the grounds that a church without a 'scripture' is unthinkable (so, e.g., Harnack, *op. cit.* p. 135 n. 129 above). Instead, what made it imperative, was the radical rejection of the whole tradition, oral and written alike.

[16] Nevertheless, this preference for a Thomas or a John etc. never, as it does for Marcion, becomes absolute rejection of the other disciples.

[17] Cf. p. 142 above. Julius Africanus even falsified lines of Homer, if the need arose: W. Bauer, *Orthodoxy*, pp. 158–164.

sort, but exclusively ancient, traditional documents, which were merely edited in his own sense and purged of supposed distortions.

We must now turn to the composition of the Marcionite bible itself. This for our purposes is significant. As is well known, Marcion's bible is in two parts. After a single 'Gospel' it contains as its second section the 'Apostle', that is, a collection of ten exclusively Pauline letters. At first sight this is surprising. A similar 'canonical' arrangement, despite all statements to the contrary, is nowhere attested and nowhere attempted before Marcion.[18] We have become accustomed to this arrangement, and therefore easily overlook the fact that in itself there is nothing whatever obvious or inevitable about it. If there was any desire at all to supplement the Gospel, it would have been far more natural to associate with it one or more apocalypses, which at that time were already circulating. These would have matched the Gospels in content, since the latter themselves contained apocalyptic sections, and would have been commended by their lofty pretensions to revelatory character.[19] Or another choice might have been an early, 'apostolic' Church order; the Didache is in fact occasionally reckoned among New Testament writings in just this way.[20] Or again, one might think in terms of a collection of psalms or hymns, such as we find later in the Marcionite church itself.[21] But even if the decision had already been taken to use letters, yet those of Paul, being real letters, and therefore frequently fortuitous in content and very much the product of the immediate moment, were of their very nature by no means the most suitable.[22] In fact the strange construction of Marcion's Bible is explicable solely in terms of his dogmatic Paulinism.[23]

[18] This discovery of Harnack's has never been refuted, and becomes entirely convincing once his (essentially independent) assumption of a pre-Marcionite 'Four-Gospel' canon is abandoned: cf. n. 6 above.
[19] Cf. pp. 214ff. below.   [20] Cf. Zahn, *op. cit.*, I, pp. 360ff.
[21] Cf. the testimony of Maruta of Maipherkat in Harnack, pp. 363*f., and the latter's critical comments (pp. 175*f.); also the Muratorian canon, p. 247 n. 211 below.
[22] For this very reason, it would seem, attempts had been made before Marcion's time to edit and 'catholicise' them here and there in order to make them more suitable as edifying literature: N. A. Dahl, 'The particularity of the Pauline Epistles as a problem in the ancient church' in: *Neotestamentica et Patristica* (Cullmann-Festschrift), 1962, pp. 266ff. We shall not go into the difficult question, how far Marcion in his compilation of the 'Apostle' was determined by already existing collections and editions of Paul's letters: cf. p. 143n. 186 above. Certainly he placed Galatians at the beginning for dogmatic reasons; and he may have been the first to put it into circulation at all: cf. Bauer, *Orthodoxy*, pp. 221f.
[23] As against Knox, *op. cit.*, p. 31, I do not believe that an attempt to secure a similarity to the bipartite arrangement of the old Bible ('Law and Prophets') was a factor here. The correspondence is too superficial, and Marcion is the very last man to whom we should attribute a purely formal adherence to a rejected

There can be no doubt that Marcion—however much or little he took over from Cerdon or other gnostic teachers—was personally convinced that in Paul he had found the meaning and true content of the 'Gospel'. From Paul come both the concepts which he employs and, to a certain extent, the problems which he poses in his teaching, neither of which could he have found in the current Gospels with such precision and clarity. But the Pauline letters, as Marcion saw them, not only confirmed him in the positive rightness of his own teaching; with their sallies against the Judaisers they also explained how the great apostasy within the Church had been able to develop. Finally, they showed that Paul had a sacred right and duty to take a stand and to assert himself against all other apostles;[24] it was for this purpose that he had been 'chosen from the womb',[25] for this that he had received the Gospel 'not from men nor by the agency of men' but directly from Christ.[26] For this reason later Marcionites allotted Paul and not a representative of the feeble first apostles the place of honour in heaven at Christ's right hand, while Marcion, as the great Reformer, received the place on the left.[27] In Marcionite thinking Paul's status is that of an essential figure in salvation-history in the strict sense.[28] For them he alone is *the* apostle and *the* evangelist of Christ.[29] 'Paul alone knew the truth;

---

model. So far as I know, Pelagius was the first to explain the structure of the N.T. in terms of the pattern of the Old: argumentum omnium epistolarum, Souter, p. 3; Wordsworth-White, *Novum Testamentum* . . . *latine* II, 1 (1913), pp. 1f.; dependent on Pelagius is the same idea in Ps.–Jerome, Wordsworth-White, pp. 5f.; cf. earlier Ep. Diogn. 11, 6.

[24] In Marcion, who here follows Galatians, the first apostles are, it is true, distinguished from the false apostles, but play 'a quite deplorable part' in events, and are the ones most to blame for the Judaistic corruption of the Gospel: Harnack, pp. 37ff., 256*ff.; cf. p. 130* n. 2.

[25] Gal. 1:15; cf. Harnack, pp. 69*f.

[26] Gal. 1:1; cf. Tertullian, Adv. Marc. V, 1 (Harnack, pp. 306*, 309*). In the Epistle to the Laodiceans, which is probably a Marcionite forgery, the same formula appears (1): Harnack, p. 139*. Cf. the significant excision of ὁ καὶ παρέλαβον from I Cor. 15:3 (Harnack, p. 91*), p. 114 n. 35 above.

[27] Origen, Hom. Luc. 25 (Rauer², pp. 150f.); cf. Harnack, pp. 252*, 340*. For further instances of Marcionite veneration of Paul cf. Harnack, p. 377*.

[28] The Marcionite Laodiceans uses the 'high' term *parousia* for Paul's arrival: Harnack, p. 142* (in Marcion himself it is a *terminus technicus* for the appearing of Christ: Harnack, p. 283*). The Marcionite Prologues (Harnack, pp. 127*ff.) also have as a major theme the exaltation of Paul's position as the one true apostle as opposed to all the false teachers, a point which they repeat again and again 'with monumental partiality' (Harnack, p. 147*). According to Tertullian, Marcion interpreted the 'adhuc' of II Cor. 3:15 ('to this day the veil hangs') of Paul—'until the time of Paul', the apostle of the new Christ: Harnack, p. 308*.

[29] That Paul was actually the only evangelist is the view which the Marcionite in Adamantius, Dial. I, 6, tries to maintain.

for to him the mystery of Christ was made known by revelation.'[30] It would be perverse to take such statements merely as the expression of an enthusiastic admiration. Some such teaching about the call and calling of the apostle was in fact an indispensable prerequisite, if for the sake of Paul one meant to dare to reject and combat all the other apostles and the whole of Church tradition.

That Marcion's bible had to contain one Gospel in addition to the Pauline letters is obvious. Naturally he could not do without the account of the normative words of the Lord.[31] It seems, however, that the content of this first section was also to a certain extent decided on the basis of Paul, and was therefore 'apostolic'.[32] Marcion understood those passages where Paul speaks simply of 'his gospel', or 'the gospel', to refer to one particular gospel book,[33] which consequently would already have been at the apostle's disposal.[34] Whence this gospel came, and who must have been its author, are questions to which Marcion,

[30] Irenaeus, Adv. haer. III, 13, 1. That was also why he was the only apostle to receive baptism: Tertullian, De bapt. 12; cf. W. Bauer in his review of Harnack's *Marcion*, *Gött. Gel. Anz.* 185, 1923, p. 2 n. 1.

[31] According to the by no means incredible tradition in Hippolytus and others, Marcion based his breach with the Roman church on the exegesis of the saying about the good and the corrupt trees in Lk. 6:43: Harnack, pp. 26, 24*ff., 194*f. Nevertheless, the Marcionite in Adamantius, Dial. II, 16f., is already citing Paul's saying about the new creation (II Cor. 5:17) in conjunction with that of Jesus about the wine and the wineskins: Harnack, p. 309*.

[32] Harnack's view (p. 250*) is as follows: 'Behind the Gospel, therefore, as he offered it to the church, stands no apostolic authority (or only an indirect one, inasmuch as Paul had acknowledged it as "his" gospel), but Christ. . . .' This is certainly not untrue; but I myself would put the emphasis the other way round, that is, on the passage in parenthesis. This relationship with Paul, and not the general confession of belief in the 'Lord', is the manifestly new element imported by Marcion. Cf. further Harnack's comment (p. 44) that Marcion 'very probably' began his purging of the text with Paul's epistles: 'for only on the basis of these could he find a criterion by which to judge the variegated tradition present in the "falsified" Third Gospel.' The Last Supper narrative in Luke Marcion may simply have supplemented from I Cor. 11:24f.: Bauer, *Gött. Gel. Anz.*, pp. 13f.

[33] This new interpretation of this phrase is not securely attested before Marcion: Harnack, p. 35 n. 1; H. Köster, *Synoptische Überlieferung bei den Apostolischen Vätern*, 1957, pp. 6ff. Roughly contemporary may be the pejorative term for the gospel in Jewish polemic, ʿawen gillayon, or ʿawon gillayon (= 'edge of wickedness' or 'edge of futility', referring to a scroll), which is best taken as a reference to a written gospel: O. Michel, art. 'Evangelium', *RAC* VI, 1966, cols. 1139f. This usage must therefore already have been possible at this time; but it was by no means the obvious one, for the older manner of speaking still continued for a considerable period.

[34] Harnack, pp. 39, 306*; cf. Eusebius, *HE* III, 4, 7. In the Marcionite Bible the characteristic phrase, κατὰ τὸ εὐαγγέλιόν μου is even interpolated at Gal. 1:7 (Harnack, pp. 45, 306*; cf. p. 309*), and, if Rom. 16:25 is Marcionite, has been supplied there as well (Harnack, pp. 45, 110*, 165*f.).

significantly enough, appears to have given no thought;[35] his mind did
not function historically.[36] But in any case its use by Paul inevitably
legitimated this mysterious gospel in his eyes as the true and original
one. It was therefore essential to rediscover it, and, once it had supposedly been recovered, to elevate it once more, in an unfalsified, that
is corrected, state, to the level of a universal norm. From this standpoint
it is possible to understand the determination with which Marcion
concentrated on one single gospel, in which alone he was prepared to
find genuine tradition. In theory it would have been possible to collect
the words of Christ from various gospels; but to all appearances
Marcion scorned such a procedure on principle.[37] To adopt it he would
have had to move back closer to the general 'tradition', and to have
modified his own strict Paulinism. But what Marcion was looking for was
not traditions but documents, and, what is more, only those documents
which actually and exclusively derived from 'the apostle'. In other
quarters it was customary to prefer this gospel or that; but such a preference did not tie one to a single text, nor were the texts as a whole
'canonical'. This makes the way in which Marcion justifies his procedure
highly significant. So far as we know, he never polemised against particular gospels. Instead, what he is attacking in the Great Church is the
teaching of the first, judaising apostles, of the false apostles, and of
other corrupting influences mentioned by Paul, that is, he is fighting
against the oral[38] tradition of the Church, which he still sees as a unity,[39]
not against individual canonical writings, which at this stage still did
not exist as canonical texts.[40]

[35] Harnack, 'Die ältesten Evangelienprologe und die Bildung des Neuen
Testaments', *Sitzungsberichte Berlin. Akad.*, 1928, p. 339 n. 5. Later Marcionites thought of Paul or even of Christ himself as the author: Adamantius, Dial.
I, 8; II, 13f.; Carmen adv. Marc. II, 29. That Marcion inferred a gospel 'not
written by any man, but bestowed directly by Christ' (Harnack, pp. 39, 249*f.),
is, to the best of my knowledge, not found anywhere in the tradition.

[36] What Harnack, pp. 35ff., relates about Marcion's supposed ideas on the
scope and nature of the judaistic 'conspiracy' is entirely psychologising conjecture: cf. n. 47 below.

[37] Marcion's disciples, however, seem occasionally to have deviated from this
principle: Harnack, pp. 43, 44 n. 2, 61 n. 2, 72, 251*ff.

[38] The Marcionite Marcus, in Adamantius, Dial. II, 12 (Harnack, p. 259*),
maintains that the first apostles left no writings behind them, but simply
preached ἀγράφως, 'sine scriptura'.

[39] Harnack's statement, which he wrongly wished to restrict to the 'apostolic'
section of Marcion's Bible, is therefore valid in this context as well: 'If Marcion
in his polemic against catholic tradition had already envisaged a canonical
collection of writings (an *apostolicum*), then that polemic would have taken
quite a different form . . .': p. 173*, cf. pp. 84f.

[40] The opposite is asserted not only by Zahn, *op. cit.* I, pp. 654ff., but also, a
little more guardedly but on the whole with equal emphasis, by Harnack:
'At the beginning of the "Antitheses" ' Marcion may have justified his rejec-

Why Marcion thought to find his supposed original gospel behind Luke in particular can no longer be determined with certainty. That Luke was associated with Paul as one of his disciples cannot have been a

---

tion of the Four Gospels and 'probably' also of the Book of Acts accepted by his opponents (pp. 256–f.). This statement recurs (pp. 40ff., 78f., 83, 249*) so definitely that one almost forgets that it is only a hypothesis. In the essay on the Prologues to the Gospels (cf. n. 35 above), p. 339 n. 6, even the qualification with regard to Acts has been dropped, and the Apocalypse has now been added; and in his 'Neuen Studien zu Marcion', 1923, pp. 21f., Harnack includes the assertion that 'Marcion found the Four Gospel canon already in existence' among those propositions about which 'there is no disagreement'. This contradicts his own earlier statement: *Das Neue Testament um das Jahr 200*, 1889, p. 50. That the hypothesis is false may be demonstrated as follows:

1. That Marcion criticised the 'Four-Gospel canon' (Harnack, p. 79 n. 1) is nowhere stated in the tradition (any more than this contains explicit mention of any single gospel apart from Luke). Of course, the polemists proceed throughout on the assumption that Marcion not only 'mutilated' Luke, but also malevolently scorned the other gospels, which were assumed to have been already canonical. Despite this, however, it is still very clear in Irenaeus that Marcion's direct polemic was aimed only at the apostles and at the apostolic preaching of the gospel (cf. Adv. haer. I, 27, 2; III, 2, 2; 13, 1f.), not against individual gospels, much less a 'Four-Gospel canon'. Harnack, who himself adduces the relevant passages, draws inadmissible conclusions from them. 'The expression used of the Marcionites—"gloriantur se habere evangelium"—which Irenaeus employs twice' certainly presupposes that Marcion regarded only his own gospel as valid, and rejected all others, but not that he named those others, nor in particular that he referred specifically to the four which were normative for Irenaeus. In the two passages which Harnack has especially in mind (III, 11, 9; 14, 4) it is Luke and the Lukan gospel alone that are explicitly mentioned on both occasions; in one instance (III, 11, 9: 'Marcion . . . *partem* gloriatur se habere evangelii'), moreover, the phrasing makes it clear that we are dealing with an insinuation on the part of Irenaeus himself. Furthermore, Tertullian's polemic adds absolutely nothing to what Irenaeus says with regard to particular gospels. The one statement to which Harnack appeals again and again (Adv. Marc. IV, 3, 2: 'Marcion . . . connititur ad destruendum statum eorum evangeliorum, quae propria et sub apostolorum nomine eduntur vel etiam apostolicorum, ut [sc. fidem] quam illis adimit, suo conferat') cannot possibly be pressed, in the absence of any other evidence, to mean that Marcion expressed in this form and carried into effect the intention which Tertullian, on the basis of his own assumptions, imputed to him.

2. Relevant here is the fact that even in Irenaeus, and most definitely in our principal source, Tertullian, we cannot as a rule distinguish between what Marcionites were currently saying and what Marcion himself—at that stage, of course, in the 'Antitheses'—may have said. This is in keeping with the normal practice of anti-heretical polemists (and of philosophical polemic before them), and is also admitted by Harnack. With regard to the arguments and texts which he has collected he explicitly concedes that 'a great deal of all this may belong to the disciples, but cannot be distinguished from the words of the master' (p. 87). Tertullian is certainly conscientious in his reporting (p. 80 n. 1), but directs his polemic 'not only against Marcion, but also in rapid alternation against the Marcionites', whom he knew from personal encounter; 'indeed, in some passages one has the firm impression that his arguments and the remarks

factor, since Marcion naturally did not regard the text of his hypothetical gospel as Lukan—indeed, Luke to him was above all the one who

---

of his opponents echo disputations which Tertullian had had with them in
Carthage' (pp. 83f.). Now it is obvious that the Marcionites, whenever the
Church's gospels were used against them, might easily be moved to express
themselves more forcefully on the subject of their worthlessness than their
master had done. Definite conclusions on this question are therefore particularly difficult. I would not like to rule out the possibility that Marcion himself
may have set his face firmly against such a saying as Matt. 5:17: οὐκ ἦλθον
καταλῦσαι, ἀλλὰ πληρῶσαι, since to reject and indeed to reverse this statement was the real platform of his whole campaign. On the basis of what Tertullian has to say (Adv. Marc. IV, 7. 9. 12. 36; V, 14) Harnack regards it as proven
that he did so (p. 80), even though, on the other hand, he thinks that it was only
later Marcionites who incorporated the inverted form of this saying (οὐκ
ἦλθον πληρῶσαι τὸν νόμον, ἀλλὰ καταλῦσαι: cited in Adamantius, Dial. II,
15) into their gospel (p. 252*). But it by no means follows that in the 'historical
and dogmatic comments' which, according to Harnack's conjecture at any rate,
introduced the 'Antitheses' Marcion specifically criticised in detail all four Gospels or even the Gospel of Matthew alone. Furthermore, he can hardly have
done so in the 'eclectic series of scholia', forming a commentary on his own
gospel, which he attached to the 'Antitheses' (p. 83), since:
   3. In the supposed extant fragments of the 'Antitheses', of which Harnack
(pp. 256*-313*) gives a 'complete, in fact more than complete' collection, the
material relevant to this point is so infinitesimally small that it can be said that,
so far as any conclusion about Marcion or the 'Antitheses' is concerned, it is in
fact as good as nothing. Leaving aside a polemical reference to the saying already
mentioned (Matt. 5:17), in which, according to Harnack (p. 41 n. 3), it is 'as
certain as can be' that Marcion also 'explicitly attacked it in the course of dealing
with other gospels', the following are the only relevant texts (pp. 80f.):
   (a) Origen, when expounding the saying about self-castration in Matt. 19:12
(a passage which for him was, of course, to be interpreted allegorically), finds
occasion to say something about the objections which inevitably arose from the
Marcionite rejection of all allegory (Comm. Matt. XV, 3: Klostermann, pp.
356*; according to Lommatzsch incompletely quoted in Harnack, p. 305*):
πρὶν δὲ ἔλθω ἐπὶ τὴν διήγησιν τῶν κατὰ τὸν τόπον, λεκτέον ὅτι, εἴπερ τι
ἀκόλουθον ἑαυτῷ ὁ Μαρκίων πεποίηκε φάσκων μὴ δεῖν ἀλληγορεῖν τὴν γραφήν,
καὶ τοὺς τόπους τούτους ἠθέτησεν ὡς οὐχ ὑπὸ τοῦ σωτῆρος εἰρημένους, νομίσας
δεῖν ἤτοι παραδέξασθαι (μετὰ τοῦ φάσκειν τὸν σωτῆρα ταῦτα εἰρηκέναι) τὸ
καὶ ἐπὶ τὰ τοιαῦτα τολμᾶν ἑαυτὸν παραδιδόναι πεισόμενον τὸν πεπιστευκότα,
ἢ μὴ ἂν εὐλόγως τολμήσαντα τὰ τηλικαῦτα, ἐσόμενα εἰς δυσφημίαν τὴν κατὰ
τοῦ λόγου, μηδὲ πιστεύειν εἶναι τοῦ σωτῆρος τοὺς λόγους, εἴ γε μὴ ἀλληγοροῦνται.
In this passage, as it seems to me, Origen is speaking only in the most general
way about Marcion's textual principles and excisions. One can hardly deduce
from it a dispute over this particular Matthaean saying, which might moreover
have come to Marcion via a different route, e.g. through Basilides (cf. p. 139 n.
159 above). Tertullian, in fact, almost makes it a case for reproach against Marcion that he did not extend his corrections to the Gospels of Matthew (and John):
Adv. Marc. IV, 5: 'cur non haec quoque Marcion attigit aut emendanda, si
adulterata, aut agnoscenda, si integra?'
   (b) 'Furthermore, it clearly follows from Tertullian, Adv. Marc. II, 12f.,
that Marcion objected to Matt. 1:23 and 2:11, since he contested the fulfilment
of the prophecy of Isa. 7:14 in Jesus on the grounds of Isa. 8:4.' So far from

distorted it.[41] Marcion supplied no attribution for his corrected text of Luke, but described it simply as 'Gospel'. Luke may already have been familiar to him from his childhood,[42] or he may have been introduced to it by his teachers.[43] Or again, Luke may have commended itself to him by its strongly Gentile Christian character, by its emphasis on the idea of grace, and by its ascetic tendencies. Matthew, which in Church circles was the most widely disseminated gospel, was out of the question from the start, because it was so palpably 'judaising', and similar objections must have been raised against the Jewish Christian gospels or the

being 'clear', this is quite unprovable, when one remembers that early Christian 'scriptural proof' in general, and even as late as Justin, felt no necessity to make use of Gospel texts.

(c) 'As regards Tertullian, Adv. Marc. IV, 34,' it seems 'very probable that Marcion, when dealing with Lk. 16:18, also considered and rejected Matt. 19:3–8.' Here Harnack calls on the support of Zahn, op. cit. I, p. 670. But all Tertullian says is that Marcion naturally did not accept (non recepisti) Matthew's gospel and its version of this saying, and that he, i.e., Tertullian, would therefore refute Marcion out of Marcion's own text (his, quae recepisti)—a method he employs throughout. This passage will seem to indicate an explicit mention of Matthew only to those who regard it as more or less self-evident a priori that such mention must have been made.

(d) 'That Johannine passages were treated in the "Antitheses" cannot be proved for certain,' even according to Harnack (pp. 81, 249*ff.), so there is no need to discuss this question further.

(e) Since Mark does not enter into the matter, there is absolutely nothing to add on that score.

When we examine the evidence for this thesis as a whole, it becomes, in my opinion, a convincing proof of the opposite. It is obvious that Marcion is concerned to justify only his own text, and to defend it against what he imagines to be distortions in the Lukan gospel. These, consequently, are the points which are considered and contested by Irenaeus (cf. p. 157 above) and Tertullian (e.g., Adv. Marc. IV, 4). Marcion had no need to accept the other gospels, and he did not do so; as a general rule, at any rate, he simply ignored them. If this were not so, it would be impossible to explain why neither Irenaeus nor Tertullian nor Origen ever mentions an explicit and reasoned critique of the 'canonical' gospels on these lines, nor why such a critique was not rejected and refuted like Marcion's other errors. If this rebuttal of Harnack's assessment of the situation is sound, then the conclusion which he draws must also be reversed. The fact that the Four Gospels are not mentioned in Marcion's polemic emphatically does not indicate that they 'were already in existence at that time as an authoritative collection' (p. 79), but precisely that such a collection was still lacking: so also Knox, op. cit., p. 156 n. 42.

[41] As against E. Amann, art. 'Marcion', DTC IX, 2, 1927, col. 2032; R. S. Wilson, Marcion, 1933, p. 134; G. Bardy, art. 'Marcion', Dict. de la Bible, suppl. V, 1957, cols. 862–877. Marcion not only suppressed the name of Luke from the gospel, but also 'very probably excised the friendly words of Paul in Col. 4:14': Harnack, pp. 51, 249*; cf. 124.

[42] Harnack, pp. 42, 250*; Knox, op. cit., pp. 136f. H. E. W. Turner, The Pattern of Christian Truth, 1954, pp. 171f., disagrees.

[43] Cf. H. Windisch, Johannes und die Synoptiker, 1926, p. 175.

Gospel of Peter, which at that time, moreover, were still recent, and in some cases were only just appearing. Mark was as yet little used, and contained too few dominical sayings. Marcion will hardly have given it much thought. On the other hand, he must have known the Gospel of John, in which there was a great deal to his taste. But here too there were offensive elements,[44] and possibly also doubts about age and authenticity.[45] All in all, Luke presented the fewest problems, and was therefore, in accordance with Marcion's conception of the original gospel, chosen in preference to all other works of the kind.

Of course, Marcion could not accept even the text of Luke as it stood without further ado.[46] First, he had to purify it of the interpolations which the Judaisers, as he thought, had smuggled into it. The same applied to the Pauline letters. What Marcion needed was a text free from what he regarded as contradictions, and purged of 'legalistic' adulterations and Old Testament references; and because such a text was not directly available, he had to construct it—or, as he would have said, restore it—himself by a rigorous dogmatic revision. In ancient times the polemists were already protesting noisily against this brutal radicalism in his heresy; and modern scholars, in their own presentation and assessment of Marcion, frequently concentrate on what is for them a particularly interesting feature. But it may be asked whether to do so is not to shift the emphasis in Marcion's methods too far in the direction of historical and philological criticism.[47] In any case, his attempts at textual criticism were not so unheard· of as they inevitably appeared to be to a later age habituated to the 'canonical' inviolability of the New Testament. Matthew and Luke had already not only expanded their Marcan source but also revised and corrected it.[48] The Fourth Evangelist reshapes his material with theological intent.[49] and it is unlikely that

---

[44] Harnack, pp. 41f.   [45] Bauer, *Gött. Gel. Anz.*, p. 12 n. 1.

[46] This will still be true, even if we assume a proto-Lukan source for his gospel.

[47] It seems to me that even Harnack overestimated this element, and ascribed to Marcion a thoroughgoing and methodical critique of primitive Christian history and tradition. Marcion may well have been content with demonstrating the objective contradictions between the Church and the 'gospel', and with excising the supposed interpolations on the authority of the anti-judaistic polemic in Paul. It is in fact, as Harnack emphasises (pp. 35f.), very striking that he never appeals to other traditions about the first apostles, of which the second century, as we know from Papias, Hegesippus, and the early apostolic 'Acts', was full. That Marcion 'recognised' that these sources of information were 'valueless', and rejected them by a conscious process of criticism (p. 207 n. 1), seems to me, however, not very probable. It is simpler to assume that he was not interested in historical information because the material in the Pauline letters was ample for his needs. This would also be in keeping with his uncritical attitude to the whole Old Testament: cf. n. 61 below.

[48] Harnack also alludes to this point (p. 68).

[49] Harnack, pp. 70f.

Basilides was much more cautious than Marcion when going to work on the composition of his gospel.[50] Tatian, too, in constructing his harmony of the 'Four' did not shrink from making major excisions.[51] The distinctive feature of Marcion's radical recension is the fact that he nowhere expands his source but on every occasion abbreviates it. This, however, is more a sign of methodological circumspection than of an arbitrary or irresponsible attitude to textual questions, and is linked with Marcion's basic assumption, namely that there had been, so to speak, only one specifically 'canonical' gospel, the text of which it was for that very reason essential to restore. If one's intention was to sift and collect the tradition, then it was permissible to draw on many different sources, and to a certain extent to handle them as one thought fit. But if one's purpose was to recover a lost document, then willy-nilly one must be satisfied with removing interpolations and with making trifling corrections, if the result was not to be falsified.[52]

It is well known that Marcion justified his bible in a dogmatic and exegetical treatise of his own, the only book, so far as we know, that he ever wrote. Unfortunately, we can no longer form any picture of the structure and character of the Antitheses;[53] but it would seem that in it the theological and systematic and the philological and, to a certain extent, text-critical argumentation were all in frequent interplay. In this respect the Antitheses formed a kind of 'Introduction to the New Testament'.[54] But even for an essay on these lines there are certain analogies in the second century. Papias had already defended the authenticity of the dominical sayings and of the exegeses of them which he had collected;[55] and before Marcion's time Basilides, with the twenty-four books of his Exegetica,[56] and then Tatian, with his Problemata,[57]

[50] Cf. pp. 139f. above. H. Windisch, 'Das Evangelium des Basilides', *ZNW* 7, 1906, p. 245, conjectures 'that his editorial work was not in principle different from that of Marcion'.

[51] Cf. p. 175 below; also Harnack, pp. 72f.

[52] In my view Harnack, pp. 61ff., did not pay sufficient attention, when characterising Marcion's methodological sense of responsibility, to the fact that this difference between Marcion and others was largely the result of his situation. R. M. Grant, *Letter*, pp. 63f., rightly argues against overestimating Marcion's methodological objectivity.

[53] Harnack himself stressed this point (p. 74), but to my mind was still much too bold in his suggestions and hypotheses.

[54] Harnack, p. 74 n. 3.   [55] Cf. p. 134 above.

[56] Cf. pp. 139f. above; so also Bauer, *Orthodoxy*, p. 190.

[57] Cf. Eusebius, *HE* V, 13, 8: (Rhodon) φησὶν δὲ καὶ ἐσπουδάσθαι τῷ Τατιανῷ προβλημάτων βιβλίον· δι' ὧν τὸ ἀσαφὲς καὶ ἐπικεκρυμμένον τῶν θείων γραφῶν παραστήσειν ὑποσχομένου τοῦ Τατιανοῦ, αὐτὸς ὁ 'Ρόδων ἐν ἰδίῳ συγγράμματι τὰς τῶν ἐκείνου προβλημάτων ἐπιλύσεις ἐκθήσεσθαι ἐπαγγέλλεται. Cf. M. Elze, *Tatian und seine Theologie*, 1960, p. 115. Though here, of course, it is primarily the O.T. Scriptures which are in mind, this does not exclude the possibility that Tatian, like Marcion, defended his gospel at the same time.

must have done much the same for their own gospel texts as Marcion did with the Antitheses for the Marcionite bible.[58] Explanatory works of this kind, aimed at justifying and confirming a particular text, are unavoidable at a period when a canon is only just beginning to emerge; and they tell us less about individual theologians than about the difficult situation in which almost everyone found himself at that time, if he wished to introduce or commend a particular document or collection of documents. For Marcion, moreover, this particular difficulty was especially great, and the necessity of dealing with it effectively correspondingly urgent. Till then no one had advanced, as he now did, the claim to present the *only* normative and authentic documents of Christianity, in order to use them for the purpose of a total transformation and renewal of the doctrine and preaching of the Church. It was therefore essential that the justification of this canon should really be convincing and incontrovertible. Obviously Marcion believed that in the Antitheses he had in principle fulfilled this task. The work was accepted by his church as a kind of basic handbook, and was always held in high honour. Naturally, it could not form part of the Canon itself;[59] but to some extent it played the part of a credal text for the Marcionite church,[60] a text which was indispensable to them as backing for their canon and their doctrine.

It was not, however, possible to maintain that every word of the canonical text could be established with absolute certainty. In this respect the Marcionite bible was not on an equality with the old Scripture which they had rejected.[61] It constituted no more than the product of painstaking critical scholarship, and at no point in its career had it been simply handed down as traditional, or 'revealed'.[62] There was,

[58] In this context it may be worth recalling the Commentaries of Theophilus: cf. pp. 174f. below. To some extent, of course, the defence of the Four-Gospel canon in Irenaeus (cf. pp. 195ff. below) and the Muratorianum (cf. pp. 249f. below) also fall into the same category; but the latter are no longer taking up the cudgels for a new order of scripture, but for one that is traditional and assumed to have obtained for a long time; and that is a new factor.

[59] The later Mesopotamian Marcionites may have formed an exception to this rule: Harnack, p. 174*.

[60] Harnack, p. 76; Bauer, *Orthodoxy*, p. 183.

[61] Cf. Harnack, pp. 67, 86: 'It is very remarkable, however, that Marcion accepted the O.T. as a whole and intact, refused to recognise any corruptions, interpolations, or anything of that sort . . . and regarded its text as absolutely reliable'—in contrast to the attempts of Jews and gnostics to excise false pericopes or to arrange the material within the Scripture in strata of differing value: cf. pp. 19f., 84f. above. (Perhaps Marcion's attitude is not so remarkable, when we remember that total and undifferentiated recognition was essential if there was also to be the total and undifferentiated condemnation called for by his two-god doctrine.—Tr.)

[62] In this respect Marcion's position is comparable with that of Luke himself: cf. pp. 126f. above.

therefore, nothing to stop Marcion's disciples from continuing their master's work, and from introducing further corrections and 'improvements' into his text.[63] It is in fact possible that—in contravention of Marcion's basic principle—they may here and there have supplemented the 'Gospel' with passages from other gospels.[64] They also canonised further Pauline letters, which they wrongly regarded as authentic.[65] The sole decisive criterion of canonical authority was apostolic origin; there was nothing sacrosanct about the collection as such. Nevertheless, both the scale and the significance of these later corrections and additions may have been exaggerated by opponents. 'Day after day they remodel their gospel, as day after day we refute them once more,' mocks Tertullian.[66] The Marcionites, however, never let themselves be deterred by such variations in the text and composition of their scripture; they remained convinced that they possessed the only reliable and original New Testament. Absolute perfection and literal inspiration did not as yet constitute the essence of the idea of a canon. But Marcion, with his 'Gospel' and 'Apostle',[67] remains 'the creator'—in conception, at any rate—'of the Christian holy scripture'.[68]

[63] Harnack, pp. 173f., 254*.

[64] Cf. n. 31 above. The complex problem of the use of Scripture in Arnobius may also be connected with this: F. Scheidweiler, 'Arnobius und der Marcionitismus', ZNW 45, 1954, pp. 45–48; also F. G. Sirna, 'Arnobio e l'eresia Marcionita di Patrizio', VC 18, 1964, pp. 39–41.

[65] This applies in the case of the Epistles to the Laodiceans and to the Alexandrians, both of which are Marcionite forgeries (Harnack, pp. 172f., 134*ff.), and possibly also of the Pastorals: Harnack, p. 43, 132* n. 2; Blackman, op. cit., pp. 52ff.

[66] Adv. Marc. IV, 5: cotidie reformant illud (sc. evangelium), prout a nobis cotidie revincuntur. Harnack, p. 254, also refers to Celsus as evidence for the Marcionite alterations of the text: 'This was so notorious and scandalous that even that out-and-out opponent of Christianity, Celsus, some years after Marcion's death, mentions it with disapproval.' The passage referred to is Origen, Contra Cels. II, 27: . . . τινὰς τῶν πιστευόντων φησὶν ὡς ἐκ μέθης ἥκοντας εἰς τὸ ἐφεστάναι αὐτοῖς μεταχαράττειν ἐκ τῆς πρώτης γραφῆς τὸ εὐαγγέλιον τριχῇ καὶ τετραχῇ καὶ πολλαχῇ καὶ μεταπλάττειν, ἵν' ἔχοιεν πρὸς τοὺς ἐλέγχους ἀρνεῖσθαι. The opinion expressed here, however, is not directly that of Celsus but rather that of his Jewish informant, and it is more probable that the reproach is meant for Christians as a whole. The rendering of μεταχαράττειν is debated, but it might be an allusion to the various church gospels: cf. R. Bader, Der ΑΛΗΘΗΣ ΛΟΓΟΣ des Kelsos, 1940, p. 69 n. 2 on II, 27; H. Chadwick, Origen: Contra Celsum², 1965, p. 90 n. 2. Celsus plainly has in mind 'a basic text, from which all Gospels originate . . . and on which the succeeding Gospels execute more, or less free variations': W. Völker, Das Bild vom nichtgnostischen Christentum bei Celsus, 1928, p. 90. Origen, it is true, preferred to deflect the accusation exclusively toward Marcion, Valentinus, and Lucan the Marcionite (on the latter cf. Harnack, pp. 401*ff.): μεταχαράξαντας δὲ τὸ εὐαγγέλιον ἄλλους οὐκ οἶδα . . .

[67] As to any single name which Marcion may have given to his bible as a whole, 'nothing can be ascertained', and it is probable that no such name existed: Harnack, p. 441*. This appears surprising, but ceases to be strange when we

M

Taking it by and large, how is this epoch-making creation to be assessed? In the present context there is no need to discuss the theological doctrines which Marcion used to justify his canon. The question may be asked, whether Marcion's teaching, for all its errors of historical fact, was not nevertheless a renewal of primitive Christian ideas and concerns, or whether, as a reaction against the Christianity of his day, it was not at least unavoidable, and so relatively a justifiable necessity. The answer will depend on how far one regards his antinomian and strictly dualistic interpretation of Pauline theology as permissible and adequate to the facts. Personally, I am not inclined to accept such an exegesis. At all events, however, one thing is certain: Marcion did not succeed, as he intended and claimed, in recovering and making known the ancient gospel and the authentic apostle Paul in their original form. The extent to which the old tradition had become corrupt and run wild before the time of Marcion is debatable; but whether Marcion with his corrections hit upon the right form of that tradition at even one single point seems doubtful in the extreme. In the majority of cases he was definitely wrong; and looked at as a whole his bible is certainly not the restoration but the complete devastation of the original text. His 'original gospel' was an *idée fixe*[69] which corresponded to nothing in reality; and a Paul who rejects the Old Testament, and knows nothing of either creation or judgment, is equally a phantom who never lived. The historical data, therefore, which Marcion thought to provide are in reality dogmatic constructs. The principle on which his work of critical purgation proceeded was supplied by those 'contradictions' in the text (the supposed antinomies which gave its name to the Antitheses) which he himself regarded as irreconcilable. Marcion's biblical text is a striking example of where a dogmatism hostile to facts and history can lead, when it is allied with formal philological criticism,[70] and pursues its way with apparently relentless logic to the ultimate conclusion. Had he succeeded in his aim, access to the sources of Christianity, so far from being opened up, would have been blocked for ever.

The theological and methodological deficiencies of the first Christian canon should not, however, prevent us from appreciating the fundamental importance of the attempt. Marcion's bible tabled once for all the question of a new canon, that is, the question of the 'authentic' witnesses to the original gospel, which were to provide the standard of

---

realise that at that time no exact designation for the O.T. as a whole was current either.

[68] Harnack, p. 151; cf. pp. 84f. Knox, *op. cit.,* pp. 19ff., rightly defends this thesis, which in Blackman, *op. cit.,* pp. 23ff., 38ff., is unjustifiably weakened.

[69] Harnack, p. 39.

[70] Marcion must have had some degree of philological training: Harnack, p. 24 n. 1.

all later tradition and the norm for the preaching of the Church. The Church as she was then situated could not ignore this question if she wished to hold her own. But there was still a long way to go, through crises and controversies of many different kinds, before an answer was found. That answer stands today in our New Testament; but at the outset of the conflict such a thing did not exist, even as an idea.

The suddenness and energy with which Marcion launched his total war against existing Christianity created a shock for which the Church everywhere was completely unprepared. This is proved by his success in founding his church, which within a very short time had established numerous Marcionite congregations throughout the Roman empire.[71] Particularly in the eastern provinces orthodox Christians were in many cases driven wholly on to the defensive.[72] Evidence of this is the flood of polemical literature which now appeared, and which is overwhelmingly directed against Marcion and the Marcionites.[73] It is true that these writings have for the most part disappeared; but a long series of titles 'Against Marcion' has come down to us, and testifies to the burning urgency which this controversy possessed for the men of its time.[74]

At first the outstanding issue, as might be expected, was the defence of the Old Testament. This book, which for the Church was normative, was the primary target of Marcion's attack; and to a greater or lesser degree all Christian groups felt themselves threatened at this point. The first reaction known to us against the forces which Marcion deployed comes not from an orthodox churchman, but from the Valentinian, Ptolemaeus.[75] His Letter to Flora gives one the impression that he felt bound to dissent more sharply from Marcion's denigration of the Law and the creation than from the high esteem in which they were held in catholic communities.[76] Ptolemaeus' attempt to disentangle the various authors and inspiratory powers in the Old Testament was meant to legitimise a critical use of the ancient Scriptures, and thus precisely to make any radical rejection of them impossible. But this gnostic solution of the problem seemed to the orthodox majority already half way to Marcionism, and made them all the more set on affirming the

[71] Justin, I Apol. 26, 5; cf. Tertullian, Adv. Marc. V, 19, 2.

[72] Harnack, pp. 153f.; Bauer, *Orthodoxy*, pp. 24ff., 169ff.

[73] Cf. Harnack, *Geschichte der altchristlichen Literatur bis Eusebius I: Die Überlieferung und der Bestand*, 1893, pp. 191ff; Bauer, *Orthodoxy*, pp. 147ff.; also M. Rist, 'Pseudepigraphic Refutations of Marcionism', *Journ. of Relig.* 22, 1942, pp. 39–62.

[74] Harnack, pp. 84f.; cf. p. 78 n. 1, and 'Neue Studien', p. 20 n. 2: 'When compared with the army of churchmen who entered the lists against Marcion, from Justin to Esnik, the number of those who were engaged in writing against the individual gnostic sects seems infinitesimally small.'

[75] Cf. pp. 82ff. above.

[76] Cf. p. 86 n. 133 above; G. Quispel, *Ptolémée: Lettre à Flora²*, 1966, pp. 12–14.

Old Testament as a totality. The holy Scripture was to be ascribed neither to a non-Christian God nor to a multiplicity of gods. It must, both as a whole and in each individual detail, be equally divine, true, and inviolable, if faith was to cleave to it and be based upon it. This was, as we have seen,[77] the attitude of Justin, who mentions Marcion by name,[78] and also wrote specifically against him.[79] What the prophets of old had said was not to be denigrated as their personal opinion, but was to be attributed directly to Christ, the Logos of God, or to the Holy Spirit.[80] The following defence is typical: 'Nothing which the scripture relates without condemnation is unimportant', says the Elder quoted by Irenaeus.[81] 'All scripture is inspired by God and profitable for teaching, for reproof, for correction, and for training in righteousness'.[82] There is no contradiction in the prophecies,[83] and it is one and the selfsame God who acts both in the old and in the new covenant.[84] We must therefore take care not to make accusations where Scripture does not do so; 'for we must not judge more strictly than God himself, nor can we be set above our Master'.[85]

If such comments were not to mean that all hope of a genuine understanding of the Old Testament had been given up,[86] then, apart from typological exegesis, which Marcion refused to recognise, there was only one hermeneutical method of salvaging the ancient Bible: it was necessary to acknowledge that there was a difference between the eras· in which one and the same God had acted, and to see in the Old Testament a stage (or various stages) of that providential guidance of salvation-history which attained its goal in Christ. In this way laws which

[77] Cf. p. 89 above.   [78] I Apol. 26, 5; 58, 1; Dial. 35, 6 (?).
[79] Irenaeus, Adv. haer. IV, 6, 2; Eusebius, HE IV, 11, 8ff.; cf. Justin, I Apol. 26, 8.
[80] I Apol. 36, 1f.; also II Pet. 1:21; and the Elder in Irenaeus, Adv. haer. IV, 32, 1; cf. Athenagoras, Suppl. 9, 1.
[81] Adv. haer. IV, 31, 1: nihil enim otiosum est eorum, quaecunque inaccusabilia posita sunt in scripturis.
[82] II Tim. 3:16 (cf. p. 181 below); the same thought occurs, only this time made more pointedly anti-heretical, in the Elder in Irenaeus: Adv. haer. IV, 27ff.
[83] Justin, Dial. 65, 2; Theophilus, Autol. II, 9.
[84] The Elder again: Irenaeus, Adv. haer. IV, 27; 32, 1. The unity of God is seen, first in Justin and then pre-eminently in Irenaeus, as dogmatically the crucial point in which Marcion was in error. In their eyes this puts him in the same category as Valentinus and the other gnostics. From the standpoint of the history of the Canon, however, this is a misleading picture. Marcion is unique.
[85] The Elder: Irenaeus, Adv. haer. IV, 31, 1: de quibus autem scripturae non increpant, sed simpliciter sunt positae, nos non debere fieri accusatores (non enim sumus diligentiores deo neque super magistrum possumus esse), sed typum quaerere.
[86] Cf. Justin, Dial. 65, 2 (pp. 97f. above).

were meant for a particular age, and temporary (or disguised) revelations could be meaningfully interpreted without having to sacrifice the unity of God and the truth of his word. Justin had already been forced to move in this direction by the pressure of the new questions raised both by philosophy and by the needs of anti-Marcionite polemic.[87] In a similar manner the Elder in Irenaeus develops against all gnostics the idea of the 'economy' of salvation-history,[88] a concept which was to be fully worked out in Irenaeus himself.

There was as yet no need to defend a New Testament, and no one did so.[89] Marcion's attack on the Church's Jesus tradition was at first answered in the same way as his onslaught on the Old Testament, namely by even more emphatic confession of its validity: the tradition proceeding from the apostles is normative and reliable,[90] and everything is to be decided in accordance with the words of the Lord, which 'alone are capable of guiding one without error to an understanding of what is right.'[91] To this extent the Valentinian and the Elder in Irenaeus are in agreement, and a generation after Marcion's apostasy Hegesippus is still citing 'the Law, the Prophets, and the Lord' as the only norms to which a right faith must conform.[92] Undoubtedly, at this period the text of the Lord's words is already usually taken from written gospels,[93] the 'memoirs of the apostles' and of their companions, as Justin calls them,[94] testifying at the same time to the fact that it was a regular

[87] Cf. pp. 97ff. above.

[88] Cf. O. Lillge, 'Das patristische Wort οἰκονομία,' TLZ 80, 1955, pp. 239f.; M. Widmann, 'Irenäus und seine theologischen Väter', ZTK 54, 1957, pp. 158–161.

[89] It is significant that Justin, I Apol. 58, 1f., could still fail completely to see the importance of the Marcionite N.T., and could flatly affirm that in putting forward their teaching the Marcionites had ἀπόδειξιν μηδεμίαν περὶ ὧν λέγουσιν. As against this Justin himself mentions (I Apol. 59, 1) τῶν αὐτολεξεὶ εἰρημένων διὰ Μωυσέως.

[90] Ptolemaeus, Flora 7, 9; the Elder, Irenaeus, Adv. haer. IV, 27, 1.

[91] Ptolemaeus, Flora 3, 8; the Elder, Irenaeus, Adv. haer. IV, 28, 1.

[92] Eusebius, HE IV, 22, 3: ἐν ἑκάστῃ δὲ διαδοχῇ καὶ ἐν ἑκάστῃ πόλει οὕτως ἔχει ὡς ὁ νόμος κηρύσσει καὶ οἱ προφῆται καὶ ὁ κύριος. In Syria the situation appears to be still much the same in the first half of the third century; cf. the references in G. Strecker (suppl. to Bauer, Orthodoxy, p. 59f.) to the Didascalia, which defines the authoritative norms as 'the sacred scriptures and the gospel of God' (Achelis-Flemming, pp. 8, 31f.), or as 'the Law, the book of the Kings and of the Prophets, and the Gospel' (pp. 5, 18f.), or even as 'Law, Prophets, Gospel' (pp. 15, 26). Similarly the Κηρύγματα Πέτρου in the Ps.-Clementines apparently 'cited only the O.T. and the four Gospels as sacred scriptures'.

[93] Significantly, however, it is still almost exclusively the sayings of Jesus which are cited, not as yet the narrative text of the gospels themselves. This is true of Ptolemaeus, the Elder, and Athenagoras, and, with very few exceptions, of Justin as well.

[94] I Apol. 66, 3: οἱ γὰρ ἀπόστολοι ἐν τοῖς γενομένοις ὑπ' αὐτῶν ἀπομνημο-

practice to read them in public worship alongside the writings of the prophets.[95] This is important; for it means that in the consciousness of the congregation these texts take their place directly on a par with the ancient sacred Scriptures, and this in a way is a stage preparatory to the coming canonisation.[96] But there is still in no sense a true canonisation, however much the situation 'cries out' for one.[97] Other edifying writings also were used in various places as reading matter in the liturgy, but that did not make them 'canonical'.[98] And most important of all: there is in practice still a wide choice of gospels to use, when the time comes in the service to open 'the Gospel'.

In this connection considerable variations in accordance with local practice and personal taste were clearly still both possible and permitted. Over a wide area Matthew had become a kind of standard gospel; it is regularly quoted both by Ptolemaeus and by the Elder. But there was no necessity to limit oneself to Matthew's text. Ptolemaeus also makes use of John—a gospel particularly valued by the Valentinians;[99]

νεύμασιν, ἃ καλεῖται εὐαγγέλια, οὕτως παρέδωκαν . . . Dial. 103, 6: ἐν τοῖς ἀπομνημονεύμασι τῶν ἀποστόλων γέγραπται . . .

[95] I Apol. 67, 3: . . . τὰ ἀπομνημονεύματα τῶν ἀποστόλων ἢ τὰ συγγράμματα τῶν προφητῶν ἀναγινώσκεται. The 'prophets' here certainly means the O.T. Scriptures as a whole: Knox, op. cit., p. 29 n. 14; cf. p. 257 n. 257 below, and Dial. 119, 6: . . . καὶ ἡμεῖς τῇ φωνῇ τοῦ θεοῦ τῇ διά τε τῶν ἀποστόλων τοῦ χριστοῦ λαληθείσῃ πάλιν καὶ τῇ διὰ τῶν προφητῶν κηρυχθείσῃ ἡμῖν πιστεύσαντες . . .

[96] Cf. Harnack, Entstehung, p. 19: 'The fact that christian writings were treated in worship on a par with those of the O.T., without however simply being incorporated into the ancient collection, was the chief (?) factor which gave rise to the idea of a second collection'; similarly Jülicher-Fascher, Einleitung in das N.T.[7], 1931, pp. 469f. But Melito's sermon, On the Pasch, is still tied only to an O.T. passage, which had previously been read aloud (1, 11). This is certainly not sufficient grounds for speaking of 'full canonical dignity', as does A. Vögtle, Das N.T. und die neuere katholische Exegese I, 1966, p. 22.

[97] Harnack, Entstehung, p. 12; Marcion, p. 174* n. 1 (on Justin); on the Elder cf. Marcion, p. 84 n. 1.

[98] According to Polycarp (Phil. 13, 2) the collected letters of Ignatius were, as a matter of course, read aloud in Philippi and other places; but they no more for that reason became part of the Canon than did the epistle of the Roman bishop Soter, which, as Dionysius of Corinth writes, was also read aloud in the Sunday liturgy, and 'which we shall read again and again to our edification, as we already do the earlier letter which was written to us by Clement' (i.e., I Clem.): Eusebius HE IV, 23, 11. Jerome, De vir. ill. 17, makes a similar comment about the Epistle of Polycarp: usque hodie in Asiae conventu legitur. The liturgical reading of the Acts of the martyrs is attested by Tertullian's preface to the Acts of Perpetua (1); on the apocalypses cf. p. 215 below.

[99] Flora 3, 6. The strong preference for Matthew in the letter may be for the benefit of the catholic recipient. That Ptolemaeus may also have made use of apocryphal gospels remains no more than a vague conjecture: Quispel, op. cit., pp. 90f.

the Elder quotes Lukan texts.[100] Justin cannot have been a stranger to the Fourth Gospel; but he avoids drawing upon it.[101] He bases himself primarily on Matthew and Luke; but it is possible that he also makes use of 'apocryphal' texts and oral traditions.[102] Mark he will have known and recognised;[103] but compared with the major gospels it plays to all intents and purposes no part in Justin's works—and the same is true, indeed, for other writers. On the other hand, the church at Rhossos at the end of the century was still reading the Gospel of Peter, and, what is more, with the explicit approval of the then bishop of Antioch, which he only later withdrew on dogmatic grounds.[104] Despite this, the Syrian

[100] Irenaeus, Adv. haer. IV, 27, 4; 30, 3.

[101] The latter point had been established as long ago as W. Bousset, Die Evangeliencitate Justins des Märtyrers, 1891, pp. 115–121; and it was confirmed in a wider context by W. Bauer, Orthodoxy, pp. 205f.; cf. also Knox, op. cit., pp. 147f. W. G. Kümmel in Feine-Behm, Einleitung in das N.T.[14], 1965, p. 357, adduces as evidence of Justin's knowledge of John an isolated quotation in I Apol. 61, 4 (Joh. 3:5), which in fact derives from liturgical tradition (A. J. Bellinzoni, The Sayings of Jesus in the Writings of Justin Martyr, Leiden, 1967, pp. 134–138), and an allegedly Johannine phrase in Dial. 100, 1, which actually comes from Matt. 11:27. This certainly is not enough to allow us to conclude, as Kümmel would have us do, that Justin had a Four-Gospel canon. Further Johannine 'echoes' will be found in F. M. Braun, Jean le Théologien et son évangile dans l'église ancienne, 1959, pp. 136–139.

[102] Cf. the detailed evidence in the unpublished thesis of H. Köster, Septuaginta und synoptischer Erzählungsstoff im Schriftbeweis Justins des Märtyrers, 1956; also id., Synoptische Überlieferung bei den Apostolischen Vätern, 1957, pp. 87ff. Bellinzoni (op. cit., n. 101 above), on the other hand, decides against the theory of apocryphal sources, and in favour of a written collection of more, or less contaminated dominical sayings, for which the synoptists served as sources.

[103] Cf. Dial. 103, 8, concerning the ἀπομνημονεύματα, which were written ὑπὸ τῶν ἀποστόλων . . . καὶ τῶν ἐκείνοις παρακολουθησάντων. By 'companions' of the apostles (in the plural!) only Mark and Luke can possibly be meant, since other gospels by disciples of the apostles are out of the question so far as Justin is concerned. The following assertion by W. C. O'Neill, The Theology of Acts in its Historical Setting, 1961, pp. 40f., made to support his theory that Justin did not use Luke, is totally arbitrary: 'The words about those who followed the Apostles need not refer to Luke, and they could equally well apply to Mark or to any other Gospel which could not claim direct apostolic authorship (?).' Cf. further the review by H. F. D. Sparks, JTS N.S. 14, 1963, pp. 457–466.

[104] Bishop Serapion himself writes to the Rhossians: ἐγὼ γὰρ γενόμενος παρ' ὑμῖν, ὑπενόουν τοὺς πάντας ὀρθῇ πίστει προσφέρεσθαι, καὶ μὴ διελθὼν τὸ ὑπ' αὐτῶν προφερόμενον ὀνόματι Πέτρου εὐαγγέλιον, εἶπον ὅτι εἰ τοῦτό ἐστιν μόνον τὸ δοκοῦν ὑμῖν παρέχειν μικροψυχίαν, ἀναγινωσκέθω· νῦν δὲ μαθὼν ὅτι αἱρέσει τινὶ ὁ νοῦς αὐτῶν ἐφώλευεν, ἐκ τῶν λεχθέντων μοι, σπουδάσω πάλιν γένεσθαι πρὸς ὑμᾶς, ὥστε, ἀδελφοί, προσδοκᾶτέ με ἐν τάχει. Serapion now procured a copy of the gospel of the docetic heretics, and stated: τὰ μὲν πλείονα τοῦ ὀρθοῦ λόγου τοῦ σωτῆρος, τινὰ δὲ προσδιεσταλμένα, ἃ καὶ ὑπετάξαμεν ὑμῖν (Eusebius, HE VI, 12, 4. 6).

Didascalia was still using the Gospel of Peter in the third century.[105] The vague picture that emerges is confirmed, after the lapse of seventy years, by the heathen polemist Celsus. Even for him, the 'Gospel' is 'still not a firmly defined entity', and 'the boundaries between canonical and apocryphal' appear to be completely 'fluid'.[106]

As a permanent arrangement, however, this simply cannot continue. In view of the growing flood of gospels of a gnostic character, and in face of the Marcionite claim to be the sole possessors of the few genuine and original documents, the catholic churches in their turn could not evade the necessity of laying down which texts were to be acknowledged as authentic and normative—'documents of the Lord'[107]— and which not.[108] This is perhaps already discernible in the emphasis with which Justin on occasion introduces a dominical saying with the words, 'It is written',[109] or when the 'Elder', who has heard and seen 'the Apostles' (or their disciples),[110] likewise refers to texts which can be 'read' in the Gospel.[111] But the basic principle that there must be an exclusively normative sacred book is still not explicit.

In theory there were three ways in which the Gospel literature could be standardised. The first was that adopted by Marcion: to select one

[105] Strecker, op. cit., p. 251; Lietzmann, Bücher des Neuen Testaments, p. 73, treats this evidence far too lightly, but in his History of the Early Church II, p. 98, expressss a more cautious judgment.

[106] Völker, op. cit., p. 90; Bauer, Orthdoxy, p. 237 n. 13. The Protevangelium Jacobi, which was written about this time, also uses its 'canonical' sources with such freedom that the formation of the Canon can certainly not have been completed by this stage: cf. O. Cullmann in: N.T. Apocrypha, I, p. 278.

[107] Thus Dionysius of Corinth mentions (Eusebius, HE IV, 23, 12) heretics among whom καὶ τῶν κυριακῶν ῥαδιουργῆσαί τινες ἐπιβέβληνται γραφῶν. The reference is still, however, solely, or at least primarily, to writings of the Old, not of the 'New' Testament: Zahn, op. cit., I, p. 97; cf. p. 188 below, on Irenaeus.

[108] Complaints about the distortion and forgery of dominical sayings are general in this period: Polycarp, Phil. 7, 1; Dionysius of Corinth in Eusebius, HE IV, 23, 12; Irenaeus, Adv. haer. I pref.; cf. Bauer, Orthodoxy, pp. 183f.

[109] This feature has not yet appeared in the Apology, but occurs in the later, anti-Jewish Dialogue: 49; 100; 105.

[110] Irenaeus, Adv. haer. IV, 27, 1. The Latin text reads: audivi a quodam presbytero, qui audierat ab his, qui apostolos viderant. The edition of A. Rousseau (Irénée de Lyon: Contre les Hérésies, Livre IV, Paris, 1965), I, p. 263 decides, in the light of Adv. haer. IV, 32, 1 (senior apostolorum discipulus and of the Armenian version, on τοῦ ἀκηκοότος παρὰ τῶν ἀποστόλων αὐτούς τε ἑωρακότος as the underlying Greek text. For the chronology the decisive point is still that Irenaeus himself had heard the Elder speak.

[111] Irenaeus, Adv. haer. IV, 29, 1: qui ergo haec imputant, non legunt in evangelio, ubi discipulis dicentibus domino "Quare in parabolis loqueris eis?" (Mt. 13, 10), respondit dominus. . . .

single gospel, to revise it in accordance with one's own ideas, and then to declare this and this alone to be *the* Gospel. To accept such a solution of the existing difficulty, however, was neither desirable nor possible; it involved altogether too savage a curtailment of the traditional deposit of sayings and stories of the Lord. Secondly, an attempt might be made to combine the trustworthy and useful elements in all texts into a single new gospel; or finally, one might select various gospels, and pronounce them valid in combination, as a complex unity. Prevailing practice had prepared the way for the last-named of these three solutions; but it too had serious obstacles to overcome, since, as is well known, the gospels do not agree at every point, and indeed, if we include John, display very considerable differences of content. Nevertheless, it was this solution which in the end prevailed, nor is it hard to guess why. It would have been quite impossible to counter those gospels which it was desired to reject and controvert as 'forgeries'—in particular, the gospel of Marcion—with a new work which had only now been artificially constructed. Such a canon would have made things all too easy for hostile criticism. The 'authentic' gospels had to be ancient books, accepted and handed down from long ago, if they were to succeed in imposing themselves and inspiring belief. It was necessary to take account of Marcion's more rigorous requirements of authenticity and originality; and in this way it was in fact possible actually to outdo him in fidelity to and preservation of the truth.[112]

It was in this situation, and against this enemy, that the set of four Church gospels must have been consolidated.[113] Marcion and Justin

[112] This is also the explanation for the acceptance of Mark, a gospel which at this period was given preference hardly anywhere, having been superseded by the great synoptic gospels, especially Matthew, and virtually suppressed in the practice of the Church. The *Epistula apostolorum,* for instance, is apparently unacquainted with it: M. Hornschuh, *Studien zur epistula apostolorum,* 1965, p. 11; and even Origen 'displays little familiarity with this gospel': P. Koetschau, in the Introduction to *Contra Celsum* (Origenes Werke, *GCS,* III, 1899), p. xxxiii. In the effort to sacrifice nothing that came from ancient and 'authentic' sources, however, it was brought out once more, and accepted.

[113] In opposition to the dominant opinion as given by Harnack, and especially by E. J. Goodspeed, *The Formation of the New Testament,* 1926, and *An Introduction to the New Testament,* 1937, this point has rightly been made not only by Knox, but also by K. L. Carroll, 'The Creation of the Fourfold Gospel', *BJRL* 37, 1954-5, pp. 68–77. Knox, *op. cit.,* p. 152, thinks in terms of the quarter-century from 150 to 175 for this development, but Carroll would prefer to settle on a date around 155. Both see the Four-Gospel canon as a Roman and anti-Marcionite creation: 'The fourfold Gospel was an answer to Marcion' (Carroll, p. 75). But even if this last statement is correct, it was inevitable that the new arrangement had at once to be turned against all other heretical gospels as well. That the new Gospel Canon was particularly directed against Marcion cannot be deduced from its composition. The theory of D. De Bruyne, 'Les plus anciens prologues latins des Évangiles', *RevBénéd* 40, 1928, pp. 193–214,

are still unacquainted with it; but for Irenaeus the Four-Gospel canon
is already an established entity, which he champions as an indispensable
and recognised collection against all the deviations of the heretics.[114]
To define the date more precisely than this is not possible.[115] As the
area of provenance Asia Minor is the most likely, but Rome is also a
possibility. Against Rome, however, is the fact that the Gospel of John,
which the Valentinians had promoted, is not only ignored by Justin,
but even a generation later could be attacked by the orthodox theologian
Caius as a forgery.[116] On the other hand, 'John' is a recognised apostle
of the churches of Asia Minor, and Irenaeus is proud of the fact that,
through Polycarp, he himself has a direct link with him.[117] On this
question of origins a definite conclusion can hardly be arrived at, because the Four-Gospel canon was not a conscious creation, 'constructed' at one blow, nor was it disseminated from a single centre. Its
formation was gradual and the result of earlier presuppositions, and it
was in the end universally accepted.[118]

The contrary has, however, again and again been asserted and defended, especially by Harnack.[119] Harnack appeals to the fact that in

---

that for the edition (also in his view Roman and anti-Marcionite) of the Four-
Gospel canon and the Pauline letters the Marcionite prologues were adopted,
being expanded in the case of the Gospels, has now rightly been abandoned. The
so-called anti-Marcionite prologues to the Gospels are not a unity, and come
from a later period: E. Haenchen, *Die Apostelgeschichte*[5], 1965, p. 8 n. 8. In
view of all that has been said in the previous chapter the theory that the Four-
Gospel canon was originally a gnostic creation seems quite inept: cf. J. N. San-
ders, *The Fourth Gospel in the Early Church*, 1943, p. 47, and R. P. C. Hanson,
Tradition in the Early Church, 1962, p. 192.

[114] This does not mean, however, that he had already become familiar with it
in Asia Minor in his 'earliest youth', as Harnack thinks, *Origin*, p. 71: 'Irenaeus is unaware that the written Gospel, organised in this way, has not always
existed, in fact he derives its fourfold structure from a divine ordinance of salvation, corresponding to the order of nature, and already foreshadowed in the
O.T.' Actually, as Knox, *op. cit.*, p. 152, rightly remarks, in the relevant passage
(Adv. haer. III, 1, 1) Irenaeus gives a purely historical account of the Canon's
gradual emergence in chronological sequence, and wisely says nothing about
when this catholic system, which he regards as the only possible one, became
general. In his day this goal had in fact not yet been completely attained: cf.
p. 174 below.

[115] Unfortunately we cannot make use of the Diatessaron for this purpose,
first because its exact dating is problematic, and secondly because its dependence on the Four-Gospel canon, though probable, is not absolutely certain:
Kümmel, *op. cit.*, pp. 354f.

[116] Cf. pp. 237ff. below.

[117] Eusebius, *HE* V, 20, 5–7; cf. H. von Campenhausen, 'Polykarp von Smyrna und die Pastoralbriefe', in: *Aus der Frühzeit des Christentums*, 1963, pp.
212–217.

[118] So also C. F. D. Moule, *The Birth of the New Testament*, 1962, p. 188.

[119] Cf. esp. Harnack, *Geschichte der altchristlichen Literatur II: Chronologie*

the manuscript tradition the collective title 'Gospel' is not repeated for the individual books, which are headed simply 'according to'[120] Matthew, Mark, and so on, that the Gospels are already cited in this way, and in a fixed sequence, by the Muratorian canon,[121] and that it is not by chance that Irenaeus speaks of a single 'fourfold' Gospel.[122] All this, it is alleged, must be the result of an earlier, normative publication of the Four-Gospel 'canon',[123] which is best understood as an official act of the Roman church. The argument, however, is full of flaws, and all probability is against it. The extant manuscript tradition of the Gospels within the framework of the New Testament is too late to allow us to draw any conclusions concerning the second century. Furthermore, any publication which established a fixed sequence of gospels is conceivable only as from the start in the form of a codex;[124] had they been recorded on scrolls, which at any time could hardly contain more than one gospel,[125] this would have been quite impossible. In fact, the codex form seems to have been the rule for biblical texts even as early as the second century;[126] but these codices were, so far

---

I, 1897, pp. 681–884; *Entstehung*, pp. 47ff.; F. C. Burkitt, *Two Lectures on the Gospels*, 1901, pp. 17f.; also Knox, *op. cit.*, p. 141. Quite pointless is the question whether the Four-Gospel canon was preceded by a collection of two or three gospels, as Leipoldt, *op. cit.*, I, p. 150, conjectures. It retrojects the idea of a quasi-canonical regulation into a period in which such a thing neither existed nor was desired.

[120] It should be noted that this construction with κατά in the superscriptions is, strictly speaking, 'a good Greek substitute for the genitive' (Bauer, *Orthodoxy*, p. 50), and should therefore be taken to imply no more than the normal ascription of authorship.

[121] Can. Murat. 2; 9; cf. p. 250 below.

[122] Adv. haer. III, 5, 1 (cf. n. 215 below); 11, 8 (cf. n. 256 below). The word εὐαγγέλιον occurs in Irenaeus almost always in the singular: A. Benoit, *Saint Irénée. Introduction à l'étude de sa théologie*, 1960, pp. 107f.

[123] According to Harnack (*Entstehung*, p. 47 n. 1) even the titles of the Gospels of Mark and Luke point to the fact that this publication took place at an early stage: had the Four-Gospel canon been a later formation, then 'in all probability care would have been taken to ensure that in the superscription Mark's Gospel was presented as that of Peter, Luke's as that of Paul'. But these ancient and presumably original titles were already long established, as Papias indicates and indeed Justin as well (cf. n. 103 above), and could no longer be altered arbitrarily at a later stage.

[124] Zahn, *op. cit.*, II, p. 364: 'One can speak of a fixed order of the Gospels obviously only from the time at which the Gospels were united in one codex'— which in Zahn's view means hardly before the time of Origen (p. 343).

[125] As they are shown, for example, in the Laurentius mosaic in the sepulchre of Galla Placidia at Ravenna, where they appear in the order: Mark—Luke—Matthew—John.

[126] C. H. Roberts, 'The Codex', *Proceedings of the British Academy* 1954, pp. 169–204. To this extent Zahn's arguments (I, pp. 65ff.) are today obsolete. P. L. Hedley, 'The Egyptian Tests of the Gospels and Acts', *CQR* 118, 1934,

as we can tell, at first still small, and hardly adequate to combine four
gospels at once in a single volume,[127] which would be necessary in order
to establish a 'canonical' order. That there was at first no such authentic arrangement is confirmed also by the variations in the sequence of
the gospels, both at that time and later.[128] The fact that Irenaeus and
the Muratorian canon regard the fourfold gospel as a spiritual unity is a
theological phenomenon and nothing to do with book production. It is
therefore impossible to discern traces of a once-for-all 'edition', definitive for all later developments. Consequently, the restriction to four
'canonical' gospels must be seen as the result of a gradual, and at first
quite limited, development which spread as a defence against the
Marcionite and other heretical gospels, and finally prevailed. This may
be seen from the toleration, already mentioned, of the Gospel of Peter
at Rhossos,[129] from the polemic against John, which could still persist
even in the third century,[130] and not least from the attempts to overcome the multiplicity of gospels with a new, composite Gospel,[131]
that is, by introducing a harmony of the Gospels.

No less a person than the bishop and apologist, Theophilus of
Antioch, who also wrote against the heretics and in particular against
Marcion, is said to have 'combined the words of the four Evangelists in
one work'.[132] The accuracy of the statement is not certain, since it occurs
only in Jerome, who is guilty of quite a number of confusions and

---

p. 228, assumed that the Church's use of the codex 'was associated with the
formation of the fourfold Gospel canon' (which at the same time created a canonical form of the text), but according to Roberts, *op. cit.*, p. 191 n. 4, he himself
later withdrew this view. Personally, I do not find Roberts' own conjectures
about the influence of Mark's gospel, which he regards as of Roman provenance,
on the codex form (pp. 187–190) particularly happy either.

[127] Roberts, *op. cit.*, pp. 191f.

[128] Zahn, *op. cit.*, II, pp. 364–375. The monarchian prologues follow an order
which is particularly to be found in other western circles as well: Matthew–
John–Luke–Mark, thus placing the apostles before those who were merely
disciples of the apostles. On Irenaeus cf. n. 244 below, also n. 264.

[129] Eusebius, *HE* VI, 12, 3–6 (cf. n. 104 above). Serapion subsequently came
to regard these Christians as heretics, but at first had no objections either to
them or to their reading of the Gospel of Peter, reading which was assuredly not
just in private.

[130] Cf. pp. 238ff. below.

[131] It is repeatedly asserted that Justin had already made use of a harmony of
the Synoptists; cf. H. Chadwick, *Early Christian Thought and the Classical
Tradition*, 1966, p. 125. But all the evidence suggests that what was involved was
a collation of dominical sayings for catechetical and apologetic use, not a full-
blown harmony; cf. the demonstration in Bellinzoni, *op. cit.*, esp. pp. 141f.

[132] Jerome, *Ep.* 121, 6: . . . Theophilus Antiochenae ecclesiae septimus post
Petrum apostolum episcopus, qui quattuor evangelistarum in unum opus dicta
compingens ingenii sui nobis monumenta dimisit, haec super hac parabola
[Lk. 16:3–14] in suis commentariis est locutus.

errors in this field. Seeing, however, that Jerome had actually read Theophilus' commentary on the Gospel, and quotes it,[133] I would not like to dismiss the information summarily as false.[134] What is quite certain is that Tatian wrote such a harmony, as 'a' chord of a fourth,[135] in which he at the same time revised the texts, cut out the infancy narratives of Matthew and Luke, and even drew on apocryphal gospels for the form of particular sayings.[136] He will probably have been acquainted with the new 'canon', but adopted a fairly free attitude toward it.[137] Because he had been a pupil of Justin at Rome, it seems very likely that Tatian too constructed his Harmony to a certain extent in opposition to the Gospel of Marcion,[138] whose doctrines he in no way shared.[139] In any case, on his home ground of Syria, his harmony of the Gospels actually established itself as the canonical gospel of the Church, and this 'Gospel of the Mixed' was dislodged only at a late date, in the fifth and sixth centuries, and that with a deal of trouble,

[133] The commentary is mentioned by him again in De vir. ill. 25, and in the Prologue to his own commentary on Matthew. On the problems connected with this commentary of Theophilus cf. O. Bardenhewer, *Geschichte der altkirchl. Literatur* I², 1913, pp. 312ff. That Tatian cannot have been the only compiler of this kind is apparently confirmed by Ambrose, who comments on Lk. 1:2: plerique etiam ex quattuor evangelii libris in unum ea quae venenatis putaverunt assertionibus convenientia referserunt.

[134] One further, though very late, witness to the existence of this work (Theophilus Antiocenus episcopus, qui prius quattuor evangelia in uno volumine rescripsit) has been adduced by B. de Gaiffier from the 'Liber Sancti Jacobi', which belongs to the high Middle Ages, and is discussed by him in 'Une citation de l'Harmonie évangelique de Théophile d'Antioche dans le "Liber Sancti Jacobi" ', in: *RevSR* (Mélanges M. Andrieu) 1956, pp. 173–179.

[135] The phrase διὰ τεσσάρων, as is well known, is a musical term (the 'fourth'), and as such is not certainly a reference to four Gospels.

[136] It is not possible, but also it is not necessary, for me to embark here on an account of the infinitely complex problems of Diatessaron studies. The ancient references to Tatian are discussed in Elze, *op. cit.*, pp. 106–126; cf. also R. M. Grant, 'Tatian and the Bible', *StudPatr* I, 1957, pp. 297–306. According to G. C. Hansen, 'Zu den Evangelienzitaten in den "Acta Archelai" ', *StudPatr* VII, 1966, p. 481, Tatian's 'substantial links with extra-canonical traditional material' are today generally acknowledged.

[137] Cf. Kümmel, *op. cit.*, p. 355.

[138] Harnack, p. 73. The doubts on this score expressed by Blackman, *op. cit.*, p. 63, seem to me to have little foundation. H. Vogels, 'Der Einfluss Marcions und Tatians auf Text und Kanon des Neuen Testaments' in: *Synoptische Studien* (Festschrift Wikenhauser), 1953, p. 289, rightly emphasises that such opposition at the same time implies dependence. Unfortunately it is still quite possible to have doubts about the connection which Vogels tries to demonstrate between the Gospel texts of the two men.

[139] It would seem that Irenaeus, Adv. haer. I, 28, 1; III, 23, 8, was biased in branding Tatian as a heretic: Elze, *op. cit.*, pp. 106ff.; also H. Langerbeck, *Aufsätze zur Gnosis* (ed. H. Dörries), 1967, pp. 168ff.

by the so-called 'Gospel of the Separated'.[140] As the translations of this work, and its effects on the history of the text show, it exerted a considerable influence even beyond the borders of Syria, although nowhere was any harmony of the gospels able to establish itself permanently as the standard gospel. How strongly the need was felt for a compendium of the Gospel material, even where a proper harmony of the gospels had been rejected, is shown by an attempt of the 'Alexandrian Ammonius'. About 220 this man wrote a kind of synopsis of the four Gospels,[141] since he apparently 'placed alongside the Gospel of Matthew those sections from the other gospels which referred to the same subject-matter, with the inevitable result that the ordered continuity of the three (other gospels) was destroyed, so far as the weft of the reading was concerned'.[142] Only Eusebius, with his Canones, succeeded in avoiding such drawbacks, and yet to some extent meeting the underlying need.[143]

So far we have considered the Four-Gospel canon and the harmonies of the Gospels in isolation. And it is true that originally they did provide a solution which for the time being was independent and in its context successful of that 'canonical' problem which most urgently needed to be cleared up. The outstanding importance of the Gospels is still very obvious in Irenacus.[144] It could therefore be said, if you like, that the first catholic canon was originally conceived as 'unicellular', having one section only.[145] Marcion's bible, however, now posed un-

---

[140] Bauer, *Orthodoxy*, pp. 29–33. H. Köster, 'ΓΝΩΜΑΙ ΔΙΑΦΟΡΟΙ: The Origin and Nature of Diversification in the History of Early Christianity', *HTR* 58, 1965, p. 304, thinks that before the time of Tatian none of the canonical gospels had yet reached Edessa. This, in my opinion, is most improbable.

[141] Eusebius, *Ep. ad Carp.* (in H. von Soden, *Die Schriften des Neuen Testaments* I, 1902, pp. 388f.): Ἀμμώνιος μὲν ὁ Ἀλεξανδρεὺς πολλὴν ὡς εἰκὸς φιλοπονίαν καὶ σπουδὴν εἰσαγηοχὼς τὸ διὰ τεσσάρων ἡμῖν καταλέλοιπεν εὐαγγέλιον, τῷ κατὰ Ματθαῖον τὰς ὁμοφώνους τῶν λοιπῶν εὐαγγελιστῶν περικοπὰς παραθείς, ὡς ἐξ ἀνάγκης συμβῆναι τὸν τῆς ἀκολουθίας εἱρμὸν τῶν τριῶν διαφθαρῆναι ὅσον ἐπὶ τῷ ὕφει τῆς ἀναγνώσεως· ἵνα δὲ σωζομένου καὶ τοῦ τῶν λοιπῶν δι᾽ ὅλου σώματός τε καὶ εἱρμοῦ εἰδέναι ἔχοις τοὺς οἰκείους ἑκάστου εὐαγγελιστοῦ τόπους, ἐν οἷς κατὰ τῶν αὐτῶν ἠνέχθησαν φιλαλήθως εἰπεῖν, ἐκ τοῦ πονήματος τοῦ προειρημένου ἀνδρὸς εἰληφὼς ἀφορμὰς καθ᾽ ἑτέραν μέθοδον κανόνας δέκα τὸν ἀριθμὸν διεχάραξά σοι τοὺς ὑποτεταγμένους.

[142] T. Zahn, 'Der Exeget Ammonius und andere Ammonii,' *ZKG* 38, 1920, pp. 3ff.; doubts about this interpretation are expressed in Harnack, *Geschichte* I, 1893, pp. 406f.

[143] J. Moreau, art. 'Eusebios von Caesarea,' *RAC* VI, 1966, col. 1063.

[144] Cf. Adv. haer. II, 27, 2: universae scripturae et prophetiae et evangelia. Here apparently 'the whole N.T. is termed "evangelia": O. Michel, art., 'Evangelium', *RAC* VI, 1966, col. 1126; cf. Hippolytus, *Elench.* VIII, 19.

[145] Jülicher-Fascher, *op. cit.*, p. 475; Harnack, *Entstehung*, p. 9 n. 2; cf. n. 162 below; Kümmel, *op. cit.*, p. 357 reaches the same conclusion on different grounds. As late as the seventh century, in the Coptic *Quaestiones Theodori*, a special curse is laid on anyone who does not believe in the four Gospels: C. D. G. Müller, "Was können wir aus der koptischen Literatur über Theologie und

avoidably the further question of the place and status of the Pauline letters. With regard to these the Church found itself in an especially difficult situation. On the one hand, she too recognised that Paul was the only apostle of whom a large and important group of writings were extant, having been handed down from the earliest days—writings, moreover, which had long enjoyed particular respect. His epistles had, indeed, already been counterfeited in the first century. Furthermore, Paul occupied a central position in the Lukan Acts; and as early as I Clement he, like Ignatius, had been celebrated as a Roman martyr, and explicit reference made to his writings.[146] When it came to the point, it was impossible to give him up. On the other hand, however, his theology with its radical faith in the miraculous power of redemption and of the Spirit, with its mysterious speculations and tendencies to asceticism, with its disregard of all natural and organisational safeguards for the Church, and its rejection of the Law and of all the systems of this world, simply did not answer to the dominant needs of catholic piety. Instead it went half way to meet the fantastic, antinomian tendencies of the gnosis, hostile to the cosmos and critical of the Church, and seemed to justify them. The use which Marcion and other sects had made of his writings appeared to discredit them completely. The Valentinians in particular regarded themselves *vis-à-vis* the great Church as the true Pauline theologians,[147] appealed to him constantly, and saw in 'the Apostle' the embodiment of a type of the Spirit of Christ himself.[148] Had Paul not in fact become, as Tertullian ironically put it, the 'apostle of Marcion' and the 'apostle of the heretics'?[149]

Frömmigkeit der Ägyptischen Kirche lernen?' *Oriens Christ.* 48, 1964, p. 200. This accords with the special honour paid to the books of the Gospels in liturgical worship. On the other hand, the hypothesis that there were originally 'two one-part canons', i.e., a Gospel canon and a Pauline canon, put forward by W. Schmithals, *Das kirchliche Apostelamt*, 1961, p. 258, proceeds from an unclear concept of canon, and ignores the decisive effect which Marcion's canon exercised on canonical development. The fantastic theories of a conjectural two-part canon of the 'early Paulinists' before Marcion, advanced by W. Hartke, *Vier urchristliche Parteien und ihre Vereinigung zur apostolischen Kirche*, 1961, pp. 582f., 599ff., will not be discussed here.

[146] Cf. pp. 144f. above.

[147] This point is emphasised (to this extent undoubtedly correctly) by Langerbeck; cf. pp. 145f. above.

[148] Clem. Alex., Exc. ex Theod. 23, 2: . . . καὶ ἐξ εὐδοκίας τῶν αἰώνων Ἰησοῦς προβάλλεται παράκλητος τῷ παρελθόντι αἰῶνι· ἐν τύπῳ δὲ παρακλήτου ὁ Παῦλος ἀναστάσεως ἀπόστολος γέγονεν. On the interpretation of this passage cf. F. Sagnard in his edition, *Extraits de Théodote*, Paris, 1948, p. 106.

[149] Adv. Marc. III, 5, 4; on what follows cf. H. von Campenhausen, 'Polykarp', pp. 242f.; W. Schneemelcher, 'Paulus in der griechischen Kirche des zweiten Jahrhunderts', *ZKG* 75, 1064, pp. 6ff.

Had he not at the end already been lost to the catholic church? About the middle of the second century, in the circles of the strenuously orthodox, this must in fact have been a widely held opinion. It is not only Papias and Justin who pass over Paul in silence, though they were of course acquainted with his writings;[150] even the pseudo-Justin, the author of a work on the Resurrection,[151] has apparently no desire to know the 'Apostle of the Resurrection',[152] and Hegesippus not only leaves him out of his list of 'canonical' authorities,[153] but even inveighs—consciously or unconsciously—against a passage which occurs in I Corinthians.[154] The precarious explanations by which the pseudonymous II Peter, which certainly dates from around this period, makes the obscurity of Paul's Epistles responsible for the fact that they have been misused by 'ignorant and unstable' people[155] are also clear enough evidence.

In opposition to this school of thought others equally decisively champion the Apostle.[156] Above all, this was the great service of Bishop Polycarp of Smyrna,[157] who emphatically commends the reading of

---

[150] A. von Harnack, *Judentum und Judenchristentum in Justins Dialog mit Tryphon*, 1913, pp. 5of.; Bauer, *Orthodoxy*, pp. 214–217; G. Klein, *Die zwölf Apostel*, pp. 192–201. The same may also be true of the *Protevangelium Jacobi*, which makes lavish use of the Gospels: É. de Strycker, *La forme la plus ancienne du Protévangile de Jacques*, Brussels, 1961, p. 426.

[151] Despite the new and interesting rescue-attempt by P. Prigent, *Justin et l'ancien Testament*, 1964, pp. 5off., I cannot bring myself to accept this work as authentic.

[152] Cf. n. 148 above. The passages from Methodius which quote Paul, and which Prigent, *op. cit.*, pp. 39ff., would like to attribute to the work in question, cannot for this very reason derive from it in their present form.

[153] Eusebius, *HE* IV, 22, 3 (cf. n. 92 above); A. Hilgenfeld, *Judentum und Judenchristentum*, 1886, pp. 43ff.

[154] I Cor. 2:9: Stephanus Gobarus in Photius, Bible, cod. 232 (Routh, I², p. 219); cf. n. 92 above; Bauer, *Orthodoxy*, pp. 213f.

[155] II Pet. 3:15f.; cf. Grant, *Letter*, p. 78. For 'Peter', therefore, the Pauline letters are already reckoned among the 'scriptures'. For criticism of Paul cf. also James 2:14–26, and the Epistle of Peter 2, 4 in the Clementine Homilies: καὶ ταῦτα ἔτι μου περιόντος ἐπεχείρησάν τινες ποικίλαις τισὶν ἑρμηνείαις τοὺς ἐμοὺς λόγους μετασχηματίζειν εἰς τὴν τοῦ νόμου κατάλυσιν.

[156] This is the element of truth in the view of J. Werner, *Der Paulinismus des Irenäus*, 1889, pp. 46–58, that the great Church was first compelled to make a 'quasi-canonical use' of the Epistles by the gnostic appeals to Paul.

[157] The theory of P. N. Harrison, *Polycarp's two Epistles to the Philippians*, 1936, that there were in fact two letters by Polycarp, the first in the time of Ignatius, the second dated (by Harrison) around 135, has rightly met with fairly general acceptance. There are, in my view, no objections to placing the principal letter substantially later; for more recent studies have shown that Polycarp suffered martyrdom certainly not earlier than 155–6, and probably not until the end of the sixth decade of the century; cf. H. von Campenhausen, 'Bearbeitungen und Interpolationen des Polykarpmartyriums', in *Aus der Frühzeit des Christentums*, 1963, pp. 253f.

'the blessed and glorious Paul' who 'taught the word of truth accurately and reliably',[158] but at the same time rejects Marcion and anyone who 'twists the Lord's words in accordance with his own desires' as 'first-born of Satan'.[159] Tatian is said to have produced his own edition of the Pauline epistles, polishing and touching up the style,[160] and then to have set them up against Marcion's 'Apostle', just as he had opposed his 'Harmony' to the latter's 'Gospel'.[161] In the process, his anti-heretical interest in 'rescuing' the Apostle seems to have lost all sense of proportion and to have overstepped the mark. A presbyter in Asia had to be deposed, because, 'from love for Paul' and even indeed using Paul's name,[162] he forged an Acts of Paul, 'as though from his own

---

[158] Polycarp, Phil. 3, 2: οὔτε γὰρ ἐγὼ οὔτε ἄλλος ὅμοιος ἐμοὶ δύναται κατακο-λουθῆσαι τῇ σοφίᾳ τοῦ μακαρίου καὶ ἐνδόξου Παύλου, ὃς γενόμενος ἐν ὑμῖν κατὰ πρόσωπον τῶν τότε ἀνθρώπων ἐδίδαξεν ἀκριβῶς καὶ βεβαίως τὸν περὶ ἀληθείας λόγον, ὃς καὶ ἀπὼν ὑμῖν ἔγραψεν ἐπιστολάς, εἰς ἃς ἐὰν ἐγκύπτητε, δυνηθήσεσθε οἰκοδομεῖσθαι εἰς τὴν δοθεῖσαν ὑμῖν πίστιν.

[159] Polycarp, Phil. 7, 1: . . . καὶ ὃς ἂν μεθοδεύῃ τὰ λόγια τοῦ κυρίου πρὸς τὰς ἰδίας ἐπιθυμίας καὶ λέγῃ μήτε ἀνάστασιν μήτε κρίσιν, οὗτος πρωτότοκός ἐστι τοῦ σατανᾶ. Cf. Irenaeus, Adv. haer. III, 3, 4; also Campenhausen, 'Polykarp', p. 238. If this passage is aimed, as it seems to be, directly at Marcion, then it is one further piece of evidence, how little 'falsification of the text' as such was regarded as the crucial offence of the arch-heretic. In order to explain it there is no need to conclude, with Knox, op. cit., pp. 112f., that Proto-Luke must have been closer to the Marcionite gospel than the canonical Luke.

[160] Eusebius, HE IV, 29, 6: . . . τοῦ δ' ἀποστόλου φασὶ τολμῆσαί τινας αὐτὸν μεταφράσαι φωνάς, ὡς ἐπιδιορθούμενον αὐτῶν τὴν τῆς φράσεως σύνταξιν. Jerome, Comm. Tit., prol., says of Tatian: nonnullas Pauli epistolas repudiavit. This may refer merely to Hebrews and Philemon, possibly also to I–II Timothy, but in any case not to the Marcionite forgeries, which Jerome also rejected; K. L. Carroll, 'The Expansion of the Pauline Corpus', JBL 72, 1953, p. 237 n. 35, disagrees, but at the same time wishes to make Tatian the creator of the enlarged canon of Pauline epistles!

[161] This is not, however, to say that he, like Marcion, had already combined the Diatessaron with the Pauline letters to make a fixed canon. (Nor had the Scillitan martyrs, even though they listed Paul's letters among their 'books': libri et epistolae Pauli, viri iusti [αἱ καθ' ἡμᾶς βίβλοι καὶ αἱ πρὸς ἐπὶ τούτοις ἐπιστολαὶ Παύλου τοῦ ὁσίου ἀνδρός]: Passio Scil. 12; cf. p. 62n. 3 above.) The isolated piece of information which Eusebius separates from his previous men-tion of the Diatessaron rather suggests the opposite. In HE IV, 29, 5f., he relates that certain Encratites, the Severians, of whom he describes Tatian as the ἀρχηγός: χρῶνται μὲν οὖν οὗτοι νόμῳ καὶ προφήταις καὶ εὐαγγελίοις . . . βλασφημοῦντες δὲ Παῦλον τὸν ἀπόστολον, ἀθετοῦσιν αὐτοῦ τὰς ἐπιστολάς, μηδὲ τὰς Πράξεις τῶν ἀποστόλων καταδεχόμενοι. The Doctrina Addai describes the Diatessaron, tout court, as the 'New Testament': 'Much people, however, assembled day by day for liturgical prayer, and for the Old Testament, and for the New (sc.), the Diatessaron' (Philipps, op. cit., p. 35; Harnack, Überlieferung, p. 494). On Tatian's exegesis of Paul, R. M. Grant, 'Tatian and the Bible,' StudPatr I, 1957, pp. 300–303.

[162] W. Schneemelcher, Acts of Paul, in: N.T. Apocrypha II, p. 323.

N

resources he was able to add something to Paul's writings'.[163] For
Theophilus of Antioch it was the divine Logos who spoke through
the teachings which Paul gives;[164] and when he expounds the parable
of the Unjust Steward (Lk. 16:1ff.) directly in terms of Paul, his conversion, and his preaching freedom from the Law,[165] one would expect
such an exegesis rather from a Marcionite[166] than from a zealous opponent of their heresy.[167] The Epistle of the Apostles also offers 'an out-
spoken defence' of Paul, in which the significance of his ministry for
salvation history is corroborated from the Old Testament prophets.[168]

The truth of the matter is that because Marcion had canonised the
Pauline epistles only in mutilated form, in their unmutilated form they
had for that very reason become all the more trustworthy and acceptable. All that was necessary was that Paul should be extricated from
his supposed opposition to the first apostles,[169] and instead associated
with and subordinated to them. They alone, as was now emphasised,

[163] Tertullian, De bapt. 17, 5: Quodsi quae Pauli perperam inscripta sunt
[exemplum Theclae] ad licentiam mulierum docendi tinguendique defendunt,
sciant in Asia presbyterum, qui eam scripturam construxit, quasi titulo Pauli
de suo cumulans, convictum atqeu confessum id se amore Pauli fecisse loco
decessisse.

[164] Ad Autol. III, 14: . . . κελεύει ἡμᾶς ὁ Θεῖος Λόγος. Cf. R. M. Grant,
'Scripture, Rhetoric and Theology in Theophilus', VC 13, 1959, p. 40. It is true
that the passage states a general rule; but the specific reference to I Tim. 2:2
is obvious. Clem. Alex., Exc. ex Theod. 23, describes Paul as ἐν τύπῳ παρακλήτου
= of Jesus.

[165] Jerome, Ep. 121, 6; cf. esp.: coepitque eos, qui prius versabantur in lege
et sic in Christo crediderant, ut arbitrarentur se in lege iustificandos, docere
legem abolitam, prophetas praeterisse et, quae antea pro lucro fuerint, reputari
stercora.

[166] Origen, Hom. Luc. XXV (Rauer², p. 151) mentions a heretical (Marcionite?) group who interpreted the Paraclete prophecy in Joh. 14:16f. of the
apostle Paul: A. von Harnack, Der kirchengeschichtliche Ertrag der exegetischen
Arbeiten des Origenes II, 1919, pp. 70f.

[167] In the case of the work entitled τὰ Ἡρακλείτου εἰς τὸν ἀπόστολον,
mentioned in Eusebius, HE V, 27, it is also possible that 'we are dealing with an
apologetic writing in favour of the apostle to the Gentiles, which is meant to
defend him against misinterpretations and even misuse on the part of the heretics': Bauer, Orthodoxy, p. 149. By contrast, the attempt of W. H. C. Frend,
'The Gnostic-Manichaean Tradition in Roman North Africa', JEH 4, 1953,
pp. 13ff., to interpret even the testimony to Paul by the Scillitan martyrs (cf.
n. 161 above) as springing from an interest that was one-sidedly gnostic in
character has rightly been refuted by G. Bonner, 'The Scillitan Saints and the
Pauline Epistles, JEH 7, 1956, pp. 141–146.

[168] Hornschuh, op. cit., pp. 73ff., 84ff. Hornschuh himself would date the
Epistle in the pre-Marcionite period: cf. p. 142 n. 177.

[169] The 'rest of the apostles' are mentioned alongside 'Paul himself' as early
as Polycarp, Phil. 9,1. That the reference is to the Twelve seems to me, despite
the objections of Klein, op. cit., p. 107, and Schmithals, op. cit., p. 228, very
much the most probable interpretation.

had 'been all the time with the Lord Jesus Christ' and Paul had simply
'handed on' the teaching he received from them, in contrast to all those
scoundrels who had so quickly gained ground by 'forging' his apostolic
words.[170] The Pauline Epistles could not be abandoned—but if they
were to be preserved they had to be balanced with needs and ideas of a
wholly different kind. It is, in my view, indisputable that it was at this
time and with this intention that the Pastoral Epistles must have been
composed.[171] Their author must at least have been intimately connected
with Polycarp.[172] With the same strength of feeling and with almost the
same phrases, they attack, as he does, 'the godless chatter and contradictions (ἀντιθέσεις) of what is falsely called knowledge (γνῶσις)',[173]
commend instruction with the help of 'scripture, all of which is inspired
by God',[174] and portray a Paul who rejects all exaggerated asceticism,
and directs his readers toward an officially organised Church life, bour-
geois virtues, and respect for the ordinance of creation. It is only within
this framework that Paul's doctrines of grace, faith, and the freedom of
the 'just'[175] are proclaimed—in other words: they portray the sort of
Paul who was needed in the fight against gnosis, and who was quite
definitely not to be found in the genuine epistles. Only when combined
with these inauthentic letters could the genuine legacy of the apostle
be tolerated by the Church and made 'canonical'.

The trends and reactions, therefore, which were trying to make
themselves heard in the troubled generation after Marcion were neither
unified nor individually clear nor thought through to their logical
conclusion. The paucity of material would make them even harder for
us to interpret, were it not that at the end of this period an outstanding
personality arose, who brought together the many different currents of

[170] So, e.g., in the 'III Corinthians' which appears in Acts of Paul 4:
ἐγὼ γὰρ ἐν ἀρχῇ παρέδωκα ὑμῖν, ἃ καὶ παρέλαβον ὑπὸ τῶν πρὸ ἐμοῦ
ἀποστόλων γενομένων τὸν πάντα χρόνον μετὰ 'Ιησοῦ χριστῷ . . . Similarly in
Ep. Apost. 31; 33; cf. Bauer, Orthodoxy, p. 114 n. 6. A tendency to some
extent similar, but as yet not essentially anti-heretical, may already be discerned
in the canonical Acts. Klein, however, in my view exaggerates the degree to
which it is present (cf. esp. op. cit., pp. 210ff.), and is wrong to compare it with
the instances just quoted.

[171] So also H. Köster, art. 'Häretiker im Urchristentum', RGG³ III, 1959,
col. 21; also, in dependence on Harrison, op. cit. (cf. n. 157 above), Rist, op.
cit., pp. 39ff., Knox, op. cit., pp. 73–76, and Carroll, 'Expansion', pp. 234f.

[172] I have attempted to prove this in my essay, 'Polykarp von Smyrna und die
Pastoralbriefe', already mentioned, and will not repeat here the arguments and
evidence there advanced. Schneemelcher, 'Paulus' (cf. n. 149 above), pp. 6f.,
agrees with me.

[173] I Tim. 6:20f.; cf. Campenhausen, 'Polykarp', pp. 205f.

[174] II Tim. 3:15f.; cf. Campenhausen, 'Polykarp', pp. 211f. Is the emphasis
on πᾶσα γραφὴ θεόπνευστος a concealed piece of polemic against the narrow
Marcionite canon?

[175] I Tim. 1:9.

thought, and directed them all into one single broad new channel: Irenaeus. He signalises the transition from the earlier period of belief in tradition to the new age of deliberate canonical standardisation—a transition in the direction of later orthodoxy in which the Canon of an Old and a New Testament was firmly laid down.[176] Irenaeus is no longer content to safeguard and expound the Old Testament alone; as the first catholic theologian he begins to appeal to the New Testament documents, that is, he explicitly names them, defends their authenticity, and declares them to be normative. It is no accident that this reminds one of Marcion. But Irenaeus is no Marcionite, calling up Scripture simply because he no longer trusts the tradition of the Church. On the contrary, according to Irenaeus Scripture and tradition, as regards their doctrinal content, are in entire agreement, and the purpose of Scripture is to confirm the teaching of the Church against all doubts. Irenaeus has no desire to be an innovator; and so, as his intention is not to correct the theological teachings and teaching methods of his predecessors nor to set them against one another, but rather to link and unify them.[177] tradition and Scripture continue legitimately side by side.

Irenaeus is not, like a later canonist, concerned with formal safeguards for their own sake, but with the one substantial truth of the Christian message, through which mankind receives salvation. Man was from the first called to be the child and the eternal partner of God. The first creation, which the gnostics so shamefully despise, was already forwarding this destiny, which later was revealed as a fact by the incarnation and death of Christ, and is now continually proclaimed and taught by the Church in the power of the Spirit, and will be so until the ultimate consummation at the end of the ages.[178] The one rule and guideline, the only 'canon' which Irenaeus explicitly acknowledges, is the 'canon of truth', that is to say: the content of the faith itself, which the Church received from Christ, to which she remains faithful, and by which she lives. By this is meant neither a *Summa* of dogmatic propositions nor an unchangeable confessional formula nor even the sacred Scripture as such, however certain it may be that the latter teaches and contains this truth.[179] The truth is alive in the Church from the begin-

[176] The conclusions of the account which follows have been summarised in my 'Irenäus und das Neue Testament', *TLZ* 20, 1965, pp. 1–8.
[177] On the general characteristics of this relationship cf. Widmann, *op. cit.* It should also be noted how Irenaeus introduces his 'Elder' as an authority (Adv. haer. IV, 27) without in any way altering the Elder's old-fashioned attitude to Scripture (cf. pp. 166, 168 above).
[178] A summary of the relevant ideas and texts will be found in: C. Hoergl, 'Die göttliche Erziehung des Menschen nach Irenäus', in: *Oikoumene, Studi paleocristiani publicati in onore del concilio ecumenico Vaticano II*, Catania, 1964, pp. 323–349.
[179] Adv. haer. I, 9, 4; 22, 1; II, 27, 1; 28, 1; III, 2, 1; 11, 1; 12, 6; 15, 1; IV,

ning; it is actualised in her, so to speak, by its own power, and is never lost to her. In Irenaeus confidence in the Church and in the Church's word exists unbroken; and, from this point of view, he had no need of a New Testament.

Irenaeus expressly defends this confidence at the very point where Church tradition might be thought most open to objection. The distant barbarians on the Rhine cannot read, yet without the external aid of a Scripture they are established in a right faith; for the Holy Spirit himself writes the true confession—'without ink and paper'[180]— on their heart.[181] Consequently the preaching of the Church has no need, provided that it proclaims Christ as he really was and is, to refer constantly to the books in which the apostolic message is recorded. The Church, in authority and obedience, simply continues the first preaching. This kind of proclamation is very much in accord with Irenaeus' own method of teaching, of which we have an interesting example in the so-called *Epideixis*, a small work extant only in an Armenian version, on the 'Proof of the Apostolic Preaching', which Irenaeus wrote down at the request of a friend.[182] This little book was written after the great work against the heresies,[183] and does not therefore reflect a youthful stage of Irenaeus' theology and method. Its content is a short summary of Christian teaching, suitable for the ordinary congregation, and presented mainly in the form of 'biblical history'. The recital of God's saving providence moves from the creation through the Law and the Prophets to Christ and the contemporary existence of the Church. Irenaeus thus follows the ancient pattern of 'prophecy and fulfilment', by which the truth of the Christian message is 'proved'.[184] The text of

---

35, 4; cf. *Dem.* 3. Today agreement may be said to have been reached on the main features of the much discussed concept, κανών τῆς ἀληθείας; cf. D. van den Eynde, *Les Normes de l'Enseignement Chrétien dans la littéra-ture patristique des trois premiers siècles*, 1933, pp. 282–291; E. Flesseman–van Leer, *Tradition and Scripture in the Early Church*, 1954, pp. 125–128; 161–170; B. Hägglund, 'Die Bedeutung der "regula fidei" als Grundlage theologischer Aussagen', *StTh* 12, 1958, pp. 4–19; J. N. D. Kelly, *Early Christian Creeds*[2], 1952, pp. 76–82; G. G. Blum, *Tradition und Sukzession. Studien zum Normbe-griff des Apostolischen von Paulus bis Irenäus*, 1963, pp. 168–173; P. Hefner, 'Theological Methodology and St Irenaeus', *JRel* 44, 1964, pp. 294–309; and esp. N. Brox, *Offenbarung. Gnosis und gnostischer Mythos bei Irenäus von Lyon*, 1966, pp. 105–113.

[180] II Joh. 12.   [181] Adv. haer. III, 4, 2; cf. I, 10, 2.

[182] The Armenian text of the Ἐπίδειξις τοῦ ἀποστολικοῦ κηρύγματος (Eusebius, *HE* V, 26) will be found in *Patrol. Orient.* XII, 5 (Paris, 1919) with an English translation; other English translations by J. Armitage Robinson, 1920, and J. P. Smith in *ACW*[16], 1952.

[183] Dem. 99.

[184] Dem. 42: 'That all these things would so come to pass, the Spirit of God declared beforehand by the prophets; that in respect of them the faith of those who worship God in truth should be confirmed. For what was an impossibility

the prophecies he naturally draws from the Old Testament, the books
and authors of which he constantly adduces by name, and quotes. By
contrast, the 'fulfilment' is either simply related in the form of the story
of Jesus or taken for granted as well known. The material used for this
purpose plainly derives from our gospels and from Acts; nevertheless
Irenaeus names not one single book nor author. It would seem that the
preaching of Christ lives on simply on the basis of oral tradition, just
as 'the Elders, the disciples of the apostles, have handed it down to us'.[185]
All this corresponds to the method of teaching and preaching in
general use down to the time of Irenaeus. If Justin had on occasion
referred in his presentation of Christianity to the 'memoirs of the
apostles', this was connected with the apologetic character of his writings, in which an 'educated' reference to the 'sources' was in keeping.[186]
By contrast, the Easter sermon of bishop Melito of Sardis, who was
almost an exact contemporary of Irenaeus,[187] in its use of Scripture
still keeps entirely to the method with which we are familiar from the
Epideixis. It follows the reading aloud of an Old Testament passage,[188]
which is expounded typologically of Christ, and appeals to many different predictions in Moses, David, Isaiah, Jeremiah, and other
prophets; but the actual story of Christ is treated as a fact that is manifestly and universally familiar[189] and needs no documentation. Here and
there this old-fashioned style of preaching continues down into the
third century;[190] but once there is a New Testament, this, strictly

to our nature, and therefore adapted to awaken only incredulity in mankind,
this God caused to be made known beforehand by the prophets; in order that,
through its having been foretold in times long before, and then at last being
fulfilled in this way, even as it was foretold, we might know that it was God who
thus proclaimed to us beforehand our redemption' (ET, J. A. Robinson, slightly
revised.) This is Justin's theology, which Irenaeus also adopts elsewhere for the
most part, when interpreting the Old Testament. There is therefore no need to
deal once again with this aspect of his theology of Scripture here. For a more
detailed account cf. Benoit. *Saint Irénée*, pp. 74–102.

[185] *Dem.* 3.
[186] M. Dibelius, *Die Formgeschichte des Evangeliums*[5], 1966, pp. 36f.; cf. pp.
167f. above.
[187] O. Perler, *Meliton de Sardes: Sur la Pâque et fragments*, 1966, pp. 23f.,
dates the homily somewhere between A.D. 160 and 170.
[188] Ex. 12:1–32. According to F. L. Cross, *The Early Christian Fathers*, 1960,
pp. 105ff., the text would first have been read in Hebrew, and then translated,
and the exposition in question would have taken the place of the Jewish Passover
haggada. This is no reason, however, to dispute that it is palpably a sermon in
character.
[189] Cf. esp. § 94, 1, ll. 721–726: εἰ μὲν γὰρ νύκτωρ γεγόνει ὁ φόνος ἢ ἐπ'
ἐρημίας ἦν ἀπεσφαγμένος, σιγᾶν εὔχρηστον ἦν· νῦν δὲ ἐπὶ μέσης πλατείας
καὶ πόλεως ἐν μέσῳ πόλεως πάντων ὁρώντων γέγονεν δικαίου ἄδικος φόνος κτλ.
[190] Cf. E. Peterson, 'Pseudo-Cyprian, Adversus Iudaeos und Melito von
Sardes', in : *Frühkirche, Judentum und Gnosis*, 1959, pp. 137–145. In this revi-

speaking, has become an anachronism. The change begins with Irenaeus—but it affects not his congregational preaching but another aspect of his work, which took shape in his polemical masterpiece. To this we must now turn.

When we open the 'Condemnation and Refutation of the Gnosis falsely so called', we find a completely different picture. It is true that even here the appeals to the Old Testament and its prophecies have not disappeared; but they are far outnumbered by the innumerable quotations from the New Testament,[191] and these too now serve to construct a formal 'proof from scripture' such as had previously been drawn only from the Old Testament. This is the really new thing which has to be explained. It can be understood only in the light of the particular goal which Irenaeus is pursuing in this work: the effectual and compelling refutation of that heresy which had as yet never been overcome.

Had Irenaeus in his fight against heresy appealed as hitherto merely to the Old Testament and the Church's own tradition, he would have accomplished very little. For the heretics countered the catholic tradition with their own allegedly better traditions; and the Old Testament had in their eyes for a long time now been of more or less doubtful value, and by Marcion had been rejected altogether. But even apart from this, the allegorising 'scriptural proofs' which it was possible to draw from the Old Testament always retained an element of the problematic when applied to the questions now at issue. Ignatius had already come to realise this.[192] The Old Testament scriptural proof had been developed originally in controversy with the Jews, in order to prove that Jesus really was the promised Messiah, and that the Christians were

---

sion of Melito's homily the 'scripturae' which Christians 'teach, know, and understand' (10) are still exclusively those of the Old Testament, and the 'New?' Testament' which Christ 'inaugurated' and 'wrote', and which his disciples 'proclaimed' throughout the whole world, is not our book of the New Testament but the new divine covenant (1; 3; 5; 7f.). The treatise is, of course, directed at the Jews, who do not recognise the Christian Scriptures, and who must therefore be brought to acknowledge the *novum testamentum* on the basis of their own (8f.). Cf. further Harnack, *Der pseudocyprianische Traktat De aleatoribus*, 1888; *Chronologie* II, pp. 375ff. This African work (H. Koch, 'Zur Schrift adv. aleatores', *Festschrift K. Müller*, 1922, pp. 58–67) is apparently prepared to quote only the Old Testament and certain apocalypses (Hermas, John) as Scripture in the strict sense. Apart from these, it is also familiar with the dominical sayings 'in the Gospel' and with the Pauline epistles. This would mean that in practice an unquestionably post-Cyprianic work was still governed in its use of Scripture by 'the oldest form of the western canon, indeed, of any canon at all, which we are able to discover' (Harnack, *Traktat*, p. 57).

[191] According to Werner, *op. cit.*, p. 7, the Adversus Haereses contains 629 O.T. quotations and allusions, and 1065 N.T.; cf. the table in Benoit, *Saint Irénée*, p. 106.

[192] Cf. pp. 71ff. above.

the new people of God. In the struggle against the false teachers this was no longer the question in dispute. The problem was the new one, which of the contending traditions in fact rightly reflected Jesus and his teaching, where the undistorted truth was to be found, and by what criteria it wàs to be determined. The important thing, therefore, was no longer to link the ancient prophecies with their Christian fulfilment; what mattered was to bridge the new and dangerous gulf which had opened up between that fulfilment and the present. For the moment there was nothing more to fill that gap than a mass of 'traditions', the confusions and contradictions of which constantly increased. It was to meet this situation that Marcion had created his New Testament, and by means of its allegedly authentic documents had at a stroke eliminated the whole oral tradition which, as he supposed, had been completely adulterated. To lay stress on an appeal to individual dominical sayings, as the Valentinians in particular did,[193] was no adequate defence against such an onslaught; for these sayings themselves derived from a 'tradition', which did to some extent certainly exist in writings, but had not been unambiguously fixed in this form, and was still not related to particular 'canonical' books. Irenaeus, so far as we can tell, was the first catholic theologian who dared to adopt the Marcionite principle of a new 'scripture' in order to use it in his turn against Marcion and all heretics.[194] In the work we are considering he is primarily fighting against the Valentinians, who at that time, thanks to their voluminous and elaborate writings, were more of a danger than other gnostics.[195] Marcion was to have had a work all to himself,[196] and there-

[193] Cf. pp. 82f. above.

[194] Irenaeus himself was well aware of the novelty of this proceeding: Adv. haer. II, 35; III, pref.: in hoc autem tertio [libro] ex scripturis inferemus ostensiones, ut nihil tibi ex his quae praeceperas desit a nobis, sed et, *praeterquam opinabaris*, ad arguendum et evertendum eos, qui quolibet modo male docent occasiones a nobis accipias; cf. also III, 12, 9: . . . et tu cum magnanimitate intende eis (sc. his ostensionibus, quae ex scripturis sunt) et noli longiloquium putare, hoc intelligens quoniam ostensiones, quae sunt in scripturis, non possunt ostendi nisi ex ipsis scripturis.

[195] Adv. haer. IV, pref. 2, explains the teaching of the Valentinians in a *recapitulatio omnium haereticorum*. They are mentioned by name as early as I pref. 2, and constantly thereafter. Cf. F. Sagnard, *La gnose valentinienne et le témoignage de saint Irénée*, 1947. That the modern usage, whereby the various heresies of the second century are all included in the general description of 'gnostics', is already present in embryo in Irenaeus, has been demonstrated by N. Brox, Γνωστικοί als häreseologischer Terminus,' *ZNW* 57, 1966, pp. 105–114.

[196] Adv. haer. I, 27, 4; III, 12, 12. In the former passage in particular Irenaeus describes the method which he proposes to adopt in his future attack on Marcion in terms very similar to those later used by Tertullian: . . . et ex iis sermonibus, qui apud eum observati sunt, domini et apostoli, quibus ipse utitur, eversionem eius faciemus.

fore the specifically anti-Marcionite problems of the mutilation and interpolation of the text are less prominent here. But this has no significant effect on the way in which Irenaeus shapes his proof from Scripture.

The outstanding role which scriptural proof plays in the Adversus haereses will be recognised, as soon as one realises the plan and structure of this complex work.[197] In detail often confusing and difficult to take in, nevertheless in broad outline it follows a simple and clearly discernible scheme. At the beginning and end of the various books Irenaeus indicates what this is. The first book is to present the doctrines of the false teachers and 'unmask' them,[198] the second to confute them out of their own contradictions and absurdities.[199] In the third book begins the really positive presentation of the truth from the normative, ancient and authentic testimonies of the apostolic age, which vindicate the Church's teachings. Irenaeus, however, takes longer to complete this demonstration than he had originally planned, so that a fourth and then a fifth book have to be added.[200] In its crucial sections, therefore which make up more than half the total work, the Adversus haereses is nothing less than a comprehensive and continuous proof from Scripture, and the Scripture in question is 'New Testament'. The picture is blurred only by the fact that Irenaeus in his characteristic manner is constantly inserting excursuses and discussions of various themes, in which the leading ideas and the scriptural proofs are oriented quite differently from those in the rest of the work. It is in these sections that the Old Testament is repeatedly brought into play,[201] and is then ex-

---

[197] For the construction and line of argument in the third Book reference should be made to the excellent edition by F. Sagnard in the *Sources Chrétiennes* series: *Irénée de Lyon, Contre les Hérésies* . . . Livre III, Paris, 1952; but cf. also the earlier work of J. Kunze, *Glaubensregel, Heilige Schrift und Kirche*, 1899, pp. 110f. At this point I would like to acknowledge the indispensable aid which B. Reynders has given us with his *Lexique comparé du texte grec et des versions latine, arménienne et syriaque de l' 'Adversus Haereses' de S. Irénée*, 1954; to which should now be added: *Vocabulaire de la 'Demonstration' et des fragments de Saint Irénée*, 1958.

[198] Adv. haer. I pref. 2; 31, 4; II pref. 1.

[199] Adv. haer. I, 31, 4; II pref. 2. Irenaeus pursues the same method with regard to the heretics' mutually contradictory exegeses of Scripture: IV, 35, 4.

[200] Adv. haer. II, 35, 4; II pref.; 11, 9; 12, 9; 25, 7; IV pref. 1; 41, 4–6; V pref.

[201] Thus the programme announced at III, 5, 1 only in fact gets under way at 9, 1. In between we have a discussion of the unity of God, in which the scriptural proof is organised in the earlier pattern: Spirit (= prophets)—Apostle (= Paul)—the Lord, in an ascending scale. In IV, 20, 2 the quotation from *scriptura*, beginning with Hermas, continues with a prophet, then the Apostle, and finally the Lord. Toward the end of the last three books the thread is again and again almost completely lost, and is taken up clearly only in the closing remarks and the prefaces.

pounded in the old-fashioned manner christologically and prophetically or in terms of 'the economy of salvation'. The crucial burden of proof nevertheless rests on the 'New Testament'.

This designation, so familiar to us, is however as yet unknown to Irenaeus. He has no name by which to distinguish the New Testament books from the ancient Scripture and to describe them collectively as a new unity. As occasion requires he speaks simply of the fourfold Gospel, of the Acts of the Apostles, or of the letters of the Apostle. Sometimes he groups these books together with the Old Testament, and refers to the whole without differentiation by the long-hallowed names of 'scriptures of the Lord', 'the scriptures', or 'the scripture'.[202] This does not, however, occur regularly,[203] but only occasionally and almost as if by inadvertence. In general these terms—as also the solemn formulas of quotation—are still confined to the books of the Old Testament.[204] From this we may learn two things: first, the actual importance which the New Testament writings already possess for Irenaeus, and secondly, the novelty of and absence of any guarantee for the standing and authority which they claim. Now, in the fight against the false teaching, they are to acquire a fundamental significance. That is why Irenaeus opens this part of his refutation with a demonstration that they are in fact reliable, and can demand our unqualified confidence in what they have to say. Irenaeus does not proceed simply by putting the new Scripture alongside the old, and then asserting its authority by analogy. He does not start from a general 'principle of scripture', which would carry over from the Old Testament to the New. His concern is solely to establish the credibility and value as witnesses of those books from which he intends to give the original teaching of Jesus and the apostles

---

[202] Cf. e.g., Adv. haer. II, 27, 2; 30, 6; 35, 4; III, 19, 2. According to J. Hoh, *Die Lehre des Hl. Irenäus über das Neue Testament*, 1919, p. 62, ἡ γραφή/αἱ γραφαί 'occur 135 times in Irenaeus, of which 57 refer to the O.T. alone, a few to the N.T. alone, and the majority to the Old and New Testaments combined'.

[203] It is especially frequent in the fourth book, which is exceptionally disorganised. The intrusion of O.T. quotations here, however, is not to be explained, as A. Bengsch, *Heilsgeschichte und Heilswissen*, 1957, p. 68, would have it, by taking Adv. haer. IV, 2, 3 to mean that the words of Moses are as the words of Christ.

[204] This has often been noted and emphasised before; cf. the detailed statistics in Hoh, pp. 60–86; 191f.; also Benoit, *Saint Irénée*, pp. 120–122; 135–141; 146f. In the few passages where the Gospels or Acts are, directly or indirectly, called 'scripture' (Paul is nowhere so termed) it should also be borne in mind that the 'technical' use of the word for the biblical 'writings' has by no means suppressed the more general 'profane' meaning, and that sometimes it is hard to draw the line between them; cf. Werner, *op. cit.*, pp. 36f.; J. Lawson, *The Biblical Theology of Saint Irenaeus*, 1948, pp. 50–52; Hanson, *op. cit.*, pp. 205–207. The instances in which Irenaeus combines Old and New Testament quotations as proofs of equal value are, however, innumerable.

a status so exalted that even the heretics will not be able to gainsay it. For this purpose he does not need to defend the Pauline epistles; they are recognised even by his opponents. But reasons must be given for confidence in the 'historical books' of the New Testament. Irenaeus is the first to attempt anything of this kind.[205] He opens the third book straightaway with a historical statement setting out his basic principle:

> The Lord of all things gave his apostles authority to preach the Gospel. Through them we have learned the truth, that is, the teaching of the Son of God. And it was to them that the Lord said: 'He who hears you, hears me; and he who despises you, despises me and him who sent me.'[206] For we have not learned the plan of our salvation through any other men than those through whom the gospel came to us. The gospel which they then proclaimed, they afterwards by the will of God handed down to us in writings, as the future foundation and pillar[207] of our faith.[208]

Now we may not assume, continues Irenaeus in clear opposition to the heretics both Valentinians and Marcionites, that the apostles would have begun to preach before they had acquired full knowledge, with the result that we would have had to correct the apostles.[209] Instead, after the resurrection they were all endowed with the Holy Spirit, and each of them equally had received the whole gospel.[210] Their authority is thus unassailable. The false teachers would like to evade the unambiguously anti-gnostic confession of faith which the apostles have made

---

[205] That the views expressed by Irenaeus in Adv. haer. III, 1, 1–18, 6, are in substance completely his own, is rightly stressed by F. Loofs, *Theophilus von Antiochien Adversus Marcionem und die anderen theologischen Quellen bei Irenäus*, 1930, p. 342. It cannot, of course, be established with absolute certainty that nothing of the kind had anywhere been attempted before Irenaeus; but nothing indicates that it had, and since Irenaeus is not elsewhere in the habit of concealling the fact that he is making use of tradition, there is all the less reason to assume secret indebtedness here, when he is breaking new ground. 'The compulsion always to be searching for forerunners in history falls into the category of monomania': C. J. Burckhardt, *Gestalten und Mächte*², Zurich, 1961, p. 59.

[206] Lk. 10:16.   [207] I Tim. 3:15.

[208] Adv. haer. III pref. 1, 1: Etenim dominus omnium dedit apostolis suis potestatem evangelii, per quos et veritatem, hoc est dei filii doctrinam, cognovimus. quibus et dixit dominus: 'Qui vos audit, me audit; et qui vos contemnit, me contemnit et eum, qui me misit.' Non enim per alios dispositionem salutis nostrae cognoviumus quam per eos, per quos evangelium pervenit ad nos. quod quidem tunc praeconaverunt, postea vero per dei voluntatem in scripturis nobis tradiderunt, fundamentum et columnam fidaei nostrae futurum.

[209] Adv. haer. III, 1, 1: nec enim fas est dicere, quoniam ante praedicaverunt, quam perfectam haberent agnitionem, sicut quidam audent dicere, gloriantes se emendatores esse apostolorum.

[210] Adv. haer. III, 1, 1: . . . qui quidem et omnes pariter et singuli eorum habentes evangelium dei.

in their writings. They therefore allege that the Scriptures are corrupt, are not binding, and contradict one another; and that therefore no one can discover the truth there who does not at the same time adhere to the living, oral tradition.[211] By this they mean their own secret traditions which they pit against the tradition of the Church. But, for Irenaeus, these are empty sophistries. In a wide-ranging historical excursus he brings proof that the only reliable, ancient and credible tradition is to be found in the catholic church and from of old has been publicly taught within that church. If there were no Scriptures, then it would be to her teachings alone that men would have to hold fast.[212] But in fact we do have the Scriptures, and out of them the original truth can be far more clearly and incontrovertibly brought to light.[213] The teaching of the Church is thus in substance identical with the teaching of the Scriptures,[214] and it is out of these Scriptures that the heretics are now finally to be convicted and refuted. This brings Irenaeus back to his real purpose, that of providing scriptural proof from the New Testament,[215] and from now until the end of the work this remains his sole object.[216]

211 Adv. haer. III, 2, 1: Cum enim ex scripturis arguuntur, in accusationem convertuntur ipsarum scripturarum, quasi non recte habeant neque sint ex auctoritate et quia varie sint dictae et quia non possit ex his inveniri veritas ab his, qui nesciant traditionem. non enim per litteras traditam illam, sed per vivam vocem, quam ob causam et Paulum dixisse: 'sapientiam autem loquimur inter perfectos—sapientiam autem non mundi huius' (I Cor. 2:6) et hanc sapientiam unusquisque eorum dicit, quam a semetipso adinvenerit, fictionem videlicet. . . . Cf. the examples from gnostic literature (Ptol., Ad Floram 3, 8; 7, 9; Hom. Clem., Epist. Petri) in Quispel, op. cit., pp. 77f.

212 Adv. haer. III, 4, 1: quid autem si nec apostoli quidem scripturas reliquissent nobis, nonne oportebat ordinem sequi traditionis, quam tradiderunt his, quibus committebant ecclesias? The importance of this hypothetical question is rightly stressed by J. Beumer, 'Die mündliche Überlieferung als Glaubensquelle', Handbuch der Dogmengeschichte I, 4, 1962, p. 24.

213 Adv. haer. III, 12, 14: manifestius autem hoc ostenditur ex apostolorum epistula . . . (Acts 15:7-11); cf. II, 35, 4: quoniam autem dictis nostris consonat praedicatio apostolorum et domini magisterium et prophetarum annuntiatio et apostolorum dictatio et legislationis ministratio unum eundemque omnium deum patrem laudantium . . . arbitror quidem sufficienter ostensum et per haec tanta uno ostenso deo patre factore omnium. sed ne putemur fugere illam quae ex scripturis dominicis est probationem ipsis scripturis multo manifestius et clarius hoc ipsum praedicantibus, his tamen qui non prave intendunt eis proprium librum, qui sequitur has scripturas, reddentes, ex scripturis divinis probationes apponemus in medio omnibus amantibus veritatem.

214 Rightly pointed out by J. N. Bakhuizen van den Brink, 'Traditio im theologischen Sinne', VC 13, 1959, pp. 74-76; Flesseman–van Leer, op. cit., pp. 100f., 128; Blum, op. cit., pp. 178f. Lawson, op. cit., pp. 87-93 disagrees.

215 Adv. haer. III, 5, 1: traditioni igitur, que est ab apostolis, sic se habente in ecclesia et permanente apud nos revertamur ad eam, quae est ex scripturis ostensionem eorum, qui evangelium conscripserunt apostolorum. . . .

216 The whole section on tradition is thus only an interpolation provoked by

Let us now consider the sequence in which the individual books and testimonies of the 'New Testament' are taken up and consulted. In accordance with Irenaeus' own clearly described plan they are adduced in the following order:

1. the teaching of all the apostles—as given in the four Gospels and in Acts;
2. the sayings of the Lord;
3. the apostolic letters of Paul.[217]

At first sight this is a surprising arrangement. Why are the words of Jesus separated from the Gospels in which they have been handed down, and why is Paul separated from the other apostles, in whose company he undoubtedly belongs? And why is Jesus inserted between the apostles and Paul instead of either opening or crowning the sequence, as is customary elsewhere?[218] The explanation is simple, as soon as one realises that the Gospels and Acts as 'canonical books' constitute a new entity, which now has to be combined with those ancient authorities of long standing, 'the Lord' and 'the Apostle'. The Gospels are not thought of as sources for the words of Jesus; their purpose is simply to provide documentary evidence of the teaching of 'that apostle' who wrote down the gospel.[219] For this reason the examination is restricted to the 'beginnings' of the Gospels,[220] that is,

the heretics' objections to scriptural proof, and its significance should not be overestimated. Hefner, *op. cit.*, p. 308 n. 27. ignores the overall structure of the work and wrongly attempts to qualify this statement. On the problem of tradition in Irenaeus cf. Kunze, *op. cit.*, pp. 120ff.; B. Reynders, 'Paradosis. Le progrès de l'idée de tradition jusqu'a saint Irénée, *'RTAM* 5, 1933, pp. 174ff.; E. Molland, 'Irenaeus of Lugdunum and the Apostolic Succession', *JEH* 1, 1950, pp. 20–22; Flesseman–van Leer, *op. cit.*, pp. 100–106; 139–144; and especially A. Benoit, 'Écriture et tradition chez S. Irénée,' *RHPR* 40, 1960, pp. 32–43, with whose comments I am in entire agreement.

[217] Cf. the passages cited in n. 200 above, esp. Adv. haer. V pref.: quaestionibus omnibus solutis, quae ab haereticis nobis proponuntur, et apostolorum doctrina explanata et manifestatis pluribus, quae a domino per parabolas et dicta sunt et facta in hoc libro quinto operis universi, quod est de traductione et eversione falso cognominatae agnitionis, ex reliquis doctrinae domini nostri et ex apostolicis epistolis conabimur ostensiones facere. . . .

[218] This is normal practice even in other passages in Irenaeus, as well as in the sources he employs; thus, e.g., in the excursus inserted at Adv. haer. III, 6–8, the scriptural proof is organised in an ascending scale in the form: prophets—Paul—the Lord. Further examples of the various permutations will be found in H. Holstein, 'Les témoins de la révélation d'après Saint Irénée', *RSR* 41, 1953, pp. 410–420.

[219] Adv. haer. III, 5, 1 (cf. n. 215 above). It is still a question of 'the' gospel—id quod ab apostolis nobis datum (IV, 36, 1)—which has taken literary shape uniformly in the four Gospel books. Cf. n. 122 above.

[220] Adv. haer. III, 11, 7. 9 (principia evangelii). In III, 10, 6 a quotation from the end of Mark (16:19) is also used as evidence for that gospel.

to those parts which contain no words of Jesus but only the voices of the apostolic witnesses. The testimony of 'the other apostles' is supplied by Acts.[221] As against this, the 'words of the Lord' form a group on their own, which from as far back as Paul down to Hegesippus are drawn without ascription of source from the 'tradition', whether oral or written. That is why even in Irenaeus they still exist in a special category and apparently in isolation,[222] although in fact of course he quotes them in the form in which they appear in the four Gospels,[223] and there are occasions when this provenance is not passed over in silence.[224] If they drop into the background when Scripture is being used to refute the heretics, this is done quite deliberately. Naturally Irenaeus does not mean to say that the words of Jesus are less important or binding than the preaching of those apostles who after all received their doctrine and commission from him and from him alone. But it is obvious that, as regards the immediate purpose, namely the refutation of the gnostic doctrines of God and of Christ, the apostolic witness places much more abundant and much more apposite material at his disposal than do the dominical sayings. Of the latter it is now no longer the moral instructions but above all the parables, interpreted generally as dogmatic allegories, which are given prominence.[225] Unfortunately,

[221] Adv. haer. III, 11, 9: examinata igitur sententia eorum, qui nobis tradiderunt evangelium ex ipsis principiis ipsorum, veniamus et ad reliquos apostolos. . . .

[222] Irenaeus repeatedly names the Evangelists when he is adducing them as apostolic witnesses to sound doctrine; by contrast, the words of the Lord, which he quotes as such, are normally given without indication of source. Cf. the list of 'explicit quotations' in Hoh, op. cit., pp. 190ff.

[223] Apocryphal traditions, however, are not wholly absent from Irenaeus: I, 20, 2; II, 34, 3; V, 33, 3f.; 36, 2. But their significance for the Irenaean 'canon' is, in my opinion, overestimated by W. L. Dulière, 'Le Canon néotestamentaire et les écrits chrétiens approuvés par Irénée', Nouv. Clio 6, 1954, pp. 199–224.

[224] E.g., when he comes to speak about Luke's special material (cf. p. 201 below), or in conjunction with the historical accounts refers also to the 'magisterium', quod ad divites dictum est (III, 14, 3) and one or two other texts. Nevertheless, there is absolutely no attempt to confirm the authority and reliability of the dominical sayings by referring to the fact that they occur in a recognised Gospel.

[225] This is true also of Irenaeus himself: cf. e.g., Adv. haer. IV, 26, 1 (on the Greek tradition cf. L. Doutreleau in: Rousseau, op. cit., n. 110 above, I, pp. 81f.): si quis igitur intentus legat scripturas, inveniet in iisdem de Christo sermonem et novae vocationis praefigurationem. hic est enim thesaurus absconsus in agro—id est: in isti mundo ('ager enim mundus est')—absconsus vero in scripturis thesaurus Christus, quoniam per typos et parabolas significabatur; cf. Matt. 13:38, 44. But Irenaeus' interpretations of the parables are, in accordance with the principle which he repeatedly emphasises, and in contrast to the gnostics, intended 'in all cases as no more than a supplement to arguments based on clear and unambiguous passages of scripture': A. Jülicher, Die Gleichnisreden Jesu I², 1910, p. 212. That Irenaeus is no gnostic in his methods of

however, they have already been explained in this sense by the Valentinians, and to a great extent commandeered by them to support their
heretical speculations.[226] These texts must, therefore, first be wrested
from their grasp, and for this purpose an assured starting-point is
needed. Irenaeus had thus made his task quite extraordinarily difficult
by beginning on this dangerous ground.

Much the same is true of the Pauline epistles. Irenaeus in no way
shares the prevailing tendency to rank Paul below the first apostles or
even to ignore him altogether.[227] On the contrary, it is on Paul in particular that he bases his position, feeling himself to be the legitimate
heir of Pauline theology. The full agreement of the one apostle whose
teaching has always been available in literary form with all the other
apostles, represented in the Gospels and in Acts, is just as much a
fundamental 'catholic' concern of his exposition as the agreement
of all the apostles with the Lord, with the predictions of the ancient
prophets, and with the contemporary preaching of the Church. It is
precisely to this point that he comes back again and again in his rejection of the heretics' critique of the Old Testament, namely their preference for Paul or for other apostles supposedly endowed with higher
knowledge.[228] Yet even Paul, in his genuine epistles, is not a comfortable ally against the Valentinians and Marcionites, who in their turn
claim his support against the Church.[229] The Gospels and Acts must

---

scriptural exegesis is rightly stressed by Bengsch, *op. cit.*, pp. 26–31; cf. further
Lawson, *op. cit.*, pp. 82–86.

[226] Cf. Irenaeus, Adv. haer. I pref.; 3, 6; 8, 1; II, 10, 2; 27, 1f.; III, 5, 1;
IV pref. 2–4; Tertullian, De carn. res. 33: ad evangelia nunc provoco; hic
quoque occursus prius eidem astutiae eorum, qui proinde et dominum omnia in
parabolis pronuntiasse contendunt . . . ; cf. *De pudic.* 8f. On this subject cf.
Turner, *op. cit.*, pp. 195f.; J. B. Bauer in W. C. van Unnik, *Evangelien aus dem
Nilsand*, 1960, pp. 108–150; Brox, *op. cit.*, p. 62; cf. also Theodotus in Clem.
Alex., Exc. ex Theod. 66; Theophilus, *op. cit.* n. 164 above; and the discussion
of the 'spiritual' meaning of the parables in Adamantius, Dial. 7. Further ex-
amples from orthodox writers are listed in Hanson, op. cit., pp. 208f.; also A.
Adam, 'Gnostische Züge in der patristischen Exegese von Luk. 15', *StudEvang*
III, 1964, pp. 299–305.

[227] The opposite view, forcibly expressed by J. Wagenmann, *Die Stellung des
Apostels Paulus neben den Zwölf in den ersten zwei Jahrhunderten*, 1926, pp. 202–
217, is rightly attacked by Schmithals, *op. cit.*, pp. 255–258: 'In Irenaeus (and
all church writers after him) we find therefore exactly that concept of the aposto-
late which to this day dominates the unreflecting thinking of the Christian community, including their theologians. Both the Twelve and Paul count as apostles,
without distinction of rank . . .' (p. 256); cf. also the pertinent comments of Lawson, *op. cit.*, pp. 31, 46–48, 52; and Kunze, *op. cit.*, pp. 112f.

[228] On the formal combination and association of authorities the valuable
statistics in Holstein, *op. cit.*, are instructive.

[229] Adv. haer. IV, 41, 4: necessarium est autem conscriptioni huic in sequenti
post domini sermones subiungere Pauli quoque doctrinam et examinare senten-

therefore provide the fixed dogmatic framework within which his teachings—like the words of Jesus—find their 'correct' setting, and can, as occasion arises, be elucidated and defined. This task is made substantially easier for Irenaeus by the fact that for him the Pastorals also belong to the Pauline corpus. As with the equally helpful Acts,[230] it is in Irenaeus' work that they appear, so far as we can see, for the first time in Church use. Its very title derives in part from a phrase in I Timothy,[231] and in the wider controversy the Pastorals are deployed not indeed very frequently but all the more vigorously against 'the knowledge falsely so called' of the heretics.[232]

By contrast, the so-called 'catholic' epistles figure hardly at all in Irenaeus. It is true that he quotes I Peter,[233] and is acquainted with at least two of the Johannines,[234] and regards all of them as genuine letters of the relevant apostle. But they do not serve to reinforce his chorus of original witnesses, and in the design of his great proof from Scripture they are left out of account. This is very remarkable. It is clear that these works have not yet acquired sufficiently general recognition and importance for it to be possible to use them in controversy with the heretics as of indisputable, 'canonical' authority.[235] Only the Apocalypse, written by 'John, the disciple of the Lord'[236] is brought in at all frequently, and that toward the end of the work, with the particular purpose of

---

tiam eius et apostolum exponere, et quaecumque ab haereticis in totum non intelligentibus, quae a Paulo dicta sunt, alias acceperunt interpretationes explanare et dementiam insensationis eorum ostendere et ab eodem Paulo, ex quo nobis quaestiones inferunt, manifestare illos quidem mendaces, apostolum vero praedicatorem esse veritatis et omnia consonantia veritatis praeconio docuisse. . . .

[230] It is possible that an indirect knowledge of Acts can be proved for Justin; all earlier 'echoes' are quite indeterminate; cf. Haenchen, *op. cit.*, pp. 1ff.; H. Conzelmann, *Die Apostelgeschichte*, 1963, pp. 1f.

[231] I Tim. 6:20.

[232] The whole work begins with a quotation from I Tim. 1:4: Ἐπεὶ τὴν ἀλήθειαν παραπεμπόμενοί τινες ἐπεισάγουσι λόγους ψευδεῖς καὶ γενεαλογίας ματαίας, αἵτινες ζητήσεις μᾶλλον παρέχουσι, καθὼς ὁ ἀπόστολός φησιν, ἢ οἰκοδομὴν θεοῦ ἐν πίστει . . .

[233] Adv. haer. IV, 9, 2; 16, 5; V, 7, 2. I Peter is already used repeatedly in Polycarp's Philippians, but is nowhere explicitly named.

[234] Adv. haer. I, 16, 3; III, 16, 5.8.

[235] James seems to be used in Adv. haer. IV, 13, 4; 16, 2; V, (1, 1?); 10, 1, but is never mentioned by name.

[236] In dependence on Papias this description—discipulus domini, not 'apostolus'—is Irenaeus' regular usage for John the Apocalyptist, despite the fact that John had already been designated ὁ ἀπόστολος by Ptolemaeus (Ad Floram 3, 6), quite unambiguously in the light of the context, and that Irenaeus himself believed him to be the son of Zebedee. Cf. however, the significant sequence in Adv. haer. V, 36, 3: Johannes praevidit . . . consonanter . . . prophetae prophetaverunt . . . et dominus docuit . . . et apostolus (= Paulus) . . . confessus est. John is plainly classified among the prophets, and Paul alone is 'the Apostle'.

defending the Church's eschatology.[237] As a prophetic book it is vested with an authority of its own, and stands in a class by itself.[238] But all these witnesses pale into insignificance beside the multitude of quotations from Paul.[239] Nevertheless, the overall dogmatic interpretation of the new Scripture rests decisively on the opening exposition of the Gospels, and in particular of Acts. These above all call for a detailed justification. The various 'Introductions' offered in their defence are the first essay in a 'doctrine of holy scripture' which goes beyond the Old Testament.

The Four Gospels stand out, and at first are the only works under consideration.[240] According to Irenaeus they contain the direct record of the apostolic proclamation. This is proved by the historical circumstances of their appearance. First Matthew wrote his Gospel in Hebrew[241] and for the Hebrews, at a time when Peter and Paul were already working in Rome. After their deaths their disciples, Mark and Luke, came next with their record of what they had heard from their apostles; and still later John, when he was already in Ephesus, published a final Gospel.[242] This sequence, the one familiar to us, is followed by Irenaeus only in this passage;[243] it is obviously intended as a chronological order.[244] What matters is to show that these basic documents

[237] Almost without exception quotations from the Apocalypse occur in the Fourth and especially in the Fifth Book.

[238] Cf. pp. 217f. below. Nevertheless John (as a 'disciple of the Lord'?) ranks at any rate far above Hermas, whose 'scripture' is also quoted: Adv. haer. II, 30, 9; IV, 20, 2; cf. Eusebius, *HE* V, 8, 7; also p. 219 below.

[239] The 248 direct Pauline quotations (cf. Hoh, *op. cit.*, p. 38 n. 4) should be compared with the 8 from the catholic epistles and a total of 19 from the Apocalypse (*ibid.*, p. 194).

[240] Cf. p. 188f. above.

[241] The phrase, τοῖς Ἑβραίοις τῇ ἰδίᾳ αὐτῶν διαλέκτῳ (cf. n. 242 below) can refer only to the language. The doubts raised by J. Kürzinger, 'Das Papiaszeugnis und die Erstgestalt des Matthäusevangeliums', *BZ* N.F., 1960, pp. 35f., are unfounded.

[242] Adv. haer. III, 1, 1: Ὁ μὲν δὴ Ματθαῖος ἐν τοῖς Ἑβραίοις τῇ ἰδίᾳ αὐτῶν διαλέκτῳ καὶ γραφὴν ἐξήνεγκεν εὐαγγελίου, τοῦ Πέτρου καὶ τοῦ Παύλου ἐν Ῥώμῃ εὐαγγελιζομένων καὶ θεμελιούντων τὴν ἐκκλησίαν· μετὰ δὲ τὴν τούτων ἔξοδον Μάρκος, ὁ μαθητὴς καὶ ἑρμηνευτὴς Πέτρου, καὶ αὐτὸς τὰ ὑπὸ Πέτρου κηρυσσόμενα ἐγγράφως ἡμῖν παραδέδωκεν καὶ Λουκᾶς δὲ, ὁ ἀκόλουθος Παύλου, τὸ ὑπ' ἐκείνου κηρυσσόμενον εὐαγγέλιον ἐν βιβλῳ κατέθετο· ἔπειτα Ἰωάννης, ὁ μαθητὴς τοῦ κυρίου, ὁ καὶ ἐπὶ τὸ στῆθος αὐτοῦ ἀναπεσών, καὶ αὐτὸς ἐξέδωκεν τὸ εὐαγγέλιον, ἐν Ἐφέσῳ τῆς Ἀσίας διατρίβων.

[243] When explaining the symbols of the Evangelists (III, 11, 8) he arranges them in the order: John–Luke–Matthew–Mark, because here they have to correspond to the various epochs of salvation history (cf. p. 197 below). Elsewhere (III, 9, 1–11, 6; 11, 7; IV, 6, 1) the sequence is always: Matthew–Luke–Mark–John, which would seem therefore to be the order most familiar to Irenaeus himsslf. The theory of Bauer, *Orthodoxy*, pp. 211f., that the canonical order reflects the gradual adoption of the Gospels by the 'Church'—first Matthew

O

are authentic, and in view of their dates of composition far older than all the subsequent discoveries of the false teachers (the fact that they emerge so very much later in terms of Church history is noted in another passage[245]). The Church's documents all with one voice teach 'us the one God, Creator of heaven and earth, proclaimed by the Law and the Prophets, and the one Christ, the Son of God',[246] that is, they show that the contrary constructions of the heretics have not preserved, but distorted and betrayed the original truth.

Their reproaches against the Gospels are not to be taken seriously, and can easily be refuted. Irenaeus does this with some skill by letting the various sects which each recognise only one gospel testify against one another, and thus confirming the security and completeness of the Church's Four-Gospel canon: 'These gospels possess such a degree of certainty, that even the heretics themselves testify to them, and every apostate strives to maintain his own teaching with their assistance.'[247] The fourfold Gospel is one, and all the Evangelists possessed 'equally and individually this Gospel of God'.[248] It is wrong to try to restrict oneself simply to one or other of them—as the Ebionites do with Matthew, Marcion with Luke, certain Docetists with Mark, and Valentinus with John (which again is just the Gospel that others reject[249]).

---

and Mark, then, 'hesitantly and not without opposition', Luke, and finally John—and that the chronological interpretation is 'simply an attempt to account for a state of affairs for which the original reason was quite different', consequently seems to me unconvincing.

[244] This has been clearly demonstrated by Hoh, *op. cit.*, pp. 5–18 in opposition to J. Chapman, 'St Irenaeus on the dates of the Gospels', *JTS* 6, 1905, pp. 563ff., and Harnack, *Neue Untersuchungen zur Apostelgeschichte und zur Abfassungszeit der synoptischen Evangelien*, 1911, pp. 90–92; though he is in the wrong in arguing against the view of Zahn, *op. cit.*, II, pp. 364ff., that it was a practical impossibility to include all four gospels on a single roll: cf. p. 173 above. Benoit, *Saint Irénée*, p. 113 n. 3, also rightly regards the list given in Adv. haer. III, 1, 1, as chronological. On the sources from which Irenaeus' information about the authors of the gospels came to him only conjectures are possible: cf. R. Heard, 'The Apomnemoneumata in Papias, Justin and Irenaeus', *NTS* 1, 1954–5, pp. 122–129. Dependance on Papias remains the likeliest hypothesis; it is emphatically adopted by Loofs, *op. cit.*, pp. 325–338, and J. Kürzinger, Irenäus und sein Zeugnis zur Sprache des Matthäusevangeliums', *NTS* 10, 1963–4, pp. 108–115.

[245] Adv. haer. III, 4, 3.   [246] Adv. haer. III, 1, 2; cf. 4, 2; 11, 7.

[247] Adv. haer. III, 11, 7: tanta est autem circa evangelia haec firmitas, ut et ipsi haeretici testimonium reddant eis et ex ipsis egrediens unusquisque eorum conetur suam confirmare doctrinam.

[248] Adv. haer. III, 1, 1: . . . qui quidem at omnes pariter et singuli eorum habentes evangelium dei.

[249] Adv. haer. III, 11, 9. This last group is not heretical but catholic, and is therefore given no name. Those referred to are catholics who because of the Montanist claim to possess the 'Paraclete' had fallen into error on the subject of the Fourth Gospel (. . . illam speciem non admittunt, quae est secundum Iohan-

Moreover, it is not permissible to introduce another Gospel in addition to these four—a practice for which the Valentinians, with their 'Gospel of Truth', once again serve as an example.[250] These four are 'the only true and reliable' Gospels.[251] 'There may be neither a greater nor a lesser number of gospels'[252] than those which the catholic church recognises and venerates.

Mere assertion, however, is not enough to make the *de facto* position in the church into a dogmatic necessity; and so Irenaeus girds himself for his famous proof, which is meant to justify the fact that the Gospels are four in number on the higher, so to speak, speculative and typological plane as an aspect of salvation-history:

> Since there are four regions of the world we live in, and four universal winds (καθολικὰ πνεύματα), and the Church has been thickly sown all over the earth, and pillar and prop of the Church (is) the Gospel and spirit (πνεῦμα) of life; it is only reasonable that she has four pillars, from every quarter breathing incorruption and giving fresh life to men. From which it is clear that the Logos, Artificer of all things, he who is seated upon the cherubim and holds all things together, when he had been manifested to men, gave us the gospel in four forms but united by one spirit.

This is why Scripture tells of the fourfold face of the cherubim; each face corresponds to a mode of operation of the Son of God.[253] 'And the

---

nis evangelium, in qua 'paracletum' se missurum dominus promisit, sed simul et evangelium et propheticum repellunt spiritum). Cf. pp. 238f. below.

[250] Adv. haer. III, 11, 9. Only just previously (11, 7) Irenaeus has been rebuking the Valentinians for the opposite reason, namely that they concentrated on a single Gospel, that of John. This shows how arbitrarily Irenaeus makes these judgments, simply in order to be able to carry through his scheme. What he says about the Docetists in the same passage, alleging that they prefer Mark, sounds, highly improbable. In these circumstances perhaps one ought not to worry one's head too much about the Ebionite Matthew (Ebionaei etenim eo evangelio, quod est secundum Matthaeum solo utentes); on this point cf. most recently Strecker, *op. cit.*, pp. 277f. Irenaeus' concern is to find for each Gospel a heresy which is supposed to base itself on that gospel alone—a connection which arises naturally only in the case of Luke and the Marcionites. The Valentinians, against whom Irenaeus is primarily fighting, are the only other group to use a more restricted, though still fairly wide, quasi-canonical Scripture. I do not wish to discuss the problem of their 'Gospel of Truth' here; cf. p. 140 above.

[251] Adv. haer. III, 11, 9: quoniam autem sola illa vera et firma et non capit neque plura, praeterquam praedicta sunt, neque pauciora esse evangelia . . .

[252] Adv. haer. III, 11, 8: οὔτε πλείονα τὸν ἀριθμὸν οὔτε ἐλάττονα ἐνδέχεται εἶναι τὰ εὐαγγέλια.

[253] Irenaeus is thinking of the 'cherubim' of Ezek. 1, which he equates with the ζῷα of Rev. 4:6ff., despite the fact that, in contrast to the ancient cherubim, the latter are four individual beings, each of whom bears one of the four faces only. In addition he appeals to Ps. 80:2.

Gospels therefore accord with those on whom Christ sits enthroned.'[254] The exalted origin of the Son with the Father is described in the Prologue to John's Gospel (once again it is the 'beginning' of each Gospel with which we are concerned); hence the royal lion is proper to him. To Luke, who begins with the priestly liturgy of Zacharias, corresponds the bull, the sacrificial animal. Matthew tells of the conception of the man Jesus, and therefore has the human face; and finally Mark has the face of the eagle, who like the Spirit comes from on high and begins his Gospel with the Spirit's predictions abruptly, as if in mid-flight, as a prophet should.[255] At the same time, all four symbols in this series also correspond to the great epochs of salvation-history: the Word of God spoke to the patriarchs in his divine glory, in the Law he established the priestly liturgy, then he became Man, and finally he sent the Holy Spirit to cover us with his wings. And again, for the last time, this fourfold scheme is taken up in the four covenant-makings —those with Adam, Noah, and Moses, and that by Christ himself. Triumphantly Irenaeus sums up his reflections: 'As is the operation of the Son of God, so is the form of the beasts; and as is the form of the beasts, so is the nature of the Gospel. Quadriform are the beasts and quadriform is the Gospel and the operation of the Lord.'[256] 'Since this is so, all those are futile, ignorant, and presumptuous who disregard the ideal form of the Gospel, and wish to introduce either more or fewer faces than the Gospels of which we have been speaking possess, the former thinking to have discovered additional truth, the latter to set aside the saving ordinances of God.'[257]

There is no need to examine here the long subsequent history of this symbolism.[258] In Irenaeus it makes its first appearance; and despite

---

[254] Adv. haer. III, 11, 8: καὶ τὰ εὐαγγέλια οὖν τούτοις σύμφωνα, ἐν οἷς ἐγκαθέζεται χριστός.

[255] Here, therefore, the allocations of the lion and eagle have been exchanged when compared with the later order, made 'canonical' by Jerome.

[256] Adv. haer. III, 11, 8: 'Οποία οὖν ἡ πραγματεία τοῦ υἱοῦ τοῦ θεοῦ, τοιαύτη καὶ τῶν ζώων ἡ μορφή, καὶ ὁποία ἡ τῶν ζώων μορφή, τοιοῦτος καὶ ὁ χαρακτὴρ τοῦ εὐαγγελίου· τετράμορφα γὰρ τὰ ζῶα, τετράμορφον καὶ τὸ εὐαγγέλιον καὶ ἡ πραγματεία τοῦ κυρίου.

[257] Adv. haer. III, 11, 9: Τούτων δὲ οὕτως ἐχόντων μάταιοι πάντες καὶ ἀμαθεῖς προσέτι δὲ καὶ τολμηροὶ οἱ ἀθετοῦντες τὴν ἰδέαν τοῦ εὐαγγελίου καὶ εἴτε πλείονα εἴτε ἐλάττονα τῶν εἰρημένων παρεισφέροντες εὐαγγελίων πρόσωπα, οἱ μὲν ἵνα πλείονα δόξωσι τῆς ἀληθείας ἐξευρηκέναι, οἱ δὲ ἵνα τὰς οἰκονομίας τοῦ θεοῦ ἀθετήσωσιν.

[258] Cf. T. Zahn, Forschungen zur Geschichte des neutest. Kanons II, 1883, pp. 257–275 ('Die Tiersymbole der Evangelisten'); X, 1929, pp. 63f.; J. Kunze, Die Übergabe der Evangelien beim Taufunterricht, 1909, pp. 3–11; H. Leclercq, art. 'Évangélistes (Symboles des),' DACL V, 1, 1922, cols. 845–852; and esp. J. Michl, Die Engelvorstellungen in der Apokalypse des Hl. Johannes I, 1937, pp. 88–103; also W. Neuss, Das Buch Ezechiel in Theologie und Kunst, 1912, pp, 26ff.; on the astrological and cosmological background cf. P. Janzon, 'Evange-

the fact that it is already elaborately developed, there is no reason to search for earlier models. As a 'New Testament' theologian Irenaeus was compelled to break his own trail; and this highly original typology of the Four Gospels is so closely bound up with his fundamental concerns, his polemic, and especially his exegesis of the 'beginnings' of the Gospels, that for this very reason it is extremely difficult to believe in an earlier provenance.[259] It cannot in any case be much earlier than Irenaeus himself; for it presupposes the Four-Gospel canon. The mythology of numbers, so bizarre to our way of thinking, is entirely in keeping with the theological taste of his age and environment,[260] though it is appreciably different from the numerical speculations common among the gnostics[261] by virtue of its clear connection with salvation-history. Certainly the way in which the four apocalyptic beasts are matched to the various Gospels is somewhat violent. It has, of course, been introduced only *a posteriori*,[262] and in the succeeding period was frequently

---

listensymbolerna och deras ursprung', *Svenska Jerusalems föreningens Tidskrift* 59, 1960, pp. 68–77.

[259] According to Zahn, *Forschungen* II, 265, the orginator of this widely ramifying tradition was 'an exegete or homiletic writer of the second century unknown to us'; according to Kunze, *Übergabe*, pp. 46ff., none other than John, the author of Revelation, himself. The most likely candidate is Papias; but here too nothing whatever can be proved—even if it should turn out to be true that Papias once described the heathen god Janus as τετραπρόσωπος, as J. Sykutris, 'Ein neues Papiaszitat', *ZNW* 26, 1927, pp. 210–122, believes. That the remarks attributed to Polycarp in Victor of Capua (*Patres apostolici*, ed. Gebhardt–Harnack–Zahn, II, 1876, pp. 171f.) are inauthentic, despite Zahn, *op. cit.* I, pp. 782f., is today very generally agreed.

[260] In the N.T. it is to be found in the arithmetical analysis of Jesus' genealogical tree in Matt. 1:17. In Origen, Comm. Ps. 1 (= Philoc. III), Hilary, In psalmos prol. 15, and Jerome, Praef. Sam. et Malach. the books of the O.T., in accordance with earlier Jewish practice, are made to match the 22 letters of the Hebrew alphabet. Cf. Zahn. *op. cit.*, II, pp. 318ff. ('Zählungen der biblischen Bücher'); F. Dornseiff, *Das Alphabet in Mystik und Magie²*, 1925, p. 73, and generally, art. 'Buchstaben', *RAC* II, 1954, pp. 775–778; some very superficial observations on the connection with earlier cosmic numerical speculations will also be found in F. Israel, 'Der Kanon als Zwilling der Schöpfung', *ZNW* 10, 1909, pp. 239–245.

[261] Cf., e.g., Adv. haer. I, 1, 1; 14, 1 on the τετράς of the Valentinians and Marcosians; also II, 23, 3f.; and on the specific subject of the four apocalyptic beasts, the 'Unnamed' gnostic text in Codex II from Nag Hammadi, 152, 33ff., on which cf. A. Böhlig, 'Der jüdische und judenchristliche Hintergrund in gnostischen Texten von Nag Hammadi', in: *Le Origini dello Gnosticismo (Supp. Numen XII)*, 1967, p. 118; also, 'Die himmlische Welt nach dem Ägyptere-vangelium von Nag Hammadi', *Muséon* 80, 1967, pp. 369ff.; further material on the symbolism of the number four will be found in A. Hermann, 'Porphyra und Pyramide', *JAC* 7, 1964, pp. 133–135.

[262] Cf. F. S. Gutjahr, *Die Glaubwürdigkeit des irenäischen Zeugnisses über die Abfassung des vierten kanonischen Evangeliums*, Graz, 1904, pp. 8–10.

corrected and given a different exegetical basis.[263] But the actual method applied remained part of the accepted convention, and found imitators everywhere. After the canonical status of the Four Gospels was firmly established, the artificial symbolism did, it is true, lose much of its original topicality, and became more or less lighthearted ornamentation.[264] For Irenaeus, however, it was still a matter of an extremely serious and necessary defence of those exclusive rights which the Four-Gospel canon had either to retain or to acquire. Hence he takes the proof completely seriously: 'Since God has made all things in good and fitting order, it was necessary also that the form of the Gospel should be well designed and put together.'[265] 'To conclude that Irenaeus supplies the lack of a historical proof of the exclusive validity of the church's collection of Gospels with dogmatic assertions and theosophical fancies is to misunderstand' both him and his contemporary situation.[266] Historical proof is very much present in his approach; by means of allegorical interpretation it is merely removed from the appearance of contingency, and on the basis of 'scripture', which from of old must have served such purposes, it is 'theologically' incorporated into the eternal saving plan of God. Irenaeus may not, therefore, be reproached with wishing to evade the 'scandal of the human mediation of revelation.[267]

Be that as it may, the four traditional Gospels had now been success-

[263] Hippolytus, *Frag. Ezech. 1* (Achelis, p. 183) makes Matthew the lion and Mark the man; Epiphanius, Mens. et pond. 35, Ambrose, Exp. Luc., prol. 8, and Jerome, In Ezech. I, 1 (on 1:6–8a and 1:10) adopt the modern arrangement, to which Augustine, too, (De cons. evang. 1, 6, 9) would like to give the preference. Yet variations continue right down into the Middle Ages; cf. the data assembled in Michl, *op. cit.*, p. 100. They correspond to the kaleidoscopic changes in the order in which the texts of the Gospels are arranged; on this subject cf. J. Brinktrine, 'Nach welchen Gesichtspunkten wurden die einzelnen Gruppen des neutestamentlichen Kanons geordnet?' *BZ* 24, 1938–9, pp. 130ff.

[264] Nevertheless, the details of the arguments involved are not without interest. How significant for example, is Augustine's biblicistic reticence with regard to speculations about the *partes terrae* (De cons. evang. I, 6, 9), in sharp contrast to the parallels drawn between the fourfold Gospel and the cosmos in Origen (Comm. Joh. I, [6]) and to the extensive elaboration of nature analogies in the Middle Ages. The only constant factor throughout is that 'analogical, not causal connections' are the only ones required: A. Nitschke, in his 'Diskussionsbeitrag' on H. Fuhrmann, 'Fälschungen im Mittelalter', *HZ* 197, 1963, p. 575.

[265] Adv. haer. III, 11, 9: etenim cum omnia composita et apta deus fecerit, oportebat et speciem evangelii bene compositam et bene compaginatam esse.

[266] So, pertinently, Zahn, *op. cit.*, I, p. 153.

[267] O. Cullmann, 'Die Pluralität der Evangelien als theologisches Problem im Altertum' in: *Vorträge und Aufsätze 1925–1962*, 1966, p. 563, directs this reproach less against Irenaeus in person than against the method as such which he adopted; Moule, *op. cit.*, p. 196, following Cullmann, is more sharply critical.

[268] Benoit, *Saint Irénée*, p. 105.

fully linked in such a way that they had an incontrovertible, final and exclusive right to be heard as the God-intended historical documentation of the one Gospel. Thanks to Irenaeus they had become a single canonical book in the strict sense. Yet as such they still, to begin with, stand on their own, and are not to be understood without further ado as 'part' of a greater unity. This is in line with the importance which they possess for Irenaeus in particular: three-fifths of his 'New Testament' quotations derive from the fourfold Gospel.[268] For his fight against the heretics, however, even this basis turns out to be still too narrow; and in the continuation of his proof, therefore, Irenaeus deliberately seeks to widen it.

Acts is his second text; and out of it—after his examination of the Evangelists—it is possible to discover the same orthodox teaching in the case of the 'other apostles'.[269] The speeches, which even at this early date already have a marked 'anti-gnostic' slant,[270] are naturally a particularly fertile source for his campaign. In addition Acts makes it easier to achieve a corresponding, urgently desired interpretation and incorporation of the apostle Paul. For not only does Acts, so Irenaeus asserts, agree in substance with the Pauline epistles,[271] but also, by the way in which Paul here acts and teaches in harmony with all the other apostles, finally makes it clear that neither the Marcionite claim for the exclusive validity of his theology, nor the Ebionite rejection of it, nor its reinterpretation by the Valentinians has any justification.[272]

Here, however, as in the case of the Gospels, the important thing first of all is to show that Acts is really reliable, and thus no less normative and binding than they.[273] Again Irenaeus starts by bringing forward historical grounds: Luke was an eyewitness of the things he describes—the 'we'—passages already play a part here; Luke had to be faithful to the truth in his account, because what he related was at that time common knowledge; finally, Paul himself gave him the very best testimonial.[274] Luke with his truthful and at the same time sober presentation is a far earlier witness than any of the heretics who today pretend to know better than he.[275] To these Irenaeus adds a further argument, so to speak, from canonicity: Luke, the author of Acts, is

[269] Adv. haer. III, 11, 9: veniamus et ad reliquos apostolos.
[270] Irenaeus quite rightly detected this tendency in, for example, Paul's farewell speech at Miletus (Acts 20): Adv. haer. III, 14, 2.
[271] Adv. haer. III, 12, 9; 13, 3.   [272] Adv. haer. III, 15, 1f.
[273] A. C. Sundberg, 'Dependent Canonicity in Irenaeus and Tertullian', StudEvang III, 2, 1964, pp. 403–409, has failed to understand Irenaeus' intentions, since he wrongly refers the latter's remarks in justification of Acts to the person of Luke the Evangelist and his presumed lack of apostolic status.
[274] Since Irenaeus is already making use of the Pastorals, he can (Adv. haer. III, 14, 1) cite in support of this point not only Col. 4:14 but also II Tim. 4:10f.
[275] Adv. haer. III, 14, 1.

also above all else the author of the Gospel of Luke. Whoever doubts his authority and knowledge in the former instance[276] must also reject his testimony in the latter—and that would be impossible. The heretics cannot bring themselves to renounce the Gospel of Luke; for how many vital dominical sayings and how many pieces of information about the Lord—Irenaeus gives a whole list of them—are known to us solely from the Lukan gospel! But if Luke as an Evangelist is indispensable and true, then it is impermissible to accept what he has to say on one occasion and on another arbitrarily to reject it. The heretics must therefore either renounce everything, including the Gospel, or accept everything, which means that they must recognise Acts.[277] The authority of Acts therefore depends on the authority of the Gospel, and this in its turn has its firmly established place in the fourfold 'Gospel' as a whole. Luke confirms Paul, and Paul confirms Luke—the one interlocks with the other,[278] and this combination appears nothing short of providential: 'For perhaps God so arranged it that a great many things in the Gospel which all need to use should be recorded by Luke, in order that all men, following his subsequent testimony about the deeds and teaching of the apostles, and possessing therein an uncorrupted norm of truth, might be saved.'[279]

In this way Irenaeus has fashioned a new, solid block of canonical Scriptures, and enlarged the Four-Gospel canon, as it were, with a fifth book. This brings him to his goal. There is no need for him to discuss further problems of 'Introduction' in the course of his great proof from Scripture. Both the 'words of the Lord' and 'the letters of the Apostle' are of undisputed validity, and are respected even by the Valentinians; these therefore require no vindication. That the words of the Lord are treated on their own without reference to the Gospels is, in view of what has been said earlier, to be regarded as an archaic survival, a practice which derives from the time when the tradition of the faith formed an unbroken unity, and which occurs for the last time in this form in Irenaeus. By contrast this is the first occasion on which the Pauline letters are linked with other literary testimonies, representing the rest of the apostles. Nevertheless, they are still the only apostolic

[276] This has in mind the kind of heretical mistrust which previously (adv. haer. III, 1, 1; 5, 1) had been directed against the apostles.

[277] Adv. haer. III, 14, 3.4: necesse est igitur et reliqua, quae ab eo dicta sunt, recipere eos aut et his renuntiare. non enim conceditur eis ab his, qui sensum habent, quaedam quidem recipere ex his, quae a Luca dicta sunt, quasi sint veritatis, quaedam vero refutare, quasi non cognovisset veritatem (4).

[278] Benoit, Saint Irénée, p. 130.

[279] Adv. haer. III, 15, 1: fortassis enim et propter hoc operatus est deus plurima evangelii ostendi per Lucam, quibus necesse haberent omnes uti, ut sequenti testificationi eius, quam habet de actibus et doctrina apostolorum, omnes sequentes et regulam veritatis inadulteratam habentes salvari possint.

letters bearing the writer's name.[280] The Apocalypse stands, as already remarked, on its own, and does not form an integral part of Irenaeus' scriptural proof. Strictly speaking, therefore, we are still dealing with a series of independent writings or groups of writings, not with a 'New Testament', for which an overall designation is also lacking for this very reason. Nevertheless, *de facto* the new 'scriptures' do belong together; they agree as to the teaching of the apostles, which they reproduce as it originally was. The use which Irenaeus makes of them against the heretics allows their absolute spiritual unity to become apparent. There need be no hesitation, therefore, in designating Irenaeus as the first catholic theologian, the first man to know and acknowledge a New Testament both in theory and in practice.[281]

Thus in the history of the Canon Irenaeus takes his place alongside the heretic Marcion as the latter's catholic counterpart, the man who first demanded and realised a new Christian Canon. It cannot be denied that the concept of a catholic 'New Testament' was stimulated by Marcion's production, and was shaped, defended, and established in the fight against him and against all other heretical writings and traditions. But in fulfilling this function the new Canon changed its significance. It is true that like Marcion's canon its purpose was to confirm what was originally Christian, and to that extent it shared his concept of authenticity and documentary character; there is also an undeniable similarity to Marcion in structure and content. Nevertheless, even in Irenaeus it already displays a new kind of spirit and understanding: from being a Marcionite it has become a catholic canon.

What we mean is this: Marcion's canon had been in the strictest sense an 'apostolic' canon, that is, it was based exclusively on the one apostle, Paul, and was controlled by him even in its 'Gospel'. The canon which Irenaeus supplies can equally be called apostolic; as a result of the new canon the earlier, vague use of apostolic authority within the

[280] Adv. haer. I, 3, 6: καὶ οὐ μόνον ἐκ τῶν εὐαγγελικῶν καὶ τῶν ἀποστολικῶν πειρῶνται τὰς ἀποδείξεις ποιεῖσθαι..., ἀλλὰ καὶ ἐκ νόμου καὶ προφητῶν... 8, 1: ... ἀξιόπιστα προσαρμόζειν πειρῶνται τοῖς εἰρημένοις ἤτοι παραβολὰς κυριακὰς ἢ ῥήσεις προφητικὰς ἢ λόγους ἀποστολικούς... (on both occasions said about heretics); V pref.: ex reliquis doctrinae domini nostri et ex apostolicis epistolis. I, 8, 1 is the only passage at most of which it could be asked whether other writings than the Pauline letters are not in mind; but this is hardly to be assumed. Hoh, *op. cit.*, pp. 36f., who rightly rejects Werner's interpretation of ἀποστολικά as referring to the Gospels (p. 28), does not pay sufficient attention to Irenaeus' linguistic usage and the scheme which he is following, when he himself wishes to include Acts and the catholic epistles within this term.

[281] Furthermore, the heart of the Irenaean 'New Testament' (leaving out the Apocalypse) corresponds exactly to the definitive list which the *Doctrina Addai* required for Syria as late as the third century: Gospel (= Diatessaron), Pauline epistles, Acts of the Twelve Apostles; cf. Zahn, *op. cit.*, I, pp. 373f.

catholic church acquires a more precise, normative meaning.[282] But by comparison with Marcion the concept has been changed—both enlarged and softened.[283] It is enlarged to the extent that now in addition to Paul the rest of the apostles, that is, the Twelve, are given equal status as witnesses to the original truth; and it is softened to the extent that, while it is still the original teaching of these first disciples of Christ which stands behind the canonical Scripture as such, there is no longer an unconditional requirement that each individual document should be written or legitimated by an apostle. Mark and Luke are no less reliable and binding than Matthew or John,[284] and the testimony of the evangelist Philip[285] or of the martyr Stephen[286] is considered quite as good as that of an apostle. Irenaeus trusts the Church and her tradition, which were precisely the things Marcion wished to combat; hence for Irenaeus the apostles, despite their outstanding greatness and holiness, are from the standpoint of the Canon basically no more than the men who were first called and empowered to be witnesses to Christ's teaching. Since their day this teaching has been kept alive in the Church.[287] Everywhere there is but one truth, 'which the prophets predicted and Christ fulfilled and the apostles handed on, and which the church proclaims to her children throughout the world.'[288] That is why one

[282] Adv. haer. III, 1, 1 (cf. n. 208 above); 5, 1f.; 12, 13f.; 13, 1; 16, 9; 35, 2; IV, 35, 2. In a more general sense the apostles had, of course, long been regarded as the source of all church order and preaching (cf., e.g., Acts 2:42; Did. Inscr.; I Clem. 42, 1f.; II Clem. 14, 2), and the criticisms of heretics had further strengthened this tendency to distinguish them: Ignatius, Magn. 13,1; Jude 17; II Pet. 3: 2; Polycarp, Phil. 6, 3; Serapion in Eusebius, *HE* VI, 12, 3. Nevertheless, the exclusiveness with which in Irenaeus the apostles are made the starting-point of all teaching is something new (Reynders, *Paradosis,* pp. 178ff.). Bengsch, *op. cit.,* p. 66, comments pertinently: 'The apostolic tradition acquires within the *oikonomia* a place similar in importance to that of the Old Testament predictions.' Now, like the testimony of the ancient prophets it too appears in written form. This relation of the tradition to the Canon proceeding—directly or indirectly—from the apostles is to be regarded primarily as 'a catholic counter-concept' in the fight against Marcion (Harnack, *Neue Studien,* p. 23 n. 1).

[283] That Marcion's canonical apostolism cannot, conversely, be a caricature of that of the Church follows automatically from the view of the development of the Canon adopted here; Hanson, *op. cit.,* p. 214, takes the opposite view.

[284] Significant is the carefree way in which on the one hand it is alleged that the Gospels were written by the apostles (Adv. haer. III, 5, 1: ostensionem eorum qui et evangelium conscripserunt apostolorum), while on the other it is explained with equal candour that Mark and Luke had written down the teaching of Peter and Paul only 'after the death' of these apostles (III, 1, 1; cf. n. 242 above). For Acts even this source of information is lacking; but here it is sufficient that Luke is speaking in part from his own experience, and was unquestionably a reliable witness (cf. p. 201 above).

[285] Adv. haer. III, 12, 8.   [286] Adv. haer. III, 12, 10.13.

[287] Cf., e.g., Adv. haer. III, 14, 2: sic apostoli simpliciter et nemini invidentes, quae didicerant ipsi a domino, haec omnibus tradebant.

[288] Dem. 98; cf. Adv. haer. V pref.

can appeal equally well either to the apostles or to yet other leading men of the earliest days. It is certainly necessary that the normative writings should be ancient and authentic, in order to demonstrate what the apostolic teaching originally was; but it is not essential that these Scriptures should without exception derive solely from the apostles. It is enough if they reproduce the apostolic proclamation conscientiously and without misrepresentation.[289] Irenaeus does not yet think in terms of a specific 'inspiration' of the New Testament writers.[290]

[289] In this sense even Polycarp can be called an 'apostolic elder' (Eusebius, *HE* V, 20, 7), because he 'always taught that which he had learned from the apostles' (Adv. haer. III, 3, 4).

[290] Benoit, *Saint Irénée*, p. 139; A. Souter, *The Text and Canon of the N.T.*[2], 1954 (rev. C. S. C. Williams), p. 158; and hesitantly also Lawson, *op. cit.*, pp. 26–32, who, following P. Beuzart, *Essai sur la théologie d'Irénée*, Paris, 1908, p. 138, contents himself with the expectation 'that had S. Irenaeus lived in later times he would probably have been an upholder of the doctrine of Literal Inspiration' (p. 32). Indisputably correct, however, is the following statement: 'The doctrine typical of and general to Irenaeus is not that of a Spirit who comes to dwell in an individual prophet and inspires him to declare new truth, but of a Spirit who indwells and lifts to perfection those who faithfully adhere to the established tradition of truth' (p. 29). Naturally the writings of the apostles and the record of their spoken words are not to be doubted, since they contain their original preaching and the true revelation which from that day forward has been unalterably valid: Flesseman–van Leer, *op. cit.*, p. 130. But this has not yet resulted, as Blum, *op. cit.*, p. 176, would have it, in 'the concept of verbal inspiration' to be subordinated only to 'the concept of the apostolic'; for a similar view cf. K. Stendahl, 'The Apocalypse of John and the Epistles of Paul in the Muratorian Fragment', in: *Current Issues in N.T. Interpretation* (Festschrift O. Piper), London, 1962, p. 244. Beumer, *op. cit.*, p. 23, refers to Adv. haer. II, 28, 2: scripturae quidem perfectae sunt, quippe a verbo dei et spiritu eius dictae, in order to rescue the status of the N.T. scriptures as 'inspired Word of God', but overlooks the fact that here only the O.T. Scriptures can be meant. The only text which could possibly be adduced in support of his thesis is Adv. haer. III, 16, 2. This shows how easily the conception of the prophetic inspiration of the O.T. can be transferred to the New. Nevertheless, this passage is a special case in Irenaeus. It concerns Isaiah's prediction (Isa. 7:14) of the Virgin Birth—and thus a text already hotly debated in Justin (Dial. 44), which the Gospel of Matthew is to confirm. That explains why it is here asserted that the Spirit spoke through Matthew: ceterum potuerat dicere Matthaeus: 'Jesu vero generatio sic erat;' sed providens spiritus sanctus depravatores et praemuniens contra fraudulentiam eorum per Mattaeum ait: 'Christi autem generatio sic erat' . . . All the other passages which Hoh, *op. cit.*, pp. 90ff., adduces in support of a doctrine of inspiration fall short of actual proof. In Irenaeus the Spirit is in principle linked not with the records but with the person of the apostle, and therefore cannot be separated from the preaching, on the one hand, and on the other from faith in and preservation of the rule of truth, which the Scriptures for their part merely confirm. By contrast the Old Testament, which for their part merely confirm. By contrast the Old Testament, which for Irenaeus naturally means the Septuagint, really is, as in Judaism and for Justin, an inspired divine book: cf. Sagnard in his edition, pp. 432ff.

He never calls the New Testament books, 'apostolic writings',[291] nor, conversely, is he concerned to unite everything deriving from the apostles in a canonical collection.[292] His canon is thus not guaranteed and constituted, in the later manner, on the basis of a formal principle, but rather is in the Lukan sense 'historical'.[293]

That the dominant interest, as a result of which the documents were collected and studied, was not historical but dogmatic is obvious. In this respect Irenaeus was no different from Marcion or any other theologian of his time. But, in contrast to Marcion, his 'dogma' was not so narrowly framed that he had to concentrate on one single apostolic witness, and even then resort to deletions and corrections to bring order into his material. Irenaeus lets the documents stand as they are. With an easy mind he juxtaposes the four different Gospels, places Acts next to both authentic and inauthentic Paulines, and explains that they all witness to the same Christ and to one and the same truth proclaimed by Christ. It would be wrong to see in this proceeding nothing more than an uncritical naïveté, doing violence to the texts. Certainly Irenaeus is no critical philologist such as both Marcion and Ptolemy were in some degree; he is indeed even less of one than Justin who—in the Old Testament—strove as best he could to explain and reconcile the obvious contradictions. But that which sustains his capacity for the comprehensive view and his serene freedom and confidence in face of the conflicting voices of the texts is not blindness to the detailed and particular but a feeling for the essential and unitary: the One God, the one

---

[291] For Irenaeus the 'apostolic writings' are the Pauline epistles, as being letters 'of the Apostle'; cf. n. 280 above. The adjective ἀποστολικός, both in Irenaeus and generally in the early period, is still extremely rare: L.-M. Dewailly, 'Notes sur l'histoire de l'adjectif "apostolique",' MelScRel 5, 1948, pp. 141–152. 'Apostolica traditio' occurs once in Adv. haer. III, 3, 3, 'apostolica doctrina' in IV, 32, 1; and Irenaeus' short popular work is called Ἐπίδειξις τοῦ ἀποστολικοῦ κηρύγματος (Eusebius, HE V, 26). Almost all modern scholars attempt all the more eagerly, when paraphrasing Irenaeus, to make good the deficiency by inserting the word. Typical, for instance, is the way in which Blum, op. cit., pp. 162f., at first rightly observes that 'the abstract concept of the apostolic' generally 'occurs only in weak rudimentary forms' in Irenaeus, but then in his own presentation constantly speaks of 'apostolic writings', and on p. 173 even makes the assertion that their 'legitimacy' was established for Irenaeus by the 'criterion of apostolicity'.

[292] This to some extent explains the slight attention paid to the catholic epistles. Zahn, op. cit., I, p. 447, rightly attacks the 'remarkable persistence' with which 'right down to recent times it has been maintained, with reference to Irenaeus, that "the N.T. came into being on the basis of the simple principle of the apostolic origin of its parts".'

[293] In this connection Adv. haer. III, 14, 2 refers to the prologue to the Gospel of Luke: sic igitur et Lucas nemini invidens ea, quae ab eis didicerat, tradidit nobis, sicut ipse testificatur dicens: 'Quemadmodum tradiderunt nobis, qui ab initio contemplatores et ministri fuerunt verbi' (Lk. 1:2).

Christ, and the one salvation, which God has given to mankind, and which the Church, in accordance with the 'canon of truth', has taught and guarded. Certainly his selection of controlling viewpoints is determined by his hostility to gnosticism; but it can hardly be said, nevertheless, that this has made Irenaeus' living understanding of Scripture empty or shallow. His scriptural theology is not conceived one-sidedly, as a result of his opposition to the gnosis; it collects the traditions, and is able now for the first time not merely to affirm Paul and John and the Synoptists simultaneously but actually to make room for them. It rests on a broad foundation and a rich experience, which allows it to grasp the One in the Many and again and again to bring it out forcefully and afresh. The spaciousness which Marcion's dogmatism had obstructed has, thanks to Irenaeus, become a basic feature of the New Testament, never to be lost again.

The framework for the overall interpretation is provided by the salvation-history scheme of divine covenant makings, which Irenaeus took over from Justin and indeed from other predecessors as well. It had originally—that is to say, as early as Paul—been forced on Christianity by the retention of the Old Testament. Marcion, who rejected this, and whose thinking in other ways also was quite unhistorical, did not develop even the most rudimentary form of such a view. Irenaeus, on the other hand, extended the old concept, and was able at the same time powerfully to deepen it: in this context belong his observations on the relationship of creation to redemption, of redemption and new life, and on the threefold development of the knowledge of God, first in the prophetic spirit, then through the Son, and finally one day in the kingdom of the Father. We cannot here survey the whole of Irenaean theology. What is important is that the idea of God's providential government is now from beginning to end linked and permeated with the testimonies of Scripture. Hitherto, when warding off the Marcionite attacks on the Old Testament, it had been only the first, pre-Christian stage which had been defended biblically in the strict sense. Now in addition the story of Christ and the tradition of the Church, leading on from Christ, are given a scriptural basis, and thus safeguarded against all subsequent reinterpretations. And at the end, with the help of John's Apocalypse, Irenaeus draws one last enormous curve which reaches right to the consummation of history in the millenial kingdom and into God's own eternity. In this way the Scriptures as dogmatic texts become simultaneously a witness to and themselves part of the great saving history which from the creation has been enacted between God and men, and at whose penultimate stage stands the contemporary Church.

The Bible accompanies the Church on its journey through the ages and to its eternal goal. One cannot, it is true, say on Irenaeus' terms

that the Church lives 'by Scripture alone'; for in his view it lives from
the beginning in the power of the Spirit and of the truth which is its
perpetual possession and familiar study. But Irenaeus does indeed understand the necessity, where this truth is obscured, contested or denied,
to verify it no longer by general references to the tradition or the ancient
Scriptures, but by solid documents which go back to Christ and his
disciples.[294] These agree in every respect with that the Church teaches;
but nevertheless they derive their power to compel and convince not
from the Church but from that which they are in themselves and to
which they bear witness, independently of any tradition. Indeed, they
for their part are able to buttress tradition without, as it would seem,
themselves requiring support of any kind.[295] As yet this scriptural
principle is applied almost exclusively outside the Church, against the

[294] These stand alongside the Old Testament particularly in the context of
scriptural proof, which presupposes their unqualified validity. The theoretical
question of their 'rank' apart from this context, and whether they are already
in every respect of equal value with the older Scriptures, is one with which
Irenaeus, in contrast to modern historians of the Canon, was not concerned.
It is the wrong question to ask, and therefore, as one might expect, has no correct answer. On the O.T. cf., e.g., A. Camerlynck, *Saint Irénée et le Canon du
Nouveau Testament*, Louvain, 1896, pp. 55ff.; A. Jacquier, *Le Nouveau Testament dans l'église chrétienne* I³, Paris, 1911, pp. 183f.; also Leipoldt, *op. cit.*,
I, pp. 37, 156, 198.
[295] It is hard to understand how Blum, who in general is very much to the
point in his development of the relation between Scripture and tradition, can
then make the statement that according to Irenaeus the correct exegesis of the
Scriptures cannot 'be arrived at on the basis of the scriptures themselves, but is
guaranteed by the tradition of the church' (p. 185; similarly pp. 179, 182:
'the kerygma preached by the church proves the truth of the scriptures'). This
sort of statement does, it is true, correspond to a certain extent to modern catholic views (to which Bengsch, *op. cit.*, pp. 72f., also, though with caution, makes
Irenaeus accede); but a rejection of proof resting on the Scriptures alone—
quia non possit ex his inveniri veritas ab his, qui nesciant traditionem—occurs
in Irenaeus (Adv. haer. III, 2, 1; cf. n. 211 above), as Molland has already emphasised and Flesseman-van Leer (*op. cit.*, esp. pp. 139–144) has shown in
detail, only as a heretical plea which Irenaeus in no way regards as valid; cf.
also H. Karpp, 'Viva Vox' in: *Mullus* (Festschrift T. Klauser, 1964, pp. 190–
198), p. 196. We must agree with Lawson, *op. cit.*, p. 103, when he stresses that
the question of the relation between Scripture and tradition has not yet arisen
for Irenaeus himself, and thus is one that can hardly be put to him direct: 'The
truth hangs by two cords, and he can speak of either as self-sufficient without
intending to deny or subordinate the other.' I consider, however, that the way
in which in the *Proof* he connects the tradition of the Church with proclamation
by the living word, and in his polemic in favour of the Scripture leaves the latter
out almost entirely, does in fact allow us to determine the trend of his remarks in
practice, 'when "the Written Word" was pitted against "priestly tradition".'
The affirmation of what the Church's 'Elders' teach seems, it is true, to be taken
for granted by Irenaeus; but cannot in his thinking be made into an absolute
principle against the Scripture; cf. Campenhausen, *Ecclesiastical Authority*,
1969, pp. 169–173.

heretics; what the New Testament means for the Church itself is rather taken for granted and occasionally touched upon than demonstrated and emphasised. But the idea of a new, normative scripture, deriving from Christ and 'his true disciples',[296] has been discovered, and no longer left to the Marcionites or to a more or less accidental process of regulation. It is true that the limits of the new collection have not yet been sharply drawn, and as yet their unity is hardly comprehended as such;[297] but the first steps have been taken. After Irenaeus there was never again to be a church which did not affirm the bipartite Christian Bible, containing the Old and, parallel with this and controlling it, the New Testament.

[296] Adv. haer. II, 32, 4: οἱ ἀληθῶς αὐτοῦ μαθηταί.

[297] I do not know how Flesseman–van Leer, *op. cit.*, pp. 132f., can assert on the basis of Adv. haer. V, 30, 1 and IV, 33, 8 that 'Irenaeus knows and uses an apparently fixed, well defined collection of New Testament apostolic writings to which nothing may be added and from which nothing is to be deleted'. In this passage, as happens elsewhere, she incorrectly extends what Irenaeus says about the Four Gospels to a New Testament.

CHAPTER SIX

Defining the Limits of the New Testament Canon

THE INFLUENCE which Irenaeus exercised on his contemporaries and on the succeeding generation was unquestionably strong. Clement, Tertullian, and Hippolytus were familiar with him, and took up his idea of a new canon and developed it further. In detail, however, the pattern which he set was not followed,[1] and the very rapidity with which this pattern prevailed forbids us to see it as the only source of the emergent catholic New Testament. Irenaeus is but the pioneering representative of a method and approach which everywhere met an urgent need. Once provoked by Marcion, and set in train, the consolidation of the new canon could nowhere be checked, and was carried through as it were by its own momentum. In its essential content the New Testament collection of early writings from the start displayed no innovation. The majority of the items had been known for a long time, and had certainly for the most part also already been put to liturgical use. Nowhere—not even among heretics—do we hear of a protest directed against the New Testament as such. To begin with, however, only the hard core of the collection was in any way firmly established. The further selection of books in the running was undecided, and nowhere as yet had been intentionally defined.

At once there began a period of swift expansion of the number of works felt to be normative. A collection of sacred books, even if they are of the highest authority, does not for that reason have also to be a 'closed' collection.[2] Moreover, there was a particular desire for a many-

---

[1] Clement did not understand the implications of Irenaeus' scriptural principle, even though he appeals to it (cf. pp. 291, 305f. below). Gaius attacked the Apocalypse and, above all, the Four-Gospel canon (cf. pp. 236ff. below), and the Muratorian Canon uses different arguments from those of Irenaeus to justify it (cf. pp. 251f. below). When Didascalia 24f. follows up the first missionary preaching of the Apostles with a second journey in the course of which these 'Didascalia' were delivered, then its theology stands, 'of course, in clear contradiction to Irenaeus's theology of the Canon': G. Kretschmar, 'Die Konzile der alten Kirche' in: H. J. Margull, Die ökumenischen Konzile der Christenheit, 1961, p. 17 n. 10.

[2] A. von Harnack, Entstehung, p. 24: 'A mere "collection" of writings need not be "closed"; instead it may even intentionally—to a greater or lesser degree—

sided witness to the 'genuine' tradition to set against the narrow and mutilated bible of Marcion. Attempts were made to secure as comprehensive and solid a collection as possible; and in the process people naturally liked to adopt such books as confirmed their own points of view. There was thus a danger that even recent, tendentious works would find their way into the Canon, as, for example, II Peter or the Shepherd of Hermas. But this development did not continue for long unhindered. Only one generation after Marcion[3] the whole prevailing structure of the Church was jeopardised by a very differently oriented movement, the 'New Prophecy' of Phrygian Montanism. In the struggle against the enthusiasm of this movement the significance of the Canon changed. The contemporary Church was sharply separated from that of the primitive period, and what now mattered was that the Canon should be a closed, final, and immovable datum. Consequently a brake was put on further expansion, and it was finally brought to a halt. It was in the course of this double movement, at first expansive but then restrictive, that the basic features of our present New Testament were formed.

We shall begin by considering the evidence pointing in the direction of expansion. It is in the first part of the new 'scripture', the 'Gospel', that fewest traces of these tendencies are to be found. The fourfold Gospel had itself been the product of a move to provide an enlarged collection, and it is no accident that Irenaeus defended it in such detail. The Gospel of Mark must have become or remained almost completely unknown to many congregations at that time, because it was ousted by Matthew,[4] and John could still be thought of as all too new and alien in character.[5] The attempts that were made, therefore, were rather to replace the multiplicity of Gospels by a single 'Harmony',[6] or, as in Jewish Christian circles, to stop at a single Gospel.[7] There was in general little inclination to introduce extra gospels. Where such were in use, they now had hardly any prospect of recognition, and, like the Gospel of Peter, despite their relative antiquity easily fell under suspicion of being heretical fabrications.[8]

---

be left open, especially if it serves purposes which do not preclude an enrichment from contemporary sources ("lectionary").'

[3] On the disputed question of date I do not follow Epiphanius, but Eusebius whose Chronicle places the first appearance of Montanus in the year 172, not as early as 156/7.

[4] Cf. p. 171 n. 112 above.   [5] Cf. pp. 160, 168 above; 237ff. below.
[6] Cf. pp. 174ff. above.   [7] Eusebius, HE III, 25, 5; cf. 27, 4.

[8] Bishop Serapion of Antioch refused the inhabitants of Rhossos permission, which he had earlier granted, to use the Gospel of Peter for liturgical reading (cf. p. 169 above), even though he himself acknowledged that the greater part of it was predominantly orthodox (τὰ μὲν πλείονα τοῦ ὀρθοῦ λόγου τοῦ σωτῆρος,

P

The Epistles present quite the opposite picture; here progressive enlargements are everywhere observable.[9] In the beginning it had contained only Paul's letters to the churches (plus Philemon), and consequently was also given his name, 'the Apostle', ὁ ἀπόστολος.[10] Paul is quite generally referred to, among catholics as well as Marcionites and Valentinians, as 'the' Apostle. This designation cannot derive from Paul's own statements about himself—there he is certainly the 'apostle of the *Gentiles*' but never simply 'the Apostle'—but must be the result of his outstanding literary significance. Paul was at first the one and only apostle who was available for quotation and whom men wished to quote.[11] Even Irenaeus, in his efforts to collect additional apostolic testimony, still appeals only to Acts and the Gospels, not to the Catholic Epistles, even though he is acquainted with some of them.[12] By contrast, the Pastoral Epistles, which had then only just appeared, he accepts at once and includes them in his 'canon'.[13] Others are starting to cite Hebrews as Pauline;[14] and towards the end of the second century comes the forged 'III Corinthians',[15] and possibly also an Epistle

---

τινὰ δὲ προσδιεσταλμένα: Eusebius, *HE* VI, 12, 6), and the docetic-gnostic tendency which he claimed to find in it is, in the light of the extant fragments, not really credible: C. Maurer in *N.T. Apocrypha* I, pp. 179f.

[9] Only Syria, even to some extent in later times, refused to recognise any epistles other than those of Paul: W. Bauer, *Der Apostolos der Syrer in der Zeit von der Mitte des vierten Jahrhunderts bis zur Spaltung der syrischen Kirche*, 1903, pp. 40ff., esp. 67–69, 70.

[10] So far as Marcion's bible is concerned, the tradition preserved in Epiphanius and Jerome does, it is true, mention only the neutral form, ἀποστολικόν, *apostolicum*: A. von Harnack, *Marcion*[2], 1924, p. 67*. According to the evidence —to my mind not altogether unequivocal—listed in (ed.) Lampe, *Patristic Lexicon*, 1961ff., the corresponding use of ἀπόστολος does, however, already occur in Origen (Hom. Jerem. I, 7; XX [19], 3; in Eusebius, *HE* VI, 38). It is not his creation.

[11] Cf. pp. 143ff., 176ff. above.   [12] Cf. p. 194 above.
[13] Cf. pp. 193f. above.

[14] Irenaeus is acquainted with Hebrews (Eusebius, *HE* V, 26), but is said to have disputed its Pauline origin: Stephanus Gobaros in Photius, Bibl. 232: Ἱππόλυτος καὶ Εἰρηναῖος τὴν πρὸς Ἑβραίους ἐπιστολὴν Παύλου οὐκ ἐκείνου εἶναί φασι (cf. Zahn, *op. cit.*, I, p. 296 n. 1). The first whom we know to have accepted it as Pauline was, according to the testimony of Clement, 'the blessed Elder', that is, Pantaenus: Eusebius, *HE* VI, 14, 4. Clement followed his teacher on this point, but regards the extant form of the epistle as a translation undertaken by Luke from the 'Hebrew': *ibid.*, 13, 6; 14, 2f.; Adumbr. in Ep. Petri 5, 13; Zahn, *op. cit.*, I, pp. 283ff.

[15] It formed a part of the Acts of Paul, and from there found its way into the canon of the Syrian and Armenian churches, and also into various Latin biblical MSS: A. von Harnack, *Apocrypha* IV[2], 1931, pp. 6f.; K. Pink, 'Die pseudo-paulinischen Briefe', *Biblica* 6, 1925, pp. 70–91. Nevertheless, the epistle itself seems to be older: A. F. J. Klijn, 'The apocryphal correspondence between Paul and the Corinthians', *VC* 17, 1963, pp. 10–16.

to the Laodiceans.[16] Clement of Alexandria is, so far as we know, the first, Egypt being an enthusiastically receptive milieu, to make a start by treating and quoting the letters of other apostles as 'scripture'. I Peter and I John, but also Barnabas and Jude and II John are formally expounded in his Hypotyposes.[17] I Clement, to which Irenaeus had already made one reference,[18] and the Preaching of Peter are almost as important.[19] There is even, it would seem, a readiness to ascribe canonical status to an ancient Church order which is alleged to go back to the twelve apostles.[20]

In the case of the apocryphal Acts more caution is shown. It is for

[16] The catholic (?) Epistle to the Laodiceans cannot unfortunately be dated with certainty: Harnack, *Apocrypha* IV, p. 2, would place it 'before the middle of the third century', Pink, *op. cit.*, p. 192, between 250 and 350, and W. Schneemelcher, in *N.T. Apocrypha* II, p. 131, in 'the period between the second and fourth century'.

[17] Eusebius, *HE* VI, 14, 1 (and the extant translated Fragments). In Strom. II, 31, 2 Barnabas is in fact termed 'apostle' (cf. II, 116, 3: ἀποστολικός).

[18] Adv. haer. III, 3, 3 (cf. n. 52 below); Hegesippus also seems to have adduced it for a similar anti-heretical purpose: Eusebius, *HE* IV, 22, 1.

[19] The 'apostle' Clement (Strom. IV, 105, 1) and his epistle are quoted with exceptional frequency; the Preaching of Peter also makes repeated appearances, is regarded as the work of Peter hmself, and as a sacred text is not only quoted but even expounded in commentary: Strom. VI, 39–41. The gnostic Heracleon may already have anticipated Clement of Alexandria in this: Origen, Comm. Joh. XIII, 17, 104. Cf. further the Index in Stählin's *GCS* edition of Clement. By contrast II Peter and James appear by name for the first time in Origen, as 'disputed' texts (in Eusebius, *HE* VI, 25, 8; Origen, Comm. Joh. XIX, 23, 152; XX, 10, 66). The so-called II Clement occurs for the first time in Eusebius, *HE* III, 38, 4.

[20] Unfortunately it cannot be decided with certainty whether Clem. Alex., Strom. I, 100, 4, really intends to make a formal citation of the text of the Didache (3, 5), but it is highly probable: J. M. Creed, 'The Didache', *JTS* 39, 1938, pp. 373ff. The *Stichometria* of Nicephorus lists it among the τῆς νέας διαθήκης ἀπόκρυφα. It is first mentioned explicitly by Athanasius in his thirtyninth Easter letter, excluded from the canonical Scriptures, but sanctioned for church use in company with the Wisdom of Solomon, Ben Sira, Esther, Judith, Tobit, and the Shepherd of Hermas. In view, however, of the earlier attestation in the Oxyrhynchus papyri, and of the use of the Didache in the Didascalia, we may conclude that at an earlier period—in Egypt at any rate—the Didache enjoyed quasi-canonical respect. Thus, J. P. Audet, *La Didachè—Instructions des Apôtres*, 1958, p. 216, thinks that in this case we must reckon with 'a kind of strictly ecclesiastical, official, and controlled transmission, in the ambit of the Old and New Testament writings. We must therefore assume that from time immemorial it has been held in very high esteem, and that no serious doubt had ever been cast upon it as regards its ultimate purpose.'

Perhaps I may be allowed at this point to remind the reader once more that our concern throughout the present work is not with the first use or attestation of the works in question but only with establishing their formal citation as canonical or quasi-canonical authorities. In studies of the history of the Canon these two standpoints are unfortunately very often confused.

the most part not until this period that they are published,[21] and they are designed more to meet a popular need for edification and instruction than to pursue any serious theological purpose. Nor are they written to compete with the canonical Acts of Luke.[22] All the same, even here some material makes a bid for canonical standing. It is true that in the catholic church it is—significantly—once again only the Acts of Paul, a work which, it would seem, was attributed to Paul himself,[23] that had any marked success,[24] though even in the lifetime of its actual author it was exposed as a forgery.[25] Later on, however, in the sacred scriptures of the Manichaeans appeared a whole corpus of apostolic Acts, and these gnosticising works were also in use in other sects. From the time of Eusebius onwards[26] they are constantly condemned and rejected in catholic literature and in various lists of canonical works.[27] Developments in this area too, therefore, were not without their dangers.

One final group of writings which were candidates for inclusion in the Canon is that of the early Christian apocalypses. They had had an independent pre-history of their own, and could be disregarded in our discussion hitherto. Only now, in connection with the Montanist

[21] E. Peterson, 'Einige Beobachtungen zu den Anfängen der christlichen Askese' in: *Frühkirche, Judentum und Gnosis*, 1959, p. 211, wishes to place the Acts of Andrew, John, and Thomas in the time of Hadrian (117–138); but this is neither demonstrable nor probable. Against Peterson's view cf. M. Hornschuh, in *N.T. Apocrypha* II, p. 396.

[22] Cf. the introductory survey by W. Schneemelcher/K. Schäferdiek in: *N.T. Apocrypha* II, pp. 167–187.

[23] Cf. W. Schneemelcher in: *N.T. Apocrypha* II, pp. 323f.

[24] Tertullian, De bapt. 17; 5 (cf. n. 25 below) indicates the standing (which he himself challenged) of the work in Africa; Hippolytus made use of it (Comm. Dan. III, 29), and Origen (Comm. Joh. XX, 12, 91), cited it as quasi-canonical, though with the cautious comment, εἴ τῳ δὲ φίλον παραδεξασθαι τὸ ἐν ταῖς Παύλου Πράξεσιν ἀναγεγραμμένον; a further quotation occurs in De princ. I, 2, 3.

[25] Tertullian, De bapt. 17, 5: quodsi quae Pauli perperam scripta sunt [exemplum Theclae] ad licentiam mulierum docendi tinguendique defendunt, sciant in Asia presbyterum, qui eam scripturam construxit quasi titulo Pauli de suo cumulans, convictum atque confessum id se amore Pauli fecisse loco decessisse. This was a case, therefore, not of a heretical but, in its motives, of a relatively harmless forgery. 'It may be assumed that the author was familiar with the Lukan Acts. His work, however, is dependent not on Acts but on the tradition in circulation concerning Paul and his doings': W. Schneemelcher, 'Die Apostelgeschichte des Lukas und die Acta Pauli' in: *Apophoreta* (Festschrift Haenchen), 1964, p. 250.

[26] In *HE* III, 25, 4 Eusebius classifies the Acts of Paul with the Shepherd of Hermas, the Apocalypse of Peter, the Epistle of Barnabas, the Didache, and the Revelation of John, under the head of disputed writings, but sharply rejects all other apostolic Acts as heretical concoctions: *ibid.*, III, 25, 6f.

[27] Cf. K. Schäferdiek, *op. cit.* n. 22 above, pp. 118f., and the material in Zahn, *op. cit.*, II, pp. 840ff.

Prophecy, does their canonical status become a problem. Debate on this issue then has its effect on the understanding of the idea of the canonical in general.

Prophecy and apocalyptic played a part in the Christian Church from the beginning.[28] In this Christians were the heirs of Later Judaism, which had produced an abundant apocalyptic literature. These productions were without exception pseudonymous, and mostly circulated under the names of extremely ancient biblical figures. They contained predictions about the course of world history and the end of the world, linked with exhortations to repentance and all kinds of teachings about heavenly things. These writings were read in the early Church, and not infrequently cited as authoritative.[29] It is true that the religious interest of Christians no longer attached to the future alone, and had very largely turned away from the universal destiny of the world and its people; now it centred on the present and on the present salvation of the community in Christ. But the history of Christ and of Christians had not yet reached its goal. The Return of the Lord, the Judgment, and the Coming of the Kingdom of God were still outstanding and eagerly awaited. What Jesus had said on this subject was now combined with earlier Jewish traditions concerning the time of the End and the signs which were to precede it. For the most part these predictions were put into the mouth of Jesus himself; soon too, actual Jewish writings were given Christian revisions and additions. Apocalyptic writings of their own, however, under the name of a Christian prophet or apostle, did not at first appear.

The Revelation of John, therefore, was a new phenomenon which opened a new phase in Christian apocalyptic.[30] It was conceived from the start as a book with which the author came before the Christian public under his own name.[31] It tells of the visions and auditions which John himself received and which are shortly to come to pass: 'Blessed

[28] The reader is referred to the masterly introductory survey by P. Vielhauer in *N.T. Apocrypha* II, pp. 581–642. In what follows, however, we shall be concerned not with the form-critical problem of the apocalypses but only with the distinctive character of their quasi-canonical claim to authority.

[29] Cf., e.g., the list in A. Oepke, *TWNT* III, 1938, pp. 988–993.

[30] Vielhauer, *op. cit.*, p. 582: 'Here the word ἀποκάλυψις is used for the first time with the meaning "revelation of that which must shortly take place". We meet it for the first time as the designation of a book in the title of the Johannine Apocalypse, ᾿Αποκάλυψις ᾿Ιωάννου. Because of the significance of this Apocalypse the word ἀποκάλυψις became a literary title and the designation of related Christian books—about A.D. 200 the Muratori Canon mentions "apocalypse . . . Johannis et Petri" (II. 71f.)—and was then assigned to Jewish works of this type, oddly enough by Christians.'

[31] Rev. 1:3, as the change from singular to plural shows, was thought of in terms of a liturgical reading. The book is addressed to the 'congregations' (cf. n. 33 below).

is he who reads aloud the words of the prophecy, and blessed are those who hear, and who keep what is written therein; for the time is near'.[32] John has been instructed by the Lord himself; it is 'the Spirit' who through him speaks to the churches.[33] His revelations are backed by the highest authority known to Christianity, and the apocalyptist explicitly transfers to his own book the sacred validity of that authority. The apocalypse closes with an appalling threat intended to maintain and protect its immovable right: 'I warn everyone who hears the words of the prophecy of this book: if any one adds to them, God will add to him the plagues described in this book, and if any one takes away from the words of the book of this prophecy, God will take away his share in the tree of life and in the holy city, which are described in this book. He who testifies to these things says, "Surely I am coming soon." Amen. Come, Lord Jesus!'[34] A claim such as belongs to every inspired text by its very nature is here given conscious, conceptually precise formulation.[35]

About one generation later there appeared in Rome a new apocalyptic book, 'the Shepherd', the author of which, Hermas, likewise mentions himself. It is in every respect more jejune and superficial than the Johannine Revelation, and in the main is filled up with exhortations to repentance and general teaching, in comparison with which the element of apocalyptic expectation and prediction recedes into the background.[36] But Hermas too presents himself as a prophet endowed by Christ and by the divine Church, tells of visions, and concerns himself with world-wide dissemination of and attention to his book.[37] By contrast, in the Apocalypse of Peter, which may be only a little later in date, the prophetic claim has now virtually disappeared. There is a return to pseudonymity, and only in one branch of the tradition do we still have a genuine account of a vision. In the Ethiopic version of the text the description of rewards and punishments in the world to come, which forms the major part of the book, no longer occurs as prediction but simply as instruction which Jesus gives to Peter and the other disciples. The situation recalls the way in which the 'Conversations of Jesus

---

[32] Rev. 1:3.   [33] Rev. 2:7, 11, 17, 29; 3:6, 13, 22; cf. 22:6, etc.
[34] Rev. 22:18–20; cf. Deut. 4:2; 12:32.
[35] There is no need, however, with E. Lohmeyer, *Die Offenbarung des Johannes*², 1953, p. 182, to contrast this 'claim to holiness and completeness' with the traditional formulas intended to 'protect a work against impermissible expansion or abridgement'; cf. n. 115 below.
[36] E. Molland, art. 'Hermas', *RGG*³ III, 1959, p. 242: 'In form the "Shepherd" is an apocalypse, but in content a penitential sermon'; similarly Vielhauer, *op. cit.*, pp. 630, 634ff. It is, however, going too far to say, as Vielhauer does (p. 641), that the author has chosen the apocalyptic 'form' only to serve his own purposes: 'it lends to it the character of a revelation, that is, a divine authority for the claims put forward in it, an authority which the author could not lay claim to for himself.'

with his Disciples' are presented in the Epistle of the Apostles.[38] In this way the whole document makes itself out to be a piece of tradition about Jesus, apostolically guaranteed, supplementing the existing Gospels.[39] In the second century, alongside Christian revisions of Jewish apocryphal works and of the ostensibly pagan Sibylline Oracles, gnostic apocalypses also appear in great numbers. These works too are pseudonymous, and for the most part more didactic than prophetic or apocalyptic. They include yet another Apocalypse of Peter.[40] The apocalypses of John, Hermas, and Peter already discussed, however, remain the ones most respected and familiar among Christians at large.[41]

What was the nature of their authority? This is the question which concerns us. It goes without saying that any prophetic text, regardless whether it is transmitted orally or in writing, is bound to demand unqualified acceptance as a word revealed by God. In this sense every apocalypse is 'sacred scripture'. But this authority is self-authenticating, that is, it is based on the claim of its author to be inspired and has nothing to do either with a canon or with earlier testimony of any kind: 'He who has an ear, let him hear what the Spirit says to the churches.'[42] One characteristic expression of this prophetic self-consciousness is

[37] Herm. 8, 2f. (*Vis.* II, 4, 2f.).

[38] Nevertheless, I can hardly believe that the date (the first half of the second century) which M. Hornschuh, *Studien zur Epistula Apostolorum*, 1965, pp. 116ff., attempts to give this document can be maintained. This, if nothing else, would tell against it, namely that this letter of the eleven apostles 'to the churches of the east and the west, the north and the south' is, as Hornschuh himself rightly observes (p. 4), a 'catholic epistle' in the strict sense of the word—something which is only approximately true of I Peter, I John, and James. With such a form the Epistle of the Apostles would, in the first half of the century, be virtually unparalleled.

[39] J. Daniélou, 'Les traditions secrètes des Apôtres', *Eranos-Jahrbuch* 1962, Zurich, 1963, p. 203. The narrative of the Apocalypse of Peter is at many points dependent upon the Synoptics, though naturally these are not cited.

[40] Four new gnostic apocalypses (those of 'Paul', 'James' I and II, and 'Adam') have been published by A. Böhlig and P. Labib: *Koptisch-gnostische Apokalypsen aus Codex V von Nag Hammadi*, 1963.

[41] It would, however, be wrong to give the impression that these three apocalypses had been combined to form a fixed 'collection', a threefold apocalyptic canon comparable to the fourfold Gospel, one which might possibly have 'formed the basis of a distinctive New Testament' that was then nipped in the bud (so Harnack, *Entstehung*, p. 58). According to H. Lietzmann, 'Wie wurden die Bücher des Neuen Testaments heilige Schrift?' in *Kleine Schriften* III, 1958, p. 96, such a canon 'is elusive'—but the assumption that it existed at all is quite unfounded. I would therefore prefer to say that it is purely 'illusory'. The right comment is that of H. B. Stonehouse, *The Apocalypse in the Ancient Church*, 1929, p. 86: 'The whole construction that at one time the Church possessed a canon of apocalypses, which were accepted apart from any question as to their authorship and time of their origin, is not grounded in fact, and particularly looks in vain to the Canon Muratori for support.'

[42] Rev. 2:7, 11, 17, 29; 3:6, 13, 22; 13:9.

the absence of any biblical quotations in support of the message.[43] The standing of the Christian prophet is not inferior to that of the prophets of old; he steps up alongside them with equal authority.[44] Thus, the Revelation of John is indeed formally saturated with Old Testament phrases and reminiscences; but the new prophetic 'servant of God'[45] nevertheless cites not one single passage of Scripture as such. He does not count as a scribe, and has no need to defend himself, as they do, with scriptural examples. Hermas too, in the whole of his voluminous book, nowhere cites a passage of canonical Scripture; his one explicit quotation derives from the Prophecy of Eldad and Modad, probably a late judaistic work, now lost.[46] Only in the Apocalypse of Peter does this principle start to become blurred, in that twice there are references to passages of Scripture which are to be 'fulfilled' at the end of the days. This is in keeping with the work's unclear stylistic character.[47]

In the earliest stages of forming the new canon the apocalypses played no important part, and attracted hardly any attention.[48] The process

[43] Sextus Julius Africanus had already correctly recognised this in principle, when he wrote in his letter to Origen: ἐπὶ δὲ πᾶσι τοσούτων προωδοιπορηκότων προφητῶν ἑξῆς οὐδεὶς ἑτέρου κέχρηται ῥητῷ ἢ νοήματι· οὐ γὰρ ἐπτώχευσεν ὁ λόγος αὐτῶν ἀληθὴς ὤν: (ed.) W. Reichardt, Die Briefe des Sextus Julius Africanus an Aristides und Origenes, 1909, p. 80.

[44] Nevertheless, as Lietzmann, Bücher des N.T., pp. 30f., rightly remarks, John, the author of Revelation, did not 'of course, bother himself about his status relative to the Old Testament'.

[45] Rev. 1:1.

[46] Herm. 7, 4 (Vis. II, 3, 4). Apart from this, Hermas contains only 'similar ideas, echoes, Old Testament language, while verbatim quotations . . . are nowhere contemplated': M. Whittaker in her edition, 1956, p. XXII.

[47] The quotations occur only in the sections which have come down to us in Ethiopic: in ch. 4 Jesus refers to Ezek. 37:4, and in ch. 17 the author himself gives prominence to the eschatological consummation with an allusion to Ps. 24:6f.

[48] Against the views of Leipoldt, op. cit., I, pp. 33ff., Harnack, Entstehung, p. 58, and especially H. Windisch, 'Der Apokalyptiker Johannes als Begründer des neutestamentlichen Kanons', ZNW 10, 1909, pp. 148–174, this needs to be stated decisively. Windisch thinks that, on the whole, it was John the seer who 'gave the impulse to the formation of the Canon . . . first of all by the fact that he wrote and published the first new canonical book, and secondly, because his book both in form and content legitimated the canonisation of other writings' (p. 172). 'It is easy to understand how, in those circles which accepted the Apocalypse, the Gospels too were able to attain canonical status as earlier records of the Lord's words'—for the apocalyptist also sought to provide genuine words of Jesus (pp. 162f.). W. Hartke, Vier urchristliche Parteien, 1961, pp. 566ff., has an even more fantastic idea of the situation. All this is speculation which has absolutely nothing to do with the course of the actual historical development which we have attempted to portray in the foregoing chapters. Equally unprovable, though, is the opposite assumption of C. Clemen, 'Die Stellung der Offenbarung Johannis im ältesten Christentum', ZNW 26, 1927, p. 173, that the

began with the Gospels and Paul, and interest in the original teaching
and tradition was its most prominent feature. The apocalypses, however,
were above all paraenetic in purpose, and spoke of the future, not of the
past. In addition, Marcion rejected this whole class of writings, and
had not considered them for his canon.[49] There was therefore no need
to provide an orthodox substitute. Irenaeus undoubtedly prized the
Revelation of John, the Lord's disciple, highly, and based the last book
of his great work chiefly on its statements;[50] but he does not cite it
among the normative 'canonical' books, of decisive weight in the fight
against false teaching.[51] He also quotes the 'Shepherd', but considers
this even less as 'scripture' in the strict sense.[52] The Apocalypse of
Peter he apparently never draws upon. Nevertheless, these three apocalypses must, as we know from Clement and Tertullian, have at the time
still enjoyed high respect.[53] Two of them seem to have been legitimated
by their apostolic names.[54]

Apocalypse 'from the start was accepted only by a small circle' and elsewhere
came up against strong resistance. Against this view cf. W. Bousset, *Die Offenbarung Johannes*[6], 1906, pp. 19ff., also Stonehouse, *op. cit.*, pp. 7ff.

[49] Tertullian, Adv. Marc. III, 14; Ps.-Tertullian, Adv. omnes haer. 6, 1:
acta apostolorum et apocalypsin quasi falsa reicit. Nevertheless we cannot deduce from this, as Harnack, *Marcion*, pp. 172*f. wishes to do, 'an explicit condemnation'.

[50] Even stronger is the emphatic phrase used in the letter, which may derive
from Irenaeus, to the church of Vienne-Lyon, given in Eusebius, *HE* V, 1, 58,
where ἵνα ἡ γραφὴ πληρωθῇ is followed by Rev. 22:11.

[51] Cf. pp. 194f. above.

[52] Adv. haer. IV, 20, 2: καλῶς οὖν ἡ γραφὴ ἡ λέγουσα· πρῶτον πάντων
πίστευσον, ὅτι εἷς ἐστιν ὁ θεὸς κτλ (Herm. 26, 1 = Mand. I, 1). For the correct
interpretation cf. A. Rousseau, *Irénée de Lyon, Contre les Hérésies, Livre IV* I,
Paris, 1965, pp. 248–250. The prevailing opinion, that here Irenaeus treats
Hermas as a 'canonical' book, proves to be incorrect. The introductory formula is definitely not typical, and in the light of the parallel in Adv. haer. I, 22,
1, cannot be meant in a technical sense. In line with this is the fact that in
every other passage where Hermas is used (I, 15, 5; 22, 1; II, 10, 2; 30, 9; Dem.
4), the book is never referred to by its name.

[53] For Hermas in the West: Tertullian, Orat. 16; De pudic. 10 (cf. p. 247
n. 13 below), also the Muratorian Canon and Ps.–Cyprian, De aleat., who
among other instances, in ch. 2 cites Herm. 108, 5f. (Sim. IX, 31, 5f.) explicitly
as 'scriptura divina': A. von Harnack, '*Der pseudocyprianische Traktat De
aleatoribus,* 1888, pp. 54ff., 126ff.; *Geschichte der altchristlichen Literatur II:
Die Chronologie der altchristlichen Literatur bis Eusebios* II, 1904, p. 376; in the
East, the numerous quotations from Clement and Origen, the latter of whom
became more cautious in his recourse to Hermas only after 231: Harnack,
Geschichte der altchristlichen Literatur I: Die Überlieferung und der Bestand, 1893,
pp. 53ff.; *Der kirchengeschichtliche Ertrag der exegetischen Arbeiten des Origenes*
II, 1919, pp. 34–36; on the whole problem of dissemination and recognition cf.
H. Chadwick, 'The New Edition of Hermas', *JTS* N.S. 8, 1957, pp. 274–280.
The Apocalypse of Peter was recognised in the West by the Muratorian Canon
(cf. p. 239 below); in the East it was used by Theophilus of Antioch (cf.

In an earlier period it may have been the natural thing to do to put the writings of Christian prophets on a par with those of the prophets of the Old Testament, and to attach the one to the other. Only we have virtually no evidence that any serious attempt was ever made to annex the Christian apocalypses to the Old Testament and its prophetic books.[55] (The greatest possibility of this happening was in the case of those books which had been written under Old Testament names.)[56] Once the concept of a Christian canon existed, however, such a solution was, of course, no longer even considered. The only question now was whether apocalyptic writings should be incorporated in the new Scriptures, and if so which. In Irenaeus' time no decision had as yet been reached on this point, and it seems quite conceivable that the emerging New Testament would have concluded with two or three

---

G. Quispel and R. M. Grant, 'Note on the Petrine Apocrypha', *VC* 6, 1952, pp. 31f.), was included by Methodius (Symp. II, 6, 45) ἐν θεοπνεύστοις γράμμασι, and according to Sozomenos (HE VII, 19, 9) was still in his day read publicly in some places in Palestine during Holy Week; cf. Harnack, *Die Petrusapokalypse in der alten abendländischen Kirche,* 1895; C. Maurer in: *N.T. Apocrypha* II, p. 664.

[54] Cf. Serapion of Antioch in Eusebius, *HE* VI, 12, 3 (with reference to the Gospel of Peter, cf. n. 8 above): ἡμεῖς γάρ, ἀδελφοί, καὶ Πέτρον καὶ τοὺς ἄλλους ἀποστόλους ἀποδεχόμεθα ὡς χριστόν. τὰ δὲ ὀνόματι αὐτῶν ψευδεπίγραφα ὡς ἔμπειροι παραιτούμεθα γινώσκοντες, ὅτι τὰ τοιαῦτα οὐ παρελάβομεν.

[55] The Muratorian Canon seems (ll. 78f.) to want to ensure that Hermas shall not be placed 'inter prophetas completo numero'; cf. pp. 256f. below. From the 'striking fact' that 'in Codex Sinaiticus of the Greek bible the "Shepherd" is plainly written in the same hand as the books of the O.T. prophets' we can, of course, conclude absolutely nothing—as against Leipoldt, *op. cit.,* I, p. 34 n. 1— and the evidence of certain mediaeval MSS which include it among the O.T. Apocrypha (cf. Harnack, *Patrum apostolicorum opera* III, 1877, pp. LXIXf.; *Entstehung,* p. 62) hardly allows us to argue with certainty back to our period. That Ps.–Cyprian, *De aleatoribus,* 2, cites Hermas as 'scriptura divina' is emphasised in this context by Leipoldt, *op. cit.* I, p. 37, following Harnack (cf. n. 53 above), but this would be of significance only if the work belonged to the pre-Cyprianic period. In my view, however, such a dating has, despite the doubts expressed by Chadwick, *op. cit.,* p. 279 n., been finally refuted by H. Koch, 'Zur Schrift adversus aleatores' in: *Festgabe . . . Karl Müller,* 1922, pp. 58–67, and *Cyprianische Untersuchungen,* 1926, p. 78.—When Justin, *Dial.* 81, 3f., cites the Revelation of John as containing a prediction related to one of Isaiah's (Leipoldt, *op. cit.* I, p. 34 n. 1), his purpose is to stress the identity of the one Spirit which has passed from the Jews to the Christians and now continues his work in them, not to recommend that their writings should be grouped together.

[56] Cf. Tertullian, De cult. fem. I, 3 (cf. p. 276 n. 45 below); De carn. res. 32, 1. In fact the Ethiopic Enoch, a late judaistic work, has kept its place in the Abyssinian canon of the O.T. to this day.—In the Stichometry of Nicephoros (Zahn, *op. cit.* II, p. 300; Preuschen, *Antilegomena²,* p. 64) and in the list of the sixty canonical books (Zahn, *op. cit.* II, p. 292; Preuschen, p. 69) the Apocalypse of Zephaniah and that of 'Zacharias, the father of John', are, among others, included in the O.T. Apocrypha.

apocalypses.[57] But at that very moment the crisis had already begun which was to call a halt to the uncontrolled growth of the New Testament, and more especially to that of the apocalyptic literature. To this development we must now turn.

The factor which brought about the concentration of the Canon in a 'New Testament' was, as we have already said, Montanism, the enthusiastic revival movement of a 'New Prophecy' which, for reasons unknown to us but possibly connected with a local persecution, suddenly broke out in Phrygia, quickly captured the rest of Asia Minor, and spread through the whole Church, both East and West. It was as though, in a Church that had become slack, the spirit of primitive Christianity had awoken at a stroke to new life. Once again the return of Christ seemed immediately at hand; and then, after the great judgment, the new age of the promised glory would begin on a transformed earth, starting from Phrygia. All Christians were summoned by Montanus to repentance, renewal of life, and martyrdom. And once again the divine spirit with his miraculous gifts was poured out upon all those congregations which did not shut their ears to his call. The 'women' who accompanied Montanus were his miraculous mouthpieces—independent of any human or ecclesiastical authority that might obtain elsewhere.[58]

It is clear that Montanism, considered as a whole, despite some peculiar ideas and practices, did not break out of the framework of earlier apocalyptic hopes and demands. It was more a reactionary than a revolutionary movement. The continuing influence which here finds exaggerated and abrupt actualisation is that of the old prophetic and apocalyptic traditions in the style of the Revelation of John, which also comes from Asia Minor.[59] Like John, the Montanist prophets too speak in their own name, and demand strict belief in their proclamations and obedience to their commands; for the authority which they have

[57] In the opinion of Harnack, *Entstehung*, p. 59: 'There is no doubt about it—a corpus of Christian prophetic writings, forming a new collection, was to be expected.'
[58] The classic account of Montanism is still that of P. de Labriolle, *La crise montaniste*, Paris, 1913; cf. also the same author's convenient and very nearly exhaustive collection of sources, *Les sources de l'histoire du Montanisme*, 1913, and A. Faggiotto, *L'eresia dei Frigi*, Rome, 1924. For more recent literature cf. n. 59 below.
[59] That Montanism is not to be derived from 'Phrygian cults' but from the traditions of Jewish and Christian apocalyptic, and in particular is intimately connected with Revelation, has been convincingly demonstrated by W. Schepelern, *Der Montanismus und die phrygischen Julte—eine religionsgeschichtliche Untersuchung*, 1929, pp. 159ff. The important study by H. Kraft, 'Die altkirchliche Prophetie und die Entstehung des Montanismus,' *TZ* 11, 1955, pp. 149–271, and the essay by K. Aland, 'Bemerkungen zum Montanismus und zur frühchristlichen Eschatologie' in: *Kirchengeschichtliche Entwürfe*, 1960, have further verified and illuminated these connections.

received is of no human sort—they are simply organs of Christ or the voice of the Holy Ghost.[60] Again, their utterances likewise make no appeal to Scripture, and contain not one single instance of explicit quotation.[61] But this, of course, does not imply any rejection of Scripture. The leaders of the movement know themselves to stand in the succession of Old and New Testament prophets,[62] and like all Christians recognise the Old Testament as a matter of course. That the Revelation of John was held in high honour among the Montanists there is also no doubt; and the same may be assumed to be true of the Gospel of John[63] and in fact of yet other gospels and epistles. At that time a complete 'New Testament' was as yet unknown;[64] but we hear nothing of any Montanist resistance to its formation. The Montanists plainly joined in the general development.[65] Soon they are indistinguishable from their opponents in their citing of New Testament texts both in attack and defence.[66] The critical point beyond which Montanism became a sect is thus not directly connected with their attitude to the Canon; it lies instead in the movement's estimate of its own position in salvation-history, which was of course bound to clash with the concept

[60] Cf. (following de Labriolle's numbering) in particular Oracles 5, 12, 13, 14, 17 (Aland: 5, 16, 14, 15, 12).

[61] An utterance which has been preserved in Epiphanius, Panar. XLVIII, 10, 3 (Labriolle 4; Aland 6) has points of contact with Matt. 13:43 and Dan. 12:3; but it is still not possible to agree with Kraft, op. cit., p. 264, that 'This is a case of the exegesis of a passage in Daniel', even if this is the way in which Epiphanius must have understood it (ἀσύστατα κατὰ τῆς θείας γραφῆς διηγεῖται).

[62] Eusebius, HE V, 17, 4 (the Antimontanist): εἰ γὰρ μετὰ Κοδράτον καὶ τὴν ἐν Φιλαδελφίᾳ Ἀμμίαν, ὥς φασιν, αἱ περὶ Μοντανὸν διεδέξαντο γυναῖκες τὸ προφητικὸν χάρισμα ... Since the Antimontanist (ibid., V, 17, 3) introduces an even longer series of prophets, beginning with Agabus, with the words, τοῦτον δὲ τὸν τρόπον οὔτε τινὰ τῶν κατὰ τὴν παλαιὰν οὔτε τῶν κατὰ τὴν καινὴν πνευματοφορηθέντα προφήτην δεῖξαι δυνήσονται, it may be assumed that this series too, including the O.T. link, derives from the Montanists or can count on their approval. Cf. Epiphanius, Panar. XLVIII, 3, 3–10; 8, 1.

[63] On the Montanist appeal to the prophecy of the Paraclete, however, cf. pp. 225f. below.

[64] Harnack, Entstehung, p. 25 n. 1: 'There is no need to point out that Montanism and its pretensions could never have arisen, if there had already been a New Testament'; cf. an earlier essay by the same writer: 'Das Muratorische Fragment und die Entstehung einer Sammlung apostolisch-katholischer Schriften', ZKG 3, 1879, pp. 406f.; similarly Leipoldt, op. cit. I, p. 50.

[65] This is later explicitly attested by Epiphanius, Panar. XLVIII, 1, 3: οὗτοι γὰρ οἱ κατὰ Φρύγας καλούμενοι δέχονται καὶ αὐτοὶ πᾶσαν γραφὴν παλαιᾶς καὶ νέας διαθήκης.

[66] The earliest instance is the appeal to Matt. 23:34 at the Disputation of Ancyra: Eusebius, HE V, 16, 12; cf. also the polemic of Apollonius (n. 103 below). For the later period it will be enough to remind the reader of Tertullian (De monog. 4, 1: secedat nunc mentio Paracleti, ut nostri alicuius auctoris, evolvamus communia instrumenta scripturarum pristinarum) and the Μοντανιστοῦ καὶ ὀρθοδόξου διάλεξις in Labriolle, Sources, no. 79, pp. 93–108.

of a canonical norm. Because the Montanists were not prepared to give up attaching absolute value to the extravagant authority of their spirit and their founding prophets, they necessarily exempted them from any further test,[67] even from scrutiny in the light of the 'testimony of Jesus', which for the John of Revelation was still identical with 'the spirit of prophecy'.[68] In this way they went behind Christian 'beginnings', and thus beyond the Canon which was meant to determine and preserve those beginnings. These consequences of the 'New Prophecy', however, were at first hidden from both its opponents and its adherents.

Defensive action against Montanism began in the episcopal churches of Asia, among which there was a high degree of solidarity. Several synods took a stand against the unsettling and dubious movement and its inordinate claims.[69] Offence was taken at all sorts of externals: the unusual role of women,[70] the claims for Pepuza, a town in the back of beyond, as the destined site of the 'new Jerusalem',[71] ascetic rigorism,[72] arrogance characteristic of martyrs,[73] and dangerous pressures toward martyrdom.[74] Soon began the usual slanders, alleging motives of ambition[75] and in particular—as constantly happens in such cases—'unscriptural' avarice and venality on the part of the Montanist leaders,[76] who are said in some cases to have come to an ignominious end.[77] There is nothing to be gained from reading through this tittle-tattle.[78]

[67] As is well known, this is a reproach that was early made against them: Eusebius, *HE* V, 16, 17 (the Antimontanist); V, 19, 3 (Aelius of Debeltum, according to Serapion), without too much importance being attached to such accusations in detail. Nevertheless, Montanism's distinctive form of inspiration, excluding all use of reason, is relevant in this connection; cf. Schepelern, *op. cit.*, pp. 17ff.

[68] Rev. 19:10.   [69] Eusebius, *HE* V, 16, 10.12 (the Antimontanist).

[70] Eusebius, *HE* V, 16, 9 (the Antimontanist); 18, 3 (Apollonius).

[71] Eusebius, *HE* V, 18, 2 (Apollonius).

[72] Eusebius, *HE* V, 18, 2 (Apollonius); cf. Tertullian, De ieiun. 1; De monog. 2. It was only later that the consequences for penitential practice became a problem: cf. H. von Campenhausen, *Ecclesiastical Authority and Spiritual Power*, 1969, pp. 220 ff.

[73] Eusebius, *HE* V, 16, 12. 20–22 (the Antimontanist); 18, 5–9 (Apollonius).

[74] *Mart. Polyc.* 4; cf. M. Simonetti, 'Alcune osservazioni sul martirio di S. Policarpo', *Giorn. Ital. di Filol.* 9, 1956, pp. 338ff.; H. von Campenhausen, 'Bearbeitungen und Interpolationen des Polykarpmartyriums', *Aus der Frühzeit des Christentums*, 1963, pp. 268–271.

[75] Eusebius, *HE* V, 16, 7 (the Antimontanist).

[76] Eusebius, *HE* V, 18, 2.4 (δοκεῖ σοι πᾶσα γραφὴ κωλύειν προφήτην λαμβάνειν δῶρα καὶ χρήματα;)—7 (with reference to Matt. 10:9f.), 11 (Apollonius); cf. Ascension of Isaiah III, 21–31 (?).

[77] Eusebius, *HE* V. 16, 13f. (the Antimontanist).

[78] This is sufficiently proved by the miserable comment with which the Antimontanist himself concludes, Eusebius, *HE* V, 16, 15: ἀλλὰ μὴ ἄνευ τοῦ ἰδεῖν ἡμᾶς ἐπίστασθαί τι τῶν τοιούτων νομίζωμεν, ὦ μακάριε· ἴσως μὲν γὰρ οὕτως, ἴσως δὲ οὐχ οὕτως τετελευτήκασιν Μοντανός τε καὶ Θεόδοτος καὶ ἡ προειρημένη γυνή.

At the heart of the controversy stands the question of the authenticity of the Montanist prophetic spirit and of the strange forms taken by Montanist ecstasy.[79] Was this a case, as the Montanists would have it, of genuine prophecy or of demonic possession? (That the ecstasy was nothing but sham and trickery no one dared to maintain.) In this context appeals to earlier examples and to the witness of Scripture at first took on increased importance. The adherents of the 'New Prophecy'[80] asserted that their leaders were the prophets promised by Jesus, and the opponents of those leaders 'the killers of the prophets';[81] they stood in the succession of the prophets of old.[82] This was energetically disputed by the catholics: the Montanists' mindless ecstasy had been unknown in earlier times, and was a sign of demonic origin; they were false prophets, and prophesied in a manner directly contrary to tradition and to the prophetic succession as this had existed and still did exist in the Church.[83] A 'prophet ought not to speak in ecstasy'.[84] The Montanists were not at a loss for a retort, pointing to Peter who under the impact of the Transfiguration 'knew not what he said'.[85] In course of time the whole Bible, both Old and New Testaments, was scrutinised from this angle.[86] But naturally enough this produced no unambiguous results. The decisive step by which the Montanists sought in one move to justify themselves on the basis of the Bible and to establish that the authority of their prophecy was superior to all previous revelation started from one single promise in the Gospel of John: the New Prophecy is the Paraclete. The concept of the Paraclete, the Intercessor and Advocate, already

---

[79] On this cf. Schepelern, *op. cit.*, pp. 10ff., 17ff., 130ff.; H. von Campenhausen, *Ecclesiastical Authority*, pp. 187ff.

[80] Ἡ νέα προφητεία is the proper self-designation used by those whom only their opponents termed Phrygians, Kataphrygians, or Montanists: cf. Schepelern, *op. cit.*, pp. 10f.

[81] Eusebius, *HE* V, 16, 12 (the Antimontanist). E. Schwartz in his edition wrongly refers here to Joh. 14:26 in addition to Matt. 23:34; cf. even so early a work as I. Döllinger, *Hippolytus und Kallistus*, 1853, p. 302; also A. Faggiotto, 'I Catafrigi e il IV. Vangelo' in: *La Scuola Cattolica*, Anno LIV, Serie VI, Vol. VII, 1 (Milan, 1926), p. 99.

[82] Cf. n. 62 above.

[83] Eusebius, *HE* V, 16, 7 (the Antimontanist: . . . Μοντανόν . . . παρὰ τὸ κατὰ παράδοσιν καὶ κατὰ διαδοχὴν ἄνωθεν τῆς ἐκκλησίας ἔθος δῆθεν προφητεύοντα. The appeal to Scripture did not, of course, *vis-à-vis* the Montanists exclude the customary appeal to the παράδοσις; cf. the Antimontanist in Eusebius, *HE* V, 17, 4; Apollonius, *ibid.*, V, 18, 14; and even Gaius, *ibid.*, II, 25, 7.

[84] Miltiades personally wrote a work entitled Περὶ τοῦ μὴ δεῖν προφήτην ἐν ἐκστάσει λαλεῖν: Eusebius, *HE* V, 17, 1.

[85] Tertullian, Adv. Marc. IV, 22, on Lk. 9:33.

[86] Epiphanius, Panar. XLVIII, 3–7, whose comments probably derive from Hippolytus: Schepelern, *op. cit.*, pp. 21f. On the reference to Ps. 116:11 cf. M.-J. Rondeau, 'Les polémiques d'Hippolyte de Rome et de Filastre de Brescia concernant le Psautier', *RHR* 171, 1967, p. 29.

had a fairly lengthy history[87] before the author of John applied it to the Holy Spirit, who was to console and guide the disciples as 'another Counsellor' in place of the departing Counsellor, Jesus.[88] Moreover, it was explicitly added that he would one day teach the disciples everything which as yet they could not 'bear', and 'guide them into all truth'.[89] The strange choice of term[90] had already led to all kinds of speculations within gnosticism; it had, for example, been applied to Paul who in place of the Paraclete and as his 'image' was to take over the preaching 'immediately after the Passion of the Lord'.[91] Now the Montanists took up the idea once again, and interpreted the promise of the Paraclete as referring to the 'New Prophecy', which was thus exalted over all pre-Montanist sendings of the Spirit, and proclaimed as a last, definitive fulfilment—in exactly the same way as had once been done with the Spirit of Pentecost in the New Testament.

Unfortunately it is impossible to discover when this exegesis was first invented and put forward. In the early disputes with the Montanists it still plays no part;[92] but Irenaeus seems to have been acquainted with it,[93] and in Tertullian, Hippolytus, and Origen this justification of Montanist authority is already a fixed traditional dogma, which is regularly defended by the adherents of the 'New Prophecy', and contested

[87] On this subject cf. most recently O. Betz, *Der Paraklet—Fürsprecher im häretischen Spätjudentum, im Johannesevangelium und in neu gefundenen gnostischen Schriften,* 1963.
[88] Joh. 14:16–18, 26; 15:26; 16:7.
[89] Joh. 16:12f.; 14:26; cf. Tertullian, De monog. 2.
[90] In I Joh. 2:1 it is also used of the exalted Jesus.
[91] Clem. Alex., Exc. ex Theod. 23, 1f.
[92] Faggiotto, *op. cit.* n. 81 above, has clearly demonstrated this, and it has also been recognised independently by Schepelern, *op. cit.,* pp. 16f., 169f. The earlier assumption that the character of Montanism was already dictated when it first began by the Johannine Paraclete prophesy, indeed that this must be regarded as virtually 'the programme of Montanism, implemented in a spirit of enthusiasm' (Harnack, *Lehrbuch der Dogmengeschichte* I⁴, 1909, p. 431 n.), rests, on the other hand, on conclusions and general considerations which fail to recognise the spontaneous and elemental character of the movement: Zahn, *op. cit.,* I, p. 16 n. 13; Harnack, *Dogmengeschichte* I, p. 427; Aland, *op. cit.,* pp. 131f., 139f. The hostile presentation by E. Benz, 'Creator Spiritus', *Eranos-Jahrbuch* 1956, pp. 293–305, allows of no critical discussion. The only source which can be adduced in support of a Johannine influence on Montanism in its early period is a saying of Montanus, cited for the first time in the fourth century in Didymus, Trin. III, 41, and with slight variations in the Dial. Mont et Orthod., which uses the word 'Paraclete' in place of 'Holy Spirit': Ἐγώ εἰμι ὁ πατὴρ καὶ ὁ υἱὸς καὶ ὁ παράκλητος (Labriolle, *Sources,* p. 97, 25 and no. 3; Aland, *op. cit.,* nos. 1 and 2); but in view of the fact that the same saying is quoted twice more in the Dialexis but with πνεῦμα (Labriolle, *Sources,* p. 101, 17) or ἅγιον πνεῦμα (*ibid.,* p. 103, 30) in place of παράκλητος, the mention of the Paraclete here ought certainly to be understood as secondary adaptation to the later, developed Montanist doctrine.
[93] Adv. haer. III, 11, 9 (cf. n. 159 below).

by the catholic 'Psychics'.[94] As a Montanist Tertullian did not shrink
from drawing the inevitable conclusions for salvation-history. With the
Paraclete divine revelation was destined to go beyond the earlier, New
Testament stage, and a new, third epoch has begun. Just as the Old
Testament was not abrogated by the predicted manifestation of Christ,
but fulfilled and surpassed, so also the final revelation of the Spirit had
already been proclaimed by Christ, and had from the very beginning
been the true goal of God's providence. Nevertheless, Tertullian deliberately keeps this view within bounds. Even in the final stage of the
salvation-history Christ remains the true Lord, and that which his
apostles once taught is not revoked by the new revelation, but simply
carried to its conclusion. In principle the new endowment of the Spirit
was not meant to occasion any alteration of any kind in doctrine, but
only in morals and men's way of life: now at last the Church is given the
power to endure the full stringency of the commandment and to carry
it out.[95] In practice Tertullian restricts himself to justifying certain
more rigorous requirements in respect of married life, fasting, the
duty of martyrdom, and suchlike, with sayings of the Paraclete;[96]
and he is always anxious so far as possible to confirm this objective
justification with biblical testimony. There can be no doubt that
his conception of an era of salvation-history beyond that of Christ and
the apostles is not in practice compatible with primitive Christian belief; in form it is reminiscent of the later teaching of the Manicheans,
of Islam, and of the mediaeval 'Third Kingdom'. But his motives are
more moralistic and disciplinary than enthusiastic and genuinely
'heretical'. In any case Tertullian is not prepared to allow the old, common foundation of the 'earlier writings'[97] to be shaken at any point
in favour of the new Spirit. He joyfully embraces both the Spirit and
the additional prescriptions which the Spirit lays upon the Church;

[94] Cf. esp. Tertullian, De monog. 2, and the further texts collected in Labriolle
Sources, pp. 12ff.; Hippolytus, Elench. VIII, 19; Origen, De princ. II, 7, 3;
Comm. Matt. XV, 30. Tertullian cannot possibly, as surmised by S. A. Fries,
'Die Oden Salomos—Montanistische Lieder aus dem zweiten Jahrhundert',
ZNW 12, 1911, p. 117, have 'given rise to the idea by the language he uses'.
[95] Cf. Labriolle, Crise, pp. 17ff.; H. Karpp, Schrift und Geist bei Tertullian,
1955, pp. 58–67; and, for the theological context of Tertullian's concept, H.
von Campenhausen, 'Urchristentum und Tradition bei Tertullian', ThBl 8,
1929, pp. 193–200.
[96] Cf. Adv. Marc. I, 29, 4; De pudic. i, 20; Monog. 1ff.; Virg. vel. 1; Ieiun.
1, 10, 13. The commandment of most serious consequence was the one that
grievous sins after baptism should no longer be forgiven: De pud. 21 (cf. n.
72 above). In addition there are some small supplementary points and confirmatory conclusions in respect of individual doctrinal matters, such as the millenial kingdom (Adv. Marc. III, 24, 4) or the resurrection of the flesh (De anim.
9), which are arrived at not on the basis of the old oracles but of a visionary experience within the Montanist church.
[97] De monog. 4, 1 (cf. n. 66 above).

but his Montanism makes no difference to his basic attitude toward and opinion of the biblical canon.

The picture of the Montanist sect afforded by our other sources is not essentially different. The spirit-oracles of the great Montanist prophets were collected and written down at an early stage: it was possible to quote them from books,[98] and the prophets themselves were in many cases regarded as the authors of these books.[99] But nowhere do we hear that these writings were described as a 'new Gospel', were cited as 'scripture', or were combined as a third section with the old bible to form a new Montanist canon.[100] The process does not therefore

[98] The earliest evidence of this is provided by the Antimontanist (Eusebius, *HE* V, 16, 17), who quotes one utterance in the following characteristic form: μὴ λεγέτω ἐν τῷ αὐτῷ λόγῳ τῷ κατὰ ᾿Αστέριον Οὐρβανὸν τὸ διὰ Μαξιμίλλης πνεῦμα. Later we have Apollonius (*ibid.*, V, 18, 1): τὰς φερομένας αὐτῶν προφητείας ψευδεῖς οὔσας κατὰ λέξιν εὐθύνων. Further instances in Tertullian, Fuga 9, 4 ('alibi'), and Epiphanius, Panar. XLVIII (ἐν τῇ αὐτῇ λεγομένη προφητείᾳ) *et. al.*; cf. Zahn, *op. cit.*, I, p. 6 n. 1; Schepelern, *op. cit.*, pp. 13f. Certainly, when we hear of the innumerable books of the Montanists, about which Hippolytus complains (Elench. VIII, 19, 1), and which are often mentioned elsewhere until the time of the imperial decrees ordering the destruction of the Montanist codices, 'scelerum omnium doctrinam ac materiam contintentes' (Cod. Theod. XVI, 5, 34, 1), we should think primarily of such collections of oracles. Nevertheless, W. Schneemelcher (*N.T. Apocrypha* II, p. 685 n. 2) is absolutely unjustified, in view of Tertullian, Proclus (Eusebius, *HE* II, 25, 6; VI, 20, 3; Photius, Bibl. 48; cf. n. 126 below), and possibly the Asterius Urbanus mentioned by the Antimontanist, as well as an anonymous opponent of Miltiades (Eusebius, *HE* V, 17, 1), in the doubt which he expresses, against the views of Aland, *op. cit.*, pp. 105f., whether there was such a thing as a Montanist literature at all. On the other hand, the conjectures of Zahn, *op. cit.* I, pp., 11f.; II, pp. 119ff., concerning Montanist psalms remain completely unconvincing.

[99] Hippolytus, Elench. VIII, 19, 1; Dial. Mont. et orth., in Labriolle, *Sources,* pp. 106f.; Didymus, Trin. III, 41, 3; Theodoret, Haer. fab. comp. III, 2; and, in the lists of apocrypha in the Decretum Gelasianum, 5, 7 no. 6; cf. 5, 9 no. 9 (Dobschütz). It seems to me not inconceivable that the prophets did in fact to some extent write down their auditions and visions themselves; cf. n. 104 below, and H. Weinel, *Die Wirkungen des Geistes und der Geister im nachapostolischen Zeitalter*, 1899, p. 103. It may be that these collections were brought together in a 'canonical' collection; but it is no longer possible to prove this. Likewise the title of such a collection remains uncertain. Harnack, *Überlieferung und Bestand*, p. 238, assumed on the basis of Epiphanius, Panar. XLVIII, 10, 3, that it was called ἡ τοῦ Μοντανοῦ προφητεία; but we cannot be sure of this: Labriolle, *Crise*, pp. 35f.

[100] A. von Harnack, *Das Neue Testament um das Jahr 200*, 1898, pp. 26–32, severely criticising the view of Zahn, *op. cit.*, I, pp. 6, 20. For a correct view cf. A. F. Walls, 'The Montanist "Catholic Epistle" and its New Testament Prototype', *StudEvang* III, 1964, pp. 443ff. The fact that Tertullian occasionally describes the 'old', agreed Scriptures of the Old and New Testaments as 'pristina instrumenta' (Carn. res. 63, 7; similarly Monog. 4, 1 [cf. n. 6 above], 7) in no way implies 'the view that the most recent revelation also has its corre-

reach its conclusion at this point. It is clear that the oracles of the Paraclete, without prejudice to their unassailable authority, remain in a separate category—as had originally been the case with the earlier apocalypses. The real authority to which appeal was made in the Montanist camp was not a new canon, but the Spirit and his 'gifts'; and it was recognition of these which was demanded from the catholic church.[101]

This Spirit, newly poured forth, was held to be not less but even greater than the Spirit of past ages,[102] which had produced the holy Scriptures. Hence he could hardly be prevented from doing something equally great in the present. Thus, in Asia Minor a certain Themison, conscious of his dignity as a martyr, published a 'catholic' didactic epistle, in which he imitated the style of the apostle Paul, and expressed correspondingly lofty pretensions.[103] Later on, moreover, the Mon-

---

sponding *instrumenta*' (Zahn, *op. cit.*, I, p. 20 n. 2; but cf. also Harnack, *Entstehung*, pp. 120f.). Just as little does the way in which Asterius Urbanus's writing is cited in good classical Greek make him into an Evangelist (Zahn, *op. cit.*, I, p. 5).

[101] Cf. the appropriate phrases in Tertullian, Adv. Prax. 1, 5 (propositum recipiendorum charismatum); *anim.* 58, 8 (ex agnitione promissorum charismatum); *monog.* 1, 2 (agnitio spiritalium charismatum), and Epiphanius, Panar. XLVIII, 1, 4 (δεῖ ἡμᾶς, φησί, καὶ τὰ χαρίσματα δέχεσθαι) in Zahn, *op. cit.*, I, p. 7 n. 2.

[102] Epiphanius, Panar. XLVIII, 8, 1: οὐχ ὅμοια τὰ πρῶτα χαρίσματα τοῖς ἐσχάτοις. Similarly Passio Perpetuae I, 3, n. 106 below.

[103] Eusebius, *HE* V, 18, 5 (Apollonius): Θεμίσων... ὡς μάρτυς καυχώμενος ἐτόλμησεν, μιμούμενος τὸν ἀπόστολον, καθολικήν τινα συνταξάμενος ἐπιστολήν, κατηχεῖν τοὺς ἄμεινον αὐτοῦ πεπιστευκότας, συναγωνίζεσθαι δὲ τοῖς τῆς κενοφωνίας λόγοις, βλασφημῆσαι δὲ εἰς τὸν κύριον καὶ τοὺς ἀποστόλους καὶ τὴν ἁγίαν ἐκκλησίαν. The question which 'apostle' is meant here is an old point of controversy. N. Bonwetsch, *Die Geschichte des Montanismus*, 1881, p. 18, thought it referred to the circulation of the Apocalypse; Harnack, *Das Neue Testament um das Jahr 200*, 1889, p. 28, W. Bauer, *Orthodoxy and Heresy in Earliest Christianity*, 1972, p. 136 n. 13, and others, though of I John as a possible model, Labriolle, *Crise*, p. 28, of II Peter and Jude, Walls, *op. cit.*, p. 441, of I Peter. To my mind there is no doubt that Zahn, *op. cit.*, I, pp. 9 n. 1, 263; II, p. 75 n. 1, is correct when he strictly insists that really only Paul can be meant. It can in fact not be proved that 'in the Early Church the term ὁ ἀπόστολος, when not more precisely defined by the context, ever denoted anyone other than Paul'. That Paul wrote no 'catholic epistles' does not, on the other hand, constitute a serious objection, since at this time the term still did not possess its later meaning, which was not firmly defined until Origen, and could certainly be applied to Paul's letters to particular churches as well; cf. the examples in Walls, *op. cit.*, pp. 439f., the controversy over the canonicity of the 'private' letter to Philemon, and the 'catholicising' revisions of the Pauline Epistles themselves: N. A. Dahl, 'The particularity of the Pauline Epistles as a problem in the Ancient Church' in: *Neotestamentica et Patristica* (Cullmann Festschrift), 1962, pp. 261–271. Tertullian, Adv. Marc. V, 17, 1, rightly remarks: nihil autem de titulis interest, cum ad omnes apostolus scripserit dum ad quosdam.. These compelling arguments

tanists did not refrain from writing down their visions and the stories of their martyrs, giving them worldwide circulation as edifying documents of their Spirit, and having them read aloud in public worship.[104] Tertullian explicitly defends this arrogant proceeding. It is, he says,[105] mere prejudice to heed and value only past demonstrations of power and grace. 'Those people who condemn the one power of the one Holy Spirit in accordance with chronological eras should beware.' It is the recent instances to which far higher respect ought to be paid; for they already belong to the time of the End, and are to be prized as a superabundant increase of grace, 'which God, in accordance with the testimony of scripture, has destined for precisely this period of time'.[106] In fact the practice of circulating works of spiritual exhortation and

can also be supported by more general considerations relating to the history of the Canon: at this time only the Pauline Epistles already formed a firmly established part of the 'canonical' Scriptures, whereas the 'catholic epistles' had as yet by no means attained an equally secure place. (This explains why even Gaius [cf. n. 126 below] to all appearance discusses the number of the Pauline letters only; on the Muratorian Canon cf. p. 246 below.) That developments in Asia Minor were different, and went more in favour of the Johannines, is an easy enough conjecture; but there is not one single clear piece of evidence to support it. Lawlor and Oulton in their translation of Eusebius (vol. II, p. 177) rightly connect with Asia Minor the Antimontanist's practice of referring to Paul as 'the Apostle' (*HE* V, 17, 4); cf. similarly Abercius (n. 113 below). By contrast the Johannines figure not at all in the utterances either of the Montanists or of their radical opponents, who rejected both the Gospel and the Apocalypse; cf. A. Bludau, *Die ersten Gegner der Johannesschriften*, 1925, pp. 129-131. In my view, this silence does not entitle one to draw the conclusion that the 'Alogi' may possibly have recognised these Epistles, an opinion apparently favoured by A. Jülicher and E. Fascher, *Einleitung in das Neue Testament*[7], 1931, p. 485, and R. Schnackenburg, *Die Johannesbriefe*[2], 1963, p. 47 n. 12.

[104] Cf. Tertullian, anim. 9, 4, concerning a Montanist prophetess, who after her vision was asked, 'quae viderit; nam et diligentissime digeruntur, ut etiam probentur'; cf. Zahn, *op. cit.*, I, p. 10 n. 1. Pass. Perp. 2 says of Perpetua: haec ordinem totum martyrii sui iam hinc ipsa narravit, sicut conscriptum manu sua et suo sensu reliquit; cf. 10, 7 and 11, 1: sed et Saturus benedictus hanc visionem suam edidit, quam ipse conscripsit; cf. 14.

[105] That Tertullian edited the Passio Perpetuae, and wrote the Introduction and Conclusion, seems to me established.

[106] Pass. Perp. 1, 1f.: Si vetera fidei exempla, et dei gratiam testificantia et aedificationem hominis operantia, propterea in litteris sunt digesta, ut lectione eorum quasi repraesentatione rerum et Deus honoretur et homo confortetur, cur non et nova documenta aeque utrique causae convenientia et digerantur? vel quia proinde et haec vetera futura quandoque sunt et necessaria posteris, si in praesenti suo tempore minori deputantur auctoritati, propter praesumptam venerationem antiquitatis. sed viderint qui unam virtutem spiritus unius sancti pro aetatibus iudicent temporum, cum maiora reputanda sunt novitiora quaeque ut novissimiora, secundum exuperationem gratiae in ultima saeculi spatia decretam. There follows the quotation from Joel, as given in Acts 2:17. Cf. Tertullian, virg. vel. 1; carn. res. 63.

narrative, and of holding them in high esteem, signified no new departure, but corresponded to normal custom elsewhere.[107] Now, however,
it was linked with the intentionally exalted claims of the new Paraclete,
and therefore appeared as an attack on the original, fundamental revelation, and thus as impudent 'blasphemy against the Lord, the Apostles,
and the holy Church'.[108] Hence the emergent catholic canon, which
preserved the evidence of the beginnings, acquired all the greater importance. No longer was it regarded, as it had been in the confrontation with gnosticism, simply as a source and, when occasion required, a
guideline of Christian truth; now it was seen as a sacred borderline
beyond which no teaching or preaching ought ever to pass. Most particularly, the composition of new authoritative writings was now thought
of as outrageous presumption.[109]

The 'innumerable books' of the Montanist prophets, declares
Hippolytus, only confuse the minds of those who are unable to test
them, and for anyone of sound mind they are unworthy of attention.[110]

[107] It will suffice to mention the 'catholic' church letters of Bishop Dicnysius
of Corinth: Eusebius, *HE* IV, 23 1. A late echo, polemical in tone, of the high
value anciently put on stories of martyrs is afforded by a prologue, deriving from
the fifth or sixth century, prefixed to such a text, which has been published and
discussed by B. de Gaiffier, 'Un prologue hagiographique hostile au Décret de
Gélase', *AnalBoll* 82, 1964, pp. 341–353. Here it is bluntly asserted: interrogo
vos, qui ista inter apocryphas litteras abolendo censetis: per quos constat canon
scripturarum omnium divinarum? numquid non per eos, qui ipso canone occidi
magis optavere quam vinci? quid enim tenuerunt martyres? fidem rectam, quae
sacris voluminibus certo librorum numero continetur. This entity is now fixed
down to the last detail. It is explicitly stated: nihil praeter scripturas canonicas
recipientes, ista studiose conscripsimus, ostendentes dogma catholicum per
catholicos martyres custoditum.

[108] Apollonius in Eusebius, *HE* V, 18, 5 (cf. n. 103 above); cf. Hippolytus,
Elench. VIII, 19, 1f., on the credulity of the Phrygians toward their prophets.
The same sort of unfair argument as Apollonius uses against the Montanists is
perpetrated by Dionysiu⌐ of Alexandria against the chiliastic adherents of Nepos:
Eusebius, *HE* VII, 24, 5.

[109] The general significance of Montanism for the formation of the Canon has
already been stated more, or less decisively, in particular by Harnack, e.g.,
Entstehung, pp. 24ff., and recently by A. Ehrhardt, 'Christianity before the Apostles' Creed', *HTR* 55, 1962, p. 107. The doubt expressed by G. Strecker, in the
Appendix to the new edition of Bauer's *Rechtgläubigkeit* (p. 303), whether 'the
controversy with Montanism was of decisive importance for the emergence of
the N.T. Canon', I personally am unable to share. Nevertheless, that other
factors were also involved in this development is, of course, not ruled out.
Sooner or later the Canon was in any case bound to reach a limit of some kind.

[110] Hippolytus, Elench. VIII, 19, 1: ὧν βίβλους ἀπείρους ἔχοντες πλανῶνται,
μήτε τὰ ὑπ' αὐτῶν λελαλημένα λόγῳ κρίναντες μήτε τοῖς κρῖναι δυναμένοις
προσέχοντες . . . 4: ἱκανὰ μὲν οὖν καὶ τὰ περὶ τούτων εἰρημένα κρίνομεν, δι'
ὀλίγων τὰ πολλὰ φλύαρα αὐτῶν βιβλία τε καὶ ἐπιχειρήματα πᾶσιν ἐπιδείξαντες
ἀσθενῆ ὄντα καὶ μηδενὸς λόγου ἄξια, οἷς οὐ χρὴ προσέχειν τοὺς ὑγιαίνοντα
νοῦν κεκτημένους.

Their apocalyptic expectations have not been fulfilled,[111] and have caused only bewilderment. 'This is what happens to uninstructed and thoughtless people, who do not keep carefully to the Scriptures, but pay more heed to human traditions, to their own fancies, dreams, inventions, and old wives' tales than to them'.[112] In controversy the disputants studiously emphasise that they have read every single Scripture,[113] and in contrast to the Montanists lay stress precisely on the great difference between a contemporary author and the early witnesses to the Gospel. 'Till now', writes one polemist with priggish dignity,[114] 'I have held back, not from lack of ability to refute the lie and to testify to the truth, but because I was fearful and anxious lest I might seem to some to be making additions or interpolations to the word of the Gospel of the New Covenant, when the man who is determined to live in accordance with the Gospel itself cannot possibly either add anything to it or take anything from it.'[115] It is obvious that such an attitude can no longer be content with recognising a rough list of sacred writings and with rejecting others as heretical forgeries; it now has to be clearly decided which books are to belong to the 'New Testament'

[111] Hippolytus, Comm. Dan. IV, 19f. This argument had already been advanced by the Antimontanist (Eusebius, HE V, 16, 19. It naturally features later on as well, in Apollonius (ibid., 18, 12), Gaius of Rome (cf. p. 242 below), Epiphanius, Panar. XLVIII, 2 et al.

[112] Hippolytus, Comm. Dan. IV, 20, 1: ταῦτα συμβαίνει τοῖς ἰδιώταις καὶ ἐλαφροῖς ἀνθρώποις, ὅσοι ταῖς μὲν γραφαῖς ἀκριβῶς οὐ προσέχουσιν, ταῖς δὲ ἀνθρωπίναις παραδόσεσιν καὶ ταῖς ἑαυτῶν πλάναις καὶ τοῖς ἑαυτῶν ἐνυπνίοις καὶ μυθολογίαις καὶ λόγοις γραώδεσι μᾶλλον πείθονται. Cf. Elench. VIII, 19, 1; X, 25.

[113] So Polycrates of Ephesus in the Paschal Controversy, opposing Victor of Rome (Eusebius, HE V, 24, 7): ἐγὼ οὖν, ἀδελφοί, ἑξήκοντα πέντε ἔτη ἔχων ἐν κυρίῳ καὶ συμβεβληκὼς τοῖς ἀπὸ τῆς οἰκουμένης ἀδελφοῖς καὶ πᾶσαν ἁγίαν γραφὴν διεληλυθώς, οὐ πτύρομαι ἐπὶ τοῖς καταπλησσομένοις. Abercius, who is certainly the Antimontanist Avirkios Markellos (Eusebius, HE V, 16, 3) similarly emphasises in his grave inscription that Paul had accompanied him on all his journeys (l. 23: Παῦλον ἔχων ἐπ'ὀχῶν). To my mind there can be no doubt of the Christian character of the inscription, the garland on the reverse of the cippus notwithstanding: contra E. Dinkler, 'Älteste christliche Denkmäler' in: Signum Crucis (Ges. Aufs.), 1967, pp. 159f.

[114] Probably the 'Antimontanist' was none other than Polycrates of Ephesus: W. Kühnert, 'Der antimontanistische Anonymus des Eusebius,' TZ 5, 1949, pp. 436–446.

[115] Eusebius, HE V, 16, 3 (the Antimontanist): . . . ἐφεκτικώτερόν πως μέχρι νῦν διεκείμην, οὐκ ἀπορίᾳ τοῦ δύνασθαι ἐλέγχειν μὲν τὸ ψεῦδος, μαρτυρεῖν δὲ τῇ ἀληθείᾳ, δεδιὼς δὲ καὶ ἐξευλαβούμενος, μή πη δόξω τισὶν ἐπισυγγράφειν ἢ ἐπιδιατάσσεσθαι τῷ τῆς τοῦ εὐαγγελίου καινῆς διαθήκης λόγῳ, ᾧ μήτε προσθεῖναι μήτε ἀφελεῖν δυνατὸν τῷ κατὰ τὸ εὐαγγέλιον αὐτὸ πολιτεύεσθαι προῃρημένῳ. The concluding phrase has no direct connection with the Revelation of John (22:18f.) or the corresponding words in Deuteronomy (4:2; 12:32): W. C. van Unnik, 'De la règle Μήτε προσθεῖναι μήτε ἀφελεῖν dans l'histoire du Canon', VC 3, 1949, pp. 1–36.

and which are not. At this point the final stage of the formation of the Canon has begun. It did not at once reach its goal; but the necessity of a 'closed' canon had been grasped in principle.[116]

The only attempt of this kind known to us from earlier times is the regulation of the Old Testament.[117] The new efforts to arrive at an exact list and sequence of books closely parallel those of Judaism in the corresponding situation.[118] For the New Testament Irenaeus had already precisely defined the Four-Gospel canon, and rejected any attempt to enlarge or reduce it.[119] Now similar lists for the Epistles and the Apocalypses were the question of the moment. This meant that the trend was not to enlarge the corpus of normative books but to restrict it. Only in the latter part of the third century, primarily under the influence of Origen, was there a return to a more broad-minded assessment of the traditional material.

Unfortunately we are not fully briefed on the subject of these discussions, and in particular on the reasons for the various exclusions. That the rejection of Hebrews in the West is linked with anti-Montanism seems certain: for what it has to say about the hopelessly lost condition of the apostate must have had the effect of justifying Montanism's harsh penitential practice.[120] Moreover, it was not clear who was the author of this epistle: Barnabas, Luke, Clement of Rome[121]—all are mentioned with a greater or lesser degree of confidence. It was apparently in Egypt that it was first counted as a Pauline epistle.[122] Irenaeus is said to have explicitly disputed its Pauline origin, but he valued and made use of it all the same.[123] This is in keeping with his mediating, wait-and-see attitude toward the Montanists.[124] By contrast, Hippolytus not only declared Hebrews to be non-Pauline, but would

---

[116] Cf. further pp. 242f. below.

[117] Melito carefully examined in the Holy Land τῶν ὁμολογουμένων τῆς παλαιᾶς διαθήκης γραφῶν κατάλογον (Eusebius, HE IV, 26, 12ff.): cf. n. 286 below.

[118] Cf. pp. 2f. above. Also A. C. Sundberg, The Old Testament of the Early Church, 1964, pp. 133ff. Origen is entirely typical when at the beginning of his Commentary on the Psalms he enumerates τοὺς ἐνδιαθήκους βίβλους, ὡς Ἑβραῖοι παραδιδόασιν (Eusebius, HE VI, 25, 1).

[119] Cf. pp. 195ff. above.

[120] Heb. 6:4ff.; 10:26f.; 12:16f. This rigorism, which, however, reminds later writers no longer of the Montanists but of the Novatianists, is explicitly made a ground of complaint against Hebrews by Filastrius (89). That the Montanists appealed to Hebrews against catholic penitential practice is attested not only by Tertullian (cf. n. 128 below) but also Jerome, Adv. Jovin. II, 3 (in Labriolle, Sources, no. 126, p. 176).

[121] Barnabas: Tertullian, De pudic. 20, 2; cf. Zahn, op. cit., I, p. 293 n. 1. Clement or Luke: Origen in Eusebius, HE VI, 25, 14.

[122] Cf. n. 14 above.   [123] Cf. n. 14 above.

[124] Eusebius, HE V, 3, 4; 4, 1f.; cf. Labriolle, Crise, pp. 230ff.; Faggiotto, L'eresia, pp. 15ff.

seem to have refused to quote from it.[125] Even before his time the Roman anti-Montanist polemical writer, Gaius, had explicitly recognised only thirteen Pauline epistles, thus excluding Hebrews.[126] The Muratorian Canon, too, passes it over in silence.[127] Only Tertullian, as a Montanist, makes an attempt to rescue the canonicity of the epistle, though even he does not regard it as Pauline, but ascribes it to Barnabas, 'a companion of the apostles', who as such was well qualified to hand on their ideas about discipline.[128] For Tertullian, therefore, the crucial issue is precisely the disputed statements on penitential discipline, which he tried to press in a sense opposite to that of catholic 'laxity'. For this very reason he did not succeed in imposing his high opinion of the epistle outside Montanist circles. Only in the fourth century was Hebrews recognised in the West as Pauline, after it had already long been canonised in the East, first under the influence of Origen and finally as a result of the conflict with Arianism.[129]

[125] Photius, Bibl. 121; 232. There are clearly numerous echoes of the epistle, which was of course well known to him: N. Bonwetsch, *Studien zu den Kommentaren Hippolyts zum Buche Daniel und Hohen Liede*, 1897, p. 25; Lagrange, *op. cit.*, pp. 62f. At the most it may be, as Zahn, *op. cit.*, I, p. 297, would have it, that these echoes provide 'indications, not to say proofs' of the fact that Hippolytus had read the epistle 'with great respect, and had appropriated a good deal from it'; but they do not imply more than this.

[126] Eusebius, *HE* II, 25, 6; VI, 20, 3:ἦλθεν δὲ εἰς ἡμᾶς καὶ Γαΐου, λογιωτάτου ἀνδρός, διάλογος, ἐπὶ ʻΡώμης κατὰ Ζεφυρῖνον πρὸς Πρόκλον τῆς κατὰ Φρύγας αἱρέσεως ὑπερμαχοῦντα κεκινημένος· ἐν ᾧ τῶν δι' ἐναντίας τὴν περὶ τὸ συντάττειν καινὰς γραφὰς προπέτειάν τε καὶ τόλμαν ἐπιστομίζων τῶν τοῦ ἱεροῦ ἀποστόλου δεκατριῶν μόνων ἐπιστολῶν μνημονεύει, τὴν πρὸς ʻΕβραίους μὴ συναριθμήσας ταῖς λοιπαῖς ... The term συντάττειν makes one think of the composition of new (revelatory) books (cf. n. 98 above); but Rufinus must be rightly interpreting the substance of the passage when he translates it: quod novas sibi quasdam scripturas praesumeret. In Tertullian (*Adv. Valent.* 5, 1) 'Proculus noster' is mentioned with the greatest honour alongside Justin, Miltiades, and Irenaeus, 'quos in omne opere fidei, quemadmodum in isto, optaverim adsequi'. He is to be identified with Proklos.

[127] Cf. p. 246 below. There are no grounds for questioning or minimising the importance of this negative evidence, as is done by D. Guthrie, *New Testament Introduction*, 1964, pp. 12f.

[128] Tertullian, *De pudic.* 20, 1ff.: volo tamen ex redundantia alicuius etiam comitis apostolorum testimonium superducere, idoneum confirmandi de proximo iure disciplinam magistrorum. exstat enim et Barnabae titulus ad Hebraeos, a deo satis auctoritati viri, ut quem Paulus iuxta se constituerit in abstinentiae tenore . : . (*I Cor.* 9:6). et utique receptior apud ecclesias epistula Barnabae illo apocrypho 'Pastore' moechorum. monens itaque discipulos . . . 'impossibile est enim', inquit . . . (*Heb.* 6:4–8). hoc qui ab apostolis didicit et cum apostolis docuit, numquam moecho et fornicatori secundam paenitentiam promissam ab apostolis norat.

[129] On this cf. Zahn, *op. cit.*, I, pp. 283ff.; Leipoldt, *op. cit.*, pp. 219ff. etc.; Lietzmann, *Bücher des N.T.*, pp. 82ff. It should not be overlooked that even in the East the testimony in favour of Hebrews in the pre-Origen period is exclusively Egyptian.

Even the Pastoral Epistles had to suffer as a result of the general reaction against 'apocryphal' writings. From the very first several heretical groups had refused to recognise them; indeed, in their own day they had been written for the purpose of combating heresy.[130] Origen, however, tells us that there were also orthodox circles which refused to accept II Timothy. The reason is revealing: the epistle refers to a 'secret' writing not recognised by the Church, namely the 'Book of Jannes and Mambres'—an objection which, as Origen remarks, should then strictly be applied to I Corinthians as well, since that likewise contains an extra-canonical quotation.[131] Nevertheless, Origen regards these radical views as having already had their day. The right course, in his view, is rather to make a positive use of such Jewish works in order with their help to throw light on the words of Christ and of his disciples.[132]

The apocalyptic writings were, of course, the ones bound to be most strongly affected by the anti-Montanist backlash. For it was in this group of works that the dangerous 'Spirit', which expressed itself in inspirations, visions, raptures, and ecstasies, and which was attacked as something demonic in Montanists, found support and justification. Irenaeus was already lamenting the fact that from anxiety about false prophets many people were no longer prepared to recognise any prophetic gifts at all.[133] Prophecy is confined to the writing prophets of the Old Testament and, at most, to primitive Christianity.[134] There is

---

[130] Cf. Clem. Alex., Strom. II, 52, 6; Jerome, Comm. Tit. prol.; and pp. 180f. above.

[131] *Comm. Ser. Matt.* 117 (ed. Klostermann, p. 250): item quod ait: '. . . sicut Iamnes et Mambres restiterunt Moysi' (II Tim. 3:8) non invenitur in publicis libris, sed in libro secreto, qui suprascribitur liber Iamnes et Mambres. unde ausi sunt quidam epistolam ad Timotheum repellere quasi habentem in se textus alicuius secreti, sed non potuerunt; primam autem epistolam ad Corinthios propter hoc aliquem refutasse quasi adulterinam, ad aures meas numquam pervenit. Cf. Harnack, *Der kirchengeschichtliche Ertrag* II, pp. 43ff., esp. p. 49. On 'Jannes and Jambres' cf. J. Daniélou, art. 'Exodus', *RAC* VII, 1969, col. 31; cf. also K. Koch, 'Das Lamm, das Ägypten vernichtet', *ZNW* 57, 1966, pp. 79–93, and contra, C. Burchard, 'Das Lamm in der Waagschale', *ibid.*, pp. 219–228; B. Murmelstein, 'Das Lamm in Test. Jos. 19, 8,' *ibid.*, 58, 1967, pp. 273–279. Later (?), according to Didymus of Alexandria (Jud. brev. enarr.) on Jude 9, the Epistle of Jude was also rejected by some, because it contains a quotation from the Assumption of Moses: K. H. Schelkle, 'Der Judasbrief bei den Kirchenvätern' in: *Abraham unser Vater* (Michel Festschrift), Leiden/Cologne, 1963, pp. 413f.

[132] *Comm. Ser. Matt.* 28 (ed. Klostermann, p. 50): propterea videndum, ne forte oporteat ex libris secretioribus, qui apud Iudaeos feruntur, ostendere verbum Christi, et non solum Christi, sed etiam discipulorum eius Stephani protomartyris et Pauli apostoli. Cf. Harnack, *Der kirchengeschichtliche Ertrag* II, pp. 42f.

[133] Irenaeus, *Adv. haer*, III, 11, 9: cf. n. 159 below.

[134] That the line of prophets was closed and could not be further extended is

now a general mistrust of all more recent writings of this kind. It was in the 'East', that is to say, in the area of the early Church which, apart from Egypt, was linguistically Greek-speaking, that the most radical inference was drawn from this change of mood. Here there was an almost total refusal to admit apocalyptic works into the new Canon. Even the Revelation of John hardly constitutes an exception to this rule. Only in its Asia Minor homeland was it upheld even by anti-Montanists, and enlisted by them in the fight against Montanism.[135] Elsewhere its status was not more than that of a 'disputed' or at best a tolerated book.[136] Only in the fourth century, under Western influence, does opinion gradually begin to veer round; and in the course of the Middle Ages Revelation to some degree wins general, securely established recognition even in the East.[137]

During the critical years apocalyptic literature ran into resistance even in Egypt. The Apocalypse of Peter is completely ignored by

---

emphasised by the Muratorian Canon: cf. n. 255 below. In Hippolytus the term 'prophet' is restricted entirely to the biblical prophets: A. Hamel, *Kirche bei Hippolyt von Rom*, 1951, p. 122. It may be that the disappearance of the loan-word 'charisma', which is still used by Novatian, is linked with anti-Montanism: C. Mohrmann, 'Les origines de la latinité chrétienne a Rome', *Études sur le latin des chrétiens* III, Rome, 1965, pp. 115f. Cf. H. von Campenhausen, *Ecclesiastical Authority*, pp. 187–191, and on the whole problem, Labriolle, *Crise*, pp. 555ff.

[135] In the case of the anti-Montanists (contra Zahn, *op. cit.*, I, pp. 112, 115) the use of Revelation cannot be proved: cf. n. 115 above; but Eusebius, *HE* V, 18, 14 relates of Apollonius: ἔτι δὲ ὡς ἐκ παραδόσεως τὸν σωτῆρά φησιν προστεταχέναι τοῖς αὑτοῦ ἀποστόλοις ἐπὶ δώδεκα ἔτεσιν μὴ χωρισθῆναι τῆς Ἱερουσαλήμ, κέχρηται δὲ καὶ μαρτυρίαις ἀπὸ τῆς Ἰωάννου Ἀποκαλύψεως, καὶ νεκρὸν δὲ δυνάμει θείᾳ πρὸς αὑτοῦ Ἰωάννου ἐν τῇ Ἐφέσῳ ἐγηγέρθαι ἱστορεῖ, καὶ ἄλλα τινὰ φησιν, δι' ὧν ἱκανῶς τῆς προειρημένης αἱρέσεως πληρέστατα διηύθυνεν τὴν πλάνην. Despite this phrase, which concludes the whole chapter, it is quite unclear whether the story in Apollonius of John's raising the dead was really held to serve as proof of the 'trustworthiness' of Revelation against 'all doubts', as Bauer, *Orthodoxy*, pp. 141, 145, thinks. In this passage Eusebius in his usual manner excerpts various pieces which for him were of historical interest, and we cannot determine for certain in what context they were placed by Apollonius. If Bauer's conjecture is correct, then it would show that even at this stage the Revelation of John was already challenged. Melito, as a chiliast, may have spoken up for Revelation in his work, Περὶ τοῦ διαβόλου καὶ τῆς Ἀποκαλύψεως (Eusebius, *HE* IV, 26, 2). Later Methodius recognised it without reserve, and drew heavily upon it. By contrast, in the interior of Asia Minor it was still rejected in the fourth century: Lietzmann, *History of the Early Church* II, p. 103.

[136] Cf. Eusebius, *HE* III, 25, 4, who in his cautious grading of the work is compelled also to take account of the more positive valuation attached to it by Origen and in the West. The Apocalypse is omitted both in the whole of Eastern Syria and in Armenia as well as in Wulfila's bible.

[137] Cf. Leipoldt, *op. cit.*, I, pp. 95ff. A broad survey of this well-known development may be found in Lietzmann, *Bücher*, pp. 92ff.

Origen.[138] Bishop Dionysius of Alexandria has told of earlier attacks on the Revelation of John. He himself sought to adopt a mediating position; but 'certain representatives of the older generation', as he tells us, absolutely rejected the book and refused to have anything to do with it. 'They criticised every single chapter, declared that the text was obscure and full of contradictions, and that the superscription was untrue. They say in fact that the book not only is not by John but also is not even a "Revelation", in view of the way in which it is so thickly veiled by the curtain of incomprehensibility. The author of the writing was no apostle, indeed not even a holy man or a churchman, but Cerinthus, the founder of the sect of Cerinthians named after him, which wanted to give his fabrication a name that would inspire confidence'; and the crudely sensual notions of the Apocalypse were in keeping with his teachings.[139] Dionysius gives this information in the course of a dispute with the millenarians,[140] and his chief desire is to show that the Apocalypse should on no account be expounded absolutely literally.[141] But very clearly discernible behind his cautious utterances are reservations which go a good deal further. He confesses that this book still contains much that is completely opaque to himself as well,[142] and that the author, though certainly someone called John, cannot possibly have been the apostle.[143] Here the new spiritual approach, Origenist in character, has inherited the anti-Montanist criticism of the prophets. The old arguments have been weakened, but they are still influential.

The West in general adopted a far less harsh attitude toward apocalyptic literature. Nevertheless, here too anti-Montanist reactions were not

---

[138] This can only be a sign of tacit rejection, because Clement knew the Apocalypse and in fact commented it: Eusebius, *HE* VI, 14, 1.

[139] Eusebius, *HE* VII, 25, 1–3: τινὲς μὲν οὖν τῶν πρὸ ἡμῶν ἠθέτησαν καὶ ἀνεσκεύασαν πάντη τὸ βιβλίον, καθ' ἕκαστον κεφάλαιον διευθύνοντες ἄγνωστόν τε καὶ ἀσυλλόγιστον ἀποφαίνοντες ψεύδεσθαί τε τὴν ἐπιγραφήν. Ἰωάννου γὰρ οὐκ εἶναι λέγουσιν, ἀλλ' οὐδ' ἀποκάλυψιν εἶναι τὴν σφόδρα καὶ παχεῖ κεκαλυμμένην τῷ τῆς ἀγνοίας παραπετάσματι, καὶ οὐχ ὅπως τῶν ἀποστόλων τινά, ἀλλ' οὐδ' ὅλως τῶν ἁγίων ἢ τῶν ἀπὸ τῆς ἐκκλησίας τούτου γεγονέναι ποιητὴν τοῦ γράμματος, Κήρινθον δὲ τὸν καὶ τὴν ἀπ' ἐκείνου κληθεῖσαν κηρινθιανὴν συστησάμενον αἵρεσιν, ἀξιόπιστον ἐπιφημίσαι θελήσαντα τῷ ἑαυτοῦ πλάσματι ὄνομα· τοῦτο γὰρ εἶναι τῆς διδασκαλίας αὐτοῦ τὸ δόγμα, ἐπίγειον ἔσεσθαι τὴν τοῦ χριστοῦ βασίλειαν καὶ ὧν αὐτὸς ὠρέγετο, φιλοσώματος ὢν καὶ πάνυ σαρκικός, ἐν τούτοις ὀνειροπολεῖν ἔσεσθαι γαστρὸς καὶ τῶν ὑπὸ γαστέρα πλησμοναῖς, τοῦτ' ἐστι σιτίοις καὶ ποτοῖς καὶ γάμοις καὶ δι' ὧν εὐφημότερον ταῦτα ᾠήθη περιεῖσθαι, ἑορταῖς καὶ θυσίαις καὶ ἱερείων σφαγαῖς.

[140] Eusebius, *HE* VII, 24.

[141] His comments throughout are redolent both in attitude of mind and in manner of speech of a thoroughly scientific philological training: F. H. Colson, 'Two examples of literary and rhetorical criticism in the Fathers', *JTS* 25, 1924, pp. 365–374.

[142] Eusebius, *HE* VII, 25, 4f.

[143] Eusebius, *HE* VII, 25, 6–27.

altogether absent.[144] The apocalypse of Hermas was the work chiefly affected.[145] Because on account of its mild views on penance it was odious even to the Montanists,[146] it soon completely disappeared from view in the West.[147] The standing of the Apocalypse of Peter too was challenged, despite its apostolic attribution, in which plainly there was no longer much confidence;[148] and even the Revelation of John was suspect. Gaius of Rome, who has already been mentioned,[149] at any rate rejected it out of hand, and regarded it as a work of the heretic Cerinthus.[150] (The remarks of Dionysius quoted earlier refer to him[151]). This polemic must be seen in a wider context. Gaius already brings us down to the third century.[152] He composed a Dialogue against the Montanist Proclus, and seems to have been a spokesman for the extreme anti-Montanists. As such he was not content with rejecting the 'new scriptures' of the Montanists, but strove for a revision and reduction of the whole New Testament.[153] In his works its limits were drawn

[144] Later the fight against Priscillianism once more produced very similar repercussions. Filaster (88), when writing against them, details the canonical Scriptures, but omits the Apocalypse, and in its place inserts the following sentence: scripturae autem absconditae, id est apocrypha, etsi legi debent morum causa a perfectis, non ab omnibus debent, quia non intelligentes multa addiderunt et tulerunt quae voluerunt haeretici.

[145] Cf. pp. 256f. below on the Muratorian Canon.

[146] Tertullian, De pudic. 20, 2 (cf. n. 128 above). Tertullian's opinion as a Montanist stands in contrast to his use of the 'Shepherd' in his pre-Montanist days: Orat. 16.

[147] Jerome, vir. ill. 10, can write of the 'Shepherd': apud Latinos paene ignotus est; cf. further Leipoldt, op. cit., I, pp. 51ff., who attaches more importance to the echoes in Hippolytus and Novatian than they deserve.

[148] Can. Murat. 71ff.: apocalypses etiam Iohannis et Petri tantum recipimus, quam quidam ex nostris legi in ecclesia nolunt. Tertullian cites the Apocalypse of Peter only in his Montanist period, and then without explicitly mentioning it by name (cf. n. 53 above).

[149] From Eusebius's characterisations of him in HE II, 25, 6, as ἐκκλησιαστικὸς ἀνήρ, and in VI, 20, 3 (cf. n. 126 above), not even Jerome (contra Bludau, op. cit., p. 40) but Photius, Bibl. 48, in his largely confused account, groundlessly makes him a presbyter.

[150] Dionysius Bar Salibi, Comm. Apoc. (CSCO Syr.), CI, 1f.: Hippolytus Romanus dixit: apparuit vir nomine Gaius, qui asserebat Evangelium non esse Iohannis nec Apocalypsin, sed Cerinthi haeretici ea esse. Et contra hunc Caium surrexit beatus Hippolytus et demonstravit aliam esse doctrinam Iohannis in Evangelio et in Apocalypsi et alium Cerinthi. On the text of Dionysius bar Salibi cf. P. Nautin, Le dossier d'Hippolyte et de Méliton, Paris, 1953, pp. 145ff.

[151] Zahn, op. cit., I, p. 230. To my mind there is no need, with Bludau, op. cit., pp. 40ff., and others to think of further sources and intermediate links.

[152] According to Eusebius, HE VI, 20, 3 (n. 126 above) Gaius wrote under Pope Zephyrinus (198/9–217).

[153] The conjecture of Rondeau (cf. n. 86 above) that the criticism of the Psalter to which Hippolytus and Filaster bear witness may also derive from the anti-Montanist circles around Gaius seems to me extremely precarious.

not only more precisely but also more narrowly than in Irenaeus. Gaius not only attacked Hebrews[154] and the Revelation of John, which since Justin's day had always been held in high regard in the West;[155] he did not shrink even from laying hands on the Four-Gospel canon, inasmuch as he pronounced the Gospel of John likewise to be the work of Cerinthus and a wicked forgery.[156] This is all the more interesting in view of the fact that Gaius was a respected theologian, and that even Eusebius—who does admittedly keep quiet about the attack on the Gospel—expresses no doubts about his orthodoxy.[157]

Unfortunately, we do not know where the polemic against the Johannine writings first arose, but this may already have happened in Asia Minor.[158] At any rate, even Irenaeus knows of a rejection of the Gospel of John by orthodox Christians; and since this was the result of anxiety over the spirit inspiring false prophets, it is obviously anti-Montanist circles which were involved.[159] The Gospel of John did

[154] Cf. p. 233 above.   [155] Dial. 81, 4.

[156] Cf. n. 150 above. There is no reason, on the basis of the positive characterisation given by Eusebius (cf. n. 149 above), to regard a rejection of the Gospel of John by Gaius as 'inconceivable' (so Harnack, *Chronologie* II, pp. 227, *et al.*), or to assume, with E. Schwartz, 'Über den Tod der Söhne Zebedäi', *Ges. Schr.* V, 1963, pp. 106f., that Eusebius possessed only an incomplete copy of the Dialogue against Proclus, in which the rejection of the Gospel had been deleted, or to postulate in place of Gaius an anonymous author of the second century, whose work would then have antedated Irenaeus (cf. n. 159 below), as the same scholar with tortuous argumentation suggests elsewhere (Schwartz, 'Johannes und Kerinthos', *Ges. Schr.* V, pp. 173f.); contra even Rondeau, *op. cit.*, p. 36 n. 3. Eusebius' opinion may be surprising, but that does not make it inconceivable. From the standpoint of a history of the Canon, that the Gospel of John should be contested is by no means to be ruled out, when the beginnings of the Four-Gospel canon are placed, as they must be, only in the second half of the second century: cf. pp. 171ff. above.

[157] Cf. n. 149 above.

[158] This is the confident assumption of Labriolle, *Crise*, pp. 191, 202, 285, and Stonehouse, *op. cit.*, p. 60.

[159] Irenaeus, Adv. haer. III, 11, 9: alii vero ut donum spiritus frustrentur, quod in novissimis temporibus secundum placitum patris effusum est in humanum genus, illam speciem non admittunt, quae est secundum Iohannis evangelium, in qua paracletum se missurum dominus promisit, sed simul et Evangelium et propheticum repellunt spiritum. infelices vere, qui pseudoprophetae quidem esse nolunt, propheticam vere gratiam repellunt ab ecclesia, similia patientes his, qui propter eos, (qui) in hypocrisi veniunt, etiam a fratrum communicatione se abstinent. (The replacement of the MS 'volunt' by 'nolunt' or some equivalent correction is generally agreed to be indispensable: Zahn, *op. cit.*, I, p. 244; Labriolle, *Crise*, pp. 230–238; Bludau, *op. cit.*, pp. 28–32). This is clearly a case of radical anti-Montanists who reject the Gospel of John on account of the prediction of the Paraclete, and have also become mistrustful of other expressions of 'spirit'. It is indeed, as Zahn, *op. cit.*, I, p. 240, remarks, 'hard to understand how scholarly exegetes can imagine that Irenaeus is here combatting Montanism or a Montanist tendency'. On the detailed reasons put forward for rejecting this

after all contain the dangerous prediction of the Paraclete, the text with which the Montanists gave their claims biblical justification.[160] Likewise the rejection of the Apocalypse, wherever it occurs in this period, is conditioned or partly conditioned by fear of the ecstatic and apocalyptic false spirit of the 'Phrygians'. It is now denied that either book can be the work of John the Apostle, and instead both are ascribed to an arch-heretic.[161] It is by no means certain that Gaius was the first to hit upon this attribution. For all the pungency of his polemic the figure that Gaius cuts is that of a scholar, unruffled in argument, and basing his case more on objective and philological grounds than on tendentious whims.[162] Unfortunately, the problem of sources for the whole complex web of opposition to John is an extremely difficult one, since the crucial texts, namely the writings of Hippolytus—or, more probably, his work specifically attacking Gaius[163]—have been lost, and have laboriously to be reconstructed from later reports and quota-

---

erroneous interpretation from Tillemont to Harnack cf. Bludau, *op. cit.*, pp. 13–27. Dem. 99 clearly refers to the same group. Here, in a list of various errors all involving rejection of trinitarian belief, we are told: 'Others do not accept the gifts of the Holy Spirit, and repudiate the grace of prophecy, which enables men to bring forth the fruit of divine life. These are they of whom Isaiah (1:30) said: "You shall become like a terebinth stripped of its leaves, and like a garden that has no water." These are good for nothing to God, for they are incapable of bearing fruit.' Among these anti-Montanists—who are of course catholics— there is as yet no mention of Cerinthus; but it can hardly be doubted that they just as much as Gaius rejected not only the Gospel but also the Revelation of John. The reason why Irenaeus says nothing in this passage concerning the latter work is simply the context, which deals exclusively with the Four-Gospel canon: Schwartz, 'Söhne Zebedäi', p. 89. On the other hand, we are not of course to take Irenaeus's words literally, as though he thought that these people with their hostility to everything charismatic actually wanted to repudiate even the apostle Paul, when in the passage from the *Adv. haer.* he continues: datur autem intellegi, quod huiusmodi neque apostolum Paulum recipient; in ea enim epistula, quae est ad Corinthios de propheticis charismatibus diligenter locutus est et scit viros et mulieres in ecclesia prophetantes. per haec igitur omnia peccantes in spiritum dei in inremissibile incidunt peccatum.

[160] In considering this question it is important to take into account the fact that it was only later that the Gospel of John came into general use. At this stage therefore it was still suspect, and Justin made no use of it at all: cf. p. 168 above.

[161] Why precisely Cerinthus was named by Gaius as the author can hardly be determined with certainty. Probably the fact that Cerinthus and John were contemporaries, and that tradition made them out to be enemies (Irenaeus, Adv. haer. III, 3, 4), was the sole reason for the attribution: Stonehouse, *op. cit.*, pp. 98f. Anyway, all speculations about possible theological reasons or connections fail to lead to any tangible result: Bludau, *op. cit.*, pp. 59–66; 131–136.

[162] Schwartz, 'Söhne Zebedäi', p. 93, sees him as 'a shrewd and sober-minded man, who wishes to use his criticism to do the church a service'.

[163] It does in fact seem to be a question of *one* polemical treatise only: Nautin, *op. cit.*, pp. 146f.

tions.[164] But the main lines of his defence, and by the same token those of Gaius's attack, can nevertheless still be established.[165]

Gaius's criticism of the Gospel of John was not apparently based on dogmatic grounds but on comparison with the Synoptists.[166] Whereas the three earlier Gospels tell first of the birth, the flight into Egypt, the stay in Nazareth, and only then of the baptism and, connected with that, of a forty-day sojourn by Jesus in the wilderness, the soi-disant 'John' begins with a double visit to the Baptist, followed by the marriage at Cana.[167] The Johannine account thus contradicts the recognised witnesses. Furthermore, John tells of two Passovers during the public ministry of Jesus, while the Synoptists know of only one.[168] Traditio-historical or literary-critical explanations of such discrepancies are naturally not available to Gaius. Consequently the Gospel of John must simply be wrong; it 'lies',[169] and ought not to be included among books recognised by the Church.[170] In the extant fragments there is no specific reference to the Paraclete prediction; yet there can hardly be any doubt that it was emphatically condemned by Gaius, the anti-Montanist polemical writer.[171]

In waging his campaign against the Apocalypse Gaius seems to have made use of more weighty, spiritual arguments.[172] He undoubtedly

[164] The relevant sources are: (1) the account and quotations given by Eusebius in his History; (2) the quotations which Dionysius bar Salibi uses in his Commentary on Revelation, based on Hippolytus; and (3) the observations of Epiphanius on the subject of the 'Alogi', which probably also derive from Hippolytus. Irenaeus did not yet know Gaius, and when W. von Loewenich, *Das Johannes-Verständnis im zweiten Jahrhundert*, 1932, p. 141, gives as his opinion that the Church 'primarily' has Irenaeus to thank 'that the Gospel of John remained extant,' he is on the whole rather overestimating the importance of his opposition.

[165] I do not wish to resume the debate here in detail, and refer the reader to the full discussions in Bludau, *op. cit.*, and, for Revelation only, Stonehouse, *op. cit.*, pp. 59–71.

[166] Here again, as in Irenaeus (cf. p. 191 above) and in the Muratorian Canon (cf. pp. 250f. below), it is the 'beginnings' of the Gospels which are of prime importance.

[167] Epiphanius, Panar. LI, 4; 17, 11; 18, 1.6.

[168] Epiphanius, Panar. LI, 22, 1f.

[169] Epiphanius, Panar. LI, 18, 1: τὸ δὲ εὐαγγέλιον τὸ εἰς ὄνομα 'Ιωάννου, φασί, ψεύδεται. Cf. Eusebius, *HE* III, 28, 2 (n. 181 below).

[170] Epiphanius, Panar. LI, 18, 6: λέγουσι δὲ τὸ κατὰ 'Ιωάννην εὐαγγέλιον ἀδιάθετον εἶναι. The word ἀδιάθετος should not be translated 'without order'; it signifies the opposite of ἐνδιάθετος = ἐνδιάθηκος, i.e., not belonging to the canon: Schwartz, 'Söhne Zebedäi', p. 91 n. 2.

[171] Cf. n. 126 above.

[172] According to E. Schwartz, 'Johannes und Kerinthos', p. 175, it must be 'clear' that the attack on the Apocalypse was Gaius's main concern from the start. But we may suspect that what has happened is simply that, because the attacks on this book were still of topical interest at a later date, fuller excerpts were made from these parts of his work.

rejected apocalyptic literature *in toto*.[173] Moreover, he was able to reinforce his specific polemic against Revelation by comparing what it has to say with contrary statements from the recognised canonical Scriptures. Had not Paul expressly stated that the final catastrophe would break in suddenly and unexpectedly, 'like a thief in the night', and that until then the godless were to live on secure and undisturbed? By contrast the terrifying false predictions of Cerinthus,[174] allegedly proclaimed by the mouth of an angel, made out that the appearing of Christ would be preceded by protracted plagues,[175] during which a third of mankind would be destroyed by locusts alone.[176] Such pictures were spiritually completely worthless, indeed 'laughable'.[177] 'What good does the Revelation of John do me when it tells me of seven angels and seven trumpets,[178] or of four angels who are to be let loose at the River Euphrates, and of the mighty host of ten thousand myriads of warriors and of a thousand times ten thousand horsemen in flame-red, dark, and hyacinth-blue armour?'[179] Even more revolting is the idea of a kingdom to last for a thousand years, when Satan will be bound,[180] and those who have been resurrected are, as Gaius caricatures the situation, to live in lust and sensual pleasures and to enjoy a 'marriage feast'.[181] We are here concerned, therefore, with the same grounds of

---

[173] There is no theologian known to us who rejected Revelation but retained Hermas or the Apocalypse of Peter.

[174] Eusebius, *HE* III, 28, 2 (cf. n. 181 below).

[175] Dionysius bar Salibi on Rev. 8:8: Caius haereticus impugnavit hanc visionem et dixit: Impossibile est, ut ista fiant; nam, 'sicut fur qui venit noctu' (I Thess. 5:2; cf. Matt. 24:43; II Pet. 3:10; and even Rev. 3:2), ita erit adventus domini. Hippolytus, who will not allow Gaius's arguments against Revelation to be valid, nevertheless himself uses Matt. 24:27 in an exactly similar way against the apocalyptic prophets of his own time: Comm. Dan. IV, 18.

[176] Dion. bar Sal. on Rev. 9:2ff.: hic obiicit Caius: quomodo scelesti percutientur locustis, cum dicat scriptura peccatores prosperaturos et iustos persecutioni obnoxios fore in mundo (Ps. 73:12–14), et Paulus: fideles persecutionem patientur a scelestis et mali prospere agent, errantes et decipientes (II Tim. 3:12f.).

[177] Epiphanius, Panar. LI, 34, 3: ἐνόμισαν γὰρ οἱ τοιοῦτοι, μή πη ἄρα γελοῖόν τί ἐστιν ἡ ἀλήθεια.

[178] Epiphanius, Panar. LI 32, 2.   [179] Epiphanius, Panar. LI 34, 2.

[180] Dion. bar Sal. on Rev. 21:2f.: Caius haereticus obiicit: Satanas hic vinctus est secundum quod scriptum est: ingressus est Christus domum fortis et ligavit eum et rapuit nos, vasa eius (Matt. 12:29).

[181] Eusebius, *HE* III, 28, 2: ἀλλὰ καὶ Κήρινθος ὁ δι' ἀποκαλύψεων ὡς ὑπὸ ἀποστόλου μεγάλου γεγραμμένων τερατολογίας ἡμῖν ὡς δι' ἀγγέλων αὐτῷ δεδειγμένας ψευδόμενος ἐπεισάγει, λέγων μετὰ τὴν ἀνάστασιν ἐπίγειον εἶναι τὸ βασίλειον τοῦ χριστοῦ καὶ πάλιν ἐπιθυμίαις καὶ ἡδοναῖς ἐν Ἰερουσαλὴμ τὴν σάρκα πολιτευομένην δουλεύειν. καὶ ἐχθρὸς ὑπάρχων ταῖς γραφαῖς τοῦ θεοῦ, ἀριθμὸν χιλιονταετίας ἐν γάμῳ ἑορτῆς, θέλων πλανᾶν, λέγει γίνεσθαι. There can be no doubt that Gaius does here have the Revelation of John in mind: Bludau, *op. cit.*, pp. 40–60.

offence that later made acceptance of the Apocalypse so difficult for the Greek church, and, even before Origen, moved the anti-Montanist Hippolytus to his more or less spiritualising reinterpretation.[182] But Gaius was able to bring forward yet another argument, which at that time must have been particularly telling: the predictions in Revelation had not been fulfilled, and so were false prophecy. In at least one passage this could now be proved: Christ had had a letter written to the angel of the church of Thyateira which contained certain promises—and so was patently unaware that before long this church would cease to exist. This odd statement should be taken to mean that in Gaius's time there was no longer in Thyateira a genuine, that is an orthodox, congregation, since it had wholly fallen away to Montanism.[183] This argument naturally would not have made any impression on a Montanist: but this shows us all the more clearly for what public and with what intention Gaius was writing. What he wanted to do was not to convert the Montanists, but to urge the catholic church to which he belonged to abandon the Johannine writings.

Such an attempt is symptomatic, even though the immediate effects of Gaius's polemic were probably small. It is true that Epiphanius, in the polemic which he derived from Hippolytus, makes up some tale about a formal sect of anti-Johannists, for whom he invents the nickname 'Alogi', on the grounds, that together with the Gospel of John they have disowned the 'Logos' of which that Gospel speaks, and so are people who have no Logos, that is, no understanding. But it is hardly possible to accept that such a sect ever existed.[184] On the contrary, the efforts during the third century to fix the New Testament Canon exactly were universally approved. The limits could not yet be precisely drawn; there were differences of opinion, and between the hard core of the collection and those works which were unequivocally rejected there was still a number of pieces, the assessment of which fluctuated, and which in many areas were not recognised at all, while in others they were acknowledged only with reservations. Nevertheless, this group was no longer large either in number or in importance. It was of concern primarily to scholarly theologians who were acquainted with the situation in the churches in several different areas, and so could compare their various collections with one another. The relevant lists of biblical books in Origen[185] and Eusebius,[186] to which at a later date

---

[182] Cf. Stonehouse, *op. cit.*, pp. 105ff.

[183] Epiphanius, Panar. LI 33, 1. The correct interpretation of this difficult and disputed passage has been established by Bludau, *op. cit.*, pp. 122–124.

[184] Gaius, as Irenaeus (cf. n. 159 above) makes clear, was certainly not the only 'Alogos' but he may nevertheless have been the last; on the whole question cf. Bludau, *op. cit.*, pp. 220–230.

[185] Lagrange, *op. cit.*, pp. 93–103; Harnack, *Ertrag* I, 1918, pp. 7–30; II,

was added that of Jerome,[187] are well known. In fact the discussion on this subject never really reached a conclusion;[188] but the earliest 'list' of this kind must antedate even Origen. After the crucial debates of the second century it presents the first formal attempt at a definitive standardisation, and in principle marks the end of the long period of the formation of the Canon. We refer, of course, to the 'Muratorianum', that document which, after the name of the scholar who first discovered and published it, is ordinarily referred to as the 'Muratorian Canon'.

As is well known, the Muratorian Canon, 'a *catalogue raisonné* of the canonical writings of the New Testament',[189] is a fragment; the beginning and end are lost. The eighty-five extant lines start in the middle of a sentence with the second Gospel, Mark, and break off quite abruptly after an enumeration of heretical works. The text itself affords us no information about either its author or its provenance or its date of composition. It is also unclear in what context its statements originally belonged. What is more, the Latin in which it is set out is so barbarous and slipshod, and disfigured by such a multitude of scribal errors, that in the case of many of the sentences no assured interpretation is possible. The literature on the Muratorianum long ago became quite unmanageable,[190] and there is little hope that the forest of hypotheses will ever be cleared. Fortunately for us there is no need here to discuss all the detailed points; we can be content with characterising the nature and particular tendencies of the document. These too are admittedly just as much in dispute; but in my own view the basic features can be very adequately determined.[191]

What is certain is that the Muratorianum is a Western production,[192]

---

pp. 34–50; J. Ruwet, 'Les "Antilegomena" dans les oeuvres d'Origène', *Biblica* 23, 1942, pp. 18–42.

[186] Lagrange, *op. cit.*, pp. 105–110; M. Müller, 'Die Überlieferung des Eusebios in seiner Kirchengeschichte über die Schriften des Neuen Testaments und deren Verfasser', *ThStKr* 105, 1933, pp. 425–455.

[187] Lagrange, *op. cit.*, pp. 152–156; L. Schade, *Die Inspirationslehre des Heiligen Hieronymus*, 1910, pp. 211–218.

[188] Cf. Leipoldt, *op. cit.*, II, pp. 3ff.

[189] F. Overbeck, *Zur Geschichte des Kanons*, 1880 (reprinted 1965), p. 95.

[190] S. Ritter (cf. n. 191 below) had already compiled a bibliography with some 150 items as early as 1926.

[191] I shall content myself here with referring the reader to some of the comprehensive treatments of the subject: Zahn, *op. cit.*, II, pp. 1–143; S. Ritter, 'Il Frammento Muratoriano', *RivAC* 3, 1926, pp. 215–263; Lagrange, *op. cit.*, pp. 66–84; H. Leclercq, art. 'Muratorianum', *DACL* XII, 1, 1935, pp. 543–560. The most convenient edition of the text is that of Lietzmann in his *Kleinen Texten*², 1933, no. 1; it is his reconstruction which will normally be used here. The most recent English translation is that in *N.T. Apocrypha* I, pp. 43ff.

[192] To mention only one indication, this follows from the fact that Revelation
R

and must have been written not long before or after the year 200.[193] The theory, advocated by Harnack in particular, that we are dealing with an official document of the Bishop of Rome, cannot be maintained, and has today been almost universally abandoned.[194] Official regulations of this kind do not begin until one and a half centuries later,[195] and can nowhere be demonstrated for our period. We are dealing here with the private work of a theologian whose thought is strongly catholic and ecclesiastical,[196] and who may, of course, also have been a bishop.

---

is accepted without question, while at the same time there is no mention whatever of Hebrews.

[193] At a later period it is hardly conceivable that the Catholic Epistles would be limited to three or four, with no mention of those attributed to Peter, or, on the other hand, that the Apocalypse of Peter and the Wisdom of Solomon would have been acknowledged as part of the N.T. Canon. Furthermore, the heretics and heresies named by the Muratorianum all still belong to the second century. Nevertheless, the limits of the Canon were not yet so firmly fixed at the beginning of the third century as is often supposed (cf. n. 156 above), and the comments about Hermas cannot, in my opinion, be pressed too strongly for chronological purposes (cf. n. 258 below). A date toward the end of the second century, as assumed by G. Strecker, art. 'Muratorisches Fragment', *RGG*[3], IV, 1960, 1191, and many others, is intrinsically the most probable; but a later date, at the beginning of the third century, cannot be excluded, as Zahn, *op. cit.*, II, p. 134, rightly observes.

[194] An exception is A. Ehrhardt, 'The Gospels in the Muratorian Fragment', *Ostkirchliche Studien* 2, 1953, pp. 121–138 (= *The Framework of the New Testament Stories*, Manchester, 1964, pp. 11–36), who in fact elaborates Harnack's position even further. Cf. contra, Zahn, *op. cit.*, II, pp. 132ff., and decisively H. Koch, 'Zu A. v. Harnacks Beweis für den amtlichen römischen Ursprung des Muratorischen Fragments', *ZNW* 25, 1926, pp. 154–160. The untenable character of Harnack's arguments is now recognised also by Roman Catholic scholars, e.g., B. Altaner and A. Stuiber, *Patrologie*[7], 1966, p. 94; J. Schmid, art. 'Muratorisches Fragment', *Lexicon für Theol. u. Kirche* VII, 1963, p. 693; and even H. Höpfl and L. Leloir, *Introductio in sacros utriusque testamenti libros* I[6], Naples-Rome, 1958, p. 174. On the other hand there is still a tendency to consider seriously an origin in Rome or within the Roman sphere of influence, in view of the statements about Hermas's having been the brother of Pius, bishop of Rome, and having written during the latter's pontificate (cf. n. 255 below). 'Roman bishops would hardly have been used for dating purposes in a remote period' (Jülicher-Fascher, *Einleitung*, p. 491). But because Hermas was by his own testimony a Roman, such a note—backed up perhaps by legend—could have been composed anywhere, and tells us nothing about the provenance of the Muratorianum.

[195] Cf. pp. 330f. below.

[196] The phrase 'catholica ecclesia', which at this time was by no means common parlance, occurs twice in quick succession (ll. 61f., 66), in addition to one instance of 'catholica' by itself (l. 69). 'This concise designation arose first in popular speech, and then gradually found its way into literary usage': H. Koch, *Cyprianische Untersuchungen*, p. 105 n. Probably, however, in the last-named instance the predicate refers not to the catholic church but to I John: cf. n. 205 below.

There has been a tendency to think in particular of Hippolytus as the author;[197] but serious objections can also be raised against this attribution.[198] In any case the text we possess must be the translation of a Greek original.[199] In character the Fragment recalls the 'fly-leaves' which occur in many early biblical MSS, and on which the reader is given brief indications, in the manner of our 'Introductions', concerning the authors and contents of the individual books and the circumstances in which they originated.[200] The earliest example of this type

[197] So esp. J. B. Lightfoot, *S. Clement of Rome* II, 1890, pp. 405–413; T. Zahn, 'Hippolytus der Verfasser des Muratorischen Kanons', *Forschungen zur Geschichte des neutestamentlichen Kanons* X, 1929, pp. 58–75; Lagrange, *op. cit.*, pp. 78–84 (= 'Le Canon d'Hippolyte et le fragment de Muratori', *RB* 42, 1933, pp. 161–186.

[198] J. Chapman, 'L'auteur du Canon Muratorien', *RevBen* 21, 1904, pp. 240f.; A. von Harnack, 'Über den Verfasser und den literarischen Charakter des Muratorischen Fragments', *ZNW* 24, 1925, p. 14; G. Bardy, art. 'Muratori (Canon de)', *Dict. de la Bible* V, 1954, cols. 1406–1408; N. A. Dahl, 'Welche Ordnung der Paulusbriefe wird vom Muratorischen Kanon vorausgesetzt' *ZNW* 52, 1961, p. 45. The principal objection remains the one that it is simply impossible to ascribe to a man like Hippolytus the muddle-headed remarks to be found in the Muratorian Canon—a point which Zahn, *op. cit.*, II, pp. 137f., once insisted on against Lightfoot, and never abandoned later even when advancing the most extraordinary hypotheses. In addition there is the remarkable recognition of the Apocalypse of Peter; Lagrange's assumption (*op. cit.*, p. 84) that Hippolytus's opinion here was dictated by the overriding influence of Origen, is, as he himself felt, 'une ressource désespérée', a typical counsel of despair.

[199] This is not undisputed, but seems to me absolutely certain. Around the year 200 Greek was still the predominant ecclesiastical language in the West. Of course, a theologian in the age of Tertullian, the Acts of the Scillitan Martyrs, and the Passio Perpetuae, may very well have written in Latin; but such precedents do not entitle us to imagine him capable of the kind of Latin perpetrated by the Fragmentist. Finally, there is the notorious misunderstanding by which the Wisdom of Solomon, written 'by Philo' (ὑπὸ φίλωνος) in honour of Solomon (or of the Church: cf. n. 205 below), is said to have been written 'ab amicis' (ὑπὸ φίλοις), 'by the friends' of Solomon, an error already correctly recognised by P. S. Tregelles, *Canon Muratorianus, the earliest catalogue of the Books of the New Testament*, Oxford, 1867, pp. 51f., and which points incontrovertibly to a Greek original; since the Latin text of the Muratorianum at this point hardly makes any sort of reasonable sense, and moreover there is independent testimony that Philo was supposed to be the author; cf. n. 208 below. On the other side of the argument, the alleged Latin pun in ll. 67f.: 'fel enim cum melle misceri non congruit,' is of no significance; cf. Hermas 33, 5 (Mand. V, 1, 5). Cf. further n. 205 below.

[200] So Lietzmann, *Bücher*, pp. 52f.; also Schneemelcher, *N.T. Apocrypha* I, p. 42; cf. the brief survey of this literary form by B. Kraft, art. 'Argumentum', *Lex. f. Theol. u. Kirche* I, 1957, pp. 839f.; 'Prologe, biblische', *ibid.*, VIII, 1963, pp. 790f., and for its further development, M. Schild, *Abendländische Bibelvorreden bis zur Lutherbibel* (TS Diss. Heidelberg 1964). To the best of our knowledge the only instance in which the Muratorianum has had a direct influence occurs, certainly not accidentally, in a Prologue to the Pauline Epistles preserved in MSS of the 11th and 12th centuries: A. von Harnack, 'Exzerpte

is the Marcionite prologues to the Pauline Epistles.[201] The Muratorianum appears to be acquainted with them, and it is certainly possible that its intention was to counter them directly with its own sound catholic observations.[202] We may also recall the kindred comments with which Irenaeus had earlier prefaced the four Gospels with brief notes on their authors and date of composition, before going on to establish their exclusive validity in more detail.[203] Such texts are constantly couched in purely objective terms, even when they are meant to serve to justify a particular polemical and apologetic intention.

The corpus of works for church reading recognised by the Muratorianum contains, taken as a whole, little that our own day finds surprising. The four Gospels, the Lukan Acts, and the thirteen Pauline epistles are firmly established. The Pastorals are mentioned only at the end of the Pauline series, after the letter to Philemon, and like the latter, as 'private' documents, require a special justification.[204] By contrast the catholic epistles constantly give the impression of a loosely connected appendix—only Jude and two, or perhaps three, Johannine epistles are cited.[205] There is not a single mention of I Peter.[206] In its

---

aus dem Muratorischen Fragment (saec. XI et XII)', *TLZ* 23, 1898, pp. 131–134.

[201] The early Marcionite origin of the oldest prologues to Paul was first recognised by D. de Bruyne, 'Prologues bibliques d'origine Marcionite', *RevBén* 24, 1907, pp. 1–16, and P. Corssen, 'Zur Überlieferungsgeschichte des Römerbriefes', *ZNW* 10, 1909, pp. 1–45; 97–102. The doubts expressed by W. Mundle, 'Die Herkunft der "marcionitischen" Prologe zu den paulinischen Briefen, *ZNW* 24, 1925, pp. 56–77, and Lagrange, 'Les prologues prétendus Marcionites', *RB* 35, 1926, pp. 161–173, to which even Schneemelcher, *N.T. Apocrypha* II, pp. 130f., attaches weight, have in my view done nothing to shake this position; cf. A. von Harnack, *Marcion*, pp. 127*–134*, and 'Der marcionitische Ursprung der ältesten Vulgata-Prologe zu den Paulusbriefen', *ZNW* 24, 1925, pp. 204–218.

[202] This is an attractive conjecture by Dahl, 'Ordnung', pp. 52f., remodelling a somewhat too sweeping theory of Harnack's ('Die Marcionitischen Prologe zu den Paulusbriefen, eine Quelle des Muratorischen Fragments', *ZNW* 25, 1926, pp. 160–163). Harnack had thought that the Fragmentist already regarded the Prologues as a part of the Epistles themselves: E. Haenchen, *Die Apostelgeschichte*[5/14], 1965, pp. 8ff.

[203] Irenaeus, Adv. haer. III, 1, 1 (cf. pp. ooof. above). It is not possible, however, to assume with Harnack, 'Die ältesten Evangelien-Prologe und die Bildung des Neuen Testaments', *Sitzungsberichte Berl. Akad.*, 1928, pp. 331f., and A. Strobel, 'Lukas der Antiochener', *ZNW* 49, 1958, p. 132 n. 5, that Irenaeus here was already in his turn dependent upon the so-called 'anti-Marcionite Gospel prologues'. These are in no sense a unity, and must be considerably later in date: Haenchen, *op. cit.*, pp. 8ff. n. 2.

[204] Cf. n. 234 below. The fact that they are included in a supplementary section brings out the fact that the sevenfold scheme of Paul's letters to his churches fits neither them nor the letter to Philemon. Cf. p. 252 below.

[205] Ll. 68ff.: epistola sane iude et superscrictio [superscripti = ? mentioned in ll. 9ff. above] iohannis duas in catholica habentur et sapientia ab amicis

place we find, oddly enough, the Wisdom of Solomon, which apparently is regarded as the work of Philo of Alexandria,[207] but which nevertheless takes its place between the apostles and prophets of the New Covenant.[208] The list is closed by 'only' two apocalypses, those of John and Peter. It is noted that some of the brethren in the faith, however, have objections to the Apocalypse of Peter.[209] On the other hand, the Shepherd of Hermas is unequivocally excluded: it is certainly permissible to read it, but it is no longer to be used in public for Christian liturgical worship.[210] Finally (lumped together in a fairly confused and obscure way) we find listed Marcion and some other leading gnostic heretics and the 'Kataphrygians' (here given this name for the first time), that is, the Montanists. 'Nothing whatever' of their writings is of interest to the Church.[211] The Marcionite Epistles to the Laodiceans and to the Alex-

---

salomonis in honore[m] ipsius scripta. The text is plainly corrupt, and the mention of only two Johannine epistles instead of one or all three is somewhat puzzling. There is therefore something to be said for the ingenious conjecture of P. Katz, 'The Johannine Epistles in the Muratorian Canon', *JTS* N.S. 8, 1957, pp. 273f., who would read 'dua(e) sin catholica', corresponding to an original δύο σὺν καθολικῇ; or that of C. F. D. Moule, *The Birth of the New Testament*, 1962, p. 206 n.1: δύο πρὸς καθολικήν. This solution is adopted by R. Schnackenburg, *Die Johannesbriefe²*, 1963, pp. 302f. I John, which in other quarters too has a more secure place in the Canon than I Peter, is also referred to by Dionysius of Alexandria in Eusebius, *HE* VII, 25, 7.10, as ἡ ἐπιστολὴ ἡ καθολική, and the Muratorianum would then afford the first formal mention of the two less securely attested epistles along with the established one. In that case, the words, 'in honorem ipsius' in l. 70 can no longer apply, as Harnack thought, to the catholic church, but must refer, as Zahn suggested, to Solomon. Another possibility would be to explain the exclusion of III John by its private character (Γαίῳ τῷ ἀγαπητῷ): Harnack, 'Muratorisches Fragment', p. 379; cf. n. 232 below. Lagrange, *op. cit.*, p. 74 n. 3, takes 'ipsius' as referring to Wisdom itself.

[206] The violent attempt of Zahn, *op. cit.*, II, pp. 105ff., to substitute it for the Apocalypse of Peter in ll. 71ff. of the text no longer calls for refutation.

[207] Personally I regard the correction mentioned in n. 199 above as convincing. According to Zahn's rendering back into Greek (*op. cit.*, II, p. 142) the text (cf. n. 205 above) would then run: ἡ Σοφία Σαλομῶντος, ὑπὸ Φίλωνος εἰς τιμὴν αὐτοῦ συγγραφεῖσα.

[208] Even later still, however, Wisdom, together with other doubtful works, is occasionally mentioned in conjunction with the New Testament writings, as a kind of appendix to both Testaments: Zahn, *op. cit.*, II, pp. 103f.; Lagrange's attempt (*op. cit.*, pp. 74f.) to transfer the words referring to Wisdom to a point after the mention of the Shepherd of Hermas is purely arbitrary. On the general theological significance of Wisdom cf. R. M. Grant, 'The Book of Wisdom at Alexandria', *StudPatr* VII, 1966, pp. 462–472.

[209] Ll. 71ff.: Apocalypses etiam Iohannis et Patri tantum recipimus, quam quidam ex nostris legi in ecclesia nolunt. 'Quidam' is best understood if we supply 'fratres'; but the question is of no importance.

[210] Cf. n. 255 below.

[211] Ll. 81ff.: Arsinoi autem seu Ualentini uel Mi[l]itiadis nihil in totum recipimus, qui etiam nouum psalmorum librum Marcioni conscripserunt, una cum

andrians had already been rejected, together with all other forgeries
of the same sort, a few lines earlier in connection with the Pauline
epistles.[212]

One thing is clear: a decisive effort to secure the exclusion of unde-
sirable material and a conclusion to the debate is the determining factor behind the whole list. The Four Gospels, and very particularly the
Gospel of John,[213] the one history 'of all the Apostles',[214] no more than
thirteen Pauline epistles, and 'only' two prophetic books now form the
inviolable corpus—together with a couple of catholic epistles and the
Wisdom of Solomon.[215] All fabrications by heretics or of recent date

---

Basilide Assianom Catafrycum constitutorem. Lietzmann in his edition (p.
11) rightly remarks on these lines that their contents are 'partly unknown, partly
false: but neither fact justifies emendation'; cf. Labriolle, *Crise*, pp. 287f. The
interesting attempt of A. Adam, 'Die ursprüngliche Sprache der Salomo-Oden',
ZNW 52, 1961, p. 152 n. 30; *Lehrbuch der Dogmengeschichte* I, 1965, p. 142, to
explain the 'psalm-book' as the (Valentinian) Odes of Solomon must remain
simply a hypothesis.

[212] Ll. 63ff.: fertur etiam ad Laodicenses, alia ad Alexandrinos Pauli nomine
finctae ad haeresem Marcionis et alia plura, quae in catholicam ecclesiam recipi
non potest.

[213] Ll. 9ff.: quartum euangeliorum Iohannis ex discipulis. cohortantibus condiscipulis et episcopis suis dixit: 'conieiunate mihi hodie triduo, et quid cuique
fuerit revelatum, alterutrum nobis enarremus.' eadem nocte reuelatum Andreae
ex apostolis, ut recognoscentibus cunctis Iohannes suo nomine cuncta describeret.
This strange legend of the origin of the Gospel is admittedly not without parallels, but is nevertheless extremely surprising in this particular context (Zahn,
op. cit., II, pp. 34ff.), and, as Lietzmann, *Bücher*, p. 55, says, in a way presents
this Gospel as 'the proper one, revised by the apostolic college'. (It is not, however, in my opinion necessary to assume, with O. Cullmann, 'Die Pluralität
der Evangelien als theologisches Problem im Altertum' in: *Vorträge und Aufsätze
1925–1962*, 1966, p. 558, and O. Michel, art. 'Evangelium', *RAC* VI, 1966,
col. 1129, that the legend originally sought to make out the Gospel of John to be
the only Gospel; and even more unnecessary, with J. H. Crehan, 'The Fourfold
Character of the Gospel', *StudEvang* I, 1959, pp. 3–13. to think in terms of a
redaction of all four Gospels by John.) If we also take into account the emphasis
with which John is presented as belonging to the 'discipuli', i.e., the disciples,
meaning the Apostles (not forgetting the further reference back to John in l.
68: cf. n. 205 above), then it would seem that what we have here is a defence
against anti-Johannine tendencies such as had already been noted by Irenaeus
(cf. n. 159 above); cf. Zahn, *op. cit.*, II, pp. 46–49. There is no need, with Lagrange, *op. cit.*, pp. 78ff., and T. W. Manson, 'The Fourth Gospel' in: *Studies
in the Gospels and Epistles*, Manchester, 1962, p. 107, to suppose that Gaius also
is referred to.

[214] This exaggerated title (acta omnium apostolorum) may be directed against
either Marcion's exclusive faith in Paul or other 'inauthentic' Acts of apostles or
both. To my mind the former interpretation is the more probable.

[215] A concessive *sane* admits these after the detailed discussion of the Pauline
epistles and the rejection of all counterfeit Pauline letters and of forgeries in
general (cf. n. 212 above). (In those mediaeval texts which excerpt the Muratorianum [cf. n. 200 above] the heretical works mentioned at the end are also

are excluded. With its trend toward finality and hard-and-fast definition the Muratorianum breathes the spirit of the new, anti-Montanist era.[216] Its orientation is especially discernible in its assessment of the apocalyptic literature.[217] Nevertheless, the Canon is not directed against the Montanists alone. Just as in its beginnings the New Testament, though occasioned by Marcion, was also at the same time meant to counter the Valentinians and all other gnostic false teachers, so now, at its completion, the attempt is made to set it up also once for all as a solid bulwark against all known heresies and heretical writings.

Because the opening lines are missing we do not know under what name this list originally appeared. But that the Muratorianum was meant to be a complete list of all normative writings of the New Covenant, binding upon the whole Church, that is, that it sets out to describe the substance of a New Testament Canon, is not open to doubt.[218] Only in one passage—that relating to the Apocalypse of Peter—does the document admit to a degree of uncertainty; and from the force with which the decision about the 'Shepherd' is underlined and justified we may conclude that on this point there was still opposition to be overcome.[219] Everything else—even the tacit exclusion of Hebrews—is

---

inserted here; but this order cannot be original: Harnack, 'Exzerpte', col. 133.) The situation in fact, as Zahn, *op. cit.*, II, pp. 88, says, is that 'from the last' (i.e., the preceding) 'sentences the reader might receive the impression that with Paul's private letters the list of writings acknowledged by the Church had come to an end'. The extraordinary inclusion of the Wisdom of Solomon confirms the impression that here, in contrast to the rejection of all other epistles, we are dealing with certain exceptional cases, works which were recognised but which in comparison with the Paulines, the really important documents, clearly take a humbler place. According to F. H. Hesse, *Das Muratorische Fragment neu untersucht und erklärt*, 1873, pp. 230ff., the wording must mean that the catholic works are mentioned solely as permitted reading, so that 'the Epistolary which formed the second part of the sacred collection consisted only of Pauline letters' (p. 304). It is, however, out of the question to expound 'in catholica habentur' (l. 69) in such a way.

[216] One may even say, with Overbeck, *op. cit.*, p. 107, that the Muratorianum already adopts the 'normal catholic standpoint', which throughout ancient times, ever since the Canon came into existence, maintained its solidarity in principle, and disregarded it only under pressure when the feeling of uncertainty about particular items became too great. Such a summary characterisation, however, irons out the distinctive features of the various periods far too drastically.

[217] It is hard to understand how E. Schwartz, for whom the Muratorian Canon stands 'at the same stage of tradition' as Papias ('Söhne Zebedäi', p. 87), can state—admittedly in a different context—that the Muratorianum 'has no concern with Montanism' ('Johannes und Kerinthos', p. 175).

[218] N.B. also the emphasis with which in ll. 26ff. (cf. n. 245 below) I Joh. 1:1–4 is expounded—without any support in the text—to stress the completeness of John's narrative (scriptorem omnium mirabilium domini per ordinem).

[219] Harnack, 'Die ältesten Evangelien–Prologe', p. 341: 'One has the clear impression that the formation of the N.T. is on the brink of completion, but

apparently taken for granted. Moreover, the enumeration of the valid Scriptures is not proclaimed as a new regulation by any sort of ecclesiastical court, but is presented as a statement of what already confessedly obtains and must obtain in the 'catholic church'.[220] The term used in this context—*recipere*—meaning to 'accept' or 'recognise', has a positive technical sense; in practice it means no less than that a book is confirmed as authorised reading in the public worship of the Church.[221] The books of the Christian Canon, therefore, now occupy a position of complete equality with the Scriptures of the Old Testament, indeed they are superior rather than inferior to them. As the Fragment remarks somewhat pointedly against Marcion, Paul had not only already set out at considerable length in Romans the right context of the ancient Scriptures, but had also stressed that these were to be understood as referring to Christ as their principal subject-matter[222]— and this Christ is known from the sure testimony of the four 'Books of the Gospels'.[223] This requirement corresponds in fact to the christological exegesis of the Old Testament as practised by Paul and in the Church from time immemorial; but enunciated in so general a form as a basic principle the statement is nevertheless something new. It recalls the related hermeneutical rule of the Valentinians.[224] Only now it has been stripped of its critical connotation, and so 'catholicised'.

The New Testament is thus in complete agreement with the Old, when the latter is rightly understood. Moreover, there must be an equally complete absence of discord between the various statements of the New Testament itself; after all, that is obviously what a 'canon' implies. Yet this principle—as in Irenaeus—is discussed only in relation to the Gospels; for it is here that the problem was inherent from the start, that is to say, from the formation of the Four Gospel 'canon' onwards, and plainly it is still a living issue. The Muratorian Canon,

---

that the line has not yet been drawn across the page—indeed, it is still necessary to make an explicit rejection of notoriously heretical writings. On the other hand, the house which in Irenaeus's time had not yet been completely roofed is now considered as much of a dwelling-place and fortress as the O.T.'

[220] L. 66: . . . in catholicam ecclesiam recipi non potest; l. 69: . . . in catholica habentur (cf. n. 205 above); ll. 77f.: se publicare in ecclesia (cf. n. 256 below); l. 82: . . . nihil in totum recipimus.

[221] Ll. 72f.: . . . . (Apoc. Pet.) quidam ex nostris legi in ecclesia nolunt. Ll. 77f. (Shepherd) . . . legi eum quidem oportet, se publicare vero in ecclesia populo neque inter prophetas . . . neque inter apostolos . . . potest. Cf. P. Glaue, *Die Vorlesung heiliger Schriften im Gottesdienst* I, 1907, pp. 79–83.

[222] Ll. 44ff.: Romanis autem ordinem scripturarum, sed et principium earum esse Christum intimans prolixius scripsit. Cf. Zahn, *op. cit.*, II, pp. 63–65.

[223] So l. 2: tertium evangelii librum secundum Lucam; l. 9: quartum evangeliorum Iohannis; ll. 16f.: singulis evangeliorum libris: cf Zahn, *op. cit.*, II, p. 40 n. 1, and pp. 172ff. above.

[224] Cf. pp. 84f. above.

like Irenaeus[225] and Gaius as well,[226] takes as its starting-point in particular the 'beginnings', that is, the opening sections, of the Gospels,
in which the differences between them are most starkly clear. It does
not, however, follow up the attempts at typological and symbolic interpretation which Irenaeus had put forward, but is content with flatly
asserting the essential agreement of the Gospels in face of all objections and difficulties: what is provided in all the Gospels is one and the
same testimony to Christ. 'And therefore, though various "beginnings"
are taught in the several Gospel books, yet that matters nothing for
the faith of Christians, since by the one guiding Spirit everything is
made known in all of them: the birth, the passion, the resurrection, the
intercourse with his disciples, and his twofold coming, first despised in
lowliness, which has already taken place, then in the splendour of kingly
power, which is still in the future.'[227] Hence it can hardly be maintained
that the writer of the Muratorianum must have known and read
Ireaneus;[228] the course of his argumentation is anyway quite
different.[229]

Nevertheless, it would be wrong to think of this difference as a positive contrast:[230] the same symbolic-sacral play on numbers which the
Muratorianum avoids in the case of the Gospels it applies in very

---

[225] Cf. p. 191 above.   [226] Cf. n. 166 above.

[227] Ll. 16ff.: licet varia singulis evangeliorum libris principia doceantur,
nihil tamen differt credentium fidei, cum uno ac principali spiritu declarata
sint in omnibus omnia: de nativitate, de passione, de resurrectione, de conversatione cum discipulis suis ac de gemino eius adventu, primo in humilitate de-
spectus, quod fuit, secundo in potestate regali praeclaro, quod futurum est.
The meaning of the word 'principia' is disputed. One suggestion is that it refers
to the 'principles' or 'tendencies' expressed in the various Gospels, in support
of which one might perhaps cite Tertullian, Adv. Marc. IV, 2, 2: viderit enim
si narrationum dispositio variavit, dummodo de capite fidei conveniat . . . To
my mind, however, there can be no doubt that the interpretation given by Harnack, 'Muratorisches Fragment', p. 394 n. 1, and Zahn, op. cit., II, pp. 42–44,
who supports it with numerous parallels, even though from a later period, is
the only correct and indeed possible one. The apparently intentional pun which
results from the translating of πνεῦμα ἡγεμονικόν by 'principalis spiritus',
is quite fortuitous (Zahn, op. cit., II, p. 41 n. 1). The 'conversatio cum discipulis'
is an allusion to the 'Conversations of Jesus with his disciples after the Resurrection'; the purpose is to exclude heretical literature of this sort. The order of
the items in the list is therefore strictly chronological.

[228] So Zahn, Forschungen zur Geschichte des neutestamentlichen Kanons X,
1929, p. 64.

[229] Later, e.g., Adamantius expresses himself in a way very similar to that of
the Muratorianum: Dial. I, 6: si vero toti quattuor de uno Christo loquuntur,
non sunt quattuor, sed unum est evangelium.

[230] As Cullmann, op. cit., pp. 562ff., tends to do; cf. p. 203 n. 267 above.
Furthermore, we cannot be absolutely certain that the lost opening section of
the Muratorianum did not speak of the significance of the fact that the Gospels
are four in number.

Irenaean fashion to the corpus of Paul's letters to the churches. Here, it is true, the point at issue is not so much that of inner unity as the universal validity and completeness of the collection. Paul, the argument runs, did not bestow his epistles on precisely seven churches simply by accident. He was following the example of his predecessor John, who likewise at the beginning of his Revelation wrote to no more than seven churches specifically.[231] But although Paul addresses only seven churches, that mysterious number shows—to complete the thought— that this definitely did not come about by chance, and that what was taught to particular churches 'nevertheless was said to all'.[232]

The author of the Muratorianum is here wrestling with a problem of which others too had been aware, and which was responsible, among other things, for the 'catholicising' corrections to the Pauline epistles: namely that the particularity of the occasions which had given rise to the epistles seemed to be an obstacle to their universal relevance and their liturgical use.[233] But it is obvious that the sevenfold pattern, which may also have determined the form of the collection of Ignatius's Epistles, can be applied to the Pauline letters only with some difficulty, since it accords not with the number of the epistles but only with the

[231] Ll. 46ff. : . . . de quibus singulis necesse est a nobis disputari, cum ipse beatus apostolus Paulus sequens prodecessoris sui Iohannis ordinem non nisi nominatim septem ecclesiis scribat. . . . The odd statement that the Apocalypse served as a model for Paul should not be pressed to imply deliberate imitation on Paul's part (so Zahn, *Geschichte*, II, p. 69) but neither should it be denied that it is there (*id.*, *Forschungen* X, p. 71). In any case what cannot be disputed is Zahn's statement (*Geschichte* II, pp. 73f.) that the Muratorianum 'asserts that the fact that Paul's letters to the churches are seven in number has a symbolic significance which is evidence of their importance as catholic documents.'

[232] Ll. 54ff.: verum Corinthiis et Thessalonicensibus licet pro correptione iteretur, una tamen per omnem orbem terrae ecclesia diffusa esse dinoscitur. et Iohannes enim in apocalypsi licet septem ecclesiis scribat, tamen omnibus dicit. For an explanation of the grammar of these sentences which 'condensed expression has made obscure' cf. Lietzmann in his edition, pp. 7f.; Dahl, 'Welche Ordnung', p. 44 n. 12, expresses a more cautious view. The idea developed in this passage is also to be found in substance in Hippolytus, Cyprian, Victorinus and others, and there is therefore no necessity to regard it as 'conceived for the first time by the author of the Fragment' (*ibid.*, p. 45); cf. earlier Tertullian, Adv. Marc. V, 17, 1: nihil autem de titulis interest, cum ad omnes apostolus scripserit, dum ad quosdam.

[233] Cf. N. A. Dahl, 'The particularity of the Pauline Epistles as a problem in the Ancient Church', in: *Neotestamentica et Patristica* (Cullmann-Festschrift), 1962, pp. 261–271. A less happy suggestion is put forward by K. Stendhal, 'The Apocalypse of John and the Epistles of Paul in the Muratorian Fragment' in *Current Issues in New Testament Interpretation* (Piper Festschrift), 1962, pp. 239–245, who follows Leipoldt (cf. n. 48 above) in thinking of a legitimation of the Pauline Epistles by the inspired Apocalypse. At a later period there were still some who disputed the right of Philemon to be in the Canon on these grounds: Zahn, *op. cit.*, I, pp. 267ff.; Bauer, *Der Apostolos der Syrer*, pp. 23f.; Leipoldt, *op. cit.*, I, pp. 207ff.

number of different churches addressed. But even with this expedient the symbolic arrangement still causes some trouble, because it works only for those letters addressed to churches, and cannot allow for Philemon and the Pastorals.[234] This the author himself admits. These private documents, it is asserted, were, it is true, originally composed only out of personal 'goodwill and love', but were later 'held sacred for the glory of the catholic church' and 'for the ordering of church discipline', that is, for the sake of their contents.[235] In other words: 'Paul did not write them as "canonical" documents, but the Church soon recognised their value for ecclesiastical order, and honoured herself by canonising these important writings.'[236]

For us it is important to note that this sevenfold pattern, like the fourfold pattern of the Gospels, is patently something already existing which the Muratorianum took over, and not something which it created. Each of the individual groups of 'sanctified' writings was first arranged separately, and defended in this particular arrangement, before they were brought together in a new and greater whole. Hence only the individual sections—the Gospels, the Pauline epistles, even the Apocalypses—were enumerated on their own;[237] there was still no continuous numbering of all the books of the Bible, and even less was there any idea of a symbolic interpretation of the total number, such as already existed for the Old Testament in the Judaism of the time.[238] Nevertheless, we can now detect the desire to treat the new collection of Scriptures as a single and—and this is the really new element—as a closed corpus which is to remain in force universally and for ever.

By what criterion was the selection made? What is the basis of the sacred authority of those writings which the catholic Church has 'accepted', while banning others from official use, and not only heretical

---

[234] K. L. Carroll, 'The Expansion of the Pauline Corpus', *JBL* 72, 1953, p. 235, conjectures as regards the Pauline epistles that in Irenaeus there may already be some consideration of a gematria relating to the number thirteen; but such an assumption has no foundation in fact.

[235] Ll. 59ff.: verum ad Philemonem unam et ad Titum unam et ad Timotheum duas pro affectu et dilectione (sc. scripsit), in honorem tamen ecclesiae catholicae in ordinationem ecclesiasticae disciplinae sanctificatae sunt. On the semantic history of *sanctificare* cf. C. Mohrmann, 'Quelques traits caractéristiques du latin des chrétiens,' *Études sur le latin des Chrétiens* I², Rome, 1961, p. 25; R. Braun, "*Deus Christianorum*". *Recherches sur le vocabulaire doctrinal de Tertullien*, Paris, 1962, pp. 524–526.

[236] Lietzmann, *Bücher*, p. 58. According to Harnack, 'Über den Verfasser', p. 11 n. 1, Lagrange, *op. cit.*, p. 73 n. 6, and Bardy, *oop. cit.*, col. 1402, these letters would have been 'sanctified' for church use not by the Church but already by Paul himself.

[237] The numbering of the Gospels is clear enough; on the enumeration of the Pauline letters cf. n. 253 below.

[238] Cf. p. 260 n. 199 above.

ones at that? This is the crucial question for the theological understanding of the Muratorian Canon. In recent scholarly literature it
receives, so far as I can see, almost always the same answer: the Muratorianum keeps to the 'apostolic', or, to be more precise, the 'prophetic-
apostolic' principle. In other words: as the author saw it, the Old
Testament was written by prophets, the New by apostles. Apostolic
origin is thus the basis of the New Testament's title and the criterion
by which its limits are determined. 'In principle nothing belongs in
the New Testament which does not derive from the apostles,' is the
verdict of, for example, Lietzmann: 'that is the theoretical standpoint'.[239]

Harnack's interpretation of the document as an official production
of the Roman see has not been able to hold its ground; but it would
seem that this theory enabled him to prevail over Zahn.[240] His view
should, of course, be seen in a wider context, and affects the whole
question of how the New Testament Canon came into being. We
have already had to take issue in the present work with similar modern
interpretations in the case of Papias and Irenaeus, even indeed of Paul
and Luke.[241] Now it is a matter of arriving at an impartial understanding of the Muratorian Canon and of what it has to tell us. In my own
opinion the Muratorian Canon is not primarily interested in the apostolic 'principle', but is merely asking for documents which are ancient
and reliable. The apostles are naturally the most notable authors of
such works, but they owe that position to their status not as apostles
but as witnesses to the Christ-event and to the teaching which in the
first instance was entrusted to them.[242] On this point the Muratorianum
is in complete agreement with Irenaeus. Its method of proceeding may
be dogmatic, but the critical principle in accordance with which the
sources are scrutinised is nevertheless determined by historical or, if
preferred, dogmatic-salvation-history considerations.

This concern with historical certainty comes out clearly in the (un-

[239] Lietzmann, *Bücher*, p. 59.
[240] On this point he agrees with the even more dogmatic Overbeck; cf. in
addition to the latter's *Zur Geschichte des Kanons*, M. Tetz, *Overbeckiana* II,
1962, pp. 159f. (A 345). What is more, Harnack, in his early work, 'Über das
Muratorische Fragment', p. 369, sees just as clearly as Zahn that any inversion
of the supposed principle, that is to say, any 'idea that everything apostolic
must be canonical', is completely alien to the Muratorianum.
[241] Cf. pp. 114ff., 126ff., 131ff., 195ff. above.
[242] Even Lietzmann, *Bücher*, p. 56, contrary to his overall interpretation,
rightly remarks about the Gospels: 'Our Fragmentist is concerned simply to
demonstrate or defend their value as historical sources.' Similarly E. Flesseman-
van Leer, 'Prinzipien der Sammlung und Ausscheidung bei der Bildung des
Kanon', *ZTK* 61, 1964, p. 411: like Irenaeus the Muratorian Canon principally
attaches 'value to the testimony of eyewitnesses. Apostolicity as a sign of canonicity is thus primarily a historical, not a dogmatic, concept.'

fortunately incomplete) discussion of the Gospels. Neither Mark nor Luke were apostles, and it may be that it is in contrast to them that John is expressly described as 'one of the disciples'.[243] But—apart from the miraculous commissioning and the co-operation of all the other disciples[244]—what particularly distinguishes his presentation is simply this, that it rests on the evidence of his own eyes and experience. This is the angle which the Muratorianum expressly emphasises: John himself said of himself, that he wrote what he had seen with his eyes, heard with his ears, and handled with his own hands. In other words, he really was a genuine witness whose account of 'all the marvellous acts of the Lord' is therefore worthy of confidence.[245] Conversely, Mark and Luke are not reproached with lacking apostolic authority. It is true that their testimony is at second hand. But this does not lessen their value for us, since all the Gospels, it is argued, agree in substance.[246] Mark in his Gospel followed the teaching discourses of Peter,[247] while Luke was a companion of Paul, which certainly implies that his Gospel was basically constructed in accordance with the latter's teaching.[248]

---

[243] L. 9: quartum evangeliorum Iohannis ex discipulis. Probably, however, this more precise definition of his person was formulated only in opposition to those who disputed the Gospel of John: cf. n. 213 above.

[244] For the text cf. n. 213 above.

[245] Ll. 26ff.: quid ergo mirum, si Iohannes tam constanter singula etiam in epistulis suis profert dicens in semetipsum: "quae vidimus oculis nostris et auribus audivimus et manus nostrae palpaverunt, haec scripsimus vobis" (I Joh. 1:1, 3f.). sic enim non solum visorem et auditorem, sed et scriptorem omnium mirabilium domine per ordinem profitetur. Cf. also the emphasis which II Peter, which is fairly close to the Muratorianum in date, lays on the status of eye-witness (1:16, 18).

[246] Cf. n. 227 above. As against Zahn, op. cit., II, p. 40, the text (declarata in omnibus omnia) must be taken to mean what it says, namely that in each Gospel everything of importance about Jesus is related—however remiss such a sweeping assertion may seem in fact to be in view of many of the items detailed. This point was long ago made by G. Kuhn, Das muratorische Fragment und die Bücher des Neuen Testaments, Zurich, 1892, p. 53 n. 1.

[247] As is well known, all we have about Mark is a fragment of one sentence: 'quibus tamen interfuit, et ita posuit.' Zahn, op. cit., II, 17ff., and, among others, also Lietzmann, Bücher, p. 53 n. 2, think that here we may have an assertion that Mark was an eyewitness of at least some of the events of the life of Jesus. It is far more probable, however, that the reference in this passage, as in Papias (Eusebius, HE III, 39, 15) and Irenaeus (Adv. haer. III, 1, 1), is to Peter's discourses which Mark recorded just as he had heard them; so, among others, Lagrange, op. cit., p. 71, and Schwartz, 'Söhne Zebedäi', pp. 81f.; Bardy, op. cit., col. 1401; Schneemelcher, N.T. Apocrypha I, p. 42, and Ehrhardt, 'Gospels', pp. 12f.

[248] It would be safe to say this if, with Overbeck, op. cit., pp. 135ff., or Schwartz, 'Söhne', pp. 82 n. 1, we could expand the enigmatic prase 'ex opinione' into 'ex opinione Pauli' = Παύλου γνώμη. This, however, is by no means certain, as is shown by the wealth of suggested emendations and translations (cf. Ritter, op. cit., pp. 255f.). The strongest contrast to this would be the inter-

The idea, however, is not elaborated. The text at this point is unfortunately somewhat obscure. What is clear is that Luke wrote in his own name and on the basis of all the sources accessible to him, but that he himself had not seen the Lord in the flesh.[249] Obviously the Muratorianum, like Irenaeus, is here keeping to the data of the Lukan prologue.[250] The Gospel accordingly is seen as a historical work, and not as merely reproducing 'apostolic' instruction; and no more for Luke than for Mark is there any idea of a special authorisation in the form of subsequent inspection or approval on the part of the apostles.[251] It is enough that their account is reliable and can be trusted. In the same way the bold assertion is made with regard to Acts that here Luke's intention was to record only what he himself had experienced, and that this is why he conscientiously kept silent about Peter's martyrdom and Paul's journey to Spain.[252] Even in the case of Paul himself the historical orientation is apparent: his epistles are listed by the Muratorianum not in the 'canonical' sequence, but chronologically,[253] though in defining their content it is, of course, once again the contemporary concerns of the Church which are given expression.[254]

Of decisive importance for our present concern are the reasons given for excluding the 'Shepherd'. It is precisely these which the champions of the 'apostolic principle' particularly advance in favour of their

---

pretation of 'opinio' as ἀκοή, proposed by H. Rönsch, *Das Neue Testament Tertullians,* 1871, p. 152 n., and adopted, among others, by Lietzmann, *Bücher,* p. 53; cf. his edition, p. 5 *ad loc.* Zahn, *op. cit.,* II, p. 29, rightly as it seems to me, is firmly opposed to this solution.

[249] Ll. 3 ff.: Lucas iste medicus, post ascensum Christi cum eum Paulus quasi iuris (litteris? itineris?) studiosum secum adsumpsisset, nomine suo ex opinione conscripsit, dominum tamen nec ipse vidit in carne et ideo prout assequi potuit ita et a nativitate Iohannis incipit dicere.

[250] Cf. p. 206 n. 293 above. When the Muratorianum in the case of Luke emphasises his independence, this is in agreement with Irenaeus, and does not, as Harnack, 'Muratorisches Fragment', p. 368 n. 1, thought, represent 'an earlier, more impartial view than that of Irenaeus'.

[251] Later on such suppositions occur regularly.

[252] Ll. 34ff.: acta autem omnium apostolorum sub uno libro scripta sunt. Lucas 'optimo Theophilo' comprendit, quae sub praesentia eius singula gerebantur, sicuti et semota passione Petri evidenter declarat, sed et profectione Pauli ab urbe ad Spaniam proficiscentis.

[253] That the author of the Fragment must 'have thought, judging by the form of his list, that his sequence really was chronological', had already been stated by Harnack, 'Über den Verfasser', p. 11 n. 3, as also by Zahn, *op. cit.,* II, pp. 59f. Dahl, *op. cit.* n. 198 above, has shown that in doing so, however, he was not following the order of the epistles in the collection he was using.

[254] Ll. 42ff.: primum omnium Corinthiis schismae haereses interdicens, deinceps Galatis circumcisionem, Romanis autem ordinem scripturarum, sed et principium earum esse Christum intimans prolixius scripsit.

theory.[255] The passage runs: 'But Hermas wrote the Shepherd only recently, in our time in the city of Rome, when on the throne of the church of the city of Rome Bishop Pius, his brother, was seated. Therefore it must indeed be read, but cannot be publicly recited to the people in church—neither among the prophets, whose number is filled, nor among the apostles, who taught at the end of the times.'[256] Here, so we are assured, it is bluntly stated that the New Testament liturgical Scriptures must derive from the apostles. But if the text were really to be taken in this sense, then the author of the Muratorianum would be contradicting what he himself had said earlier; for neither Mark nor Luke were apostles, and yet no attempt is made to compensate in any way for this supposed deficiency in their case. The fact is that the designation of 'apostle', as is also true elsewhere, has more an *a parte potiori* sense—in exactly the same way that the parallel term 'prophet' is used to cover the writers of the Old Testament.[257] Were it otherwise, and

[255] Overbeck, *op. cit.*, p. 109: 'The view of the Muratorian Fragment on the principle of the apostolicity of the New Testament is most directly indicated by the section on the apocalypses (ll. 71–80)'; cf. Leipoldt, *op. cit.*, I, pp. 47f.; Lietzmann, *Bücher*, pp. 58f.; Kümmel, *op. cit.*, p. 362 *et al.* K. L. Carroll, 'The Earliest New Testament', *BJRL* 38, 1955–6, p. 56, however, prefers to base his case on the insertion of the word 'omnium' (i.e., apostolorum) into the title of Acts, l. 34; on this cf. n. 214 above.

[256] Ll. 73ff.: Pastorem vero nuperrime temporibus nostris in urbe Roma Hermas conscripsit sedente cathedra urbis Romae ecclesiae Pio episcopo fratre eius; et ideo legi eum quidem oportet, se publicare vero in ecclesia populo neque inter prophetas completo numero neque inter apostolos in fine temporum potest. For a detailed discussion of the linguistic problems cf. Zahn, *op. cit.*, II, p. 111 n. 1. Against the superfluous theory of 'extra services', in which Hermas was banned, cf. Glaue, *op. cit.*, pp. 82f.

[257] As Kuhn, *op. cit.*, p. 101 rightly observes: 'It is extremely probable that *prophetae* here signifies the O.T. in general, not merely the Prophets in the narrower sense. . . . In the same way *apostoli* must here signify the N.T. in general, since even the Gospels rest on apostolic authority. *Prophetae et apostoli* = Old and New Testament.' (That 'the Gospels rest on apostolic authority' is not however stated by the Muratorianum with that degree of exactitude.) Cf. so early a work as II Clem. 14, 2: καὶ ἔτι τὰ βιβλία τῶν προφητῶν καὶ οἱ ἀπόστολοι, where 'apostles' admittedly does not yet clearly refer to written documents, but by the same token has even less in mind an *apostolos* as a mere part of the N.T., which is the sense in which Zahn, *op. cit.*, I, p. 809, wishes to take it: H. Köster, *Synoptische Überlieferung bei den Apostolischen Vätern*, 1957, p. 68 n. 7. Cf. further Polycarp, *Phil.* 6, 3: . . . καθὼς αὐτὸς ἐνετείλατο καὶ οἱ εὐαγγελισάμενοι ἡμᾶς ἀπόστολοι καὶ οἱ προφῆται, οἱ προκηρύξαντες τὴν ἔλευσιν τοῦ κυρίου ἡμῶν. The semantic usage of 'prophets' in Justin and his 'prophetic' proof from Scripture is clear: E. Flesseman van Leer, *Tradition and Scripture in the Early Church*, 1954, pp. 72, 98, and earlier, Glaude, *op. cit.*, p. 67: 'It admits of no doubt that Justin uses the designation τὰ συγγράμματα τῶν προφητῶν (cf. similarly αἱ βίβλοι τῶν προφητῶν: I Apol. 31, 7; 44, 12) for all the O.T. writings, even the Hagiographa. In doing so he is guided by the principle of *a potiori fit denominatio*.' But we also find in Justin the precise parallelism of the συγγράμματα τῶν προφητῶν with the ἀπομνημονεύματα τῶν ἀποστόλων (I Apol.

had the author really wished to base his exclusion of Hermas on the apostolic principle, he would have been able to save himself all those more detailed comments; for no one ever imagined that Hermas was an apostle.[258] What the passage is meant to point out is something quite different: by the time of Hermas the old, apostolic period has come to an end. The chronological angle is stressed no fewer than three times, and it alone constitutes the reason for excluding the Shepherd from the Canon.[259] This is all the more significant, since there are no valid

---

67, 3; cf. p. 168 n. 95 above), where the important point to note is that for Justin this phrase covers not only apostolic writings in the strict sense but also the works of 'companions' of the apostles (Dial. 103, 8; similarly Irenaeus, cf. p. 204 n. 284 above). The same meaning occurs in Irenaeus, Adv. haer. III, 19, 2; 24, 1; and Hippolytus, Comm. Dan. IV, 12, 1 (ἐπεὶ οὖν τοῦτον πάντες οἱ προφῆται καὶ ἀπόστολοι μαρτυροῦσιν); cf. N. Bonwetsch, Studien zu den Kommentaren Hippolyts, pp. 20f. Cf. also Tertullian, De pudic. 12, 2: non in apostolis quoque veteris legis forma soluta . . . ; Origen, De princ. IV, 2, 7: . . . τοὺς διακόνους τῆς ἀληθείας, προφήτας καὶ ἀποστόλους . . .

[258] Nevertheless, Origen did wish to identify the Hermas mentioned once in Rom. 16:14, in a list of what Origen calls 'disciples of the apostle' with the author of the Shepherd, clearly with the desire of thus raising the status of the book. In Comm. Rom. X, 31, he gives as his opinion: quod Hermas iste sit scriptor libelli illius, qui Pastor appellatur, quae scriptura valde mihi utilis videtur et puto divinitus inspirata; cf. Harnack, in the Prolegomena to his edition of Hermas, p. LVI n. 1. But this is a purely isolated instance, and does not indicate that the Muratorianum was in any way aware of such ideas, to say nothing of being prepared to champion them. It is true that as regards the testimony of the Fragment in the abstract one may 'perhaps have certain suspicions that the author wanted to discredit the "Shepherd", and was therefore quite clearly glad to date it as late as possible' (Dibelius, Kommentar, p. 421; similarly Chadwick, op. cit., pp. 276ff.). Nevertheless, this is no reason for regarding the ascription to the brother of Pius (so also Ps.–Tertullian, Carm. adv. Marc. III, 294) as simply a tendentious invention in the style of a 'definite form of scholarly polemic', as is the view of E. Peterson, 'Kritische Analyse der fünften Vision des Hermas', Frühkirche, Judentum und Gnosis, 1959, pp. 271, 283; cf. contra E. Molland, art. 'Hermas', RGG III³, 1959, p. 242; P. Vielhauer in N.T. Apocrypha II, p. 642. St. Giet, Hermas et les Pasteurs: Les trois auteurs du Pasteur d'Hermas, Paris, 1963, pp. 287–289, maintains that the information in the Fragment is historically correct at least as regards one of the authors; similarly L. W. Barnard, VC 18, 1964, p. 186.

[259] Zahn, op. cit., II, p. 113: 'He [sc. the Fragmentist] justifies his decision simply by this statement that the book is of recent origin, and by this alone . . . '; p. 116: 'The number of the apostolic writings was not something settled, unalterable, and everywhere the same. . . . Acceptance of the Shepherd could not be contested on those grounds; nor with the argument that the author of the Shepherd had not been an apostle. . . . The only grounds on which the Sheperd was to be excluded for ever from this circle were these: that it was a recent book, written no earlier than the year 145'; cf. id., I, pp. 116f. In addition there is controversy about the meaning and grammatical status of the phrase in the text, 'in fine temporum'. Hesse, op. cit., pp. 270, 300, and Zahn, op. cit., II, p. 113 et al. take it to mean that public reading of the work is forbidden until 'the end

practical objections raised; indeed, for private reading it is actually recommended. In taking this line the Muratorianum is adopting the same anti-Montanist stance as the polemical writer who disputed the right of Themison, with the authority of the Spirit, to imitate 'the Apostle' and to write 'catholic' documents for circulation. Hermas no longer lives in the 'apostolic age', he is no longer a representative of the classical era, and therefore he does not belong in a canon which collects and gives binding force to the documents of this primitive period.[260] 'Primitive Christianity' finally belongs to the past, and may not be extended.[261] This is the determining and delimiting principle behind the new Canon.

The predominant importance of the apostles is, of course, disputed by no one. They are the first and most notable witnesses to Jesus, and possess outstanding authority and holiness. This status is already theirs in Irenaeus, and within the catholic church it is absolutely taken for granted. But what everywhere, including the Muratorianum, is of decisive importance is not the apostolic but the original tradition, of the written record of which the apostles are certainly, the first but not necessarily the only guarantors. For after all they themselves are not the

---

of time'. Lietzmann and others see it as referring to the fact that the author is a contemporary, as opposed to those who lived in the apostolic age: 'now, at the end of the ages, this book written *nuperrime* cannot be included among the ancient apostles' (edn., p. 11). In fact, however, we are dealing here with a classic expression from the language of Christian eschatology, embracing the whole period from Christ's appearing down to the Last Day; cf. W. C. van Unnik, 'Der Ausdruck "In den letzten Zeiten" bei Irenäus' in: *Neotestamentica et Patristica* (Cullmann Festschrift), 1962, pp. 293–304. The note of time is therefore to be understood as contrasted with the era of the Old Covenant and of the 'Prophets'; and the apostles in particular are to be thought of only as falling *within* this all-embracing period: G. Rauschen, *Monumenta minora saeculi secundi* (Florilegium patristicum 3², 1914), p. 34 ('fortasse'), and Lagrange, *op. cit.*, p. 74 n. 6.

[260] Conversely this explains the acceptance of the 'Philonic' Wisdom of Solomon (cf. n. 207 above).

[261] In addition to Zahn this view was put forward among earlier scholars by Kuhn, *op. cit.*, p. 102: 'For catholic Christians the corpus of revelatory documents was closed with the apostolic age.' Cf. also K. Aland, 'The Problem of Anonymity and Pseudonymity in Christian Literature of the first two Centuries', *JTS* N.S. 12, 1961, pp. 39–49: 'The apostolic age was a closed epoch of the distant past fundamentally different from the present. Writings belonging to that age must be distinguished from those which did not belong to it.' Aland rightly identified the view taken by the Muratorianum, when in 'Das Problem des neutestamentlichen Kanons', *Studien zur Überlieferung des Neuen Testaments und seines Textes*, 1967, p. 11, he wrote: 'Canonical books must be old (ll. 73f.)—in the end that is the only principle which is adhered to.' But in order to be able to retain the concept of apostolicity, on p. 10—in very much the same way as Lietzmann—he nevertheless contradicts the principle which he has rightly proclaimed by also asserting that 'the authors of canonical scriptures must be apostles'.

S

origin of the tradition, but witnesses to the story and teaching of Christ. (In the Muratorianum there is a striking preference for the history; compared with Irenaeus, the anti-gnostic interest in the teaching is much less prominent.) The Gospels contain the essential data of the life of Jesus, which are the direct concern of faith;[262] the Acts of the Apostles is a faithful, though not quite complete, presentation of the deeds of 'all' the apostles; John and Paul moreover, as time and circumstances dictated, supplied in their epistles instructions in accordance with which the Church everywhere is to teach and live. The reliability, the universality and the accuracy of the documents is stressed; and in the case of the Gospel of John, against which objections had been raised, a particularly impressive account of its origin is provided: not only did all the apostles share in its composition, but there is especial emphasis on the fact that John himself was an eyewitness. Nowhere, however, is apostolic authorship as such made a reason for or a precondition of canonical status, nor conversely is the absence of such authorship a motive for rejecting those works which are 'not received'.[263] It is significant that the concept of the apostle, which in later times is so frequently stressed, is only once used with emphasis in the whole of the Muratorianum, and that is for the 'blessed apostle Paul',[264] the apostle *par excellence*, for whom this designation is traditional. In some few other passages the title of apostle, used unemphatically, is for no discernible reason interchangeable with that of disciple; and in the great majority of instances the 'apostolic' personalities are simply mentioned by name without any indication of rank.[265] If their apostolic status had been determinative for the validity of their writings, then one would have expected a quite different picture.

Nevertheless, even in the Muratorianum it is not age and authenti-

[262] Cf. the text quoted in n. 211 above. There is no longer any mention of the sayings of Jesus, and even the dogmatic 'teachings' take a secondary place compared with the history. This can hardly be regarded, with Harnack, 'Muratorisches Fragment', p. 396, as indicating a particular anti-gnostic interest; rather is it a sign that directly theological controversy is receding in importance.

[263] The opponents of the Apocalypse of Peter cannot have regarded it as Petrine; but this was the consequence and no more the starting-point of their criticism than in the case of the rejection of the Gospel of Peter by Bishop Serapion (cf. p. 169 above).

[264] Ll. 47f.; cf. n. 231 above.

[265] L. 9: Johannes ex discipulis; 10: cohortantibus condiscipulis; 22: de conversatione cum discipulis. By contrast, 'apostle' as a title occurs once only for Paul (cf. n. 264 above), in l. 14 for Andrew (ex apostolis), in l. 34 in the title of Acts, and in l. 80, in the passage about Hermas under discussion (n. 256 above). In all other passages the apostles are mentioned simply by name, without title. The view of Ehrhardt, *Gospels*, p. 14, that John is here deliberately included among the disciples and not the apostles, comes to grief on ll. 10 and 22 (de conversatione cum discipulis): 'apostoli' and 'discipuli' are obviously used at random.

city alone which win respect for the canonical Scriptures. In practice the crucial factor is clearly the usage and judgment of the one true Church, spread throughout the world.[266] Here she is seen not in an official, but very much in a universal, 'catholic' light, as a sacred reality. What is held in esteem in her is not imposed by arbitrary decree; there are objective reasons for it, proved by practical experience. It is not exempt from all discussion; the Muratorianum does not altogether deny that differences of opinion still exist, and it exerts itself to overcome them. But where the Church has arrived at a final acceptance or rejection, a decision has been made which is henceforth unalterable.[267] This certainly does not set the Church 'over' the Canon nor make it into the real source of the Canon's authority. But the Church is indeed the place in which the definitive verdict on the worth or worthlessness of individual writings is handed down; for the Church—if one may complete the thought along Irenaean lines—has within her the living Canon, the Spirit of truth which has been active from the beginning, and to which she remains faithful.

In saying this, however, we have ascribed to the Muratorian Canon a theological attitude which goes beyond the direct statements of the text. Nowhere is there any mention of the Spirit and the life which it creates, nor of the continuing effectual power of the ancient tradition. In its utterances we can discern only 'catholic', not genuinely theological concerns. Interest in 'doctrine' seems remarkably feebly developed, even where the subject under discussion is the content of the Pauline epistles. Only the anti-Marcionite affirmation of the Old Testament, and the boundary-lines against Judaism and heresy, are everywhere clearly set out; but beyond that all we hear on the positive side is merely something about the holiness of Christian discipline.[268] The theological poverty of the Muratorianum is not solely the result of the brevity of its text; it must be characteristic of the anti-heretical spirit of vulgar Catholicism in the Western church around the turn of the century. For us, nevertheless, the Muratorianum is a valuable document: it displays for the first time the concept of a collection of New Testament

---

[266] Ll. 55ff.: una tamen per omnem orbem terrae ecclesia diffusa esse dinoscitur; 61ff.: in honorem tamen ecclesiae catholicae in ordinationem ecclesiasticae disciplinae sanctificatae sunt; 66: in catholicam ecclesiam recipi; 69: in catholica (cf. n. 205 above); 73: legi in ecclesia; 75f.: cathedra urbis Romae ecclesiae; 77f.: se publicare in ecclesia populo.

[267] Nevertheless, Harnack, 'Tertullians Bibliothek christlicher Schriften', *Sitz. Berl. Akad.* 1914, p. 305, goes a great deal too far when he asserts that the author of the Muratorian Fragment 'pronounces' the new collection 'to be still open to enlargement (at the discretion of the Church)'. This is to make the Church's necessity not just into a virtue but into a positive capability.

[268] Ll. 42ff., n. 254 above; ll. 61ff., n. 266 above; cf. also ll. 54f.: verum Corinthiis et Thessalonicensibus licet pro correptione iteretur.

scriptures, which has deliberately been closed, and the individual books of which are regarded as 'accepted' and ecclesiastically 'sanctified',[269] that is to say, that—as Gaius may already have intended—they have been 'incorporated' into the valid corpus.[270] We have thus arrived at the end of the long journey which leads to a New Testament thought of as 'canonical' in the strict sense. Only one thing is still lacking: the precise name for this collection, which will make it possible to refer to the new Scripture as a unity, and thus at one and the same time both to distinguish it from the old Scriptures and to combine it with them in a new totality. This terminological process was, it would seem, already set in train during the fight against Montanism, and was almost complete before the middle of the third century. This is the last feature still wanting to the accomplishment of the bipartite Christian Bible.

We must realise that at this time the format of the Scriptures, from the technical angle of book production, did not as yet suggest any need for a comprehensive nomenclature of this kind.[271] There was no such thing as an Old Testament or a New Testament as a single physical entity. To the eye the whole Canon was still fragmented into a series of separate rolls or volumes. It is true that expert opinion today considers that the Church of the second century was already using the 'Codex'—sometimes even illustrated—in place of the less handy and permanent scroll.[272] But even such a codex certainly did not as yet comprise the whole 'New Testament', but at most separate groups of writings, such as 'the Gospel' or the Pauline Epistles,[273] and these then all counted as the 'scriptures' or the 'scripture' in the wider sense.[274] Even Marcion, despite his pronounced sense of canonicity, apparently still had no common name for his Gospel and Apostle.[275] But in addition he made no use of the Old Testament; the Church, which knew and recognised different kinds of 'scripture' could not let matters rest at that stage.

There was no reason why in themselves the two parts of the Bible should not have different names. In the early period one possibility suggested itself almost automatically: if one had the New and the Old Testament in mind, one could speak of the 'Gospel' and the 'Law'.[276]

---

[269] Cf. n. 235 above.

[270] Cf. n. 170 above. To my mind it is not fair to say, as K. Aland, 'Das Problem', p. 10, wishes to do with regard to the basis of this selection, that 'the only principle is that there is no principle'.

[271] Zahn, *op. cit.*, I, pp. 110f.

[272] L. Koep, art. 'Buch I,' *RAC* II, 1954, cols. 681–684; and above all C. H. Roberts, 'The Codex', *Proceedings of the British Academy* 1954, pp. 185ff.

[273] Zahn, *op. cit.*, I, pp. 70ff.; Roberts, *op. cit.*, p. 192.

[274] Cf. pp. 226f., 237 above. Later examples in Lampe, pp. 322f.

[275] Cf. p. 163 n. 67 above.

[276] Zahn, *op. cit.*, I, p. 103; Harnack, *Entstehung*, pp. 14ff.; cf. p. 176 n. 142 above.

Already in Judaism the Old Testament had repeatedly been called simply 'the Law' after its most important section, and this terminology had to some extent penetrated the Church.[277] So long as 'the Gospel' remained in practice an exclusively theological concept, then it would certainly have been possible to apply this word in a similar way to the whole collection of Christian Scriptures. But as time went by the 'Gospels' and the 'Gospel' became also a literary entity, and in this sense could form only a part of the 'New Testament'.[278] This made it impossible to extend the term to cover the whole corpus. There was also the further factor that, so far as the Old Testament was concerned, the church was less interested in the Law than in Prophecy. It came more naturally, therefore, to speak of 'the Prophets' and 'the Apostles', if the Old or New Testament was meant. We have seen that the Muratorianum comes at least very close to such a technical usage; nor is it uncommon elsewhere.[279] This terminology too, however, was inexact in both cases, and could not suffice. The designations 'Old' and 'New Testament' had no such defects. They denoted a comprehensive and theologically very significant dual concept, in which nevertheless each group of Scriptures had its clearly defined place. This is one of the reasons why it defeated all competing concepts. But it is still not enough to explain how it came into existence. The usage was by no means a simple datum; it presupposes the views of a particular theology, in the context of which it arose and in which it must have had its roots.

Originally the idea of a new compact superseding the old covenant order, of a new ordinance and institution at the end of the ages embodying the divine will,[280] derives from the great prophets of the Old Testament.[281] Paul took it up, and proclaimed its fulfilment in Christ and in the Christian Church.[282] On one occasion he does indeed speak

[277] W. Gutbrod, art. νόμος, *TWNT* IV, 1942, pp. 1047, 1062f. (Paul), 1075 (John); cf. p. 144 n. 187 above (? I Clement).

[278] Their pre-eminence is, however, at first very clear: cf. p. 176 n. 143 above; and in the Antimontanist the Gospel, as Harnack, *Entstehung*, p. 69 n. 1, remarks, is still discernibly 'the dominant factor'. In the admittedly late MS of the Muratorianum (8th cent.) they alone are written in red.

[279] Cf. n. 257 above.

[280] This is the meaning of διαθήκη which obtains in the N.T.: J. Behm, *TWNT* II, 1935, pp. 132ff.; W. Bauer (tr. Arndt and Gingrich), *Greek–English Lexicon of the N.T.*, *sub voc.*; Lampe, *Patristic Lexicon*, p. 348; a slightly differing view is put forward by H. Pohlmann, art. 'Diatheke', *RAC* III, 1957, pp. 982–990. In what follows we shall use the more current rendering, 'covenant'.

[281] Isa. 55:3; 61:8; Jer. 32:40; Ezek. 16:60.

[282] Rom. 11:27; II Cor. 3:6, 14; Gal. 3:17; 4:24; (Eph. 2:12); cf. Heb. 8:8; 9:15ff.; 12:24; 13:20 etc. The further dissemination and the pre-history of this concept in primitive Christianity need not concern us here. The language

of a 'reading' of the Old Covenant.[283] Nevertheless the later understanding of the term as referring to a book does not derive from him; this
wider use first becomes current simply in imitation of the 'Old Testament'.[284] It was from this starting-point that, toward the end of the
second century, a developed theology of the covenants in salvation-
history was elaborated, which had as its centre the 'new covenant'
effected through Christ and the Church. This theology is known to us
primarily from the work of Irenaeus;[285] but it seems certain that in this
respect he was only extending earlier theological traditions, and that
the usage of contrasting the old and the new covenant originally came
from Asia Minor.[286] At any rate, it is here, in Asia, that we come across
the first rudimentary forms of an extension of this manner of speaking to
the books of the old and the new scriptures. It is a matter of a gradual
process, which cannot be pinpointed with precision; but for understanding what is involved in practice this is not important. The new
phraseology develops alongside the consolidation of the New Testament; and as with the latter, while the period of formation was tentative,
then—sweeping aside all other candidates—it prevailed in short space
and wellnigh universally.

The earliest traces indicative of the new phraseology occur in Melito
of Sardis, the older contemporary and fellow-countryman of Irenaeus.
As a bishop in Asia Minor he had rejected Montanism more decisively
than Irenaeus, and had written works against it. Among other things
Melito compiled a list of the Old Testament books, and on this occasion
refers to them once in the usual way as 'the Law and the Prophets',
then simply, 'the old books', and finally, 'the books of the old cove-

---

of the Synoptists (and of Acts) does not emphasise the contrast between the two
covenants, and was therefore less directly determinative of later developments
than was Paul.

[283] II Cor. 3:14: ἐπὶ τῇ ἀναγνώσει τῆς παλαιᾶς διαθήκης. Here the παλαιὰ
διαθήκη is 'undoubtedly thought of as a written document': H. Windicsch,
Der zweite Korintherbrief[9], 1924, p. 121. That in this Paul was already following
an existing usage, as D. Georgi, Die Gegner des Paulus im 2. Korintherbrief,
1964, p. 265, seems to think, is in my view improbable. According to S. Schulz,
'Die Decke des Moses', ZNW 49, 1958, p. 12 n. 58, 'the phrase should not be
pressed'. P. Katz, 'The early Christians' use of Codices instead of Rolls',
JTS 46, 1945, p. 64 n. 3, puts forward the strange conjecture that the disappearance of the scroll in the Church in favour of the codex might be connected with
this passage.

[284] This was pertinently emphasised by W. C. van Unnik, Ἡ καινὴ διαθήκη—
a Problem in the early history of the Canon, StudPatr IV, 1961, p. 220, in opposition to the hitherto prevailing opinion: 'However many quotations are given
in the post-apostolic writings, never is there any influence of this passage of
Paul's.'

[285] Cf. pp. 207f. above.   [286] Van Unnik, Διαθήκη, pp. 224ff.

nant'.[287] From such fluidity of usage we can hardly as yet deduce a fixed designation for the Old Testament, and it must remain even more questionable whether Melito spoke in corresponding fashion of the 'Books of the New Covenant';[288] in fact at that time these books were not yet, so far as we know, thought of as a unity. But all the same the road in this direction was open, and some may already have struck out along it. Only a little while afterwards we arrive at the so-called 'Antimontanist', who is probably to be identified with Bishop Polycrates of Ephesus,[289] and in any case belongs to the last decade of the second century, and once again to Asia. In a work against the Montanists this writer speaks of the word of the 'new covenant'[290] with a nuance which leaves no doubt that what he has in mind is the writings of the 'New Testament'. As the sentence in question, which has already been quoted in an earlier context,[291] lays down, nothing is to be added to this word (in writing), nor is any instruction to be given that goes beyond it. The collection described in such terms is therefore already felt to be final—at least in the sense that works of more recent date are not to be admitted into it.[292] Nevertheless, this author does not yet give the name 'New Testament' to this book as such, but simply speaks of the word of the new Gospel covenant, which for him is a written text. The word *diatheke* still retains its broad sense, covering

[287] Eusebius, *HE* IV, 26, 13f.: ἐπειδὴ πολλάκις ἠξίωσας . . . γενέσθαι σοι ἐκλογὰς ἔκ τε τοῦ νόμου καὶ τῶν προφητῶν περὶ τοῦ σωτῆρος καὶ πάσης τῆς πίστεως ἡμῶν, ἔτι δὲ καὶ μαθεῖν τὴν τῶν παλαιῶν βιβλίων ἐβουλήθης ἀκρίβειαν, πόσα τὸν ἀριθμὸν καὶ ὁποῖα τὴν τάξιν εἶεν . . . ἀκριβῶς μαθὼν τὰ τῆς παλαιᾶς διαθήκης βιβλία, ὑποτάξας ἔπεμψά σοι.

[288] Zahn, *op. cit.*, I, p. 104; similarly Van Unnik, 'Règle', p. 1; *id.*, Διαθήκη, pp. 218f., against Harnack, *Entstehung*, p. 69 *et al.*

[289] Cf. n. 114 above.

[290] Linguistically this is the only possible translation of τῷ τῆς τοῦ εὐαγγελίου καινῆς διαθήκης, not, for example, a word 'of the New Testament good news' (as, among others, P. Haeuser suggests in his translation, 1932, p. 238): Van Unnik, 'Règle', p. 36 n. 122.

[291] Cf. p. 231 above.

[292] So esp. Van Unnik, 'Règle', p. 4, in agreement with Zahn. In his definition of the 'classical period', therefore, the Antimontanist is entirely at one with the Muratorianum, even if, however, the 'openness' of his canon may be greater than in the case of the latter. The explanation for this, however, does not lie where Van Unnik, Διαθήκη, pp. 217f., attempts to find it: 'On the one hand it seems as though he speaks about a closed number of sacred books, but this list is not yet watertight, because there could be a chance that his own book would be reckoned with it.' Harnack, *Das Neue Testament um das Jahr 200*, p. 43, expresses a similar view. But this, as it seems to me, is to take the high-flown phrases of the Antimontanist too seriously. I agree with Lagrange, *op. cit.*, p. 112, when, following Labriolle, *Crise*, p. 189, he offers the alternative view: 'It is obvious that we have here a *captatio benevolentiae* which is not to be taken too literally; but in the last analysis the man who expressed himself in these terms had very fixed ideas on the subject of a group of sacred writings. . . .'

the whole epoch and reality of salvation and of the Church. Another passage, in which the same author lists the prophets of the 'new covenant', makes this completely clear.[293] Their line does not stop at the borders of the New Testament, but is continued quite unconcernedly down to the prophetess Ammia of Philadelphia and the 'prophet' Quadratus, that is, to the very eve of the writer's own day.[294] We have not yet arrived at the purely literary meaning of the word.[295]

The direct passage from the old to the new meaning of the word can be detected in Clement of Alexandria. Clement, who has read Irenaeus,[296] speaks very frequently of the two covenants, the old and the new, and of the higher unity which they constitute together.[297] This is still along conventional lines. In addition, however, there are passages in which it would be arbitrary not to refer this same word *diatheke* directly to the old and new Scriptures. Thus, on one occasion he says that we have to believe in the Son of God even 'without probable and compelling proofs', since this is 'proclaimed and described by the old and by the new *diatheke*'.[298] Or again: what Paul wrote may be considered wholly dependent upon the old *diatheke*, and as deriving from that source the power of its speech; for 'the knowledge of the Gospel is an exegesis and fulfilment' of the Law.[299] But the dividing-line be-

---

[293] Here the language is even more strongly formalised, but only to the extent that it speaks of prophets κατὰ τὴν παλαιάν and κατὰ τὴν καινήν. διαθήκην, which is obviously the word to be supplied, has already become dispensable in theological parlance.

[294] Eusebius, *HE* V, 17, 3: τοῦτον δὲ τὸν τρόπον οὔτε τινὰ τῶν κατὰ τὴν παλαιὰν οὔτε τῶν κατὰ τὴν καινὴν πνευματοφορηθέντα προφήτην δεῖξαι δυνήσονται, οὔτε Ἄγαβον οὔτε Ἰούδαν οὔτε Σίλαν οὔτε τὰς Φιλίππου θυγατέρας οὔτε τὴν ἐν Φιλαδελφίᾳ Ἀμμίαν οὔτε Κοδράτον οὔτε εἰ δή τινας ἄλλους μηδὲν αὐτοῖς προσήκοντας καυχήσονται.

[295] This is rightly stressed by Van Unnik, Διαθήκη, p. 218, against Zahn and the somewhat vacillating attitude of Harnack (cf. the references in 'Règle', pp. 1–3) and his own earlier view ('Règle', p. 36). But even Lagrange, *op. cit.*, p. 112, and Kümmel, *op. cit.*, p. 360, believe that the Antimontanist supplies assured evidence for the 'New Testament.'

[296] Eusebius, *HE* VI, 13, 9.

[297] Cf., e.g., Strom. II, 29, 2: "ὁ δὲ δίκαιος ἐκ πίστεως ζήσεται" (Rom. 1:17), τῆς κατὰ τὴν διαθήκην καὶ τὰς ἐντολάς, ἐπειδὴ δύο αὗται ὀνόματι καὶ χρόνῳ καθ' ἡλικίαν καὶ προκοπὴν οἰκονομικῶς δεδόμεναι, δυνάμει μία οὖσαι, ἡ μὲν παλαιά, ἡ δὲ καινή, διὰ υἱοῦ παρ' ἑνὸς θεοῦ χορηγοῦνται. For further instances in abundance cf. the concordance in the *GCS* edition by O. Stählin, pp. 330f., though the entry does not distinguish between the narrrower technical sense and the general meaning, 'covenant of God with men'. For an exposition of the passage of Clement just quoted cf. pp. 303f. below.

[298] Strom. V, 85, 1: πιστευτέον ἄρα τοῦτο καὶ κατὰ Πλάτωνα, κἂν "ἄνευ γε εἰκότων καὶ ἀναγκαίων ἀποδείξεων" (Timaeus 40E) διά τε τῆς παλαιᾶς διά τε τῆς νέας διαθήκης κηρύσσηται καὶ λέγηται.

[299] Strom. IV, 134, 2f.: . . . ἀλλ' οὖν ἡ γραφὴ αὐτῷ ἐκ τῆς παλαιᾶς ἤρτηται διαθήκης, ἐκεῖθεν ἀναπνέουσα καὶ λαλοῦσα· ἡ γὰρ εἰς χριστὸν πίστις καὶ ἡ τοῦ εὐαγγελίου γνῶσις ἐξήγησίς ἐστι καὶ τοῦ νόμου πλήρωσις.

tween the two senses still remains fluid.[300] Even Origen, for whom *diatheke* in the sense of 'book' was a perfectly normal usage, still felt something strange in such a term, when he wrote of the 'divine scriptures of the *so-called* Old and of the *so-called* New *Diatheke*'. The documentation of the covenant is not itself the covenant.[301] Nevertheless, in the Greek-speaking world it always remained possible to discern the connection between the two, and to make it directly understood theologically.

By contrast, the transition into Latin made it virtually impossible to prevent what was now a technical term from becoming rigid and lifeless. The normal rendering for the *diatheke* of the Greek bible was *testamentum*, a term which with its hard, juristic overtones could really comprehend only the idea of a 'testamentary' deposition or instrument, but not the whole breadth and elasticity of the Greek concept. In ecclesiastical usage *testamentum* is a typical example of Christian translator's jargon; and by applying it, on the Greek model, to the parts of holy Scripture the Church deprived it of all flexibility, and merely made its meaning totally obscure. Tertullian, who attests the early spread of the loan-rendering 'vetus et novum testamentum'[302] himself uses it only infrequently, and prefers to speak of the 'vetus et novum instrumentum'.[303] In this he is certainly following earlier Jewish terminology for the Old Testament.[304] 'Instrumentum' can denote the document—in this case, therefore, the document (or, in the plural, the relevant passages in the text) of the old and new divine covenants; but it also, according to the context, allows of interpretation in the sense of the 'resources' or 'backing' for preaching and instruction.[305] The choice

---

[300] As P. Dausch, *Der neutestamentliche Schriftcanon und Clemens von Alexandrien*, 1894, p. 46, rightly remarks: 'Clement thus applies the word, it is true, to Old and New Testament books, yet gives it no definite, fixed content' (in this sense).

[301] Origen, De princ. IV, 1, 1: ... Θείων γραφῶν, τῆς τε λεγομένης παλαιᾶς διαθήκης καὶ τῆς καλουμένης καινῆς; *Comm. Joh.* V, 8: ... συμφωνίας δογμάτων κονιῶν τῇ καλουμένῃ παλαιᾷ πρὸς τὴν ὀνομαζομένην καινὴν διαθήκην. Augustine too was conscious of the fact that these terms, 'ex consuetudine, qua iam loquitur ecclesia' (Retract. II, 30, 3) were not entirely unproblematic: Zahn, *op. cit.*, II, pp. 103f.

[302] Adv. Marc. IV, 1, 1: alterius instrumenti vel quod magis usui est dicere testamenti.

[303] Zahn, *op. cit.*, I, pp. 105ff.; Harnack, *Entstehung*, pp. 137–144, and exhaustively, Braun, *op. cit.*, pp. 463–473. Tertullian is familiar with yet other variant descriptions of the Scripture and its two component parts: Rönsch, *op. cit.*, pp. 47f.; Braun, *op. cit.*, p. 472 n. 2.

[304] Braun, *op. cit.*, pp. 470–472, with whom agrees V. Loi, ' "Scripturae sacramentum" ', *RivBibl* 14, 1966, p. 277.

[305] Cf. esp. *praescr.* 38, 3: alias enim non potuissent aliter docere, nisi aliter haberent per quae docerent, sicut illis non potuisset succedere corruptela doc-

of this term therefore offered notable advantages and potentials which were lacking in the case of 'testamentum'. Despite this, however, Tertullian did not succeed in having the word accepted.[306] The decisive factor in this failure was simply that 'instrumentum' had no biblical overtones. Precise and sober as it was, it would have been more serviceable and in any case clearer than the clumsy term 'testamentum', which, though it certainly evoked theological associations, yet was an obstacle rather than a help to meaningful interpretation.[307]

But the immediate and most important requirement has now been met, whether by *diatheke* or by *testamentum*: each part of the Scripture has acquired a new name which simultaneously unites the two and distinguishes between them. It is no longer possible to divorce the New Testament from the Old, as Marcion had tried to do; but it is even less possible simply to put the two collections on the same level, as if there were no difference between them. At least, this is the consequence which is bound to follow constantly from the predicates 'Old' and 'New', so long as these are not completely ignored.[308] They recall to mind the great historical movement in the course of which the documents of God's saving will came into being, their permanent givenness, and the fact that the Person and Spirit of Jesus, who is their consummation, are eternally new. Behind the name of the holy Scripture, there will always stand to this extent the theology of an Irenaeus and of those who in Asia Minor were his fathers in the faith, and who in their turn drew upon the ancient prophets and Paul. But the name by itself is not adequate to open up the meaning of that which it denotes and protects, nor to make it a living reality.

---

trinae sine corruptela instrumentorum. Cf. further Zahn, *op. cit.*, I, p. 108 n. 1. Tertullian also uses *paratura* in the same sense: Braun, *op. cit.*, pp. 468f.

[306] 'Instrumentum' does not occur in Cyprian, but isolated instances are to be found in the fourth century in Optatus, Jerome, Rufinus, and Augustine: Zahn, *op. cit.*, I, p. 108 n. 2. These examples may, however, be influenced less by Tertullian than by a more general usage of Jewish origin: cf. n. 304 above.

[307] An early example of interpretation on the basis of the meaning of the Latin word occurs in Lactantius, Inst. IV, 20, 2f.: idcirco Moyses et idem ipsi prophetae legem, quae Iudaeis data est, testamentum vocant, quia nisi testator mortuus fuerit, nec confirmari testamentum potest (cf. Heb. 9:16) nec sciri, quid in eo scriptum sit, quia clausum et obsignatum est. itaque nisi Christus mortem suscepisset, aperiri testamentum, id est: revelari et intelligi mysterium dei non potuisset.

[308] The qualitative, not merely chronological significance of the predicates παλαιά (as opposed to ἀρχαία) and καινή (as opposed to νέα) διαθήκη has already been almost lost in Latin, and is impossible to convey in German; for English cf. A. Souter, *The Text and Canon of the New Testament*[2] (rev. C. S. C. Williams), 1954, p. 144. In Clement, however, we do also find νέα (Paed. I, 59, 2; Strom. III, 71, 3) or καινὴ καὶ νέα διαθήκη (Paed. I, 59, 1). For isolated later examples of the same kind cf. Lampe, p. 348.

CHAPTER SEVEN

The New Canon in Post-Irenaean Theology and in Origen

FROM THE beginning of the third century onwards no one anywhere knew of a different arrangement: the sacred Scripture of the orthodox Church consisted of an Old and a New Testament. In the preceding chapters we have set out the process which led to this result. It took place so gradually, and in such close association with the way in which the traditional new testament writings were used and valued in earlier times, that the formation of the New Testament and of the new bipartite Canon was nowhere either remarked or experienced as an innovation or as an alteration of what had gone before. Even outside the Great Church the new Bible was seriously contested only by Marcionites, and their resistance was directed primarily against the Old Testament, the position of which had already long been secure. The New Testament was affected only to the extent that the selection and the text of the received writings, not the existence of the new collection as such, were the object of criticism.

It is virtually impossible to make a detailed assessment of the significance of the bipartite Canon for the age that now dawned. It touched the whole of theological endeavour, and its effect was constant and universal. The new Bible freed theology from its one-sided commitment to the Old Testament,[1] made possible a less arbitrary justification of the propositions of Christian belief, clarified and safeguarded the deposit of what was dogmatically important, and in general created a solid 'catholic' community of interest. It also purified polemic—at least in its better exponents—of its worst irrelevances and futile insults,[2]

---

[1] The immediate and outstanding effect of this was a perceptible relief. A. von Harnack, *Lehrbuch der Dogmengeschichte* I⁵, 1931, p. 373 (and similarly, *Die Entstehung des Neuen Testaments und die wichtigsten Folgen der neuen Schöpfung*, 1914, pp. 82–86) thinks that as a result of the addition of the New Testament the Old Testament 'became a complicated book for Christianity'. Nevertheless, for a long time now the Old Testament had been the Old Testament as interpreted by Christians. The formation of the New Testament as a literary entity gave this interpretation a fixed point at which to aim, and in this way simplified matters far more than it complicated them.

[2] This angle is rightly stressed by W. Bauer, *Orthodoxy and Heresy in Earliest*

by providing what was now an agreed basis for all controversies.[3]

In the present context there is no need for us to go further into this more general influence of the Bible, which in essence would involve us in a history of its exegesis. Nevertheless, it seems sensible to pursue briefly the question of the way in which the new Canon was regarded and theologically understood in the decades immediately after Irenaeus. Irenaeus himself had taken only the first steps in this direction, and the fully formed concept of a 'New Testament' had taken shape during the fight against Montanism. Only then—very quickly, it is true, but almost anonymously—did it sweep the board. It should not be thought that this impression is the result simply of a lack of fuller sources. It is striking how little part conscious reflection plays in the influence of the concept of the Canon even in the succeeding generation, and how different again and again is the understanding of it in the 'early Catholic Fathers' after Irenaeus. Only in Origen does the picture change. To grasp this is more important than to retail the minor variations which can be detected in the definition of the biblical corpus, and which, though indefatigably discussed in all studies of the history of the Canon, remain virtually meaningless for the understanding of the Canon itself.[4] The sketch which follows is restricted entirely to the theological definition and interpretation of the Canon, and with this limited concern brings our historical investigation of the formation of the Canon to a close. It is not intended as a contribution to the customary questions of canon statistics, nor should it make any attempt to assess the great exegetical and hermeneutical achievements of those Fathers whom we shall be considering. Our concern is solely with the way in which the biblical Canon as such was conceived and understood.

I begin my survey not in chronological sequence but with *Hippolytus*. Hippolytus's activity as an author falls almost entirely within the third

---

Christianity, 1972, p. 145; but elsewhere he has described the process by which the unified catholic church and its Scripture came into being much too one-sidedly in terms of 'ecclesiastical politics'.

[3] Cf. Harnack, *Entstehung*, pp. 90–94.

[4] So Harnack, *Dogmengeschichte* I, p. 395: 'The differences which still existed in the scope of the Canon remained essentially devoid of influence on its use or on the respect in which it was held'; cf. *Entstehung*, pp. III, 64f., 77.

[5] In what follows I shall treat all the works traditionally ascribed to Hippolytus as in fact his, excluding only the Church Order, which for our purposes is hardly essential. The persistent attempts of Nautin to distinguish between a Roman Josippus and a Hippolytus from Asia Minor have, so far as I can see, despite arguments which in some respects are weighty, nowhere carried conviction, and so far from 'shaking the unity of Hippolytus's literary output, have simply confirmed it': G. Kretschmar, *JLH* I, 1955, p. 93.—That the textual tradition, and in particular the various translations of Hippolytus are often unreliable is well known, and unfortunately often means that we must have reservations as to the wording of the passages quoted.

century,[5] yet no one stayed so close to 'the blessed presbyter Irenaeus'[6] as he. It is true that he lacks the simple greatness of his teacher—Hippolytus is more pretentious, more verbose, and wearisomely dull, an obtuse thinker; but zealous conviction, integrity, and seriousness one cannot deny him. The new age brought forth new heresies, and thus new controversies, and Hippolytus enters into them all. He thinks of himself with pride as an orthodox bishop[7] and as an outstanding theological investigator and scholar;[8] but if one examines the substance of his writings, there is hardly anything to be found which does not occur also in Irenaeus, or which goes in any significant point beyond the latter's suggestions. This is true, at any rate, of Hippolytus's concept of the Canon and of his whole outlook on holy Scripture.[9]

The predominance in principle of the Old Testament continues; it is also observable in practice. In addition to numerous individual treatises Hippolytus as the senior theologian of the Great Church also wrote continuous biblical commentaries; but his efforts in this field were devoted almost exclusively to the Old Testament.[10] Normally too it is the Old Testament alone which is meant when he speaks of 'the scripture' or 'the divine scriptures'.[11] In the usual manner they are interpreted 'prophetically', and Hippolytus further elaborates the typological and allegorical proof from Scripture deriving from Justin.[12] He frequently talks about the inspiration of the Scriptures; but, so far as I can see, in every case it is exclusively the Old Testament texts which

[6] Elench. VI, 42, 1; 55, 2.

[7] H. von Campenhausen, *Ecclesiastical Authority and Spiritual Power*, 1969, pp. 175–177.

[8] K. Engelhardt, *Der Ort der Theologie bei den griechischen Vätern um 200* (TS Diss. Heidelberg 1960), pp. 101–131.

[9] Research into this group of problems has been stagnant for a long time. Still fundamental are the studies of N. Bonwetsch: (I) *Studien zu den Kommentaren Hippolyts zum Buche Daniel und Hohen Liede*, 1897; (II) *Hippolyts Kommentar zum Hohenlied*, 1902; (III) *Drei georgisch erhaltene Schriften von Hippolytus*, 1904; cf. also Lagrange, *op. cit.*, pp. 58–66.

[10] The fragments on Matthew probably do not derive from a complete commentary, those on John are not authentic: P. Nautin, *Le dossier d'Hippolyte et de Méliton*, Paris, 1953, pp. 141f. If the fragments on the Apocalypse do in fact come from a commentary, then this is an exceptional case: in subject-matter they belong in the context of the controversy with Gaius: cf. pp. 236ff. above.

[11] Bonwetsch (I), p. 21; Lagrange, *op. cit.*, p. 60.

[12] Bonwetsch (III), p. VIII, especially notes as characteristic of Hippolytus 'his treatment of the O.T. scripture as throughout predictive of Christ, and his fondness for giving his views on the nature and function of prophecy'. Numerous examples of his method of exegesis will be found in Bonwetsch (I), pp. 31ff., and A. D'Alès, *La théologie de Saint Hippolyte*, Paris, 1906, pp. 118–134; also cf. G. Bardy in the Introduction to the French edition of the Commentary on Daniel by M. Lefèvre (*Hippolyte, Commentaire sur Daniel*, Paris, 1947), pp. 38ff.

are in question.[13] Within the New Testament the Four Gospels unquestionably take pride of place.[14] They are frequently set alongside 'the Law and the Prophets'.[15] Hippolytus stresses more than Irenaeus that they contain the complete account of the story of Jesus, his birth, his baptism, and his crucifixion.[16] Yet when the words of Jesus are quoted the source is hardly ever given.[17] In addition, Hippolytus relies on Acts, and on 'the Apostle', whom he loves to quote.[18] Catholic epistles are also used, it is true, but not cited by name.[19] On the other hand, Hippolytus, as we have seen,[20] defends the Apocalypse at great length against the attacks of Gaius. All these features correspond completely to Irenaeus's 'Canon'.[21] His reticence with regard to other New Testament writings is very strange in a third-century writer; it may help to explain it if we remember that Hippolytus had been a zealous campaigner against the Montanists and their 'innumerable' new books.

Whence the New Testament writings derive, and on what their special status is based, is nowhere discussed in Hippolytus's extant works.

[13] As Lagrange, *op. cit.*, p. 60, long ago complained, there is no detailed study devoted specifically to Hippolytus's exegesis of the N.T.

[14] Comm. Dan. I, 17, 11: 'A stream of unceasing water flows (sc. in Paradise), and from it divide "four streams", watering the whole earth. As may be seen in the Church. For Christ, who is the stream, is proclaimed throughout the world by the fourfold Gospel, and sending forth his waters over the whole earth he sanctifies all who believe in him, as also the prophet says: "Streams flow from his body" (Joh. 7:38).' For further passages cf. Bonwetsch (I), pp. 24f.

[15] Cf., e.g., Elench. V, 23, 1: Ἰουστῖνος πάντῃ ἐναντίος τῇ τῶν ἁγίων γραφῶν γενόμενος διδαχῇ, προσέτι δὲ καὶ τῇ τῶν μακαρίων εὐαγγελιστῶν γραφῇ ἢ φωνῇ . . . ; VIII, 19. 1: . . . πλεῖόν τι δι' αὐτῶν (sc. βίβλων ἀπείρων) φάσκοντες μεμαθηκέναι ἢ ἐκ νόμου καὶ προφητῶν καὶ τῶν εὐαγγελίων.

[16] Elench. VII, 27, 8; VIII, 10, 7; X, 16, 6: πάντα δὲ συμβεβηκέναι αὐτῷ (sc. Ἰησοῦ) φασι, καθὰ ἐν τοῖς εὐαγγελίοις γέγραπται.

[17] The normal introductory formulas are ὁ κύριος λέγει and suchlike: Bonwetsch (I), p. 23.

[18] On the use of this designation in Hippolytus cf. Bonwetsch (I), pp. 23f. Even in the O.T. we find numerous typological indications of the pre-eminent position of Paul: A. Hamel, *Kirche bei Hippolyt von Rom*, 1951, pp. 34f.

[19] Cf. the evidence collected in Lagrange, *op. cit.*, pp. 61f., who as usual fails to distinguish between use and canonicity. In a fragment on Rev. 7:4–8, preserved in Arabic, we find, oddly enough, 'a saying of Jude in his first Epistle to the twelve tribes'; the passage in question is James 1:1.

[20] Cf. pp. 239ff. above.

[21] That Hippolytus occasionally makes use of O.T. and N.T. Apocrypha (IV Esdras, Hermas, Barnabas, Acts of Paul) tells us nothing about his 'Canon'; cf. Lagrange, *op. cit.*, pp. 63–66; D'Alès, *Hippolyte,* pp. 112–118; also M. J. Rondeau, 'À propos d'une prophétie non canonique citée par Epiphane', *RechSR* 55, 1967, pp. 209–216. Hippolytus very frequently makes use of Hebrews, but is said nevertheless to have expressly excluded it: cf. pp. 232f. above.

[22] Hamel, *op. cit.*, pp. 32ff.

It is clear that they are backed by the authority of the Apostles. These were the first bearers of that proclamation which in accordance with God's will was published throughout the world.[22] It is to them, therefore, that the New Testament, just as much as the living tradition of the Church, goes back.[23] Especial stress is laid on the tradition in official and ecclesiastical contexts.[24] Yet Hippolytus never reflects on the relation between Scripture and tradition.[25] It is to be understood in the Irenaean sense. Moreover, the concept of the 'canon of truth' has been retained unaltered.[26] But the understanding of the Spirit, which goes with this, has become in general decidedly more jejune, and certainly more clerical and liturgical. It is stated often enough that the passage from the Old Covenant to the New brought with it an advance in spiritual understanding and the revelation of divine mysteries. But for all Hippolytus's chronological interests and studies Irenaeus's great conception of salvation-history is no longer a living reality to him. In his world of thought it has no further part to play.[27]

So far as the history of the Canon is concerned, therefore, the progress represented in Hippolytus comes down to this: that he supports the fully developed conception of a bipartite Bible. To him this is something to be taken absolutely for granted. There are two Testaments, presented in the allegory of the Song of Songs as the two breasts of Christ, from which his devout children suck the milk of the commandments and of the Gospel.[28] The monotony of the terms in which

[23] This is shown by the terminology which Hippolytus uses to refer to the two Testaments collectively: cf. p. 257 n. 257 above; also Lagrange, *op. cit.*, p. 60: 'When he names them separately, the first is the "prophets", the second the "apostles".'

[24] G. G. Blum, 'Apostolische Tradition und Sukzession bei Hippolyt', *ZNW* 55, 1964, pp. 95–110.

[25] That in *De antichristo* 56 Luke is called an 'Apostle and Evangelist' (Zahn, *op. cit.*, I, p. 263 n. 1; Leipoldt, *op. cit.*, I, p. 153 n. 5) is, according to the critical edition of H. Achelis, 1897, p. 37, irrelevant, and to be regarded simply as a secondary variant.

[26] D. van den Eynde, *Les Normes de l'Enseignement Chrétien dans la littérature patristique des trois premiers siècles*, 1933, pp. 289–291; J. Kunze, *Glaubensregel, Heilige Schrift und Kirche*, 1899, pp. 129–131; Hamel, *op. cit.*, pp. 93–98, 109; Blum, 'Tradition', p. 96.

[27] N. Brox, 'Kelsos und Hippolytus zur frühchristlichen Geschichtspolemik', *VC* 20, 1966, pp. 150–158.

[28] Slavonic fragment of Comm. Cant. on 1:2, 4: Bonwetsch (II): II, 3; III, 3; cf. XII; XXII; cf. Ben. Mos., Joseph, on the typology of milk and honey (Bonwetsch, III, p. 67; *Patrol. Orient.* XXVII, p. 169). In Comm. Dan. I, 17, 12 the two trees planted in Paradise point to 'the Law and the Word in the Church'. Other different typologies are listed in Bonwetsch (III), p. x; but for the most part they are to be referred not to the 'testaments' in the literary sense, but only to the two covenants. Evidence for Bonwetsch's statement (I, p. 41) that 'Law and Gospel in Hippolytus are not in opposition to one another, but complementary' is plentiful.

Hippolytus constantly praises the holy Scriptures is in its way very significant.[29] They are the source from which every man must draw;[30] here and nowhere else is the true knowledge of God to be learned,[31] and nothing which the Bible teaches is superfluous.[32] This is by no means a proposition emphasised merely in opposition to heresy, but is universally valid. Scripture exists also for the edification of the faithful,[33] and particularly for all those who desire to penetrate more deeply into theological truths.[34] In style these perpetual exaggerated commendations of Scripture belong to a slightly later period than that of Irenaeus—Hippolytus is a contemporary of Origen. Their solemn praises, however, though certainly matched by detailed study, do not betoken a keener insight into the essence of the Bible or its distinctive character.

If Hippolytus shows us how canonical development could stagnate even as early as the third century, virtually disregarding all the more profound suggestions which Irenaeus had put forward,[35] *Tertullian* demonstrates the opposite possibilities. Tertullian too is familiar with

---

[29] Cf. D'Alès, *Hippolyte,* pp. 118ff. It is impossible to cite all the relevant passages; cf., e.g., the indications of contents at Elench. V, 3.5; VI, 3; VII, 5.7; VIII, 7.

[30] Antichr. 1: Βουληθέντι σοι κατ' ἀκρίβειαν ἐκμαθεῖν τὰ προτεθέντα ὑπὸ σοῦ ἡμῖν κεφάλαια, ἀγαπητέ μου ἀδελφὲ Θεόφιλε, εὔλογον ἡγησάμην, ἀφθόνως ἀρυσάμενος ὡς ἐκ ἁγίας πηγῆς ἐξ αὐτῶν τῶν θείων γραφῶν καταστῆσαί σοι κατ' ὀφθαλμὸν τὰ ζητούμενα· ἵνα μὴ μόνον ταῖς τῶν ὤτων ἀκοαῖς ἐγκαταθέμενος ταῦτα εὐφρανθῇς, ἀλλὰ δυνάμει καὶ αὐτὰ τὰ πράγματα ἐνιστορήσας κατὰ πάντα τὸν θεὸν δοξάσαι δυνηθῇς. The reminiscence of the Lukan Theophilus in the Prologue may not be accidental; but what is significant is the difference between the two passages: Luke's historical witnesses and numerous sources have been replaced by 'the Scripture'.

[31] Noet. 9 (Text following P. Nautin, *Hippolyte, Contre les Hérésies,* 1949, p. 251): εἷς θεός, ὃν οὐκ ἄλλοθεν ἐπιγινώσκομεν, ἀδελφοί, ἢ <ἐκ> τῶν ἁγίων γραφῶν. ὃν γὰρ τρόπον ἐάν τις βουληθῇ τὴν σοφίαν τοῦ αἰῶνος τούτου ἀσκεῖν, οὐκ ἄλλως δυνήσεται τούτου τυχεῖν, ἐὰν μὴ δόγμασιν φιλοσόφων ἐντύχῃ, τὸν αὐτὸν δὴ τρόπον καὶ ὅσοι θεοσέβειαν ἀσκεῖν βουλόμεθα, οὐκ ἄλλοθεν ἀσκήσομεν ἢ ἐκ τῶν λογίων τοῦ θεοῦ. ὅσα τοίνυν κηρύσσουσιν αἱ θεῖαι γραφαὶ ἴδωμεν, καὶ ὅσα διδάσκουσιν ἐπιγνῶμεν· καὶ ὡς θέλει πατὴρ πιστεύεσθαι πιστεύσωμεν, καὶ ὡς θέλει υἱὸν δοξάζεσθαι δοξάσωμεν, καὶ ὡς θέλει πνεῦμα ἅγιον δωρεῖσθαι λάβωμεν, μὴ κατ' ἰδίαν προαίρεσιν μηδὲ κατ' ἴδιον νοῦν μηδὲ βιαζόμενοι τὰ ὑπὸ τοῦ θεοῦ δεδομένα, ἀλλ' ἢ ὃν τρόπον αὐτὸς ἐβουλήθη διὰ τῶν ἁγίων γραφῶν δεῖξαι, οὕτως ἴδωμεν.

[32] Comm. Dan. I, 7, 2: '. . . the holy scriptures make known nothing that is useless to us, but (all is) for our encouragement, and moreover, in the case of the prophets, for blessedness and to prove everything said by them.'

[33] Comm. Dan. IV, 26, 1: πρὸς οἰκοδομὴν τῶν πιστευόντων.

[34] Noet. 9 (cf. n. 31 above).

[35] Bonwetsch (III), p. IX, rightly speaks of the 'archaising character of Hippolytus's exegesis'; but how far was this archaism still dominant, if not in Africa (cf. n. 36 below), at any rate in Rome and even more in the rest of the West?

Irenaeus, and we encounter the latter's influence, so to speak, at every turn in Tertullian's defence of the new Canon. But here a man of completely different temperament has at the same time consciously toiled and striven to surpass Irenaeus. Tertullian takes the traditional arguments, refines them and adds to them, he reforges and rearranges them in order to smite all enemies of the truth, both old and new. Tertullian does not study the Bible in order to derive from it personal enlightenment, edification, or secret knowledge. He loves it for its hard, practical realism, he loves in particular the inexorable clarity of its demands on which salvation depends. These are the things which he seeks constantly to champion and to proclaim, and it is in making this proclamation that he simultaneously teaches and upholds the rightness and authenticity of his holy Scripture. He knows it inside out;[36] but it is not just that he is continually quoting it,[37] he sees it as a whole, the parts of which are to be understood, divided and defined in accordance with their individual character. It is astonishing what definite form and contour the Canon has already acquired in this way in Tertullian's writings only one generation after Irenaeus. And the way in which he appeals to it shows us that it was already familiar in this aspect to Tertullian's church as well.[38]

'The bipartite bible is found in all Tertullian's writings as an established possession of the church; nothing points back to an earlier period.'[39] The 'divine' or 'sacred scripture'[40] comprises an Old and a New Testament (or 'Instrument'[41]). There is no longer any suggestion that the Old Testament takes precedence;[42] on the contrary the precedence of the Gospel and the apostolic writings over the Law and the Prophets is repeatedly declared with the utmost emphasis: Christ,

[36] Some mistakes, collected by Harnack, 'Tertullians Bibliothek christlicher Schriften', *Sitz. Berl. Akad.*, 1914, I, pp. 332–334, imply nothing to the contrary; Tertullian was simply quoting from memory (*ibid.*, p. 308 n. 2): *idol.* 4, 5; Adv. Marc. IV, 14, 3.

[37] Harnack, 'Bibliothek', p. 308 n. 1, estimates that there are between 3000 and 4000 quotations. Frequently Tertullian translates direct from the Greek 'original text', and attaches importance to the nuances of meaning to be found there: cf., e.g., Adv. Marc. II, 9, 1f.; IV, 14, 1; cf. G. J. D. Aalders, *Tertullianus' Citaten uit de Evangelien en de oud-latijnsche Bibelvertalingen* (Diss. Amsterdam), 1932, p. 200; S. Rossi, 'La citazione dei testi sacri nell' "adversus Praxeam" di Tertulliano', *Giorn. Ital. di Filol.* 13, 1960, pp. 252f.

[38] Harnack, *Entstehung*, pp. 128–137.

[39] Harnack, 'Bibliothek', p. 306.

[40] On the various terms for the Bible cf. R. Braun, *'Deus Christianorum.' Recherches sur le vocabulaire doctrinal de Tertullien*, Paris, 1962, pp. 454–473; also H. Rönsch, *Das Neue Testament Tertullians*, 1871, pp. 47f.

[41] Cf. pp. 267f. above.

[42] The old terminological contrast between *scriptura* and *evangelium* does in fact reappear once: Adv. Hermog. 22, 5 (cf. n. 54 below).

T

who had once established the old order, has himself simplified, enhanced, and perfected it in the new covenant.[43]

Over the essential contents of the Bible there is no longer any dispute.[44] Tertullian would certainly have liked to add Enoch to the Old[45] and Hebrews to the New Testament;[46] but he contents himself with commending the testimony of these works and with justifying his own appeal to them. He is not striving for any 'reform' of the Bible. Variations of this kind on peripheral questions persisted throughout ancient times. 'Of an apocryphal literature to be used by the church Tertullian knows absolutely nothing'.[47] In his mind the Bible consisting of the Old and New Testaments is in principle 'closed'.[48]

As in Irenaeus the unity and structure of Scripture are seen in terms of salvation-history. Tertullian takes over Irenaeus's concept of the progressive revelation which God bestowed first on his own people and finally on the whole world. But it must be admitted that his understanding of this movement is essentially more superficial. The growing richness of Man's knowledge of God now consists in an ever clearer insight into the divine nature and, above all, an ever more stringent

[43] Cf., e.g., Adv. Marc. IV, 1, 3 (cf. n. 50 below), or, predicated of God, Jud. 2, 7.

[44] Tertullian's bible coincides almost entirely with ours (including the 'O.T. Apocrypha'): A. D'Alès, La théologie de Tertullien, 1905, pp. 223–230. Only 'II Peter, III John, and James were completely missing in Tertullian's day and church': Rönsch, op. cit., p. 572. Harnack, 'Bibliothek', p. 306 n. 2, with a reference to the silence of the Muratorian Canon on the subject (cf. pp. 246f. above), regards it as 'not quite certain' that 'I Peter had a place in the church's collection'.

[45] Cult. fem. I, 3, 1: scio scripturam Enoch . . . non recipi a quibusdam, quia nec in armarium Iudaicum admittitur. opinor non putaverunt illam ante cataclysmum editam post eum casum orbis omnium rerum abolitorem salvam esse potuisse. After refuting this assumption, Tertullian continues, 3, 3: sed cum Enoch eadem scriptura etiam de domino praedicarit, a nobis quidem nihil omnino reiciendum est, quod pertineat ad nos. et legimus omnem scripturam aedificationi habilem divinitus inspirari (II Tim. 3:16), [et] a Iudaeis postea— iam videri(s) propterea—reiectam, sicut et cetera fere quae Christum sonant. nec utique mirum hoc, si scripturas aliquas non receperunt de eo locutas quem et ipsum coram loquentem non erant recepturi. eo accedit, quod Enoch apud Iudam apostolum testimonium possidet (Jude 14). Cf. Harnack, 'Bibliothek,' pp. 310f. In carn. res. 32, 1 a quotation from I Enoch 61, 5 is introduced with 'habes scriptum': D'Alès, Tertullien, p. 147 n. 7; also 225f.

[46] Cf. p. 233 above; on the rejection of the Shepherd of Hermas, cf. p. 237 n. 146 above, and on the Acts of Paul, p. 214 n. 25.

[47] Harnack, 'Bibliothek', p. 309. 'Apocrypha' for Tertullian are virtually equivalent to forgeries, and 'no trace has yet been discovered in Tertullian's writings of the use of any non-canonical Gospel': Zahn, op. cit., I, p. 170.

[48] The statement to the contrary in Harnack, 'Bibliothek', p. 305, is concerned more with the actual variations in the cases of Enoch, Hebrews, and Hermas, than with the general attitude of Tertullian, who never says anything to this effect.

application of the divine commands.[49] Tertullian knew how to make intensive exegetical use of the implications of this salvation-history approach. No one before his time had taken such a down-to-earth view of the historical character of the Bible, without prejudice to its divine unity and perfection, or emphasised so strongly that it was something to be taken for granted. 'I do not deny', he declares in his attack on Marcion, 'the diversity of language, of moral counsels, and of legal ordinances; but all this variety belongs nevertheless to one and the same God'.[50] Tertullian puts forward reflections on the circumstances in which the individual biblical books originated, on their chronology, and on their mutual relationships. He also reveals a surprisingly keen eye now and then for the individuality of the writers. Whereas he makes his opponents for preference confine themselves to a wooden 'it is written', he himself customarily refers to the biblical authors by name: Moses and the prophets, Paul, John, Jesus himself—for him all are distinctive faces. For the most part Tertullian presents his quotations in historical sequence;[51] occasionally he runs through the entire Bible in this way, collecting his evidence.[52] His concerns are, of course, never 'historical' in the modern sense; they remain throughout didactic and dogmatic, and accordingly are also quite often dictated by dogmatic considerations.[53] But dogmatic thinking does not deprive him of his eye for what is concrete and particular in the Bible. 'I worship the fulness of scripture, which manifests to me both the Creator and his creatures; but in the Gospel I find more, the one who acts as servant and judge for the Creator, the Word.'[54]

[49] The approach to Scripture which articulated and interpreted it in terms of salvation-history was clearly already fully established before Montanism. As a Montanist Tertullian went further and developed the formal theory that faith remained in essentials always the same, and that only morality was progressively improved; cf. H. Karpp, *Schrift und Geist bei Tertullian*, 1955, pp. 48f., 54–57, and e.g., orat. 1; bapt. 13; uxor. I, 2.

[50] Adv. Marc. IV. 1, 3: non nego distare documenta eloquii, praecepta virtutis, legis disciplinas, dum tamen tota diversitas in unum et eundem deum competat. . . .

[51] Karpp, *op. cit.*, pp. 22f.   [52] Cf., e.g., scorp. 2ff.; ieiun. 2ff.

[53] This gets Tertullian into difficulties *vis-à-vis* Marcion, for example, over the dispute between Peter and Paul at Antioch: praescr. 23f.; Adv. Marc. I, 20, 3; IV, 3f.; V, 3, 7; but it is enough for him if the true preaching of the apostles is salvaged as a unity; on this subject cf. the not altogether satisfactory treatment of F. Overbeck, *Über die Auffassung des Streits des Paulus mit Petrus in Antiochien (Gal. 2, 11ff.) bei den Kirchenvätern* (Progr. Basel), 1877, pp. 10–13. Similarly, with regard to the secret traditions of the gnostics, Tertullian concedes the possibility that in theory there could have been special utterances of Jesus in private. What one may not assume is that these would have affected the substance of the public teaching: praescr. 26, 9 (cf. n. 67 below).

[54] Hermog. 22, 5: adoro scripturae plenitudinem, qua mihi et factorem manifestat et facta; in evangelio vero amplius et ministrum atque arbitrum factoris invenio, sermonem.

For Tertullian, Scripture is quite simply the fundamental book—the textbook of belief and the manual and law for all human actions. As such it requires no support from outside, neither from heathen philosophy[55] nor from the official structures of the Church nor, moreover, from any secret tradition. The validity of the Bible is absolutely supreme. This does not, of course, mean that Tertullian is unfamiliar with philosophical concepts and makes no use of them, any more than it means that he is unacquainted with or refuses to acknowledge an episcopal teaching office;[56] and in his writings too the tradition of the Church—exactly as in Irenaeus—has its proper status.[57] This same teaching, which is now to be found in the New Testament, was handed on by the apostles to their churches right back at the time when they were founded. In championing the original revelation and, in this sense, the tradition[58] the Church is also upholding the teaching of Scripture.[59] Catholic tradition may be followed and trusted with good reason—but that does not make it either an indispensable pre-condition or a criterion of the understanding of Scripture.[60] Where Scripture is silent, there certainly it is permissible to appeal to the practice prevailing in

[55] The wider question of 'natural theology' and natural law cannot be discussed here. These, as is well known, play a prominent part in Tertullian, especially in the Apologetic, but also elsewhere. But they are never a substitute or even a qualification of the truth as revealed in Scripture; at the most they can prepare the way for and commend what Scripture itself has to say *plenius et impressius* (apol. 18, 1).

[56] Nevertheless, he himself, who to all appearances was a layman, lays astonishingly little stress on its importance. 'In the extant writings of Tertullian', says J. K. Stirnimann, *Die Praescriptio Tertullians im Lichte des römischen Rechts und der Theologie*, 1949, p. 156, 'there is unfortunately only one fairly detailed passage which gives us more precise information on his concept of the teaching vocation of the bishop: praescr. haer. 32.' This passage has moreover been given an apologetic slant in the direction of the proof of succession as derived from Irenaeus. On Tertullian's general attitude toward the bishops, which later became strongly 'anti-clerical', cf. Campenhausen, *Ecclesiastical Authority*, pp. 227–233.

[57] Cf. on this point esp. E. Flesseman-van Leer, *Tradition and Scripture in the Early Church*, 1954, pp. 145–150, 180–185.

[58] J. N. Bakhuizen van den Brink, 'Traditio im theologischen Sinne', *VC* 13, 1959, pp. 70f.

[59] Cf. praescr. 38, 50: quod sumus, hoc sunt scripturae ab initio suo. ex illis sumus, antequam nihil aliter fuit quam sumus.

[60] Completely off the mark is the first half of the following statement by G. G. Blum, 'Der Begriff des Apostolischen im theologischen Denken Tertullians', *Kerygma und Dogma* 9, 1963, p. 114: 'The mutual relation between *instrumentum* and *doctrina* is so close, that on the one hand doctrine is the criterion of undistorted scripture, and on the other even authentic doctrine can be demonstrated only by scripture whole and intact.' In support of this he appeals to praescr. 38, 3 and 14, 14 (cf. n. 108 below), neither of which is sufficient to substantiate the existence of the modern catholic concept of 'mutual relationship' in Tertullian.

the Church,[61] and thus in this broader and more general sense to its tradition, or rather, to its traditions.[62] But this does not make such traditions normative without qualification.[63] In every controversy, whether inside or outside the Church, Tertullian regularly insists even more emphatically and as a matter of principle than Irenaeus on proof from Scripture.[64]

Tertullian is a keen logician and jurist. He is no longer content to assert the divine origin and authority of the Canon in general terms; he has a more precise conception of Scripture as a norm, and as occasion requires he brings out the formal presuppositions and the practical consequences of biblical infallibility with a decisiveness hitherto unknown. If the New Testament contains the whole truth as this was proclaimed by the apostles in virtue of their commission from Jesus, then it cannot possibly contain any contradictions,[65] such as those alleged by Marcion, nor can it tolerate any supplementation from secret traditions in the gnostic manner. One may never assume that John permitted something which Paul forbade,[66] and even if it is conceivable that in private the apostles discussed matters of which we know nothing, yet this can in no way have affected their public preaching.[67] On occasion his insistence on these points forces Tertullian to assume formal inspiration not only of the Old but now also of the New Testament.[68]

---

[61] Cor. 3, 1: hanc (sc. observationem inveteratam) si (nulla scriptura determinavit, certe consuetudo corroboravit, quae sine dubio de traditione manavit.

[62] On this point cf. Flesseman-van Leer, op. cit., p. 147.

[63] Virg. vel. 1, 1: sed dominus noster Christus veritatem se, non consuetudinem cognominavit; ibid. 2, 1: consuetudo sit tantisper, ut consuetudini etiam consuetudinem opponam; cf. Cyprian, Ep. 63, 14; 71, 3; 73, 13; 75, 19 (Firmilian).

[64] Cf., e.g., Hermog. 22, 5: si non est scriptum, timeat vae illud adicientibus aut detrahentibus destinatum (Rev. 22:18f.); carn. Chr. 6, 10: certum est. sed nihil de hoc constat, quia scriptura non exhibet.—The same principle seems to have been equally common among his opponents; cf., e.g., cor. 2, 4: expostulantes enim scripturae patrocinium in parte diversa praeiudicant suae quoque parti scripturae patrocinium adesse debere.

[65] Consonantia scripturarum divinarum: Iud. 11, 11; 14, 11; Adv. Marc. III, 20, 1.

[66] Pudic. 19, 3: totius itaque sacramenti interest nihil credere ab Iohanne concessum, quod a Paulo sit denegatum.

[67] Praescr. 26, 9: quamquam etsi quaedam inter domesticos, ut ita dixerim, disserebant, non tamen ea fuisse credendum est, quae aliam regulam fidei superducerent, diversam et contrariam illi quam catholicae in medium proferebant. . . .

[68] A comparable development is likewise already beginning in Theophilus of Antioch: cf. pp. 316f. below. The miraculous, inspired perfection of the Old Testament was something which all the Apologists had emphasised (cf. esp. Athenagoras, Suppl. 7 and Ps.-Justin, Cohort. 8), and is, of course, a commonplace with Tertullian as well; cf., e.g., Apol. 18ff.; Hermog. 22; anim. 35, 6; carn. Chr. 23, 6.

Here, too, the Holy Spirit with prescient wisdom has so arranged the words that they cannot be misunderstood.[69] Whoever contradicts Paul, in some sense contradicts the Holy Spirit himself;[70] for Paul speaks under the influence of the Holy Spirit, who controls the whole of sacred Scripture.[71] As an apostle he possesses the Spirit in a special, that is, a more far-reaching sense,[72] like all the apostles whom Christ chose.[73] Not to trust the men whom Christ sent out, and to seek to correct their Gospels as Marcion did, would be an affront to Christ himself.[74] In principle, therefore, Tertullian considers the predictions and utterances of the Holy Spirit through the apostles in the New Testament exactly as authoritative as those given through the Prophets in the Old.[75] The formal status of the Canon is already beginning to enforce a correspondingly formal and unqualified concept of inspiration.[76]

From here it is but a step to the fully developed conception according

[69] Adv. Marc. V, 7, 1 (on I Cor. 4:9): immo, ne ita argumentareris, providentia spiritus sancti demonstravit, quomodo dixisset "spectaculum facti sumus mundo"—dum "angelis", qui mundo ministrant, "et hominibus", quibus ministrant.

[70] Adv. Marc. V, 7, 2: (Paulus) tantae constantiae vir, ne dicam spiritus sanctus; cf. uxor. II, 2, 4; Valent. 3, 4; praescr. 7, 7; carn. res. 24, 8.

[71] Orat. 22, 1: apostolus eodem utique spiritu actus, quo . . . omnis scriptura divina . . . digesta est.

[72] Exh. cast. 4, 5f., with reference to I Cor. 7:40: spiritum quidem dei etiam fideles habent, sed non omnes fideles apostoli. cum ergo qui se fidelem dixerat, adiecit postea spiritum dei se habere, quod nemo dubitaret etiam de fideli, idcirco id dixit, ut sibi apostoli fastigium redderet. proprie enim apostoli spiritum sanctum habent, qui plene habent in operibus prophetiae et efficacia virtutum documentisque linguarum, non quasi ex parte, quod ceteri.

[73] Praescr. 8, 14f.; 22; 28, 1.

[74] Adv. Marc. IV, 3, 4: si apostolos praevaricationis et simulationis suspectos Marcion haberi queritur usque ad evangelii depravationem, Christum iam accusat accusando, quod Christus elegit.

[75] Tertullian refers to N.T. prophecies in his apologetic in connection with both persecutions and heretics; they are an example of a direct 'providentia spiritus sancti'; cf. W. Bender, Die Lehre über den heiligen Geist bei Tertullian, 1961, pp. 115–123. In praescr. 39, 7 Tertullian applies this idea even to the heretical misuse of Scripture: nec periclitor dicere ipsas quoque scripturas sic esse ex dei voluntate dispositas, ut haereticis materias subministrarent, cum legam oportere haereses esse (I Cor. 11:19), quae sine scripturis esse non possunt.

[76] In the opinion of Lagrange, op. cit., p. 54, Tertullian is, however, still not sufficiently punctilious: 'He has not distinguished clearly enough . . . between the personal inspiration bestowed on a pious author, and the official inspiration which gives the inspired writings their normative character.' He is here referring to Tertullian's opinion of the Book of Enoch, and to the mistaken use which he makes in connection with it of II Tim. 3:16 (cf. n. 45 above). From the historian's point of view, however, it is the opposite, precisian tendency which is the really significant thing about Tertullian—and by Lagrange's standards pretty well all the writers of the Early Church of the first three centuries are at fault so far as the New Testament is concerned.

to which only the apostles, who had been singled out for this purpose in some unique way, were called to write infallible works. Mark and Luke, the blatant exceptions in the Canon, must therefore have been commissioned for their tasks by their apostolic teachers, and have recorded nothing except what they had learned from that source. It is in Tertullian that we meet for the first time observations which point in this direction. Nevertheless, they occur on only one occasion, and are elaborated with obviously polemical intent. The passage in question occurs in the great work against Marcion. Here at one point Tertullian declares mockingly that there is really no need to go into details about Marcion's Gospel, because it is even silent about its own name. However, it is in fact Luke's Gospel mutilated, and one may ask in vain why of all the Gospels Marcion chose this one for his exercises in textual devastation. 'Luke is not even an apostle, but the disciple of an apostle, not a teacher but a pupil and so decidedly a lesser figure than the teacher, and certainly as much later on the scene as the apostle whom he followed was a later apostle.'[77] Even if Paul had been an Evangelist himself, he could not have sufficed on his own without the earlier Gospel of his predecessors, which he found already in existence and to which he in his turn gave his belief.[78] Certainly recognition on the part of the apostolic churches bestowed validity on the Gospel of Luke as it did on the rest, and it is therefore justifiable to regard this as the Pauline Gospel just as Mark is regarded as the Petrine.[79] But it is precisely this recognition which the Marcionite version lacks—in every respect, therefore, it is worthless.

[77] Adv. Marc. IV, 2, 4: porro Lucas non apostolus, sed apostolicus, non magister, sed discipulus, utique magistro minor, certe tanto posterior, quanto posterioris apostoli sectator. According to F. Winkelmann, 'Grosskirche und Häresien in der Spätantike', FF 41, 1967, p. 243 n. 5, Clem. Alex., Strom. VIII, 107, 2f. also expresses a similar idea, namely that heresies are of later date than the Great Church, which 'is to be equated directly with the apostles' because 'they derived from the disciples of the apostles'. But this is not to be found in the text, and simply results in misunderstanding and displacement of its traditional point.

[78] Adv. Marc. IV, 2, 4f. (following on the passage quoted in n. 77 above): Pauli sine dubio, ut et si sub ipsius Pauli nomine evangelium Marcion intulisset, non sufficeret ad fidem singularitas instrumenti destituta patrocinio antecessorum. exigeretur enim id quoque evangelium, quod Paulus invenit, cui fidem dedit, cui mox suum congruere gestiit, siquidem propterea Hierosolymam ascendit ad cognoscendos apostolos et consultandos, ne forte in vacuum cucurrisset (Gal. 2:2), id est ne non secundum illos credidisset et non secundum illos evangelizaret.

[79] Adv. Marc. IV, 5, 3f.: eadem auctoritas ecclesiarum apostolicarum ceteris quoque patrocinabitur evangeliis, quae proinde per illas et secundum illas habemus, Iohannis dico atque Mathei, licet et Marcus, quod edidit Petri adfirmetur, cuius interpres Marcus. nam et Lucae digestum Paulo adscribere solent. capit autem magistrorum videri, quae discipuli promulgarint.

The trend of such arguments is clear. The attack is stepped up, phase by phase, in a form very typical of Tertullian. From the very start Marcion's gospel is unworthy of credence because it is nameless. But even the slightest investigation will show his pretensions to be hollow, while any serious examination proves them totally null and void. Luke is no apostle, but a disciple of Paul; Paul is a latecomer, and likewise would be quite insufficient by himself; and even if he did suffice, yet Marcion's version of him still lacks the essential qualification of acceptance by the Church. All this is so much polemical swordplay.[80] It is not Tertullian's custom elsewhere to pay less attention to Luke than to Matthew, or to demote Paul to a status below that of the first apostles,[81] and even the traditional argument about the 'apostolic churches' is dragged in simply as an extra.[82] It would be completely perverse to deduce from this isolated passage the conclusion that Tertullian was already championing the 'apostolic principle', on which acceptance into the Canon or exclusion from it are supposed to have been decided.[83] What Tertullian is demanding here is much more the traditional 'catholic' acknowledgement of the *communis sensus* and of the agreement of witnesses; and what he really has in mind, and seeks to defend, is simply the validity of the Four-Gospel canon as opposed to Marcion's artificially constructed single Gospel.[84] The permanent

[80] A point to which A. C. Sundberg, 'Dependent Canonicity in Irenaeus and Tertullian,' StudEvang III, 1964, pp. 403-409, in my view pays far too little attention.

[81] Even the interpretation of Gal. 2 in this passage is deliberately tendentious; we need only compare it with the correct account which Tertullian gives in praescr. 23, 7: dehinc, sicut ipse enarrat, ascendit Hierosolymam cognoscendi Petri causa, ex officio et iure scilicet eiusdem fidei et praedicationis.

[82] It is of especial weight in this context, because the apostolic churches in the primitive period must have known which Gospels rightly reflected the apostolic preaching; cf. nn. 85, 87 below. Nevertheless, first in Adv. Marc. IV, 5, 2 and then in praescr. 28, 8 the right is extended explicitly to all churches, on the grounds that the identity of their belief is the surest guarantee that it is the original faith. This argument has absolutely nothing in common with modern ideas of ecclesiastical ' "catholic" legitimation', as Blum, 'Begriff des Apostolischen', p. 110 supposes. Such a notion is completely alien to Tertullian.

[83] So, e.g., Blum, 'Begriff des Apostolischen', p. 109.

[84] It is easy to overlook the fact that Tertullian's arguments—in keeping with their purpose—are directed exclusively to the Gospels; Adv. Marc. IV, 2, 1: constituimus imprimis evangelicum instrumentum apostolos auctores habere, quibus hoc munus evangelii promulgandi ab ipso domino sit impositum. si et apostolicos, non tamen solos, sed cum apostolis. . . . In Tertullian's assessment of the Shepherd of Hermas, for example, the question of apostolicity plays not the slightest part, either positive (orat. 16, 1f.) or negative (pudic. 10, 12). The assertions of Lagrange, *op. cit.*, p. 51, about a supposed confirmation of Acts by the Twelve and about the slight embarrassment which Tertullian is presumed to have felt with regard to this book are without foundation. Harnack, *Entstehung*, p. 37, is absolutely right when he concludes that in prasecr.

privileged position of the Gospels is based ultimately once again simply on the reliability with which they have preserved the original—which, of course, means the apostolic—message.[85] The apostles themselves are not yet seen as 'creative' originators of the tradition,[86] but simply as the earliest and outstanding source for the teaching and acts of Jesus.[87] It is true that they were chosen for their vocation by the Lord, and thus strengthened and empowered in a unique degree; all the accounts of Jesus depend upon them. But this does not mean that the apostles alone received the endowment needed for the composition of canonical Scriptures. Given knowledge of and unanimity about the facts,[88] pupils or companions of the apostles may just as properly take up the pen as the apostles themselves.[89]

23, 3f. it is no longer (as it was in Irenaeus) Paul who confirms Acts, but Acts which is already confirming Paul: possum et hic acta apostolorum repudiantibus dicere: "prius est, ut ostendatis, quis iste Paulus et quid ante apostolum et quomodo apostolus", quatenus et alias ad quaestiones plurimum eo utuntur. neque enim, si ipse se apostolum de persecutore profitetur sufficit unicuique examinate credenti, quando nec dominus ipse de se testimonium dixerit (Joh. 5:31). But, of course, this too is adduced only as a polemical tactic against the Marcionites, and by no means as the expression of a genuine doubt on Tertullian's part with regard to Paul and the canonicity of his epistles.

[85] This is the sense in which such assertions as the following are made; Adv. Marc. IV, 5, 1: in summa. si constat id verius, quod prius, id prius, quod (ab initio), id ab initio, quod ab apostolis, pariter utique constabit id esse ab apostolis traditum, quod apud ecclesias apostolorum fuerit sacrosanctum; *ibid.*, 4: atquin haec magis a primordio fuisse credibile est, ut priora, qua apostolica, ut cum ipsis ecclesiis dedicata.

[86] As Blum, 'Begriff des Apostolischen', p. 113, rightly points out with reference to the *regula fidei*.

[87] Cf. Adv. Marc., IV, 2, 1: . . . praedicatio discipulorum suspecta fieri posset de gloriae studio, si non adsistat illi auctoritas magistrorum, immo Christi, quae magistros apostolos fecit; Apol. 47, 10: . . . illam esse regulam veritatis, quae veniat a Christo transmissa per comites ipsius, quibus aliquanto posteriores diversi isti commentatores probabuntur. In the De praescriptione the following thought occurs with especial frequency, e.g., 6, 4: apostolos domini habemus auctores, qui nec ipsi quicquam ex suo arbitrio, quod inducerent, elegerunt, sed acceptam a Christo disciplinam fideliter nationibus adsignaverunt; 21, 4: . . . constat perinde omnem doctrinam, quae cum illis ecclesiis apostolicis matricibus et originalibus fidei conspiret, veritati deputandam, id sine dubio tenentem, quod ecclesiae ab apostolis, apostoli a Christo, Christus a deo accepit.

[88] This is the dominant thought, emphasised again and again. By contrast, there is absolutely no idea that the evangelists Mark and Luke were specially commissioned or sanctioned for their work by their apostolic teachers.

[89] In this connection cf. Tertullian's comments on the Epistle of Barnabas (= Hebrews), p. 271 n. 128 above. That Tertullian, for all that he set high value on Hebrews, did not wish to see it in his N.T. 'because Barnabas, under whose name Tertullian was acquainted with the Epistle, was not an apostle in the strict sense', is asserted by Harnack, 'Bibliothek', p. 306, simply on the basis of a preconceived notion.

Despite his efforts to secure a strict interpretation of biblical authority, Tertullian is no biblicist.[90] Over and over again he stresses that the words of the Bible are to be understood and interpreted not in isolation and mechanically, but in accordance with their meaning and context, the intention of the author, and the spirit of the whole sacred Scripture. This requirement is all the more serious—and all the harder to meet— because Tertullian is very well aware of the dangers of an unbridled allegorism.[91] For him the Bible does not all the time and in every verse consist of allegories and parables, which can be brought into play at will in order to resolve every difficulty, but only in quite definite passages and in quite definite circumstances.[92] In principle the literal interpretation deserves to take precedence so long as is at all possible.[93] Tertullian keeps to this rule. In fact he adopts the allegorical method almost exclusively in those places where it is sanctified by tradition, or seems in practice to be quite unavoidable, that is, primarily in the interpretation of the 'prophetic' and especially the legal texts of the Old Testament.[94] Here, moreover, he can appeal to the apostle[95] who by his example has already refuted the 'Jewish error' of a Marcion.[96] It is true that there are certain passages, the interpretation of which is difficult, and cannot be established straight away; it is right to take pains over these.[97] But this does not mean that Scripture in general is inherently obscure, or that its really important statements are not perfectly comprehensible.[98] 'Scripture', says Tertullian at one point in the

[90] On Tertullian's hermeneutic cf. A. Jülicher, *Die Gleichnisreden Jesu* I[2], 1910, pp. 215–220; G. Zimmermann, *Die hermeneutischen Prinzipien Tertullians* (Diss. phil. Leipzig, 1937); Karpp, *op. cit.*, esp. pp. 21ff.; O. Kuss, 'Zur Hermeneutik Tertullians,' in: *Neutestamentliche Aufsätze* (Festschrift Jos. Schmid), 1963, pp. 138–160.

[91] It is, as he emphasises, the favourite method of the gnostic heretics; so, e.g., Valent. 1; pudic. 8, 12.

[92] Carn. res. 33, 3: si (non) ad omnes in parabolis, iam non semper nec omnia parabolae, sed, quaedam, cum ad quosdam . . .; cf. pudic. 2, 1of. (termini, condiciones, causa).

[93] Scorp. 11, 5: siquidem tunc aliud significabitur in scripturis, si non id ipsum reperiatur in rebus. (In the word *res* what is here immediately in mind is the fulfilment of Christ's predictions of persecution for his followers.)

[94] Kuss, *op. cit.*, p. 153, seems to me to pay too little attention to this point when, following Zimmermann, he states that 'allegorical and typological exegesis' are 'of great importance' for Tertullian. I would be hard put to it to name even one Church Father, let alone theologian, of the second century who so drastically minimises their importance as he does.

[95] Adv. Marc. III, 5, 4; V, 7, 11; idol. 5, 4.

[96] Adv. Marc. III, 6, 2 (Iudaicus error).

[97] Praescr. 14, 1f.

[98] Cf., e.g., carn, res. 21, 2: et utique aequum sit, quod et supra demandavimus incerta de certis et obscura de manifestis praeiudicari, vel ne inter discordiam certorum et incertorum, manifestorum et obscurorum fides dissipietur, veritas periclitetur, ipsa divinitas ut inconstans denotetur; 21, 6: et puto deo nec

course of a heated anti-monarchian controversy, 'is in no danger, and there is no need for you to come to her help with your sophistry, in order to save her from seeming contradictions. She is equally in the right when she teaches one God alone, and when she shows that the Father and the Son are two Persons. She is self-sufficient (*sufficit sibi*)'.[99]

It is, admittedly, only too obvious that Tertullian himself was far from adhering faithfully to his own principles. His polemical writings swarm with exegetical swindles and with examples of violence to the text. This does not mean that Tertullian had never been in earnest about his declarations. But Tertullian is a barrister, and to the Roman barrister a great deal was permitted which seems shocking to the modern exegete, accustomed to impartial objectivity.[100] Tertullian is much too passionate and much too brilliant to be always 'objective'. He never misses an opportunity, nor does he consider any means unjustified which will reduce his opponent to silence, even where the exegesis of the Bible is involved.[101] Nevertheless, his concern for correct understanding and exegesis is by no means mere humbug, nor did it remain unfruitful. We need only recall the monumental and on the whole unrivalled work in which—admittedly in the spirit of the Old Testament—he refuted Marcion. But Tertullian had neither the opportunity nor the patience to be content with scholarly works of this kind. He suffered under the awareness of how little his arguments really achieved—when one considered the obdurate prejudice and empty sophistries which, as he thought, were always and everywhere to be found whenever his lead was not followed. But in addition there was a second far more serious consideration. Tertullian saw the helplessness of the catholic congregations when faced with the skilful seductions of the heretics, particularly when the latter made use of their exegesis of the

---

livorem nec dolum nec inconstantiam nec lenocinium adscribi posse, per quae fere promulgatio maiorum cavillatur.

[99] Prax. 18, 2: porro non periclitatur scriptura, ut illi de tua argumentatione succurras, ne sibi contraria videatur. habet rationem, et cum unicum deum statuit et cum duos patrem et filium ostendit, et sufficit sibi.

[100] The harsh judgments which Tertullian has had to endure at the hands of scholars from Jülicher to Kuss on this subject do not seem to me always justified. The church historian K. Holl, 'Tertullian als Schriftsteller', *Ges. Aufs. zur Kirchengeschichte* III, 1928, p. 5, gives a more adequate and understanding assessment.

[101] It cannot, however, be said that this was always true of the polemic of the early Church. Both Origen and Augustine sincerely strove to do justice to the reasoning and motives of their opponents—with the result that they frequently succeeded in convincing them. Tertullian has no use for such efforts: duritia vincenda est, non suadenda (scorp. 2, 1). Even when he is disputing with his fellow-believers his tone is for the most part so sharp that virtually no one is willing to listen to him, and he meets with rejection—proprium iam negotium passus meae opinionis (virg. vel. 1, 1).

Scripture, allegorising and reinterpreting to produce what they alleged to be a profounder meaning. He himself never tired of refuting them again and again; but when he thought of his Church, he longed for a simpler and more effective method which would allow him to 'deal summarily' with these intruders and enemies of the truth. In the famous treatise *De praescriptione haereticorum* he found the way to achieve this, and in his own manner vindicated it convincingly with his accustomed shrewdness.

To hope to find in this work something akin to Tertullian's doctrine of Scripture or even a biblical hermeneutic is to misunderstand it from the start.[102] Its aim is precisely to avoid further controverisies on this subject. Experience has shown that the endless disputes and hot air about the surface meaning and inner meaning of the various biblical texts, so dear to the heretics, achieve nothing except constant unrest and confusion in the congregation. The latter know perfectly well that they are in possession of the true faith, and they must draw the logical conclusion from that: heretics are no longer to be given any kind of a hearing; they must be shown the door at once. It can, after all, be proved that the catholic Church and she alone possesses complete and undistorted the original teaching of Christ and his truth, which means the teaching and truth of God himself. She received it from the authorised apostles, and following the lead of the first apostolic churches she has unanimously preserved it to this day in a fixed, unbroken tradition. Hence she also knows what is and always will be the real meaning and content of the holy Scripture. By contrast, the heretics have crept in at a later stage, falsifying and perverting the text and its meaning to suit their own fancy,[103] and so have absolutely no right to trespass on the Bible, which simply does not belong to them. Consequently—and this is the upshot of the whole discussion[104]—heretics are no longer to be admitted, if they wish to start a dispute about Scripture; for it can

---

[102] Harnack, *Entstehung*, p. 136 n. 3: 'One should beware of defining Tertullian's attitude to holy Scripture on the one-sided evidence of that polemical work, the *De praescriptione*'; Kuss, *op. cit.*, p. 152 n. 60, agrees. It is not, however, the case that Tertullian was here saying anything that he had not maintained elsewhere; all that is necessary is to see that here he is restricting himself wholly to one idea, and why he is doing so.

[103] It should be noted that in the De praescriptione Tertullian almost always brings forward the charges of falsification and misinterpretation of the Scripture simultaneously. The brutal demand that heretical exegeses should not even be given a hearing appears more justified when it is asserted at the same time that they have also destroyed the only basis on which a discussion is possible, namely the Canon itself.

[104] There is no need to reproduce here the whole argument of the praescriptio; cf. on this subject Stirnimann, *op. cit.* (n. 56 above), and R. F. Refoulé in his edition: *Tertullien, Traité de la prescription contre les Hérétiques*, Paris, 1957, pp. 20–45.

be established even without the help of Scripture that they are cut off from the Scriptures.[105] This is the sense of the 'address to the court' which, as Tertullian sees it, means that the controversy, like a legal action, can be cut short at the very beginning and dispensed with.

The purport of the basic idea behind these observations is misrepresented if it is taken to mean that Tertullian has turned against the use of Scripture in argument altogether, simply because he has been able to propose a more effective ecclesiological method of proceeding in its place. What Tertullian wants is an estoppal of all further controversy and dispute with heretics, *tout court*. In his eyes they are no longer Christians;[106] quarrelling of this sort can therefore lead absolutely nowhere. The demonstration that the catholic church alone can be and is in possession of the truth serves merely to explain this unequivocal situation and the harsh attitude which inevitably follows from it.[107] The futility of discussing Scripture is given such strong emphasis solely because Tertullian is quite unaware of any other form that controversy might take. 'With what else can the false teachers conduct their arguments in matters of faith,' he asks explicitly, 'apart from the scripture on which faith is founded?'[108] Now it may certainly be said that it is a limitation of the sovereignty and judicial function of the Bible to make it, as Tertullian does, the private property of the orthodox community, and to dismiss any heretical appeal to its verdict as invalid and unworthy of attention. But this impression is at best only half correct and, if the whole of Tertullian's writings is taken into account, not much better than an illusion. The last sentence of the De praescriptione already tells us as much: with God's help Tertullian will yet give a detailed answer to the various heretics,[109] and this promise he kept. All his great anti-heretical writings—and equally the kindred polemical works of his Montanist period against the Great Church—

[105] Praescr. 37, 1: ... constat ratio propositi nostri definientis non esse admittendos haereticos ad ineundam de scripturis provocationem, quos sine scripturis probamus ad scripturas non pertinere.

[106] Praescr. 32, 8. This rigorist view constitutes a presupposition of the whole dispute, and in its implications is in accord with the hard line on church unity which obtained throughout ancient times; Refoulé, *op. cit.*, p. 41 n. 3: 'These conclusions are not peculiar to Tertullian, but express the viewpoint of all the Fathers of the early centuries.'

[107] This important explanation of the train of thought in the De praescriptione was first clearly set out by Flesseman-van Leer, *op. cit.*, esp. pp. 182f.

[108] In Praescr. 14, 14 Tertullian promptly replies to the objection, 'sed ipsi de scripturis agunt et de scripturis suadent', with the words: aliunde scilicet loqui possent de rebus fidei nisi ex litteris fidei? (the various minor variants and conjectural emendations do not alter the sense of this passage); cf. 39, 7 (n. 75 above)

[109] Praescr. 44, 13f.: sed nunc quidem generaliter actum est nobis adversus haereses omnes certis et iustis et necessariis praescriptionibus repellendas a conlatione scripturarum. de reliquo, si dei gratia adnuerit, etiam specialiter quibusdam respondebimus.

were published after the De praescriptione,[110] and all of them endeavour to refute his opponents with objective arguments and with reasons based on faith, which means in effect, with the Scriptures. Tertullian does not give up the position he has won, and continues to insist that the heretics manifestly and 'in principle' have no claim to be heard at all. Nevertheless, 'of his bounty' he repeatedly enters into debate with them,[111] in order thus to destroy them not merely on formal legal grounds but in earnest and all the more effectively. This method is authentic Tertullian. Tertullian loves to demand and to prove everything, to begin by stripping his enemies—and the heretics are his enemies—of all their rights in order that he may then yield with seeming magnanimity and smite them all over again on the assumptions he has conceded.[112] If concealed behind the terse reserve of the De praescriptione we seem to sense something like dejection or a secret resignation, this in no way concerns the Scripture but arises from despair chiefly of the rationality and teachability of the heretics but also of the assurance and steadfastness of the faith of his own church. For this very reason the latter have to be protected at any price from the sophistries of these seducers, and in particular from their subtle appeals to Scripture.

This leads to the distinctive use of the *regula*, to which Tertullian refers fairly frequently, and in the De praescriptione repeatedly and with great emphasis. It is called the rule and guideline of truth (*regula veritatis*), or, even more often, of faith (*fidei*) and likewise of moral discipline (*disciplinae*); and on one occasion, against Marcion, it is even referred to as the 'rule of the scriptures' (*scripturarum regula*).[113] It is precisely this multiplicity of aspects which is significant, and which shows that what Tertullian has in mind is no different from what Irenaeus meant by his 'canon of truth'.[114] To render Irenaeus's term κανών in this way is entirely correct. The expression signifies the essential content of the Christian faith itself, 'the content of faith as a totality',[115] as this is alive in the Church and finds expression in her tradition and her witness and is therefore also to be found, identically as regards its

[110] Stirnimann, *op. cit.*, p. 143.

[111] Carn. Chr. 2, 6: sed plenius eiusmodi praescriptionibus adversus omnes haereses alibi iam usi sumus. post quas nunc ex abundanti retractemus . . . ; Adv. Marc. IV, 38, 7: ex abundanti nunc et post praescriptionem retractabo adversus argumentationes cohaerentes.

[112] On this point cf. the pertinent comments of Holl, *op. cit.*, p. 6.

[113] Adv. Marc. III, 17, 5: oportet (et) actum eius (sc. Christi) ad scripturarum regulam recognosci, duplici, nisi fallor, operatione distinctum: praedicationis et virtutis.

[114] Cf. pp. 207ff. above.

[115] B. Hägglund, 'Die Bedeutung der "regula fidei" als Grundlage theologischer Aussagen,' *StTh* 12, 1958, p. 29.

substance, in the Bible.[116] Tertullian, in his usual manner, has laid especial stress on the normative, binding character of this canon of faith, has outlined its content on the model of the baptismal confession and roughly in the sense of the later Apostles' Creed[117] more clearly than Irenaeus, and on occasion has even given it special emphasis in definite propositions. But it is impossible to speak in his case of a rigid, sacral 'formula' in the sense of the Apostles' or any other comprehensive creed of the later period.[118] In the context of the De praescriptione Tertullian was especially concerned to stress the independence and sufficiency of the *regula*, which (as in Irenaeus) is sufficient even without scriptural support. The *regula dei*[119] was given to the Church by Christ through the apostles, and it is this to which faith adheres. 'It is your faith, says Christ, which has made you whole, not busying yourself with the scriptures'.[120] The contrast here is with the empty arguments and debates in which difficulties are raised about this or that passage of Scripture, and which according to Tertullian the heretics practise simply in order to undermine men's faith—not with Scripture and the reading of Scripture as such. Now as always Scripture may be studied in faith and among the faithful—in such a way, in other words, that the rule of faith is never called in question.[121] As Tertullian understands the situation, this is by no means to imply that the exegesis of Scripture must be subjected to an external norm, laid down by the Church,[122]

---

[116] On this subject cf., in addition to Van den Eynde, *op. cit.*, pp. 291–297, and J. N. D. Kelly, *Early Christian Creeds*[2], 1952, pp. 82–88, esp. Flesseman-van Leer, *op. cit.*, pp. 161–170; R. P. C. Hanson, *Tradition in the Early Church*, 1962, pp. 102–114, as well as the systematic examination by Hägglund, *op. cit.*, pp. 19–29; cf. also Refoulé, *op. cit.*, pp. 50–53; Bakhuizen, *op. cit.*, pp. 71–73.

[117] Cf. the material in F. Kattenbusch, *Das apostolische Symbol* I, 1894, pp. 141–145.

[118] The opposite view, which formerly held the field, was unfortunately the one which I adopted in my portrait of Tertullian in *Fathers of the Latin Church*, 196–.

[119] So Adv. Marc. I, 21, 4; 22, 3.

[120] Praescr. 14, 3f.: fides, inquit, tua te salvum fecit, non exercitatio scripturarum. fides in regula posita est, habet legem et salutem de observatione legis. On the last part of this quotation Hägglund, *op. cit.*, p. 20, rightly comments: 'What is referred to here is not the moral law, the "ordo" or the "regula disciplinae", but simply the fact that the "regula fidei" supplies the normative form of the doctrine necessary for salvation.'

[121] Praescr. 12, 5: quaeramus ergo in nostro et a nostris et de nostro—idque dumtaxat, quod salva regula fidei potest in quaestionem devenire; cf. Irenaeus, Adv. haer. V, 20, 1.

[122] In this case we would never be able to answer 'the quite simple and absolutely basic question, what is the use of scripture if in the end the only thing that matters is the rule of faith': Kuss, *op. cit.*, p. 158. Despite its comparable starting-point Tertullian's little book should not be interpreted in the same sense as the exhortation of a Vincent of Lerins: ut propheticae et apostolicae interpretationis

but that Scripture is to be read from within the faith with which the believer is already familiar, and that when it is so read scripture itself simply confirms that faith over and over again. The closest modern counterpart to this definition of the *regula veritatis* is the concept of the 'canon within the canon'—but only if this is understood as a 'guide' to a right understanding, and not as a critical principle by which to scrutinise the Scripture. The indestructible unity and homogeneity of the Scriptures of the Old and New Testaments is for Tertullian, as for all the Fathers from Irenaeus onwards, the fundamental biblical dogma in their fight against the gnostics. It is a dogma which was not seriously imperilled until the rise of modern historical criticism, and it gave Tertullian, like most of the theologians of the early Church, relatively little trouble.

Tertullian found it much more difficult to maintain the sufficiency of Scripture.[123] So far as the area of 'dogmatic' truths about God, Christ, and Christian salvation were concerned, he defended it at all times and, as he believed, triumphantly. But Tertullian was also a moralist and a rigorist; and it was equally important to him to regulate the whole of Christian life by means of clear standards, and to answer every practical question of decisive importance which faced the Church with unambiguous commands. Could the bible really satisfy this desire permanently? Tertullian tries his utmost. Not only does he expound the various commandments from time to time in accordance with his own understanding of them; as regards the many different examples and 'models' occurring in Scripture he tries at one time to give them the status of indirect commands, and then at another to rule them out altogether as exceptions dictated by the age in which they occurred. The scheme of salvation-history, with its eras of moral progress even within the new covenant itself, is often intolerably overworked in order to arrive at the desired result. It becomes clear, however, that the Bible does not

---

linea secundum ecclesiastici et catholici sensus normam dirigatur (Commonit. II, 2).

[123] Karpp, *op. cit.*, p. 41, however, goes much too far when he expresses the opinion that Tertullian 'did not constantly adhere to the concept of the sufficiency of scripture'. He is here thinking of the alleged supplementation of Scripture by the 'rule of faith', giving this what is, in my view, a false connotation which Tertullian did not intend. Kuss, *op. cit.*, p. 146 n. 39, is perhaps right to doubt whether the concept of 'sufficiency' (Prax. 18, 2: cf. n. 99 above) was meant in so radical a sense; but it cannot be doubted that in substance it underlies everything that Tertullian ever wrote.

[124] Cf. esp. Cor. 2f. (on the concept of tradition employed here cf. Flesseman-van Leer, *op. cit.*, p. 147); also virg. vel. 1f. (cf. n. 63 above). The counsel of despair of an unwritten tradition for the practical ordinances of the Church appears for the first time in the late works of Tertullian: Van den Eynde, *op. cit.*, p. 274, and especially F. de Pauw, 'La justification de traditions non écrits chez Tertullien', *EThL* 19, 1942, pp. 5–46.

always have an answer ready to casuistic problems about situations in daily work or the duty of confessing the faith, about married life or theatregoing, about wearing garlands or veils; and even Tertullian is obliged—though it goes against the grain—to admit it.[124] Here we have one vital reason why he went over to Montanism: the Paraclete with his stringent orders seemed at last to afford some real help and to bring the full seriousness of Christian discipline to perfection.[125] But even this is a delusion. 'The growing inner unrest is clearly reflected in the ever more violent tone of his writings. Indeed, the conflict is now quite impossible to resolve; Tertullian wears himself out, but can never make up his mind.'[126] It may be that he himself felt this, but could never bring himself to admit it. To do so would for him have been equivalent to a moral capitulation.

The limitations which Tertullian here fails to transcend are not those of his concept of the Canon, which he continued to use even as a Montanist.[127] They are those of his Christianity, which sees the Gospel merely as a perfect *lex* and *disciplina*, and which is therefore unable to surmount the obstacle of a rigorist casuistry. From this starting-point there can be no hope of arriving at the inner unity of salvation-history and the Scriptures. The failure to establish a clear definition of Law and Gospel certainly caused trouble throughout the history of the early Church; but it is significant that even where other and better theological approaches were sought and found, there was never any need to change either Tertullian's canon or his concept of the canon. The Canon remains the same totality, articulated in terms of salvation-history, formally complete, and inherently inviolable, and the standard of everything which the Church teaches and believes.

With *Clement of Alexandria* we move into a different world. Clement is a contemporary of Tertullian, and roughly one generation younger than Irenaeus. He knew the latter's writings and used them, as he did those of Justin,[128] and occasionally he even mentions Irenaeus by name.[129] Clement too is a fighter for the true Church against the error of heresy,[130] and in his own way no less of a 'scriptural theologian'[131]

[125] A sketch of this development in its context will be found in my earlier essay: 'Urchristentum und Tradition bei Tertullian', *ThBl* 8, 1929, pp. 193–200; on Tertullian's statements in his Montanist period which are of particular interest for the history of the Canon cf. Lagrange, *op. cit.*, pp. 55–57.

[126] Holl, *op. cit.*, p. 12.

[127] This point has been unanimously established by all scholars; cf. esp. Karpp, *op. cit.*, pp. 58ff.; also Kuss, *op. cit.*, p. 157.

[128] For both writers cf. the list of quotations in the Index to the great edition by O. Stählin (*GCS* IV), 1936, p. 28.

[129] Eusebius, *HE* VI, 13, 9.

[130] T. Rüther, 'Die eine Kirche und die Häresie bei Klemens von Alexandrien', *Catholica* 12, 1958, pp. 37–50.

[131] As Harnack, *Dogmengeschichte* I, p. 391 emphasises.

U

than Tertullian. He too lives and moves and has his being in the words of the Bible.[132] Nevertheless, this extremely general similarity apart, in relation to the Canon and to canonical thinking in general it is hardly possible to think of two men more different than Clement and Irenaeus, and in the case of Clement and Tertullian completely impossible. Clement is a different personality from either; he lives in a different intellectual environment, and comes from a different, almost diametrically opposite, ecclesiastical and theological tradition. In his interpretation of Scripture he is working in a direction the dangers of which Irenaeus had already weighed, and which both he and Tertullian had used the new Canon precisely to combat. Clement remained content with roughly the same 'canonical' stock of Scripture which he found already existing in his day and milieu; and in the intellectual interpretation of the Canon and of the necessity for it, he never, taken by and large, remotely reached the position maintained by Irenaeus and Tertullian— indeed, perhaps we have to say that he deliberately took good care not to reach it.

Irenaeus had been a bishop; in everything he thought as a churchman, and as a theologian his concerns were basically dogmatic. His thinking was spiritual, and in his acceptance of diverse traditions far from narrow; but what he was constantly seeking was the essential and the permanent, that which was common to all Christians. This was what the witness of the Bible was primarily meant to confirm, and thus to provide the decisive support needed to combat all false teachers. Because the Old Testament by itself no longer sufficed, Irenaeus had moved away from the precarious allegorical and typological exegeses of the ancient texts to the clear christological utterances of the primitive Christian documents, and with painstaking argument had presented the most important and useful books from this period as a sure and unmistakable standard of what was valid. When both Tertullian and the Muratorian Canon describe and delimit more precisely the stock of 'received' books to which the catholic Church adheres, this is simply an extension of the line which he had laid down. The target was a final selection which could never thereafter be disturbed.

In Clement there is no trace of such endeavours. Clement is an independent, 'academic' teacher, with barely any interest in the 'objective' norms and ordinances of the Church. When he expounds the Scripture, he wants above all to awaken a living understanding, to decipher its deeper mysteries, and in this way to make it possible for men to appropriate personally the scriptural truth which leads to perfection. To stop at the universal and seemingly self-evident is precisely what he does not want; his desire is to press on to the heights of knowledge, where the true 'gnostic' lives in inner freedom. In this he is an heir of the Alexandrian-gnostic tradition. His attitude does not require of him unqualified opposition to the datum of a canon: but, rather than being able to reinforce and advance a fixed 'canonical' commitment, he inevitably feels it as a trammelling problem.

This much at any rate is clear: Clement too is at home with the concept that the sacred Scriptures which the Church possesses fall into two parallel groups which belong together, and which are linked to the old and new divine covenants. It was precisely in his writings that we found the first instances of the usage whereby these writings could themselves be described as the old and the new covenant, the 'Old' and the 'New Testament'.[133] But in Clement's case this is still very much the exception, and not at all characteristic of his particular manner. Clement rarely considers the bipartite Bible as a literary unity. Although in fact he strongly prefers the 'New Testament',[134] the solemn emphasis of the sacral concept of 'scripture' for him falls time after time on the Old Testament—which was, after all, largely put together in Alexandria. As in Hippolytus, when Clement speaks of 'the scripture', 'the divine scriptures' or the 'scriptures of the Lord' it is in most cases the Old Testament alone, or at any rate primarily, which is meant.[135] Marcionites and other heretics are still directing their attacks against the Old Testament, and, as Clement complains, are distorting the Scripture and refusing to listen to its instruction.[136] And yet 'faith in Christ and the knowledge of the Gospel are the exposition and fulfilment of the Law'.[137] Paul, in what he writes, is entirely dependent both in spirit and in language on the Old Testament,[138] and it is the Old Testament which above all he expects his pupils to understand.[139] These are ancient, traditional ideas, in keeping with a predominantly oral, not literary, understanding of the 'Gospel' and the 'new covenant': 'The church's guideline is the harmony and agreement between the

---

[132] C. Mondésert, *Clément d'Alexandrie. Introduction a l'étude de sa pensée religieuse à partir de l'Écriture,* 1944, pp. 65ff.

[133] Cf. pp. 266f. above.

[134] The index of O.T. quotations in Stählin's edition comprises 30 columns as against more than 46 for the New. This corresponds to the practice of the great Valentinian theologians: cf. pp. 80f. above.

[135] H. Kutter, *Clemens Alexandrinus und das Neue Testament,* 1897, p. 147. His judgment on this point is confirmed by the verification which the passages listed in Stählin's index (pp. 319f.) provide. Nevertheless, the borderline between instances is fluid, and in view of the imprecise style which Clement employs even in this context, is sometimes almost impossible to define.

[136] So, e.g., Strom. III, 38, 1; 39, 2; 71, 1f.; IV, 2, 2; VI, 123, 3; 125, 3; VII, 94ff.; 101ff.

[137] Strom. IV, 134, 3 (cf. p. 266 n. 299 above).

[138] Strom. IV, 134, 2–4 (cf. p. 266 n. 299 above); cf. *hypot.* frag. 21, on II Tim. 2:2: "Διὰ πολλῶν μαρτύρων", τουτέστι νόμου καὶ προφητῶν. τούτους γὰρ <ὁ> ἀπόστολος ἐποιεῖτο μάρτυρας τοῦ ἰδίου κηρύγματος.

[139] Strom. VII, 105, 2.

Law and the Prophets on the one hand and the new covenant which
springs from and accords with the appearing of the Lord'.[140]

The only group of New Testament writings which Clement regularly
cites as 'scripture',[141] and to that extent equates with the Old Testament, is once again the Gospels, or more frequently, as they are called
in Irenaeus and even in the Muratorian Canon: 'the Gospel'. On occasion—in the same way as in Hegesippus[142] and Hippolytus—this is
mentioned alongside 'the Law and the Prophets' as a single, formal
authority.[143] Clement also prefers to quote the 'word of the Lord'
directly, without citing any source,[144] although he is, of course, perfectly familiar with the individual Gospels and evangelists, and occasionally even takes an interest in their provenance.[145] In one passage
'the four Gospels which have been handed down to us' are marked out
as such, and given decisive precedence over the 'Gospel of the Egyptians'.[146] Nevertheless, this occurs only on this one occasion, and
although Clement also indicates elsewhere an unambiguous preference
for the four canonical Gospels, yet he has no misgivings about employ-
ing other, 'apocryphal' Gospels (though he does not call them that)
to supplement them.[147]

What apart from the four Gospels belongs in Clement's eyes to the
'New Testament' can be only approximately determined. It is clear
that 'the Apostle' takes a predominant place;[148] but other epistles, as
well as apocalypses and other books, occur alongside him. All of these

---

[140] Strom. VI, 125, 3: κανὼν δὲ ἐκκλησιαστικὸς ἡ συνῳδία καὶ ἡ συμφωνία
νόμου τε καὶ προφητῶν τῇ κατὰ τὴν τοῦ κυρίου παρουσίαν παραδιδομένῃ
διαθήκῃ.

[141] Cf. Harnack, *Dogmengeschichte* I, p. 391 n. 4.

[142] Cf. p. 167 above.

[143] In these cases it is admittedly not always clear whether it is really the written and not rather the oral, preached Gospel which is meant; cf. Strom. IV,
2, 2: . . . ἕνα δεικνύναι θεὸν καὶ κύριον παντοκράτορα τὸν διὰ νόμου καὶ
προφητῶν, πρὸς δὲ καὶ τοῦ μακαρίου εὐαγγελίου γνησίως κεκηρυγμένον.
Also II, 29, 3; III, 76, 1. Yet we also find the bald counterpoint of prophets and
apostles (cf. p. 257 n. 257 above), e.g., Strom. I, 45; V, 135, 1, and the complete
formula in VI, 88, 5: . . . μουσικὴν συμφωνίαν τὴν ἐκκλησιαστικὴν νόμου καὶ
προφητῶν ὁμοῦ καὶ ἀποστόλων σὺν καὶ τῷ εὐαγγελίῳ. Similarly V II, 97, 2.

[144] So, e.g., Strom. I, 2, 3; 32, 4; 41, 2; 56, 2; 85, 2; 87, 6; 100, 3; 169, 2;
II, 108, 3; III, 27, 3; 31, 1; 33, 3; 36, 4; 56, 3, etc.

[145] Cf. the fragments of the *Hypotyposes* in Eusebius, *HE* II, 15, 1f.; VI, 14,
5-7.

[146] Strom. III, 93, 1: πρῶτον μὲν οὖν ἐν τοῖς παραδεδομένοις ἡμῖν τέτταρσιν
εὐαγγελίοις οὐκ ἔχομεν τὸ ῥητόν ἀλλ᾽ ἐν τῷ κατ᾽ Αἰγυπτίους.

[147] For the detailed evidence the reader is referred, in addition to Stählin's
Index and the various histories of the Canon, to the study by J. Ruwet, 'Clément
d'Alexandrie—Canon des Écritures et Apocryphes', *Biblica* 29, 1948, pp. 77-99;
240-268; 391-408, which is extremely thorough, though it shows little understanding of the real nature of Clement's concept of Scripture.

[148] Cf. n. 153 below.

can be referred to as 'apostolic' in the wider sense;[149] yet neither apostolic authorship nor restriction to the 'classical' period of primitive Christianity constitutes, so far as one can tell, the principle on which they are selected.[150] Quite obviously Clement took no interest in these particular problems. Despite his anti-Montanism he nowhere advocates a restriction of the Canon. In his writings the 'apostles' Barnabas and Clement stand side by side with Paul, Peter or Jude; Hermas and the Apocalypse of Peter beside the Revelation of John; and apocryphal apostolic Acts alongside the canonical Acts, which though certainly quoted more frequently and with greater emphasis than the others is also on the whole only sparingly employed.[151] It is impossible to compile a definite 'list' of those books which Clement regarded as 'authentically' belonging to the New Testament[152]—to some extent he still

[149] Cf. n. 143 below.

[150] The opposite view is taken by Kutter, *op. cit.*, pp. 127–138, who concentrates on a supposedly normative principle of 'apostolicity', which is impossible to substantiate. For a correct assessment cf. P. Dausch, *Der neutestamentliche Schriftcanon und Clemens von Alexandrien*, 1894, pp. 44f. The apostles are, it is true, frequently mentioned as witnesses to the secret, oral tradition (cf. n. 186 below), but so far as the Canon is concerned they do not constitute a body of guarantors. They represent much more an ideal of perfection which in principle every Christian can attain (Strom. VI, 106, 1). It is in this context that they are contrasted with the heretics (Strom. VII, 103, 6f.) and represented by the true gnostics (Strom. VII, 77, 1). Were this not so, it would be impossible to explain the extraordinarily lavish way in which Clement uses the concept of 'apostle'. He applies the title even to Clement of Rome (Strom. IV, 105, 1) and Barnabas (Strom. II, 31, 2; 35, 5). (In Strom. II, 116, 3, on the other hand, Barnabas is called ἀποστολικός, and is included among the seventy disciples; cf. n. 189 below.) In Exc. ex Theod. 74, 1 the evangelist Luke is also apparently called an apostle.

[151] According to Kutter, *op. cit.*, p. 100, it is quoted about ten times; and according to Harnack, *Dogmengeschichte* I, p. 392 n. 3, is used to roughly the same extent as the 'Preaching of Peter' (seven quotations), from which it is 'completely doubtful what degree of authority' Clement attaches to it; cf. further Harnack, *Entstehung*, p. 74, with the reference to Leipoldt, *op. cit.*, I, p. 200: 'Clement does not regard Acts as canonical.' This may be somewhat overstated (Dausch, *op. cit.*, p. 15); yet the fact that so much less attention is paid to it is undoubtedly very significant when we consider the value which Irenaeus attached to precisely this work as a source of what he regarded as the essential 'apostolic' testimony. Nevertheless, the question of 'degrees' of authority is one which it is not really appropriate to ask about Clement. Clement, as Harnack, *Dogmengeschichte* I, p. 391, himself emphasises, thinks of all 'writings which contain religious and moral truths as inspired', and in his quotations he is concerned far less with sacral authority than with the living witness of the Spirit. Only, as Kutter, *op. cit.*, p. 108, rightly comments, 'it is the people who make the scriptures significant'. Stählin's translation in the *Bibliothek der Kirchenväter* (1934ff.) unintentionally somewhat blurs this vital feature by constantly supplementing the indefinite φησί with the German, 'die heilige Schrift' ('holy scripture').

[152] This is admitted, cautiously, even by Lagrange, *op. cit.*, pp. 90f., and con-

has an 'open' canon. If, taken by and large, his apposite quotations fall mostly within the scope of our New Testament, this is in part to be explained by the ecclesiastical practice of his own church, but is primarily to be attributed to his strong sense of what is intellectually and spiritually essential. Consequently, as in Irenaeus, it is the four great Gospels and the apostle Paul—without Acts, though—which for him constitute the hard permanent core of a New Testament which at its edges is fluid.[153]

This impression that Clement's use of Scripture is open, without any hard edges, is strengthened even further when we remember that he by no means treats his biblical quotations in a separate category of their own. At every step they are intertwined with the words of classical philosophers and poets, with heathen oracles and wisdom sayings. The non-Christian quotations in Clement's writings are more numerous than all the biblical quotations put together.[154] But even this is in a wider sense part of his use of Scripture. For the citations from pagan literature are not simply secular; they may confirm and supplement the biblical insights, and help to defend and interpret them. Even Plato was 'as it were, inspired', when he determined to follow only the Logos,[155] or 'almost prophetic' when he spoke of the crucifixion of the righteous man.[156] It is true that the heathen 'prophets' were not themselves aware of the implications of their utterances; they testified to the coming Christ only unconsciously and to a certain extent 'against their will'.[157] There are times, however, when Clement even goes so far as to

---

firmed by every specialist; cf. esp. R. P. C. Hanson, *Origen's Doctrine of Tradition*, 1954, pp. 127–133. In the light of this, it is certainly no accident that Clement is almost the only writer to make no use of the otherwise widely disseminated formula μήτε προσθεῖναι μήτε ἀφελεῖν, as W. C. van Unnik has established ('De la règle Μήτε προσθεῖναι μήτε ἀφελεῖν dans l'histoire du Canon',*VC* 3, 1949, p. 9). Clement is also often very free in his quotation: Kutter, *op. cit.*, pp. 31–45.

[153] In Stählin's Index of Quotations there are over 21 columns of references to the Gospels, and almost 20 from Paul, as against less than 6 for the whole of the N.T.—to which, admittedly, Clement would add some further works, such as Barnabas (½ col.), I Clement (1 col.), Hermas (½ col.), and possibly also other less used 'apocrypha' (Didache, Apocalypse of Peter, 'Preaching of Peter', etc.).

[154] In Stählin's Index 46 cols. of N.T. passages and a good 10 cols. for 'Christian writers and heretics (including apocrypha)' are followed by 90 cols. for 'non-Christian writers' (of which a good 7 are devoted to Philo).

[155] Strom. I, 42, 1: οἷον θεοφορούμενος.

[156] Strom. V, 108, 2: μονονουχὶ προφητεύων; on this subject cf. E. Benz, *Der gekreuzigte Gerechte bei Plato, im Neuen Testament und in der alten Kirche*, 1950, p. 41.

[157] Strom. VI, 127, 3. Thus, it is said of Homer, Paed. I, 36, 1: τοιοῦτόν τι καὶ ῞Ομηρος ἄκων μαντεύεται, and of the Epicurean, Metrodoros, Strom, V,

speak of a formal 'covenant', which God made with the Greeks through philosophy, corresponding to the Old Covenant made with the Jews.[158] In thinking along such lines Clement is undoubtedly following 'gnostic' influences and traditions. The 'religio-historical' conviction that God's revelatory activity is universal, a conviction which in gnostic circles had blocked the formation of a strict canon,[159] still works effectually upon him. It is true that the influence of Justin, whose concept of the *logos spermatikos* was certainly well known to Clement, should also be borne in mind. Like Justin, Clement in his reflections on the universal activity of the Logos has no intention of weakening the unique claim of Christ; on the contrary, his aim is precisely to extend it in this way to cover all truth and to make its dominion complete. The full knowledge of God is to be found only where it has been revealed by God through his Son.[160] But similar views are also advanced by Valentinus and the Valentinians,[161] who were definitely conscious of the wide area of agreement between their Christian conviction and the philosophers;[162] and on this point Clement—with slight reservations—agrees with them.[163] He never goes so far as simply to equate the words of Plato or Homer with the words of Scripture; but he takes over the gnostic method of unrestricted quotation and the technique of constructing catenas of quotations, and with supreme skill brings them to perfection.[164] The only thing which always distinguishes him from the

---

138, 2: Μητροδώρου τε, καίτοι ʼΕπικουρείου γενομένου, ἐνθέως ταῦτά γε εἰρηκότος . . . ; cf. W. Schmid, art, 'Epikur', *RAC* V, 1962, col. 812.

[158] Strom. VI, 42, 1; cf. 161, 5f. Clement, however, is by no means being consistent in making this declaration. He is also familiar with the traditional explanation of heathen wisdom, namely that it was stolen by the Greeks from the O.T.; cf. J. Munck, *Untersuchungen über Klemens von Alexandria*, 1933, pp. 134, 151; A. Méhat, *Étude sur les "Stromates" de Clément d'Alexandrie*, 1966, pp. 356–361; and on the whole problem, together with further texts, E. Molland, 'Clement of Alexandria on the Origin of Greek Philosophy,' *Symb. Osloens.* fasc. V-XVI, 1936, pp. 57–85, and *The Conception of the Gospel in the Alexandrian Theology*, 1938, pp. 40–69.

[159] Cf. pp. 74ff., 135ff. above.

[160] Strom. I, 98, 4; cf. 28, 2f.; 29, 9; II, 122, 1; 134, 1, etc. It is also no accident that 'Clement . . . never, like Justin, calls Christianity a philosophy and nothing more': J. W. Waszink, 'Der Platonismus und die altchristliche Gedankenwelt' in: *Entretiens sur l'antiquité classique III: Recherches sur la tradition Platonicienne*, 1955, p. 153.

[161] Cf., e.g., Strom. II, 114, 3, or the Epistle to Rheginos XXIII[6], 3ff.

[162] Strom. VI, 52, 4.

[163] Strom. VI, 53; cf. Dausch, *op. cit.*, p. 53.

[164] In doing so he keeps for the most part to a deliberate sequence, e.g. O.T.–N.T.–pagan witnesses. Frequently there is significant sub-division, e.g., within the O.T., first the Law, then the Prophets; within the N.T., first Gospels, then Paul, then the rest. The whole procedure and its history ought sometime to be studied in its context.

heretical gnosis is that he never impugns the divine revelation in the Old Testament. He regards the complete accord of the old and new covenants as virtually a guiding principle of orthodox scriptural exegesis, and defends it with determination.[165] For it is Christ himself who speaks in the Old as well as in the New Testament.[166] Indeed, the Lord stands and teaches alone and free above every Scripture as the one without whom first and last there can be no faith; and he himself cannot be exhausted by any written statement.[167] He in his own person is absolute truth, reason, and knowledge; he is also the Law[168] and the Covenant[169] and the perfect teacher whom all instruction must follow.[170]

The old-fashioned attitude which Clement displays toward the process by which the idea of canonicity came into being is to be seen not only in his use of Scripture; it comes out even more clearly in his corresponding ideas about oral tradition, on which living knowledge of Christ and of the Scriptures vitally depends. But Clement's concept of tradition is not merely archaic; older views are also reinforced by definite concepts from the Alexandrian gnostic tradition. These create difficulties in the way of coming to terms with the new scriptural principle, and render its complete victory in any stringent form impossible.

In itself the affirmation of the New Testament was, if we disregard Marcion, nowhere understood as a renunciation of the 'living' tradition out of which it had sprung. Irenaeus himself had explicitly defended the permanent rights of oral tradition in the orthodox Church, and even in the struggle against Montanist prophetism he had made no change in his stand on this principle. The assumption which made it possible to juxtapose Scripture and tradition in this way had always been simply that the two could not diverge because in content they were identical. That was why in dealing with the gnostics Irenaeus had rejected any 'secret' tradition which went beyond the Scripture, and had deliberately restricted his proof that catholic teaching was the original teaching to the written witness of the Old and especially of the New Testament. This seemed to him the most appropriate and completely satisfactory method of securely setting up the whole of Christian truth and establishing it irrefutably against the heretics. In this Hippolytus and Tertullian followed him.

[165] Cf. n. 140 above; also Strom. VI, 88, 5.
[166] This traditional conception is in no way diluted in Clement's writings: Mondésert, *op. cit.*, pp. 82f.
[167] On this point cf. P. T. Camelot, *Foi et gnose. Introduction à l'étude de la connaissance mystique chez Clément d'Alexandrie*, Paris, 1945, pp. 114–120; E. F. Osborn, *The Philosophy of Clement of Alexandria*, 1957, pp. 114f.
[168] Eclog. proph. 58.
[169] Strom. I, 182, 2.
[170] Protr. 3ff.; Strom. I, 9, 3; 12, 3; 16, 2f.; II, 12, 1; 16, 2 etc.; cf. also Frag. 68.

In Clement we find a completely different picture. It is true that Clement is no less of a believer in Scripture than Irenaeus or Justin,[171] and in the struggle against heresy refers constantly to the Scriptures in which God has spoken.[172] They provide the surest proofs 'that the sects have gone astray, and that in the true, ancient Church alone can we find knowledge which is really well-founded and the sect which is truly the best'.[173] Nevertheless, polemical statements of this sort still do not contain his full convictions. Clement is by no means of the opinion that Scripture will actually reveal its truth—leaving aside perhaps the most general sort—to everyone. Quite the contrary. The full truth of Scripture, like any religious knowledge, is a mystery, which is disclosed slowly and only to those who follow the laborious path of learning and toil, of mental purification, education and self-education. To find this path what is needed above all is the right teacher, one who knows the truth and has himself received it in the same way from instructors who have attained enlightenment. This is something that can be done only by word of mouth—simply because it is a mystery which is involved. Divine truth should be revealed and passed on only step by step with constant reference to the mental and moral maturity of the hearer. To give away the ultimate knowledge too quickly would be to ruin everything; error and heresy would be the results of such a betrayal.[174]

Behind such expressions lies a living experience. Clement knows something of the existential seriousness of an authentic encounter with truth, which cannot be conveyed merely 'objectively' and as a matter of theory. Consequently he fights not only against the anxiety of the pious in face of philosophic and scientific culture but also against the superficiality of an instant pseudo-gnosis and the arrogance of heretics who think they know everything 'without having learned or searched or laboured, and before they have discovered the inner coherence' of truth.[175] It would, however, be absurd, where Clement is stressing the need for a secret and oral tradition, to think that the desire of the teacher or pastor to do his work effectively is all that is involved. When Clement speaks of the unwritten gnostic or Church[176]

[171] Cf. Mondésert, op. cit., pp. 81–87.
[172] Strom. V, 5, 4; for further evidence on his attitude to Scripture cf., e.g., Strom. II, 12, 1; III, 42, 5; IV, 2, 2; VI, 128; VII, 93, 1; 95, 1.9; 98, 2; 104, 6; 105.
[173] Strom. VII, 92, 3, reading ἀληθεῖ for ἀληθείᾳ with O. Stählin, Des Clemens von Alexandria ausgewählte Schriften, aus dem Griechischen übersetzt V, 1938, ad loc.
[174] For a fuller discussion, with evidence, of this complex of ideas cf. Campenhausen, Ecclesiastical Authority, pp. 201–211.
[175] Strom. VII, 103, 1.
[176] As Hanson, Tradition, pp. 59, 61, rightly maintains, the two concepts can-

tradition, he is in fact thinking of particular doctrines and insights which are indispensable for a complete grasp of the truth and for an ultimate understanding of Scripture. It is true that Clement defends the faith of the simple Christian against the arrogant criticism of the pneumatics; but at the same time he is not prepared, as Origen was later, to say that faith can comprehend everything in its own way, and that 'knowledge' only reworks the same material at a higher level.[177] Christianity full and free, reposing in God and doing the works of love, he sees instead as really possible only where there is perfect knowledge such as that possessed by the true Christian gnostic. Such a man is therefore the proper, professional expositor of holy Scripture,[178] which demands far more for an understanding of its essential message than a mere knowledge of its contents. Christ, the Prophets, and the Apostles all followed this method and no other whenever they spoke or wrote of spiritual things: the heart of the matter had to be concealed, and reserved for the oral instruction of the few. In other words, they too followed the immemorially sacrosanct principles of the *disciplina arcani*.

This is absolutely firmly laid down. 'Neither the prophetic writings nor the Saviour himself simply proclaimed the divine mysteries point-blank, in such a way that any listener could understand them, but they spoke in parables'.[179] Even Paul or Barnabas did not dare entrust the profoundest knowledge to their epistles, but at most referred to it allusively.[180] And when Paul offered his congregations only milk and not as yet solid food,[181] in doing so he was following the same 'prophetic and venerable system of concealment' which Plato and innumerable other wise men had practised from of old.[182] If anyone in reply wishes to appeal to the dominical saying that 'there is nothing hidden that will not be revealed',[183] then he ought to know that this was precisely a prediction made to the few who discern the truth behind the veil while to the many it remains obscured.[184]

It follows that the oral traditions to which Clement appeals consist primarily of exegeses of Scripture, or are at any rate derived from such exegeses and associated with them. It is no accident that Clement

---

not be sharply distinguished: the true *gnosis* is found in the Church, and 'church' does not connote merely the standard attained by the average congregation.

[177] The relation between πίστις and γνῶσις is a problem with which Clement is constantly struggling, and to which he returns again and again, because, being motivated by opposing impulses, he can never really solve it on the basis of his own assumptions.

[178] Strom. VI, 82, 3; 92, 3; VII, 93f.; 95, 9; 104, 1 etc.

[179] Strom. VI, 124, 6.   [180] Strom. V, 26, 5; 62–64.

[181] I Cor. 3:2.   [182] Strom. V, 65f.   [183] Cf. Matt. 10:26.

[184] Strom. I, 13, 3; cf. VI, 124, 6.

celebrates his teacher Pantaenos as above all a skilled exegete, who knew how to suck honey from the 'flowers of the prophetic and apostolic meadow'.[185] These traditions go back in their turn to other, earlier Church fathers and to the apostles themselves.[186] Clearly it is from these teachers that Clement derives a good part of his own 'knowledge'.[187] Papias had already concerned himself with such 'exegeses' of the words of Jesus, which had been orally—but not secretly—transmitted.[188] The way in which Clement bases himself on the secret tradition is most closely in agreement with the Valentinian principle of equating their own special doctrines with supposedly apostolic traditions.[189] Here again it is the dominical sayings, and especially the parables of Jesus, which are the focus of attention and a particularly tempting occa-

[185] Strom. I, 11, 2, on which cf. Munck, op. cit., pp. 175–185.

[186] The early fathers and teachers are referred to in this connection in Protr. 113, 1; Strom. I, 11; Ecl. proph. 11, 1; 27, 1.4; 50, 1; Hypot. cited in Eusebius, HE VI, 14, 4; de pascha cited ibid. VI, 13, 9; adumbr. frag. III on I Joh. 1:1. The link with the very first apostles is, by contrast, cursorily assumed rather than conceived in precise detail: cf., e.g., Strom. VI, 61, 3; 124, 4. The same applies to Strom. I, 11, 3, where three apostles are mentioned by name. In view of the comprehensive and shifting character of gnosis in Clement, it seems difficult to follow J. Daniélou, 'Les Traditions secrètes des Apôtres', Eranos-Jahrb. 1962, Zurich 1963, pp. 199–215 (cf. also id., Theology of Jewish Christianity, 1964), in restricting the content of the secret traditions to quite definite themes; but cf. also M. Hornschuh, 'The apostles as bearers of the Tradition' in: N.T. Apocrypha II, pp. 79–86.

[187] Clement knows of no teaching which could ever disregard Scripture: Strom. VII, 1, 3f.; but it is precisely in the biblical expositions in his Hypoty-poses, which was not a continuous commentary but simply elucidated selected passages from the Old and New Testaments, that according to Photius, bibl. cod. 109, there occurred alongside orthodox views the most serious lapses and 'godless and invented doctrines'.

[188] Cf. pp. 130ff. above.

[189] Campenhausen, Ecclesiastical Authority, pp. 156ff. The passage from Book VII of the Hypotyposes, quoted in Eusebius, HE II, 1, 4, has a very 'gnostic' ring: Ἰακώβῳ τῷ δικαίῳ καὶ Ἰωάννῃ καὶ Πέτρῳ μετὰ τὴν ἀνάστασιν παρέδωκεν τὴν γνῶσιν ὁ κύριος, οὗτοι τοῖς λοιποῖς ἀποστόλοις παρέδωκαν, οἱ δὲ λοιποὶ ἀπόστολοι τοῖς ἑβδομήκοντα· ὧν εἷς ἦν καὶ Βαρναβᾶς. The methodological agreement between the Valentinians and Clement had already been rightly emphasised by Jülicher, op. cit., I, p. 220. Clement (on this point a good catholic) recognises no objective difference between the apostles. Nevertheless, the whole conception of secret oral tradition derives, like so much else in Clement, from the common background of Alexandrian gnostic theology, as this is understood by H. Kraft, Die Kirchenväter bis zum Konzil von Nicäa, 1966, pp. 79ff., or H. Langerbeck, Aufsätze zur Gnosis, 1967, pp. 38ff. et passim. It is, in my view, completely misguided to explain Clement's mysterious lan-guage and world of ideas by assuming instead that 'the disciplina arcani had already found its way into the Alexandrian liturgy' (of which at this period we know absolutely nothing!); contra O. Perler, art. 'Arkandisziplin', RAC I, 1950, col. 672.

sion of speculative exegesis.[190] We know that Clement had read, and to some extent indeed excerpted, the explanatory comments of the Valentinians Heracleon and Theodotus.[191] From these predecessors—and from Philo—he also took over an unqualified acceptance of the allegorical method. The idea of a hidden and multiple meaning of Scripture, calling for special elucidation, is for Clement the hermeneutical correlative of the doctrine of the secret oral tradition.[192] We must now briefly state the repercussions which inevitably followed from this for the Canon.[193]

Two points are principally involved. The first concerns the relationship between the Old and New Testaments, and is a direct result of the adoption of the allegorical principle. Originally Christian allegorical and typological exegesis was virtually exclusively concerned with the Old Testament. Here it seemed indispensable to a precise understanding of the obscure prophecies of Christ and their present fulfilment in the scheme of salvation-history. Furthermore it mitigated—as it had already done for Philo—the difficulties which had been experienced with a strictly literal exposition of the old Law. One crucial assumption, however, behind all allegorical exegesis of the Old Testament was always the certainty that the unfathomable 'mystery' of redemption had in fact been made manifest by Christ[194] and that on this basis the meaning of the ancient Scriptures had finally been revealed. Now as always the exposition of these Scriptures remained, it is true, a particular spiritual skill, which was the pride of the body of professional Christian teachers;[195] but the Gospel of Christ himself required nothing for its essential message to be understood other than faith and obedience, and it remained hidden only to those 'who are perishing', because 'the god of this world has blinded their minds'.[196] Of course, as soon as 'the

[190] Cf. p. 192 above.

[191] Cf. the conclusive evidence in Stählin, *op. cit.*, Register, pp. 28f., and, for the *Excerpta ex Theodoto*, the edition of F. Sagnard, *Clément d'Alexandrie: Extraits de Thééodote*, Paris, 1948.

[192] Camelot, *op. cit.*, p. 94: 'This preoccupation . . . with linking himself to a secret tradition, to a succession of *didaskaloi* is an example of the same concern to justify his esotericism which inspired Clement's reflections on allegory and on the hidden sense of Scripture.'

[193] The material on the recently much discussed problem of allegorical interpretation will be found, so far as Clement is concerned, in the following works: W. den Boer, *De Allegorese in het Werk van Clemens Alexandrinus* (Diss. Leiden), 1940 (unfortunately written in Dutch); Mondésert, *op. cit.*, pp. 131–162; 237ff.; and above all in R. P. C. Hanson, *Allegory and Event. A Study of the Sources and Significance of Origen's Interpretation of Scripture*, 1959.

[194] 'Consequently μυστήριον occurs (in the N.T.) almost always in conjunction with words denoting revelation': G. Bornkamm, art. μυστήριον, *TWNT* IV, 1942, p. 827.

[195] Cf. Campenhausen, *Ecclesiastical Authority*, pp. 201–203.

[196] II Cor. 4:3f.

Gospel' underwent development into a wider, didactic entity, matters ceased to be quite so simple; and after it had become 'scripture', they were no longer simple at all. For all that, however, the refutation of heresy from Scripture in Irenaeus, and indeed the whole of theology before Origen, continues to proceed on the assumption that the New Testament contains a clear and unambiguous testimony sufficient for a true faith. Clement is the first church theologian to abandon this principle, and to follow gnostic ideas in extending the allegorical method to the New Testament as well, and in particular to the words of Jesus.[197] In his opinion 'almost the whole of scripture' speaks in riddles[198] and symbols,[199] in order to make it more difficult for the casual reader to break in upon its wisdom, to stimulate us to deeper reflection, and to demonstrate how indispensable it is to have special instruction to introduce one to and guide one in the study of Scripture.[200]

In this way the original contrast between Then and Now, which had supplied the rationale of the bipartite Bible, was once more obscured and to a large extent ironed out. Clement is certainly aware of the old pattern of prophecy and fulfilment, of the Old Testament oracle and its New Testament resolution, and speaks of it not infrequently.[201] But at bottom this distinction, which takes cognisance of the gulf between the two eras, has lost its significance for the contemporary moment. In the old covenant Christ spoke through the Law and the Prophets 'in parables', and in the new covenant at his appearing he again spoke in parables, in veiled language.[202] In the last analysis there

[197] This distinctive position of the Gospels was especially emphasised by Harnack, *Dogmengeschichte* I, p. 392 n. 1, and Kutter, *op. cit.*, p. 29 n. 1; 149 n. 2. In my opinion the principal reason for this is the primacy which the Gospels enjoy within the N.T., and it should not therefore be assumed that it does not apply in principle equally to the other texts. The assertion of R. M. Grant, *The Letter and the Spirit*, 1957, p. 89, that on the whole Clement gave an allegorical interpretation only of the O.T. is quite impossible to accept, and would totally contradict Clement's own statements about the mysterious character of the N.T.; cf. Hanson, *Allegory*, pp. 117ff.

[198] Strom. V, 32, 1 (δι' αἰνιγμάτων); cf. VI, 127, 1.

[199] Strom. V, 56, 1 (συμβολικῶς).

[200] Strom. V, 56, 2–4; VI, 126, 1–3: διὰ πολλὰς τοίνυν αἰτίας ἐπικρύπτονται τὸν νοῦν αἱ γραφαί, πρῶτον μὲν ἵνα ζητητικοὶ ὑπάρχωμεν καὶ προσαγρυπνῶμεν ἀεὶ τῇ τῶν σωτηρίων λόγων εὑρέσει, ἔπειτα <ὅτι> μηδὲ τοῖς ἅπασι προσῆκον ἦν νοεῖν, ὡς μὴ βλαβεῖεν ἑτέρως ἐκδεξάμενοι τὰ ὑπὸ τοῦ ἁγίου πνεύματος σωτηρίως εἰρημένα. διὸ δὴ τοῖς ἐκλεκτοῖς τῶν ἀνθρώπων τοῖς τε ἐκ πίστεως εἰς γνῶσιν ἐγκρίτοις τηρούμενα τὰ ἅγια τῶν προφητειῶν μυστήρια ταῖς παραβολαῖς ἐγκαλύπτεται· παραβολικὸς γὰρ ὁ χαρακτὴρ ὑπάρχει τῶν γραφῶν . . .

[201] Mondésert, *op. cit.*, pp. 101–104; cf. 249–251.

[202] Strom. VI, 125, 1f.: λέγουσιν γοῦν οἱ ἀπόστολοι περὶ τοῦ κυρίου, ὅτι "πάντα ἐν παραβολαῖς ἐλάλησεν καὶ οὐδὲν ἄνευ παραβολῆς ἐλάλει αὐτοῖς" (Matt. 13:34)· εἰ δὲ "πάντα δι' αὐτοῦ ἐγένετο καὶ χωρὶς αὐτοῦ ἐγένετο οὐδὲ ἕν" (Joh. 1:3), καὶ ἡ προφητεία ἄρα καὶ ὁ νόμος δι' αὐτοῦ τε ἐγένετο καὶ ἐν παραβολαῖς ἐλαλήθησαν δι' αὐτοῦ.

is in fact only one single covenant, one single Testament, which was given at various periods, and which now belongs to the elect in the one Church and under the one Lord.[203] The meaning of this fulfilment, however, is still a mystery, and does not become clear even to Christians simply from the Scripture alone; it can be made known only by special initiation and instruction, orally communicated. In practice, therefore, concern for the personal progress of the individual Christian and for his growth in 'knowledge' has replaced the salvation-history approach. On this basis Clement finds no difficulty in rebutting the criticism of the Old Testament by Marcionites and heretical gnostics and in asserting the full *symphonia* of the Bible.[204] Allegorical exegesis has apparently done away with the difficulties of the historical past, with which Justin and Irenaeus had had to wrestle, and with which Tertullian was still wrestling. For faith there is only the present.

The second logical conclusion from a theology of Scripture based on mystery affects the normative status of the Canon itself. Here it is less a matter of the effect of allegorical interpretation as such than of the idea which goes with it, namely that the oral tradition is indispensable for the elucidation of Scripture. If we say that on principle a text cannot be understood and explained purely on the basis of what it itself contains but only with the help of a supplementary tradition, then is not that text from the start restricted as to its sovereignty, subordinated to an alien authority, and thus robbed of its properly 'canonical' significance? It is 'plain to see', says Ferdinand Christian Baur (here very much the Protestant), that Clement 'sets above Scripture something else which alone, as the gnostic would have it, makes it possible for Scripture to be rightly understood'.[205] And the Catholic scholar Dausch is prepared to see in Clement's doctrine of *gnosis*, which makes tradition antecedent to Scripture, 'without difficulty the rudiments of those principles which still obtain today in the Catholic church'.[206] Both writers here have in mind the 'gospel' or 'church standard' or 'standard of truth', to which Clement repeatedly refers, and which for him is identical with the 'living', oral tradition of his teachers.[207]

---

[203] Strom. VII, 107, 5: κατά τε οὖν ὑπόστασιν κατά τε ἐπίνοιαν κατά τε ἀρχὴν κατά τε ἐξοχὴν μόνην εἶναί φαμεν τὴν ἀρχαίαν καὶ καθολικὴν ἐκκλησίαν, εἰς ἑνότητα πίστεως μιᾶς, τῆς κατὰ τὰς οἰκείας διαθήκας, μᾶλλον δὲ κατὰ τὴν διαθήκην τὴν μίαν διαφόροις τοῖς χρόνοις, ἑνὸς τοῦ θεοῦ τῷ βουλήματι δι' ἑνὸς τοῦ κυρίου συνάγουσαν τοὺς ἤδη κατατεταγμένους: cf. VI, 106f.

[204] Cf. nn. 140, 165 above.

[205] F. C. Baur, *Vorlesungen über die christliche Dogmengeschichte* I, 1, 1865, p. 369, quoted in Kutter, *op. cit.*, p. 120 n. 3.

[206] Dausch, *op. cit.*, p. 56. Even more exaggeratedly identified with the ideas of the Catholic church is the exposition given by P. Smulders, 'Le mot et le concept de tradition chez les Pères Grecs', *RechSR* 40, 1952, pp. 54f.

[207] In addition to the not altogether happy comments of Van den Eynde, cf.

What Clement means by this term, however, is first and foremost exactly the same as Irenaeus had in mind when he spoke to the same effect of the 'rule' or canon 'of truth', that is to say, not a fixed ecclesiastical profession of faith[208] nor even the content of Scripture as such[209] but the spiritual essence of Christian faith, which is alive in the Christian community. Neither the fact that for Clement this community is not co-terminous with the clearly defined entity of the Church but on occasion looks more like a private 'school' of disciples, nor the fact that the biblical content of his teachings is determined in a completely different, more elastic manner, is here of decisive significance. Both men live by the same conviction, namely that they themselves learned their Christianity within their Church, from their teachers, and had personal experience of its truth, and that it was this which for them opened up the way to the Scripture and enabled them rightly to grasp its meaning. The crucial difference between them is simply this: in Irenaeus Scripture of itself confirms this truth for everyone, heretics not excepted; Clement, however, makes acceptance of the gnostic or ecclesiastical canon instead a necessary precondition of being able properly to appreciate Scripture at all and of making it truly one's own. The authentic tradition is the 'key' to the Scripture, and it is this key which the heretics have distorted.[210] To this extent Clement—though under a catholic flag—stands by the Valentinian principle which Irenaeus had rejected: that the Bible can be understood only by those who at the same time also know and accept the tradition—that is to say the special secret tradition of their school and community.[211] Only thus does the tradition become an essentially superior, indispensable norm controlling the norm of the Bible itself, which comes to men in written form.

It hardly needs to be said that this is not the intention which Clement really had in mind when he appealed to the secret tradition. When in his polemic he has recourse over and over again to the Scripture as the supreme and decisive, the truly normative source of all knowledge, and summons the heretics to be converted and hearken to it, he is very much in earnest.[212] Exactly as Irenaeus had done,[213] he explains that

---

esp. Hanson, *Tradition*, pp. 59–66. The work entitled Κανὼν ἐκκλησιαστικὸς ἢ πρὸς τοὺς Ἰουδαΐζοντας (Eusebius, *HE* VI, 13, 3), which Clement dedicated to Bishop Alexander of Jerusalem, has unfortunately not survived.

[208] This has, in my view, been established by F. Kattenbusch, *Das apostolische Symbol* II, 1900, pp. 102–134, the misgivings of W. Völker, *Der wahre Gnostiker nach Clemens Alexandrinus*, 1952, p. 357 n. 2, notwithstanding; but cf. Hanson, *Tradition*, pp. 65f.

[209] Kutter, *op. cit.*, p. 115, comes very close to this conception when he defines the κανών as 'the mutual συνῳδία of the sacred scriptures, as this is set out by the church'.

[210] Strom. VII, 106, 2.   [211] Cf. p. 189 above.

[212] Cf. esp. Strom. VII, 92–106.

Scripture ought to be elucidated only by Scripture,[214] just as, according to Paul,[215] it is only the Spirit that can recognise the Spirit,[216] and that mere men can never be reliable teachers when it is a question of comprehending God's truth.[217] Truth is recognised by means of the Truth[218] —in other words: Christ as the Truth is himself the starting-point which confirms the truth. He speaks in the Scripture, and he in turn is proclaimed and attested by Scripture.[219] To this extent it can virtually be said that for Clement Scripture is αὐτόπιστος; for its vindication cannot 'be proved from any other source, but it contains within itself the demonstration of its own truth.'[220]

Nevertheless, it is significant that Clement confined himself to this occasional statement. His preference for mystery and for the ideas of personal direction and training did not fit him to deduce from the autonomy of Scripture the further necessary concept of its clarity for faith. To this extent his teaching is fragmentary; at the very least it is marked on this point by a permanent lack of clarity which the concept of tradition is no longer adequate to overcome. The clearly discernible tendency to base the truth of Scripture on Scripture alone and to declare it to be self-sufficient clashes with the simultaneous assertion of its need to be supplemented by spiritual instruction and a secret tradition.

---

213 Adv. haer. III, 12, 9. Cf. Kunze, *op. cit.*, p. VI: 'In the anti-heretical sections Clement resembles Irenaeus.'

214 Strom. VII, 96, 4; 104, 1; *Quis dives* 4, 2.   215 I Cor. 2:10, 14.

216 Strom. VI, 166, 3.   217 Strom. VI, 165, 5; VII, 95, 7 *et al.*

218 Strom. V, 1, 4.

219 Strom. VII, 95, 3–96, 1: ἔχομεν γὰρ τὴν ἀρχὴν τῆς διδασκαλίας τὸν κύριον διά τε τῶν προφητῶν διά τε τοῦ εὐαγγελίου καὶ διὰ τῶν μακαρίων ἀποστόλων "πολυτρόπως καὶ πολυμερῶς" (Heb. 1:1) ἐξ ἀρχῆς εἰς τέλος ἡγούμενον τῆς γνώσεως. τὴν ἀρχὴν δ᾽ εἴ τις ἑτέρου δεῖσθαι ὑπολάβοι, οὐκέτ᾽ ἂν ὄντως ἀρχὴ φυλαχθείη. ὁ μὲν οὖν ἐξ ἑαυτοῦ πιστὸς τῇ κυριακῇ γραφῇ τε καὶ φωνῇ ἀξιόπιστος εἰκότως <ὡς> ἂν διὰ τοῦ κυρίου πρὸς τὴν τῶν ἀνθρώπων εὐεργεσίαν ἐνεργουμένη· ἀμέλει πρὸς τὴν τῶν πραγμάτων εὕρεσιν αὐτῇ χρώμεθα κριτηρίῳ· τὸ κρινόμενον δὲ πᾶν ἔτι ἄπιστον πρὶν κριθῆναι, ὥστ᾽ οὐδ᾽ ἀρχὴ τὸ κρίσεως δεόμενον. εἰκότως τοίνυν πίστει περιλαβόντες ἀναπόδεικτον τὴν ἀρχήν, ἐκ περιουσίας καὶ τὰς ἀποδείξεις παρ᾽ αὐτῆς τῆς ἀρχῆς περὶ τῆς ἀρχῆς λαβόντες, φωνῇ κυρίου παιδευόμεθα πρὸς τὴν ἐπίγνωσιν τῆς ἀληθείας. οὐ γὰρ ἁπλῶς ἀποφαινομένοις ἀνθρώποις προσέχοιμεν <ἄν>, οἷς καὶ ἀνταποφαίνεσθαι ἐπ᾽ ἴσης ἔξεστιν. εἰ δ᾽ οὐκ ἀρκεῖ μόνον ἁπλῶς εἰπεῖν τὸ δόξαν, ἀλλὰ πιστώσασθαι δεῖ τὸ λεχθέν, οὐ τὴν ἐξ ἀνθρώπων ἀναμένομεν μαρτυρίαν, ἀλλὰ τῇ τοῦ κυρίου φωνῇ πιστούμεθα τὸ ζητούμενον, ἣ πασῶν ἀποδείξεων ἐχεγγυωτέρα, μᾶλλον δὲ ἡ μόνη ἀπόδειξις οὖσα τυγχάνει· καθ᾽ ἣν ἐπιστήμην οἱ μὲν ἀπογευσάμενοι μόνον τῶν γραφῶν πιστοί, οἱ δὲ καὶ προσωτέρω χωρήσαντες ἀκριβεῖς γνώμονες τῆς ἀληθείας ὑπάρχουσιν, οἱ γνωστικοί, ἐπεὶ κἄν τοῖς κατὰ τὸν βίον ἔχουσί τι πλέον οἱ τεχνῖται τῶν ἰδιωτῶν καὶ παρὰ τὰς κοινὰς ἐννοίας ἐκτυποῦσι τὸ βέλτιον. οὕτως οὖν καὶ ἡμεῖς, ἀπ᾽ αὐτῶν περὶ αὐτῶν τῶν γραφῶν τελείως ἀποδεικνύντες, ἐκ πίστεως πειθόμεθα ἀποδεικτικῶς. For an explanation of the difficulties of this passage cf. Hägglund, *op. cit.*, pp. 30–34.

220 So Hägglund, *op. cit.*, p. 33, following Kunze, *op. cit.*, pp. 133ff.

It is highly questionable whether as a result of his gnosticising presuppositions Clement was ever aware of this logical difficulty; at any rate he never overcame it. It is therefore no accident that he got no further than he did in developing and creating a rationale for the new Canon— he was unable to provide a theological solution to the problem of the normativeness of Scripture. Consequently Clement, though a sensitive friend and a great teacher of the Bible, is of no significance for the history of the concept of the Canon. It was Origen who was the first to overcome, both in principle and in practice, the crippling influence of the gnostic traditions in this sphere.

'There has never been a theologian in the church who was (and wished to be) so exclusively a biblical exegete as Origen'.[221] As a matter of principle *Origen* took his stand on the ground of an 'unqualified biblicism'.[222] As the principal and, for a considerable period, the only theologian of the early Church he made the Bible one of the subjects of dogmatic theology. In his speculative and apologetic textbook, the De principiis, 'Concerning first things',[223] the chapters on the Scripture form a solid block, planned from the start, which systematically concludes the complicated and occasionally wavering train of thought of the whole work.[224] Similarly, therefore, the picture of the canon as Origen defined it may fitly bring to a close our story of the formation of the Bible in the early Church.[225]

The tentative uncertainties of the earlier period, when it became necessary for the first time to form and consolidate the new Canon, have, by the time we come to Origen, been in principle overcome and belong to the past. The sacred and divine Scriptures of the Old and New Testaments[226] are for him a datum which God has bestowed on the Church. The faith of Christians lives by the Scripture and cleaves to it

---

[221] A. von Harnack, *Der kirchengeschichtliche Ertrag der exegetischen Arbeiten des Origenes* II, 1919, p. 4 n. 3.

[222] Harnack, *Dogmengeschichte* I, p. 781 n. 4.

[223] Following Hal Koch, *Pronoia und Paideusis*, 1932, pp. 251ff., I continue to regard this as the correct translation.

[224] Princ. IV, 1–3; cf. I pref. 8; IV, 4 simply adds an ἀνακεφαλαίωσις. On this question cf. the excellent analysis by M. Simonetti, 'Osservazioni sulla struttura del "De principiis" di Origene', *Riv. di Filol. e di Istruz. class.* N.S. 40, 1962, pp. 273–290; 372–393, which now supersedes the distinguished study by B. Steidle, 'Neue Untersuchungen zu Origenes' Περὶ ἀρχῶν, 'ZNW 40, 1941, pp. 236–243; but cf. also M. Harl, 'Recherches sur le Περὶ ἀρχῶν d' Origène en vue d'une nouvelle édition: la division en chapitres', *StudPatr* III, 1961, pp. 57–67.

[225] What is offered here is by no means an exhaustive account of material so vast as to be virtually impossible to survey. I shall confine myself to a selection from the evidence and a number of references to the literature, though unable to engage in a detailed discussion.

[226] Θεῖαι γραφαί is the expression which Origen prefers when speaking of the Bible.

X

alone. It is a work of providence. Just a the visible works of the creation
are meant to teach us about the invisible and to guide us to what is
heavenly, so—indeed, much more so—was scripture fashioned and
made wholly perfect for our salvation.[227] Whoever maintains that the
sacred Scriptures are the writings of the Creator of the universe must be
convinced that the divine Reason is to be found in them as much as in
the creation.[228] 'It is proper to believe that the sacred scriptures contain not a single dot that is devoid of the wisdom of God'.[229] All the
doctrines of the Church, all the wisdom of knowledge, and all faith are
to be founded on Scripture.[230] The heart of the Christian ought, so to
speak, to be a 'library' of the sacred writings.[231] For Christ, the eternal
Logos of God, dominates the whole Bible; he has, as it were, incar-
nated himself in it, and thus, clothed in its letters, he remains a present
reality for us.[232] There is nothing wrong with a knowledge of philosophy

[227] Comm. Cant. III (ed. Baehrens, p. 212): . . . ut ipsa creatura mundi tali
quadam dispensatione condita intelligatur per divinam sapientiam, quae rebus
ipsis ex exemplis invisibilia nos de visibilibus doceat et a terrenis nos transferat
ad caelestia. haec autem rationes non solum in creaturis omnibus habentur,
sed et ipsa scriptura divina tali quadam sapientiae arte conscripta est.

[228] Comm. Psalm. I (= Philoc. II, 5): χρὴ μέντοι γε τὸν ἅπαξ παρδεξάμενον
τοῦ κτίσαντος τὸν κόσμον εἶναι ταύτας τὰς γραφὰς πεπεῖσθαι, ὅτι ὅσα περὶ
τῆς κτίσεως ἅπαντα τοῖς ζητοῦσι τὸν περὶ αὐτῆς λόγον, ταῦτα καὶ περὶ τῶν
γραφῶν.

[229] Hom. Hierem. 21, 2 (= Philoc. I, 28): πρέπει δὲ τὰ ἅγια γράμματα
πιστεύειν μηδεμίαν κέραιαν ἔχειν κενὴν σοφίας θεοῦ.

[230] Cf., e.g., Comm. Matt. Ser. 18: debemus ergo ad testimonium omnium
verborum, quae proferimus in doctrina, proferre sensum scripturae quasi
confirmantem quem exponimus sensum.

[231] Hom. Gen. II, 6: si quis est, qui crescentibus malis et inundantibus vitiis
convertere se potest a rebus fluxis ac pereuntibus et caducis et audire verbum
dei ac praecepta coelestia, hic intra cor suum arcam salutis aedificat et biblio-
thecam, ut ita dicam, intra se divini consecrat verbi; Hom. Exod. IX, 4 (Baehrens, p. 242): habeat et arcam testamenti, in qua sint tabulae legis, ut "in lege
dei meditetur die ac nocte" (Ps. 1:2) et memoria eius arca et bibliotheca efficia-
tur librorum dei . . .

[232] Philoc, XV, 19 (= Cels. VI, 77?): ἀεὶ γὰρ ἐν ταῖς γραφαῖς ὁ λόγος σάρξ
ἐγένετο, ἵνα κατασκηνώσῃ ἐν ἡμῖν. Comm. Matt. frag. 11: ὅταν ἐν βίβλῳ γραφῇ
καὶ οἱονεὶ σωματωθῇ. Comm. Matt. Ser. 27: arbitror, sicut Christus celatus
venit in corpore, ut a carnalibus quidem speciem corporis eius aspicientibus et
non virtutes considerantibus homo videretur, a spiritalibus autem non speciem
corporis adtendentibus, sed opera virtutum eius considerantibus deus intelligatur
—sic est et omnis scriptura divina incorporata, maxime autem veteris testamenti. A number of other similar texts will be found in R. Gögler, Zur Theologie
des biblischen Wortes bei Origenes, 1963, pp. 301–304. Analogising similes such as
these, which are typical of Origen's thinking, hardly justify one, however, in
talking about his 'basic conviction of the christological and incarnational structure of scripture' (ibid., p. 304), or, with H. U. von Balthasar, Origenes², 1938,
pp. 30, 38, in reinterpreting Origenistic symbolism to imply a 'sacramental
realism'; cf. id., 'Le Mysterion d' Origène', RechSR 26, 1936, pp. 535–562, and,
Parole et Mystère chez Origène, Paris, 1957, where Origen's thought on this

—indeed, the advanced Christian or the apologist for Christianity must study it. But it can never be God's revelation for us; this is to be found in Scripture alone.[233] This book is everything, and we possess everything through the medium of this one book.

Origen, like Clement, comes from the Alexandrian tradition, from which as a theologian and in particular as an exegete he took over a great deal. But he is far more church-minded and more correct in his attitude to Church doctrine than Clement. Origen's whole desire is to be a churchman and a teacher within the Church. It would seem that he regarded Clement, whom he can hardly have known personally, as more or less a Valentinian, and rejected him for this reason. His total silence about him and his works is virtually inexplicable on any other basis.[234] Origen cannot possibly have approved of the enthusiasm which Clement displays for philosophy and for secret traditions. His view seems to have been that while it was admittedly astonishing that the heathen philosophers should also here and there have presaged and taught about a 'Son' of God, we now know him from Scripture, and need no additional means to enable us to believe in him and proclaim him.[235] The belief of a Papias that some information about the original teaching of the apostles could still be received along oral channels is finally laid to rest.[236] Origen no longer wants to know about 'apostolic'

---

subject is summarised in systematic outline. The tendency to interpret Origen in sacramental–'mystical' and ecclesiological terms seems to me entirely a modernising anachronism, which it is incorrect to apply to the concept of Scripture, as is done even by H. de Lubac, *Histoire et Esprit. L'intelligence de l'Écriture d'après Origène*, Paris, 1950, pp. 364ff. The 'sacramental' analogy is precisely the one which is never drawn by Origen himself, as M. Barth, *Vom Geheimnis der Bibel*, 1962, pp. 13f., rightly observes.

[233] Koch, *op. cit.*, pp. 176ff.; Molland, *Gospel*, pp. 86ff.; more cautiously Hanson, *Tradition*, pp. 162–173; J. H. Waszink, 'Bemerkungen zum Einfluss des Platonismus im frühen Christentum', *VC* 19, 1965, pp. 159–161.

[234] Hanson, *Tradition*, pp. 88–90. It is, however, true that Origen does not often mention any of his predecessors by name.

[235] Princ. I, 3, 1: huic (sc. deo) tamen esse filium non nos soli pronuntiamus, quamvis satis hoc et mirum et incredulum videatur his, qui apud Graecos vel barbaros philosophari videntur; tamen a nonnullis etiam ipsorum habita eius videtur opinio, cum verbo dei vel ratione creata esse omnia confitentur. nos vero secundum fidem doctrinae eius, quam divinitus adspiratam procerto habemus, eminentiorem divinioremque rationem de filio dei nullius alterius possibilitatis esse credimus exponere atque in hominum cognitionem proferre, nisi eius solius scripturae, quae a spiritu sancto inspirata est . . . ; cf. III, 6, 6; Dial. Heracl. 25: παραστῆσαι πειράσομαι, ὅσα σημαίνεται (sc. τὸ ὄνομα τοῦ θανάτου) οὐ καθ᾽ Ἕλληνας, ἀλλ᾽ ὅσα σημαίνεται κατὰ τὴν θείαν γραφήν.

[236] Origen now derives from tradition only isolated 'historical' data about the lives of the apostles, geographical details and suchlike, of dubious reliability; cf. the summary in Hanson, *Tradition*, pp. 145f.; also G. Frankowski, *Origenes über die Urgemeinde* (Diss. theol. Heidelberg, 1955, TS).

traditions, secret or otherwise;[237] nor does he any longer mention, as Clement had done, any successions of teachers or bearers of the tradition. These for Origen are simply heretics who seek by such methods to get beyond Scripture to their 'inexpressible mysteries'.[238] Origen is determined never to allow himself to come into conflict with the 'church Canon'[239] of valid teachings; he respects it as, so to speak, the framework for his theological labours.[240] But, without realising it, he has changed the meaning of the concept which he has taken over. 'Canon' now no longer designates the living truth itself, by virtue of which the Church lives in the power of the Spirit, but has become the sum of those dogmatic propositions and convictions which are universally upheld by her in her public teaching. These acknowledged truths are now derived from Scripture as their self-evident source.[241]

Nevertheless, the picture of Origen as a theologian which this presents is not complete. Origen is not simply the teacher of a comfortable orthodoxy, which confines itself with equanimity within the framework of what is given. He too, like Clement, strives after a higher and more comprehensive knowledge which the average Christian piety has not yet attained; the only difference is that now the Bible takes the place of the special secret tradition. The Bible contains far more than the customary Church catechesis has to offer, and points beyond this to an immense mountain range, an illimitable ocean of hidden truth[242] which it is vital to sound to its very depths. This concept of the doc-

---

[237] Hanson, *Tradition*, p. 73. The opposite view is maintained by R. C. Baud, 'Les "Règles" de la Théologie d'Origène', *RechSR* 55, 1967, p' 189. Starting from the (correct) statement that it was Rufinus's practice to translate Origen's term κανών punctiliously by *regula*, he allows himself (incorrectly) to interpret Origen throughout in accordance with Rufinus's renderings, which over-simplify Origen's position. It is no accident that the 'apostolic' traditions appear only in Rufinus's translations; cf., e.g., Princ. I pref. 2: . . . illa sola credenda est veritas, quae in nullo ab ecclesiastica et apostolica traditione discordat.

[238] Comm. Pss. frag. on Ps. 41:6 (ed. Lommatzsch, vol. XII, p. 310): ἁρμόζει δὲ τὸ ῥητὸν (sc. Ps. 41:7: καὶ εἰ εἰσεπορεύετο τοῦ ἰδεῖν μάτην ἐλάλει) καὶ πᾶσι τοῖς ἀπόρρητα ἐπαγγελλομένοις τοῖς ἑτεροδόξοις. Comm. Matt. Ser. 47: sola autem ecclesia neque subtrahit huius fulguris (Matt. 24:27, allegorically interpreted as referring to Scripture) verbum et sensum, neque addit quasi prophetiam [Montanism!] aliud aliquid.

[239] In the Latin versions we find also *regula pietatis, regula fidei*, and *regula veritatis*. Nevertheless, 'it is remarkable how extraordinarily sparse the directly relevant' (i.e., for the use of κανών/*regula*) 'material is': Kattenbusch, *op. cit.*, II, p. 142; cf. the evidence cited there and in E. Stuiber, 'Einiges zur Schrifttauffassung des Origenes', *IKZ* 13, 1923, pp. 147f.

[240] Cf. the observations in Princ. I pref.

[241] On this point cf. esp. Hanson, *Tradition*, pp. 91–113. Baud lays a one-sided emphasis on the importance of the Church as the regulative factor, and has fallen himself, though in the opposite sense, into the danger against which he warns his readers (*op. cit.*, p. 199), of posing the problem in an anachronistic form.   [242] Hom. Gen. IX, 1.

trine of Scripture Origen had already developed and demonstrated at an early stage.[243] Consequently, there are not a few truths which are not spelled out in the Bible but at best indicated allusively; and there are questions which inevitably occur to the thinking mind, and which Scripture deliberately leaves open in order that the 'lover of truth' may concern himself with them and seek an answer. This is the task of the true teachers, endowed with the Spirit, who 'have made themselves both worthy and capable of receiving wisdom'.[244] In Origen we find for the first time something like a proper task for theology, which as biblical study does not simply minister to the piety and instruction of the Church, but is independent of these things and of a higher status. He sees this work of spiritual exploration and discovery, it is true, not as a purely theoretical affair, but as one requiring simultaneously personal effort and the training, purification and elevation of the moral life. The 'inexpressible mysteries' of the faith are accessible only to the perfect, and cannot be revealed just to anyone.[245] Nevertheless, the theoretical and didactic elements, when compared with Clement, have been noticeably strengthened: Origen demands a methodical course of study and training lasting several years, and including among other things instruction in heathen philosophy.[246] The result is plainly a two-

---

[243] Origen always remained faithful to the basic hermeneutical principles which he developed in the De principiis and followed in the Commentary on John. Slight shifts of position may have occurred in the course of time, but these can be disregarded in the present context. Cf. Grant, *Letter,* p. 104: 'It seems likely that as he grew older Origen adhered less closely to his basic theory as set forth in the De principiis and reflected in the Commentary on John.' There is still, however, a lack of adequate studies on this topic.

[244] Princ. I pref. 3: illud autem scire oportet, quoniam sancti apostoli fidem Christi praedicantes de quibusdam quidem, quaecumque necessaria crediderunt, omnibus credentibus, etiam his, qui pigriores erga inquisitionem divinae scientiae videbantur, manifestissime tradiderunt, rationem scilicet assertionis eorum relinquentes ab his inquirendam, qui spiritus dona excellentia mererentur et praecipue sermonis, sapientiae et scientiae gratiam per ipsum sanctum spiritum percepissent; de aliis vero dixerunt quidem quia sint, quomodo autem aut unde sint, siluerunt, profecto ut studiosiores quique ex posteris suis, qui amatores essent sapientiae, exercitium habere possent, in quo ingenii sui fructum ostenderent, hi videlicet, qui dignos se et capaces ad recipiendam sapientiam praepararent.

[245] Cf., e.g., Cels. I, 7; Comm. Matt. X, 6, and—a particularly characteristic passage—*Dial. Heracl.* 15. Origen has not altogether forgotten the special importance of oral communication: Princ. IV, 2, 4: οὐκέτι δὲ διὰ γραμμάτων ἀλλὰ διὰ λόγων ζώντων αὐτὸς ὁ μαθητὴς τοῦ πνεύματος προστάσσεται ἀναγγέλλειν κτλ. (on Hermas VIII, 3 = Vis. II, 4, 3); Hom. Jes. N, 20, 5; cf. H. Karpp, 'Viva vox', in: *Mullus* (Festschrift T. Klauser), 1964, pp. 197f.

[246] Koch, *op. cit.,* pp. 302–304. H. J. Marrou, *Histoire de l'Education dans l'antiquité classique,* 1953, speaks of a 'university training in theology' with the 'characteristic methods of university education in the hellenistic manner'.

level structure of spiritual and theological knowledge and tuition. Origen is aware, so to speak, of two methods of spiritual formation; and he studiously emphasises that they are not mutually incompatible and have no need to be in conflict.[247] Simple faith in the straightforward word of the Bible has and always will have its rightful place. Each man receives from the Scripture—as from Christ himself—whatever is best for him in the light of his state of faith and maturity.[248] Behind such assurances we seem already to detect a certain anxiety. Origen is familiar with the narrow-mindedness of the ordinary congregation, to which he also wishes to be of service, and he knows the intolerance and thirst for power of its leaders,[249] whom he not infrequently criticises.[250] But even so the difficulties which inevitably arise from such a position had already caught up with him in his own lifetime.[251]

The mistrust which Origen's theology aroused was not unjustified. From the teaching and preaching of primitive Christianity and of the Bible itself[252] the gnosticising, idealist concepts of the world and God which Origen upholds, and the shallow moralistic and pedagogic nature of his doctrine of redemption are, for all their emphatically Christian and indeed christocentric character, in reality far removed.[253] Posterity has condemned his writings on inadequate grounds but, to this extent anyway, correctly. Origen himself, however, was wholly unaware of the discrepancy. He was convinced that never at any time had he done anything except bring out the meaning of Scripture and champion its truth; and his disciples—and indeed a marvelling world—believed him. The reason for this error of judgment is to be found in the most dangerous inheritance which Origen received from the Alexandrian-gnostic tradition and pressed to its ultimate implications, namely, the assumption that Scripture contained a variety of meanings, with a resultant virtually unrestricted dominance of the allegorical method.[254] Without

---

[247] J. Lebreton, 'Les degrès de la connaissance religieuse d'après Origène', RechSR 12, 1922, pp. 265–296.

[248] This view of Scripture is completely in line with the gnostic doctrine, docetic in tendency, of the polymorphous character of Jesus, a doctrine which, as is well known, Origen also upheld.

[249] On this point cf. most recently F. H. Kettler, Der ursprüngliche Sinn der Dogmatik des Origenes, 1966, who nevertheless in my opinion overestimates the extent to which Origen's ambiguity of utterance is a conscious tactical expedient.

[250] Cf. Campenhausen, Ecclesiastical Authority, pp. 256–261.

[251] Cf. J. Lebreton, 'Le désaccord de la foi populaire et de la théologie savante dans l'Eglise chrétienne de III° siècle', RHE 19, 1923, pp. 481–506; 20, 1924, pp. 5–37, esp. 13–26.

[252] Its words are constantly the starting-point but hardly ever the true source of Origen's seemingly exegetical insights: Harl, Origène et la fonction révèlatrice du Verbe incarné, Paris, 1958, pp. 348f.

[253] This has been decisively, one-sidedly, but nevertheless rightly stressed by Koch, op. cit., pp. 305ff. in particular.

[254] In addition to the fundamental chapters of the De principiis (IV, 2–4) cf.

deliberate intent this becomes the universal method of obscuring the 'literal' sense of Scripture to suit one's own convenience, and of allowing in it only those things which the pious reader already expects and desires to find in advance.[255]

In the rigorousness of his methodological principles and also in the comprehensive manner in which he applied them Origen goes far beyond Clement of Alexandria. He alone makes allegorical and typological exegesis into an all-embracing hermeneutical principle which it is both right and necessary to apply at all times and in all instances to the exposition of the Bible. For Origen allegorical exegesis means nothing less than the truly appropriate and scientific method of expounding holy Scripture. He explains his theory in the De principiis, and later returns repeatedly to the subject in order to defend his views against doubters and critics.[256] His life's work as a biblical scholar is based on acceptance of the allegorical method.

Moreover, for him—as for the gnostics—this is not an isolated phenomenon but forms part of his total, 'allegorically' structured worldview. 'Just as man consists of body, soul, and spirit, so also has Scripture been designed by God in order to give salvation to men.'[257] Consequently in addition to its literal sense it is axiomatic that a biblical passage also possesses a higher spiritual meaning and yet another, highest of all (though in practice the latter two mostly coincide), and it is precisely this higher meaning which is of primary importance. As Origen sees it, this is not a view based on purely extraneous considerations; the Bible itself in various places unmistakably indicates this hidden sense,

---

also, in connection with his appeals to the example of Paul and his *intelligentiae regula*, Hom. Exod. V, 1; propterea ergo ipse in nonnullis intelligentiae tradit exempla, ut et nos similia observemus; and Hom. Lev. XV, 3: si quando scripturas divinas legimus et sanctorum patrum in his delicta aliqua recensemus, si secundum apostoli Pauli sententiam dicimus, quia: "haec omnia in figura contingebant illis, scripta sunt autem propter commonitionem nostram" (I Cor. 10:11).' Cf. further n. 316 below.

[255] Such a summary judgment of course over-simplifies a complex problem. I am not saying that typological, nor even (in the narrower sense) allegorical exegesis was always bound to be in contradiction with the text and could never lead to any but distorted results. In practice, however, these methods almost without exception led Origen into error. Nevertheless, even in his writings one can detect from time to time a 'genuine tension between the conflicting principles' of historical and allegorical-typological exegesis; so D. Lerch, *Isaaks Opferung, christlich gedeutet*, 1950, pp. 64–66. Cf. also the interesting observations of W. den Boer, 'Hermeneutic Problems in early Christian Literature', *VC* 1, 1947, pp. 150–167.

[256] It is clear that there was no lack of such people among his hearers; cf. Harnack, *Ertrag* I, 1918, pp. 8f.; II, p. 4 n. 3.

[257] Princ. IV, 2, 4: ὥσπερ γὰρ ὁ ἄνθρωπος συνέστηκεν ἐκ σώματος καὶ ψυχῆς καὶ πνεύματος, τὸν αὐτὸν τρόπον καὶ ἡ οἰκονομηθεῖσα ὑπὸ θεοῦ εἰς ἀνθρώπων σωτηρίαν δοθῆναι γραφή. Cf. Hom. Gen. II, 6.

and Paul explicitly taught it.[258] This now makes it possible to deal more or less easily with any biblical statement which contains theological difficulties: all one has to do is to understand it 'more profoundly'. Another result is that now there are no longer any trivialities or unprofitable passages in the Scriptures. Even the numbering of the psalms,[259] the various stopping-places of the Israelites on their journey through the wilderness,[260] the names of which are pregnant with meaning,[261] can be allegorically expounded and thus made spiritually fruitful. The only reason why heretics discover allegedly scandalous or contradictory passages in Scripture is that they have failed to use the right method of exposition.[262] Thus, for example, all the discrepancies between the Gospels, right down to the smallest variants in the text, if rightly expounded involve no contradiction but instead prove to be meaningful.[263] What had once been an embarrassment and a difficulty has now become a beneficent source of higher knowledge.[264] If the literal sense appears to be utterly intolerable, then it may even be abandoned altogether.[265] Origen can give an impressive explanation of why there must be such passages in Scripture, namely, that this is the only way in which men's attention can be drawn to the fact that the higher meaning, the one really intended, is indispensable.[266] Examples of this are.by no means confined to the Old Testament; they occur also in the New. A mountain from which, as in the Temptation narrative, one could survey the whole world is an impossibility—consequently it is there simply as a symbol.[267] The story of the Cleansing of the Temple too, in view of

---

[258] Princ. IV, 2, 4–6; cf. n. 254 above.

[259] Comm. Pss. pref. (ed. Lommatzsch, vol. XII, pp. 370f.).

[260] Hom. Num. 27; cf. W. Völker, *Das Vollkommenheitsideal des Origenes*, 1931, pp. 62f.

[261] R. P. C. Hanson, 'Interpretations of Hebrew Names in Origen', *VC* 10, 1956, pp. 103–123.

[262] Princ. IV, 2, 2.

[263] Comm. Joh. VI, 34, 171f.; Comm. Matt. XVI, 12: ὁ μὲν οὖν τῇ ἱστορίᾳ ψιλῇ παριστάμενος καὶ μὴ βουλόμενος διαφωνεῖν τοὺς εὐαγγελιστάς, ἐρεῖ οὐχ ἅμα γεγονέναι τὸ κατὰ τὸν Ματθαῖον καὶ τὸν Μάρκον . . . ὁ μέντοιγε ὅλων τούτων ζητῶν βαθυτέραν διήγησιν φήσει, ὅτι ἕν καὶ τὸ αὐτὸ πρᾶγμα διαφόροις λέξεσι παρίσταται. Hanson, *Allegory*, pp. 259f.

[264] Cf. Hom. Jes. N. XVI, 3: putasne contraria sibi scriptura contineat? hoc nec leviter suspicandum est. sed redeamus ad intelligentiam spiritalem et in ea nihil invenies esse contrarium.

[265] Comm. Joh. X, 5, 20: προέκειτο γὰρ αὐτοῖς ὅπου μὲν ἐνεχώρει, ἀληθεύειν πνευματικῶς ἅμα καὶ σωματικῶς, ὅπου δὲ μὴ ἐνεδέχετο ἀμφοτέρως, προκρίνειν τὸ πνευματικὸν τοῦ σωματικοῦ, σωζομένου πολλάκις τοῦ ἀληθοῦς πνευματικοῦ ἐν τῷ σωματικῷ, ὡς ἄν εἴποι τις, ψεύδει.

[266] Princ. IV, 2, 9; examples of this, 3, 1ff.; Comm. Joh. X, 5, 20 (cf. n. 265 above); Hom. Gen. II, 6.

[267] Princ. IV, 3, 1. Cf. K. P. Köppen, *Die Auslegung der Versuchungsgeschichte unter besonderer Berücksichtigung der Alten Kirche*, 1961, pp. 51f.

the contemporary situation and Jesus's position, is in the highest degree improbable, and in fact never occurred: it is an image of the purifying activity of the Lord, and teaches yet other, higher truths.[268] Such explanations would have been quite unthinkable not only in Tertullian but also in Irenaeus and Hippolytus.

The most important contribution which Origen made to the theory of the Canon was his doctrine of the inspiration of Scripture.[269] This is intimately linked with his use of the allegorical method. For only on the assumption that Scripture is directly divine in character is there any justification for looking for a higher meaning behind the literal sense of the words; and conversely, the profounder sense thus disclosed is a proof of the divinity of the text. To this extent faith in the inspiration of the Canon depends on arguing in a circle; but it is a circle which, for the man who has once settled for it, can never again be broken.[270] Origen also appeals to direct experience: the man who reads the Scriptures feels himself inspired by them, and so apprehends that they are the work not of man but of God.[271] The books of the Bible were 'written down and came to us as a result of the inspiration of the Holy Spirit in accordance with the will of the Father of all things through Jesus Christ'.[272] Origen gives detailed reason for and proofs of this statement. Only its incontrovertible validity saves the Christian faith from being built on sand.

The idea of the inspiration of the Bible was, of course, not completely new. The 'prophetic' exegesis of the Old Testament had taken account of it long since; and the oracular miracle of the fulfilment of its predictions had led Justin to regard the whole Old Testament as inspired in the strict sense of that word.[273] Origen, too, takes up this line of argument

---

[268] Comm. Joh. X, 20–34; on this passage cf. S. Leuchli, 'The Polarity of the Gospels in the Exegesis of Origen', Church History 21, 1952, pp. 215–224; further instances in Hanson, Allegory, pp. 264ff.

[269] In his own judgment also this was the crucial point in his doctrine of Scripture: cf. the summary of contents in Princ. I pref. 8: Tum deinde quod per spiritum dei scripturae conscriptae sint et sensum habeant non eum solum, qui in manifesto est, sed et alium quendam latentem quam plurimos. On Origen's doctrine of inspiration cf. what follows, and the evidence in A. Zöllig, Die Inspirationslehre des Origenes, 1902; Lubac, op. cit., pp. 139ff.; Hanson, Allegory, pp. 187ff.; Gögler, op. cit., pp. 282ff.

[270] Hom. Hierem. 39, 1 (= Philoc. X, 1): πίστευσον πρῶτον, καὶ εὑρήσεις ὑπὸ τὸ νομιζόμενον σκάνδαλον πολλὴν ὠφέλειαν ἁγίαν.

[271] Princ. IV, 1, 6: παθὼν ἐξ αὐτοῦ τοῦ ἀναγινώσκειν ἴχνος ἐνθουσιασμοῦ. Further passages in Hanson, Allegory, p. 189.

[272] Princ. IV, 2, 2: διόπερ τοῖς πειθομένοις μὴ ἀνθρώπων εἶναι συγγράμματα τὰς ἱερὰς βίβλους, ἀλλ' ἐξ ἐπιπνοίας τοῦ ἁγίου πνεύματος βουλήματι τοῦ πατρὸς τῶν ὅλων διὰ Ἰησοῦ χριστοῦ ταύτας ἀναγεγράφθαι καὶ εἰς ἡμᾶς ἐληλυθέναι, τὰς φαινομένας ὁδοὺς ὑποδεικτέον, ἐχομένοις τοῦ κανόνος τῆς Ἰησοῦ Χριστοῦ κατὰ διαδοχὴν τῶν ἀποστόλων οὐρανίου ἐκκλησίας.

[273] Cf. p. 89 above.

and carries it (on the basis of New Testament fulfilment) to its conclusion in traditional style.[274] For him, however, the whole Bible is now a
unity, and inspiration is as much a fact about the New Testament as
about the Old.[275] But this was a conclusion which Irenaeus had not yet
been capable of drawing, even though on one occasion, when in an
exegetical quandary, he did allow the wording of Matthew's Gospel
to have been directly determined by the Holy Spirit.[276] Nevertheless,
ever since the New Testament had achieved equality with the Old,
this inference followed almost automatically. Theophilus of Antioch
had already drawn it quite unambiguously in this sense, for the Gospels
at any rate.[277] Clement of Alexandria likewise had spoken of 'men filled
by the Spirit of God',[278] but at the same time understood the concept
of inspiration in such general terms that it could be applied to more or
less any religiously significant book,[279] and did not exclude the possibility of criticism on detailed points.[280] Only Tertullian makes a start
on a formal, thought out concept of inspiration for the whole Bible.
Origen, however, goes far beyond his sober lawyer's reflections, and,
in particular, he develops the idea not simply on an *ad hoc* basis, in
order to extract the truth he wants from a particular text, but in principle, as an established article of belief. The sacred text of the Bible
is as such unique, divine, and miraculous; even in the most fortuitous
letter of the Scripture the wisdom of God is to be found.[281] Origen is
thus a champion of verbal inspiration,[282] and in principle hardly less

---

[274] Princ. IV, 1, 2ff.   [275] Princ. I, pref. 4; IV, 3, 4.
[276] Cf. p. 205 n. 290 above.
[277] Theophilus, Ad Autol. III, 12: ἔτι μὴν καὶ περὶ δικαιοσύνης, ἧς ὁ
νόμος εἴρηκεν, ἀκόλουθα εὑρίσκεται καὶ τὰ τῶν προφητῶν καὶ τῶν εὐαγγελίων
ἔχειν, διὰ τὸ τοὺς πάντας πνευματοφόρους ἑνὶ πνεύματι θεοῦ λελαληκέναι.
[278] Cf. Theophilus, Ad Autol. II, 22: διδάσκουσιν ἡμᾶς αἱ ἅγιαι γραφαὶ καὶ
πάντες οἱ πνευματοφόροι. The 'holy scriptures' here may mean no more than the
O.T.; cf. R. M. Grant, 'The Bible of Theophilos of Antioch', *JBL* 66, 1947,
pp. 173–196, who thinks (p. 188) that for Theophilus the New Testament,
despite its inspired character, was not on a par with the Old (?). This, however,
certainly does not apply to the Gospels; cf. H. Lietzmann, 'Wie wurden die
Bücher des Neuen Testaments heilige Schrift?' in: *Kleine Schriften* II, 1958,
pp. 50–52.
[279] Cf. pp. 296f. above.
[280] Paed. II, 83, 4; Strom. II, 67f.; cf. Harnack, *Dogmengeschichte* I, p. 392
n. 2. On Theophilus cf. Lietzmann, *op. cit.*, pp. 51f.
[281] Comm. Pss. I (= Philoc. II, 4): . . . ἐπὶ πᾶσαν ἔφθασε γραφὴν θεόπνευστον
ἡ σοφία τοῦ θεοῦ μέχρι τοῦ τυχόντος γράμματος. Cf. n. 229 above.
[282] The objections of Gögler, *op. cit.*, p. 293, to this view, made in the course
of explicit polemic against Zöllig, Hanson and others, seems to me unfounded,
and are certainly not adequately supported by reference to occasional rudimentary attempts at textual criticism, and suchlike, on Origen's part. What advocate
of a doctrine of verbal inspiration was ever consistent in this respect if at the
same time he engaged in exegesis! The principle that it is 'not the text as such,
not the letters and the phrasing, which should be considered inspired, but the

strictly so than his Jewish contemporaries, with whom he was also associated.[283] Consequently his whole exegetical technique is bound up with the single word,[284] and indeed never balks even at finding a meaning 'in the most accidental letters'.

Even Origen, however, was not always absolutely consistent in practice. It was a help to him that, unlike Philo, he did not understand the process of inspiration as involving an automatic elimination of human consciousness.[285] Origen rejected the Montanist concept of ecstasy, and 'for the idea of a mere passivity substituted that of a heightening of the natural mental powers', effected by the touch of the Holy Spirit.[286] Accordingly he is on occasion also able to take into account, 'under the uniform whitewash of inspiration'[287] the circumstances and the subjective condition of the writer, and even to reckon with varying degrees of inspiration. Despite this, however, the problems are still sufficiently great, and without the resource of allegorical interpretation would in most cases be impossible to overcome. Origen reads and explains the Bible not simply as a dogmatic theologian or an edifying preacher but as a scholar. He brings the whole armoury of contemporary scholarship to bear on his work. He enquires into the data of history and folklore, he notes linguistic peculiarities, he knows about the difficulties of translating and translations, he even makes allowance for corruptions in the text. Origen evades none of these problems; he himself refers frankly to possible objections, in order to discuss them from every angle.[288] This shows his seriousness as a scholar, but no less also his rocklike confidence in the unshakeable truth of the inspired Scripture, which can never really be imperilled. His normal practice is to use the Septuagint version, which in the manner of the legend in the *Letter of Aristeas* he regards as inspired—even at those points where it deviates from the original text with later additions, though he was not blind to the importance of the Hebrew. Nevertheless, he came out against Julius Africanus on behalf of the broader canon of the Old

---

kerygmatic intention' (p. 188) is typically modern, and is never expressed in such terms by Origen.

[283] Origen was acquainted with Jewish scholars and exegetes, and we must therefore reckon with direct influence in that quarter; cf., e.g., Harnack, *Ertrag* II, pp. 10ff.; R. Cadiou, *La jeunesse d'Origène*, Paris, 1935, pp. 56ff.; Hanson, *Tradition*, pp. 182ff.; *Allegory*, pp. 154ff.

[284] Cf. Harl, *Origène*, p. 350; numerous examples in Lubac, *op. cit.*, pp. 113–125.

[285] Zöllig, *op. cit.*, pp. 63–76; Hanson, *Allegory*, pp. 194–197; on Gögler, *op. cit.*, pp. 287–294 cf. n. 282 above.

[286] Baur, *op. cit.*, p. 387.   [287] Harnack, *Ertrag* I, p. 11 n. 3.

[288] Zöllig, *op. cit.*, pp. 63–76. Origen considers it important not to do violence to the text; in contexts of this kind ἀβιάστως is one of his favourite terms: Hanson, *Allegory*, p. 197 n. 4.

Testament, and defended the authenticity of the story of Susanna. The 'eternal landmarks' which the Fathers had set up (Prov. 22:28) ought never to be moved;[289] and here, in addition to other, more objective arguments, Origen enlists the dangerous assistance of Providence, which could not have allowed the Christians to possess a worse text than the unbelieving Jews.[290]

A necessary consequence of the idea of inspiration is the doctrine that holy Scripture nowhere contradicts itself.[291] As a doctrine of the consonance of the Old Testament with the New this too was a long-standing affirmation of the apologetic literature, and one which had had to be particularly asserted against Marcionite and gnostic criticisms.[292] In this context Irenaeus and Tertullian in particular had made use of the idea of progress in the course of salvation-history, thus explaining rather than removing the discrepancies; and the possibility of an allegorical reinterpretation of the obsolete Law or of dealing with offensive stories by typology was brought in only as a supplementary measure. Origen pursues the traditional polemic with vigour;[293] but the relation between its two elements has been inverted. Allegorical interpretation dominates, and history has become virtually insignificant.[294] Like Clement, Origen is, of course, familiar with the old

---

[289] Ep. ad Afric. 5 (ed. Lommatzsch, vol. XVII, p. 26); cf. Comm. Cant. prol. (ed. Baehrens, p. 28).

[290] Ep. ad Afric. 4 (ed. Lommatzsch, vol. XVII, pp. 25f.): "Ὥρα τοίνυν, εἰ μὴ λανθάνει ἡμᾶς τά τοιαῦτα ἀθετεῖν τὰ ἐν ταῖς ἐκκλησίαις φερόμενα ἀντίγραφα καὶ νομοτεθῆσαι τῇ ἀδελφότητι, ἀποθέσθαι μὲν τὰς παρ' αὐτοῖς ἐπιφερομένας ἱερὰς βίβλους, κολακεύειν δὲ Ἰουδαίους καὶ πείθειν, ἵνα μεταδῶσιν ἡμῖν τῶν καθαρῶν καὶ μηδὲν πλάσμα ἐχόντων. Ἄρα δὲ καὶ ἡ πρόνοια ἐν ἁγίαις γραφαῖς δεδωκυῖα πάσαις ταῖς χριστοῦ ἐκκλησίαις οἰκοδομὴν οὐκ ἐφρόντισε τῶν τιμῆς ἀγορασθέντων, ὑπὲρ ὧν χριστὸς ἀπέθανεν . . . ;

[291] This does not mean, however, that all parts of it are of absolutely equal value. Even in Origen the Gospels enjoy a discernible precedence: Comm. Joh. I, 4, 21.23: ἐγὼ δ' οἶμαι, ὅτι καὶ τεσσάρων ὄντων τῶν εὐαγγελίων οἰονεὶ στοιχείων τῆς πίστεως τῆς ἐκκλησίας, ἐξ ὧν στοιχείων ὁ πᾶς συνέστηκε κόσμος ἐν Χριστῷ καταλλαγεὶς τῷ θεῷ . . . τολμητέον τοίνυν εἰπεῖν ἀπαρχὴν μὲν πασῶν γραφῶν εἶναι τὰ εὐαγγέλια, τῶν δὲ εὐαγγελίων ἀπαρχὴν τὸ κατὰ Ἰωάννην . . . Cf. Zöllig, op. cit., pp. 51ff.

[292] From the time of the emergence of the Four-Gospel canon onwards the controversy then spread to the question of contradictions between the four Gospels, as we can see from Irenaeus, Gaius, and the Muratorian Canon.

[293] The unity of the old and new covenants and Testaments is, together with the doctrine of the three natures, the most vital point in his dispute with the Valentinian Heracleon: M. Simonetti, 'Eracleone e Origene', Vetera Christ. 3, 1966, pp. 3–75; on the conflict with the Marcionites cf. Hanson, Allegory, pp. 135ff.; also Lubac, op. cit., pp. 166ff.

[294] In the problem of the old and new covenants, of Law and Gospel, it can, of course, never be entirely omitted. In these contexts Origen speaks of preparation and fulfilment, shadow and reality, letter and spirit. Everything reaches its climax in Christ, and Christ also speaks through the Old Testament—spiritually

pattern of prophecy and fulfilment; but what he himself likes to emphasise is not the continuity of an actual history but the inner harmony of a self-contained book, the Bible. Spiritually assessed, the Bible is in fact just one single book.[295] All that is needed is to peel away the husk of the letter, and then everywhere one comes across the same truths and the same Christ, who is the One who really speaks in both Testaments. Seen in this way, there is indeed in the last analysis no 'Old' Testament; to the 'spiritual' understanding both Testaments have become one new Testament—not chronologically, in which respect they are still distinct, but in the full understanding of the One who is proclaimed equally in each.[296] Whereas unbelief thinks to discern discrepancies and 'fighting' in the Scripture, faith recognises 'peace' and the perfect 'harmony' of the whole sacred volume. Peace reigns not only between the Old and New Testaments, but in just the same way between the individual sections and groups of writings within the Old and the New: the legal texts agree with the prophetic, the Gospels agree among themselves and at the same time with the apostolic writings, just as these in their turn are in agreement with one another. Everywhere rings out the voice of the same Good Shepherd, and the same eternal Logos holds sway, making of Scripture a single, miraculously unified divine instrument for teaching salvation to those of mankind who are prepared to listen.[297] Similarly Origen finds absolutely no

---

understood. Cf. Molland, *Gospel*, pp. 101–136; also J. Daniélou, 'L'unité des deux Testaments dans l'oeuvre d'Origène,' *RevSR* 22, 1948, pp. 27–56; V. E. Hasler, *Gesetz und Evangelium in der Alten Kirche bis Origenes*, Zurich, 1953, pp. 78–85.

[295] Comm. Joh. V, 7: ἀλλὰ καὶ ὁ ἐσθίων Ἰωάννης (Rev. 10:10) . . . τὴν πᾶσαν νενόηκε γραφὴν ὡς βίβλον μίαν.

[296] Hom. Num. IX, 4: sic ergo invenitur et evangelii virtus in lege et fundamento legis subnixa intelliguntur evangelia; nec vetus testamentum nomino ego legem, si eam spiritaliter intelligam. illis tantummodo lex vetus efficitur testamentum, qui eam carnaliter intelligere volunt; et necessario illis vetus effecta est et senuit, quia vires suas non potest obtinere. nobis autem, qui eam spiritaliter et evangelico sensu intelligimus et exponimus, semper nova est; et utrumque nobis novum testamentum est, non temporis aetate, sed intelligentiae novitate; cf. Clem. Alex., Strom. VII, 107, 5 (n. 203 above). In the same way the distinction between Law and Gospel is defined in Origen only in a very colourless way to mean shadow and reality, or preparation and fulfilment.

[297] Comm. Matt. II, on Matt. 5:9 (= Philoc. VI, 1): γίνεται δὲ καὶ τρίτος εἰρηνοποιός, ὁ τὴν ἄλλοις φαινομένην μάχην τῶν γραφῶν ἀποδεικνὺς εἶναι οὐ μάχην καὶ παριστὰς τὴν συμφωνίαν καὶ τὴν εἰρήνην τούτων, ἤτοι παλαιῶν πρὸς καινὰς ἢ νομικῶν πρὸς προφητικὰς ἢ εὐαγγελικῶν πρὸς εὐαγγελικὰς ἢ εὐαγγελικῶν πρὸς ἀποστολικὰς ἢ ἀποστολικῶν πρὸς ἀποστολικάς. Comm. Matt. Ser. 47, on Matt. 24:47: Christus verbum esse et veritas et sapientia dei ostenditur a primo initio creaturae mundi usque ad novissimam apostolorum scripturam (id est a Genesi usque ad apostolicos libros), post quos nullis scripturis ita credendum est sicut illis.

difficulty in combining any passage of Scripture which he happens to be discussing with any other, and in explaining the whole in the light of each part; allegorical interpretation creates a universal equality. Origen's commentaries live by this 'biblical alchemy',[298] and as a result proliferate in monotonous detail to infinity.

Where Scripture is understood in this way as a unity, it is essential that the Canon should be strictly defined in a clear and unambiguous manner. Here, however, Origen runs into a problem which even he cannot resolve: such a clearly demarcated canon does not as yet exist. It is precisely in Egypt that, despite the fact that their essential core is firmly established, there are still variations in the peripheral contents of both the Old and New Testaments, and these variations cannot be wished away.[299] The one thing that Origen can do is to try for his part to clarify the situation as far as possible. It would seem that for the most part, and ever more decisively, his efforts tended in a restrictionist direction, something which did not come naturally to him.[300] For him as for Clement the Epistle of Barnabas remained a part of the New Testament; but Hermas, which Origen had at first accepted without question as sacred Scripture, he came in time to assess more cautiously.[301] Even the Revelation of John, it would seem, he eventually regarded as problematic, after he had left the more generously receptive atmosphere of Egypt, and had settled in Palestine.[302] On the other hand, he in the end accepted the disputed Epistle to the Hebrews regardless of the problem of authorship.[303] There were as yet no established formal criteria for determining what was 'canonical'—a word which Origen does not use in this sense.[304] Furthermore, Origen is unacquainted with

[298] Harnack, *Dogmengeschichte* I, p. 665 n. 2, following C. Bigg, *The Christian Platonists of Alexandria*, 1886, pp. 137f.

[299] I shall not here go into the much-discussed problems of Origen's canon. It is frequently too closely equated with the standard catholic canon—not without the assistance of Rufinus' translations, and by presenting even that evidence one-sidedly; cf., e.g., for the O.T., A. Merk, 'Origenes und der Kanon des Alten Testaments', *Biblica* 6, 1925, pp. 200–205, and for the N.T., in particular Lagrange, *op. cit.*, pp. 93–103. By contrast Hanson, *Tradition*, pp. 133–145, in his incisive discussion of the problem seems to me to go too far in the opposite direction, when in the case of the N.T. he lays great stress on the (scholarly) use of apocrypha, and in that of the O.T. will hardly allow Origen to have gone beyond Clement's position (p. 137). Cf. further Harnack, *Ertrag* I, pp. 17–21; II, pp. 4–9, 34–50.

[300] His general attitude is very well characterised by Lagrange, *op. cit.*, p. 98: 'In his thinking, therefore, he was content to confine himself to the minimum, but he did not consider that he had any authority to reject the maximum, since the minimum was the work of certain writers only.'

[301] Cf. the evidence in Hanson, *Tradition*, pp. 139f.

[302] Lagrange, *op. cit.*, pp. 94f.   [303] Hanson, *Tradition*, pp. 141f.

[304] It is imported into Rufinus' translation: Zöllig, *op. cit.*, p. 83. The word occurs for the first time in this sense in the fourth century.

any 'principle of apostolicity' as a means of arriving at a correct selection.[305] It is clear that for him the factor of supreme importance was universal acceptance by the Church, and to this he frequently refers.[306] He commonly describes the canonical scriptures simply as 'writings that are in use in the churches of God', or refers to the 'incontrovertible testimony of the inspired books in customary use'.[307] But in addition to the 'universally acknowledged'[308] authentic Scriptures, and the manifestly 'inauthentic' there is a further 'mixed' group[309] of works which are not universally accepted but are doubtful or 'disputed'.[310] In such cases Origen makes painstaking efforts to determine the historical and traditional, the philological, and not least the theological data in order to arrive at a reasoned judgment. For all this, however, he never achieved a firm definition of the content of the canon such as Tertullian already possessed.

The conscientious care with which Origen, 'discussing everything and deciding nothing that still called for a decision',[311] examined and defended the accepted canon was something new. From Marcion's time until now critical investigation had almost always figured purely as an opponent of the Canon. Even in Origen's day doubts and outright

[305] The contrary is often asserted but without justification. Origen uses Hermas (cf. n. 301 above) and the disputed 'catholic epistle' of Barnabas (Cels. I, 63: cf. Zahn, op. cit., I, pp. 348f.), and discusses the problem of the authorship of Hebrews (Hom. Hebr. in Eusebius, HE VI, 25, 11–14), without drawing any conclusions from this for the question of canonicity. Conversely, he rejects the Doctrina Petri, and considers that it can be proved, quia neque Petri est ipsa scriptura neque alterius cuiusquam, qui spiritu dei fuerit inspiratus (Princ. I praef. 8). Hanson, Tradition, p. 142, rightly comments: 'This frank statement' (i.e., about Hebrews) 'makes perfectly clear what we might infer from Origen's references to other works whose authority was disputed, that the question of authorship was not the only test, in his eyes, of a book's authority.'

[306] E. Flesseman-van Leer, 'Prinzipien der Sammlung und Ausscheidung bei der Bildung des Kanons', ZTK 61, 1964, p. 415, rightly remarks: 'The crucial point in his view is not apostolicity but inspiration'; cf. also Zöllig, op. cit., pp. 84f.; and Rufinus' translation of Comm. Matt. Ser. 47, quoted in n. 297 above. Hom. Jes. VII, 4, like the Muratorian Canon, stresses that there is a chronological limit to the N.T. era, only now this is applied to a N.T. already existing and complete.

[307] Cels. VI, 20: αἱ φερόμεναι ἐν ταῖς ἐκκλησίαις τοῦ θεοῦ γραφαί: In Psa. 4, 2 (ed. Lommatzsch, vol. XII, p. 429): κατὰ τὰ ἀναντίρρτα τῶν ἀναφερομένων βιβλίων θεοπνεύστων κτλ.; cf. Hanson, Tradition, p. 138.

[308] Ὁμολογούμενα: Comm. Joh. V, 3 (= Eusebius, HE VI, 25, 8); Hom. Hebr. (in Eusebius, HE VI, 25, 12); Comm. Matt. XIV, 21; XVII, 35.

[309] Comm. Joh. XIII, 17, 104: . . . ἐξετάζοντας καὶ περὶ τοῦ βιβλίου (sc. Πέτρου κηρύγματος) πότερόν ποτε γνήσιόν ἐστιν ἢ νόθον ἢ μικτόν.

[310] Ἀμφιβαλλόμενα: Comm. Joh. V, 3 (= Eusebius, HE VI, 25, 8); Orat. 14, 4. 'The usual opposite of "Homologumena" is "Apocrypha" ': Harnack, Ertrag II, p. 5 n. 2; cf. Ep. ad Afric. 9.

[311] T. Zahn, Grundriss der Geschichte des neutestamentlichen Kanons², 1904, p. 43.

attacks had by no means been silenced.[312] Gaius had denounced the Johannine writings,[313] cultivated Monarchians were attempting radical corrections of the text,[314] Julius Africanus had demanded the excision of the story of Susanna from the text of the book of Daniel.[315] To all these critics Origen replied not merely with empty dogmatic postulates, but also with solid scholarly arguments.[316] To this extent it may be said that together with the final formulation of the catholic canon he also founded orthodox biblical scholarship. Nevertheless, it is still suspicious that what he stands up for is always just the existing, given situation in the Church. Such a proceeding is typical of his personal style, and unfortunately has never been without its imitators. On the other hand, however, his writings also supplied a Eusebius and a Jerome with an inexhaustible fund of solid, objective information.

Origen never pursued his philological and archaeological studies, any more than his philosophical ones, simply for their own sake.[317] His only concern is to illuminate God's truth, which lies hidden in Scripture for men's salvation. It is his modest pride to possess, as a genuine teacher, the gift of the spiritual understanding of Scripture. The divine Scriptures, he remarks on one occasion, using an image borrowed from a Jewish scholar, are like a house which contains within itself many houses, each of which has to be opened with a different key. It is not always easy to hit upon the right key at the right time. Many obscure passages must be compared with one another in order

[312] Cf. in Grant, *Letter*, pp. 143-145, Appendix III: Textual and literary criticism.

[313] Cf. pp. 238ff. above.

[314] Eusebius, *HE* V, 28, 13-19; cf. H. Schöne, 'Ein Einbruch der antiken Logik und Textkritik in die altchristliche Theologie', in: *Pisciculi* (Festschrift F. J. Dölger), 1939, pp. 252-265.

[315] Ep. ad Orig. In his Letter to Aristides he discusses, in a similarly critical manner but with a harmonising conclusion, the divergent genealogies of Jesus. Both letters may be read in the critical edition of W. Reichardt, *Die Briefe des Sextus Julius Africanus an Aristides und Origenes*, 1909. In this context mention may also be made of certain critics of the Psalter seemingly referred to by Hippolytus: cf. p. 237 n. 153 above.

[316] Cf. the astonishing judgment of Harnack, *Die Briefsammlung des Apostels Paulus und die anderen vorkonstantinischen christlichen Briefsammlungen*, 1926, p. 47, on Origen as contrasted with the 'flashy philologist' (p. 52), Africanus. Harnack concludes that 'although Origen as a biblicist and churchman feels himself tied to the tradition, and defends a mistaken thesis, yet in solidity of scholarship he far surpasses Africanus, and his reply affords a far more valuable specimen of ancient scholarship than Africanus' letter'.

[317] Cf. Hom. Exod. II, 1. After a hair-splitting explanation that Ex. 1:17 cannot be taken in its literal sense, Origen continues: haec interim propter eos, qui amici sunt litterae et non putant legem spiritalem esse et spiritaliter intelligendam. sed nos, qui omnia, quae scripta sunt, non pro narrationibus antiquitatum, sed pro disciplina et utilitate nostra scripta didicimus. . . . Further passages in Gögler, *op. cit.*, pp. 288f.

to find it. But there is no other, simpler way of gaining access to this great house.[318] The Bible is meant to be explained from within itself, and it does so explain itself to those who diligently obey its wishes. For this reason Origen will have none of the note of mystery and the solemn language of the *disciplina arcani* with which Clement attracted his hearers to the Scripture, in order to communicate 'knowledge' to them.[319] He speaks like a sober scholar who, in his role of exegete, has nothing to hide, and who equally promises nothing except what the Bible itself has to say. Moreover it is Christ himself who must bestow the Spirit on both teacher and hearer and open their ears to understand what in truth is being said by means of the simple sentences of the text.[320]. No tradition, no formulary,[321] no ecclesiastical tribunal[322] thrusts itself between the teacher and the divine word of the Lord.

It is not altogether a simple matter to arrive at a fair assessment of Origen's importance for the history of the Canon. His doctrine of Scripture undoubtedly exercised—primarily in the East—an enormous influence; but it was not the only factor controlling developments, and his hermeneutical theories ran into opposition at an early stage. Nevertheless, the concept of the Canon was at least affected by him, above all as regards the discussion of its limits and content. Here Origen influenced posterity in a way which paradoxically ran almost exactly

---

[318] Comm. Psa. 1 (= *Philoc.* II, 3). Origen ends with the words: νοεῖσθαι τοίνυν καὶ τὰς γραφὰς οὔσας ἀσαφεῖς οὐκ ἄλλοθεν τὰς ἀφορμὰς τοῦ νοεῖσθαι λαμβανούσας ἢ παρ᾽ ἀλλήλων ἐχουσῶν ἐν αὐταῖς διεσπαρμένον τὸ ἐξηγητικόν. There follows a reference to 'the Apostle' Paul (I Cor. 2:13). Cf. Princ. I pref. 1 (non aliunde quam ab ipsis Christi verbis doctrinaque).

[319] In Origen the word γνῶσις does not in general have the same exalted pretensions as in Clement, but simply means religious information and spiritual education: Cadiou, *op. cit.*, p. 96; Hanson, *Tradition*, p. 84.

[320] Cf. Lubac, *op. cit.*, pp. 315–325.

[321] As is well known, the question whether Origen even considers the possibility of a fixed confession of faith is disputed, and should probably be answered in the negative. In any case it exercised no influence on his exegesis: Hanson, *Tradition*, p. 126.

[322] That Origen, though both a churchman and a man of the Bible, was anything but a clericalist is proved by the disaster which overtook him in Alexandria and by his critical and never blindly subservient assessment of those who held spiritual office; cf. further the unfortunately corrupt passage in Dial. Heracl. 4f., together with the comments in B. Capelle, 'L'Entretien d'Origène avec Héraclide', *JEH* 2, 1951, pp. 150f., and by J. Scherer in his edition, 1960, p. 64 n. 2, who makes a problematic attempt to soften the tone of the passage. Against the latter's interpretation (p. 64 n. 1) of συνθῆκαι as 'common formulas of agreement, governing liturgical prayer in all the various types of christianity', cf. Hanson, *Tradition*, p. 181: 'The evidence therefore in Clement of Alexandria and Origen is quite insufficient for us to conclude that either of these writers regarded Christian institutions or sacraments or worship as capable of providing a fund of doctrine from which the Bible could be interpreted or modified to any important extent.'

Y

counter to his own efforts. His concern was to restrict and, so far as possible, to remove existing uncertainties. But because the discussion of these questions was continued by Eusebius and noted by Jerome, the effect was to perpetuate the memory of doubts that had once existed, whether and how far particular books belonged to the Canon or not. These doubts did not shake the conviction that it was right to have an ecclesiastical canon as such; but they did stand in the way of its absolute sacralisation as something directly given by God, and this obstacle only an extreme, positivistic recognition of the absolute power of the Church authorities to decide the issue was able to overcome. Moreover, the critique of the canon first by the Humanists and then by the Reformers was directly linked with these debates in the early Church.

Much more important was the decision as to the fundamental unity and homogeneity, the inspiration and infallibility of the Canon, and its complete sufficiency as a norm of church doctrine and preaching. Here Origen gave final substantive shape to the preliminary efforts of his predecessors; but he did so by using different methods and in a highly dubious manner. The one man whose gnosticising theology had not fitted into the pattern of catholic work on the scriptures hitherto had been Clement of Alexandria. And it is precisely in comparison with him that the advance which Origen made is, from one angle, particularly clear. But on the other hand it is also from him, or at any rate from the Alexandrian-gnostic tradition common to both him and Origen, that those hermeneutical views derive which chiefly provide the rational basis for regarding the Canon as unified, infallible and inexhaustible. It was his doctrine, developed along gnostic lines, of the manifold sense of Scripture which first made it possible within the Church to allegorise the Bible in the style of Clement and the Valentinians. To the Fathers before Origen such a proceeding was wholly alien. Instead, these men had explained the Scripture in terms of salvation-history; and they had put up with the tensions which inevitably resulted from such an approach in view of the unevennesses and contradictions within the Bible, and had adjusted them on dogmatic grounds only at a number of isolated points. For Origen, thanks to the allegorical method, all the problems which had hitherto existed were done away at a stroke; but in the process history was completely annulled, or at least rendered theologically meaningless. The allegorical approach robbed the Bible of its distinctive significance. The inescapable historical gulf which yawned between every part of the Bible and the contemporary existence of the Church had simply vanished, and there was no longer any need to overcome it in faith by the power of the Spirit. Its place was taken by the false immediacy of an unvarying teaching on the subject of God's nature and goodness, of the meaning of the world and of the way of redemption, and an exhortation and encouragement to self-improvement, virtue, and holiness which was identical on every page. These universal truths are central to Origen's christianity. The constant reference to Christ made not the slightest difference to this; for he too is brought in only as one who makes his appeal to men and instructs them, not as a historical act of redemption but as the eternal truth of God—the same in the past as in the present, in the Law as in the Gospel. The historical Lord of the believers has himself become an allegory of the Logos.

Once this is understood, it will be seen that it is certainly no accident that the Irenaean concept of the canon of truth as a permanent reality in the present life of the Church should in Origen be so drastically stunted into something merely dogmatic and didactic. Although Origen loves to follow Paul in emphasising the charismatic nature of the Church, his devout belief in the Bible is directed not to the spiritual freedom and personal responsibility of a congregation steadfast in the faith but to an ever closer connection of all knowledge and of the whole of ethical behaviour to what the Bible has said uniquely and once for all. For Origen Scripture is no longer just the controlling standard, but the direct source of faith itself. In this way his idealistic didacticism converges strangely with the otherwise totally different nomistic biblicism of Tertullian—indeed, even more than the latter Origen made Christianity, in an almost Philonic sense, once again into a 'religion of the Book'.[323] It was not least the absolute biblicism of this concept of Scripture which favoured, if it did not actually provoke the later reaction to a no less one-sided church consciousness and to a renewed, equally absolute concept of tradition, now set in opposition to Scripture.

It was a dangerous legacy that Origen bequeathed to posterity—both as dogmatic theologian and as exegete and as the founder of a principle of Scripture which now brought to a close the era of crises and conflicts. Origen's theory of the canon is in fact very closely connected with his exegetical method and his total conception of the Christian message. But while disputes over his method of scriptural exegesis and over the doctrine contained in Scripture raged for centuries, and finally resulted in the unjust condemnation not merely of his writings but of his person, the Origenist dogma of Scripture itself remained in substance unshaken. It was regarded as the final and legitimate outcome of the struggles which had been carried on for so long with

[323] Cf. Harnack, *Entstehung*, p. 83, who, however, regards the Origenist attitude to the Bible as far more widespread than it really was. It is true, nevertheless, that the tendency toward a 'canonical' collection of Scriptures and to a correspondingly 'exegetical' style of thinking was universal at that time; and similar trends are observable in contemporary philosophical and juristic training.

Jews and pagans, with Marcionites and gnostics, with Montanists and with the sceptics within Christianity's own camp. There are, it is true, still occasional discussions and minor differences of opinion about the content and significance of the Canon, but no more real conflicts. The definition and meaning of the Canon, its unity and essential content, its inspiration and its normative significance for the whole of the Church's faith and life are from henceforward firmly established.

Retrospect

I HAVE brought this history of the formation of the Christian Canon[1]—a term which was still not used of the Bible during the period we have surveyed—to a close with Origen, and have deliberately refrained from carrying it beyond him. It is undisputed that both the Old and the New Testaments had in essence already reached their final form and significance around the year 200. The minor variations which still persist, and are occasionally the subject of further discussion,[2] co-exist perfectly happily with the overriding conviction that Christians everywhere possess one and the same Bible.[3] For the fundamental understanding of the Canon they are of no importance. If, therefore, we wish to form some picture of the motives behind the formation of the Canon, and to assess its significance, then the best course is to choose a standpoint not later than the beginning of the third century, and to survey the earlier development from there.[4]

I

The Christian Bible—and this is the first and absolutely unshakeable fact that we know about it—comes into existence from the start as the

---

[1] The technical use of this word to denote the 'canonical' Scriptures does not begin before the fourth century, and acquires its precise significance only as a loan-word in the vocabulary of Latin theology: T. Zahn, *Grundriss der Geschichte des neutestamentlichen Kanons*[2], 1904, pp. 1–11. On the earlier history of the term cf. H. Oppel, *KANΩN, Zur Bedeutungsgeschichte des Wortes und seiner lateinischen Entsprechungen*, 1937; H. W. Beyer, art. κανών, *TWNT* III, 1938, pp. 600–606; L. Wenger, *Canon in den römischen Rechtsquellen und in den Papyri*, Vienna, 1942.

[2] The points at issue are principally the status of Revelation and of the Epistle to the Hebrews, and to some extent also Philemon and the Catholic Epistles. 'Whereas in the West our canon is complete by about 400, in the East this process lasted some 200 years longer': E. Fascher, art. 'Testament, Altes und Neues' in: Pauly-Wissowa, *Realencyklopädie* (2nd series), vol. V A 1, 1934, col. 966.

[3] The only exception was the national church of Syria, which for a long time substituted the Diatessaron for the Four-Gospel canon in the N.T., and in addition to Revelation also excluded the Catholic Epistles.

[4] The objection to this procedure raised by A. C. Sundberg, 'A Revised History of the New Testament Canon' in: *StudEvang* IV, 1, 1968, pp. 46of., derives in part from a somewhat different conception of what is meant by 'canonical', and has failed to convince me. In other respects his sketch has repeated points of contact with the theses of the present work.

book of Christ. The 'scriptures of the Lord' testify to the Lord—the
Old Testament prophetically, the New Testament historically. Christ
speaks in both Testaments and is their true content. This alone is what
makes the Bible the Christian Bible, the book of the Christian Church.

At first it is the Old Testament alone—only later to be given this name
—which is involved. For the primitive Jewish Christian Church its
validity and the need to preserve it are taken for granted, and present
no problem; but this Scripture is understood in a new way, with the
emphasis on its prophetic testimony to the suffering and risen Lord.
In early Gentile Christianity recognition of the ancient Bible is complicated by the Law: the fact that (for the Gentile Christian Church)
this is no longer valid has to be substantiated. Nevertheless, this problem is quickly mastered, and soon is no longer a living issue.

The crisis of the Old Testament, which begins in the second century,
is also christologically determined, and precipitated by the Law: it is
discovered that its prescriptions are incompatible with the moral and
religious 'teachings' of Christ. The Great Church overcomes this
difficulty by on the one hand emphasising in addition to the prophetic
character of the Old Testament the change from the old era to the new,
while at the same time emphatically maintaining that it is one and the
same God who established the old covenant and then brought into
being the way which led to Christ. Old and New Testament are linked
in terms of salvation-history.

The New Testament does not emerge as a supplement to or continuation of the Old. Its content is the historical message about Christ, and
its purpose is to safeguard the oral tradition of the Church in its original
form against the threat of distortion. To this extent it is documentary
and historical in character.[5] The man who made a start here was the
heretic Marcion. He rejected in its entirety the living tradition about
Christ as it was in his day, and tied his church to a small, dogmatically
revised selection of primitive Christian documents, which he alone
regarded as authentic. This compelled the Great Church in its turn to
establish in opposition to him and to all other false teachers a corresponding but considerably wider and uncorrected collection of genuine
documents. In the course of defending the Church against Montanist
enthusiasm, which proclaimed new prophecies and commandments

[5] Nevertheless, the idea that there is a special security in having a written text
plays hardly any part in this. It occurs to Clement of Alexandria to mention the
point in general terms in Strom. I, 1; with specific reference to the N.T. the
earliest instance known to me in which stress is laid upon it is Adamantius, *Dialogue* I, 12 (ed. Van den Sande Bakhuyzen, pp. 82f. = *Buchheit*, p. 37): τὰ γὰρ
ἀγράφως λεγόμενα παύεται μετ' ὀλίγον, οὐκ ἔχοντα τὴν ἀπόδειξιν. (quod enim
sine scriptura dictum est paulo post desinit, quia nullum sui continet moni-
mentum.) This sweeping confidence in oral tradition is characteristic of early
Christianity and in marked contrast to Jewish ideas.

surpassing the earlier revelation, the limits of this collection were finally marked out. Now all recent works, and in particular almost all prophetic books of late date, were rejected. The New Testament was strictly confined to the testimonies about Christ and to the original preaching.

II

The Bible is never regarded as the sole source of Christian faith. It is constantly accompanied by the living preaching and teaching about Christ, which began simultaneously with the foundation of the Church and is the work of the Holy Spirit. In this sense the Church always lives by *tradition* as well as the Bible, just as in the first instance she lived by tradition alone.

As far as the Old Testament is concerned this is obvious. Its christological meaning can be understood and revealed only with the help of the new testimony to Christ.[6] But even the New Testament can be reached only by way of the living preaching which awakens true faith, even though the content of the book is in itself plain enough. The book, however, is permanently indispensable—first, to refute effectively the false assertions of heretics concerning Christ and the apostolic teaching, and secondly, to decide with equal authority the disputes which arise within the orthodox Church.

Scripture, however, never suppresses or replaces the living, public proclamation of the Church, which holds to the original 'canon of truth'. This canon or 'standard', when directed against the gnostics, emphasises the trinitarian and historical-christological aspects of the faith roughly in the manner of the Apostles' Creed. It is, however, not identical with any credal formula as such, but denotes the essence of the Church's teaching as a whole. It is not a norm placed over the sacred Scripture; it shares a common origin with the latter in the original preaching of the apostles, and is therefore in material agreement with it. Even less is there any question of a special exegetical authority vested in the clergy and restricting free access to the Bible; and so holy Scripture remains without qualification the supreme authority, and the one fixed norm of teaching and morals for the orthodox church.[7]

---

[6] The exaggerated assertion of some apologists that they attained to faith simply by reading the O.T. (cf. p. 88 above) was an isolated phenomenon, and was never applied to the complete Christian Bible.

[7] The concept, which Harnack popularised, of 'Early Catholicism' is characterised by the validity of three constitutive norms—Bible, Creed, and Episcopate. It is, however, a misleading abstraction which in no way corresponds to the self-understanding of the early Church. Even in later antiquity there is not a single text known to me which links these three things as normative.

III

The *authority* of the biblical writings is based on the fact that they reliably record the predictions of Christ in the prophets and the testimony to Christ of the apostles. The role of the apostles in this connection is not that of creative originators of Christian doctrine and tradition, but that of the only witnesses to Christ's own teaching and story who were called and accredited by Christ himself.[8] Consequently the dogma of their complete agreement, formulated in opposition to Marcion and the gnostics, is regarded as essential, and is even applied to the literary expression of their teaching, the New Testament—despite the difficulties which this dogma encountered, in particular from the divergent opening sections of the various Gospels.

For short the two Testaments are referred to simply as 'the Prophets' and 'the Apostles'. This, however, does not imply that the books of the Old Testament must have been written only by prophets in the strict sense, and those of the New exclusively by apostles (or at least at their commission and under their supervision). It is the content of the prophetic or apostolic testimony which is decisive, not the question of direct authorship or authorisation.[9] The opposite view, dominant today, that the principle for deciding whether a work should be admitted into the New Testament was that of its authorship by an apostle, is devoid of all foundation.[10] So far as any 'principle' can be discerned behind the sources, it appears to be one simply of chronological limitation: the normative testimonies must derive from the period closest to Christ, namely that of Christian origins, the age of the apostles and their disciples. This is in keeping with the 'historical' character of the New Testament, and to a certain extent also with the corresponding principle on which the Old Testament was defined within the Jewish synagogue.[11]

[8] Here we see the effects of the picture of history presented by the Lukan Acts. Paul, however, was always given equal status alongside Luke's 'twelve apostles'.

[9] Zahn, *op. cit.*, I, p. 449, pertinently comments: 'The concept of what was "apostolic", to the extent that it coincided with what we call "canonical" or "New Testament", was not derived directly from the idea of a special official dignity attaching to the twelve apostles and to Paul, but from the conviction that complete sections of the traditional New Testament were written by apostles and companions of the apostles, and thus were reliable documents for the apostolic age, and in particular for the apostolic preaching and tradition.'

[10] The view was first put forward on a scholarly basis by Erasmus; cf. W. Maurer, 'Luthers Verständnis des neutestamentlichen Kanons' in: *Die Verbindlichkeit des Kanons* (Fuldaer Hefte 12), 1960, pp. 55f.

[11] Nevertheless, the principle of restriction to an ancient 'classical' era seems to throw less light on the rationale behind the O.T. than it does in the case of the N.T., the interest of which is from theological necessity concentrated on a single person and so also on a single, correspondingly limited period of time.

IV

The main contents of both the Old and New Testaments were never officially instituted or determined. The Old Testament had come with the Church at her birth;[12] the New was consolidated in the process of the use which individual churches—with the critical and controlling participation of their intellectual leaders—made of the corpus of primitive Christian writing.[13] The regular use of a book for liturgical reading was a pre-condition of its later *reception*, but did not exclude an investigation in doubtful cases of its 'authenticity' and right to a place in the Canon. In a case of exclusion from the Canon in particular, historical and philological considerations played a part in addition to doubts of a more practical and theological kind. By contrast, in the period under review official decisions by the Church are not involved.[14] Synodal judgements and episcopal pastoral letters concerning the contents of the Bible become usual only in the later fourth century,[15]

[12] The problems of the O.T. Canon hardly made any impression on the general body of Church people; discussion of the subject remained scientific and scholarly. More important than the discussion of the considerable variations in content was the question of the status of the LXX, which had been rejected by the Jews, *vis-à-vis* the original Hebrew text and the other versions.

[13] The New Testament (considered as a 'canonical' collection) may therefore properly be described as a creation of the post-Marcionite church. On the other hand, the content of this N.T. collection of writings, and to a certain extent the writings themselves were something with which the Church was presented as an already existing 'apostolic testimony'. The Church knew that she had been called into life by this testimony, and had not herself created the Scriptures. She could merely accept, affirm, and confirm them. Hence one could also say, with equal or even greater justification, that the Canon (thought of in terms of its content) imposed itself, and was in any case not a product of the Church on which it was binding.

[14] Tertullian's famous statement about the Shepherd of Hermas (pudic. 10, 12) does not tell against this: sed cederem tibi, si scriptura Pastoris, quae sola moechos amat, divino instrumento meruisset incidi, si non ab omni concilio ecclesiarum, etiam vestrarum, inter apocrypha et falsa iudicaretur. . . . It is true that this passage is constantly taken to refer to supposed conciliar decisions, on the, as I believe, false assumption that the work is addressed to the Bishop of Rome, with indeed, especially urgent insistence on a Roman initiative in the matter; so, most recently, P. Meinhold, *Konzile der Kirche in evangelischer Sicht*, 1962, pp. 34f. But the word, *concilium*, here as elsewhere in Tertullian, patently is not to be understood in its later technical significance, but simply means the (liturgical) congregation of the churches: the Shepherd of Hermas is rejected by every church community, by the community of all the churches, including even the catholics. There is thus no question of conciliar decisions 'to establish the N.T. canon'; cf. G. Roethe, *Zur Geschichte der römischen Synoden im 3. und 4. Jahrhundert* (Geistige Grundlagen römischer Kirchenpolitik II), 1937, pp. 112–114.

[15] It is for this reason that Lagrange, *op. cit.*, p. 134, places 'the first fixing of the Canon' in the period which begins around 350 and ends with an opinion

and at first are of only local importance. They encourage uniformity between the various areas of the Church, but are unable to bring about a completely uniform canon until the Middle Ages.

V

The *holiness* of the 'divine scriptures' is taken for granted, and is nowhere affected by this trifling uncertainty over the exact limits of the Canon. They are regarded universally and without qualification as the attestation, consistent in substance and completely reliable, of Christian truth. Yet the individual Scriptures vary nevertheless in importance according to their historical and religious significance. The prophecies of the Old Testament are fulfilled and made plain only by 'the Gospel'; and even the Scriptures of the New Testament constitute no uniform mass, but display a unity with its own internal structure. The pre-eminence of the Gospels, which witness directly to Christ, is everywhere assumed; and in the same way the Pauline epistles take universal precedence over the later letters of the other apostles, which enjoy an uneven reception. This is not at all an effect of the gradual, step-by-step process of canonisation; on the contrary, it is the latter which follows the enduring theological judgment and awareness of the early Church.

The concept of a formal inspiration of Scripture attaches first of all to the 'prophetic' Old Testament, and makes its way only hesitantly into the understanding of the New. Origen was the first to extend it as a matter of principle to the whole Bible. For him the 'spiritual' sense of Scripture was no longer a consequence of the christological reference of its predictions or testimonies (I Cor. 12:3) but of the formal givenness of the divine revelatory book in the abstract. This unhistorical concept of inspiration was to some extent modified in the succeeding period but never really overcome.[16]

---

from Pope Innocent I in 405 (Ep. 6). With reference to the 'definitive settlement' by the Council of Trent he adds: 'It is only then that adherence to the Canon becomes a necessary act of faith.' Such formalist and juristic dogmatism is, however, wholly alien to the spirit of the early Church.

[16] This view received its most thoroughgoing development at a later period, in Protestant orthodoxy with its dependence on the scholasticism of the High and Late Middle Ages. It is this abstract concept of inspiration which is above all responsible for the severity with which historical and critical thought from the seventeenth century onwards clashed with the scriptural and canonical principle of both Catholic and Evangelical Christianity. Of course, even without the rigidity of a doctrine of verbal inspiration (and the allegorical interpretation that went with it) there would inevitably have been serious upheavals; but these would have been much easier to overcome if the significance of the Canon, with its preparation for and testimony to Christ, had been understood in a fundamentally historical sense, as was predominantly the case in the period before (Clement and) Origen.

VI

Discussion of the contemporary problem of the Canon does not fall within the scope of the present work. Nevertheless, the historical presentation of the circumstances and motives which brought it into being is itself of theological importance. For it would certainly not be 'legitimate' to support the traditional Canon with arguments which played no part in its formation.[17] An impartial investigation of its history saves us from this danger, and points us to the right road. Certainly, judged by modern historical standards, the way in which the infallibility, consistency, and unity of the Scriptures were once asserted and defended, is extremely naïve and cannot be retained. The *critical approach* has meant that the biblical testimony now has only relative value as documentary evidence, and to that extent has altered our understanding of it. But it has not deprived it of all value; and despite this academic revolution there is, in my opinion, no need to change the essential significance of the Canon and its theological meaning. Even an Old Testament read with critical eyes is still the book of a history which leads to Christ and indeed points toward him, and without him cannot itself be understood. Even on a critical reading the New Testament is still the only source from which we can discover who and what Christ really was—and it is precisely historical investigation which helps us for the first time to a full knowledge of his distinctive character and uniqueness. It is true that—as in the early Church—faith never comes simply from reading the holy Scriptures, and that Christ, not the Canon, is the true object of faith; but the Scripture, read in faith and with the aid of reason, still remains the canon, the 'standard'. Without adherence to the Canon, which—in the widest sense—witnesses to the history of Christ, faith in Christ in any church would become an illusion.

[17] E. Flesseman-van Leer, 'Prinzipien der Sammlung und Ausscheidung bei der Bildung des Kanons', *ZTK* 61, 1964, p. 419.

INDEX OF ANCIENT AUTHORS
AND SOURCES

INDEX OF MODERN AUTHORS